THE
bon appétit
fast *easy* fresh
COOKBOOK

THE
bon appétit
fast *easy* fresh
COOKBOOK

BARBARA FAIRCHILD

JOHN WILEY & SONS, INC.

Photographs by France Ruffenach
Illustrations by Jessica Allen
Design by Vertigo Design, NYC

Published by John Wiley & Sons, Inc., Hoboken, New Jersey
Published simultaneously in Canada

For general information on our other products and services or for technical support, please contact our Cus-
tomer Care Department within the United States at (800) 762-2974, outside the United States at (317) 572-
3993 or fax (317) 572-4002.

Wiley also publishes its books in a variety of electronic formats. Some content that appears in print may not be
available in electronic books. For more information about Wiley products, visit our web site at www.wiley.com.

LIBRARY OF CONGRESS CATALOGING-IN-PUBLICATION DATA:

Fairchild, Barbara, 1951-
Bon appétit : fast easy fresh / Barbara Fairchild; photographs by France Ruffenach.
    p. cm.
Includes index.
ISBN 978-0-470-22630-8 (cloth : alk. paper)
ISBN 978-0-470-39912-5 (special edition)
1. Cookery. I. Bon appétit. II. Title.
TX714.F3358 2008
641.5--dc22

                            2007044562

Printed in the United States of America

10 9 8 7 6 5 4 3 2 1

contents

Recipes

CHAPTER 4
Salads 101

CHAPTER 5

Sandwiches, Burgers, and Pizzas 145

SANDWICHES 148

BURGERS 171

CHAPTER 6
Pasta and Rice 197

CHAPTER 8
Salmon and More Fish 301

SALMON 304

SCALLOPS 355

CLAMS AND MUSSELS 360

LOBSTER AND CRAB 362

CHAPTER 10

Beef, Pork, and Lamb 367

BEEF 370

VEAL 393

CHAPTER 11
Potatoes, Grains, and Beans 429

CHAPTER 12
Vegetables 455

CHAPTER 13

Breakfast and Brunch 489

CHAPTER 14

Quick Breads 529

CHAPTER 16

Cookies and Brownies, Pies and Tarts, and Easy Cakes 593

COOKIES AND BROWNIES 597

PIES AND TARTS 613

EASY CAKES 623

CHAPTER 17

Custards, Puddings, and Fruit Desserts 633

acknowledgments

There is a word in the title of this book that really exemplifies everything about it.

That word is *fast*.

When we first discussed putting together a book of quick, easy, every-night-type recipes—with a modern sensibility that reflects the terrific fresh ingredients that are so accessible these days—we knew that timing was everything. We wanted to get a book like this into the marketplace as soon as possible. The topic is timely, there wasn't another cookbook like it, and the book would carry the credibility, care, and trustworthiness of the BON APPÉTIT name.

We also knew that we wanted it to be big—very big—a book that could be referred to again and again. So why not more than 1,000 recipes? Why not, indeed? We do dream big around here.

Believe it or not, that discussion took place less than two years ago—a fast track in the book publishing world if there ever was one. We took inspiration from the similarly titled column that runs in the magazine every month. "Fast Easy Fresh" has been around for only four years or so (a youngster relative to BON APPÉTIT's 52-year history), but it quickly became the go-to destination of busy home cooks. Reader feedback was instant: Readers were instantly in love. In my opinion, the secret ingredient is that all of the recipes are developed and created by our veteran test kitchen staff. Who better than Sarah Tenaglia, Lena Cederhan Birnbaum, Selma Brown Morrow, and Janet Taylor McCracken—with a combined total of 62 years at the magazine—to know what our readers want to cook? Under the expert direction of food editor Kristine Kidd (with 25 years on staff herself), this team continues to amaze and impress with their delicious, sophisticated takes on weeknight cooking. Their stellar work planted the seed for this stellar volume.

As you may have surmised by now, I tend to specialize in staff people with Type-A personalities. We had plenty of them on this project, all of them dedicated to it from the very beginning. Many of them were also instrumental in putting together our first big book—the very successful The Bon Appétit Cookbook—that debuted in 2006, the magazine's 50th anniversary. Sarah Tenaglia helped bring this book to fruition with her thoughtful evaluation and selection of our very best fast-easy-fresh recipes. Bon Appétit editors Amy Albert, Nina Elder, Camille Hahn, and Managing Editor Katie O'Kennedy—along with contributors Jeanne Thiel Kelley, Monica Parcell, and Rochelle Palermo—wrote the recipe headnotes, tips, and sidebars, helping to put the unique Bon Appétit imprint on every page. Much of the groundwork came from Bon Appétit magazine staff putting in extra time—late nights, weekends, whatever it took. On pages 704–707, you'll find the names of all the individuals who made this book what it is, contributing and testing recipes, writing, copy editing and proofreading, checking the facts. I am fortunate to work with such a talented and involved group of people who care so much about Bon Appétit and its reputation for quality.

It was Executive Editor Victoria von Biel who put together the initial proposal, tackling the project with enthusiasm, clarity and, frankly, a vested interest: As my superstar right-hand at the magazine, this very busy mother of two daughters clearly has a demanding job. She's also a foodie: She loves to cook, try new recipes, and experiment with ingredients she finds at farmers' market. So Victoria knew exactly what she wanted in a book like this. That personal view helped focus and inform the book from the outset.

Taking the compiled recipe list, clearing rights, obtaining any necessary permissions, liaising with attorneys, dotting all the i's and crossing all the t's (and then some) is the specialty of Marcy MacDonald, our Editorial Business

Director. Sometimes I feel as if Marcy has ten hands, six telephones, and four fax machines: She is a wonder, and I always know that she'll put the interests of BON APPÉTIT above all. Her assistant, Zoë Adnopoz, has Marcy's back; she and staffer Marcia Hartmann Lewis were invaluable in securing each of the 1,000+ recipes in this book.

The calm, even hand for me on a daily basis is Susan Champlin, the editor of this book (and the 2006 50th anniversary "bible") and a smart, trusted colleague and friend. Susan always manages to bring my own craziness down a few notches on particularly busy days. I can't begin to thank her enough and to tell her how much that means to me. She has my utmost respect.

Of course, a BON APPÉTIT cookbook wouldn't be complete without stunning visuals—from the beautifully clean, user-friendly design by Alison Lew and her staff at Vertigo Design, to the charming illustrations by Jessica Allen, and, of course, the beautiful and inspiring photography of France Ruffenach. I thank BON APPÉTIT's gifted, hard-working Photo Editor, Liz Mathews, and our talented Design Director Matthew Lenning, who enriched this book with their expertise.

On the publishing side, over at John Wiley & Sons, I was fortunate enough to once again have as my editor—well, my partner and guide, really—the unflappable Pamela Chirls. Pam is a terrific advocate for all things BON APPÉTIT: She makes us feel special and so well taken care of. I have such admiration for her work and her knowledge of the cookbook business. Pam has my everlasting gratitude for the hours of brainpower she has put into our books.

A few other personal notes. Special thanks to Condé Nast chairman Si Newhouse for his continuing passion for and commitment to magazines in an increasingly digital/Internet world; sincere appreciation to Condé Nast President and CEO Chuck Townsend; and gratitude beyond measure to Condé Nast editorial director Tom Wallace—for his support and counsel, as well as for his sense of humor. Our monthly meetings are always stimulating and fun.

There are four other men in my life who provide a caring and consistent presence. David Black says that he is a book agent, but to me he is mentor, book-business guru, and, yes, even wine advisor. Also a dear friend. Dennis O'Brien is the executive assistant everyone wishes they could have. He knows my schedule better than I do, and he has never failed to point me in the right direction, at the right time, to the right place. And this is while fielding all the phone calls, e-mails, and faxes that punctuate a typical day at the office.

Finally, words really can't adequately express my thanks to the two Pauls—Jowdy and Nagle: The former my valued business partner at the office; the latter my cherished life partner, always and forever.

BARBARA FAIRCHILD
Editor-in-Chief

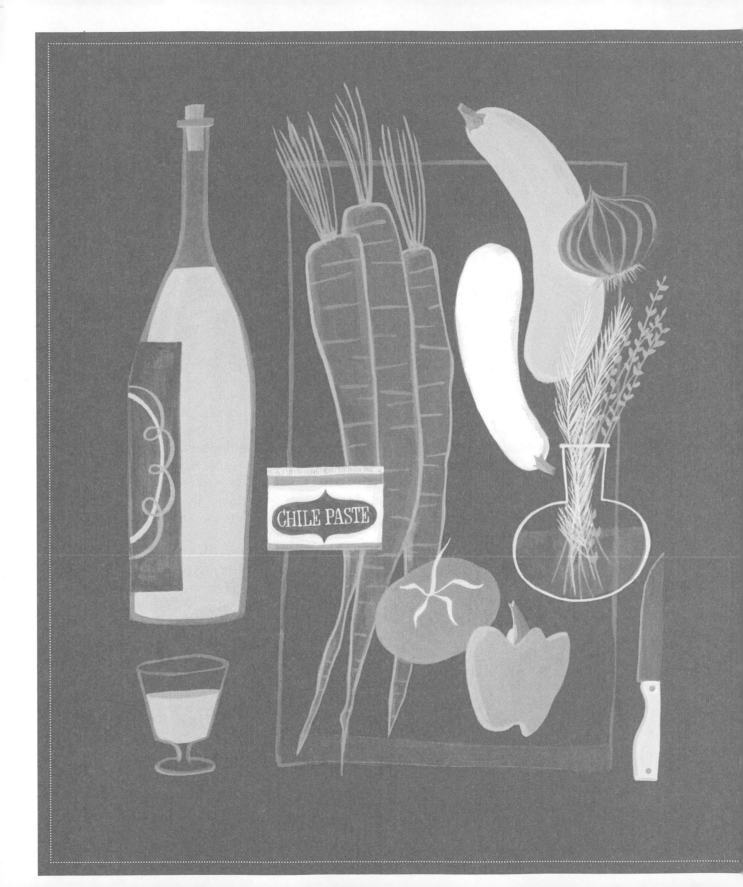

introduction

Even if you love to cook as much as I do, getting a meal on the table can seem like running a marathon. And no one lacks for excuses to stay out of the kitchen: the kids' soccer practice, answering e-mail, quick pizza delivery, good cable TV. We're busy, our families have crazy schedules, and grocery shopping is seldom a chore we look forward to. The simple ritual of sitting around the table and sharing a meal, like friends and families should, is not so simple to carry off.

Well, I'm here to tell you that it can be done. In fact, the inspiration behind this book was to prove that you *can* create a delicious, fresh meal that takes minimal effort to prepare—and you won't be up until midnight cleaning dishes afterward. Yes, even on a Tuesday night when life seems out of control and the cupboard is (almost) bare.

Part of the fast, easy, fresh strategy comes down to how you prefer to put together your meals. Are you a planner by nature, someone who likes to make lists and sort out the week's meals in advance? You can use the book that way: Sit down with it on a Saturday or Sunday and map out several dinners. Then hit the supermarket or (even easier) order your groceries using an online service like FreshDirect or Peapod. We've provided plenty of tips and ideas for making things ahead of time, so that all you have to do is assemble the components right before supper.

Or are you, like me, a spur-of-the-moment cook, someone who suddenly starts wondering at four in the afternoon what to make for dinner? My usual strategy—and I know I'm not alone—is to head to the supermarket or farmers' market and see what looks good. Sometimes it's a pile of gorgeous heirloom tomatoes or some crisp winter greens; sometimes it's the Copper River salmon just flown in from Alaska or a plump free-range chicken; sometimes it's a jar of Thai red chile paste that suddenly reminds me I'd love to make a spicy dish tonight.

If that's how you like to cook, then *Fast Easy Fresh* is perfect for you. Unlike traditional cookbooks that are organized by course, we've put this book together a little differently, organizing it by ingredients and types of dishes, as well as by course. If you've got a freezer full of chicken breasts or shrimp, a bumper crop of zucchini, or a family who will only eat burgers on Wednesday night, no problem. We've made it easy for you to find just the right recipe—and pull it together fast.

What makes these recipes special is that they've all been tested (and retested and then tested again) by the expert cooks in the BON APPÉTIT Test Kitchen. And we've kept in mind what's most important when time is short: You won't find long lists of hard-to-find ingredients. Recipe preparation is streamlined with plenty of shortcuts. And every meal will have your own touch and taste magnificent.

And a variety of handy features help make your time in the kitchen even more efficient and productive:

Our **"Shopping Guide"** shows you how to select, store and use the freshest fruits, vegetables, herbs, meats, fish and shellfish, and cheeses.

"Tool Kit" sidebars in each chapter are packed with ideas and information—mini recipes, ingredient substitions and pairings, kitchen science—that will expand your cooking repertoire even beyond the recipes in the chapter.

Recipe headnotes provide the background info you need to prepare each dish, as well as serving suggestions, ingredient info and shopping tips.

Test kitchen tips and sidebars offer the trademark BON APPÉTIT insights that simplify and amplify the recipes: easy-to-follow technique explanations, short-cut hints, suggested ingredient substitutions, and more.

Here's the bottom line: Every meal will have your own touch and taste magnificent.

Whether you are a long-time BON APPÉTIT reader or new to our fast, easy, fresh philosophy, look at this book as an invitation to come back to the kitchen. Your Tuesday nights will never be the same.

BARBARA FAIRCHILD

shoppingguide

Who doesn't love the idea of preparing fast, easy, fresh meals? The recipes in this cookbook have you covered on the "fast" and "easy" fronts. Now how about the "fresh?" Following is an overview on shopping for produce, cheeses, fish, poultry, and meats, as well as a guide to the ingredients used most frequently in this book. This should help you to select the freshest possible ingredients—and obtain the best possible results—as you prepare these fast and easy recipes.

FRUITS AND VEGETABLES

There has been an exciting boom in the growth of farmers' markets and CSAs (community supported agriculture) across the country, offering an expanding variety of fresh, local, and often organic produce. The food at farmers' markets has generally been picked that morning—it's hard to beat this kind of freshness unless you have your own garden.

But farmers' markets aren't available to everyone year-round, and for some they're not available at all. When shopping in a supermarket, opt for seasonal and local produce wherever possible; if it's organic, so much the better.

But beware of out-of-season organic produce: Most likely it has been shipped from another continent, so it is not only a few days older, but a lot of fossil fuels were used to get it to you.

A note on seasonality: In the ingredient guide on the following pages, we list the seasons in which fruits and vegetables are fresh. Many of these items are now available year-round (grapes, for instance)—but be aware that these fruits and vegetables do have a natural season during which the quality and variety will be at their peak.

FISH AND SHELLFISH

Years ago, we never thought twice about what kind of fish to have for dinner: We just bought what we liked or what was on sale. Now there are concerns about dwindling fish supplies, and questions about whether to buy farm-raised or wild-caught fish. The best guidelines come from the Monterey Bay Aquarium Foundation, available at mbayaq.org. There are even region-specific printable pocket guides (updated every few months) that you can take to the store. The guides (or a knowledgeable fishmonger) can suggest substitutes for overfished or endangered fish—fortunately, there are still plenty of varieties in abundant supply.

POULTRY

Chicken, turkey, and egg production have become highly industrialized over the last few decades, but we're now witnessing a backlash against the use of antibiotics. We have found in the Bon Appétit Test Kitchen that organic chicken not only helps to keep the environment and our bodies healthier, it actually tastes better. If your market doesn't carry organic chicken, look for chicken that is antibiotic-free. Kosher chicken is a great choice, but do not use kosher chickens in recipes that call for brining. Part of the koshering process entails a soak in a saltwater bath, and a second brining could make the dish too salty.

BEEF

Grass-fed and organic beef are becoming more and more popular—and for good reason: Cattle are *supposed* to eat grass. Studies are beginning to show that meat from grass-fed cattle is not only lower in fat, but the fat has more of the healthy omega-3 fatty acids. If grass-fed or organic beef isn't available (or is too expensive), look for beef that has been raised without hormones and antibiotics, often labeled "natural beef," which is much easier to find.

Those are the broad strokes—now here's a guide to selecting many of the individual ingredients you'll find in this book.

FRUITS

Apples

SEASON: Late summer and fall.

SELECTING: There are thousands of varieties of apples, with colors varying from deep green to rosy pink to dark burgundy. Each variety has its own flavor and texture, so it's important to use the type of apple called for in a recipe. Choose firm, heavy fruit without any wrinkles or bruises. Avoid any apples with tears or holes in the skin.

STORING: Apples will last for several weeks stored unwrapped in the refrigerator.

USING: Apples tend to brown quickly once exposed to the air, so cut them up just before using.

Bananas

SEASON: Fall and winter.

SELECTING: Perfectly ripe bananas are firm with yellow skin. Don't worry if there are only green bananas at the market. They will ripen when allowed to stand at room temperature for a few days.

STORING: Keep bananas in a well-ventilated spot at room temperature.

USING: If bananas are being used in baked goods like banana bread, use overripe bananas or bananas with lots of brown spots all over them. They will be very soft and sweet, and will impart the deep banana flavor desired in baked goods. Peeled overripe bananas can be stored in the freezer in resealable plastic bags for later use.

Berries

SEASON: Spring (strawberries), summer into fall (blackberries, blueberries, raspberries).

SELECTING: The freshest berries will have a deeply sweet and floral aroma and look like they are bursting with juices. Avoid any with green on them—they're underripe.

STORING: Store berries in the refrigerator. If you need to hold them for more than a day, line an airtight container with paper towels, add unrinsed berries in a single layer, and top with another paper towel or two to absorb additional moisture and prevent molding. Seal the container and chill; the berries should last up to five days.

USING: Rinse berries just before using, not before storing, to help prevent mold from developing. Remove the hull, if necessary, before using.

Citrus

SEASON: Late spring and summer (limes), year-round (oranges, lemons, grapefruit).

SELECTING: Select fruit that feels heavy for its size—a sure sign that it is fresh and packed with juice. The fruit should be firm, especially if the peel is being used in a recipe. Softer fruits are difficult to grate and peel, but may be perfect for juicing.

STORING: Citrus fruits can be stored uncovered at room temperature for several days or can last for several weeks when stored uncovered in the refrigerator.

USING: Scrub the fruit if using the peel in a recipe. When the peel is required, use only the colored part, leaving the bitter white pith behind.

citrus fruits

Cranberries

SEASON: Fall.

SELECTING: Color will vary in this classic holiday fruit. The whiter berries tend to be a bit milder, while the dark red ones have a deep cranberry flavor. Cranberries should be full and firm, and show no signs of brown or soft spots. Fresh cranberries will bounce when dropped.

STORING: Store cranberries in plastic bags in the refrigerator for up to one month.

USING: This is one fruit that freezes beautifully. Keep the fruit frozen and use as directed in the recipe.

Dates

SEASON: Late summer to mid-fall, year-round for dried dates.

SELECTING: There are many varieties of dates, but the Medjool (large and very moist) and the Deglet Noor (medium size, slightly firm, with drier skin) are the most common. There are many other varieties available, especially if you visit a Middle Eastern market or a farmers' market.

STORING: Fresh dates, wrapped in plastic, can last in the refrigerator for about two weeks. The more commonly found dried dates can be stored in a cool dry place for about one month or in the refrigerator for several months.

USING: Remove the pit before using.

Figs

SEASON: Summer and fall, year-round for dried figs.

SELECTING: Fresh figs have a sweet scent and should feel soft when they are pressed with your fingertip. The best dried figs are sticky and moist.

STORING: Fresh figs can be stored at room temperature for a few days and up to a week in the refrigerator. Dried figs can be stored tightly wrapped at room temperature for several months.

USING: Trim the stem before using. Except for the stem, the entire fruit is edible.

Grapes

SEASON: Summer and fall.

SELECTING: Check grapes where the stems and the fruit meet: There should be no wrinkling or browning. Avoid any bunches with brown or mushy grapes attached.

STORING: Place the grapes in plastic bags and store them in the refrigerator for up to one week.

USING: Remove the stems before using.

Kiwis

SEASON: Winter.

SELECTING: Ripe kiwis should be firm without any soft spots, but should yield slightly when pressed gently with your thumb.

STORING: If the kiwis are still a bit firm, let them stand at room temperature for a few days or until ripe. Once ripe, store kiwis in the refrigerator for up to a week.

USING: Peel the fuzzy skin from the kiwi before using. Or for a quick snack, cut the kiwi in half crosswise and scoop out the green flesh with a spoon.

Mangoes

SEASON: Spring.

SELECTING: Mangoes should give just a bit when pressed with your thumb and should feel heavy for their size when held in your hand. The green-and-orange variety most commonly available in stores can often be stringy, but many supermarkets now carry other varieties, such as Champagne and Honey, which are worth trying.

STORING: Store mangoes at room temperature until ripe, then refrigerate for up to five days.

USING: Cut the flesh away from the large narrow pit in the center of the fruit, then peel and use as directed.

Melons

SEASON: Summer into fall.

SELECTING: There are two different types of melons, and each has its own test for ripeness. The ribbed or scaly skin varieties, such as cantaloupe, have net-like or scaly ridges that cover the skin. These melons are the easiest to choose because they will smell sweet when fully ripe. The stem end of the melon should give slightly when pressed with your thumb. With smooth-skinned melons, such as watermelon and crenshaw, the best bet is to pick one that is heavy for its size, and to listen for a hollow sound (not a dull thud) when you thump it. For both types, check for a yellow (not white) spot on one side of the melon. This shows that the melon rested longer on the ground, indicating that it had a chance to ripen on the vine.

STORING: Melons can be stored at room temperature for a few days to ripen. When ripe, transfer to the refrigerator. If you'd like, cut up the melon before refrigerating it, place melon pieces in a bowl, then cover and chill for a day or two.

USING: Except for watermelon, scoop out the seeds from the center of the melon before using. Remove the peel before eating.

Papayas

SEASON: Spring and fall.

SELECTING: Ripe papayas give slightly when pressed at the narrow end of the fruit, or the whole fruit may give slightly when squeezed. The skin will be yellow and may have a few small brown spots on it.

STORING: Store papayas at room temperature until ripe. Once ripe, they can be stored in the refrigerator for a day or two.

USING: Cut the papaya in half and scoop out the small round black seeds. Remove the skin before eating.

Pears

SEASON: Late summer through early spring.

SELECTING: There are many varieties of pears, each with its own distinct beauty, flavor, and season. Choose pears with a delicate aroma and no blemishes or soft spots. The skin should be taut without any wrinkling around the stem end. Ripe pears feel heavy for their size and give slightly when pressure is applied to the stem end.

STORING: Pears can be stored at room temperature until ripe and then transferred to the refrigerator for a few days.

USING: Remove the core before using. Peeling is optional.

Pineapples

SEASON: Winter to midsummer.

SELECTING: A ripe pineapple has a splendid aroma and yellow skin with tinges of brown, along with green leaves.

STORING: Store pineapples at room temperature to ripen if necessary.

USING: Cut away the thick skin and remove the core before using. Fresh pineapple chunks can be stored in a sealed container in the refrigerator for a few days.

pomegranate

Stone fruits

SEASON: Late spring into midsummer (apricots), summer (cherries, nectarines, peaches).

SELECTING: Stone fruits should be firm and plump with juices and feel heavy. They should smell sweet and floral. Look for deep rich color. Cherries should have supple stems attached. Peaches, nectarines, and apricots should not have any green spots on them, even at the stem end; this is a sign that the fruit was picked too early and may never ripen properly.

STORING: Store stone fruits at room temperature for a day or two if not completely ripe, then refrigerate for up to three days.

USING: Remove the pits before using. Peeling is optional.

VEGETABLES

Asparagus

SEASON: Spring.

SELECTING: Asparagus tips should be tightly bundled and show no signs of sprouting or softening. Look for firm stalks without any wrinkles. The cut ends of fresh asparagus will be moist.

STORING: If not using asparagus right away, cut the bottom inch off the stalks and place cut side down in a glass filled with an inch of water. Cover loosely with a plastic bag and store in the refrigerator for a few days.

USING: Trim the ends of the stalks. Peel thick asparagus with a vegetable peeler to remove the tough skin. Thin asparagus does not need to be peeled. They're both delicious; just be sure to cook thin and thick stalks separately, as cooking times will vary.

Pomegranates

SEASON: Fall.

SELECTING: Since some varieties of pomegranate have pink skin and others have deep red skin, and because they don't smell sweet when they are ripe, it can be tricky to pick out a ripe one. The best method is to select fruit that is heavy for its size. Pomegranates do not ripen after being picked.

STORING: Whole pomegranates can be stored in a cool dry place for up to one month or in the refrigerator for up to two months. The seeds can be removed and frozen for several months.

USING: The seeds are the only edible part of the pomegranate. The skin is tough and leathery, and the white membrane that covers the seeds is bitter and astringent. Wear an apron and gloves when removing seeds from a pomegranate—the juices can stain clothes and skin. Prepackaged seeds are available at many supermarkets and are a great time-saver.

avoCado

Avocados

SEASON: Year-round.

SELECTING: Avocados are picked when still hard and green, but they will ripen when allowed to sit at room temperature. The skin of some avocado varieties will darken to almost black when ripe. The fruit should feel firm and give slightly when pressed gently with your thumb. Avoid any avocados with hollow pockets between the skin and the flesh.

STORING: Let avocados stand at room temperature until they are ripe, and then transfer them to the refrigerator. Ripe avocados will last several days when chilled.

USING: Avocados brown rapidly once they are cut. A good, simple do-ahead trick when using diced or sliced avocados in a recipe: Run the cut avocados under water, then cover and chill. The avocado will not brown for several hours. If the avocado is mashed, as for guacamole, a squirt of lemon or lime juice will help prevent it from turning brown. Store any leftovers in the refrigerator with plastic wrap pressed directly on top of the guacamole.

Beans (Green and Yellow)

SEASON: Spring through summer.

SELECTING: Fresh beans will snap crisply in two, and may even have small white flowers still attached. Avoid any beans with brown spots.

STORING: Beans can be stored in plastic bags in the refrigerator for three to five days.

USING: The stem end needs to be trimmed just before using, either by snapping it off or trimming it with a knife. The slender wispy end can be trimmed or left intact as a matter of preference.

Beets

SEASON: Summer.

SELECTING: They aren't just purple anymore. Now there are golden, white, red, and Chioggia beets, sometimes called "candy cane" for their interior pink and white stripes. With the fabulous variety available at many supermarkets and farmers' markets, any recipe calling for beets can become a thing of colorful beauty. Look for beets with their greens still attached. The beets should have smooth skins without blemishes, cracks, or many hairy roots attached.

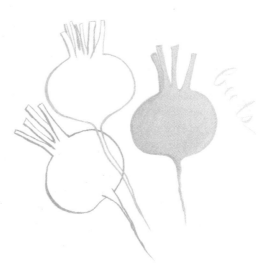

STORING: Just after purchasing, cut off all but two inches of the greens—but don't discard them. They are delicious when quickly sautéed, and are packed with vitamins and minerals. Store the beets and greens separately in the refrigerator for several days.

USING: Cook beets unpeeled. Leave a few inches of the stems and the root end attached to prevent loss of color and flavor. Peel and trim beets after cooking. It's a good idea to put on a pair of plastic gloves before peeling red beets to avoid staining hands.

Broccoli

SEASON: Year-round.

SELECTING: The freshest broccoli has firm stalks with tender skin. The cut end should be moist. The buds on top should be tight and show no signs of yellow flowering.

STORING: Store unwashed broccoli for a few days in a plastic bag in the refrigerator.

USING: Trim the stalks before using. If the skin on the stalks is woody and tough, it can be peeled off and discarded. Otherwise the stalk can be peeled, sliced, and cooked along with the florets.

Broccoli Rabe

SEASON: Fall through spring.

SELECTING: Broccoli rabe (also called *rapini*) looks like leafy underdeveloped broccoli, although it is not related. Look for bunches with long stalks and leaves that aren't wilted or yellowing. The stalks may have a few yellow flowers attached.

STORING: Wrap in plastic bags and refrigerate for a few days.

USING: Trim the ends of the stalks and remove any yellowed leaves before cooking. Use both the stalks and the pungent-tasting leaves.

Cabbages and Brussels Sprouts

SEASON: Summer (Chinese cabbages), fall and winter (cabbages and brussels sprouts).

SELECTING: The heads of round cabbages, such as red and green cabbage, as well as brussels sprouts, should be tightly packed and give only slightly when squeezed. Chinese cabbages, such as bok choy and Napa cabbage, are leafier and will be tight only at the base. The leaves should be crisp and show no signs of wilting or browning around the edges.

STORING: Place cabbages in plastic bags and store in the refrigerator. Chinese cabbages can be stored for several days. Although best within a few days of purchase, large round cabbages and brussels sprouts can be refrigerated for up to two weeks.

USING: Cabbage can be eaten raw, cooked in a variety of ways, and pickled. Remove any wilted outer leaves, if necessary.

brussels sprouts

Carrots

SEASON: Year-round.

SELECTING: Here's another vegetable that can now be found in a variety of colors such as white, yellow, red, and purple. The freshest carrots are brightly colored with the greens still attached. The tops should be vibrant green, not yellow or limp. If you stick your thumbnail into a fresh carrot, it should be juicy. Be wary of packages marked "baby carrots"; often they are just large older carrots cut into small pieces.

STORING: Remove the greens, leaving about two inches from the top of the carrots. Store carrots in plastic bags in the refrigerator for up to two weeks.

USING: Whether to scrub or peel carrots before cooking is a matter of preference, but do not peel baby carrots or you may find that there's not much left afterward. However, it is important to scrub and not peel red carrots: Their beauty really is only skin deep—peeling them will leave you with an orange carrot.

Cauliflower

SEASON: Year-round.

SELECTING: Purchase cauliflower without any brown or black spots. The leaves should be crisp and pale green, and the cut end should be moist. Cauliflower comes in the standard white, as well as in purple, orange, and green.

STORING: Cauliflower can be stored in plastic bags in the refrigerator for a few days.

USING: Remove the core and leaves of large heads of cauliflower and separate the head into florets. Baby varieties can be steamed or roasted whole with leaves intact.

Celery Root (Celeriac)

SEASON: Fall.

SELECTING: It's hard to believe that underneath all of that rough, gnarly skin lies a versatile vegetable with such a delicate flavor. Try to find celery root with the dark green leaves attached and showing no signs of wilting or browning. Avoid any with soft spots on the outside, as this is a sign of rotting. Choose roots that are about 4 to 5 inches in diameter and heavy for their size. Very large ones tend to have woody cores.

STORING: Keep uncovered celery root in the refrigerator for a day or two.

USING: Celery root browns quickly once exposed to air. Either cut celery root just before using or place cut pieces into a bowl of cold water with a splash of lemon juice to prevent browning.

Corn

SEASON: Summer.

SELECTING: The freshest corn will have bright green husks that show no signs of browning at the edges. The silks should be golden at the tips, not brown or black. Peel down the husk just an inch or two to check that the kernels are fully developed and are formed in straight, tight rows. The kernels should be plump, and juicy if pierced with your nail.

STORING: Corn is best cooked the day it is picked. Store unwrapped in the refrigerator.

USING: Since the husk helps to keep the corn moist, it is best to wait and husk corn just before using.

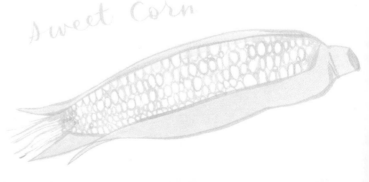

Sweet Corn

Cucumber

SEASON: Summer.

SELECTING: Choose firm cucumbers that aren't wrinkled at the ends.

STORING: Cucumbers can be stored, unwashed, wrapped in plastic for a few days in the refrigerator.

USING: Cucumbers with dark thick skin are often waxed to prevent moisture loss. The skin can be unpleasant to eat, so it is best to peel this variety. These cucumbers often have large seeds that are easily scraped out with a spoon. Thin-skinned cucumbers, such as Persian, Japanese, and English hothouse cucumbers, do not need to be peeled or seeded. Be sure to wrap any unused portions tightly in plastic before refrigerating.

Eggplant

SEASON: Summer.

SELECTING: Eggplant that is heavy for its size is the freshest. Look for firm, taut skin without any bruising or discoloration. (Eggplant is actually a fruit but is usually thought of as a vegetable—hence the categorization.)

STORING: Eggplant will last about four days when stored in the refrigerator wrapped in plastic.

USING: Eggplant is always cooked. The skin is edible, so peeling is a matter of preference.

Fennel

SEASON: Fall to spring.

SELECTING: Choose white bulbs with pale green accents. Avoid any bulbs that have brown spots. When purchasing fennel from the supermarket, the tops will have been removed. If the fronds are needed for a recipe, ask the produce manager for tops. They usually have some available in the back of the store.

STORING: If bulbs are purchased with tops attached, cut tops away and store leafy green fronds and bulbs separately in the refrigerator for a few days.

USING: If any small brown spots develop, they can be removed with a vegetable peeler, if necessary.

garlic press

Garlic

SEASON: Summer.

SELECTING: The whole head of garlic should feel firm when given a good squeeze in the palm of your hand. There should be no sign of green sprouts emerging from the top of the bulb. Check to be sure that there are no cloves that look brown or concave.

STORING: Store garlic in a dark, well-ventilated area at room temperature.

USING: Garlic that has been smashed or chopped needs to be refrigerated if not being used right away.

Ginger

SEASON: Fall.

SELECTING: Look for firm knobs with dry, pale yellow skin that shows no sign of wrinkles or mold.

STORING: Ginger can be stored at room temperature for several days or unwrapped in the refrigerator for about two weeks.

USING: Peel ginger before using.

ginger root

Greens (Swiss Chard, Collard Greens, Dandelion, Kale, Mustard Greens)

SEASON: Winter into spring (collard greens, dandelion, mustard greens), summer (Swiss chard), winter (kale).

SELECTING: Purchase crisp, vibrantly colored greens that don't have any brown spots or signs of wilting.

STORING: Store greens in plastic bags in the refrigerator. If there is moisture on the leaves from supermarket misters, wrap them in a paper towel first, then in plastic to keep them crisp and fresh and to prevent rotting. Greens will last three to five days in the refrigerator.

USING: Trim the tough stalk from greens before using. The stalks can be eaten, but need a very long cooking time, whereas the leaves cook quickly.

Lettuces

SEASON: Spring (baby lettuces, watercress), summer into fall (arugula, escarole), fall to spring (Belgian endive), winter to spring (chicory, mâche, radicchio).

SELECTING: Purchase lettuces that are pert and crisp and show no signs of wilting or browning around the edges.

STORING: All lettuce should wrapped in plastic and stored in the refrigerator, except for watercress, which should be stored in the refrigerator, leaves down in a bowl of cold water. If lettuce has any moisture clinging to the leaves, place a paper towel in the plastic bag to absorb moisture and prevent the lettuce from wilting and browning. Some lettuces, such as endive, are sold in containers with absorbent pads inside to soak up any excess moisture.

USING: Tender lettuce leaves, such as butter and red leaf lettuce, need to be torn gently to prevent damage to the leaves. Tougher leaves, such as romaine and iceberg, can be chopped with a knife if being used within a few hours. Be sure to check the expiration date on prepackaged lettuce before using.

Onions and Leeks

SEASON: Spring to summer (Vidalia onions, green onions), summer to fall (red, white, yellow storage onions), winter (leeks).

SELECTING: Choose onions that are firm and heavy for their size. There shouldn't be any green sprouts coming out of the tops. The skin should be dry without any sign of black mold. Green onions and leeks should be chosen for their fresh root ends and deep green tops.

STORING: Most onions can be stored at room temperature in a dark, well-ventilated area for about a month. Green onions and leeks should be stored in plastic bags in the refrigerator for up to five days.

USING: Before using, remove peel and root end from onions. The root ends of green onions and leeks should also be trimmed and discarded just before using. Leeks require thorough washing, as the leaves trap grit.

Parsnips

SEASON: Fall and winter.

SELECTING: Choose parsnips that are pale yellow in color, firm, and clean of any hairy root sprouts. Purchase parsnips that are less than ten inches long, as larger parsnips tend to be tough and woody.

STORING: Store parsnips in plastic bags in the refrigerator for up to two weeks.

USING: Parsnips are always cooked. Trim and peel parsnips before using.

Mushrooms

SEASON: Commercially cultivated year-round; spring (wild morels), fall (oyster mushrooms).

SELECTING: Choose mushrooms with smooth caps and edges that curl under; a flat top is a sign of age. Mushrooms should not feel at all slimy, but rather smooth and slightly moist.

STORING: Store mushrooms in brown paper bags in the refrigerator for just a few days.

USING: There is a lot of debate about how to clean mushrooms. Never soak mushrooms in water: They are like sponges and will soak up the water. Instead, quickly rinse dirty mushrooms under cold running water, or use a damp towel to wipe off cleaner mushrooms. Pat mushrooms dry before using. Avoid mushroom brushes—not only are they ineffective, but they also tend to cause scratching.

Mushroom stems are edible, with the exception of shiitake mushroom stems, which must be removed before using, as they become tough and inedible when cooked. All other mushroom stems simply need to be trimmed.

Peas

SEASON: Spring.

SELECTING: Sugar snap pea, snow pea, and English pea pods should be crisp and snap easily in half. The pods should show no signs of wrinkling, but don't worry if they are a bit scratched. Pea sprouts and their older siblings, pea shoots, should be bright green and show no sign of wilting. If possible, purchase pea shoots with flowers on them. Not only are they pretty, but they are delicious, too, with the flavor of fresh peas.

STORING: All peas, pea sprouts, and pea tendrils should be wrapped in plastic and stored in the refrigerator after purchasing. Pea shoots, pea sprouts, and English peas should be used the same day that they are purchased. The sugar in English peas begins to turn to starch as soon as it is picked, but chilling will slow down this transformation. Sugar snap peas and snow peas can be stored for a few days wrapped in plastic in the refrigerator.

USING: It's best to shuck and cook English peas the same day that they are purchased. Be sure to pull the strings from along the sides of sugar snap and snow peas before cooking.

Peppers (Sweet and Hot)

SEASON: Summer into fall.

SELECTING: Choose peppers that are deeply colored—they will be more flavorful (this is especially true of red peppers). All peppers should be firm when squeezed, and free of wrinkles or cracks.

STORING: Store peppers in plastic bags in the refrigerator. They should last about one week.

USING: Stem and seed peppers before using. Hot peppers, such as jalapeños, can vary in heat. It's a good idea to start by adding a small amount to the recipe, and then taste and add more as desired. The seeds of hot peppers are often used in recipes.

Potatoes

SEASON: Fall, except russets (year-round), new potatoes (spring to early summer), and specialty potatoes (check supermarkets and farmers' markets).

SELECTING: Purchase potatoes with smooth skins that are not sprouting or beginning to turn green. Avoid potatoes with any nicks or brown spots.

STORING: Keep potatoes in a cool, dark, well-ventilated place away from onions. Do not store potatoes in the refrigerator. Chilling turns the starches into sugar, producing unappetizing flavors.

USING: Scrub potatoes before using. Be sure to scrub freshly dug potatoes gently, as the skin will come off easily.

Radishes

SEASON: Winter and spring.

SELECTING: Choose radishes with vibrant dark green tops that do not have any brown or wilted leaves. The radishes should not be cracked, and should feel firm when squeezed.

STORING: Place radishes in a plastic bag in the refrigerator for up to a week. If not using right away, cut the greens off before storing.

USING: Be sure to lightly scrub the radishes just before using to remove any soil.

radish

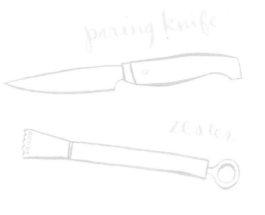

Spinach

SEASON: Spring.

SELECTING: Fresh spinach should be vibrant green without any dark spots. It should be crisp and show no signs of wilting. A great convenience product of the last decade is the prewashed spinach sold in plastic bags. Be sure to check the expiration date printed on the bag.

STORING: Store spinach wrapped in plastic bags in the refrigerator, where it will last for a few days. If the spinach is damp from supermarket misters, place a paper towel inside the bag to absorb moisture and prevent rotting.

USING: Trim any tough stems. If purchasing fresh spinach, be sure to wash the spinach well. Fill a sink with water, then place trimmed spinach leaves into the water. The sand will settle to the bottom of the sink. Lift the spinach out of the sink, and repeat until the water is clean.

Squash (Summer)

SEASON: Summer.

SELECTING: Although large squash look dramatic, they are very disappointing when cooked. Choose small- to medium-size squash for the best flavor and texture. Fresh squash will have smooth skin absent of any nicks or wrinkling.

STORING: Keep squash wrapped in plastic bags in the refrigerator. They should last for several days and up to one week. Place squash blossoms in plastic and store in the refrigerator. Squash blossoms must be used the day that they are picked.

USING: Rinse well and trim stem ends of squash before cooking. The stamen should be removed from inside squash blossoms before using.

Squash (Winter)

SEASON: Fall and winter.

SELECTING: Choose squash that are heavy for their size and without any damage to the skin. If the recipe calls for butternut squash, you can buy time-saving precut and peeled squash in plastic-wrapped packages at many supermarkets.

STORING: You can store most whole squash in a cool dark place up to one month, but thinner-skinned squash like delicata need to be eaten within a week. Be sure to store cut squash in the refrigerator and use it within a day or two.

USING: The seeds of winter squash can be removed either before cooking or after.

Sweet Potatoes

SEASON: Fall.

SELECTING: Choose small- or medium-size sweet potatoes with smooth skin—avoid those with bruises, tears, or wrinkles.

STORING: You can keep them in a cool, dark, dry place for up to one month (don't refrigerate them), but it's best to use them within a week.

USING: Pale-skinned sweet potatoes with pale yellow flesh can substitute for regular potatoes in recipes. Dark-skinned sweet potatoes with bright orange flesh (often mistakenly called yams) have a much moister texture and sweeter flavor. Both varieties should be scrubbed before using.

Tomatoes

SEASON: Summer.

SELECTING: Tomatoes (another fruit that's usually thought of as a vegetable) come in all different colors and sizes. Choose firm plump tomatoes that are heavy for their size and give slightly when pressed with your thumb. Avoid any with wrinkles or bruises. Aside from the Green Zebra tomato (an heirloom variety that is green when ripe) avoid tomatoes with green on them, a sign that they were picked too early—unless you're making fried green tomatoes, in which case you want the greenest, firmest tomatoes you can find.

STORING: Keep tomatoes at room temperature, avoiding direct sunlight. Do not store tomatoes in the refrigerator: This will give them a mealy texture and will alter their flavor.

USING: Remove stem and core from tomatoes before using.

HERBS

SEASON: Spring and summer.

SELECTING: Choose herbs that are aromatic. The leaves should be pert without any brown spots or signs of wilting. Avoid herbs that have begun to flower, which causes the flavor to diminish. The flowers on herbs are edible, however, and can make a lovely garnish.

STORING: Basil, cilantro, and parsley should be stored at room temperature with the trimmed stems submerged in a glass of water. If herbs such as chives, thyme, and rosemary will be used within a day, wrap in a damp paper towel, then place in a sealed plastic bag and chill. If not, trim ends and place them in a glass of water. Tent with a plastic bag and refrigerate for up to five days.

USING: Remove the tough stems from fresh herbs before using. Any tender stem ends can be chopped up and used.

cheeses, such as Havarti, Gorgonzola, and Muenster, in parchment or waxed paper to allow it to breathe. You may need to rewrap it occasionally to keep it fresh. Unless it is in a shrink-wrap package (as with fresh goat cheese) or already in a plastic resealable container (as with mascarpone), soft cheeses, such as Brie, young blue cheese, and fresh mozzarella, should be stored in plastic resealable containers. It is important to check cheese occasionally for signs of molding. If there is any mold, trim it away and store the cheese in fresh, clean wrappers or containers.

USING: Remove any hard rinds from cheeses such as Parmesan. Store the rinds wrapped tightly in plastic and freeze for later use in soups or sauces. If grating or cutting up a soft or semi-soft cheese, a 30-minute stint in the freezer makes the job a lot easier. If serving cheese on a cheese plate or as part of a composed salad, let the cheese come to room temperature for the best flavor.

CHEESES

SELECTING: Follow the sell-by dates on packaged cheese. Avoid cheese that looks dry or brittle, or that has any sign of molding, which can show itself with yellow or green streaking or coating. If possible, get to know a cheesemonger. They are often eager to offer samples and will help you choose the right cheeses for a recipe or a cheese plate.

STORING: If storing cheese for periods of time longer than a day or two, remove it from the original wrapper. Hard cheeses, such as Parmesan and ricotta salata, need to be wrapped in plastic or stored in plastic resealable bags to retain moisture. Semi-hard cheeses, such as cheddar and Swiss, can be stored in either waxed or parchment paper, or if you are concerned about the cheese drying out, it can also be wrapped in plastic wrap. Wrap semi-soft

SHELLFISH

SELECTING: Be sure to purchase fish from a reliable source. All shellfish still in their shells must be alive before cooking. A sign that shellfish in the shell are still alive is to give the shell a tap; it will close up quickly. Shells should not be cracked. When purchasing shellfish out of the shell, the freshest will smell sweet, not fishy. When purchasing scallops, try to find dry pack scallops. These are scallops that haven't been soaked in a solution that artificially plumps them up and turns the scallops white. Look for scallops that are plump, moist, and slightly translucent-looking. Most shrimp have been frozen and defrosted, so don't turn your nose up if it's labeled "frozen/defrosted." (It's also handy to have bags of frozen shrimp available to add to all kinds of dishes.)

STORING: Store all fresh shellfish over ice and covered in the refrigerator. Use within one day.

USING: Scrub shells well to remove any algae and sand. Remove the beard from mussels. Remove the small side muscle from scallops, since it gets tough when cooked. Discard any shellfish that do not open after cooking. This is a sign that they were dead before cooking.

FISH

SELECTING: It is important to purchase fish from a reliable source, where you know you are getting the freshest top-quality fish. Purchase fillets that look moist and smell fresh—there should be no fishy or ammonia odor. Whole fish should have eyes that are bright, not cloudy or sunken. The gills should be bright red, and the fish should not feel slimy.

STORING: Store fish in the refrigerator wrapped in plastic over a bed of ice for no more than a day or two.

USING: Rinse and pat fish dry before using.

POULTRY

SELECTING: If purchasing prepackaged poultry, be sure that it is tightly wrapped without any tears or holes in the packaging. Chicken should not be sticky to the touch or have any off odor.

STORING: Follow the sell-by date on wrapped packages of chicken. Poultry purchased from a butcher can be stored in the coldest part of the refrigerator for two to three days.

USING: Pat chicken dry before using.

MEATS

SELECTING: Beef and lamb should be a deep—but not cherry—red. There should be no signs of gray or purple colored flesh. Pork and veal should be rosy pink, not pale or gray. All meat should be firm; avoid any that feels soft or mushy. Look for nicely marbled cuts of meat, with fine lines of white fat throughout, ensuring a moist and flavorful dish. If purchasing prepackaged meat, be sure that it is tightly wrapped without any tears or holes in the plastic wrap.

STORING: Meats should be tightly wrapped and stored in the coldest part of your refrigerator.

USING: Use meat on or before the sell-by date listed on the package. If purchasing meat from a butcher, use within three days. Ground meats and fresh sausages should be used within one day of purchase. Be sure to follow the use-by dates on fully cooked sausages. Because different cuts of meat can require different cooking methods, it's important to use the cut that is called for in the recipe to ensure a successful result.

Making the grade When buying beef, veal, and lamb in retail stores, you'll find them categorized by USDA grades, which indicate (among other things) marbling (the streaks and speckles of fat within the meat) and therefore their expected tenderness, juiciness, and amount of flavor.

Beef may be marked Prime, Choice, or Select. Most veal and lamb in retail stores is marked either Prime or Choice. Pork isn't given USDA quality grades, as it generally comes from young animals that produce uniformly tender meat.

— Prime grade meat has the best marbling, which means it will be supremely tender, juicy, and flavorful. Only a small percentage of meat is prime—so it's more expensive and usually snapped up by restaurants—but you can find it at high-quality butcher shops and specialty markets. **PREPARATION:** Season minimally with salt, pepper, and a light drizzling of olive oil so that the flavor of the meat is not disguised, and use a quick, dry-heat cooking method.

— Choice grade is very high-quality meat, but has less marbling. **PREPARATION:** Choice roasts and steaks from the loin and rib are quite tender, juicy, and flavorful, and work well with dry-heat cooking. Even many less-tender cuts, such as those from the rump or round, can be cooked with dry heat, as long as you don't overcook them.

— Select grade beef is leaner than Prime and Choice, but still very good quality and widely available at supermarkets. **PREPARATION:** It is fairly tender, but with less marbling the meat has less flavor and juiciness, making it well suited for marinades, rubs, and barbecue sauces, which bolster the flavor.

quickstarters

SMALL BITES AND DIPS

Sweet Potato Ribbon Chips

Sugar and Spice Pepitas

Black Pepper Almonds

Marinated Olives with
Tangerine and Rosemary

Warm Spinach-Parmesan Dip

Garlic and Anchovy Dip
with Vegetables

Guacamole with
Roasted Tomatillos

Guacamole with Fresh
Corn and Chipotle

Dukkah

Preserved Lemon Dip

Black and White Bean Salsa

Salsa Verde

Mango and Red Onion Salsa

Beet, Chickpea, and Almond
Dip with Pita Chips

Parsley Hummus with
Cauliflower Crudités

Eggplant-Cilantro Spread

SMALL-PLATES APPETIZERS

Grilled Pesto Breadsticks with
Goat Cheese-Pesto Spread

Three-Cheese Fondue
with Champagne

Camembert with Blue
Cheese, Figs, and Port

Broiled Feta with Honey
and Aniseed

Grilled Chicken Skewers
with Red Pepper Pesto

Lamb Kebabs with
Pomegranate-Cumin Glaze

Deviled Cocktail Sausages with
Chutney and Lime Dipping Sauce

Herbed Goat Cheese with
Roasted Chiles and Olive Oil

Seared Ahi Tuna and
Avocado Tartare

Sliced Radishes and Watercress
on Buttered Ficelles

Smoked Salmon with
Mustard-Dill Sauce

PASSED APPETIZERS

White Cheddar Puffs
with Green Onions

Pizzette with Fontina, Tomato,
Basil, and Prosciutto

Black and Gold Pizzas

Grilled Prosciutto-Wrapped
Shrimp with Marsala Glaze

Skewered Shrimp with
Apricot-Curry Glaze

Crab Crostini with Green
Onions and Crème Fraîche

Mini Crab Cakes

Banana-Black Bean Empanadas

Zucchini Fritters

Wild Mushroom Crostini

Chorizo-Filled Dates
Wrapped in Bacon

Tomato-Coriander Bruschetta

Mushroom-Ham Brochettes
with Garlic Mayonnaise

Skirt-Steak Quesadillas

Spicy Pico de Gallo

Crabmeat, Corn, and Cumin
Salad in Endive Spears

Pancetta Crisps with
Goat Cheese and Pear

Prosciutto-Wrapped Figs with
Gorgonzola and Walnuts

Sesame Wonton Triangles with
Smoked Salmon and Wasabi

Shrimp Mousse Crostini with Dill

Beef Carpaccio Crostini with
Black Truffle Vinaigrette

Crostini with Burrata Cheese,
Pink Pepper, and Arugula

Bruschetta with Tomato,
Avocado, Basil, and Mint

FIRST COURSES

Mussels in Wine, Mustard,
and Saffron Broth

Steamed Clams with Spicy
Sausage and Tomatoes

Calamari Fritti with Creamy
Ponzu Dipping Sauce

Grilled Peaches with
Pecorino and Prosciutto

Parsnip and Pear Latkes

Chestnut Pancakes with
Bacon and Crème Fraîche

Goat Cheese and Herb Soufflés

Glazed Smoked Duck with
Candied Kumquats

Black Pepper Sabayon
on Asparagus

Fried Tofu with Spicy Miso Sauce

Honeydew and Prosciutto with
Greens and Mint Vinaigrette

Prosciutto with Persimmon,
Pomegranate, and Arugula

Asparagus with Gingered
Orange-Sesame Dressing

Antipasto Salad

Bresaola with Shaved Brussels
Sprouts and Horseradish

tool kit When it comes to starters, nothing is quicker, simpler, or more flavorful than a good salsa. Okay, so what makes a *good* salsa?

Ripe tomatoes (for red salsas) or tomatillos (for green salsas), combined with aromatic onions, garlic, cilantro, and tangy lemon or lime juice, form the foundation of most salsas. Chiles—fresh, dried, or ground— bring the heat, and salt intensifies all these vibrant flavors. Salsas range in spiciness and can be raw or cooked, pureed or chunky.

THE CHILE FACTOR

As a rule of thumb, the smaller the chile, the more piquancy it delivers, so keep this in mind when substituting chiles in any of your favorite salsa recipes. For less fire, remove the seeds and membranes. If using dried chiles such as anchos or chiles de árbol, first toast them in a dry skillet until slightly darker in color, then soak them in very hot water for 15 minutes or until they soften. Be careful not to touch your eyes after handling chiles, since the oils left behind on your fingers can cause a burning sensation.

MORE TO TRY

The salsas in this chapter provide great building blocks for your own creations. Here are a few twists:

— To bring out a full-bodied, roasted flavor in the **Salsa Verde,** broil the tomatillos, garlic, and serrano chile on a rimmed baking sheet until they blister and blacken before using them.

— Add a hot smoky flavor to the **Spicy Pico de Gallo** by using a chipotle chile (packed in a can with adobo sauce) in place of the jalapeño chiles.

— In the **Mango and Red Onion Salsa,** switch out the mango for other tropical fruits like pineapple or papaya, and use minced red jalapeño chile instead of the cayenne pepper.

QUICK FIXES

— When using purchased salsas, make them your own by adding fresh ingredients such as chopped cilantro, green onions, lemon or lime juice, finely grated lemon or lime peel, and minced garlic.

— Take chips and salsa to a whole new level by serving them warm. Bake the chips on an ovenproof terra-cotta platter at 300°F for about 8 minutes. Warm the salsa in the microwave for a minute or two.

— For a quick and easy dinner, spoon salsa over fish fillets, bake them in a casserole dish at 400°F until the fillets are tender, and serve them with warm tortillas.

SMALLBITESANDDIPS

Sweet potato ribbon chips

4 SERVINGS *Much better than plain old potato chips, these snacks are great with beer. A V-slicer makes quick work of slicing the potatoes thinly. If you prefer, slice the potatoes into rounds instead. A sharp vegetable peeler can also be used for slicing, but will take a little longer.*

- 2 **medium red-skinned sweet potatoes (yams), peeled**
  Vegetable oil (for deep frying)
  Salt

USING V-slicer and starting at 1 wide side of 1 potato, thinly shave potato lengthwise into long, wide ribbons. Repeat with remaining potato.

POUR enough oil into heavy large pot to reach depth of 2 inches. Heat oil to 375°F. Add handful of potatoes to oil; do not crowd. Fry until crisp and slightly golden, stirring frequently, 30 to 60 seconds. Using slotted spoon, transfer potatoes to paper towels to drain. Sprinkle with salt. Repeat with remaining potatoes in batches.

DO AHEAD *Can be made 6 hours ahead. Cover and store at room temperature.*

Sugar and spice pepitas

MAKES 2 CUPS Pepitas *(edible pumpkin seeds) are popular in Mexican cooking. They're available at many supermarkets and at natural foods stores. The addictive, spicy-sweet coating on these seeds pairs well with beer.*

- **Nonstick vegetable oil spray**
- 2 **cups shelled pepitas**
- ⅓ **cup sugar**
- 1 **large egg white, beaten until frothy**
- 1 **tablespoon chili powder**
- 1 **teaspoon ground cinnamon**
- ½ **teaspoon salt**
- ¼ **teaspoon ground cumin**
- ¼ **to ½ teaspoon cayenne pepper**

PREHEAT oven to 350°F. Spray baking sheet with nonstick spray. Mix pepitas and next 6 ingredients in medium bowl. Stir in ¼ to ½ teaspoon cayenne, depending on spiciness desired. Spread pepitas in single layer on rimmed baking sheet.

BAKE until pepitas are golden and dry, stirring occasionally, about 15 minutes. Remove from oven. Separate pepitas with fork while still warm. Cool.

DO AHEAD *Can be made 2 days ahead. Store airtight at room temperature.*

Black pepper almonds

MAKES 2⅔ CUPS *Brown sugar and black pepper give the almonds a sweet and spicy flavor. Serve with Champagne.*

1 tablespoon ground black pepper
2 teaspoons salt
¼ cup (½ stick) butter
¾ cup (packed) golden brown sugar
4 teaspoons water
2⅔ cups blanched whole almonds

PREHEAT oven to 350°F. Line large rimmed baking sheet with foil. Lightly butter foil. Mix pepper and salt in small bowl. Melt butter in large nonstick skillet over medium-low heat. Add sugar and 4 teaspoons water; stir until sugar dissolves. Add almonds; toss to coat. Cook over medium heat until syrup thickens and almonds are well coated, stirring occasionally, about 5 minutes. Sprinkle half of pepper mixture over almonds.

TRANSFER almonds to baking sheet. Using spatula and working quickly, separate almonds. Sprinkle remaining pepper mixture over almonds. Bake until deep golden brown, about 10 minutes. Transfer sheet to rack; cool.

DO AHEAD *Can be made 4 days ahead. Store airtight at room temperature.*

Marinated olives with tangerine and rosemary

MAKES ABOUT 3 CUPS *The olives need to be marinated at least two days (and up to five days) in advance, so plan ahead.*

1 pound assorted olives (such as Kalamata, Gaeta, and picholine)
1 small tangerine, cut into 4 wedges, each wedge thinly sliced crosswise
1 tablespoon coarsely chopped fresh rosemary
1 teaspoon fennel seeds, lightly crushed
1 teaspoon coriander seeds, lightly crushed
⅛ teaspoon dried crushed red pepper

DRAIN olives if in brine. Combine all ingredients in glass jar with lid; mix well. Cover and refrigerate 2 days, turning and shaking jar several times.

DO AHEAD *Can be made 5 days ahead. Keep chilled.*

OLIVE ME Kalamatas are rich and fruity eggplant-colored olives from Greece. Gaeta olives are a small, black Italian variety. Picholines are green and torpedo-shaped. You can also marinate the very small, purplish-black Niçoise or the green Lucques olives. You'll find a variety of olives at well-stocked supermarkets and at specialty foods stores.

Warm spinach-Parmesan dip

MAKES ABOUT 3 CUPS *This classic party dip has been updated with fresh ingredients. In addition to the baguette slices, tortilla chips would also be good for dipping.*

  2 tablespoons (¼ stick) butter
  2 tablespoons olive oil
1¾ cups chopped onion
  6 large garlic cloves, minced
  2 tablespoons all purpose flour
  ½ cup low-salt chicken broth
  ½ cup heavy whipping cream
  1 9-ounce bag fresh spinach leaves
  1 cup (packed) grated Parmesan cheese
  ¼ cup sour cream
  ½ teaspoon cayenne pepper
    Baguette slices, toasted

MELT butter with oil in heavy large pot over medium heat. Add onion and garlic; sauté until onion is tender, about 6 minutes. Add flour; stir 2 minutes. Gradually add broth and whipping cream, whisking constantly until mixture thickens and boils, about 2 minutes. Remove from heat. Stir in spinach, cheese, sour cream, and cayenne (spinach will wilt). Season to taste with salt and pepper. Transfer dip to bowl. Serve warm with toasted baguette slices.

Garlic and anchovy dip with vegetables

4 SERVINGS *A warm, buttery dip, bagna cauda (literally "hot bath") is often part of Christmas Eve celebrations in Italy's Piedmont region, but it's also great in late summer when peppers are at their peak. Fondue forks can be used to spear the vegetables, and cooked shrimp, other raw vegetables such as radishes and cauliflower, and cubes of bread can be served along with the bell peppers, celery, and green onions.*

  1 cup extra-virgin olive oil
  ½ cup (1 stick) unsalted butter
  8 anchovy fillets, chopped
  3 garlic cloves, minced
  1 red bell pepper, cut into strips
  1 yellow bell pepper, cut into strips
 10 celery stalks, cut in half crosswise
  6 green onions, trimmed

HEAT first 4 ingredients in heavy medium skillet over medium-low heat until butter melts and mixture simmers, about 3 minutes. Season to taste with salt and pepper. Transfer to flameproof bowl. Place over candle or canned heat burner. Serve with vegetables.

Guacamole with roasted tomatillos

MAKES ABOUT 4 CUPS *The acidity of the tomatillos and the lime juice helps prevent the guacamole from turning brown. Tomatillos (fresh green fruits covered in a papery husk) can be found in the produce section of some supermarkets and at Latin markets.*

- 12 medium tomatillos (about 1¼ pounds), husked, rinsed
- ½ cup finely chopped white onion
- ½ cup finely chopped fresh cilantro
- 4 serrano chiles, seeded, minced (about 2 tablespoons)
- 2 tablespoons fresh lime juice
- 3 large avocados (about 2 pounds), peeled, pitted, coarsely chopped

PREHEAT broiler. Line rimmed baking sheet with foil. Place tomatillos on prepared baking sheet. Broil until tomatillos are just blackened in spots and tender, about 8 minutes per side.

COMBINE onion, cilantro, chiles, and lime juice in large bowl. Add roasted tomatillos and any juices from baking sheet to onion mixture. Using fork, mash coarsely. Add avocados and mash until mixture is very coarsely pureed and some chunks remain. Season guacamole to taste with salt.

DO AHEAD *Can be prepared 4 hours ahead. Cover and chill.*

GREAT GUACAMOLE If possible, use Hass avocados when making guacamole—they're richer and creamier than the other varieties. Don't bother placing the avocado pit in your guacamole: It won't stop the dip from turning brown. The best way to preserve leftover guacamole is to place plastic wrap directly on its surface, or to sprinkle lemon juice over the top.

Guacamole with fresh corn and chipotle

MAKES ABOUT 2 CUPS *Chipotle chiles (dried, smoked jalapeños canned in a spicy tomato sauce called adobo) give this dip an appealing smoky taste. Fresh corn kernels add crunch. Canned chipotles in adobo can be found at some supermarkets and at specialty foods stores and Latin markets.*

- 2 large ripe avocados (about 1½ pounds), halved, pitted, peeled
- 1 tablespoon fresh lime juice
- 1 ear of fresh corn, husked
- 1 plum tomato, seeded, diced
- 2 green onions, chopped
- 1 canned chipotle chile in adobo, finely chopped
- ¼ cup sour cream

MASH avocados with lime juice in medium bowl. Using sharp knife, remove corn kernels from cob and add to avocado mixture. Stir in tomato and green onions. Combine chipotle and sour cream in small bowl; whisk to blend. Stir cream mixture into avocado mixture. Season to taste with salt.

DO AHEAD *Can be made 4 hours ahead. Place plastic wrap directly onto surface of guacamole and chill.*

Dukkah

10 TO 12 SERVINGS *One of the most unusual dips you'll ever try, this delicious Egyptian blend of coarsely ground nuts and spices is often used as a topping for meats and vegetables, too. Instruct guests to dip slices of bread in olive oil first so the dukkah will adhere.*

¾ **cup whole blanched almonds**
¾ **cup hazelnuts**
½ **cup (scant) coriander seeds**
¼ **cup cumin seeds**
6 **tablespoons sesame seeds**

Olive oil
Crusty bread slices

PREHEAT oven to 300°F. Bake nuts on heavy small rimmed baking sheet until golden, stirring occasionally, about 25 minutes. Cool on sheet. Maintain oven temperature. Bake coriander and cumin on another small rimmed baking sheet until aromatic, stirring occasionally, about 10 minutes. Transfer to processor; cool. Maintain oven temperature. Toast sesame seeds on same sheet, about 3 minutes; cool. Blend spice mixture and sesame seeds in processor to coarse powder; transfer to medium bowl.

COARSELY grind nuts in processor; mix into sesame-spice mixture. Season dukkah to taste with salt and pepper.

DO AHEAD *Dukkah can be made 1 week ahead. Store airtight at room temperature.*

SPOON oil onto plates. Dip bread into oil and dukkah.

Preserved lemon dip

MAKES ABOUT 2½ CUPS *Serve this spicy-tangy-salty Moroccan dip with flatbread or crusty rolls. It also makes a great salad dressing or sauce for fish. Preserved lemons have been soaked in salt and lemon juice for several weeks. Harissa is a spicy North African red chile paste. Look for both at specialty foods stores, Middle Eastern markets, or online at igourmet.com. You can also make your own quick preserved lemons: Combine 1 thinly sliced lemon, ½ cup lemon juice, and 4 teaspoons coarse sea salt in a small skillet. Bring to boil; reduce heat and simmer, covered, until almost tender, about 10 minutes. Cool.*

6 **tablespoons red wine vinegar**
6 **garlic cloves, minced**
3 **tablespoons minced fresh Italian parsley**
2 **tablespoons minced anchovies**
2 **tablespoons minced cornichons**
2 **tablespoons harissa sauce**
Peel from 1 preserved lemon, rinsed, minced (about ¼ cup)
1 **teaspoon salt**
1¼ **cups vegetable oil**
1 **cup olive oil**

WHISK first 8 ingredients in large bowl. Gradually whisk in both oils. Chill at least 2 hours.

DO AHEAD *Can be made 2 weeks ahead. Cover and keep chilled. Rewhisk before serving.*

Black and white bean salsa

MAKES ABOUT 6 CUPS *For a creamier salsa, lightly mash some of the beans before adding them to the rest of the ingredients. Serve with tortilla chips or as the filling for a vegetarian burrito.*

3	tablespoons corn oil, divided
1¼	cups fresh corn kernels or frozen, thawed
1	15- to 16-ounce can black beans, rinsed, drained
1	15- to 16-ounce can Great Northern beans, drained
1	cup chopped red bell pepper
¾	cup chopped red onion
2	tablespoons fresh lime juice
3	garlic cloves, pressed
1	large jalapeño chile, seeded, minced
1	tablespoon minced fresh oregano
1	tablespoon chili power
1½	teaspoons ground cumin

HEAT 1 tablespoon oil in heavy large skillet over high heat. Add corn and sauté until light brown, about 3 minutes. Transfer to large bowl. Add remaining 2 tablespoons oil and all remaining ingredients to skillet. Season salsa generously with salt and pepper.

DO AHEAD *Can be made 2 days ahead. Cover and chill. Bring to room temperature before serving.*

Salsa verde

MAKES ABOUT 2 CUPS *A very small amount of cream is added to this version of the classic cooked tomatillo salsa. It can be served warm or at room temperature. The salsa can be used as a dip for tortilla chips, as the sauce for chicken enchiladas, or as a topping for pork tacos. If desired, add a little fresh lime juice to the salsa. Tomatillos are green, tomato-like fruits covered in a papery husk. You can find tomatillos and Anaheim chiles (also known as California chiles) in the produce section of some supermarkets and at Latin markets.*

2	large fresh Anaheim chiles
½	pound tomatillos, husked, rinsed, diced
1½	cups low-salt chicken broth
2	large green onions, chopped
1	large serrano chile, seeded
1	garlic clove
¼	cup (firmly packed) fresh cilantro leaves
1	tablespoon heavy whipping cream

CHAR Anaheim chiles directly over gas flame or in broiler until blackened on all sides. Enclose chiles in paper bag; let stand 10 minutes. Peel, seed, and chop chiles.

COMBINE tomatillos, broth, green onions, serrano chile, and garlic in medium saucepan; bring to boil over medium-high heat. Reduce heat to medium-low; simmer until mixture is reduced to 1⅔ cups, stirring occasionally, about 18 minutes. Cool slightly. Transfer mixture to blender. Add Anaheim chiles, cilantro, and cream. Puree until smooth. Season salsa to taste with salt and pepper.

DO AHEAD *Can be made 1 day ahead. Cover and chill. Rewarm before serving.*

Mango and red onion salsa

MAKES ABOUT 1¾ CUPS *Buy small Ataulfo (sometimes labeled "Champagne") mangoes if you can find them. They're sweeter and less fibrous than the standard supermarket mango. For a fresher flavor, add one chopped jalapeño in place of the cayenne pepper. Serve the spicy-sweet salsa over fish tacos, grilled chicken, or roast pork.*

 2 small mangoes, peeled, pitted, diced
 ¾ cup chopped red onion
 ¼ cup chopped fresh cilantro
 2 tablespoons fresh lime juice
 1 teaspoon minced peeled fresh ginger
 ½ teaspoon finely grated lime peel
 ⅛ teaspoon cayenne pepper

COMBINE all ingredients in medium bowl; toss to blend. Season to taste with salt and pepper. Let stand 20 minutes.

DO AHEAD *Salsa can be made 3 hours ahead. Cover and chill.*

Beet, chickpea, and almond dip with pita chips

MAKES ABOUT 2 CUPS *Beets give this hummus-like dip a brilliant color. The pita chips are very versatile and easy to make: Try them with some of the other dips in this chapter.*

 1 large (8-ounce) beet, peeled, cut into ¾-inch cubes
 1 cup drained canned garbanzo beans (chickpeas)
 ¾ cup extra-virgin olive oil plus more for chips
 ¼ cup slivered almonds
 5 garlic cloves, peeled
 1½ tablespoons (or more) red wine vinegar

 6 7-inch-diameter pita breads

COOK beet cubes in medium saucepan of boiling salted water until tender, about 12 minutes. Drain; place in processor. Add garbanzo beans, ¾ cup oil, almonds, and garlic. Blend until smooth. Add 1½ tablespoons red wine vinegar and blend well. Season to taste with salt, pepper, and additional vinegar, if desired. Transfer dip to medium bowl.

DO AHEAD *Can be made 1 day ahead. Cover and chill. Bring to room temperature before serving.*

PREHEAT oven to 400°F. Brush pita breads on both sides with oil; sprinkle lightly with salt and pepper. Cut each bread into 8 wedges. Arrange wedges on rimmed baking sheets. Bake until lightly brown and crisp, about 12 minutes. Cool chips on sheets. Serve with dip.

Parsley hummus with cauliflower crudités

8 SERVINGS *The bright green dip looks very attractive paired with purple, white, and green cauliflower florets. Tahini is available at some supermarkets, natural foods stores, and Middle Eastern markets.*

- ½ cup (packed) fresh parsley leaves
- 1 garlic clove, peeled
- 1 15- to 16-ounce can garbanzo beans (chickpeas), rinsed, drained
- ¼ cup sour cream
- 3 tablespoons tahini (sesame seed paste)
- 2 tablespoons Asian sesame oil
- 1½ teaspoons finely grated lemon peel
- 1½ teaspoons ground cumin
- 1½ teaspoons salt
- ¼ teaspoon cayenne pepper

- 2 heads cauliflower, cut into florets

COARSELY chop parsley and garlic in processor. Add garbanzo beans and process 30 seconds. Add sour cream and next 6 ingredients and process until smooth. Transfer to bowl.

STEAM cauliflower florets in 3 separate batches until crisp-tender, about 3 minutes. Cool.

DO AHEAD *Hummus and cauliflower can be made 6 hours ahead. Cover separately and chill. Bring both to room temperature before serving.*

Eggplant-cilantro spread

MAKES ABOUT 3 CUPS *Serve the spread with pita bread, tortilla chips, or flatbread.*

- 1 large eggplant (about 1¾ pounds), unpeeled, cut into ½-inch-thick rounds
- ⅓ cup (about) olive oil

- 1 cup finely chopped onion
- ½ cup chopped fresh cilantro
- 3 tablespoons fresh lemon juice
- 3 garlic cloves, minced
- 1 teaspoon paprika
- ½ teaspoon ground cumin

PREPARE barbecue (medium-high heat). Place eggplant slices on 2 baking sheets. Brush both sides of eggplant slices with oil. Sprinkle with salt and pepper. Grill eggplant until tender and golden, 4 minutes per side. Cool.

COARSELY chop eggplant and transfer to medium bowl. Mix in onion and all remaining ingredients. Season to taste with salt and pepper.

DO AHEAD *Can be made 8 hours ahead. Cover and chill. Serve cold or at room temperature.*

SMALL-PLATESAPPETIZERS

Grilled pesto breadsticks with goat cheese-pesto spread

10 TO 12 SERVINGS *Store-bought pesto works two ways: as a glaze for the bread and, when mixed with goat cheese, as a spread. Look for prepared pesto by the canned pasta sauces or in the refrigerated aisle near the fresh pastas. Any extra spread can be served with pita chips or used in place of mayonnaise on a turkey sandwich. The breadsticks are best served hot.*

11	ounces soft fresh goat cheese, room temperature
2	7-ounce containers prepared pesto, divided
1	1-pound baguette, cut crosswise into 6-inch lengths
¼	cup olive oil

PUREE goat cheese in processor. Mix in 7 ounces pesto. Transfer to medium bowl.

DO AHEAD *Can be made 1 day ahead. Cover and chill. Bring to room temperature before serving.*

PREPARE barbecue (medium-high heat) or preheat broiler. Halve each bread piece lengthwise, then cut each half lengthwise into 1¼-inch-wide strips. Combine remaining 7 ounces pesto and oil in small bowl. Brush bread all over with pesto mixture. Grill or broil until lightly browned, about 30 seconds per side. Serve with cheese spread.

Three-cheese fondue with Champagne

4 SERVINGS *In this fun and substantial starter, the cornstarch and lemon juice mixture is the key to success. Cornstarch prevents the cheese and wine from separating, and the lemon juice's acidity prevents the cheese from forming clumps or becoming stringy as it melts. Roasted or steamed new potatoes, cubes of apples and pears, and steamed broccoli are also good for dipping. Be sure to keep the fondue over a candle or burner.*

4	teaspoons cornstarch
1	tablespoon fresh lemon juice
1¼	cups dry (brut) Champagne
1	large shallot, chopped
2	cups coarsely grated Gruyère cheese (about 7 ounces)
1⅓	cups coarsely grated Emmenthal cheese (about 5 ounces)
½	cup diced rindless Brie or Camembert cheese (about 3 ounces)
	Generous pinch of ground nutmeg
1	baguette, crust left on, bread cut into 1-inch cubes

STIR cornstarch and lemon juice in small bowl until cornstarch dissolves. Combine Champagne and shallot in fondue pot or heavy medium saucepan; simmer over medium heat 2 minutes. Remove pot from heat. Add all cheeses and stir to combine. Stir in cornstarch mixture. Return fondue pot to medium heat and stir until cheeses are melted and smooth and fondue thickens and boils, about 10 minutes. Season fondue with nutmeg and pepper to taste. Place over candle or canned heat burner to keep warm. Serve with bread cubes.

Camembert with blue cheese, figs, and Port

4 SERVINGS *A round of Camembert cheese is breaded, browned, and topped with blue cheese and a fig-Port sauce. The Camembert is best fresh off the stove, but it can sit on a table or buffet for up to an hour.*

1   8-ounce (4½-inch-diameter) firm Camembert cheese with rind
1   large egg, beaten to blend
1   cup fresh breadcrumbs made from crustless French bread

1   cup ruby Port
1   cup dried black Mission figs, halved lengthwise
1   tablespoon sugar

2   tablespoons (¼ stick) butter
⅓   cup crumbled blue cheese
    Chopped fresh chives
1   baguette, sliced into rounds, lightly toasted

BRUSH Camembert on all sides with egg, then coat with breadcrumbs. Place coated cheese on foil-lined plate and cover.

BRING Port to simmer in heavy small saucepan over medium heat. Add figs; simmer until slightly softened, about 5 minutes. Using slotted spoon, transfer figs to small bowl. Add sugar to Port in pan; boil until reduced to thick syrup, stirring occasionally, about 5 minutes. Pour syrup over figs.

DO AHEAD *Cheese and figs can be made 3 hours ahead. Chill cheese. Let figs stand at room temperature.*

MELT butter in heavy medium skillet over medium-high heat. Add Camembert and cook until breadcrumbs are brown and cheese is warm, about 2 minutes per side. Transfer to platter. Top with blue cheese, figs, and syrup. Sprinkle with chives and surround with toasts.

Broiled feta with honey and aniseed

4 SERVINGS *Warm, browned feta is topped with an aromatic mixture of aniseed and honey in this salty-sweet dish inspired by the flavors of the Greek island of Crete. Use an attractive baking dish that can go straight from the oven to the table, and serve with grilled or toasted bread. Encourage guests to eat this right away—don't let it sit or the feta can get rubbery.*

14   ounces feta cheese, cut into twelve 3×1×1½-inch sticks
4   teaspoons extra-virgin olive oil

3   tablespoons honey
1½   teaspoons whole aniseed

PREHEAT broiler. Arrange feta in single layer in shallow broilerproof baking dish; brush with oil. Broil until golden, about 3 minutes.

MEANWHILE, combine honey and aniseed in heavy small saucepan. Stir over medium heat until hot.

DRIZZLE 4 teaspoons honey mixture over cheese in dish. Sprinkle feta with ground black pepper. Serve with remaining honey mixture alongside.

CHILL OUT To easily remove the rind from a soft cheese like Brie or Camembert, chill it in the freezer until firm to touch (about 15 to 30 minutes depending on thickness of cheese) before cutting the rind off with a paring knife.

Grilled chicken skewers with red pepper pesto

10 SERVINGS *This delicious pesto would also be nice tossed with cooked pasta, spread on small toasts, or used as a dip for pita chips.*

- 1 **7-ounce jar roasted red peppers, drained well**
- ½ **cup fresh cilantro leaves**
- 3 **tablespoons balsamic vinegar**
- 1 **garlic clove, peeled**
- ½ **teaspoon dry mustard**
- ½ **teaspoon ground coriander**
  Pinch of ground cinnamon
- 8 **tablespoons olive oil, divided**
- ½ **cup whole almonds, toasted (about 2½ ounces)**

- 4 **skinless boneless chicken breast halves**

BLEND first 7 ingredients and 6 tablespoons oil in processor until almost smooth. Add almonds and process until finely chopped but not ground. Season to taste with salt and pepper.

DO AHEAD *Pesto can be made 2 days ahead. Cover and chill. Let stand at room temperature 1 hour before serving.*

PREPARE barbecue (medium-high heat) or preheat broiler. Brush chicken with remaining 2 tablespoons oil. Sprinkle with salt and pepper. Grill until cooked through, about 5 minutes per side. Cut chicken into 1-inch pieces. Skewer each piece with toothpick. Arrange on platter and serve with pesto.

Lamb kebabs with pomegranate-cumin glaze

MAKES 24 *Marinated in pomegranate molasses, oregano, cinnamon, and cumin, these kebabs have a definite Middle Eastern flavor. Add a little hummus and some lettuce and any leftovers can be turned into pita sandwiches. Pomegranate molasses is a rich, tart syrup made by reducing pomegranate juice. Look for it at Middle Eastern markets and online at adrianascaravan.com, or make your own by boiling 2 cups pomegranate juice in a heavy small saucepan until reduced to a thick syrup, about ⅓ cup. Stir often to prevent burning; it should take about 20 minutes. Let it cool before using ¼ cup in the recipe.*

- ¼ **cup pomegranate molasses**
- ½ **cup extra-virgin olive oil**
- 3 **garlic cloves, pressed**
- 1½ **teaspoons ground cumin**
- 1 **teaspoon dried oregano**
- 1 **teaspoon salt**
- ½ **teaspoon ground black pepper**
- ½ **teaspoon ground cinnamon**
- 1¼ **pounds trimmed boneless leg of lamb, cut into twenty-four ¾-inch cubes**

- 1 **large red bell pepper, cut into twenty-four ¾-inch squares**
- 24 **small metal skewers or wooden skewers, soaked in water 30 minutes, drained**

MIX first 8 ingredients in 1-gallon resealable plastic bag. Add lamb and seal; turn to coat with marinade. Chill at least 1 hour and up to 4 hours.

REMOVE lamb from marinade. Thread 1 lamb piece and 1 red pepper piece on each skewer; place on baking sheet.

DO AHEAD *Can be prepared 2 hours ahead. Cover and chill.*

PREPARE barbecue (medium-high heat) or preheat broiler. Sprinkle kebabs with salt and pepper. Grill or broil, turning often, about 4 minutes for medium-rare.

Deviled cocktail sausages with chutney and lime dipping sauce

MAKES 50 *This retro starter updates an old favorite: Small, cooked sausages are glazed with a spicy-sweet mixture of Worcestershire sauce, brown sugar, and mustard, and served with a tart mango-chutney sauce. The sausages are best when hot or warm.*

¾ cup mango chutney, such as Major Grey (from 11- to 12½-ounce jar)
¼ cup fresh lime juice
1 tablespoon finely grated lime peel
¾ cup mayonnaise

50 fully cooked smoked cocktail-size sausages
⅓ cup (packed) dark brown sugar
3 tablespoons ketchup
2 tablespoons Worcestershire sauce
2 tablespoons Dijon mustard
1 teaspoon hot pepper sauce

COMBINE chutney, lime juice, and lime peel in processor; blend until almost smooth. Transfer to bowl. Whisk in mayonnaise. Season chutney sauce to taste with salt and pepper.

PREHEAT oven to 425°F. Place sausages in 8×8×2-inch glass baking dish. Mix brown sugar, ketchup, Worcestershire sauce, mustard, and hot pepper sauce in small bowl to blend. Pour over sausages and toss to coat.

DO AHEAD *Chutney sauce and sausages can be made 1 day ahead. Cover separately and chill.*

BAKE sausages until heated through and brown in spots, turning occasionally, about 25 minutes.

TRANSFER sausages to platter. Place toothpick in each. Place chutney sauce alongside.

Herbed goat cheese with roasted chiles and olive oil

4 SERVINGS *The blackened chiles add a smoky flavor to this rustic dish. Also known as California chiles, Anaheims can be found at many supermarkets and at Latin markets. If you don't like goat cheese, use a fresh cow's milk cheese, such as* queso fresco, *instead.*

3 large fresh Anaheim chiles

2 garlic cloves, peeled
1 5-ounce log soft fresh goat cheese, crumbled
1 tablespoon chopped fresh cilantro
2 teaspoons chopped fresh oregano

¼ cup extra-virgin olive oil
1 baguette, sliced, toasted

CHAR chiles over gas flame or in broiler until blackened on all sides. Enclose in paper bag; let stand 10 minutes. Peel and seed chiles, then cut into strips.

BLANCH garlic in small saucepan of simmering water 3 minutes. Drain and cool. Chop 1 garlic clove; thinly slice remaining garlic. Mix cheese, cilantro, oregano, and chopped garlic in small bowl. Season mixture to taste with salt and pepper. Crumble cheese mixture onto plate. Top with roasted chiles and sliced garlic.

DO AHEAD *Can be made 1 day ahead. Cover and chill. Let stand at room temperature 1 hour before continuing.*

DRIZZLE oil over chiles and goat cheese. Serve with toasted baguette slices.

Seared ahi tuna and avocado tartare

MAKES ABOUT 2½ CUPS *Use the tartare as a dip or offer it on toasted baguette slices. If you want to serve a raw, restaurant-style tartare, buy sushi-grade tuna and quickly sear it on each side. For a party, keep the tartare on a plate or platter set over ice.*

- 1 6-ounce ahi tuna steak
- 3½ tablespoons extra-virgin olive oil, divided

- 1 large avocado, peeled, pitted, diced
- 1 serrano or jalapeño chile, seeded, deveined, minced
- ⅓ cup chopped fresh cilantro
- ⅓ cup chopped red onion
- ¼ cup fresh lime juice
- 2 teaspoons chopped fresh oregano

HEAT heavy small skillet over high heat 2 minutes. Brush tuna with ½ tablespoon oil; sprinkle with salt and pepper. Place in skillet and sear until brown outside and almost opaque in center, about 3 minutes per side. Cool tuna; dice finely.

COMBINE tuna, remaining 3 tablespoons oil, and all remaining ingredients in medium bowl. Mix with fork just to blend. Season tartare to taste with salt and pepper and chill until cold.

Sliced radishes and watercress on buttered ficelles

MAKES 18 *These little open-faced sandwiches are perfect for afternoon tea. Because* ficelle *is a slender demi-baguette, it slices prettily—but any narrow baguette will do. Fleur de sel (fine French sea salt), edible flowers, and daikon radish sprouts can be found at some supermarkets and at specialty foods stores. Coarse kosher salt can be used in place of fleur de sel.*

- ¼ cup (½ stick) unsalted butter, room temperature
- 18 thin diagonal slices ficelle or other narrow baguette
  Fleur de sel (fine French sea salt)
- 1 small bunch watercress, trimmed
- 4 watermelon radishes or other large radishes, very thinly sliced
  Edible flowers or daikon radish sprouts (optional)

SPREAD some butter over bread slices. Sprinkle with fleur de sel. Top each bread slice with 2 watercress sprigs. Spread 1 side of each radish slice with butter. Place 2 radish slices atop watercress, buttered side down, overlapping slightly if necessary to fit. Top with flowers or sprouts, if desired.

DO AHEAD *Can be made 1 hour ahead. Cover and let stand at room temperature.*

Smoked salmon with mustard-dill sauce

6 SERVINGS *Turn this into a bountiful platter by adding smoked trout and cod, sliced pumpernickel and whole-grain bread, and caper berries.*

- ¼ cup corn oil
- ¼ cup honey mustard
- 4 teaspoons Dijon mustard
- 1 tablespoon sugar
- 2 teaspoons white wine vinegar
- 3 tablespoons chopped fresh dill
- 1 pound sliced smoked salmon

WHISK first 5 ingredients in medium bowl to blend. Stir in dill. Season sauce to taste with salt and pepper.

DO AHEAD *Can be made 2 days ahead. Cover and chill.*

SERVE salmon with sauce.

PASSEDAPPETIZERS

White cheddar puffs with green onions

MAKES ABOUT 4 DOZEN *These luscious puffs (also known as gougères) are traditionally made with Gruyère cheese. Be sure to use high-quality cheddar for the best flavor. For easy last-minute entertaining, keep some puffs on hand in the freezer, and bake them straight from the freezer just before serving.*

1 cup water
¼ cup (½ stick) butter, cut into 4 pieces
½ teaspoon coarse kosher salt plus additional for sprinkling
1 cup plus 2 tablespoons all purpose flour
4 large eggs
1½ cups (packed) grated extra-sharp white cheddar cheese (about 6 ounces)
⅔ cup minced green onions

LINE 2 baking sheets with parchment paper. Bring 1 cup water, butter, and ½ teaspoon salt to boil in heavy medium saucepan. Remove from heat; mix in flour. Stir over medium heat until mixture becomes slightly shiny and pulls away from sides of pan, about 3 minutes. Transfer to stand mixer fitted with paddle. Add eggs 1 at a time, mixing well after each addition to form sticky dough. Mix in cheese and green onions.

USING 2 teaspoons, form dough into 1¼- to 1½-inch ovals; drop onto baking sheet 1 inch apart.

DO AHEAD *Can be made ahead. Wrap in plastic, then foil. Refrigerate up to 2 days or freeze up to 2 weeks.*

PREHEAT oven to 375°F. Bake cheese puffs until golden, about 30 minutes if at room temperature and 35 minutes if chilled or frozen. Serve immediately.

Pizzette with fontina, tomato, basil, and prosciutto

MAKES 16 *These tiny little pizzas are perfect finger food. Cut the dough with a few different cookie cutters to give your appetizer platter a bit of whimsy (first dip the cookie cutters into flour to make the dough easier to cut out).*

1 13.8-ounce package refrigerated pizza dough
¾ cup grated Fontina cheese (about 3 ounces)
8 cherry tomatoes, quartered
2 tablespoons grated Parmesan cheese

2 teaspoons extra-virgin olive oil
⅓ cup thinly sliced fresh basil
1½ ounces thinly sliced prosciutto, coarsely torn into strips

PREHEAT oven to 475°F. Lightly sprinkle rimmed baking sheet with flour. Roll out pizza dough ¼ inch thick on lightly floured surface. Using 2½-inch-diameter cookie cutter, cut 16 dough rounds (reserve any remaining dough for another use). Arrange rounds on prepared baking sheet. Sprinkle rounds with Fontina cheese, dividing equally. Place 2 tomato quarters on each round, pressing gently into dough. Sprinkle tomatoes with grated Parmesan cheese.

DO AHEAD *Can be made 2 hours ahead. Cover and chill.*

BAKE pizzette until golden brown, about 12 minutes. Drizzle pizzette with olive oil, then top with basil and sprinkle lightly with salt and pepper. Drape prosciutto strips over. Arrange on platter and serve immediately.

Black and gold pizzas

2 SERVINGS *These aren't really pizzas—they're classy little crostini topped with golden and black caviar. Champagne is the perfect accompaniment. Look for crème fraîche at some supermarkets or at specialty foods stores.*

8 ⅓-inch-thick slices baguette
   Butter, room temperature

½ cup crème fraîche or sour cream
1 bunch fresh chives, minced
2 ounces golden caviar
2 ounces black caviar

PREHEAT broiler. Arrange bread on small baking sheet; broil until lightly toasted, about 1 minute. Turn bread slices over; spread second side with butter and sprinkle with ground black pepper. Broil bread until golden brown, about 2 minutes.

SPREAD crème fraîche over bread slices. Sprinkle chives in diagonal line across center of each. Spoon golden caviar on one side of chives and black caviar on other side.

BUDGET CAVIAR If beluga and imperial caviar are out of the question pricewise, American black and golden caviar are now good substitutes. An unopened jar can be stored in the coldest part of the refrigerator for about a month. Once opened, the caviar should be eaten within 3 days.

Grilled prosciutto-wrapped shrimp with Marsala glaze

10 SERVINGS *If it's too cold for grilling, broiling works, too. Arrange the shrimp on a rack set on top of a baking sheet. Broil them for 4 to 5 minutes, turning once and brushing with glaze, until they're opaque in the center.*

3 cups imported dry Marsala
¾ cup currant jelly
3 tablespoons balsamic vinegar

   Nonstick vegetable oil spray
15 very thin prosciutto slices, each about 3×7 inches, cut lengthwise in half
30 large uncooked shrimp, peeled, tails left intact, deveined
2 tablespoons chopped fresh thyme

BOIL first 3 ingredients in heavy medium saucepan until reduced to 1⅓ cups, about 15 minutes. Cool glaze 15 minutes.

SPRAY grill rack with nonstick spray; prepare barbecue (medium-high heat). Place 1 prosciutto strip (½ slice) on work surface. Dip 1 shrimp into glaze; place almost at 1 end of strip. Sprinkle with thyme. Wrap prosciutto around shrimp, enclosing completely. Dip into glaze; place on platter. Repeat with remaining prosciutto, shrimp, thyme, and glaze as needed. Grill shrimp 2 minutes; brush with glaze. Turn shrimp over; brush with glaze. Grill until shrimp are opaque in center and prosciutto is charred, about 2 minutes longer.

Skewered shrimp with apricot-curry glaze

6 SERVINGS *Add steamed rice and these skewers become a quick main course.*

    3 tablespoons olive oil
    3 tablespoons apricot preserves
 1½ tablespoons white wine vinegar
 2¼ teaspoons Dijon mustard
 2¼ teaspoons curry powder
    2 garlic cloves, minced
   18 uncooked large shrimp, peeled,
        tails left intact, deveined

    6 10- to 12-inch metal skewers
        Shredded iceberg lettuce
        Lemon wedges

WHISK first 6 ingredients in large bowl to blend. Add shrimp and toss to coat. Cover and refrigerate at least 2 hours.

PREHEAT broiler. Thread 3 shrimp on each skewer. Broil shrimp just until cooked through, about 2 minutes per side. Place shredded lettuce on platter; arrange shrimp skewers on top. Garnish with lemon wedges.

SHRIMP AND CURRY While any curry powder can be used for the glaze, sweet curry and very fragrant maharajah-style curry powders are particularly good partners for shrimp.

Crab crostini with green onions and crème fraîche

MAKES ABOUT 30 *These warm, gooey toasts are great for a large party. Both the crab topping and the toasted bread can be prepared 1 day ahead. Crème fraîche is available at some supermarkets and at specialty foods stores.*

    1 pound fresh lump crabmeat
   ¼ cup minced celery heart (including leaves)
    3 green onions, minced
 1½ teaspoons finely grated lemon peel
    3 tablespoons mayonnaise
    2 tablespoons crème fraîche or sour cream
    3 tablespoons fresh lemon juice
    8 drops hot pepper sauce

    1 2½-inch-diameter baguette, cut
        into scant ½-inch-thick slices
        Olive oil

    1 cup shredded dry Monterey Jack cheese
        or Cheshire cheese (about 4 ounces)

SHRED crabmeat into medium bowl removing any small pieces. Add celery, green onions, and lemon peel; toss to blend. Mix in next 4 ingredients. Season to taste with salt. Cover and chill at least 2 hours.

DO AHEAD *Can be made 1 day ahead; keep chilled.*

PREHEAT oven to 350°F. Arrange baguette slices in single layer on rimmed baking sheet. Brush both sides of bread with oil. Bake until lightly browned, turning once, about 16 minutes.

DO AHEAD *Can be made 1 day ahead. Cool. Store in resealable plastic bags at room temperature.*

PREHEAT broiler. Arrange toasts on baking sheet. Spread 1 heaping tablespoon crabmeat mixture onto each; sprinkle with cheese. Broil until cheese melts, about 2 minutes. Serve warm.

Mini crab cakes

MAKES ABOUT 32 *Tiny crab cakes are great passed hors d'oeuvres. For a more elegant presentation, top each one with a little dollop of the garlicky French mayonnaise known as aioli and garnish with fresh parsley sprigs.*

¼ cup mayonnaise

2 tablespoons chopped fresh Italian parsley

2 tablespoons Dijon mustard

1 teaspoon Worcestershire sauce

½ teaspoon hot pepper sauce

½ teaspoon salt

¼ teaspoon garlic powder

1 pound fresh lump crabmeat, patted dry

10 tablespoons plus 1 cup finely crushed crackers (such as Ritz)

4 green onions, finely chopped

1 large egg, beaten to blend

6 tablespoons (about) olive oil

WHISK first 7 ingredients in large bowl to blend. Mix in crabmeat, 10 tablespoons cracker crumbs, green onions, and egg. Shape mixture by rounded tablespoonfuls into ½-inch-thick cakes. Place remaining 1 cup cracker crumbs in shallow bowl. Roll cakes in crumbs to coat; arrange on baking sheet.

DO AHEAD *Can be prepared 2 hours ahead. Cover and chill.*

PREHEAT oven to 300°F. Heat 3 tablespoons oil in large skillet over medium heat. Working in batches, fry crab cakes until golden, adding more oil to skillet by tablespoonfuls as needed, about 4 minutes per side. Transfer to another baking sheet; place in oven to keep warm.

ARRANGE crab cakes on platter.

Crabmeat 101 Crabmeat (cooked crab that's been picked from the shell) is sold fresh, frozen, pasteurized (heat-treated to prolong shelf life), or canned. Of these, fresh crabmeat is the highest quality, but it's also the most expensive. At the fish counter, ask if it's fresh—often the crab displayed on ice has been frozen or pasteurized. Avoid the crab in the canned foods aisle: Its texture and flavor are generally inferior.

You'll also find that crabmeat is labeled by the size of its pieces. "Lump" contains large chunks from the body of the crab, "claw" is from the claws, and "flake" is very small pieces. Use the lumpiest crabmeat you can afford. The meat should be bright white with a bit of pink, and have no ammonia-like odor.

Banana-black bean empanadas

MAKES 12 *These Latin American turnovers are surprisingly simple to make: Frozen puff pastry and canned beans dramatically cut down the prep work. The empanadas can be served with salsa verde for a dipping sauce.*

  2 tablespoons vegetable oil
  1 firm medium banana, diced
  ¾ cup chopped onion
  1 15- to 16-ounce can black beans, drained
  ¼ cup chopped fresh cilantro
  ¾ teaspoon ground cumin
  ¼ teaspoon cayenne pepper

  1 17.3-ounce package frozen puff pastry
      (2 sheets), thawed
  1 cup (packed) coarsely grated
      Monterey Jack cheese
  1 egg, beaten to blend (for glaze)

HEAT oil in heavy medium skillet over high heat. Add banana and sauté until golden, about 1½ minutes. Using slotted spoon, transfer banana to paper towels to drain. Add onion to skillet; sauté 3 minutes. Add beans, cilantro, cumin, and cayenne; cook until mixture is hot, about 3 minutes. Using back of fork, mash bean filling to coarse paste; season to taste with salt and cool.

PREHEAT oven to 425°F. Roll out each puff pastry sheet on floured surface to 14-inch square. Cut each into 9 squares. Place 1 heaping tablespoon filling in center of 12 squares (reserve remaining squares for another use). Sprinkle each mound of filling with cheese, then top with bananas, dividing equally. Brush edges of squares with glaze. Fold 1 corner over filling to opposite corner, forming triangle. Using fork, seal crust edges. Arrange on rimmed baking sheet; brush with glaze. Bake empanadas until golden brown, about 15 minutes. Serve hot.

Zucchini fritters

6 SERVINGS *Stout gives the fritter batter a pleasant malty flavor. Look for squash blossoms at some supermarkets, farmers' markets, specialty foods stores, and Latin markets. They're available from late spring to early fall.*

       Canola oil (for deep-frying)
  1¾ cups all purpose flour
  ¼ cup cornstarch
  1 tablespoon baking powder
  1 teaspoon salt
  2 cups chilled stout or dark beer
  4 medium zucchini, cut diagonally
      into ¼-inch-thick slices
 12 squash blossoms, pistils removed (optional)

POUR enough oil into heavy large saucepan to reach depth of 3 inches. Heat oil over medium heat until deep-fry thermometer registers 350°F.

MIX flour, cornstarch, baking powder, and salt in large bowl. Add stout; whisk until smooth batter forms. Working in batches of 5 or 6 zucchini slices or blossoms and using tongs, dip zucchini slices and blossoms into batter, then add to hot oil. Cook until golden brown, about 2 minutes per side. Using slotted spoon, transfer fritters to paper towels to drain. Sprinkle with salt and serve.

Wild mushroom crostini

MAKES 36 *Sautéed mushrooms and browned, melted cheese make for a luscious appetizer—and the bulk of the work can be done 2 days in advance.*

36 ⅓-inch-thick baguette slices

2 tablespoons olive oil

⅓ cup chopped shallots

2¼ cups chopped fresh oyster mushrooms (about 6 ounces)

2¼ cups chopped fresh stemmed shiitake mushrooms (about 6 ounces)

1¼ cups chopped fresh chanterelle mushrooms (about 4 ounces)

1 garlic clove, minced

¼ cup heavy whipping cream

1 teaspoon minced fresh rosemary

½ teaspoon finely grated lemon peel

1 cup grated Fontina cheese

½ cup freshly grated Parmesan cheese (about 1¾ ounces)

PREHEAT oven to 375°F. Arrange baguette slices in single layer on large rimmed baking sheet. Toast in oven until golden, about 9 minutes. Cool.

DO AHEAD *Can be made 2 days ahead. Store in resealable plastic bag at room temperature.*

HEAT oil in large skillet over medium-high heat. Add shallots; sauté 1 minute. Add all mushrooms; sauté until beginning to brown, about 6 minutes. Add garlic; stir 1 minute. Remove from heat. Stir in cream, rosemary, and lemon peel. Season to taste with salt and pepper. Cool. Mix in both cheeses.

DO AHEAD *Can be made 2 days ahead. Cover and chill.*

PREHEAT broiler. Top each toast with about 1 tablespoon mushroom topping. Place on 2 rimmed baking sheets. Broil, 1 baking sheet at a time, until cheese is melted and begins to brown, watching closely to prevent burning, about 3 minutes. Transfer to platter and serve warm.

Mushrooms gone wild The phrase "wild mushrooms" is often a misnomer. Many of the varieties we think of as wild—such as shiitakes, oysters, and portobellos—are actually commercially cultivated. But with their earthy, nutty, spicy flavors, these exotic mushrooms are hardly tame. Whether you choose wild or cultivated mushrooms, you should always:

— Buy mushrooms that have a pleasant aroma—it indicates good flavor. Avoid those that have shriveled caps or wet spots.

— Store them in the refrigerator in a well-ventilated container loosely covered with a paper towel. Never put them in vegetable bins or plastic bags; the humidity will cause them to spoil faster.

— Before using, trim the stems and cut off blemishes. Then gently wipe the mushrooms clean with a damp paper towel, or, if they're very dirty, rinse them in cold water and pat dry with a paper towel.

Chorizo-filled dates wrapped in bacon

MAKES 12 *This addictive snack pairs two kinds of pork—applewood-smoked bacon and chorizo—with sweet fresh dates. If you can't find fresh Spanish chorizo, the Mexican kind works well, too.*

 4 ounces fresh (not smoked) Spanish chorizo sausage links, casings removed, coarsely crumbled
 1 tablespoon chopped Italian parsley

12 large Medjool dates
 6 slices applewood-smoked bacon, cut crosswise in half

 2 tablespoons olive oil

COOK chorizo in heavy small skillet over medium heat until browned and cooked through, stirring frequently and breaking up lumps with spoon, about 5 minutes. Drain off fat; transfer sausage to small bowl. Stir in parsley. Cool.

WORKING with one date at a time, cut slit along top of date. Gently pry open date and remove pit, leaving pocket. Stuff pocket with 1 scant tablespoon chorizo mixture. Wrap 1 bacon piece around each date, overlapping ends slightly; fasten ends with toothpick.

HEAT oil in medium skillet over medium heat. Add dates, toothpick-side down, and cook without moving until bacon browns, about 5 minutes. Continue to cook until bacon is brown on all sides, turning dates occasionally, about 6 minutes longer. Transfer dates to paper towels to drain. Remove toothpicks. Serve warm.

Tomato-coriander bruschetta

8 TO 10 SERVINGS *Since cherry tomatoes are quite flavorful year-round, this is one bruschetta that can be made any time. Plus, you can double the tomato topping and toss it with farfalle or penne for a great pasta salad.*

 2 tablespoons whole coriander seeds

 2 12-ounce bags or baskets cherry tomatoes, stemmed
 ¼ cup extra-virgin olive oil
 2 garlic cloves, minced
 ½ teaspoon dried crushed red pepper
 4 teaspoons chopped fresh marjoram

 1 sourdough baguette, cut crosswise into ½-inch-thick rounds

PREHEAT oven to 400°F. Stir coriander seeds in heavy small skillet over medium heat until aromatic, about 1 minute. Cool seeds 10 minutes. Enclose in resealable plastic bag; crush coarsely with mallet.

COMBINE tomatoes, oil, garlic, and crushed red pepper on rimmed baking sheet; toss to blend. Sprinkle generously with salt. Bake until tomatoes are soft, about 15 minutes, then broil until brown in spots, about 2 minutes. Mix in coriander and marjoram. Cool topping on sheet 15 minutes.

ARRANGE bread slices on another baking sheet. Bake until just beginning to color, about 5 minutes. Mound tomato topping on toasts. Arrange on platter.

Mushroom-ham brochettes with garlic mayonnaise

6 SERVINGS *These grilled Spanish tapas call for thicker slices of Serrano ham than those that come already packaged—so head to a deli that has whole legs of Spanish ham, or use prosciutto instead. The skewers are paired with a quick aioli that's made with purchased mayonnaise.*

- 6 tablespoons mayonnaise
- 2 garlic cloves, pressed
- 1 teaspoon fresh lemon juice
- 1 teaspoon plus 3 tablespoons extra-virgin olive oil

- ¼ pound ⅛-inch-thick slices Serrano ham or prosciutto, cut into thirty 1-inch squares
- 24 small mushrooms, stems removed
- 6 10-inch wooden skewers, trimmed to 6- to 8-inch lengths
  Coarse kosher salt

WHISK mayonnaise, garlic, lemon juice, and 1 teaspoon oil in small bowl to blend. Season to taste with salt and pepper.

ALTERNATE 5 ham squares and 4 mushrooms on each skewer. Brush skewers with 2 tablespoons oil.

DO AHEAD *Garlic mayonnaise and skewers can be made 6 hours ahead. Cover separately and chill.*

BRUSH heavy large skillet with remaining 1 tablespoon oil; heat over medium heat. Add skewers and cook until mushrooms are brown and softened, turning occasionally, about 12 minutes. Season skewers with salt. Serve with garlic mayonnaise.

Skirt-steak quesadillas

8 SERVINGS *Stacked on baking sheets and baked in the oven, these quesadillas are much easier to make in large quantities than those prepared one by one on the stovetop. The homemade* pico de gallo *gives a nice fresh kick, but purchased salsa is fine too.*

- 1 1- to 1¼-pound skirt steak
- 2 tablespoons fresh lime juice

- 4 tablespoons (about) olive oil, divided

- 12 5- to 6-inch-diameter corn tortillas, divided
- 2 cups (packed) grated hot pepper Monterey Jack cheese (about 8 ounces), divided
- 1½ cups Spicy Pico de Gallo (see recipe) or purchased salsa, divided

PLACE steak in glass dish. Sprinkle steak on both sides with lime juice, salt, and pepper. Let stand at least 15 minutes and up to 1 hour, turning steak occasionally.

PREHEAT oven to 375°F. Heat 1 tablespoon oil in heavy large skillet over high heat. Add steak and cook to desired doneness, about 3 minutes per side for rare. Transfer steak to cutting board. Let rest 5 minutes; slice thinly.

BRUSH 4 tortillas with oil; place tortillas, oil side down, on 2 baking sheets. Spread ¼ cup cheese and 1 tablespoon pico de gallo on each tortilla. Top each with second tortilla. Spread each with ¼ cup cheese, ¼ of steak, and 1 tablespoon pico de gallo. Press third tortilla onto each stack. Brush top tortillas with oil.

BAKE quesadillas 10 minutes. Using metal spatula, turn each over. Continue to bake until heated through and golden, about 10 minutes longer. Transfer quesadillas to plates. Cut into wedges. Serve with remaining pico de gallo.

Spicy pico de gallo

MAKES ABOUT 2½ CUPS *This all-purpose salsa is great with tortilla chips and in tacos and burritos. If you want a spicier salsa, don't seed the jalapeños.*

    1   **pound plum tomatoes, seeded, chopped**
    1   **cup chopped onion**
    6   **tablespoons (packed) chopped fresh cilantro**
    ¼   **cup fresh lime juice**
    2   **garlic cloves, minced**
    1½ **tablespoons minced seeded jalapeño chiles**

COMBINE all ingredients in medium bowl; toss to blend well. Season to taste with salt and pepper. Let stand at least 30 minutes for flavors to develop.

CHILE WISDOM Handling spicy chiles can irritate the skin, so wear latex gloves when chopping them.

Crabmeat, corn, and cumin salad in endive spears

10 SERVINGS *Crab salad becomes a classy finger food when it's spooned into endive spears. Alternate red and yellow endive spears for a colorful presentation. If desired, sprinkle each with chopped fresh parsley and a dash of paprika.*

    6   **ounces fresh lump crabmeat,
        picked over, well drained**
    ½   **cup frozen corn kernels, thawed, drained**
    ¼   **cup finely chopped red onion**
    ¼   **cup mayonnaise**
    4   **teaspoons mixed chopped fresh herbs
        (such as tarragon and parsley)**
    1   **tablespoon thawed orange juice concentrate**
    1   **tablespoon fresh lemon juice**
    1   **teaspoon finely grated lemon peel**
    ½   **teaspoon ground cumin**
    ¼   **teaspoon cayenne pepper**

    2   **heads Belgian endive, separated into spears**

MIX first 10 ingredients in medium bowl. Season to taste with salt and pepper. Cover and chill at least 4 hours and up to 1 day.

DRAIN salad and place 1 rounded tablespoon in base end of each endive spear. Arrange on platters and serve.

Pancetta crisps with goat cheese and pear

MAKES 16 *When it's baked at a high temperature, pancetta becomes a crisp bacony chip. Topped with cheese and pear slices, it's irresistible.*

- 16 thin slices pancetta (Italian bacon)
- 16 teaspoons soft fresh goat cheese (from 5-ounce log)
- 2 very ripe small pears, halved, cored, cut into ¼-inch-thick slices
  Fresh thyme leaves

PREHEAT oven to 450°F. Place pancetta slices in single layer on large rimmed baking sheet. Sprinkle with pepper. Bake until golden, about 10 minutes. Using spatula, slide pancetta crisps onto platter. Top each with 1 teaspoon goat cheese and 1 pear slice. Sprinkle with thyme.

Prosciutto-wrapped figs with Gorgonzola and walnuts

MAKES 18 *Fresh figs are in season from June to October. During the rest of the year, you can use dried black Mission figs for this recipe, but look for ones that are soft and moist. This starter can be served either warm or at room temperature.*

- 9 large fresh black Mission figs, stemmed, halved
- 18 thin strips prosciutto (about 3 ounces), each about 1×5 inches
- 3 tablespoons Gorgonzola cheese
- 18 large walnut pieces, toasted

PREHEAT broiler. Cover large rimmed baking sheet with foil. Wrap each fig half with 1 prosciutto strip; place on prepared sheet. Broil until prosciutto chars slightly on edges, about 1½ minutes. Turn figs; broil about 1½ minutes longer, watching closely to prevent burning. Place ½ teaspoon Gorgonzola atop each fig half. Top each with walnut piece.

Sesame wonton triangles with smoked salmon and wasabi

MAKES 16 *Wonton wrappers are baked into little crackers and topped with salmon, a wasabi sauce, and spicy daikon sprouts. Wasabi (Japanese horseradish) paste can be found in the Asian foods section and at the sushi counter of some supermarkets and at Japanese markets.*

- ¼ cup plus ½ teaspoon Asian sesame oil
- 1 egg white
- 8 wonton wrappers
- 2 tablespoons sesame seeds

- 2 tablespoons seasoned rice vinegar
- 2 tablespoons chopped fresh chives
- 1¼ teaspoons wasabi paste
- 1 teaspoon minced peeled fresh ginger
- 6 ounces sliced smoked salmon
  Daikon radish sprouts or other small sprouts

PREHEAT oven to 350°F. Whisk ¼ cup oil and egg white in small bowl to blend. Place wonton wrappers in single layer on work surface; brush with some of oil mixture and sprinkle with half of sesame seeds. Fold diagonally in half. Brush with more oil mixture; sprinkle with remaining seeds. Cut each into 2 triangles. Place on baking sheet. Bake until golden, about 13 minutes. Cool.

WHISK vinegar, chives, wasabi, ginger, and remaining ½ teaspoon oil in bowl. Cover each wonton with 1 salmon slice, then drizzle with wasabi mixture. Top salmon with sprouts, then fold salmon over sprouts. Top with more sprouts.

Shrimp mousse crostini with dill

MAKES 30 *Letting the shrimp stand, off heat, in the hot water prevents them from overcooking. For a pretty presentation, garnish the crostini with fresh dill sprigs before serving.*

1¼ pounds plus 15 uncooked
    medium shrimp in shells

4 teaspoons fresh lemon juice
1 tablespoon finely grated lemon peel
3 tablespoons chopped fresh dill
½ cup (3 ounces) whipped cream cheese
1 2-ounce jar fresh salmon caviar

30 ¼-inch-thick slices baguette
    Olive oil

PLACE shrimp in heavy large saucepan. Cover with cold water. Bring just to simmer over medium heat. Remove from heat. Let stand 2 minutes. Drain shrimp; peel and devein. Cut 15 shrimp in half lengthwise; wrap, chill, and reserve for garnish.

PLACE remaining shrimp in processor. Add lemon juice and lemon peel; blend until smooth. Transfer puree to medium bowl; mix in dill. Fold in cream cheese, then caviar. Season mousse to taste with salt and pepper.

DO AHEAD *Mousse can be made 4 hours ahead. Cover and chill.*

PREHEAT oven to 350°F. Brush bread slices lightly on both sides with oil. Arrange on rimmed baking sheet. Bake until beginning to color, turning once, about 8 minutes. Cool crostini completely.

SPREAD mousse on crostini. Top with reserved shrimp halves.

Beef carpaccio crostini with black truffle vinaigrette

MAKES 24 *The incredibly pungent, earthy vinaigrette makes this dish even more luxurious. Because fresh truffles are very expensive, the canned or jarred ones are much more practical. You can find them at some supermarkets, specialty foods stores, French markets, and Italian markets. Use any leftover truffles in omelets, risottos, or pasta, or paired with cheese.*

8 teaspoons walnut oil or olive oil
2 tablespoons finely chopped
    black truffle from jar
4 teaspoons red wine vinegar
2 teaspoons Dijon mustard

24 ⅓-inch-thick baguette slices

    Purchased tapenade or Kalamata olive spread
24 large fresh arugula leaves
24 wide Parmesan cheese shavings
1 8-ounce New York strip steak (about 1 inch
    thick and 2 inches wide), well-trimmed,
    cut crosswise into ⅛-inch-thick slices

WHISK oil, truffle, vinegar, and mustard in small bowl. Season vinaigrette to taste with salt and pepper.

PREHEAT oven to 350°F. Arrange bread slices on rimmed baking sheet. Bake until just beginning to color, about 8 minutes. Cool crostini on sheet.

DO AHEAD *Vinaigrette and crostini can be made ahead. Cover and chill vinaigrette up to 1 day. Cover crostini and let stand at room temperature up to 4 hours.*

SPREAD each crostini with tapenade. Top each with arugula leaf, cheese shaving, slice of beef, and some vinaigrette. Arrange on platter.

SIMPLE SLICING Partially freezing the steak will make it much easier to slice.

Crostini with burrata cheese, pink pepper, and arugula

MAKES 16 *A simple preparation is just the thing to show off these high-quality ingredients. Burrata cheese is an ultra-creamy combination of fresh moz-zarella stuffed with cream and curds. It's available at some supermarkets, cheese shops, and specialty foods stores. Fleur de sel (fine French sea salt) can be found at some supermarkets and at specialty foods stores, but coarse kosher salt can also be used. Pink peppercorns are available in the spice section of many supermarkets.*

16 ¼-inch-thick baguette slices
   Extra-virgin olive oil
½ garlic clove
   Arugula leaves (about 3 ounces)
16 tablespoons burrata cheese (about 12 ounces)
2 teaspoons pink peppercorns
   Fleur de sel (fine French sea salt)

PREHEAT broiler. Arrange bread on baking sheet. Brush with oil on both sides; rub with garlic. Broil until golden, about 1½ minutes per side. Transfer toasts to platter. Top with arugula and cheese. Drizzle with oil. Sprinkle with pink peppercorns and fleur de sel.

Bruschetta with tomato, avocado, basil, and mint

MAKES ABOUT 30 *This topping is the ultimate salsa, with beautiful heirloom tomatoes and rich, creamy avocados. Garnish the bruschetta with whole fresh mint leaves, if desired.*

1 sourdough baguette, cut crosswise
   into ¼- to ⅓-inch-thick rounds
   Olive oil

1 large garlic clove, peeled
1 cup chopped onion
¼ cup chopped fresh basil
¼ cup chopped fresh mint
2 tablespoons fresh lemon juice
1 tablespoon (packed) chopped
   jalapeño chiles with seeds
1 pound assorted heirloom tomatoes,
   coarsely chopped, juices drained
2 large avocados, halved, pitted,
   peeled, cut into small cubes

PREHEAT oven to 425°F. Arrange bread rounds on large rimmed baking sheet. Brush with oil; sprinkle with salt and pepper. Bake until crisp, about 12 minutes. Cool.

DO AHEAD *Can be made 2 hours ahead. Let stand at room temperature.*

PRESS garlic into medium bowl. Add onion, basil, mint, lemon juice, and chiles. Mix in tomatoes, then avocados; season to taste with salt and pepper. Spoon onto toasts.

FIRST COURSES

Mussels in wine, mustard, and saffron broth

6 SERVINGS *Serve the mussels with a crusty baguette or french fries to soak up the flavorful broth.*

- ½ **cup (1 stick) butter**
- 1 **cup finely chopped shallots (about 4 large)**
- 8 **garlic cloves, chopped**
- 2 **tablespoons chopped fresh thyme**
- 2 **cups dry white wine**
- 3 **tablespoons Dijon mustard**
- ½ **teaspoon saffron threads**

- ¼ **cup heavy whipping cream**
- 3 **pounds small mussels, scrubbed, debearded**
- ½ **cup chopped fresh chives or green onions**

MELT butter in heavy large pot over medium-high heat. Add shallots, garlic, and thyme; sprinkle with pepper. Sauté until shallots are soft, about 5 minutes. Mix in wine and mustard. Boil 2 minutes. Add saffron. Remove from heat and let steep 5 minutes.

DO AHEAD *Can be made 1 hour ahead. Let stand at room temperature.*

ADD cream and mussels to pot and return to boil. Cover and cook until mussels open, about 6 minutes (discard any mussels that do not open). Mix in chives. Season broth to taste with salt and pepper. Divide mussels and broth among 6 shallow bowls.

In the shell When buying live mussels or clams, choose tightly closed shells that aren't chipped or broken. Store **mussels** in a bowl covered with a damp towel in the refrigerator, and use them within one day of purchase. When it's time to cook them, scrub the mussels under cold running water with a vegetable brush to remove any sand. Debeard them by grabbing the fibers that are attached to the shell and pulling down firmly. If that doesn't work, use pliers or cut off as much as you can with kitchen scissors. **Clams** should be used within four days of their harvest. Store them in a bowl covered with a damp towel in the back of the refrigerator. Before using them, scrub the clams under cold running water with a vegetable brush.

Steamed clams with spicy sausage and tomatoes

6 SERVINGS *The combination of clams and sausages is common in the Mediterranean. This version gets an interesting flavor kick from the balsamic vinegar.*

2 tablespoons olive oil
1 pound hot Italian sausages, casings removed
½ cup chopped shallots
4 garlic cloves, chopped
¼ teaspoon dried crushed red pepper
1 14½-ounce can diced tomatoes in juice
1 cup low-salt chicken broth
2 tablespoons balsamic vinegar
4 pounds littleneck clams (about 3 dozen), scrubbed
½ cup chopped fresh basil

HEAT oil in heavy large pot over medium-high heat. Add sausages; sauté until almost cooked through, breaking up with fork, about 10 minutes. Add shallots, garlic, and crushed red pepper. Sauté until sausage is cooked through, about 5 minutes. Mix in tomatoes with juices, broth, and vinegar. Add clams; cover and boil until clams open, about 8 minutes (discard any clams that do not open). Mix in basil.

Calamari fritti with creamy ponzu dipping sauce

4 TO 6 SERVINGS *Here's an Italian appetizer updated with Asian ingredients. Ponzu is a Japanese dipping sauce made from lemon juice or rice vinegar, soy sauce, sake, mirin, seaweed, and bonito (dried tuna) flakes. It's available at specialty foods stores and Asian markets.*

Vegetable oil (for frying)
6 tablespoons mayonnaise
2 tablespoons ponzu
1½ tablespoons chopped fresh cilantro
1½ teaspoons grated peeled fresh ginger
1½ teaspoons fresh lime juice
3 pinches (or more) of cayenne pepper

1 pound cleaned calamari, thawed if frozen, bodies cut crosswise into ¼-inch-thick rings, tentacles left whole
½ cup all purpose flour

POUR enough oil into heavy large deep skillet to reach depth of 2 inches. Heat oil to 375°F. Whisk mayonnaise and next 5 ingredients in small bowl for dipping sauce. Chill.

SPRINKLE calamari with salt and pepper. Place flour in medium bowl. Working in batches, toss calamari rings and tentacles in flour to coat, then fry in oil until golden and crisp, turning occasionally, about 1 minute. Using slotted spoon, transfer calamari to paper towels to drain. Sprinkle with salt; serve immediately with dipping sauce.

Grilled peaches with pecorino and prosciutto

4 SERVINGS *Here's a new take on the classic melon and prosciutto combination. Peach halves are lightly charred on the grill, then topped with salty pecorino and prosciutto. Make sure your peaches are ripe but still firm so they won't fall apart when they're grilled.*

Nonstick vegetable oil spray

4 firm but ripe peaches, halved, pitted

2 tablespoons extra-virgin olive oil

8 very thin slices pecorino cheese (each about 2×2 inches, shaved with vegetable peeler from large wedge)

4 thin slices prosciutto, halved lengthwise

SPRAY grill rack with nonstick spray; prepare barbecue (high heat). Brush peach halves with oil and sprinkle with salt and pepper. Grill peaches until lightly charred, about 2 minutes per side. Place on large plate, skin side down. Top each with cheese slice and drape with prosciutto. Serve immediately.

Parsnip and pear latkes

MAKES 8 TO 10 *These innovative savory pancakes are made with parsnip, pear, and panko (Japanese breadcrumbs) instead of the traditional potatoes and matzo meal. Look for panko in the Asian foods section of the supermarket and at Asian markets.*

1 6- to 7-ounce underripe Bosc pear, quartered, cored

1 7- to 8-ounce parsnip, peeled, cut into 1-inch rounds

1 large egg, beaten to blend

1½ tablespoons chopped celery leaves

1½ teaspoons drained white horseradish

¾ teaspoon salt

½ cup panko (Japanese breadcrumbs)
Vegetable oil (for frying)

USING coarse grating blade, shred pear in processor. Transfer to paper towels; squeeze very dry. Transfer to large bowl. Shred parsnip in processor; add to pear. Mix in next 4 ingredients, then panko and a sprinkle of black pepper. Coat bottom of large skillet with oil; heat over medium heat. Drop batter by packed ¼ cupfuls into skillet; flatten to ½-inch thickness. Sauté until brown and cooked through, about 4 minutes per side. Drain on paper towels.

Chestnut pancakes with bacon and crème fraîche

MAKES ABOUT 24 *Topped with chopped chives, these little pancakes make a great appetizer; drizzled with maple syrup, they're ready for breakfast. Jarred, steamed chestnuts make a flavorful substitute for flour in the batter.*

6 slices thick-cut bacon, chopped

¾ cup whole milk

2 large eggs

2 teaspoons baking powder

½ teaspoon salt

1½ cups coarsely chopped jarred steamed chestnuts (7 to 8 ounces), divided

Crème fraîche or sour cream
Chopped chives or maple syrup

COOK bacon in large skillet over medium heat until brown and crisp. Using slotted spoon, transfer bacon to paper towels to drain. Transfer 2 tablespoons bacon drippings to blender; add milk and next 3 ingredients, then 1 cup chestnuts. Blend until batter is smooth. Pour batter into bowl; stir in remaining ½ cup chestnuts.

POUR remaining bacon drippings into small bowl. Brush same skillet with some drippings; heat over medium heat. Drop in batter by rounded tablespoonfuls. Cook pancakes until brown and cooked through, about 3 minutes per side. Transfer to plates. Top with crème fraîche and bacon, then chives or maple syrup.

Goat cheese and herb soufflés

6 SERVINGS *The baking dishes are coated with grated Parmesan for an extra flavor boost and so that the airy soufflé batter has something to cling to as it rises. Be sure to serve the soufflés as soon as they come out of the oven before they have a chance to deflate.*

7	tablespoons grated Parmesan cheese, divided
¾	cup whole milk
3	large egg yolks

2	tablespoons (¼ stick) butter
½	cup chopped red onion
1	teaspoon chopped fresh thyme
½	teaspoon chopped fresh rosemary
2	tablespoons all purpose flour
1	cup crumbled soft fresh goat cheese, divided
¾	teaspoon salt
¼	teaspoon ground black pepper
4	large egg whites

PREHEAT oven to 350°F. Butter six ¾-cup soufflé dishes. Place 1 tablespoon Parmesan in each dish; rotate dishes to coat with cheese, leaving excess in dishes. Place dishes on baking sheet. Whisk milk and yolks in bowl to blend.

MELT butter in medium saucepan over medium-high heat. Add onion, thyme, and rosemary; sauté 3 minutes. Add flour; whisk 1 minute. Whisk in milk mixture. Whisk soufflé base until thick and bubbling, about 2 minutes. Remove pan from heat. Add ½ cup goat cheese, salt, and black pepper; whisk until cheese melts. Beat egg whites in large bowl until stiff but not dry. Fold ¼ of whites into soufflé base in pan. Sprinkle remaining ½ cup goat cheese and 1 tablespoon Parmesan over. Fold in remaining egg whites in 2 additions. Divide mixture among dishes.

BAKE soufflés until puffed and beginning to brown on top, about 20 minutes. Serve immediately.

Glazed smoked duck with candied kumquats

6 SERVINGS *This is perfect for a special occasion: Purchased smoked duck breasts are brushed with a sweet, cinnamon-scented sauce and placed on a bed of peppery arugula. Look for the duck in the deli or meat section of the supermarket or online at dartagnan.com; slices of smoked turkey can be substituted in a pinch. If you can't find kumquats at your supermarket, buy them online at kumquatgrowers.com or melissas.com. They are generally available from mid-November through June.*

1	cup dry white wine
1	cup apricot jam
1	bay leaf
2	cinnamon sticks, broken in half
1⅓	cups kumquats, stemmed, quartered, seeded
2	teaspoons Grand Marnier or other orange liqueur

3	cups arugula
2	6-ounce smoked duck breasts, each cut into 15 thin slices

COMBINE first 4 ingredients in medium saucepan. Bring to boil over medium-high heat, stirring occasionally. Add kumquats; simmer until kumquats are tender and liquid is syrupy, about 15 minutes. Remove from heat; stir in Grand Marnier. Season to taste with salt and pepper.

DO AHEAD *Can be made 1 week ahead. Cool, cover, and chill. Rewarm over low heat before continuing.*

STRAIN glaze into small bowl. Discard cinnamon and bay leaf; reserve candied kumquats and glaze separately.

DIVIDE arugula among plates. Top each with 5 duck slices; brush with glaze. Place 1 kumquat quarter on each duck slice.

Black pepper sabayon on asparagus

6 SERVINGS *Sabayon is a classic French egg-yolk sauce; this quick version is made with mayonnaise, flavored with toasted peppercorns and used as a beautiful golden topping for asparagus. It's also great on fish and poultry or as a sandwich spread.*

- 1 tablespoon whole black peppercorns
- 2 tablespoons finely chopped white onion
- ½ cup mayonnaise
- ⅓ cup sour cream
- 2 tablespoons heavy whipping cream
- 1 teaspoon white wine vinegar

- 2 pounds large asparagus spears, trimmed
  Lemon wedges

PLACE peppercorns in heavy resealable plastic bag; crush coarsely with mallet. Heat heavy small skillet over medium heat. Add peppercorns and onion. Cook until peppercorns are fragrant and toasted, stirring occasionally, about 4 minutes. Whisk mayonnaise, sour cream, whipping cream, and vinegar in small bowl to blend. Stir in peppercorn mixture. Season sabayon to taste with salt.

PREHEAT broiler. Butter 13×9×2-inch glass baking dish or broilerproof casserole.

COOK asparagus in large pot of boiling salted water until crisp-tender, about 5 minutes. Drain well and pat dry. Arrange asparagus in single layer in prepared dish. Spread with sabayon. Broil until sauce turns golden, about 2 minutes. Divide among plates. Serve with lemon wedges.

Fried tofu with spicy miso sauce

4 SERVINGS *Red miso is a reddish-brown, fermented-soybean paste that comes from Japan. Black bean garlic sauce is a salty, flavorful mash made from fermented black beans and garlic. Sambal oelek is a fiery Asian condiment made from chiles, brown sugar, and salt. You can find the red miso at Asian markets and in the refrigerated section of the supermarket where tofu is sold. Look for black bean garlic sauce and sambal oelek in the Asian foods section of many supermarkets and at Asian markets.*

- 1 16-ounce package extra-firm tofu
  Canola oil (for frying)

- 6½ tablespoons water
- 5 tablespoons red miso (fermented soybean paste)
- 2 tablespoons sugar
- 2 garlic cloves, minced
- 1 teaspoon black bean garlic sauce
- 1 teaspoon hot chili paste (such as *sambal oelek*)
- 1 green onion, minced

CUT tofu into 1-inch cubes. Drain cubes on several layers of paper towels 15 minutes. Pour enough canola oil into heavy large saucepan to reach depth of 2 inches. Attach deep-fry thermometer to side of pan and heat oil to 350°F. Add tofu and cook until golden, stirring occasionally for even browning, about 2 minutes. Using slotted metal spoon, carefully transfer tofu to fresh paper towels to drain.

MIX 6½ tablespoons water, miso, sugar, garlic, black bean garlic sauce, and chili paste in medium saucepan to blend. Bring just to boil over medium-high heat. Add tofu and stir to coat. Divide tofu among 4 plates; sprinkle with green onion.

Honeydew and prosciutto with greens and mint vinaigrette

2 SERVINGS *Prosciutto is paired with honeydew melon instead of cantaloupe and served alongside a fresh salad with a mint- and anise-flavored dressing lightly sweetened with honey.*

- 1 tablespoon Sherry wine vinegar
- 1 teaspoon honey
- ¼ teaspoon aniseed
- 3 tablespoons thinly sliced fresh mint, divided
- 2 tablespoons olive oil
- 4 cups (packed) mixed baby greens (about 3 ounces)
- 4 honeydew melon wedges, peeled
- 6 thin slices prosciutto

WHISK first 3 ingredients and 1 tablespoon mint in small bowl; whisk in oil. Season dressing to taste with salt and pepper. Toss greens with 2 tablespoons dressing in medium bowl; divide between 2 plates.

PLACE melon next to greens; drape prosciutto over melon. Drizzle remaining dressing over prosciutto and melon. Sprinkle with remaining 2 tablespoons mint and freshly ground pepper.

Prosciutto with persimmon, pomegranate, and arugula

8 SERVINGS *This dish showcases two fall fruits: persimmons and pomegranates. Be sure to buy a Fuyu persimmon, which can be sliced and eaten while still firm. Hachiya persimmons should only be eaten when fully ripened and very soft and are not suitable for salads. You can find pomegranate vinegar at some supermarkets and at specialty foods stores; raspberry vinegar will work, too.*

- 16 thin slices prosciutto (about 8 ounces)
- ½ cup fresh pomegranate seeds
- 1 large Fuyu persimmon, peeled, pitted, cut into ¼-inch-thick slices
- 4 ounces baby arugula
- ½ cup pistachios, toasted
  Extra-virgin olive oil
  Pomegranate vinegar

ARRANGE 2 prosciutto slices on each plate. Sprinkle pomegranate seeds over. Arrange persimmon next to prosciutto. Mound arugula atop prosciutto. Scatter pistachios over. Sprinkle with pepper; drizzle with oil and vinegar.

Asparagus with gingered orange-sesame dressing

4 SERVINGS *Asparagus is dressed up and enhanced with an Asian-flavored dressing. It can also be served as an appetizer or a side dish for an Asian fusion meal.*

1   **pound asparagus, trimmed**

1   **tablespoon sesame seeds**

2   **tablespoons unseasoned rice vinegar**
2   **teaspoons Dijon mustard**
1   **teaspoon soy sauce**
1   **teaspoon grated peeled fresh ginger**
1   **teaspoon finely grated orange peel**
1   **garlic clove, pressed**
⅔   **cup corn oil**
1   **tablespoon Asian sesame oil**

COOK asparagus in large pot of boiling salted water until crisp-tender, about 4 minutes. Drain. Transfer to bowl of ice water and cool. Drain and pat dry.

STIR sesame seeds in heavy small skillet over low heat until light brown, about 3 minutes; transfer to small bowl.

WHISK vinegar, mustard, soy sauce, ginger, orange peel, and garlic in another small bowl. Gradually whisk in both oils. Season vinaigrette to taste with salt and pepper.

ARRANGE asparagus on plates. Spoon vinaigrette over. Sprinkle with sesame seeds.

D.I.Y. crostini platter Set up a festive do-it-yourself crostini platter so guests can combine their own favorite flavors. Here are a variety of toppings to offer alongside slices of grilled ciabatta bread:

— Roasted red and yellow bell peppers
— Purchased tapenade (a thick spread made from brine-cured olives, capers, anchovies, and seasonings)
— Chopped tomatoes with extra-virgin olive oil, garlic, and basil
— Marinated artichoke hearts
— Mixed chopped fresh herbs (such as thyme, rosemary, chives, parsley)
— Fresh ricotta cheese
— Soft fresh goat cheese
— Shaved Parmesan cheese
— Sliced fresh mozzarella cheese
— Thinly sliced prosciutto
— Sliced smoked salmon
— Aged balsamic vinegar and extra-virgin olive oil

Antipasto salad

2 SERVINGS *Any leftover dressing from this "before-the-meal" salad can be tossed with greens later in the week. If you like, add a few Italian meats, such as salami, prosciutto, or mortadella, to the platter.*

  2 **tablespoons fresh lemon juice**
  1 **tablespoon Dijon mustard**
  2 **anchovy fillets, minced**
  ⅓ **cup olive oil**

  4 **cups shredded romaine lettuce**
  ½ **cup roasted red bell peppers from jar, drained, cut into strips**
  ½ **small fennel bulb, trimmed, sliced**
  1 **6-ounce jar marinated artichoke hearts, drained**
     Greek-style olives
     Grated Parmesan cheese

WHISK lemon juice, mustard, and anchovies in small bowl. Gradually whisk in oil. Season dressing generously with pepper.

TOSS lettuce in medium bowl with enough dressing to coat. Divide between plates. Arrange bell pepper, fennel, artichokes, and olives over lettuce. Drizzle with more dressing. Sprinkle with cheese.

Bresaola with shaved brussels sprouts and horseradish

4 SERVINGS Bresaola, *thinly sliced air-cured beef tenderloin, is topped with a brussels sprout slaw and a bit of grated horseradish. Look for* bresaola *in the deli section of the supermarket and at specialty foods stores and Italian markets.*

  3 **tablespoons olive oil**
  3 **tablespoons Sherry wine vinegar**
  3 **tablespoons minced shallot**
 12 **large brussels sprouts, trimmed**

 12 **thin slices bresaola (about 4 ounces)**
     Grated fresh horseradish

WHISK oil, vinegar, and shallot in small bowl. Season dressing to taste with salt and pepper. Using V-slicer or mandoline, thinly slice enough brussels sprouts to measure 4 cups. Place shaved brussels sprouts in large bowl. Add dressing; toss to coat. Season with salt and pepper.

ARRANGE 3 bresaola slices over each of 4 plates. Divide brussels sprout salad among plates, mounding in center so bresaola is visible. Sprinkle horseradish over brussels sprout salad.

Create a party menu The appetizers and starters in this chapter can be combined in any number of ways to create inventively themed tapas or small-plates parties. Here are just a few examples:

MEDITERRANEAN SMALL-PLATES PARTY

Garlic and Anchovy Dip with Vegetables

Crab Crostini with Green Onions and Crème Fraîche

Chorizo-Filled Dates Wrapped in Bacon

Prosciutto-Wrapped Figs with Gorgonzola and Walnuts

Lamb Kebabs with Pomegranate-Cumin Glaze

SUPER BOWL PARTY

Deviled Cocktail Sausages with Chutney and Lime Dipping Sauce

Pizzette with Fontina, Tomato, Basil, and Prosciutto

Skirt-Steak Quesadillas

Guacamole with Fresh Corn and Chipotle

Black and White Bean Salsa

MANHATTAN COCKTAIL PARTY

Sweet Potato Ribbon Chips

Black and Gold Pizzas

Crabmeat, Corn, and Cumin Salad in Endive Spears

Crostini with Burrata Cheese, Pink Pepper, and Arugula

Beef Carpaccio Crostini with Black Truffle Vinaigrette

Sesame Wonton Triangles with Smoked Salmon and Wasabi

Pancetta Crisps with Goat Cheese and Pear

BY-THE-SEA PARTY

Mini Crab Cakes

Calamari Fritti with Creamy Ponzu Dipping Sauce

Seared Ahi Tuna and Avocado Tartare

Skewered Shrimp with Apricot-Curry Glaze

Steamed Clams with Spicy Sausage and Tomatoes

chilies, stews, and soups

CHILIES

Chicken and White Bean Chili

Weeknight Chili

Chipotle Beef Chili
with Lime Crema

Turkey and Pinto Bean Chili

Vegetarian Black Bean Chili

Black Bean Chili with Butternut
Squash and Swiss Chard

STEWS

Curried Red Lentil and Swiss
Chard Stew with Garbanzo Beans

Spiced Beef Stew with
Carrots and Mint

Roasted-Garlic Beef Stew

Ranchero Beef Stew

Super-Quick Lamb
and Barley Stew

Porcini and Sausage Stew

Chicken Bouillabaisse

Cola-Braised Pork Stew

Spicy Scallop and
Cauliflower Stew

Brazilian Seafood Stew

Crab and Corn Chowder
with Bacon

Smoked Fish Chowder

Fish Soup with Saffron and Cream

Quick Cioppino

Seafood and
Turkey-Sausage Gumbo

Thai Tofu Stew with Zucchini,
Red Bell Pepper, and Lime

SOUPS

Hot-and-Sour Soup with
Shrimp, Napa Cabbage, and
Shiitake Mushrooms

Broccoli and Cauliflower
Cheese Soup with Sausage

Lentil Soup with Lamb and Mint

French Lentil Soup

Split Pea and Green Pea
Soup with Fresh Dill

Beef, Vegetable, and Barley Soup

Creamy Bean Soup with
Fresh Herbs and Spinach

Puerto Rican–Style
Black Bean Soup

Spicy Pasta, Bean, and
Sausage Soup

Vietnamese Beef Soup

Parsnip Soup with Corned
Beef and Cabbage

Parsnip and Apple Soup

Dilled Chicken Chowder

Chicken and Escarole
Soup with Fennel

Chicken and Hominy Soup

Asian Turkey-Noodle Soup
with Ginger and Chiles

Cauliflower Soup with
Thyme Croutons

Sweet Potato Soup with Fried
Pancetta and Rosemary Croutons

Very Simple Pumpkin Soup

Potato, Leek, and Fennel Soup

Escarole Soup with
Pasta and Meatballs

Fresh Wild Mushroom Soup

Portuguese Green Soup

French Onion Soup

Miso-Ginger Consommé

Corn Soup with Potato
and Smoked Ham

Quick Tomato and Basil Soup

Asparagus Soup with
Lemon Crème Fraîche

Roasted Red Pepper Soup
with Orange Cream

Carrot and Caraway Soup

Broccoli Soup with
Chive-Cayenne Oil

Spinach and Lime Soup

Summer Garden Soup

Chilled Zucchini-Mint Soup

Chilled Avocado and Mint Soup

Chilled Corn Soup
with Adobo Swirl

Watermelon and
Cucumber Gazpacho

Speedy Gazpacho

Pineapple and Bell
Pepper Gazpacho

Chilled Beet, Orange,
and Dill Soup

Chilled Cucumber-Yogurt
Soup with Radishes

Chilled Fennel Soup with Pernod

Chilled Red Bell Pepper Soup

Chilled Carrot Soup
with Garden Herbs

Chilled Yellow Pepper
and White Bean Soup

Chilled Pea and Tarragon Soup

Chilled Summer Squash
Soup with Curry

Chilled Pea Pod Soup

tool kit Chilies, stews, and soups are every bit as deliciously doable on a weeknight as on a leisurely weekend. There are plenty of shortcuts you can take without sacrificing flavor.

Use canned beans to speed things up: They just need to simmer until heated through.

Tender cuts such as chicken breasts, pork tenderloin, filet mignon, and lamb chops, as well as sausages and ground meats, should simmer just until cooked through; don't simmer too long or they will become dry and tough. The same is true of fish and shellfish.

Chicken thighs remain succulent and tender even after cooked through, allowing you to focus on the rest of the meal.

Use meats that are already cooked, such as ham, beef pot roast, and roast chicken; this saves time and is a great way to use leftovers.

Tougher cuts of meat—such as beef chuck, beef brisket, pork spareribs, and lamb shoulder—are good for slower-cooking stews that take a bit longer to cook but need very little attention while on the stove.

In a pinch, you can even transform a purchased basic soup by adding spices, herbs, or vegetables. Add Asian flavors to chicken noodle soup, for example, by adding Asian sesame oil, minced peeled fresh ginger, and green onions. Or turn a traditional gazpacho into something more elegant by adding crabmeat, cooked shrimp, or lobster.

Here's how to be creative _and_ careful: First mix ingredients into a cup of the soup to see how they taste; you won't ruin the whole pot if you don't like the results.

CHILIES

Chicken and white bean chili

6 SERVINGS *Cornbread or cheddar-jalapeño biscuits would be an excellent accompaniment to this simple, satisfying chili.*

¼	cup olive oil
1⅓	cups chopped onion
1	large green bell pepper, chopped
6	garlic cloves, chopped
2¼	pounds skinless boneless chicken thighs, cut into ½-inch cubes
3½	tablespoons chili powder
2	tablespoons tomato paste
1	tablespoon ground cumin
1	tablespoon dried oregano
2	15- to 16-ounce cans white beans, drained, liquid reserved
2	14½-ounce cans diced tomatoes in juice
½	cup chopped fresh cilantro

HEAT oil in large pot over medium-high heat. Add onion, bell pepper, and garlic; sauté 5 minutes. Add chicken; sprinkle with salt and pepper and sauté 5 minutes longer. Mix in next 6 ingredients, including 1 cup reserved bean liquid; bring to boil. Reduce heat and simmer until chicken is cooked through, stirring occasionally, about 25 minutes. If chili is too thick, add more bean liquid by tablespoonfuls. Season to taste with salt and pepper. Mix in cilantro.

Weeknight chili

2 SERVINGS; CAN BE DOUBLED *A last-minute squeeze of lemon makes this chili even more flavorful.*

1½	tablespoons vegetable oil
1	large onion, chopped
3	garlic cloves, minced
1	pound ground beef
1	tablespoon (or more) chili powder
2	cups canned crushed tomatoes with added puree
1	15- to 16-ounce can kidney beans, drained
2	tablespoons tomato paste
1	teaspoon fresh lemon juice
	Shredded cheddar cheese
	Sour cream

HEAT oil in heavy medium saucepan over medium-low heat. Add onion and cook 5 minutes, stirring occasionally. Add garlic and cook until onion is translucent, stirring occasionally, about 5 minutes. Add beef. Sprinkle generously with salt and pepper. Cook until beef is no longer pink, crumbling with fork. Add 1 tablespoon chili powder and stir 1 minute. Add tomatoes, beans, and tomato paste. Cover and simmer 30 minutes, stirring occasionally. Season to taste with salt and pepper, adding more chili powder, if desired.

DO AHEAD *Can be made 3 days ahead. Cool slightly. Chill uncovered until cold, then cover and keep chilled.*

STIR lemon juice into chili. Serve, passing cheese and sour cream separately.

Chipotle beef chili with lime crema

6 TO 8 SERVINGS *Chipotle chiles, canned in a spicy tomato sauce called* adobo, *are available at some supermarkets and at specialty foods stores and Latin markets. Serve with tortilla chips, if desired.*

- 3 **pounds ground beef**
- 3 **cups chopped onions**
- 6 **garlic cloves, finely chopped**
- ½ **cup chili powder**
- 2 **14-ounce cans beef broth**
- 1 **cup canned crushed tomatoes with added puree**
- ½ **cup dark beer**
- 2 **tablespoons minced canned chipotle chiles**
- 2 **tablespoons yellow cornmeal**
- 2 **15- to 16-ounce cans black beans, drained, rinsed**

- 1½ **cups sour cream**
- 2 **tablespoons fresh lime juice**
- 1 **tablespoon finely grated lime peel**

HEAT heavy large pot over high heat. Add beef; sauté until cooked through, breaking up with spoon, about 8 minutes. Transfer to large bowl. Add onions and garlic to same pot. Sauté until onions are tender, about 8 minutes. Add chili powder. Sauté until fragrant, about 3 minutes. Add broth, tomatoes, beer, chiles, and beef. Cover partially; simmer until chili is thick, stirring often, about 1 hour 10 minutes. Gradually stir cornmeal into chili. Stir in beans. Simmer until heated through. Season to taste with salt and pepper.

DO AHEAD *Can be made 1 day ahead. Cool slightly. Chill uncovered until cold, then cover and keep chilled. Rewarm over medium heat.*

WHISK sour cream, lime juice, and lime peel in small bowl. Season to taste with salt. Spoon chili into bowls. Spoon lime crema atop chili.

THE CHIPOTLE FACTOR Save leftover chipotle chiles and sauce (keep them in the fridge in an airtight container) to add smoky, spicy heat to soups, stews, sauces—and even macaroni and cheese.

With the works Part of the beauty of chili is the go-withs: They're a simple way to turn a modest chili into a fast, easy party dish. Just set out bowls of chopped cilantro, salsa, sour cream, chopped avocado, and grated cheddar or Jack cheese. Let guests dress up the chili to their liking. And don't forget plenty of hot sauce for those who like it spicy.

Turkey and pinto bean chili

6 TO 8 SERVINGS *Inspired by traditional Mexican* mole, *this chili includes a touch of chocolate to add depth.*

Nonstick olive oil spray
1 large onion, chopped
2 medium red bell peppers, chopped
6 garlic cloves, chopped
2 pounds ground turkey
3 tablespoons chili powder
1½ teaspoons ground cumin
1½ teaspoons dried oregano
3 15- to 16-ounce cans pinto beans, drained
1 28-ounce can diced tomatoes in juice
3 cups low-salt chicken broth
1 ounce semisweet chocolate, chopped

GENEROUSLY spray bottom of heavy large pot with nonstick spray. Add onion, bell peppers, and garlic and sauté over high heat until vegetables begin to soften, about 8 minutes. Add turkey and sauté until no longer pink, breaking up large pieces with back of fork, about 5 minutes. Mix in chili powder, cumin, and oregano and stir 1 minute. Add beans, tomatoes with juice, broth, and chocolate. Bring chili to boil. Reduce heat to medium and simmer uncovered until chili thickens, stirring occasionally, about 1 hour. Season to taste with salt and pepper.

Vegetarian black bean chili

4 MAIN-COURSE SERVINGS *For a less spicy chili, reduce the chili powder to one tablespoon.*

¼ cup olive oil
2 cups chopped onions
1⅔ cups coarsely chopped red bell peppers (about 2 medium)
6 garlic cloves, chopped
2 tablespoons chili powder
2 teaspoons dried oregano
1½ teaspoons ground cumin
½ teaspoon cayenne pepper
3 15- to 16-ounce cans black beans, drained, ½ cup liquid reserved
1 15-ounce can tomato sauce

Chopped fresh cilantro
Sour cream
Grated Monterey Jack cheese
Chopped green onions

HEAT oil in heavy large pot over medium-high heat. Add onions, bell peppers, and garlic; sauté until onions soften, about 10 minutes. Mix in chili powder, oregano, cumin, and cayenne; stir 2 minutes. Mix in beans, ½ cup reserved bean liquid, and tomato sauce. Bring chili to boil, stirring occasionally. Reduce heat to medium-low and simmer until flavors blend and chili thickens, stirring occasionally, about 15 minutes. Season to taste with salt and pepper.

LADLE chili into bowls. Pass chopped cilantro, sour cream, grated cheese, and green onions separately.

Black bean chili with butternut squash and Swiss chard

4 MAIN-COURSE SERVINGS *This vegetarian chili doesn't stop with beans: It gets added interest, color, and nutrients from squash and greens.*

2	tablespoons olive oil
2½	cups chopped onions
3	garlic cloves, chopped
2½	cups ½-inch pieces peeled butternut squash
2	tablespoons chili powder
2	teaspoons ground cumin
3	15- to 16-ounce cans black beans, rinsed, drained
2½	cups vegetable broth
1	14½-ounce can diced tomatoes in juice
3	cups (packed) coarsely chopped Swiss chard leaves (from 1 small bunch)

HEAT oil in heavy large pot over medium-high heat. Add onions and garlic; sauté until tender and golden, about 9 minutes. Add squash; stir 2 minutes. Stir in chili powder and cumin. Stir in beans, broth, and tomatoes with juice; bring to boil. Reduce heat and simmer, uncovered, until squash is tender, about 15 minutes. Stir in chard; simmer until chard is tender but still bright green, about 4 minutes longer. Season to taste with salt and pepper. Ladle chili into bowls.

SQUASH, CUBED Cubed peeled butternut squash is sold at many supermarkets. If unavailable, here's how to cube safely: Start with a sharp chef's knife and cut a 3-inch piece off the squash's neck. Set the flat end on the cutting board and work downward with a vegetable peeler, removing the skin. With the chef's knife, cut thick slices, and then cut slices into cubes.

STEWS

Curried red lentil and Swiss chard stew with garbanzo beans

6 SERVINGS *If you can't find Swiss chard, substitute an equal amount of spinach.*

  2 tablespoons olive oil
  1 large onion, thinly sliced
  5 teaspoons curry powder
  ¼ teaspoon cayenne pepper
  3 14-ounce cans vegetable broth
  1 large bunch or 2 small bunches
     Swiss chard, tough stalks trimmed,
     coarsely chopped (about 12 cups)
  1 pound red lentils (about 2¼ cups)
  1 15- to 16-ounce can garbanzo
     beans (chickpeas), drained
     Plain yogurt

HEAT oil in heavy large saucepan over medium-high heat. Add onion; sauté until golden, about 13 minutes. Mix in curry powder and cayenne. Add broth and chard. Increase heat; bring to boil. Add lentils and garbanzo beans; reduce heat to medium. Cover; simmer until lentils are tender, stirring twice, about 10 minutes. Ladle stew into bowls. Top with yogurt.

FRESH COLOR Look for the variety of Swiss chard known as Bright Lights, whose stalks and veins can be electric shades of orange, yellow, or even hot pink. This variety is delicious (its flavor is a bit milder than red and green chards), and will add a fun touch to this gold-and-green stew.

Spiced beef stew with carrots and mint

2 SERVINGS *The spice flavors here are aromatic rather than hot. Serve the stew with couscous and glasses of slightly chilled Beaujolais.*

   2 tablespoons olive oil, divided
  12 ounces beef tenderloin, cut into 1-inch cubes
   1 cup sliced shallots (about 3 large)
   8 ounces peeled baby carrots
   2 teaspoons ground cumin
  1½ teaspoons pumpkin pie spice
   ⅛ teaspoon cayenne pepper
   1 tablespoon all purpose flour
  2½ cups beef broth
   ⅓ cup chopped fresh mint, divided

HEAT 1 tablespoon oil in large nonstick skillet over high heat. Sprinkle beef with salt and pepper. Add beef to skillet and sauté until cooked to desired doneness, about 2 minutes for medium-rare. Using slotted spoon, transfer beef to bowl. Add remaining 1 tablespoon oil to skillet. Add shallots and carrots and sauté until golden, about 3 minutes. Add all spices; stir 30 seconds. Sprinkle flour over; stir 30 seconds. Stir in broth and bring to boil. Reduce heat to medium; simmer until carrots are just tender, about 8 minutes. Return beef to skillet; cook until sauce thickens slightly, about 1 minute. Season stew to taste with salt and pepper. Stir in ¼ cup chopped mint. Ladle stew into bowls. Sprinkle with remaining chopped mint.

Roasted-garlic beef stew

4 SERVINGS *Using tenderloin, a faster-cooking cut of beef, is the secret to this quick and delicious stew.*

16 garlic cloves, unpeeled
 5 tablespoons butter, divided

 1 pound beef tenderloin, cut into 1-inch pieces
 2 tablespoons all purpose flour, divided
 2 large parsnips, peeled, cut into ½-inch pieces
 2 carrots, peeled, cut into ½-inch pieces
 1 large potato, peeled, cut into ½-inch pieces
 1 rutabaga, peeled, cut into ½-inch pieces
 1 14-ounce can beef broth
 1 cup dry red wine
 1 tablespoon dried thyme
 2 teaspoons dried rubbed sage

PREHEAT oven to 350°F. Place garlic in small baking dish. Top with 1 tablespoon butter. Bake until butter melts and garlic is tender and beginning to brown, about 15 minutes. Cool garlic 5 minutes. Peel garlic and set aside.

MELT 3 tablespoons butter in heavy large pot over high heat. Sprinkle beef with salt and pepper; dust with 1 tablespoon flour. Add beef to pot. Sauté until no longer pink, about 6 minutes. Transfer beef to bowl. Add vegetables, broth, wine, herbs, and roasted garlic to pot. Bring to boil. Reduce heat to medium-low, cover, and simmer until vegetables are tender, about 25 minutes.

RETURN beef and any juices to pot. Mix remaining 1 tablespoon butter and 1 tablespoon flour in small bowl. Whisk flour paste into stew. Simmer uncovered until sauce thickens, about 2 minutes. Season to taste with salt and pepper.

GARLIC WITH EVERYTHING While you're at it, roast some extra garlic to use the next day. It's delicious spread on toasted bread for a quick snack, or tossed with pasta, olive oil, Parmigiano-Reggiano cheese, and dried crushed red pepper for an easy lunch.

Ranchero beef stew

4 SERVINGS *Try this over rice or egg noodles, with a dollop of sour cream. Although the stew cooks for more than an hour, it requires no attention for most of that time.*

 1 tablespoon olive oil
 1 pound beef stew meat, cut into 1-inch cubes
 1 large onion, cubed
 2 medium carrots, cubed
 3 garlic cloves, chopped
 1 15- to 16-ounce can stewed tomatoes
 1 cup beef broth
 1 4-ounce can diced green chiles
 ½ cup sliced pimiento-stuffed green olives
 2 tablespoons dried oregano
 ⅓ cup chopped fresh cilantro

HEAT oil in heavy large Dutch oven over high heat. Sprinkle beef with salt and pepper. Add to Dutch oven; sauté until brown, about 5 minutes. Add onion, carrots, and garlic; sauté 5 minutes. Add tomatoes, broth, chiles, olives, and oregano. Bring to simmer. Reduce heat to low, cover, and simmer until beef is tender, about 1 hour. Uncover; simmer until juices thicken, about 10 minutes. Season to taste with salt and pepper. Stir in cilantro.

Super-quick lamb and barley stew

4 SERVINGS *This is the perfect way to take advantage of leftover leg of lamb. For more zing, add a teaspoon or two of chopped rosemary, thyme, mint, or marjoram after cooking.*

2   tablespoons (¼ stick) butter
2   carrots, chopped
2   large celery stalks, chopped
1   onion, chopped
3   garlic cloves, chopped
1   cup pearl barley, rinsed
4   cups beef broth
3   cups cooked lamb, cut into ½-inch pieces

MELT butter in heavy large pot over medium-high heat. Add carrots, celery, onion, and garlic; sauté until vegetables begin to soften, about 8 minutes. Add barley; stir until coated, about 2 minutes. Add broth and simmer until barley is tender, about 45 minutes. Add lamb and heat through. Ladle stew into bowls.

Porcini and sausage stew

4 SERVINGS *Excellent served over pasta or polenta, this stew would be great with a medium-bodied Italian red wine such as Barbera or Dolcetto d'Alba.*

1   pound sweet Italian sausages, casings removed
6   garlic cloves, chopped
4   14½-ounce cans diced peeled tomatoes with juice
2   ounces dried porcini mushrooms, reconstituted in 2 cups hot water (see note below)
¾   cup dry red wine
2   bay leaves

SAUTÉ sausage and garlic in heavy large pot over medium heat until sausage is cooked through, breaking up with back of fork, about 10 minutes. Add tomatoes with juice, mushrooms, mushroom soaking liquid, wine, and bay leaves; bring to boil. Reduce heat; simmer until sauce thickens and is reduced to about 6 cups, stirring occasionally, about 1 hour 15 minutes. Season to taste with salt and pepper. Discard bay leaves.

DO AHEAD *Can be made 2 days ahead. Cool slightly. Chill uncovered until cold, then cover and keep chilled. Rewarm over low heat.*

RECONSTITUTING PORCINI MUSHROOMS Reconstituting dried porcini is easy: Soak 2 ounces mushrooms in 2 cups boiling water for about half an hour. Strain the liquid to remove the grit, and set aside both the mushrooms and the soaking liquid (which is full of earthy mushroom flavor).

Chicken bouillabaisse

6 SERVINGS *In this unexpected take on the southern French classic, chicken (not fish) is the star. This is especially delicious served with the Garlicky Beans with Feta and Mint on page 450. Top each serving with a quick faux rouille, made by mixing ½ cup mayonnaise with 2 minced garlic cloves, 2 teaspoons fresh lemon juice, and ½ teaspoon paprika.*

 3 tablespoons olive oil plus more for brushing
 1 onion, sliced
 ¾ cup dry white wine
 2 4-inch-long orange peel strips (orange part only)
 1 teaspoon dried thyme
 ¼ teaspoon saffron threads
 1 14½-ounce can diced tomatoes in juice
 1 14-ounce can low-salt chicken broth
 6 chicken legs (split into drumsticks and thighs), skinned
 12 ½-inch-thick baguette slices
 Olive oil

PREHEAT oven to 375°F. Heat 3 tablespoons oil in large wide ovenproof pan over medium-high heat. Add onion and sauté until golden, about 8 minutes. Add wine, orange peel strips, thyme, and saffron and bring to boil. Add tomatoes with juice and broth; bring to boil. Sprinkle chicken with salt and pepper. Arrange chicken pieces in single layer in pan, submerging in sauce; return mixture to boil. Cover pan and place in oven. Bake until chicken is cooked through, about 45 minutes.

REMOVE from oven; keep covered. Maintain oven temperature.

PLACE baguette slices on baking sheet; brush with oil. Bake until golden, about 12 minutes. Spoon chicken and sauce into shallow bowls. Top each serving with 2 toasted baguette slices.

LAST-MINUTE FEAST A bottle of rosé, some crusty bread, and a mixed-greens salad is all you need to turn this quick-cooking bouillabaisse into the centerpiece of an impromptu dinner party. Pick up some grapes and soft-ripened cheese for dessert.

Cola-braised pork stew

4 SERVINGS *Southerners often use cola as an ingredient, including as a braising liquid for pork ribs or shoulder. Here's a quicker version of that traditional preparation; it simmers for about an hour and a half, but mostly unattended. The phosphoric acid in cola actually has a tenderizing effect on the meat, and the soda gives deep flavor with just a touch of sweetness. Don't use diet cola—the artificial sweetener distorts the flavor. Serve over steamed white rice.*

 1 tablespoon vegetable oil
 2 pounds boneless country-style pork ribs, excess fat trimmed, cut into 1½- to 2-inch cubes
 2 cups cola
 6 garlic cloves, minced
 3 tablespoons soy sauce
 2 tablespoons chopped peeled fresh ginger
 1 bunch green onions, chopped, divided

HEAT oil in large pot over high heat. Add half of pork; sauté until brown on all sides, about 8 minutes. Transfer pork to bowl. Repeat with remaining pork. Return pork to pot. Turn off heat and pour cola slowly into pot. Bring to boil. Reduce heat to medium-low, cover, and simmer 30 minutes. Add garlic, soy sauce, ginger, and half of green onions. Cover and simmer until pork is tender, about 50 minutes longer. Uncover and simmer until sauce is slightly thickened, about 10 minutes. Season to taste with salt and pepper. Transfer to bowl; sprinkle with remaining green onions.

Spicy scallop and cauliflower stew

2 SERVINGS; CAN BE DOUBLED OR TRIPLED *To make this come together even faster, buy bags of trimmed cauliflower florets.*

2	tablespoons olive oil
1	onion, chopped
1	large carrot, peeled, halved lengthwise, sliced
1	garlic clove, minced
¼	teaspoon ground cumin
¼	teaspoon dried crushed red pepper
1	28-ounce can Italian plum tomatoes with juice
1	8-ounce bottle clam juice
¼	cup dry white wine
½	teaspoon dried thyme
½	medium head of cauliflower, cut into bite-size florets (about 4 cups of florets)
¾	pound bay scallops
	Chopped fresh Italian parsley

HEAT oil in heavy medium saucepan over medium-low heat. Add onion and cook until translucent, stirring occasionally, about 8 minutes. Add carrot, garlic, cumin, and red pepper and cook 1 minute. Puree tomatoes with juice in processor; add to pan. Mix in clam juice, wine, and thyme. Simmer 10 minutes.

DO AHEAD *Can be made 1 day ahead. Cool slightly. Chill uncovered until cold, then cover and keep chilled. Rewarm before continuing.*

ADD cauliflower to stew and cook until tender, about 15 minutes. Add scallops and cook until just opaque, about 1 minute. Season to taste with salt and pepper. Garnish with parsley.

Brazilian seafood stew

6 TO 8 SERVINGS *Use red, orange, and yellow bell peppers as well as green to give a festive look. Canned coconut milk is available at many supermarkets and at Southeast Asian and Latin markets.*

4	tablespoons olive oil, divided
2	tablespoons fresh lime juice
1½	pounds white fish fillets (such as tilapia), cut into 1-inch pieces
1½	cups chopped onions
1½	cups chopped bell peppers
2	garlic cloves, chopped
¾	teaspoon dried crushed red pepper
2	cups chopped tomatoes
¾	cup canned unsweetened coconut milk
½	cup chopped fresh cilantro, divided
½	cup chopped green onions, divided
1¼	pounds uncooked medium shrimp, peeled, deveined

WHISK 2 tablespoons oil and lime juice in large bowl. Add fish and sprinkle generously with salt and pepper; stir to coat. Let stand 15 minutes.

HEAT remaining 2 tablespoons oil in large pot over medium heat. Add onion, bell peppers, garlic, and crushed red pepper; sauté 5 minutes. Mix in tomatoes, coconut milk, half of cilantro, and half of green onions. Add shrimp and fish with marinade. Simmer until shrimp and fish are just opaque in center, about 5 minutes. Season to taste with salt and pepper. Transfer to bowl. Sprinkle with remaining cilantro and green onions.

Crab and corn chowder with bacon

6 MAIN-COURSE SERVINGS *If fresh crabmeat isn't available, substitute shrimp or scallops.*

6	ounces bacon, cut into ½-inch pieces
1	large onion, chopped
1	pound unpeeled red-skinned potatoes, diced
2½	cups bottled clam juice
3½	cups half and half
1	pound fresh or frozen corn kernels
1	pound fresh lump crabmeat, coarsely flaked
3	tablespoons chopped fresh thyme

SAUTÉ bacon in heavy large saucepan over medium heat until brown and crisp, about 10 minutes. Using slotted spoon, transfer bacon to paper towels to drain. Pour off all but 3 tablespoons bacon drippings from pan. Add onion to drippings in pan and sauté until beginning to soften, about 3 minutes. Add potatoes and stir until coated. Add clam juice; bring to boil. Reduce heat to medium-low, cover, and simmer 10 minutes.

ADD half and half, corn, crab, thyme, and half of bacon; cook uncovered until potatoes and corn are tender, about 5 minutes. Season to taste with salt and pepper. Ladle chowder into bowls. Garnish with remaining bacon.

Smoked fish chowder

2 SERVINGS; CAN BE DOUBLED *Any kind of smoked fish—salmon, sturgeon, or bluefish—would work here. Leave the potatoes unpeeled; the skins are tender and pretty.*

1	tablespoon butter
2	cups chopped onions
1	8-ounce bottle clam juice
8	ounces red-skinned potatoes, sliced into ¼-inch-thick rounds
1	tablespoon chopped fresh thyme
2	cups half and half
1	4.5-ounce package smoked trout, flaked into small pieces

MELT butter in heavy medium saucepan over medium heat. Add onions; sauté until soft, about 5 minutes. Add clam juice, potatoes, and thyme. Cover and simmer until potatoes are tender, stirring occasionally, about 10 minutes. Add half and half and trout. Simmer 10 minutes. Season to taste with salt and pepper.

Lucky pot An enameled cast-iron pot is ideal for cooking these stews. The cast iron retains heat long after you've turned off the flame, which helps keep the stew warm as it sits. What's more, these pots come in great colors, making them pretty enough to go from stovetop to table.

Fish soup with saffron and cream

4 SERVINGS *This comes together amazingly quickly for such a special dish. It's the perfect weeknight-party standby: Start with a steamed artichoke or asparagus vinaigrette, and serve a fruit tart for dessert.*

- 3 tablespoons olive oil
- 3 medium carrots, peeled, chopped
- 2 leeks (white and pale green parts only), chopped
- 2 celery stalks, chopped
- 1 red bell pepper, chopped
- 1 bay leaf
  Generous pinch of saffron threads
- 2 cups dry white wine
- 1½ cups bottled clam juice
- 1 cup heavy whipping cream

- 1 pound skinless striped bass or halibut fillet, cut into 1-inch pieces
- 1 pound sea scallops, cut in half crosswise
  Chopped fresh chives

HEAT oil in heavy large skillet over medium-high heat. Add carrots, leeks, celery, bell pepper, bay leaf, and saffron to skillet and sauté 5 minutes. Add wine and clam juice and bring to boil. Reduce heat to medium and simmer 10 minutes. Add cream and simmer until vegetables are tender, about 5 minutes.

DO AHEAD *Can be made 1 day ahead. Cover and chill. Return to simmer before continuing.*

ADD fish and scallops to soup and simmer until just cooked through, about 3 minutes. Season to taste with salt and pepper. Discard bay leaf. Ladle soup into large shallow bowls. Sprinkle with chives.

Quick cioppino

4 SERVINGS *This is a streamlined version of the fish stew created by immigrants from Genoa, Italy, when they came to San Francisco in the late nineteenth and early twentieth centuries. Serve the stew with crusty sourdough bread to sop up all the broth.*

- 3 tablespoons olive oil
- 2 cups finely chopped onions
- 2 garlic cloves, minced
- 2 teaspoons chopped fresh rosemary
- ¼ teaspoon dried crushed red pepper
- 1⅔ cups canned crushed tomatoes in puree (from one 28-ounce can)
- 2 8-ounce bottles clam juice
- ¾ cup dry white wine
- 12 ounces halibut fillets, cut into 1-inch pieces
- ½ pound uncooked medium shrimp, peeled, deveined
- ½ pound bay scallops
- ⅓ cup chopped fresh parsley, divided

HEAT oil in large pot over medium-high heat. Add next 4 ingredients; sauté 6 minutes. Add tomatoes, clam juice, and wine; bring to boil. Reduce heat to medium; simmer 18 minutes, stirring occasionally. Add all seafood and 2 tablespoons parsley. Simmer until seafood is opaque in center, about 3 minutes. Season to taste with salt and pepper. Ladle into bowls and sprinkle with remaining parsley.

Seafood and turkey-sausage gumbo

4 SERVINGS *Here is a lighter, faster version of the New Orleans classic, but it's just as tasty. You'll find Creole or Cajun seasoning in the spice section of the supermarket.*

¼ cup all purpose flour

1 tablespoon vegetable oil
1 cup chopped onion
1 cup chopped green bell pepper
3 garlic cloves, chopped
1 teaspoon dried thyme
1 bay leaf
3 low-fat Italian turkey sausages (about 10 ounces), casings removed
1 28-ounce can diced tomatoes in juice
1 cup low-salt chicken broth or vegetable broth
2 teaspoons Creole or Cajun seasoning

8 uncooked large shrimp, peeled, deveined
2 6-ounce catfish fillets, each cut into 4 pieces

SPRINKLE flour over bottom of heavy large pot. Stir flour constantly over medium-low heat until golden brown (do not allow to burn), about 15 minutes. Pour browned flour into bowl.

HEAT oil in same pot over medium heat. Add onion and bell pepper and sauté until tender, about 7 minutes. Add garlic, thyme, and bay leaf; stir 1 minute. Add sausage and sauté until brown, breaking up with back of fork, about 5 minutes; add browned flour. Add tomatoes with juice, broth, and Creole seasoning. Bring to boil. Reduce heat, cover, and simmer 20 minutes to blend flavors, stirring frequently.

ADD shrimp and catfish to pot and simmer just until seafood is opaque in center, about 5 minutes. Discard bay leaf. Season to taste with salt and pepper.

Thai tofu stew with zucchini, red bell pepper, and lime

4 SERVINGS *This is delicious served with jasmine rice. You'll find coconut milk and red curry paste in the Asian foods section of many supermarkets.*

2 tablespoons peanut oil, divided
1 12-ounce package extra-firm tofu, drained, patted dry, cut into ½-inch cubes
1 pound yellow and/or green zucchini, cut into ½-inch cubes
1 large red bell pepper, diced
1 tablespoon minced peeled fresh ginger
1⅓ cups canned unsweetened coconut milk
3 tablespoons (or more) fresh lime juice
1½ tablespoons soy sauce
¾ teaspoon Thai red curry paste
½ cup sliced fresh basil, divided

HEAT 1 tablespoon oil in large nonstick skillet over medium-high heat. Add tofu; sauté until golden, about 4 minutes. Transfer tofu to bowl. Add remaining 1 tablespoon oil, then zucchini and bell pepper to skillet; sauté until beginning to soften, about 4 minutes. Return tofu to skillet. Add ginger; stir 30 seconds. Add coconut milk, 3 tablespoons lime juice, soy sauce, and curry paste; stir to dissolve curry paste. Simmer until sauce thickens, about 6 minutes. Season to taste with salt and more lime juice, if desired. Stir in half of basil. Sprinkle with remaining basil.

COCONUT INSIDER Unsweetened coconut milk—not to be confused with sweetened coconut cream—is sold in cans. Be sure to shake the can before you open it because the cream separates from the milk as the coconut milk sits on the shelf.

73

SOUPS

Hot-and-sour soup with shrimp, Napa cabbage, and shiitake mushrooms

6 SERVINGS *Curry paste, ginger, and lime give genuine Asian flavor—quickly. Thai red curry paste and kaffir lime leaves can be found at Asian markets.*

- 1 teaspoon vegetable oil
- ¾ teaspoon Thai red curry paste
- 3 14-ounce cans low-salt chicken broth
- 2 kaffir lime leaves or 1 teaspoon finely grated lime peel
- 1 tablespoon minced peeled fresh ginger
- 1 pound uncooked medium shrimp, peeled, deveined, halved lengthwise
- 4 ounces shiitake mushrooms, stemmed, sliced ⅛ inch thick
- 8 ounces Napa cabbage, cut crosswise into ⅛-inch-thick slices (about 4 cups)
- ¼ cup fresh lime juice
  Chopped fresh cilantro
  Chopped green onions

HEAT oil in heavy large pot over medium heat. Add curry paste and stir until beginning to stick to pan, about 4 minutes. Stir in chicken broth, kaffir lime leaves, and ginger. Bring to boil; reduce heat to medium and simmer 5 minutes. Add shrimp and mushrooms. Cook until shrimp are beginning to turn pink, about 3 minutes. Add cabbage; cook until beginning to wilt, about 30 seconds. Stir in lime juice. Ladle soup into bowls; sprinkle with chopped cilantro and green onions.

The Asian pantry Asian ingredients offer delicious ways to get great flavor fast, and they are becoming increasingly available in supermarkets nationwide. For a hit of spicy heat, look to red curry paste, made with red chiles and sold in jars. Coconut milk, sold in cans, is rich and velvety; a little goes a long way. Kaffir lime leaves (also called wild lime leaves) are most commonly found in Asian markets; lime zest is a good substitute.

Broccoli and cauliflower cheese soup with sausage

2 SERVINGS; CAN BE DOUBLED OR TRIPLED *European-style pumpernickel bread is delicious with this cold-weather soup.*

2 tablespoons (¼ stick) butter
4 ounces smoked beef sausage or kielbasa sausage, quartered lengthwise, sliced crosswise
1 medium onion, chopped
¾ teaspoon caraway seeds, crushed, divided
1 pound russet potatoes, peeled, sliced
2 14-ounce cans low-salt chicken broth
1 bay leaf

1½ cups bite-size broccoli florets
1½ cups bite-size cauliflower florets
¼ cup heavy whipping cream
¾ cup grated sharp cheddar cheese (about 3 ounces)

MELT butter in heavy medium saucepan over medium heat. Add sausage and cook until beginning to brown, about 4 minutes. Using slotted spoon, remove sausage from pan. Add onion and ½ teaspoon caraway seeds. Season to taste with freshly ground black pepper. Reduce heat to medium-low and cook 4 minutes, stirring occasionally. Mix in potatoes. Add broth and bay leaf. Simmer until potatoes are tender, stirring occasionally and breaking up potatoes with spoon, about 25 minutes.

ADD broccoli and cauliflower to soup and simmer until just tender, about 10 minutes. Stir in cream and sausage and heat through. Add cheese and stir until melted. Season to taste with salt and pepper. Discard bay leaf. Ladle soup into bowls. Sprinkle with remaining ¼ teaspoon caraway seeds.

Lentil soup with lamb and mint

8 SERVINGS *Ground lamb makes this lentil soup a satisfying one-dish meal.*

2 tablespoons olive oil
1 pound ground lamb
3 large celery stalks, chopped
2 large parsnips, peeled, chopped
1 medium onion, chopped
6 garlic cloves, chopped
¾ pound dried lentils, rinsed
4 14-ounce cans (or more) beef broth
1 28-ounce can diced tomatoes in juice
3½ teaspoons ground cumin

1 cup chopped fresh mint, divided

HEAT oil in heavy large pot over medium-high heat. Add lamb, celery, parsnips, onion, and garlic. Sauté until vegetables are almost tender and lamb is cooked through and beginning to brown, breaking up lamb with back of fork, about 15 minutes. Add lentils and stir 1 minute. Add 4 cans broth, tomatoes with juice, and cumin. Bring soup to boil. Reduce heat to medium-low, cover, and simmer until lentils are tender, about 40 minutes.

TRANSFER 2 cups soup to blender and puree until smooth; return to pot. Mix in ¼ cup mint. Thin soup with more broth, if desired. Season to taste with salt and pepper. Ladle into bowls. Sprinkle with remaining ¾ cup mint.

French lentil soup

6 SERVINGS *French green lentils, which are especially flavorful and firm (and thus hold their shape well), give best results. You can find them at natural foods stores and specialty foods stores.*

3 tablespoons extra-virgin olive oil
2 cups chopped onions
1 cup chopped celery stalks plus chopped celery leaves for garnish
1 cup chopped carrots
2 garlic cloves, chopped
4 cups (or more) vegetable broth
1¼ cups dried lentils, rinsed, drained
1 14½-ounce can diced tomatoes in juice

Balsamic vinegar (optional)

HEAT oil in heavy large saucepan over medium-high heat. Add onions, chopped celery stalks, carrots, and garlic; sauté until vegetables begin to brown, about 15 minutes. Add 4 cups broth, lentils, and tomatoes with juice and bring to boil. Reduce heat to medium-low, cover, and simmer until lentils are tender, about 35 minutes.

TRANSFER 2 cups soup (mostly solids) to blender and puree until smooth. Return puree to soup in pan; thin soup with more broth by ¼ cupfuls, if desired. Season to taste with salt, pepper, and a splash of vinegar, if desired. Ladle soup into bowls. Garnish with celery leaves.

Split pea and green pea soup with fresh dill

4 TO 6 FIRST-COURSE SERVINGS *This healthful soup gets a double hit of color and flavor from both split peas and frozen peas. The bay leaf isn't discarded in this recipe; it gets pureed along with the other solids.*

3 tablespoons extra-virgin olive oil
1½ cups chopped leeks (white and pale green parts only; about 1 large)
1 bay leaf
1 cup dried green split peas, rinsed
5¾ cups vegetable broth, divided

1 cup frozen petite green peas, thawed
5 tablespoons chopped fresh dill, divided

HEAT oil in heavy large pot over medium-high heat. Add leek and bay leaf. Sauté until leek wilts, about 3 minutes. Add split peas and stir to coat. Add 5¼ cups broth; bring to boil. Reduce heat to medium-low, cover, and simmer until split peas are just tender, about 35 minutes. Remove from heat.

TRANSFER 1 cup soup solids, bay leaf, and remaining ½ cup broth to blender. Add petite peas and 4 tablespoons dill. Puree until smooth. Return puree to soup. Season to taste with salt and pepper. Ladle soup into bowls. Sprinkle with remaining 1 tablespoon dill.

Beef, vegetable, and barley soup

6 TO 8 MAIN-COURSE SERVINGS *Once the meat and vegetables have been cut, the ingredients are combined in a pot to simmer mostly unattended.*

1 2¾-pound piece flat-cut brisket, cut into 1-inch cubes

8 cups beef broth

3 8-ounce cans tomato sauce

4 celery stalks, cut into ½-inch pieces

3 carrots, peeled, chopped

1 large onion, chopped

⅓ cup pearl barley, rinsed

6 large garlic cloves, chopped

3 bay leaves

1 1-ounce package dried stemmed shiitake mushrooms, broken into ½-inch pieces

3 15- to 16-ounce cans kidney beans, undrained

COMBINE all ingredients except beans in heavy large pot and bring to boil. Reduce heat to medium-low, cover, and simmer 1 hour, stirring once or twice. Mix beans with their liquid into soup. Cover and continue to simmer until meat is tender, about 30 minutes longer. Season to taste with salt and pepper. Ladle soup into bowls.

Creamy bean soup with fresh herbs and spinach

8 FIRST-COURSE SERVINGS *There's no cream in this soup—pureeing the bean mixture is what gives it a luxurious texture.*

3 tablespoons (or more) extra-virgin olive oil

3 cups chopped onions

3 garlic cloves, minced

1 tablespoon chopped fresh rosemary

5 cups low-salt chicken broth

2 15- to 16-ounce cans white beans, drained

2 15- to 16-ounce cans garbanzo beans (chickpeas), drained

1 6-ounce bag fresh baby spinach

1 tablespoon chopped fresh sage
Grated Parmesan cheese

HEAT 3 tablespoons oil in large pot over medium-high heat. Add onions and garlic; sauté 15 minutes. Add rosemary; stir 1 minute. Add broth and all beans. Bring soup to boil. Reduce heat to medium-low; simmer 10 minutes.

WORKING in batches, puree soup in blender until smooth; return to pot. Mix in spinach and sage; stir until spinach wilts, about 1 minute. Season to taste with salt and pepper. Ladle soup into bowls, sprinkle with Parmesan cheese, and drizzle with more oil, if desired.

Puerto Rican–style black bean soup

2 SERVINGS; CAN BE DOUBLED *Jerk seasoning is a spice mix used in Jamaican barbecue. If there's none in the spice aisle of the supermarket, you can create the same flavor profile by using what's already in your spice cabinet: Mix ground allspice with smaller amounts of dried thyme, paprika, chili powder, cinnamon, ginger, garlic, salt, and ground black pepper.*

- 1 tablespoon jerk or Caribbean-style seasoning blend
- 2 15- to 16-ounce cans Caribbean-style or regular black beans, drained
- 1¼ cups vegetable broth
- 3 tablespoons olive oil
- 2 tablespoons fresh lime juice
  Lime wedges

STIR seasoning blend in heavy medium saucepan over medium heat until fragrant and slightly darker in color, about 4 minutes. Transfer seasoning to processor. Add beans, broth, and oil to processor and puree until mixture is almost smooth, scraping down sides of bowl occasionally. Transfer puree to same pan. Bring to boil, stirring occasionally. Mix in lime juice. Season to taste with salt and pepper. Serve with lime wedges.

Spicy pasta, bean, and sausage soup

4 TO 6 MAIN-COURSE SERVINGS *For a milder soup, use sweet Italian sausage, rather than hot.*

- 2 15- to 16-ounce cans garbanzo beans (chickpeas), undrained, divided
- 2 tablespoons olive oil
- 1 pound hot Italian sausages, casings removed
- 4 teaspoons chopped fresh rosemary
- 2 large garlic cloves, chopped
- ¼ teaspoon dried crushed red pepper
- ¼ cup tomato paste
- 5 cups low-salt chicken broth
- 8 ounces (about 2⅓ cups) orecchiette (little ear-shaped pasta) or other small pasta
- 1½ cups grated Romano cheese, divided

STRAIN liquid from canned beans into blender. Add 1 cup beans and puree until smooth. Heat oil in large pot over medium heat. Add sausage, rosemary, garlic, and crushed red pepper. Sauté until sausage is cooked through, breaking up with fork, about 8 minutes. Mix in tomato paste. Add bean puree, remaining beans, broth, and pasta. Simmer until pasta is tender and mixture is thick, stirring occasionally, about 30 minutes. Mix in ¼ cup cheese. Season to taste with salt and pepper. Serve, passing remaining 1¼ cups cheese separately.

Vietnamese beef soup

8 SERVINGS *Here's a take on the Vietnamese soup known as* pho. *You'll find bean thread noodles (also called cellophane noodles) and fish sauce (such as* nam pla *or* nuoc nam) *in the Asian foods section of many supermarkets and at Asian markets. Star anise is sold in the spice section.*

10	cups beef broth
2	medium onions, thickly sliced
4	½-inch-thick slices fresh ginger
2	tablespoons fish sauce (such as nam pla or nuoc nam)
3	large garlic cloves, halved
2	whole star anise
1½	teaspoons whole cloves
8	ounces bean thread noodles
1	pound flank steak, trimmed, thinly sliced crosswise
1	head of romaine lettuce, thinly sliced
3	green onions, thinly sliced
	Lemon wedges

COMBINE first 7 ingredients in heavy large pot and bring to boil. Reduce heat; simmer 30 minutes. Strain broth into large bowl; discard solids.

DO AHEAD *Can be made 1 day ahead. Cover and chill.*

BRING large pot of water to boil. Remove from heat. Add noodles to pot; let stand until tender and pliable, about 15 minutes. Drain. Using scissors, cut noodles into 2-inch lengths. Transfer noodles to another bowl.

RETURN broth to pot and bring to boil. Remove from heat. Mix steak slices into broth (the hot broth will cook steak slices). Place soup, noodles, lettuce, green onions, and lemon wedges in center of table. Spoon noodles, steak slices, and broth into large soup bowls, then top with generous amounts of sliced lettuce and green onions and squeeze lemon juice over.

Pho: *a how-to guide* The famed Vietnamese dish *pho* is one of the best versions of noodle soup there is. Traditionally, hot broth is poured over a bowl filled with cooked bean thread noodles, thinly sliced beef, thinly sliced onions, and chopped cilantro. The hot broth quickly cooks the ingredients in the bowl. The soup is served with a plate of condiments that includes basil leaves, bean sprouts, sliced chiles, and lime wedges. Hot sauce is also served alongside. Everyone can season the soup to taste, with as much or as little hot sauce and as many herbs as desired.

Parsnip soup with corned beef and cabbage

4 FIRST-COURSE OR 2 MAIN-COURSE SERVINGS *Need something fun (and quick) for St. Patrick's Day? Here's your dish. This is also a great way to use up leftover corned beef. Instead of using butter, you can use the trimmed fat to sauté the vegetables and beef.*

- 3 tablespoons butter, divided
- 2 Turkish bay leaves
- 2 large parsnips (about 13 ounces), peeled, coarsely chopped
- 2 cups chopped onions
- 3 cups (or more) low-salt chicken broth

- 3 large savoy cabbage leaves, center ribs removed
- 3 ⅛-inch-thick slices cooked corned beef (about 4 ounces), any fat trimmed

- ¼ cup heavy whipping cream

MELT 2 tablespoons butter in large saucepan over medium-high heat. Mix in bay leaves, parsnips, and onions. Add 3 cups broth. Cover; simmer until parsnips are tender, about 10 minutes.

MEANWHILE, cut cabbage and corned beef slices crosswise into very thin strips. Melt remaining 1 tablespoon butter in medium skillet over medium-high heat. Add cabbage and corned beef. Sprinkle with salt and pepper. Toss until cabbage wilts, about 3 minutes.

WORKING in batches, puree soup with cream in blender until smooth. Return to same pan. Rewarm soup, thinning with more broth if desired. Season to taste with salt and pepper. Ladle soup into bowls. Mound corned beef and cabbage in center.

Parsnip and apple soup

6 SERVINGS *Granny Smith apples add a tangy twist, and they amp up a parsnip's natural sweetness.*

- 3 Granny Smith apples (about 1½ pounds), divided
- 1 tablespoon olive oil
- 5 large shallots, sliced
- 1¼ pounds medium parsnips, peeled, cut into ½-inch-thick rounds
- 1¼ teaspoons ground coriander
- 5 cups (or more) low-salt chicken broth

  Plain nonfat yogurt, stirred to loosen

PEEL and core 2 apples, then cut into 1-inch pieces. Heat oil in heavy large pot over medium-high heat. Add shallots; sauté 3 minutes. Add parsnips; sauté 3 minutes. Add apple pieces and coriander; stir 1 minute. Add 5 cups broth; bring to boil. Reduce heat and simmer until vegetables are very tender, about 25 minutes. Cool slightly.

WORKING in batches, puree soup in blender until smooth, thinning with more broth by ½ cupfuls, if desired. Return soup to pot; bring to simmer. Season to taste with salt and pepper.

MEANWHILE, cut remaining apple (with peel) into very thin slices. Ladle soup into bowls. Drizzle soup with yogurt. Fan several apple slices on top.

Dilled chicken chowder

2 SERVINGS; CAN BE DOUBLED *Because this is made with chicken thighs, the chowder can be made ahead and reheated — you don't have to worry about the chicken becoming overcooked.*

    3 bacon slices, coarsely chopped
    4 skinless boneless chicken thighs,
       cut into ¾-inch pieces
    1 medium onion, sliced
    1 large red-skinned potato, diced
    1 cup low-salt chicken broth
    ¾ cup half and half
    1½ tablespoons chopped fresh dill

SAUTÉ bacon in heavy large saucepan over medium heat until crisp. Using slotted spoon, transfer bacon to paper towels. Add chicken and onion to same pan; sauté about 5 minutes. Add potato and broth; bring to boil. Cover, reduce heat to medium-low, and simmer 10 minutes. Add half and half and dill; simmer uncovered until chicken is cooked through and potatoes are tender, about 5 minutes longer. Season to taste with salt and pepper. Ladle chowder into bowls; sprinkle with bacon.

Chicken and escarole soup with fennel

6 MAIN-COURSE SERVINGS *This wonderfully quick version of the Southern Italian classic is also delicious with Swiss chard—just simmer it a couple of minutes longer than you would with escarole, until tender.*

    ¼ cup olive oil
    1½ pounds skinless boneless chicken
       thighs, cut into ½-inch cubes
    1 tablespoon dried oregano
    2 cups chopped onions
    4 celery stalks, chopped
    4 garlic cloves, chopped
    1 teaspoon fennel seeds
    1 14½-ounce can diced tomatoes in juice
    8 cups low-salt chicken broth
    1 head of escarole, cut into wide strips
       Grated Pecorino Romano cheese

HEAT oil in large pot over medium-high heat. Add chicken; sprinkle with salt, pepper, and oregano. Mix in onions, celery, garlic, and fennel seeds. Sauté until vegetables begin to soften, about 4 minutes. Stir in tomatoes with juice. Add broth; bring to boil. Reduce heat to medium; simmer until vegetables and chicken are tender, about 15 minutes. Add escarole; simmer until wilted, about 3 minutes. Season to taste with salt and pepper. Ladle soup into bowls. Serve, passing cheese separately.

Chicken and hominy soup

8 MAIN-COURSE SERVINGS *To add even more flavor and texture, top with tortilla chips, avocado, and sour cream.*

- 3 tablespoons olive oil
- 3 bunches green onions, sliced
- 4 teaspoons ground cumin
- 2½ teaspoons smoked paprika or hot smoked Spanish paprika
- 10 cups low-salt chicken broth
- 2 14- to 15-ounce cans cream-style corn
- 1 14½-ounce can petite tomatoes in juice
- 1 purchased roast chicken, meat shredded, skin and bones discarded
- 4 teaspoons hot pepper sauce
- 3 15-ounce cans golden or white hominy in juice
- 1 cup chopped fresh cilantro

HEAT oil in heavy large pot over medium-high heat. Add green onions, cumin, and paprika; sauté 3 minutes. Add broth, corn, tomatoes with juice, chicken, and hot pepper sauce. Puree hominy with juice in processor or blender. Mix into soup; bring to boil. Reduce heat; simmer 20 minutes. Stir in cilantro. Ladle soup into bowls.

PERFECT HOMINY Hominy, whole corn kernels with the hulls and germ removed, is hearty and chewy, and using it is a quick way to add substance to soups and stews. It's sold in the canned goods section of the supermarket.

Asian turkey-noodle soup with ginger and chiles

6 SERVINGS *Fish sauce and rice noodles are available in the Asian foods section of most supermarkets.*

- 3½ ounces medium-wide (linguine-width) rice noodles, broken into 6-inch lengths
  Boiling water
- 6 cups low-salt chicken broth
- ½ cup thinly sliced shallots (about 3 large)
- 6 ⅛-inch-thick rounds peeled fresh ginger
- 2 tablespoons fish sauce (such as nam pla or nuoc nam) or soy sauce
- 2 cups diced cooked turkey meat (about 10 ounces)

  Fresh bean sprouts
  Fresh mint leaves
  Thinly sliced serrano chiles
  Lime wedges

PLACE noodles in large bowl. Add enough boiling water to cover noodles. Let stand until noodles are soft, about 5 minutes; drain.

COMBINE broth, shallots, ginger, and fish sauce in large pot. Bring to boil. Reduce heat to low, cover partially, and simmer 10 minutes. Discard ginger slices. Return broth mixture to boil. Stir in noodles and turkey; simmer until turkey is heated through, about 3 minutes.

LADLE soup into bowls. Serve, allowing diners to top each serving with bean sprouts, mint leaves, chiles, and lime wedges to squeeze over.

Cauliflower soup with thyme croutons

4 SERVINGS *An easy starter for Thanksgiving dinner. Minced rosemary or sage would be good substitutes for the thyme.*

1   1½-pound head of cauliflower, stem end and leaves trimmed, head coarsely chopped

3   cups whole milk

⅓   cup heavy whipping cream

4   tablespoons (½ stick) butter, divided

2   cups coarsely torn fresh bread (from crustless sourdough baguette)

½   teaspoon minced fresh thyme

BRING cauliflower and milk to boil in heavy large saucepan. Reduce heat to medium and simmer uncovered until cauliflower is tender, about 9 minutes. Stir in cream and 2 tablespoons butter. Cool slightly. Working in batches, puree soup in blender. Season to taste with salt and pepper. Keep warm.

MELT remaining 2 tablespoons butter in heavy large skillet over medium-high heat. Add bread pieces and stir until brown and crisp, about 9 minutes. Season croutons to taste with salt and pepper. Stir in thyme.

LADLE soup into bowls. Mound thyme croutons atop soup.

Sweet potato soup with fried pancetta and rosemary croutons

4 SERVINGS *Here's a great destination for leftover sweet potatoes. If you don't have any leftovers, microwave two large sweet potatoes until tender, then peel and mash. Pancetta, an Italian bacon cured in salt, is available in the refrigerated deli case of the supermarket, but good-quality, thickly sliced bacon works just as well.*

1   3-ounce package thinly sliced pancetta (Italian bacon), chopped

3   tablespoons butter, divided

1   cup (scant) sliced shallots (about 3 large)

1½   teaspoons minced fresh rosemary, divided

2   cups mashed peeled red-skinned sweet potatoes (yams)

3½   cups (or more) low-salt chicken broth

1   cup ⅓-inch cubes country-style sourdough bread

SAUTÉ pancetta in heavy large saucepan over medium-high heat until crisp, about 5 minutes. Using slotted spoon, transfer pancetta to paper towels.

ADD 1½ tablespoons butter to drippings in same pan; add shallots and reduce heat to medium. Sauté until shallots are soft and golden, about 4 minutes. Stir in 1 teaspoon rosemary, then mashed sweet potatoes and 3½ cups broth. Bring to boil. Reduce heat to medium-low and simmer 10 minutes to blend flavors, adding more broth by ¼ cupfuls to thin soup, if desired. Season to taste with salt and pepper. Puree soup in blender or processor, if desired.

MEANWHILE, melt remaining 1½ tablespoons butter in small skillet over medium-high heat. Add bread cubes and remaining ½ teaspoon rosemary and sauté until croutons are crisp and golden, about 3 minutes.

LADLE soup into bowls. Top with croutons and fried pancetta.

Very simple pumpkin soup

6 SERVINGS *Chinese five-spice powder—a mix of ground fennel seeds, Szechuan peppercorns, cinnamon, star anise, and cloves—can be found in the spice section of many supermarkets, and at Asian markets.*

- 4 cups water
- 2 15-ounce cans pure pumpkin
- 1 cup half and half
- 1 garlic clove, pressed
- ¼ cup pure maple syrup
- 4 tablespoons unsalted butter, divided
- ½ teaspoon Chinese five-spice powder

- 4 ounces fresh shiitake mushrooms, stemmed, sliced

BRING first 4 ingredients to simmer in large saucepan over medium-high heat, whisking often. Whisk in syrup, 2 tablespoons butter, and five-spice powder. Simmer soup 10 minutes, whisking often. Season to taste with salt and pepper.

DO AHEAD *Soup can be made 1 day ahead. Chill until cold, then cover and keep chilled. Bring to simmer before continuing.*

MELT remaining 2 tablespoons butter in heavy medium skillet over medium-high heat. Add mushrooms; sauté until tender, about 10 minutes. Ladle soup into bowls. Sprinkle soup with mushrooms.

Potato, leek, and fennel soup

8 SERVINGS *Look for fennel with the fronds still attached—you'll use them as a pretty garnish for this soup.*

- 2 tablespoons (¼ stick) butter
- 2 cups sliced leeks (white and pale green parts only)
- 2 cups sliced fennel bulb, fronds chopped and reserved for garnish
- 4 14-ounce cans low-salt chicken broth
- 2 pounds red-skinned potatoes, peeled, cut into ½-inch pieces (about 4 cups)

MELT butter in heavy large pot over medium-high heat. Add leeks and sliced fennel and sauté until leeks are translucent, about 7 minutes. Add broth and potatoes and bring to boil. Reduce heat to medium-low. Simmer soup until potatoes are very tender, about 25 minutes. Working in batches, puree soup in blender. Return to pot. Rewarm soup if necessary. Season to taste with salt and pepper. Ladle soup into bowls; garnish each with reserved fennel fronds.

Escarole soup with pasta and meatballs

6 FIRST-COURSE OR 4 MAIN-COURSE SERVINGS *When shaping the meatballs, use a light hand, taking care not to compact them too much. Farfallini are small bowtie-shaped pasta.*

- ¾ pound lean ground beef
- 1⅓ cups freshly grated Parmesan cheese, divided
- ½ cup fresh breadcrumbs made from crustless French bread
- 1 large egg
- 2 garlic cloves, minced
- ½ teaspoon salt
- ½ teaspoon ground black pepper

- 7½ cups low-salt chicken broth, divided
- 2 tablespoons olive oil
- 2 large celery stalks with tops, chopped
- 1 medium onion, chopped

- ½ cup farfallini or orzo
- 1 small head of escarole, coarsely torn

BLEND beef, ⅓ cup cheese, breadcrumbs, egg, garlic, salt, and pepper in medium bowl. Using moistened hands, shape meat mixture into ¾-inch meatballs.

HEAT 1½ cups broth and oil in large pot over medium-high heat. Add meatballs and simmer until firm enough to hold shape, about 5 minutes. Using slotted spoon, transfer meatballs to bowl. Boil broth until reduced to glaze, about 6 minutes. Add celery and onion to pot. Stir until vegetables are soft, about 5 minutes.

ADD remaining 6 cups broth, pasta, and meatballs with any juices. Reduce heat. Simmer until pasta is tender, about 10 minutes. Add escarole and simmer until wilted, about 5 minutes. Season to taste with salt and pepper. Ladle soup into bowls. Serve, passing remaining 1 cup cheese separately.

MAKING CRUMBS Making fresh breadcrumbs is a snap: Just whirl chunks of French bread (with the crust removed) in the food processor. Dried breadcrumbs are equally easy: Toast a slice of bread and let it cool completely before putting in the processor.

Fresh wild mushroom soup

4 SERVINGS *It's easy to turn this into cream of mushroom soup. Before adding salt and pepper, stir in ½ cup heavy cream.*

- 6 tablespoons (¾ stick) butter
- 2 cups finely chopped onions
- 6 ounces crimini (baby bella) mushrooms, chopped
- 6 ounces fresh oyster mushrooms, chopped
- 6 ounces fresh shiitake mushrooms, stemmed, chopped
- 1 tablespoon chopped fresh thyme
- 3 tablespoons brandy
- 2 tablespoons all purpose flour
- 4 cups beef broth

MELT butter in large pot over medium-high heat. Add onions; sauté until golden, about 5 minutes. Add all mushrooms and thyme; sauté until mushrooms begin to brown, about 8 minutes. Add brandy; stir 30 seconds, then mix in flour. Slowly stir in broth; bring soup to boil. Reduce heat; simmer uncovered 10 minutes. Season to taste with salt and pepper. Ladle into bowls.

Portuguese green soup

4 MAIN-COURSE SERVINGS *Chili powder or even hot Spanish paprika are good stand-ins for the dried crushed red pepper.*

  2 tablespoons olive oil
  1 medium onion, chopped
  3 garlic cloves, minced
  1 bunch collard greens, center stems cut away, leaves thinly sliced
  1 pound fully cooked spicy sausage (such as linguiça, andouille, or hot links), cut into ½-inch-thick rounds
5¾ cups low-salt chicken broth
1¾ pounds russet potatoes, peeled, diced
  ½ teaspoon dried crushed red pepper

HEAT olive oil in large pot over medium-high heat. Add onion and garlic. Sauté until onion is soft and golden, about 5 minutes. Add collard greens and sauté until wilted, about 4 minutes. Add sausage and sauté 5 minutes. Add broth and potatoes. Simmer soup uncovered until potatoes are tender, about 20 minutes. Transfer 2 cups soup (without sausage) to processor. Blend until smooth; return to pot and bring to simmer. Mix in crushed red pepper. Season to taste with salt and pepper.

French onion soup

4 SERVINGS *Any Swiss-style cheese would be great here: Gruyère, Emmenthal, or one of the artisanal American versions that are increasingly available.*

  4 tablespoons (½ stick) butter
  6 onions (about 3 pounds), sliced
  6 garlic cloves, sliced
  ½ cup dry white wine
  3 cups low-salt chicken broth
  3 cups beef broth
  1 teaspoon Dijon mustard

  4 sourdough bread slices, toasted
  1 cup grated Swiss cheese
  ½ cup grated Parmesan cheese

MELT butter in heavy large saucepan over medium heat. Add onions and garlic and sauté until very tender and brown, about 45 minutes. Add wine and simmer until reduced to glaze, about 3 minutes. Stir in chicken broth, beef broth, and mustard. Simmer 20 minutes. Season to taste with salt and pepper.

DO AHEAD *Can be made 1 day ahead. Cool slightly. Chill uncovered until cold, then cover and keep chilled. Return soup to simmer before continuing.*

PREHEAT broiler. Ladle soup into broilerproof bowls. Top each serving with slice of sourdough toast and grated cheeses. Broil until cheeses melt and bubble.

FREEZE THE CHEESE Though cheese tastes best at room temperature, it's easiest to grate when it's very cold. Put cheese in the freezer for 15 minutes or so before grating it.

Miso-ginger consommé

6 SERVINGS *To turn this into a meal in a bowl, try adding diced firm tofu, spinach, and slivered chicken breast. White miso (also known as* shiro miso*) is available in the refrigerated Asian food section of some supermarkets and at Japanese markets. Tamari soy sauce is available at some supermarkets and at specialty foods stores and natural foods stores.*

- 1 **2-inch piece peeled fresh ginger, grated**
- 6 **cups water**
- 7 **tablespoons white miso (fermented soybean paste)**
- 6 **large shiitake mushrooms, stemmed, thinly sliced (about 4 cups)**
- 2 **green onions, thinly sliced, plus more for garnish**
- ¾ **teaspoon tamari soy sauce**

PLACE grated ginger in paper towel; squeeze to yield 1½ teaspoons juice and set aside. Whisk 6 cups water and miso in heavy large saucepan to blend. Add mushrooms and 2 sliced green onions and bring to simmer. Add ginger juice and tamari; stir 30 seconds. Ladle soup into 6 bowls. Garnish with additional green onions and serve.

Corn soup with potato and smoked ham

8 SERVINGS *Lard gives great flavor and is traditional in this hearty, rustic Cuban soup. Look for lard in the meat department of well-stocked supermarkets or in Latin markets, and check the label to make sure it is not hydrogenated lard, which contains trans fats.*

- ¼ **cup lard**
- 1½ **cups diced smoked ham steak (about 8 ounces)**
- 1 **cup chopped white onion**
- ½ **cup chopped red bell pepper**
- ½ **cup chopped green bell pepper**
- 2 **garlic cloves, chopped**
- 2 **cups fresh corn kernels (cut from about 4 ears of corn) or 2 cups frozen corn kernels**
- 1 **10-ounce smoked ham hock**
- 1 **medium Yukon Gold potato, peeled, cut into 1-inch pieces**
- 5 **cups water**

MELT lard in heavy large pot over high heat. Add ham steak, onion, both bell peppers, and garlic; sauté until vegetables are tender, about 10 minutes. Add corn and stir 5 minutes. Add ham hock and potato, then 5 cups water; bring to boil. Reduce heat to medium-low; simmer partially covered 1 hour. Remove ham hock. Season to taste with salt and pepper.

DO AHEAD *Can be made 1 day ahead. Cool slightly. Chill uncovered until cold, then cover and keep chilled. Rewarm over medium heat before serving.*

Quick tomato and basil soup

2 SERVINGS; CAN BE DOUBLED *Use a fruity-style olive oil for the drizzle on this summer soup.*

- 2 tablespoons extra-virgin olive oil plus more for drizzling
- 2 garlic cloves, flattened
- 2 pounds ripe tomatoes (about 4 large), peeled, seeded, chopped
- 3 fresh basil sprigs plus thinly sliced leaves for garnish
- 2 ½-inch-thick slices Italian bread, toasted

HEAT 2 tablespoons oil in heavy large saucepan over medium-low heat. Add garlic and cook until beginning to color, about 5 minutes. Remove garlic and reserve. Add tomatoes and basil sprigs to pan. Reduce heat and simmer until soup thickens to chunky puree, mashing tomatoes with spoon, about 15 minutes. Season soup generously with salt and pepper.

BRUSH toast with oil, rub with reserved garlic, and sprinkle with salt and pepper. Discard basil sprigs. Ladle soup into bowls. Drizzle with oil. Top with toast and sliced basil leaves.

Asparagus soup with lemon crème fraîche

6 FIRST-COURSE SERVINGS *Amazingly, this vegetarian soup has a velvety texture with only small amounts of butter and sour cream per serving.*

- 4 tablespoons (½ stick) butter
- 1 cup sliced shallots (about 6 large)
- 2 pounds asparagus, trimmed, cut into 2-inch lengths
- 2 teaspoons ground coriander
- 2 14-ounce cans vegetable broth

- ¼ cup crème fraîche or sour cream
- ½ teaspoon fresh lemon juice
- ¼ teaspoon finely grated lemon peel

MELT butter in heavy large saucepan over medium heat. Add shallots; sauté until soft, about 5 minutes. Add asparagus and coriander; stir 1 minute. Add broth; simmer until asparagus is tender, about 5 minutes. Cool slightly. Working in batches, puree soup in blender. Strain into same pan, pressing on solids to release liquid. Season to taste with salt and pepper. Keep warm.

STIR crème fraîche, lemon juice, and lemon peel in small bowl. Ladle soup into bowls. Top with dollop of lemon crème fraîche.

Roasted red pepper soup with orange cream

4 FIRST-COURSE SERVINGS *A great way to use red bell peppers from a jar. Piquillo peppers are especially flavorful.*

- 1 tablespoon olive oil
- ⅔ cup sliced shallots (about 4)
- 1 15-ounce jar roasted red peppers packed in water
- 1 teaspoon sugar
- 2 cups (or more) low-salt chicken broth
- ½ cup orange juice

- 2 tablespoons heavy whipping cream
- ¾ teaspoon finely grated orange peel
  Thinly sliced fresh basil leaves

HEAT oil in heavy medium saucepan over medium-high heat. Add shallots and sauté 5 minutes. Add red peppers with their liquid. Stir in sugar; sauté 2 minutes. Add 2 cups broth and simmer 5 minutes. Cool soup slightly. Working in batches, puree soup in blender. Return soup to pan. Bring to simmer; stir in orange juice. Thin soup with more broth, if desired. Season to taste with salt and pepper.

WHISK whipping cream and orange peel in small bowl until slightly thickened. Season with salt and pepper. Ladle soup into bowls. Drizzle orange cream over soup. Sprinkle with basil.

Carrot and caraway soup

2 SERVINGS *Aquavit, a Scandinavian caraway-seed liqueur, can be found at specialty foods stores and some liquor stores.*

- 1 tablespoon butter
- 1 onion, chopped
- 12 ounces carrots, peeled, sliced
- 1 teaspoon caraway seeds, crushed in mortar with pestle
- 1 14-ounce can (or more) low-salt chicken broth

- 2 tablespoons aquavit
  Chopped fresh parsley

MELT butter in heavy medium saucepan over medium heat. Add onion and sauté 1 minute. Add carrots and sauté until onion is tender, about 8 minutes. Add caraway seeds and cook 30 seconds. Add 1 can broth. Cover and simmer until carrots are tender, about 35 minutes. Cool soup slightly.

TRANSFER soup to processor and puree. Season to taste with salt and pepper.

DO AHEAD *Can be made 1 day ahead. Cover and chill.*

RETURN soup to pan and bring to simmer, thinning with more broth, if desired. Mix in aquavit. Ladle soup into bowls. Garnish with parsley.

Bag it A mixed-greens salad served alongside can turn any soup or stew into a light supper, or even a dinner party. Greens sold in bags are a huge time-saver; to add more interest, toss in fresh herbs like parsley, chives, and tarragon. To add texture, add Belgian endive or chopped toasted nuts.

Broccoli soup with chive-cayenne oil

6 SERVINGS *The chive-cayenne oil is also delicious drizzled on poached fish.*

¼ cup plus 1 tablespoon extra-virgin olive oil
¼ cup coarsely chopped chives
    Pinch of cayenne pepper

1 medium onion, chopped
2 Turkish bay leaves
1 pound broccoli, stems and crowns cut into 1-inch pieces (about 6 cups)
4 cups low-salt chicken broth

PUREE ¼ cup oil, chives, and cayenne in blender. Season with salt.

HEAT remaining 1 tablespoon oil in large saucepan over medium-high heat. Add onion and bay leaves; cook until onion is golden, stirring often, about 7 minutes. Add broccoli; stir until bright green, about 1 minute. Add broth. Simmer until broccoli is tender, about 5 minutes. Discard bay leaves. Cool soup slightly.

WORKING in batches, puree soup in blender until smooth, about 1 minute per batch. Return soup to pot. Rewarm until hot. Season to taste with salt and pepper.

LADLE soup into six bowls. Drizzle each with chive-cayenne oil.

Spinach and lime soup

4 TO 6 SERVINGS *Baking the tortilla strips instead of frying them and using bags of fresh spinach are the time-savers in this tasty and nutritious soup.*

3 5- to 6-inch corn tortillas, cut into thin strips
1 tablespoon vegetable oil

6 cups low-salt chicken broth
½ teaspoon ground cumin
¼ teaspoon cayenne pepper
2 6-ounce bags fresh baby spinach
⅓ cup chopped fresh cilantro
3 to 4 tablespoons fresh lime juice

PREHEAT oven to 450°F. Toss tortilla strips and vegetable oil in large bowl to coat. Transfer strips to baking sheet. Bake until crisp, stirring occasionally, about 15 minutes.

BRING broth, cumin, and cayenne to simmer in heavy large saucepan over medium heat. Add spinach and cook until wilted but still bright green, about 4 minutes. Add cilantro and 3 tablespoons lime juice. Season to taste with salt and pepper, adding more lime juice, if desired. Ladle soup into bowls and top with tortilla strips.

Summer garden soup

2 SERVINGS; CAN BE DOUBLED OR TRIPLED *Serve this main-dish soup warm or at room temperature. The drizzle of pesto enhances the summery flavor.*

- 1 tablespoon olive oil
- 1 medium onion, chopped
- 1 small zucchini, diced
- 1 small yellow crookneck squash, diced
- 1 15-ounce can cannellini beans (white kidney beans), undrained
- 1 14-ounce can low-salt chicken broth
- 4 ounces ham steak, diced
- 1 medium tomato, seeded, chopped
- 1 tablespoon prepared pesto plus more for swirling

HEAT oil in heavy medium saucepan over medium-low heat. Add onion and cook until translucent, stirring occasionally, about 8 minutes. Add zucchini and yellow squash; season to taste with freshly ground black pepper. Cook until vegetables are crisp-tender, stirring occasionally, about 6 minutes. Remove from heat. Mix in beans with their liquid, broth, ham, and tomato. Mix in 1 tablespoon pesto. Cool to room temperature or bring to simmer. Ladle soup into bowls. Swirl additional pesto into each bowl.

Chilled zucchini-mint soup

8 SERVINGS *Leeks add great flavor to this soup. Because they're grown in sandy soil and trap lots of grit, they need to be washed thoroughly before using.*

- 1 tablespoon butter
- ⅓ cup extra-virgin olive oil
- 5 cups chopped leeks (white and pale green parts only; from about 6)
- 3 pounds zucchini, trimmed, chopped (about 8 cups)
- 5½ cups (or more) vegetable broth
- ⅓ cup heavy whipping cream
- 1½ tablespoons (packed) minced fresh mint leaves plus whole leaves for garnish

MELT butter with oil in heavy large pot over medium-high heat. Add leeks and sauté until soft but not brown, about 5 minutes. Add zucchini and sauté until beginning to soften, about 5 minutes. Add 5½ cups broth and bring to boil. Reduce heat to medium-low. Simmer uncovered until zucchini is very tender, about 20 minutes. Working in batches, puree soup in blender until smooth. Return puree to pot. Mix in cream and minced mint. Cover and chill until cold, at least 3 hours and up to 1 day.

THIN soup with more broth, if desired. Season to taste with salt and pepper. Ladle soup into bowls. Garnish with mint leaves.

Chilled avocado and mint soup

8 SERVINGS *This would be a great starter for a menu featuring tacos or steak fajitas from the grill.*

   4 **cups diced peeled avocados (about 4 medium)**
3¼ **cups chilled buttermilk**
   5 **tablespoons fresh lime juice**
   ¼ **cup chopped green onions**
   ¼ **cup chopped fresh cilantro**
   1 **teaspoon minced seeded serrano chile**
   1 **teaspoon chili powder**
   6 **tablespoons chopped fresh mint, divided**
   3 **cups (or more) low-salt chicken broth**

   1 **cup diced seeded tomatoes**

COMBINE first 7 ingredients in processor. Add 4 tablespoons mint; blend until smooth. Transfer to large bowl. Gradually whisk in 3 cups broth. Season soup to taste with salt and pepper. Cover; chill until cold, about 2 hours.

DO AHEAD *Can be made 6 hours ahead. Keep chilled. Thin with more broth by ¼ cupfuls, if desired. Rewhisk before serving.*

LADLE soup into bowls. Garnish with diced tomatoes and remaining 2 tablespoons mint.

Chilled corn soup with adobo swirl

4 SERVINGS *The spicy sauce that canned chipotle chiles are packed in is known as* adobo, *and it has a marvelous smoky flavor. Look for canned chipotles at supermarkets, specialty foods stores, and Latin markets. The rust-colored swirl on this golden-yellow soup is a cinch—just drizzle the oil in a spiral pattern in the center of the soup—and it looks professional.*

   3 **tablespoons olive oil, divided**
   1 **cup chopped sweet onion (such as Vidalia or Maui)**
   3 **cups fresh corn kernels (cut from about 3 ears of corn)**
   2 **cups low-salt chicken broth**
   2 **tablespoons fresh lime juice, divided**
   1 **cup (or more) water**

   1 **teaspoon adobo sauce from canned chipotle chiles**
      Fresh cilantro leaves

HEAT 1 tablespoon olive oil in heavy large saucepan over medium-high heat. Add onion and sauté until soft, about 4 minutes. Add corn kernels, broth, and 1 tablespoon lime juice; bring mixture to boil. Reduce heat to medium and simmer until corn is just tender, about 3 minutes. Working in batches, puree soup in blender until almost smooth. Stir in remaining 1 tablespoon lime juice and 1 cup water (thinning with more water, if desired). Season soup to taste with salt and pepper. Transfer soup to large bowl; cover and refrigerate until chilled, about 2 hours.

MEANWHILE, whisk remaining 2 tablespoons olive oil and adobo sauce in small bowl to blend. Ladle chilled corn soup into bowls. Drizzle soup with adobo oil, then garnish with cilantro and serve.

Watermelon and cucumber gazpacho

4 SERVINGS *For a summer grill party, this cool, colorful starter soup can't be beat. Thick Greek-style yogurt, now available in the dairy section of most supermarkets, would make a tangy, lower-fat stand-in for crème fraîche or sour cream.*

- 1 **3-pound seedless watermelon, diced (about 5 cups), divided**
- 1 **small cucumber, peeled, seeded, diced (about 1 cup)**
- 1 **medium red bell pepper, diced (about 1 cup)**
- 1 **medium yellow bell pepper, diced (about 1 cup)**
- 1 **small jalapeño chile, seeded, minced**
- 3 **pale green inner celery stalks, diced (about ½ cup)**
- ½ **small red onion, diced (about 1 cup)**
- ¼ **cup finely chopped fresh mint**
- 3 **tablespoons fresh lime juice**
- 2 **tablespoons red wine vinegar**
- ¼ **teaspoon salt**

- ½ **cup crème fraîche or sour cream**

PUREE 4 cups watermelon in blender until smooth. Transfer puree to large bowl. Add remaining 1 cup diced watermelon and next 10 ingredients; stir to combine. Cover gazpacho and refrigerate until cold, at least 1 hour and up to 4 hours.

LADLE gazpacho into bowls; top with dollop of crème fraîche.

GO SEEDLESS Be on the lookout for seedless watermelons, which are increasingly easy to find—and much easier to prepare and eat.

Cool tool For making quick pureed soups, an immersion blender can be your new best friend. Instead of pouring the soup into the blender, you can bring the tool to the soup with this blender-on-a-stick. There's no need to work in batches, and if a chunkier consistency is the aim, just puree for less time. To avoid spattering soup all over the kitchen, wait to turn the blender on until it's completely submerged, and be sure to turn the blender off before you take it out of the puree.

Speedy gazpacho

6 TO 8 SERVINGS *Top with grilled chicken or shrimp and diced avocado to turn this into a main course.*

1   English hothouse cucumber (about 12 ounces), peeled, cut into large chunks

1   large red bell pepper (about 8 ounces), halved, seeded, cut into chunks

2   cups (or more) bottled tomato juice

1   14½-ounce can diced tomatoes in juice

1   12½-ounce container refrigerated fire-roasted tomato salsa

1   cup roasted red peppers from jar

½   cup coarsely chopped fresh cilantro

2   tablespoons red wine vinegar

WORKING in 2 batches and using on/off turns, finely chop cucumber and bell pepper in processor. Add 2 cups tomato juice and all remaining ingredients; blend to coarse puree. Season to taste with salt. Transfer to bowl. Cover and chill 2 hours to allow flavors to develop. Mix in more tomato juice by ¼ cupfuls if too spicy.

Pineapple and bell pepper gazpacho

4 SERVINGS *Here's a clever alternative to traditional tomato gazpacho, and a great starter for a main-course dinner of grilled pork tenderloin.*

2   cups chopped cored peeled pineapple

2   cups chopped seeded peeled cucumber plus more for garnish

1½   cups pineapple juice

⅔   cup chopped red bell pepper plus more for garnish

⅔   cup chopped yellow bell pepper plus more for garnish

6   tablespoons chopped Maui onion

3   tablespoons chopped fresh Italian parsley

4   teaspoons minced jalapeño chile

PUREE pineapple, 2 cups cucumber, pineapple juice, ⅔ cup red bell pepper, ⅔ cup yellow bell pepper, onion, parsley, and jalapeño in blender until smooth. Transfer to bowl. Cover and refrigerate until cold, at least 2 hours and up to 6 hours. Season to taste with salt and pepper. Ladle soup into bowls. Garnish with additional chopped cucumber and bell peppers.

Chilled beet, orange, and dill soup

8 SERVINGS *This makes a great starter for a summer supper of herb-rubbed grilled chicken. Dill works especially well here, but you can substitute another tender, distinctive herb, such as cilantro or chives.*

- **3** **15-ounce cans julienne beets, drained, ¾ cup liquid reserved, divided**
- **1½** **cups fresh orange juice, divided**
- **1½** **cups reduced-fat (2%) buttermilk, divided**
- **3** **tablespoons chopped fresh dill, divided, plus more for garnish**

- **1½** **cups finely diced unpeeled English hothouse cucumber (about ½ large)**

COMBINE half of beets, half of reserved beet liquid, and half of orange juice in blender. Blend until smooth. Blend in half of buttermilk and 1½ table-spoons chopped dill. Transfer to large bowl. Repeat with remaining beets, beet liquid, orange juice, buttermilk, and 1½ tablespoons dill. Season to taste with salt and pepper. Chill at least 3 hours.

DO AHEAD *Soup can be made 2 days ahead. Cover and keep chilled.*

LADLE soup into bowls. Garnish soup with cucumber and additional dill.

Chilled cucumber-yogurt soup with radishes

6 SERVINGS *If you like the creamy, yogurt-based Indian condiment known as raita, you'll love this soup, which comes together quickly in the blender.*

- **2¼** **cups plain yogurt**
- **1¼** **pounds pickling cucumbers, trimmed, peeled, cut into 1-inch pieces**
- **2** **garlic cloves, minced**
- **1½** **teaspoons salt**
- **1½** **teaspoons ground cumin**
- **1½** **teaspoons curry powder**
- **¼** **teaspoon (generous) ground ginger**

  Thinly sliced radishes

COMBINE yogurt, cucumbers, garlic, salt, cumin, curry powder, and ginger in blender. Puree until smooth. Strain through fine sieve into large bowl. Refrigerate until well chilled, about 2 hours.

DO AHEAD *Can be made 1 day ahead. Keep chilled.*

LADLE soup into bowls. Top with sliced radishes and serve.

"CUKE" TIPS English hothouse cucumbers are long and slender, and have fewer seeds than other varieties; pickling cucumbers are short and squat, and also have few seeds. If you can't find either variety, substitute a regular cucumber and remove the seeds: Peel the cucumber and slice lengthwise, then run a tablespoon or teaspoon down the middle of each half, removing the seeds, and chop as directed.

Chilled fennel soup with Pernod

4 TO 6 SERVINGS *Pernod is a yellowish, anise-flavored liqueur from France.*

3 tablespoons olive oil

6 cups chopped trimmed fennel bulbs (about 3 large), fronds reserved if desired for garnish

2 cups chopped onions

6 cups low-salt chicken broth

2 tablespoons Pernod or other anise-flavored liqueur

Plain yogurt (optional)

HEAT oil in heavy large pot over medium-low heat. Add chopped fennel and onions; cover and cook until vegetables are soft but not brown, stirring occasionally, about 25 minutes. Add broth and bring to boil. Reduce heat to medium; simmer uncovered until vegetables are very tender, about 25 minutes. Working in batches, puree soup in blender until smooth. Transfer to bowl. Stir in Pernod. Season to taste with salt and pepper. Cover and chill until cold, about 3 hours.

DO AHEAD *Can be made 1 day ahead. Keep chilled.*

LADLE soup into bowls. Garnish with yogurt and fennel fronds, if desired.

Chilled red bell pepper soup

4 TO 6 SERVINGS *If there's no cayenne in the house, substitute a dash or two of hot sauce.*

4 tablespoons (½ stick) butter

1¼ pounds red bell peppers, coarsely chopped

2 cups sliced leeks (white and pale green parts only)

1½ cups low-salt chicken broth

1½ cups chilled buttermilk
Cayenne pepper

Chopped chives or green onion tops

MELT butter in heavy large saucepan over medium-high heat. Add bell peppers and leeks and sauté until tender, about 18 minutes. Add broth and bring to boil. Reduce heat, cover, and simmer until vegetables are very tender, about 15 minutes. Puree soup in blender in batches. Transfer soup to bowl; refrigerate until cool, about 30 minutes.

MIX buttermilk into soup. Season to taste with cayenne, salt, and pepper. Chill until very cold, at least 3 hours.

DO AHEAD *Can be made 1 day ahead. Cover and keep chilled.*

LADLE soup into bowls. Garnish with chives.

NO BUTTERMILK? If you don't have buttermilk, mix 1½ cups whole or reduced-fat milk with 1½ tablespoons lemon juice or apple cider vinegar (1 tablespoon juice or vinegar per cup of milk). Let mixture sit at room temperature for about 10 minutes. When the milk curdles, it's ready to use.

Chilled carrot soup with garden herbs

6 SERVINGS *This cold soup has a wonderfully silky texture, especially considering there's no cream in the recipe. It also tastes great served hot.*

  6 tablespoons olive oil
  5 large carrots, thinly sliced
2½ cups thinly sliced onions
  1 teaspoon dried thyme
  1 teaspoon (packed) golden brown sugar
  ½ teaspoon ground nutmeg
  4 cups low-salt chicken broth
  ¼ cup orange juice

    Chopped fresh chives

HEAT olive oil in heavy large saucepan over medium heat. Add carrots and onions and sauté 4 minutes. Add thyme, brown sugar, and nutmeg; sauté until vegetables are tender, about 6 minutes. Add broth. Cover pan; simmer until carrots are very soft, about 25 minutes. Using slotted spoon, transfer vegetables to processor. Add ¼ cup cooking liquid. Puree until smooth. Return puree to pan. Stir in orange juice. Season to taste with salt and pepper. Chill.

DO AHEAD *Can be made 1 day ahead. Keep chilled.*

LADLE soup into bowls. Sprinkle with chives.

Chilled yellow pepper and white bean soup

4 SERVINGS *A topping of arugula adds color and a fresh, peppery kick.*

  3 yellow, orange, or red bell peppers
  1 tablespoon olive oil
  1 small onion, chopped
  ⅛ teaspoon dried crushed red pepper
  2 14-ounce cans low-salt chicken broth, divided
  1 15- to 16-ounce can cannellini (white kidney beans), rinsed, drained

  1 bunch fresh arugula, sliced

CHAR bell peppers over gas flame or in broiler until blackened on all sides. Place in paper bag and let stand 10 minutes. Peel, seed, and chop peppers.

HEAT oil in heavy medium saucepan over medium-high heat. Add onion and sauté until tender, about 5 minutes. Add bell peppers and crushed red pepper and sauté 1 minute. Add broth and cannellini. Bring to boil. Reduce heat, cover and simmer 15 minutes. Strain vegetables, reserving broth. Transfer vegetables to processor; puree. Gradually mix in 2 cups of reserved broth. Transfer puree to bowl. Stir in remaining broth. Season to taste with salt and pepper. Cover; chill until cold.

DO AHEAD *Can be made 1 day ahead. Keep chilled.*

LADLE soup into bowls. Top each serving with generous amount of arugula.

Chilled pea and tarragon soup

6 SERVINGS *Tarragon is an appetizing, spring-like variation on mint, the traditional herb used to flavor cold English pea soup. The tarragon adds a nice anise-like flavor.*

- 1 tablespoon butter
- 1 small onion, chopped
- 1 tablespoon all purpose flour
- 2 14-ounce cans low-salt chicken broth, divided
- 1 10-ounce package frozen peas or 1 pound fresh peas, shelled
- 2 teaspoons chopped fresh tarragon plus whole leaves for garnish

  Crème fraîche or sour cream

MELT butter in heavy medium saucepan over medium-low heat. Add onion and sauté until tender, about 8 minutes. Add flour and stir 2 minutes. Gradually mix in broth. Add peas and chopped tarragon. Simmer until peas are very tender, about 15 minutes. Drain peas, reserving broth. Puree peas in processor. Add ½ cup reserved broth and puree until smooth. Gradually blend in remaining reserved broth. Transfer to medium bowl and refrigerate until well chilled.

DO AHEAD *Can be made 1 day ahead. Keep chilled.*

SEASON soup to taste with salt and pepper. Ladle soup into bowls. Garnish each serving with dollop of crème fraîche and tarragon leaves.

Chilled summer squash soup with curry

4 SERVINGS *Try this soup as a starter for spice-rubbed pork loin.*

- 2 tablespoons (¼ stick) butter
- 2 large shallots, minced
- 1 garlic clove, minced
- 1½ teaspoons curry powder
- 1¼ pounds yellow crookneck squash, diced
- 2 cups (or more) low-salt chicken broth, divided

  Plain yogurt
  Minced fresh mint

MELT butter in heavy large saucepan over medium-low heat. Add shallots, garlic, and curry powder and sauté 3 minutes. Add squash, cover, and cook until squash is tender, stirring occasionally, about 10 minutes. Add 2 cups broth, cover, and simmer 10 minutes. Puree in batches in blender or processor. Cover and chill until cold.

DO AHEAD *Can be made 1 day ahead. Keep chilled.*

THIN with additional broth, if desired. Season to taste with salt. Ladle soup into bowls. Top each serving with dollop of yogurt. Garnish with mint.

Chilled pea pod soup

8 SERVINGS *Using whole peas in the pod cuts prep time and adds flavor.*

- ½ cup (1 stick) butter
- 2 pounds peas in pods, ends snapped, strings removed
- 8 green onions, thinly sliced
- 8 cups low-salt chicken broth
- 2 tablespoons minced fresh tarragon plus whole sprigs for garnish
- 16 romaine lettuce leaves

- ¾ cup crème fraîche or sour cream, divided
  Pinch of sugar (optional)
  Fresh lemon juice (optional)

MELT butter in heavy large saucepan over medium heat. Sauté pods and green onions until onions are tender, about 5 minutes. Add broth and minced tarragon and bring to boil. Reduce heat and simmer 15 minutes. Mix in lettuce and simmer 5 minutes.

WORKING in batches and using on/off turns, puree soup in processor until very smooth, about 5 minutes. Strain through fine sieve into bowl. Stir in ½ cup crème fraîche. Season to taste with salt, pepper, and sugar or lemon juice, if desired.

COOL to room temperature. Cover and refrigerate until well chilled, at least 4 hours.

DO AHEAD *Can be made 1 day ahead. Keep chilled.*

LADLE soup into bowls. Top with remaining crème fraîche; garnish with tarragon sprigs.

On the go Chilled soup is a perfect starter for a picnic lunch. It's as simple as transporting the soup in a thermos and bringing along the chopped or sliced garnishes in resealable plastic bags.

salads

MAIN-COURSE SALADS

Grilled Shrimp Salad with
Corn and Avocado

Scandinavian Salad with
Dill and Cornichons

Pasta Salad with Shrimp,
Roasted Peppers, and Fennel

Greek-Italian Chopped Salad

Smoked Salmon, Beet, and
Cucumber Pasta Salad

Tuna, White Bean, and
Roasted-Pepper Salad with
Creamy Dijon Dressing

Grilled Lobster Salad with
Avocado and Papaya

Thai-Style Seafood
Salad with Herbs

Spicy Crab and Melon Salad

Cilantro-Lime Crab Salad
in Avocado Halves

Greek-Style Pasta Salad

Spicy Asian-Style Pasta Salad

Southwestern Chicken and Pasta

Buffalo Chicken Strips with
Celery and Watercress Slaw

Chicken and Mango Salad with
Ginger-Orange Dressing

Mediterranean Chicken Salad

Chicken, Walnut, and Red Grape
Salad with Curry Dressing

Chicken and Spinach Salad
with Bacon Dressing

Chicken and Caponata Salad

Turkey Chopped Salad with
Spicy Avocado Dressing

Ham and Spring Vegetable
Salad with Shallot Vinaigrette

Salad Bar Cobb

Thai Grilled Beef Salad

Asian Noodle Salad with
Eggplant, Sugar Snap Peas,
and Lime Dressing

Jicama, Radish, and Pepita Salad

Grilled Tuna with Salad Niçoise

Spinach Salad with
Italian Sausage

Curried Quinoa Salad with Mango

Farro Salad with Peas,
Asparagus, and Feta

Curried Couscous and
Garbanzo Bean Salad

STARTER SALADS

Pear and Curly Endive Salad

Fennel, Arugula, and
Smoked-Trout Salad with
Horseradish Dressing

Smoked Salmon and Cucumber
Ribbon Salad with Caraway

Frisée Salad with Bacon,
Dates, and Red Onion

Spring Greens with
Soppressata and Grapefruit

Mâche Salad with Blood Oranges,
Pistachios, and Pomegranate

Arugula Salad with Olives,
Pancetta, and Parmesan Shavings

Arugula, Blood Orange,
and Blue Cheese Salad

Green Bean, Fennel,
and Parsley Salad

Radicchio and Haricot Vert
Salad with Candied Walnuts

Winter Salad with
Hoisin Vinaigrette

Tangy Avocado-Orange Salad

Avocado and Mango Salad with
Passion-Fruit Vinaigrette

Heirloom Tomato Salad
with Blue Cheese

Heirloom Tomato and
Burrata Cheese Salad

Watermelon and Watercress
Salad with Ginger

Watermelon and Citrus
Salad with Mint

Butter Lettuce and Radicchio
Salad with Strawberries

Zucchini and Tomato Salad
with Garlic-Chili Dressing

Mixed Greens with Feta,
Almonds, and Blueberries

Radicchio and Endive Caesar
with Ciabatta Crisps

Mixed Greens with
Roasted Beets, Fennel, and
Marinated Red Onions

Iceberg Wedges with Warm
Bacon and Blue Cheese Dressing

Frisée and Radish Salad with
Goat Cheese Croutons

Bibb Lettuce Salad with
Persimmons and Candied Pecans

Green Apple and Celery
Salad with Walnuts and
Mustard Vinaigrette

Frisée Salad with Blue Cheese,
Walnut, and Cranberry Crostini

Warm Endive Salad with
Parmesan and Hazelnuts

Warm Spinach, Mushroom,
and Goat Cheese Salad

Warm Spinach Salad
with Parmesan

SIDE SALADS

Sweet Corn and Tomato
Salad with Fresh Cilantro

Summer Vegetable Salad

Savoy Cabbage and Radicchio
Slaw with Blood-Orange Dressing

South-of-the-Border Coleslaw
with Cilantro and Jalapeño

Asian-Flavored Coleslaw with
Rice Vinegar and Ginger

Spiced Carrot Salad

Thai Cucumber Salad
with Roasted Peanuts

Sweet-and-Sour Cucumbers
with Fresh Dill

Indian-Spiced Potato Salad

New Potato and Asparagus Salad

Grilled Potato and Summer
Squash Salad with Marjoram-
Lemon Vinaigrette

Pesto Potato Salad
with Green Beans

Rice Salad with Sugar Snap
Peas, Mint, and Lime

Orzo, Feta, and Tomato Salad
with Marjoram Vinaigrette

tool kit Vinaigrettes—simple to sublime: A vinaigrette is simply one part vinegar and three parts oil with salt and freshly ground black pepper added to heighten and balance flavors. But by blending different types of vinegar (such as balsamic, raspberry, or rice vinegar) with different oils (olive oil, grapeseed oil, or a little Asian sesame oil), you can build an entire repertoire of vinaigrettes. Adding garlic, shallots, herbs, spices, Dijon mustard, and citrus juices and zests creates an array of vinaigrettes with flavors from around the world.

— For a French vinaigrette, mix olive oil, Champagne vinegar, Dijon mustard, minced shallots, and fresh tarragon or ground fennel seeds.
— Use extra-virgin olive oil, balsamic or red wine vinegar, minced garlic, and dried oregano for a quintessential Italian vinaigrette.
— Think outside the vinegar bottle and mix grapeseed oil with fresh lime juice, minced garlic, fresh cilantro, and chipotle chile powder to create a vinaigrette with Latin flair.
— For an exotic Middle Eastern flavor, try olive oil, lemon juice, minced green onions, ground cumin, and dried mint.

Well-dressed: Fine-tune your dressings to keep the flavors balanced and make sure they complement the salad.
— If there's too much vinegar in a dressing or it tastes too acidic, add more oil or balance it with a little honey, maple syrup, or frozen juice concentrate (depending on the type of salad).
— To make a lighter salad dressing, use seasoned rice vinegar or white balsamic vinegar—these vinegars are less acidic, so you'll need far less oil.

— Creamy Caesar dressings should have plenty of garlic, a little Dijon mustard, and Worcestershire sauce (plus anchovies, if you like them) for classic Caesar flavor.
— For salads that include fruit, enhance the sweet flavor by adding honey or some orange or lemon peel to the dressing.
— Dress a salad just before serving it—this keeps it crisp and fresh.

MAIN-COURSE SALADS

Grilled shrimp salad with corn and avocado

6 SERVINGS *Hot smoked Spanish paprika, sometimes labeled* Pimentón de La Vera, *is available at specialty foods stores or online from tienda.com. Mâche, also known as lamb's lettuce, is found in the produce department with the other bagged lettuces. Adding half a teaspoon of truffle oil to the dressing would lend a luxurious, earthy accent. You'll need metal skewers for grilling the shrimp and onions.*

  6 tablespoons orange juice
3½ tablespoons white wine vinegar
  2 tablespoons chopped fresh chives
1½ teaspoons finely grated orange peel
 ¼ cup olive oil plus more for brushing

  2 red onions, each cut through root end into 8 wedges, peeled
  2 pounds uncooked large shrimp, peeled, deveined
  3 large ears of corn, husked
  1 ciabatta bread or pain rustique, cut crosswise into 1-inch-thick slices
  2 teaspoons hot smoked Spanish paprika (Pimentón de La Vera)

12 cups mâche (about 7 ounces)
  2 ripe avocados, halved, pitted, peeled, cut into cubes

WHISK first 4 ingredients in small bowl to blend. Whisk in ¼ cup olive oil. Season salad to taste with salt and pepper.

PREPARE barbecue (medium heat). Thread onions on metal skewers; thread shrimp on separate metal skewers. Place onion skewers, shrimp skewers, corn, and bread slices on 2 large rimmed baking sheets. Brush onions, shrimp, corn, and bread with olive oil, then sprinkle with salt and pepper. Sprinkle shrimp on both sides with smoked paprika. Grill onions and corn until cooked through, about 5 minutes per side; grill bread slices until browned, about 2 minutes per side. Grill shrimp until cooked through, about 2½ minutes per side.

TRANSFER vegetables, shrimp, and bread to work surface. Cut corn kernels off cobs; place corn kernels in very large bowl. Remove shrimp and onions from skewers and add to bowl. Add mâche and avocados to bowl. Toss salad with enough dressing to coat. Season to taste with salt and pepper. Transfer salad to large rimmed platter and serve with bread.

SMOKE FROM SPAIN Smoked Spanish paprika adds a depth of flavor that other paprikas just can't match. The mildest grade is labeled sweet (*dulce*), and from there it gets spicier. The paprika also comes in medium-hot (*agridulce*) and hot (*picante*). A good way to get to know the product is to substitute sweet smoked paprika in any recipe that calls for regular paprika, and hot smoked paprika in any recipe that calls for cayenne pepper.

Scandinavian salad with dill and cornichons

4 SERVINGS *In keeping with the Scandinavian theme, present the salad on European-style pumpernickel bread with sliced hard-boiled egg, and serve lemon wedges and dill on the side. The tiny pickles known as cornichons are widely available at supermarkets and specialty foods stores.*

⅓ cup mayonnaise

¼ cup chopped fresh dill

1 tablespoon Dijon mustard

1 tablespoon fresh lemon juice

1 pound cooked peeled deveined medium shrimp

1 cup thinly sliced halved English hothouse cucumber

⅓ cup sliced cornichons (gherkins)

8 butter lettuce leaves

WHISK mayonnaise, dill, mustard, and lemon juice in medium bowl. Add shrimp, cucumber, and cornichons and toss to coat. Season generously with salt and pepper.

NESTLE 2 lettuce leaves on each of 4 plates. Mound shrimp salad in leaves, dividing equally.

Pasta salad with shrimp, roasted peppers, and fennel

6 SERVINGS *This main-dish salad can easily be transformed into a side dish simply by omitting the shrimp.*

5 tablespoons olive oil

2½ tablespoons fresh lemon juice

4 large garlic cloves, chopped

4 teaspoons finely grated lemon peel

1 pound farfalle (bow-tie pasta), freshly cooked, rinsed, drained

1 pound cooked deveined peeled shrimp, cut lengthwise in half

3 7-ounce jars roasted red peppers, drained, sliced, juices reserved

1½ cups thinly sliced fennel bulb

¾ cup finely chopped fresh basil

⅓ cup pine nuts, toasted

WHISK first 4 ingredients in large bowl to blend. Add farfalle, shrimp, sliced red peppers, fennel, basil, and pine nuts; toss to blend. Add enough reserved roasted-pepper juices by tablespoonfuls to moisten if salad is dry. Season to taste with salt and pepper.

Greek-Italian chopped salad

6 SERVINGS *Adding a pound or so of cooked shrimp turns this salad into supper.*

- 6 tablespoons olive oil
- 3 tablespoons white wine vinegar
- 1 teaspoon dried oregano
- 1 garlic clove, minced

- 6 cups chopped romaine lettuce
- 1 15- to 16-ounce can garbanzo beans (chickpeas), drained
- 1 red bell pepper, diced
- 1 cup very thinly sliced red onion
- 1 cup very thinly sliced fresh fennel bulb
- ½ cup crumbled feta cheese (about 3 ounces)
- 2 ounces thinly sliced Italian Genoa salami, cut into strips
- ¼ cup sliced pitted Kalamata olives

WHISK oil, vinegar, oregano, and garlic in small bowl to blend. Season dressing to taste with salt and pepper.

COMBINE lettuce, garbanzo beans, bell pepper, red onion, fennel, feta cheese, salami, and sliced olives in large bowl. Pour dressing over; toss to coat. Season with salt and pepper. Mound salad on platter and serve.

Smoked salmon, beet, and cucumber pasta salad

2 SERVINGS; CAN BE DOUBLED *Fusilli lends especially nicely to pasta salads—its corkscrew shape takes on flavors well.*

- 2½ cups fusilli (spiral-shaped pasta)

- ⅓ cup sour cream
- ⅓ cup mayonnaise
- 4 teaspoons minced fresh dill
- 2½ teaspoons fresh lemon juice
- 1½ teaspoons Dijon mustard
- ⅓ pound thinly sliced smoked salmon, cut crosswise into ½-inch-thick slices
- ½ English hothouse cucumber, quartered lengthwise, sliced
- 2 celery stalks, diced
- ½ cup diced drained pickled beet slices

COOK pasta in large pot of boiling salted water until tender but still firm to bite, stirring occasionally. Drain. Rinse under cold water to cool. Drain well. Transfer to large bowl.

WHISK sour cream, mayonnaise, dill, lemon juice, and mustard in small bowl. Season dressing with salt and pepper. Add dressing, smoked salmon, cucumber, and celery to pasta; toss gently to coat. Top with beets.

Freezer stash Keep a few bags of cooked or uncooked frozen shrimp stashed in the freezer—they're a great last-minute way to turn a salad into a substantial dinner. To quickly defrost frozen shrimp, submerge the sealed bag in a bowl of cold water for 20 to 30 minutes until thawed.

Tuna, white bean, and roasted-pepper salad with creamy Dijon dressing

4 SERVINGS *This substantial tuna salad is the perfect dish to whip up when it seems like there's nothing in the fridge: Almost all of the ingredients are pantry staples.*

¼ cup mayonnaise

¼ cup olive oil

3 tablespoons Dijon mustard

2 tablespoons Champagne vinegar or white wine vinegar

5 cups mixed baby greens

1 15-ounce can small white beans, rinsed, drained

⅔ cup chopped drained roasted red peppers from jar

⅓ cup chopped red onion

1 12-ounce can chunk light tuna

⅔ cup Kalamata olives or other brine-cured black olives, pitted, halved

WHISK first 4 ingredients in small bowl. Season dressing with salt and pepper.

TOSS greens in large bowl with enough dressing to coat. Divide greens among plates. Toss beans, red peppers, and onion in medium bowl with enough dressing to coat. Top greens with bean mixture, then tuna, dividing equally. Garnish with olives.

Grilled lobster salad with avocado and papaya

4 SERVINGS *Grilled lobster gives this dish a wonderful smoke-touched flavor, but if you're short on time, simply use cooked tail meat, available at many supermarkets and at fish stores. Or substitute jumbo shrimp: Thread them onto skewers and grill until the shrimp are pink with opaque centers.*

6 lobster tails, thawed if frozen, split in half lengthwise

9 tablespoons olive oil

½ cup fresh orange juice

3 tablespoons fresh lime juice

1 tablespoon minced seeded jalapeño chile

1 tablespoon finely grated lime peel

1½ teaspoons finely grated orange peel

2 avocados, halved, pitted, peeled, diced into ½-inch pieces

4 medium tomatoes, seeded, diced into ½-inch pieces

1 large papaya, peeled, seeded, diced into ½-inch pieces

10 cups mixed baby greens

PREPARE barbecue (medium-high heat). Arrange lobster tails, cut side up, on grill. Cover; grill 6 minutes. Turn lobsters over and grill until just cooked through, about 5 minutes. Remove lobster meat from shells. Cool. Cut meat into ½-inch pieces. Transfer to large bowl.

WHISK oil and next 5 ingredients in medium bowl to blend. Season to taste with salt and pepper.

ADD avocados, tomatoes, and papaya to lobster in bowl. Pour ½ cup dressing over; toss to coat. Season with salt and pepper.

TOSS greens in another large bowl with enough remaining dressing to coat. Divide greens among plates. Spoon lobster mixture atop greens.

Thai-style seafood salad with herbs

8 APPETIZER OR 4 MAIN-COURSE SERVINGS *This oil-free salad dressing packs zingy flavor, thanks to lime juice and fish sauce. If you're not a squid fan, substitute an equal quantity of sea scallops. Or for a meaty version, try grilled beef instead of seafood. Lemongrass and fish sauce are available at some supermarkets and at Asian markets.*

- 1 stalk lemongrass or 1 tablespoon grated lemon peel
- 14 ounces uncooked cleaned squid, tentacles reserved, bodies cut into ½-inch-thick rings
- 8 ounces uncooked large shrimp, peeled, deveined
- 3 tablespoons fresh lime juice
- 2 tablespoons fish sauce (such as nam pla or nuoc nam)
- ½ teaspoon dried crushed red pepper
- ½ cup minced shallots
- 3 tablespoons chopped fresh tarragon
- 2 tablespoons chopped fresh cilantro

- 8 crisp lettuce leaves

DISCARD all but bottom 4 inches of lemongrass stalk. Peel off outer layers from stalk; discard. Thinly slice lemongrass. Combine lemongrass, squid tentacles and bodies, shrimp, lime juice, fish sauce, and crushed red pepper in heavy large skillet. Sauté over medium-high heat until squid and shrimp are just opaque, about 3 minutes. Transfer seafood mixture to medium bowl. Cool completely. Add shallots, tarragon, and cilantro to seafood mixture; toss to coat. Season to taste with salt and pepper. Chill until cold, at least 45 minutes and up to 2 hours.

ARRANGE lettuce leaves on platter. Using slotted spoon, divide seafood mixture among lettuce leaves. Spoon some of juices over each salad.

SQUID-FRIENDLY To make preparation easier and less messy, have the fishmonger clean the squid for you, and then just slice it when you get home. Or look for cleaned squid, available in the fresh fish or frozen fish section of many supermarkets.

Spicy crab and melon salad

4 SERVINGS *To make this salad the centerpiece of a summer lunch, serve it with herbed buttermilk biscuits and chilled asparagus with a lemon vinaigrette.*

- ⅓ cup mayonnaise
- 2 tablespoons chopped fresh tarragon plus tarragon sprigs for garnish
- 1 tablespoon fresh lemon juice
- 2½ teaspoons Old Bay seasoning or other seafood seasoning, divided
- 2½ cups fresh lump crabmeat, picked over (about 12 ounces)

- 1 large cantaloupe, quartered, seeded (about 4 pounds)

WHISK mayonnaise, chopped tarragon, lemon juice, and 1½ teaspoons Old Bay seasoning in medium bowl to blend. Stir in crabmeat. Season crab salad to taste with salt and pepper.

DO AHEAD *Salad can be made 4 hours ahead. Cover and chill.*

LIGHTLY sprinkle sides of cantaloupe wedges with pepper and remaining 1 teaspoon Old Bay seasoning. Place melon wedges on serving plates and mound crab salad in cavity of each. Garnish with tarragon sprigs.

Cilantro-lime crab salad in avocado halves

2 SERVINGS *With this salad, try a starter of sliced multicolored heirloom tomatoes; sprinkle them with smoked sea salt, and drizzle with your favorite extra-virgin olive oil.*

⅓ cup finely chopped red onion

3 tablespoons mayonnaise

2 tablespoons chopped fresh cilantro

2 teaspoons fresh lime juice

½ teaspoon ground cumin

½ teaspoon grated lime peel

8 ounces fresh lump crabmeat

1 ripe large avocado, halved, pitted, peeled
  Lime wedges

STIR red onion, mayonnaise, cilantro, lime juice, cumin, and lime peel in medium bowl to blend. Mix in crabmeat. Season salad with salt and pepper.

DO AHEAD *Salad can be made 4 hours ahead. Cover and chill.*

ARRANGE avocado halves, cut side up, on plates. Mound crab salad on each avocado half. Garnish with lime wedges.

Greek-style pasta salad

2 SERVINGS; CAN BE DOUBLED *Serve this with glasses of crisp, dry rosé. For dessert, serve purchased baklava, the traditional Greek sweet made of phyllo pastry and layered with honey, spices, and nuts.*

1 cup fusilli (spiral-shaped pasta)
  or large elbow macaroni

2 large tomatoes, seeded, diced

3 ounces feta cheese, cubed

1 large shallot or 2 green onions, minced

3 tablespoons olive oil

3 tablespoons chopped arugula or
  watercress plus sprigs for garnish

1 tablespoon fresh lemon juice

1 small red bell pepper, cut into strips
  Greek olives

COOK pasta in large pot of boiling salted water until just tender but still firm to bite, stirring occasionally. Drain. Rinse under cold water until cool and drain well.

COMBINE tomatoes, feta, shallot, olive oil, chopped arugula, and lemon juice in large bowl.

ADD pasta to tomato mixture; toss to coat. Season with salt and pepper.

DO AHEAD *Salad can be made 4 hours ahead. Cover and chill.*

SPOON salad into center of large plates. Garnish with bell pepper strips, olives, and arugula sprigs.

QUICK PITTING Pitted Greek olives in jars are becoming more available at supermarkets, but if you can't find them, pitting requires no special gadget. Simply press on the olive with the flat side of a chef's knife or cleaver, using the heel of your hand. You'll gently crush the olive, and the pit can be removed easily.

109

Spicy Asian-style pasta salad

6 SERVINGS *Tossing in cooked shrimp or chicken will turn this into a main dish. Asian sesame oil, made with toasted sesame seeds, can be found in the Asian foods section of the supermarket.*

1 **pound linguine, broken in half**

4 **tablespoons Asian sesame oil, divided**
3 **tablespoons honey**
3 **tablespoons soy sauce**
3 **tablespoons balsamic vinegar**
¼ **teaspoon cayenne pepper**

3 **red bell peppers, seeded, thinly sliced**
3 **cups snow peas**
1 **large red onion, thinly sliced**
¾ **cup honey-roasted peanuts, coarsely chopped**
½ **cup chopped fresh basil**

COOK pasta in large pot of boiling salted water until tender but still firm to bite, stirring occasionally. Drain very well. Transfer to large bowl.

WHISK 3 tablespoons oil, honey, soy sauce, vinegar, and cayenne in small bowl to blend. Season to taste with salt. Mix half of dressing into pasta.

HEAT remaining 1 tablespoon oil in heavy large pot over medium-high heat. Add bell peppers, snow peas, and onion; sauté until just beginning to wilt, about 2 minutes. Add vegetables to pasta. Mix in peanuts, basil, and enough dressing to coat. Season with salt and pepper. Cool completely. Serve, passing any remaining dressing separately.

Hold the oil When making a pasta salad, it can be tempting to pour on extra oil for moisture. But use caution: Pasta coats with oil very easily, especially shapes like fusilli and shells, which trap oil in nooks and crannies. The more oil you add, the heavier the salad will be (the downfall of many pasta salads). It's fine to use a dash or two of oil for added richness, but if the salad really needs moistening, it's better to use lemon juice, broth, or a little of the pasta cooking water.

Southwestern chicken and pasta

8 SERVINGS *The rotisserie chicken that's sold at supermarkets is a boon for weeknight cooks—there's no need to roast your own. Hominy is sold in the canned goods section of the supermarket.*

- 1 **pound farfalle (bow-tie pasta)**

- ¼ **cup olive oil**
- 2 **cups diced cooked chicken**
- 8 **green onions, chopped**
- 6 **plum tomatoes, chopped**
- 1 **15-ounce can golden hominy, drained**
- 1 **15-ounce can black beans, drained**
- 1 **12-ounce bottle mild green taco sauce**
- 1 **cup chopped fresh cilantro**

COOK pasta in large pot of boiling salted water until tender but still firm to bite, stirring occasionally. Drain; rinse under cold water and drain again.

TRANSFER pasta to large bowl. Add oil and toss to coat. Add all remaining ingredients; toss to coat. Season salad generously with salt and pepper.

Buffalo chicken strips with celery and watercress slaw

4 SERVINGS *The Japanese breadcrumbs known as* panko *are sold in the Asian foods section of the supermarket.*

- ¾ **cup mayonnaise, divided**
- ½ **cup buttermilk**
- 3 **ounces blue cheese, crumbled**

- 1 **tablespoon hot pepper sauce**
- 4 **skinless boneless chicken breast halves**
- 1¼ **cups panko (Japanese breadcrumbs)**

- 4 **large celery stalks, cut diagonally into paper-thin strips**
- 1 **cup shredded red cabbage**
- 3 **tablespoons unseasoned rice vinegar**
- 4 **cups small watercress sprigs**

BLEND ¼ cup mayonnaise, buttermilk, and blue cheese in processor. Season dressing with pepper. Set aside.

MIX remaining ½ cup mayonnaise and hot sauce in bowl. Sprinkle chicken with salt. Coat each side with 1 tablespoon mayonnaise-hot sauce mixture, then 2 tablespoons panko. Heat large nonstick skillet over medium heat. Sauté chicken until cooked through, about 7 minutes per side.

MEANWHILE, toss celery, cabbage, and vinegar in large bowl. Season slaw with salt and pepper. Mix watercress into slaw.

CUT chicken crosswise into strips; arrange on 4 plates with slaw. Spoon dressing into 4 small ramekins; serve with chicken.

Chicken and mango salad with ginger-orange dressing

4 SERVINGS *Chopped crystallized ginger, which can be found at many supermarkets, specialty foods stores, and natural foods stores, adds an intriguing flavor and a touch of sweetness.*

½ cup plus 1 tablespoon vegetable oil
¼ cup thawed frozen orange juice concentrate
2 tablespoons unseasoned rice vinegar
2 tablespoons finely chopped crystallized ginger

1¼ pounds skinless boneless chicken
   breast halves (about 3)

2 large bunches watercress, trimmed
1 large mango, peeled, pitted, cut
   into ½-inch-thick slices
½ small red onion, sliced paper-thin

WHISK ½ cup oil and next 3 ingredients in small bowl to blend. Season dressing to taste with salt and pepper.

HEAT remaining 1 tablespoon oil in heavy large skillet over medium-low heat. Sprinkle chicken with salt and pepper; add to skillet. Cover and sauté until cooked through, about 6 minutes per side. Transfer to cutting board. Cut crosswise into slices; cool 5 minutes.

MOUND watercress on plates; top with chicken, mango, and red onion. Drizzle with dressing.

Mediterranean chicken salad

4 SERVINGS *Dried currants play deliciously here against the salty-briny capers. Serve this nestled in leaves of butter lettuce or romaine.*

6 tablespoons olive oil
2 tablespoons plus 2 teaspoons tarragon vinegar
1 tablespoon chopped fresh tarragon
½ tablespoon fresh lemon juice
½ tablespoon Dijon mustard
3 cups diced cooked chicken (from one
   3-pound purchased cooked chicken)

½ cup orzo (about 3 ounces)
1 cup halved cherry tomatoes (about 10 ounces)
1 6-ounce jar marinated artichoke
   hearts, drained
½ cup coarsely chopped pitted Kalamata olives
⅓ cup dried currants
1½ tablespoons drained capers

WHISK oil, vinegar, tarragon, lemon juice, and mustard in small bowl. Season dressing to taste with salt and pepper. Place chicken in medium bowl. Mix in ¼ cup dressing.

COOK orzo in large pot of boiling salted water until just tender but still firm to bite, stirring occasionally. Drain. Rinse under cold water to cool; drain well. Transfer orzo to large bowl. Stir in remaining dressing and toss to coat. Add chicken mixture, tomatoes, artichoke hearts, olives, currants, and capers. Season salad to taste with salt and pepper.

Chicken, walnut, and red grape salad with curry dressing

4 SERVINGS *Madras-style curry mixes are hotter than standard curry powders, so using the full-flavored Madras blend will add a bit of spicy heat to this flavorful, low-fat dressing. Toasting the curry powder first deepens the flavors of the spices.*

- 2 teaspoons curry powder (preferably Madras-style)
- ¼ cup light mayonnaise
- ¼ cup plain nonfat yogurt
- 2 teaspoons mango chutney (such as Major Grey)
- 1 teaspoon minced peeled fresh ginger
- ½ teaspoon finely grated orange peel
- 3 cups ½-inch pieces cooked skinless boneless chicken breast
- 1 cup halved seedless red grapes plus 4 small clusters for garnish
- ½ cup thinly sliced green onions
- ⅓ cup walnuts, toasted, coarsely chopped

- 4 large curly lettuce leaves

STIR curry powder in small skillet over medium heat until fragrant, about 30 seconds. Transfer to medium bowl. Add mayonnaise, yogurt, chutney, ginger, and orange peel. Whisk to blend. Stir in chicken, grapes, green onions, and walnuts. Season salad to taste with salt and pepper.

DO AHEAD *Salad can be made 6 hours ahead. Cover and chill.*

PLACE 1 lettuce leaf on each of 4 plates. Top each lettuce leaf with salad. Garnish each plate with grape cluster.

Change-ups Going by the book is generally a good idea, especially if it's the first time you're trying a recipe. That said, don't hesitate to make substitutions in these salads. No Dijon mustard in the house? Use coarse-grained mustard instead. White wine vinegar is a perfectly good substitute for Champagne or tarragon vinegar. And if you don't have dried currants, raisins or minced dried apricots would work just as well.

113

Chicken and spinach salad with bacon dressing

4 SERVINGS *This salad gets two hits of bacon flavor: There are crunchy bacon pieces in the salad and bacon drippings in the dressing. For variety, mix in a little curly endive and radicchio with the spinach.*

 3 cups cooked chicken, cut into short strips (from 1 purchased roasted chicken)
 1 6-ounce bag baby spinach leaves
 6 bacon slices, cut into ½-inch pieces
 ½ medium red onion, sliced paper-thin
 3 tablespoons balsamic vinegar

PLACE chicken and spinach in large bowl. Cook bacon in large skillet over medium-high heat until crisp. Using slotted spoon, transfer bacon to paper towels. Pour off all but 3 tablespoons drippings from skillet. Add onion and vinegar to drippings in skillet; stir to heat through, scraping up browned bits, about 1 minute. Pour dressing over chicken and spinach. Add bacon; toss to coat (spinach will wilt slightly). Season salad with salt and pepper.

ROAST NOW, EAT LATER The cooked chicken called for in these salads is easily found, thanks to the advent of good-quality roasted chicken sold at supermarkets. And if you happen to be roasting a chicken for dinner—on a Sunday night, say—consider roasting two, so you'll have cooked chicken ready to use for main-course salads.

Chicken and caponata salad

2 SERVINGS *Caponata is a full-flavored and savory Sicilian dish served as a salad, side dish, or relish; it includes eggplant, onions, tomatoes, and olives. You can find it at the supermarket in cans or jars, usually near the tomato paste or in the condiment section.*

 5 tablespoons olive oil, divided
 3 skinless boneless chicken breast halves
 1 large shallot, minced
 ¼ cup fresh orange juice
 2 tablespoons plus 2 teaspoons balsamic vinegar
 1 tablespoon finely grated orange peel
 1½ teaspoons Dijon mustard

 ½ medium head of escarole, torn into bite-size pieces
 1 7½-ounce can purchased caponata

HEAT 1 tablespoon oil in heavy large skillet over medium-low heat. Sprinkle chicken with salt and pepper. Add to skillet and sauté until cooked through, about 6 minutes per side. Transfer to plate. Add shallot to skillet and stir 1 minute. Add orange juice and 2 tablespoons vinegar and boil until reduced to glaze. Remove skillet from heat. Whisk in orange peel, mustard, and remaining 2 teaspoons vinegar. Gradually whisk in remaining 4 tablespoons olive oil. Season dressing with salt and pepper. Cut chicken into bite-size pieces.

PLACE escarole, caponata, and chicken in large salad bowl. Add dressing and toss to coat. Season to taste with salt and pepper.

Turkey chopped salad with spicy avocado dressing

4 SERVINGS *Because jicama has a thick skin, it requires more than just a peeler to remove. The easiest way is to slip a paring knife under the skin and then peel the skin off in strips. If needed, use a vegetable peeler to finish the job. Even easier: Look for peeled jicama sticks in the supermarket produce section. Chili-garlic sauce is available in the Asian foods section of many supermarkets and at Asian markets.*

1	large avocado, halved, pitted
1½	tablespoons fresh lime juice
1½	teaspoons chili-garlic sauce
3	tablespoons olive oil
2	cups diced cooked maple-honey turkey (about 10 ounces)
1	cup diced peeled jicama
1	cup diced red onion
1	large red bell pepper, diced
½	cup plus 1 tablespoon chopped fresh cilantro
	Romaine lettuce leaves

SCOOP avocado flesh into mini processor. Add lime juice, chili-garlic sauce, and olive oil and process until smooth. Season dressing generously with salt and pepper.

MIX turkey, jicama, red onion, bell pepper, and ½ cup cilantro in large bowl. Add avocado dressing; toss to coat. Season with salt and pepper. Divide lettuce leaves among plates. Spoon salad atop leaves and sprinkle with remaining 1 tablespoon cilantro.

Ham and spring vegetable salad with shallot vinaigrette

8 SERVINGS *Fresh sugar snap peas have a little string on one side that will need to be removed before cooking. Seasoned rice vinegar—also known as sushi vinegar—is available in the Asian foods section of most supermarkets and at Asian markets.*

½	cup chopped shallots
6	tablespoons seasoned rice vinegar
1½	teaspoons Dijon mustard
1½	tablespoons olive oil
1½	pounds small red-skinned potatoes, each cut into 8 wedges
1½	pounds baby carrots, peeled, cut lengthwise in half
1½	pounds asparagus, trimmed, cut into 2-inch pieces
6	ounces sugar snap peas, trimmed
18	ounces low-fat (97% fat-free) smoked ham, cut into 2×½×¼-inch strips
1	6-ounce package fresh baby spinach

WHISK shallots, vinegar, and mustard in small bowl to blend. Gradually whisk in oil. Season dressing to taste with salt and pepper.

COOK potatoes and carrots in large pot of boiling salted water until almost tender, about 7 minutes. Add asparagus and sugar snap peas; cook until vegetables are just tender, about 3 minutes longer. Drain. Rinse with cold water; drain again. Transfer to large bowl.

DO AHEAD *Dressing and vegetables can be made 1 day ahead. Cover and chill separately.*

ADD ham to vegetables. Add dressing and toss to coat. Season salad to taste with salt and pepper.

LINE bowl or platter with spinach. Top with salad.

Salad bar Cobb

6 SERVINGS *If you're in a hurry, you can find most of the items needed for this recipe at a supermarket salad bar. If you cook the bacon yourself, whisk some of the drippings into the vinaigrette to give it even more flavor.*

- ½ cup extra-virgin olive oil
- 3 tablespoons red wine vinegar
- 1 tablespoon chopped fresh chives
- 2 teaspoons honey-Dijon mustard
- 2 teaspoons Worcestershire sauce
- 2 5-ounce packages mixed baby greens
- 2 cups diced smoked turkey or chicken (about 10 ounces)
- 2 cups diced plum tomatoes
- 1½ cups diced peeled pitted avocados
- 1 cup chopped peeled hard-boiled eggs
- 1 cup crumbled cooked bacon
- 1 cup crumbled blue cheese

WHISK first 5 ingredients in small bowl. Season dressing with salt and pepper. Divide greens among 6 plates. Place rows of turkey, tomato, and avocado atop greens. Sprinkle each salad with eggs, bacon, and blue cheese. Drizzle salads with dressing and serve.

A SALAD WITH A PAST Created in the 1930s at a Los Angeles restaurant called the Brown Derby, Cobb salad is named for the Derby's owner, Robert Cobb, who was rummaging for leftovers and came up with this memorable combination of ingredients.

Thai grilled beef salad

4 SERVINGS *Fish sauce is available in the Asian section of many supermarkets and at Asian markets; lemongrass is available at Asian markets and is increasingly easy to find in the specialty produce section of many supermarkets. When working with lemongrass, use the bottom 4 inches, and be sure to remove the tough outer husk before chopping.*

- 8 cups thinly sliced red and/or white cabbage
- 5 tablespoons fresh lime juice, divided
- 3 tablespoons fish sauce (such as nam pla or nuoc nam), divided

- 2 8- to 10-ounce rib-eye steaks
- 2 large shallots, thinly sliced
- ½ cup chopped green onion tops
- ⅓ cup chopped fresh cilantro
- ⅓ cup thinly sliced fresh mint
- 3 tablespoons minced fresh lemongrass
- 1 teaspoon minced seeded Thai chile or serrano chile

COMBINE sliced cabbage, 2 tablespoons lime juice, and 1 tablespoon fish sauce in large bowl; toss to blend. Season with salt and pepper; set cabbage mixture aside for up to 30 minutes.

PREPARE barbecue (medium-high heat). Sprinkle steaks with salt and pepper. Grill steaks until cooked to desired doneness, about 3 minutes per side for medium-rare. Transfer steaks to work surface; let rest 5 minutes. Cut steaks crosswise into thin slices. Place sliced steak in large bowl. Add shallots, green onion, cilantro, mint, lemongrass, and chile, then remaining 3 tablespoons lime juice and 2 tablespoons fish sauce. Toss to blend. Season salad with salt and pepper.

DIVIDE cabbage mixture among plates. Top each serving with beef salad.

Asian noodle salad with eggplant, sugar snap peas, and lime dressing

4 SERVINGS *Adding sliced grilled steak or chicken will turn this salad into a main course. Look for hoisin sauce and soba noodles in the Asian foods section of the supermarket.*

4	Japanese eggplants, unpeeled, cut on diagonal into ⅓-inch-thick slices
8	ounces fresh shiitake mushrooms, stemmed
2	bunches green onions, trimmed
¼	cup Asian sesame oil
1	6-ounce package dried chuka soba (Japanese-style) noodles
1	8-ounce package sugar snap peas, trimmed
7	tablespoons hoisin sauce
3½	tablespoons fresh lime juice
1½	tablespoons minced peeled fresh ginger
4	teaspoons finely grated lime peel

PREPARE barbecue (medium-high heat). Combine first 3 ingredients in large bowl; add oil and toss to coat. Sprinkle with salt and pepper. Grill vegetables until tender, turning often, about 7 minutes for eggplant and mushrooms and 5 minutes for green onions. Transfer mushrooms and onions to cutting board; cool slightly. Slice mushrooms and onions.

MEANWHILE, cook noodles in large pot of boiling salted water until almost tender but still firm to bite, about 3 minutes. Add sugar snap peas to noodles; cook 1 minute longer. Drain well. Transfer noodle mixture to large serving bowl. Add grilled vegetables.

WHISK hoisin sauce and all remaining ingredients in small bowl to blend. Toss noodle salad with dressing; season with salt and pepper.

Nutritious noodle Soba noodles are made from buckwheat flour, which is lower in calories and carbohydrates—and higher in protein and potassium—than all purpose flour.

Jicama, radish, and pepita salad

4 SERVINGS *To make this salad into a hearty meal, add grilled chicken or steak along with some diced papaya for sweetness and color. Pepitas (shelled pumpkin seeds) can be found at many supermarkets and at natural foods stores and Latin markets. Queso fresco and Cotija cheese can be found at some supermarkets and at Latin markets; feta cheese is a good substitute.*

½   cup olive oil
⅓   cup chopped fresh cilantro
1½ tablespoons white wine vinegar
1   tablespoon honey
1¼ teaspoons ground cumin

1   5-ounce package butter lettuce mix or baby spinach leaves
2   cups diced peeled jicama
1   cup (scant) thinly sliced radishes (about 8)
⅓   cup pepitas, lightly toasted
½   cup coarsely crumbled queso fresco or Cotija cheese

WHISK first 5 ingredients in small bowl. Season dressing with salt and pepper.

TOSS lettuce, jicama, and radishes in large bowl. Add dressing and toss to coat. Divide salad among 4 plates. Sprinkle with pepitas and cheese.

Grilled tuna with salad Niçoise

2 SERVINGS; CAN BE DOUBLED *The traditional version of this southern French salad actually calls for canned tuna, but using fresh makes it feel deluxe. Swordfish, salmon, or halibut would also be delicious. Niçoise olives are small, brine-cured olives available at some supermarkets and at specialty foods stores and Italian markets.*

2   6- to 8-ounce tuna or swordfish steaks or salmon or halibut fillets
7   tablespoons olive oil, divided
1   tablespoon fresh lemon juice

4   small white-skinned potatoes, halved lengthwise
½   pound green beans, trimmed, cut into thirds

1½ tablespoons white wine vinegar
1½ tablespoons Dijon mustard
2   small shallots, minced
2   teaspoons minced fresh thyme

⅓   cup Niçoise olives

1   tomato, sliced

RUB fish with 1 tablespoon oil and sprinkle with lemon juice. Let stand while preparing salad.

ADD potatoes and beans to large pot of boiling salted water. Cook beans until just crisp-tender, about 5 minutes. Remove with slotted spoon. Rinse under cold water until cool; drain well. Continue cooking potatoes until just tender, about 10 minutes longer. Drain. Cut crosswise into ½-inch-thick slices. Transfer potato slices to medium bowl.

MEANWHILE, combine vinegar, mustard, and shallots in small bowl. Gradually whisk in remaining 6 tablespoons olive oil. Mix in thyme. Season dressing with salt and pepper.

ADD ⅓ of dressing to potatoes; toss to coat. Cool. Add beans, olives, and half of remaining dressing to potatoes and toss to coat. Season to taste with salt and pepper.

PREHEAT broiler. Sprinkle fish with salt and pepper. Broil until just cooked through, about 4 minutes per side. Divide fish and salad between plates. Garnish with tomato. Serve, passing remaining dressing separately.

Spinach salad with Italian sausage

2 SERVINGS; CAN BE DOUBLED OR TRIPLED *This spinach salad gets its oomph from hot Italian sausage rather than the more traditional bacon. For a milder result, use sweet sausage instead.*

- 4 cups (packed) baby spinach
- 1 teaspoon plus 1 tablespoon olive oil
- 4 hot Italian sausages, in 1-inch pieces, filling removed from casings

- 3 green onions, sliced
- 3 tablespoons Sherry wine vinegar or red wine vinegar
- 1 teaspoon Dijon mustard

PLACE spinach in large bowl. Heat 1 teaspoon oil in heavy large nonstick skillet over medium heat. Add sausage and cook until browned and cooked through, turning frequently, about 8 minutes. Using slotted spoon, transfer sausage to paper towels.

POUR off all but 1 tablespoon drippings from skillet. Heat remaining drippings over medium heat. Add green onions and stir 1 minute. Add vinegar and bring to boil, scraping up any browned bits. Mix in remaining 1 tablespoon oil and mustard. Add sausage and toss to coat. Pour over spinach and toss to coat. Season with salt and pepper.

Curried quinoa salad with mango

2 SERVINGS *Quinoa is a delicately flavored grain that takes little time to cook and is full of protein. It can be found at some supermarkets and at natural foods stores. Be sure to rinse the quinoa to remove the bitter resinous coating.*

- 2 cups water
- ½ teaspoon salt
- 1 cup quinoa (about 6 ounces), rinsed

- ¼ cup canola oil
- 2 tablespoons white wine vinegar
- 1 tablespoon mango chutney (such as Major Grey), chopped if chunky
- 1½ teaspoons curry powder
- ¼ teaspoon dry mustard

- 1 cup chopped peeled mango plus mango spears for garnish
- 1 cup chopped unpeeled English hothouse cucumber
- 5 tablespoons chopped green onions, divided
- 2 cups (packed) baby spinach

BRING 2 cups water and ½ teaspoon salt to boil in medium saucepan. Add quinoa, cover, reduce heat to medium-low, and cook until liquid is absorbed and quinoa is tender, about 12 minutes. Transfer to medium bowl; cool.

MEANWHILE, whisk oil and next 4 ingredients in small bowl to blend. Season dressing to taste with salt and pepper.

ADD chopped mango, cucumber, 4 tablespoons green onions, and ¼ cup dressing to quinoa; toss to coat. Divide spinach between 2 plates. Spoon quinoa salad over spinach. Garnish with mango spears and 1 tablespoon green onions. Drizzle with remaining dressing.

Farro salad with peas, asparagus, and feta

4 SERVINGS *Farro (also known as "emmer") is a hearty, nutty-flavored grain that's high in protein. Italians have long simmered it in soups and cooked it risotto style. Look for the type of farro known as semi-pearled or* perlato: *The husk has been removed, so there's no need for soaking. Farro can be found at natural foods stores and at Italian markets.*

1½ cups semi-pearled farro

12 ounces asparagus, trimmed, cut into 1½-inch lengths

1 8-ounce package sugar snap peas

12 ounces grape tomatoes, halved

½ cup chopped red onion

6 tablespoons chopped fresh dill

½ cup olive oil

¼ cup Sherry wine vinegar

1 7-ounce package feta cheese, crumbled

COOK farro in large saucepan of boiling salted water until just tender, about 10 minutes. Drain. Transfer to large bowl.

MEANWHILE, cook asparagus and sugar snap peas in another saucepan of boiling salted water until crisp-tender, about 3 minutes. Drain. Add to farro; add tomatoes, onion, and dill. Whisk oil and vinegar in small bowl. Season dressing with salt and pepper. Add dressing and feta to salad; toss to coat.

Curried couscous and garbanzo bean salad

4 SERVINGS *Cutting the vegetables into small pieces so they cook quickly makes this salad come together in no time.*

2 tablespoons curry powder

2¼ cups water

½ teaspoon salt

6 cups small pieces assorted fresh vegetables (such as 2 cups each broccoli florets, cauliflower florets, and thinly sliced carrots)

1 10-ounce box couscous

1 15-ounce can garbanzo beans (chickpeas), drained

½ cup olive oil

5 tablespoons white wine vinegar

1½ tablespoons grated peeled fresh ginger

1¼ cups crumbled feta cheese (about 7 ounces)

1 cup thinly sliced green onions

STIR curry powder in heavy large saucepan over medium-high heat until fragrant and toasted, about 1 minute. Mix in 2¼ cups water and salt. Add vegetables. Bring to boil; cover and cook 1 minute. Remove from heat. Mix in couscous. Cover and let stand until couscous softens, about 5 minutes.

TRANSFER couscous mixture to large bowl. Mix in garbanzo beans, oil, vinegar, and ginger. Cool to room temperature. Add feta and green onions; toss. Season with salt and pepper.

STARTERSALADS

Pear and curly endive salad

2 SERVINGS; CAN BE DOUBLED *Discard the tough outer leaves of a head of curly endive. The paler center leaves are more tender and make a better salad.*

- 2 teaspoons Sherry wine vinegar
- 1 teaspoon Dijon mustard
- 3 tablespoons olive oil
- ¼ teaspoon dried thyme, crumbled

- 5 cups bite-size pieces curly endive (about ¼ medium head)
- 1 large ripe pear, cut lengthwise into quarters, cored, sliced crosswise

WHISK vinegar and mustard in small bowl. Gradually whisk in oil. Mix in thyme. Season dressing with salt and pepper.

COMBINE endive and pear in large bowl. Add dressing and toss to coat. Season salad with salt and pepper.

Fennel, arugula, and smoked-trout salad with horseradish dressing

2 SERVINGS *Thick Greek-style yogurt is a good substitute for the sour cream in this recipe. You'll find it at the supermarket, sold alongside the other yogurts.*

- 1½ tablespoons sour cream
- 3 teaspoons olive oil, divided
- 2 teaspoons prepared horseradish
- 2 teaspoons finely chopped fresh dill
- 1¼ teaspoons white wine vinegar, divided

- 2 cups arugula
- 1½ cups thinly sliced fennel bulb
- ⅓ cup thinly sliced red onion
- ⅔ cup smoked trout or smoked whitefish, coarsely flaked

WHISK sour cream, 1½ teaspoons olive oil, horseradish, dill, and ¾ teaspoon vinegar in small bowl. Season dressing to taste with salt and pepper.

PLACE arugula, fennel, and onion in medium bowl. Add remaining 1½ teaspoons olive oil and remaining ½ teaspoon white wine vinegar; toss to coat. Season with salt and pepper. Divide salad between 2 plates. Top with smoked fish. Drizzle horseradish dressing over.

MARKET TIP Look for smoked trout and smoked whitefish in the deli or seafood section of supermarkets and specialty foods stores, and at delicatessens.

Smoked salmon and cucumber ribbon salad with caraway

4 SERVINGS *When making cucumber ribbons for the salad, a sharp peeler with an easy-to-grip handle will be your best friend. Zyliss and Oxo make especially good ones.*

3 tablespoons olive oil
3 tablespoons minced shallot
2 tablespoons fresh lemon juice
1 teaspoon caraway seeds

1 English hothouse cucumber
2 bunches watercress, trimmed
1 small Granny Smith apple, cored, thinly sliced
8 ounces sliced smoked salmon

WHISK first 4 ingredients in small bowl; season dressing with salt and pepper.

CUT cucumber crosswise in half. Using vegetable peeler, cut cucumber into long strips to form ribbons. Scatter cucumber, watercress, and apple slices on 4 plates. Tuck in slices of salmon. Drizzle dressing over.

Frisée salad with bacon, dates, and red onion

2 SERVINGS *Try this salad as a starter for a dinner of lamb stew with spring vegetables or beef stew with pearl onions.*

3 bacon slices, chopped
2 tablespoons extra-virgin olive oil
4 teaspoons honey, divided
½ cup chopped pitted dates
½ cup thinly sliced red onion
2 tablespoons Sherry wine vinegar

1 large head of frisée, torn into bite-size pieces (about 4 cups)
½ cup crumbled soft fresh goat cheese
⅓ cup walnut halves

COOK bacon in heavy small skillet over medium heat until crisp. Using slotted spoon, transfer to paper towel. Pour off all but 1 tablespoon bacon drippings from skillet. Add olive oil, 3 teaspoons honey, dates, and onion to drippings in skillet. Stir in vinegar. Season dressing with salt and pepper.

PLACE frisée in medium bowl; add dressing and toss. Divide salad between plates. Sprinkle with bacon, cheese, and walnuts. Drizzle with remaining 1 teaspoon honey.

Spring greens with soppressata and grapefruit

4 SERVINGS *Soppressata, a dry-cured Italian sausage, is easy to find, but other Italian salamis or a dried French sausage like* Rosette de Lyon *would be good alternatives.*

2 large red grapefruits

1 small shallot, minced

1 tablespoon white wine vinegar
   Fresh grapefruit juice

1 teaspoon minced fresh tarragon

6 tablespoons walnut oil or olive oil

1 5-ounce package mixed baby greens

4 ounces thinly sliced soppressata or other Italian salami, cut into thin strips
   Parmesan cheese shavings

CUT all peel and white pith from grapefruits. Working over bowl to catch juices, cut between membranes to release segments.

COMBINE shallot and vinegar in small bowl. Let stand 15 minutes. Add enough additional grapefruit juice to collected juices to measure ¼ cup; whisk into vinegar mixture. Add tarragon. Gradually whisk in oil. Season dressing with salt and pepper.

PLACE greens in large bowl. Drizzle ⅔ of dressing over and toss to coat. Divide salad among 4 plates. Scatter soppressata over each serving. Top with grapefruit segments and Parmesan. Drizzle remaining dressing over.

Mâche salad with blood oranges, pistachios, and pomegranate

4 SERVINGS *Pomegranate seeds that have been removed from the fruit are becoming easier to find at the supermarket. If unavailable, the neatest way to remove the seeds is to halve the pomegranate and submerge the halves in a bowl of water. Remove the seeds with your fingers and transfer them to a bowl. Mâche, also known as lamb's lettuce, is found in the produce department with the other bagged lettuces.*

2 tablespoons fresh blood orange juice or regular orange juice

1 tablespoon unseasoned rice vinegar

1 tablespoon minced shallot

½ teaspoon honey

3 tablespoons pistachio oil

2 blood oranges or regular oranges

1 4-ounce package mâche

¼ cup shelled natural pistachios, toasted

¼ cup pomegranate seeds or dried cranberries

WHISK orange juice, vinegar, shallot, and honey in small bowl. Gradually whisk in pistachio oil. Season dressing to taste with salt and pepper.

USING small sharp knife, cut off all peel and white pith from oranges. Working over small bowl, cut between membranes to release orange segments. Divide mâche among plates. Divide orange segments, pistachios, and pomegranate seeds among plates. Drizzle dressing over salad.

CITRUS SAVVY To cut neat citrus segments for salads, cut off both ends of the fruit, and cut off the peel with a knife, removing all white pith and exposing the citrus pulp. Working over a bowl, use a paring knife to free each segment from the membrane.

Arugula salad with olives, pancetta, and Parmesan shavings

2 SERVINGS *To build an easy party menu around this salad, grill veal chops and radicchio for the main course. Add some roasted baby potatoes with rosemary, and uncork a bottle of sparkling rosé. To keep it no-fuss but still special, pick up chocolate truffles for dessert.*

 6 **thin slices pancetta (Italian bacon; about ⅓ of 3-ounce package)**

1½ **tablespoons extra-virgin olive oil**
 1 **tablespoon fresh lemon juice**
 4 **cups (loosely packed) arugula**
 ⅓ **cup Kalamata olives, pitted, halved**
    Parmesan cheese shavings

ARRANGE pancetta in single layer in medium nonstick skillet. Cook over medium heat until browned and crisp (do not turn), about 8 minutes. Transfer to paper towels to drain.

WHISK oil and lemon juice in small bowl. Season dressing with salt and pepper. Place arugula and olives in medium bowl; toss with dressing. Divide salad between plates. Top with pancetta and Parmesan shavings.

Arugula, blood orange, and blue cheese salad

6 SERVINGS *If you can't find blood oranges, pink grapefruit would be an excellent stand-in.*

10 **cups (packed) arugula (about 6 ounces)**
 ½ **cup crumbled blue cheese**
 2 **blood oranges**
 ¼ **cup olive oil**
 ¼ **cup fresh lemon juice**

COMBINE arugula and cheese in large bowl. Remove peel and white pith from oranges. Cut between orange membranes to release segments into bowl with arugula and cheese. Pour oil and lemon juice over; toss to blend. Season salad to taste with salt and pepper.

Green bean, fennel, and parsley salad

6 SERVINGS *Transferring the boiled green beans to a bowl of ice water is known as shocking them; this stops the cooking and keeps vegetables from becoming overdone and mushy.*

- 3 tablespoons balsamic vinegar
- 2 tablespoons fresh lemon juice
- 1 tablespoon olive oil
- 2 teaspoons finely grated lemon peel
- 2 teaspoons water
- ½ pound green beans, trimmed, cut into 1½-inch pieces (about 2 cups)
- 2 large fennel bulbs, trimmed, quartered lengthwise, thinly sliced crosswise (about 4 cups)
- 4 ounces button mushrooms, trimmed, quartered (about 2 cups)
- 2 cups chopped fresh Italian parsley
- 3 tablespoons chopped fresh chives

WHISK first 5 ingredients in medium bowl to blend. Season dressing with salt and pepper. Cook green beans in large pot of boiling water until crisp-tender, about 5 minutes. Drain. Transfer to large bowl of ice water. Drain beans. Pat dry.

DO AHEAD *Can be made 1 day ahead. Cover and chill dressing. Wrap green beans in paper towels and chill.*

PLACE beans in large bowl. Add fennel, mushrooms, parsley, and chives. Drizzle dressing over; toss. Season with salt and pepper. Cover and chill 30 minutes. Toss again and serve.

Radicchio and haricot vert salad with candied walnuts

6 TO 8 SERVINGS *Rice vinegar adds a subtle and surprising tang to the candied walnuts. To make this even easier, use purchased candied walnuts.*

- ¾ cup walnut halves
- ¼ cup (packed) dark brown sugar
- 2 teaspoons plus ¼ cup walnut oil
- 3½ tablespoons seasoned rice vinegar, divided
- 1 garlic clove, pressed
- 1 head of Bibb lettuce, coarsely torn
- ½ large head of radicchio, thickly sliced
- 2 cups frozen haricots verts or small slender green beans, thawed

COMBINE walnuts, sugar, 2 teaspoons oil, and 1 tablespoon vinegar in medium nonstick skillet. Stir over medium heat until syrup coats nuts thickly, about 2 minutes. Season with salt and pepper. Transfer walnuts to piece of foil. Separate walnuts; freeze on foil 5 minutes or cool completely at room temperature.

WHISK remaining ¼ cup oil, remaining 2½ tablespoons vinegar, and garlic in large bowl. Season dressing with salt and pepper. Add Bibb lettuce, radicchio, haricots verts, and walnuts; toss to coat.

SLIM BEANS Haricots verts—slender green beans—are found in the freezer section of the supermarket. Because they're so thin, there's no need to cook them for use in salads.

125

Winter salad with hoisin vinaigrette

6 SERVINGS *When spring arrives, sugar snap peas are a good substitute for the water chestnuts. Hoisin sauce is available in the Asian foods section of many supermarkets and at Asian markets.*

- 2 tablespoons hoisin sauce
- 1 tablespoon distilled white vinegar
- 3 tablespoons grapeseed oil or safflower oil
- 1 tablespoon Asian sesame oil

- 1 5- to 6-ounce bag mixed baby greens
- 1 8-ounce can sliced water chestnuts, drained
- 1 small red onion, thinly sliced

WHISK hoisin sauce and vinegar in small bowl. Gradually whisk in grapeseed oil and sesame oil. Season dressing with salt and pepper.

PLACE greens and water chestnuts in large bowl. Add dressing; toss to coat. Season salad with salt and pepper. Scatter onion slices over.

Tangy avocado-orange salad

4 SERVINGS *Avocados make this simple salad feel luxurious; for extra richness, drizzle with a little olive oil.*

- 2 oranges
- ½ small head of red leaf lettuce, coarsely torn
- 1 small avocado, halved, pitted, peeled, diced
- 2 tablespoons white balsamic vinegar

USING small sharp knife, cut off all peel and white pith from oranges. Working over large bowl, cut between membranes to release orange segments. Add lettuce, avocado, and vinegar to bowl; toss gently. Season with salt and pepper; divide among 4 plates.

Avocado and mango salad with passion-fruit vinaigrette

4 SERVINGS *Using passion fruit juice concentrate is an easy way to give an inventive spin to a classic vinaigrette. The concentrate is available at some supermarkets and at specialty foods stores and natural foods stores. Or you could substitute orange juice concentrate with good results.*

- 3 tablespoons frozen passion fruit juice concentrate, thawed
- 3 tablespoons minced shallot
- 4 teaspoons Sherry wine vinegar
- 1 teaspoon Dijon mustard
- 1 teaspoon coriander seeds, coarsely cracked
- 3 tablespoons olive oil

- 8 cups herb salad mix (about 4 ounces)
- 1 large ripe mango, halved, pitted, peeled, sliced
- 2 small avocados, halved, pitted, peeled, sliced

WHISK first 5 ingredients in small bowl to blend; gradually whisk in oil. Season dressing generously with salt and pepper.

TOSS salad mix in large bowl with ¼ cup dressing. Divide salad among plates. Tuck mango and avocado slices into salad; drizzle some of remaining dressing over.

Heirloom tomato salad with blue cheese

6 TO 8 SERVINGS *Heirloom tomatoes are grown in just about every color imaginable, so have fun experimenting with the different varieties you'll find at farmers' markets and at some supermarkets.*

   8   ½-inch-thick slices crusty bread

   4   large garlic cloves, halved

   3   tablespoons plus ⅓ cup extra-virgin olive oil

   1   cup currant tomatoes or halved cherry or pear tomatoes

   ½   cup chopped green onions

  10   medium heirloom tomatoes of assorted colors, cored, thinly sliced

   1   small red onion, sliced paper-thin

   3   celery stalks, thinly sliced diagonally

  1½   cups coarsely crumbled blue cheese

PREPARE barbecue (medium-high heat). Rub bread with cut garlic halves; brush bread with 3 tablespoons oil. Combine remaining ⅓ cup oil, currant tomatoes, and green onions in medium bowl; toss to coat. Season with salt and pepper. Overlap heirloom tomato slices in concentric circles on platter, alternating colors. Scatter onion and celery slices over tomatoes. Sprinkle with salt and pepper. Spoon tomato-and-green-onion mixture over. Sprinkle with crumbled cheese.

GRILL bread until golden, about 2 minutes per side. Cut each slice diagonally in half; serve with salad.

Invisible healers You can't see them, but they're there: phytochemicals, the naturally occurring compounds in fruits and vegetables that work with nutrients and dietary fiber to help protect against certain illnesses, including cancer, heart disease, and hypertension. Beta carotene, lutein, and lycopene are just some names you may have heard making news lately, and if you want to get more of these health-giving compounds, consider this: The more intensely colored the fruit or vegetable (think dark green, red, orange), the more abundant in phytochemicals it's likely to be.

Heirloom tomato and burrata cheese salad

4 SERVINGS *Burrata, a luscious treat, is fresh mozzarella filled with cream and mozzarella curds. It's available at some high-end supermarkets, and at Italian markets and cheese stores, but if you can't find it, use fresh whole-milk mozzarella.*

      4 large heirloom tomatoes (about
         2½ pounds) or 4 to 5 large tomatoes
         Fleur de sel or coarse kosher salt
         Freshly ground black pepper
      1 teaspoon dried oregano
      ¼ cup torn fresh basil leaves plus
         whole leaves for garnish
      ¼ cup extra-virgin olive oil

      4 2.5-ounce rounds burrata cheese

CUT tomatoes into wedges and place in large bowl. Sprinkle with fleur de sel and pepper. Crush oregano between palms to release flavor; add to tomatoes. Add ¼ cup torn basil leaves and olive oil; mix well. Let stand at room temperature at least 30 minutes and up to 1 hour, stirring occasionally.

PLACE 1 burrata cheese round in center of each plate. Fan tomatoes around cheese, dividing equally. Drizzle with dressing from bowl. Garnish with basil leaves.

Watermelon and watercress salad with ginger

4 SERVINGS *Watercress has a distinctive, peppery taste that's a welcome change from garden lettuces. It provides a nice contrast to the sweet watermelon.*

      2 tablespoons unseasoned rice vinegar
     1½ tablespoons vegetable oil
      2 teaspoons minced peeled fresh ginger
     1½ teaspoons finely grated lime peel
      1 garlic clove, minced
      2 cups ½-inch pieces peeled
         seedless watermelon
      1 large bunch watercress, thick stems
         trimmed (about 2 cups packed)
      1 cup ½-inch pieces peeled seeded
         cucumber (about ½ large)
      4 green onions, thinly sliced diagonally
      ¼ cup chopped fresh cilantro

WHISK vinegar, oil, ginger, lime peel, and garlic in large bowl to blend. Season dressing to taste with salt and pepper. Add watermelon and all remaining ingredients to bowl with dressing and toss to coat. Divide salad among plates.

Watermelon and citrus salad with mint

6 SERVINGS *Whole grain Dijon mustard is an especially good way to add both flavor and texture to a vinaigrette, but regular Dijon works nicely, too.*

2 tablespoons fresh lemon juice

1 tablespoon frozen orange juice concentrate, thawed

2 teaspoons whole grain Dijon mustard

1 teaspoon finely grated orange peel

½ teaspoon sugar

½ cup olive oil

2 large bunches watercress, thick stems trimmed

4 cups ¾-inch pieces seedless watermelon

4 oranges, peel and white pith removed, each cut into 6 rounds

4 thin red onion slices, cut in half

3 tablespoons thinly sliced fresh mint

WHISK first 5 ingredients in small bowl to blend. Gradually whisk in oil. Season dressing with salt and pepper.

DO AHEAD *Can be made 1 day ahead. Cover and chill. Bring to room temperature and rewhisk before using.*

DIVIDE watercress among plates. Top watercress on each plate with watermelon pieces, orange rounds, onion slices, and mint, dividing equally. Drizzle salads with dressing.

Butter lettuce and radicchio salad with strawberries

8 SERVINGS *This is the perfect spring salad: Strawberries add an unexpected pop of color and flavor, and butter lettuce, also known as Bibb, provides a deliciously sweet, tender contrast to radicchio, which is crunchy and slightly bitter.*

3 tablespoons tarragon vinegar

1 tablespoon sugar

2 teaspoons Dijon mustard

¼ teaspoon paprika

½ cup olive oil

1 large head of radicchio, torn into 1-inch pieces (about 6 cups)

1 head of butter lettuce, torn into 1-inch pieces (about 6 cups)

1 1-pint container strawberries, hulled, halved

½ cup paper-thin red onion slices

WHISK vinegar, sugar, mustard, and paprika in small bowl to blend. Whisk in oil. Season dressing with salt and pepper. Combine radicchio, butter lettuce, strawberries, and onion in large bowl. Toss with enough dressing to coat. Season to taste with salt and pepper.

Truly "grate" vinaigrettes To give vinaigrettes—and the salads you'll dress them with—even more of a gingery or garlicky kick, try grating fresh ginger or garlic cloves, rather than mincing. The best tool for the job is one of the rasp-style graters sold under several names, including the original Microplane brand.

Zucchini and tomato salad with garlic-chili dressing

6 SERVINGS *With its big chunks of baked zucchini, this salad doubles nicely as a side dish.*

 6 medium zucchini, trimmed, quartered lengthwise
 7 tablespoons olive oil, divided

 ¼ cup chopped fresh cilantro
 3 tablespoons fresh lemon juice
 3 garlic cloves, finely chopped
 2 teaspoons chili powder
 1 teaspoon ground cumin
 1 teaspoon honey

 6 large plum tomatoes, quartered lengthwise

PREHEAT oven to 400°F. Arrange zucchini on baking sheet and brush with 1 tablespoon oil. Sprinkle with salt and pepper. Bake zucchini until just beginning to brown, about 20 minutes.

WHISK remaining 6 tablespoons oil, cilantro, lemon juice, garlic, chili powder, cumin, and honey in small bowl to blend. Season with salt and pepper.

ARRANGE zucchini and tomatoes on platter. Drizzle with enough dressing to coat. Serve warm or at room temperature with remaining dressing.

Mixed greens with feta, almonds, and blueberries

4 SERVINGS *It's an unusual ingredient combo, but the feta-almond-blueberry trio here is a tasty blend of creamy, tangy, crunchy, and juicy.*

 3 tablespoons olive oil
 1½ tablespoons red wine vinegar
 1 teaspoon honey
 1 5-ounce bag mixed baby greens
 ½ cup crumbled feta cheese
 1 ½-pint container blueberries
 ¼ cup slivered almonds, toasted

WHISK oil, vinegar, and honey in small bowl. Season dressing to taste with salt and pepper. Combine greens, feta, and blueberries in large bowl. Add dressing; toss to coat. Season salad with salt and pepper. Sprinkle with almonds and serve.

CLOCKWISE FROM TOP: **Parsley Hummus with Cauliflower Crudités; Black Pepper Almonds; Marinated Olives with Tangerine and Rosemary**

Vegetarian Black Bean Chili

Chilled Corn Soup with Adobo Swirl

Beef and Gorgonzola Burgers
Bistro Oven Fries with Parsley and Garlic

Grilled Ham and Gouda Sandwiches
with Frisée and Caramelized Onions

Heirloom Tomato and Burrata Cheese Salad

Grilled Pizzas
with Tomato,
Mozzarella,
and Basil

Radicchio and endive Caesar with ciabatta crisps

6 SERVINGS *If you can't find ciabatta bread (a rustic, chewy oval-shaped Italian bread) for the crisps, use thin slices of sourdough.*

- 2 **tablespoons fresh lemon juice**
- 2 **teaspoons anchovy paste**
- 2 **teaspoons Dijon mustard**
- ½ **teaspoon Worcestershire sauce**
- 1 **garlic clove, pressed**
- ½ **cup plus 2 tablespoons olive oil**
- ¾ **cup freshly grated Parmesan cheese, divided, plus 1 cup Parmesan cheese shavings**

- 12 **⅓-inch-thick slices ciabatta bread**

- 1 **large head of radicchio, leaves torn into pieces**
- 5 **heads of Belgian endive, leaves separated**

POSITION rack in top third of oven and preheat to 450°F. Whisk lemon juice, anchovy paste, Dijon mustard, Worcestershire sauce, and pressed garlic in large bowl to blend. Whisk in ½ cup olive oil, then ¼ cup grated Parmesan cheese. Season dressing to taste with salt and pepper.

PLACE ciabatta on baking sheet; brush with remaining 2 tablespoons oil, then sprinkle with pepper and remaining ½ cup grated cheese. Bake until crisp, about 15 minutes.

TOSS radicchio and endive with dressing in large bowl. Season salad with salt and pepper. Divide among plates. Top with cheese shavings. Serve with ciabatta crisps.

Mixed greens with roasted beets, fennel, and marinated red onions

10 SERVINGS *To make this salad come together even more quickly, roast the beets and marinate the onions a day ahead.*

- 4 **small beets, tops trimmed**

- ½ **cup olive oil**
- ¼ **cup balsamic vinegar**
- 2 **tablespoons chopped fresh fennel fronds (leafy tops) plus 2 medium fennel bulbs, halved, cored, very thinly sliced**
- 2 **cups thinly sliced red onions**

- 2 **5-ounce bags mixed baby greens**

PREHEAT oven to 350°F. Rinse each beet and wrap in foil. Place on oven rack and roast until tender, about 1 hour 10 minutes. Cool beets. Peel; cut beets into wedges.

WHISK oil, vinegar, and chopped fennel fronds in medium bowl to blend. Season dressing with salt and pepper. Mix onions into dressing.

DO AHEAD *Beets and onions can be made 1 day ahead. Cover separately; chill.*

MIX baby greens and sliced fennel in bowl. Add beets. Using slotted spoon, transfer onions from dressing to salad. Toss salad with enough dressing to coat. Season salad with salt and pepper.

Iceberg wedges with warm bacon and blue cheese dressing

6 SERVINGS *Shedding its retro reputation, iceberg lettuce makes a delicious comeback in this classic salad. Warm, thickly sliced crisp bacon adds the crowning touch.*

1½ cups mayonnaise
2 tablespoons fresh lemon juice
1 tablespoon coarsely cracked black pepper
1 teaspoon hot pepper sauce
1 cup coarsely crumbled blue cheese
   Buttermilk (optional)

½ pound thick-cut bacon, cut crosswise into 1-inch pieces
1 large head of iceberg lettuce, cut into 6 wedges, each with some core attached
½ red onion, very thinly sliced

MIX first 4 ingredients in medium bowl. Add blue cheese and stir until well blended. Thin dressing with buttermilk by tablespoonfuls, if desired.

DO AHEAD *Can be made 1 day ahead. Cover and chill.*

COOK bacon in large skillet over medium heat until golden brown and beginning to crisp. Arrange lettuce on plates. Spoon dressing over. Using slotted spoon, transfer warm bacon from skillet onto salads, dividing equally. Garnish with red onion.

Frisée and radish salad with goat cheese croutons

4 SERVINGS *This would be a great starter for a dinner of whole chicken roasted with potatoes in the pan. Serve a fruit tart for dessert.*

2 tablespoons Sherry wine vinegar
2 teaspoons Dijon mustard
1 shallot, minced
⅓ cup olive oil plus more for brushing
1 small head of frisée, torn into bite-size pieces
1 bunch radishes, trimmed, thinly sliced

12 ½-inch-thick slices baguette
4 ounces soft fresh goat cheese

COMBINE vinegar, mustard, and shallot in small bowl. Whisk in ⅓ cup oil. Season dressing to taste with salt and pepper. Combine frisée and radishes in large bowl.

DO AHEAD *Can be made 4 hours ahead. Cover dressing and let stand at room temperature. Cover salad with damp towel and chill.*

PREHEAT broiler. Broil 1 side of bread until golden brown. Brush second side with olive oil. Sprinkle with salt and pepper. Spread with goat cheese. Sprinkle with pepper. Broil until bread is brown. Cut each slice into quarters.

ADD dressing to salad and toss to coat. Divide among plates. Top each with croutons and serve immediately.

Bibb lettuce salad with persimmons and candied pecans

8 SERVINGS *Widely available in fall and winter, Fuyu persimmons resemble bright orange, slightly heart-shaped tomatoes. They have a spicy-sweet flavor, with flesh that's a little like a mango in texture.*

¾ cup whole-berry cranberry sauce
¼ cup fresh lemon juice
1 tablespoon honey
1 tablespoon (packed) golden brown sugar
6 tablespoons extra-virgin olive oil

2 heads of Bibb lettuce, coarsely torn
4 Fuyu persimmons, peeled, sliced
1 cup (generous) crumbled blue cheese
Purchased candied pecans

WHISK first 4 ingredients in medium bowl; whisk in oil. Season with salt and pepper.

MOUND lettuce in center of 8 plates. Top lettuce on each plate with persimmon slices, then drizzle with dressing. Sprinkle with cheese and pecans.

Green apple and celery salad with walnuts and mustard vinaigrette

8 SERVINGS *To keep the sliced Granny Smith apples from turning brown, sprinkle with lemon juice.*

¼ cup fresh lemon juice
¼ cup Dijon mustard
5 teaspoons honey
⅔ cup extra-virgin olive oil

1 large bunch celery with leaves
2 large Granny Smith apples, peeled, quartered, cored; each quarter cut into 2 wedges, then thinly sliced crosswise into triangle shapes
¾ cup walnuts, toasted, chopped

WHISK first 3 ingredients in small bowl to blend. Gradually whisk in oil. Season vinaigrette with salt and pepper.

TRIM celery leaves and chop enough to measure 1 cup. Thinly slice stalks on deep diagonal. Combine celery, chopped celery leaves, apples, and walnuts in large bowl. Add vinaigrette and toss to coat. Season salad to taste with salt and pepper.

Frisée salad with blue cheese, walnut, and cranberry crostini

12 SERVINGS *For a sit-down dinner, serve the crostini as an accompaniment to the salad. Or, if making dinner while guests gather in the kitchen is more your thing, offer the crostini as a starter topped with a sprig or two of the dressed frisée. Ciabatta, a rustic Italian bread, can be found at many supermarkets and bakeries.*

24 ¼-inch-thick slices ciabatta bread
4 tablespoons walnut oil, divided

½ cup chopped toasted walnuts
8 ounces blue cheese, crumbled
6 tablespoons minced shallots, divided
⅓ cup dried cranberries

8 cups baby frisée, torn into thin pieces
2 teaspoons Banyuls vinegar or red wine vinegar

PREHEAT oven to 400°F. Arrange bread slices on baking sheet. Brush top side of bread slices with 2 tablespoons walnut oil. Bake until crisp, about 5 minutes.

MIX walnuts, cheese, 4 tablespoons shallots, and dried cranberries in medium bowl. Spread mixture on toasts. Bake until cheese melts, about 4 minutes.

MEANWHILE, combine frisée, remaining 2 tablespoons shallots, remaining 2 tablespoons walnut oil, and vinegar in large bowl. Sprinkle with salt; toss to coat. Serve salad with crostini.

Warm endive salad with Parmesan and hazelnuts

4 SERVINGS *Lightly cooked endive, warm dressing, and a touch of Parmesan cheese make this salad perfect for a cold-weather meal.*

2 tablespoons olive oil
1 large garlic clove, finely chopped
4 large heads of Belgian endive, halved lengthwise
¼ cup dry white wine
¼ cup low-salt chicken broth
2 teaspoons white wine vinegar
8 tablespoons freshly grated Parmesan cheese (about 2 ounces)
   Chopped toasted hazelnuts
   Chopped fresh chives

HEAT olive oil in heavy large skillet over medium heat. Add garlic and stir 30 seconds. Add endive, cut side down. Add wine and broth and bring to boil. Cover and cook 5 minutes. Using tongs, turn endive over. Cover and cook until crisp-tender, about 1 minute longer. Remove skillet from heat. Using tongs, lift endive from skillet, draining liquid from each head back into skillet; transfer 2 halves, cut side up, to each of 4 plates. Add vinegar to skillet; cook over medium heat until sauce reduces slightly, about 1 minute. Season to taste with salt and pepper; spoon over endive. Sprinkle each salad with 2 tablespoons Parmesan cheese, then hazelnuts and chives.

Warm spinach, mushroom, and goat cheese salad

4 SERVINGS *Applewood-smoked bacon would be especially delicious in this salad. Or, for an Italian touch, substitute an equal amount of pancetta (Italian bacon).*

    6   bacon slices, chopped
    1   large red bell pepper, cut
        lengthwise into thin strips
   12   ounces crimini (baby bella)
        mushrooms, coarsely chopped
    1   10-ounce bag spinach leaves
    ½   medium red onion, cut into paper-thin slices

    ⅔   cup olive oil
    ⅓   cup white wine vinegar
    2   tablespoons sugar
    4   ounces chilled soft fresh goat
        cheese, crumbled (about 1 cup)

COOK bacon in large skillet over medium heat until brown and crisp. Using slotted spoon, transfer bacon to paper towels to drain. Add bell pepper to drippings in skillet; sauté 2 minutes. Using slotted spoon, transfer bell pepper to large bowl. Add mushrooms to same skillet and sauté until tender and beginning to brown, about 4 minutes. Add mushrooms to bowl with bell pepper and reserve skillet. Add spinach and onion to same bowl.

ADD oil, vinegar, and sugar to reserved skillet; bring to boil, whisking until sugar dissolves. Season dressing with salt and pepper. Toss salad with enough warm dressing from skillet to coat. Season with salt and pepper. Divide salad among plates. Sprinkle with goat cheese.

Warm spinach salad with Parmesan

6 SERVINGS *For a change from Parmesan, try another hard cheese like Pecorino Romano, aged Manchego (from Spain), or aged Gouda (from Holland).*

    2   6-ounce packages fresh baby spinach
    1   small head of radicchio, thinly sliced
    ⅓   cup extra-virgin olive oil
    ¼   cup balsamic vinegar
    ¼   cup dry red wine
    1   shallot, minced
    ½   cup pine nuts, toasted
        Shaved Parmesan cheese

COMBINE spinach and radicchio in large bowl. Bring oil, vinegar, wine, and shallot to simmer in large saucepan. Season with salt and pepper. Immediately pour dressing over salad. Cover bowl with foil and let stand 5 minutes. Toss salad to coat. Divide among plates. Sprinkle with nuts and shaved Parmesan.

SIDESALADS

Sweet corn and tomato salad with fresh cilantro

8 TO 10 SERVINGS *This makes perfect use of summer's fresh corn and tomatoes. To safely cut kernels from the cob, cut off one end and stand the cob on its cut end in a large shallow bowl (this way, you'll catch both the juices and the kernels). Using a large knife, work downward toward the work surface, cutting close to the cob.*

- 10 ears of corn, husked
- 2 pounds plum tomatoes, cut into ½-inch cubes
- ¾ cup finely chopped red onion
- ½ cup chopped fresh cilantro
- ¼ cup extra-virgin olive oil
- 1 tablespoon red wine vinegar

COOK corn in large pot of boiling salted water until just tender, about 5 minutes. Drain; cool to room temperature. Cut corn kernels from cobs. Transfer corn to large bowl. Add remaining ingredients; toss to blend. Season salad with salt and pepper.

DO AHEAD *Can be made 2 hours ahead. Let stand at room temperature, tossing occasionally.*

Summer vegetable salad

2 SERVINGS; CAN BE DOUBLED *Ground cumin adds a touch of exotic flavor to this fresh vegetable salad.*

- 2 small zucchini, cut into ¼-inch-thick rounds
- 2 small yellow summer squash, cut into ¼-inch-thick rounds
- 8 ounces mushrooms, quartered
- 12 cherry tomatoes, halved

- 1 tablespoon Dijon mustard
- 1 tablespoon white wine vinegar
- ¼ cup olive oil
- 2 teaspoons minced fresh oregano or ¾ teaspoon dried oregano, crumbled
- ½ teaspoon ground cumin

STEAM zucchini and summer squash until just tender, about 6 minutes. Drain well. Transfer to medium bowl. Add mushrooms and tomatoes.

WHISK mustard and vinegar in small bowl. Gradually whisk in oil. Add oregano and cumin. Add dressing to vegetables; toss to coat. Season salad with salt and pepper. Cool to room temperature and serve.

THE GOOD SEED If you love the flavor of cumin, try buying cumin seeds, toasting them in a skillet until fragrant, and grinding them with a mortar and pestle or in an electric spice grinder (available for about $20 at appliance stores and some supermarkets). As with many other spices, toasted whole seeds will deliver even more flavor than the pre-ground stuff.

Savoy cabbage and radicchio slaw with blood-orange dressing

10 TO 12 SERVINGS *The dressing for this salad gets its vibrant color from blood orange juice. If there's none around, mix ½ cup pomegranate juice (available at many supermarkets and at natural foods stores) with ¼ cup orange juice.*

- 6 tablespoons fresh blood orange juice
- 1½ teaspoons rice vinegar
- 1 teaspoon honey
- ¼ cup olive oil
- ¼ cup mayonnaise
- 1½ tablespoons chopped shallot

- 1 1¼-pound head of savoy cabbage, halved, sliced ¼ inch thick
- 1 ½-pound head of radicchio, halved, sliced ¼ inch thick
- 1 large red bell pepper, sliced
- ½ cup dried cranberries

WHISK orange juice, vinegar, and honey in bowl, Whisk in oil, then mayonnaise and shallot. Season with salt and pepper.

DO AHEAD *Can be made 1 day ahead. Keep chilled. Rewhisk before continuing.*

PLACE cabbage, radicchio, and bell pepper in large bowl. Add dressing; toss to coat. Season with salt and pepper. Sprinkle with dried cranberries.

Cabbage 101 Coleslaw is the perfect excuse to experiment with different varieties of cabbage. Here are four of the most common.

GREEN: Bright green with smooth outer leaves. At the market, make sure the head you choose feels heavy for its size.

SAVOY: Round, yellow-green heads with ruffly leaves that are more delicate in flavor than that of green. Again, make sure the head feels heavy for its size.

NAPA: Also known as Chinese cabbage. The pale green, elongated heads have delicately flavored leaves with green, crinkly tips.

RED: Bright purple; similar structure to green cabbage. When very thinly sliced, red cabbage adds great color and texture to slaws and tossed salads.

South-of-the-border coleslaw with cilantro and jalapeño

4 SERVINGS *Here's the perfect side dish for a meal of grilled spice-rubbed steak, chicken, or fish. Depending on the size of the chile and the conditions in which it has been grown, one jalapeño can vary widely from another in the amount of heat it packs. Taste a tiny bit of the chile before using. If it seems really spicy, you may want to use less. For more punch, leave in the seeds and ribs—or add another chile.*

- 4   cups thinly sliced green cabbage (about ½ large head)
- 1   red bell pepper, thinly sliced
- ½   cup chopped fresh cilantro
- 1   small jalapeño chile, seeded, minced
- 3   tablespoons olive oil
- 2   tablespoons fresh lime juice
- 1½   teaspoons ground cumin

COMBINE cabbage, bell pepper, cilantro, and jalapeño in large bowl; toss to blend. Whisk oil, lime juice, and cumin in small bowl to blend. Pour dressing over cabbage mixture. Season to taste with salt and pepper.

DO AHEAD *Can be made 2 hours ahead. Cover and chill. Toss before serving.*

Asian-flavored coleslaw with rice vinegar and ginger

4 SERVINGS *Lower in acid than other vinegars, rice vinegar gives a gentler, subtler tang. It's a useful addition to any cook's vinegar selection and can be used almost like lemon juice—in far more than just Asian recipes.*

- 1   tablespoon sesame seeds
- 4   cups thinly sliced Napa cabbage (from about ½ large head)
- ½   cup thinly sliced green onions
- 3   tablespoons unseasoned rice vinegar
- 2   tablespoons peanut oil
- 1   tablespoon minced peeled fresh ginger
- 1   teaspoon Asian sesame oil
- 1   teaspoon sugar

STIR sesame seeds in small dry skillet over medium heat until light golden, about 3 minutes. Set aside.

COMBINE cabbage and green onions in large bowl. Add vinegar, peanut oil, ginger, sesame oil, and sugar; toss to blend. Season to taste with salt and pepper.

DO AHEAD *Can be made 2 hours ahead. Cover and chill. Toss before continuing.*

SPRINKLE with sesame seeds.

OPEN SESAME To make preparing this salad even easier, purchase toasted sesame seeds. They are available in jars in the Asian foods section of many supermarkets (and are sometimes labeled "roasted" sesame seeds).

Spiced carrot salad

6 TO 8 SERVINGS *Carrots cooked until just tender take on a Moroccan accent in this salad.*

- 4 garlic cloves
- ½ cup chopped fresh cilantro
- 2 tablespoons olive oil
- 2 tablespoons fresh lemon juice
- 1 tablespoon ground ginger
- 1 tablespoon ground cumin
- 5 large carrots (about 1½ pounds), peeled, cut into ¼-inch-thick rounds

FINELY chop garlic in processor. Add cilantro, oil, lemon juice, ginger, and cumin. Process until well blended.

COOK carrots in medium pot of boiling salted water until crisp-tender, about 5 minutes. Drain. Transfer to large bowl. Add dressing and toss to coat. Season salad to taste with salt and pepper. Cool to room temperature.

Thai cucumber salad with roasted peanuts

6 SERVINGS *Fish sauce is available in the Asian foods section of many supermarkets and at Asian markets.*

- ¼ cup fresh lime juice
- 1½ tablespoons fish sauce (such as nam pla or nuoc nam)
- 1½ tablespoons sugar
- 1½ tablespoons minced seeded jalapeño chile (about 1 large)
- 2 garlic cloves, minced
- 1½ English hothouse cucumbers, halved, seeded, thinly sliced
- ¾ cup sliced red onion
- 3 tablespoons chopped fresh mint
- 3 tablespoons coarsely chopped lightly salted roasted peanuts

WHISK first 5 ingredients in medium bowl. Place cucumbers, onion, and mint in large bowl. Add dressing and toss to coat. Season salad to taste with salt and pepper. Sprinkle with peanuts.

Sweet-and-sour cucumbers with fresh dill

6 TO 8 SERVINGS *The perfect do-ahead side salad for a summer lunch or supper: It can be assembled up to two hours ahead. Serve alongside grilled or broiled salmon.*

2 English hothouse cucumbers (about 1½ pounds total), unpeeled, very thinly sliced

1 tablespoon coarse kosher salt

½ cup distilled white vinegar

¼ cup finely chopped fresh dill

3 tablespoons sugar

½ teaspoon freshly ground black pepper

PLACE cucumber slices in colander. Sprinkle with coarse salt; toss to coat. Let stand 15 minutes, stirring occasionally.

MEANWHILE, for dressing, stir vinegar, dill, sugar, and pepper in large bowl until sugar dissolves.

DRAIN cucumbers well; pat dry. Add cucumbers to dressing and stir to blend. Refrigerate at least 15 minutes and up to 2 hours; serve cold.

Indian-spiced potato salad

8 SERVINGS *Ginger and cilantro give this classic summer side dish an exotic new identity.*

3½ pounds Yukon Gold potatoes

1 cup chopped shallots (about 3)

¾ cup mayonnaise

¼ cup chopped peeled fresh ginger

2 tablespoons fresh lemon juice

2 cups (packed) chopped cilantro leaves and tender stems, divided

COOK potatoes in large pot of boiling salted water until tender, about 25 minutes. Cool. Peel potatoes; cut into ½-inch cubes. Place in large bowl.

PUREE shallots, mayonnaise, ginger, and lemon juice in processor. Transfer to small bowl. Stir in 1½ cups cilantro. Season dressing to taste with salt and pepper. Add dressing to potatoes; toss to coat. Refrigerate until cold, about 4 hours.

DO AHEAD *Can be made 8 hours ahead. Keep chilled.*

SEASON to taste with salt and pepper. Garnish with remaining ½ cup cilantro.

Potato logic A common complaint about potato salads is that the potatoes fall apart when the salad is tossed. An easy way to avoid this is to use medium-starch potatoes like Yukon Gold or purple Peruvians, or low-starch potatoes (also called "waxy potatoes") such as red-skinned potatoes or fingerlings. For potato salads, it's generally best to avoid using high-starch baking potatoes, also known as Idaho or russet.

New potato and asparagus salad

2 SERVINGS; CAN BE DOUBLED *The addition of aspar-agus makes this the perfect springtime potato salad.*

- 3 medium red new potatoes (about 17 ounces), halved lengthwise
- 1 pound asparagus, trimmed

- 1 tablespoon Dijon mustard
- 1 tablespoon fresh lemon juice
- ¼ cup olive oil
- 2 tablespoons chopped fresh chives

COOK potatoes in large pot of boiling water until just tender, about 20 minutes. Drain and cool slightly. Cook asparagus in large pot of boiling salted water until just crisp-tender, about 4 minutes. Drain. Rinse under cold water to cool. Cut potatoes into wedges. Cut asparagus into 1½-inch pieces. Toss vegetables together in large bowl.

WHISK mustard and lemon juice in small bowl. Gradually whisk in oil. Pour over vegetables. Add chives and toss to coat. Season with salt and freshly ground black pepper. Serve salad warm or at room temperature.

Grilled potato and summer squash salad with marjoram-lemon vinaigrette

6 SERVINGS *Marjoram is a tender herb with a flavor similar to that of oregano, but milder.*

- 3 tablespoons fresh lemon juice
- 2 tablespoons minced shallot
- 1 tablespoon plus 2 teaspoons chopped fresh marjoram, divided
- 1 teaspoon finely grated lemon peel
- ¼ cup plus 3 tablespoons extra-virgin olive oil, divided

- ½ pound small unpeeled fingerling potatoes (such as Russian Banana), halved lengthwise

- 1 pound assorted summer squash (such as zucchini and yellow crookneck), cut on diagonal into ⅓-inch-thick slices
- 1 large red bell pepper, cut into 1-inch-wide strips

WHISK lemon juice, shallot, 1 tablespoon marjoram, and lemon peel in small bowl. Gradually whisk in ¼ cup oil. Season vinaigrette with salt and pepper.

PREPARE barbecue (medium heat). Place potatoes in large saucepan; add enough cold salted water to cover. Boil just until almost tender, about 4 minutes. Drain. Transfer potatoes to medium bowl. Add 1 teaspoon marjoram and 1½ tablespoons oil; sprinkle with salt and pepper and toss to coat.

COMBINE squash and bell pepper in large bowl; add remaining 1 teaspoon marjoram and remaining 1½ tablespoons oil. Sprinkle with salt and pepper; toss to coat.

GRILL potatoes until tender, about 5 minutes per side. Transfer to large bowl. Grill squash and bell pepper until tender, turning occasionally, about 10 minutes. Transfer squash and bell pepper to bowl with potatoes. Add vinaigrette; toss to coat. Season salad to taste with salt and pepper. Serve warm or at room temperature.

Pesto potato salad with green beans

10 SERVINGS *If baby Dutch yellow potatoes aren't available, Yukon Golds will work just as well.*

- 4 pounds 1-inch-diameter baby Dutch yellow potatoes, halved lengthwise
- 1 pound green beans, trimmed, cut into 1-inch pieces
- 1 cup purchased pesto
- ¼ cup chopped green onions
- ¼ cup white balsamic vinegar

COOK potatoes in large pot of boiling salted water until almost tender, about 10 minutes. Add beans; cook until beans are crisp-tender, about 4 minutes longer. Drain well. Transfer vegetables to large bowl and cool 10 minutes. Mix in pesto and green onions, tossing to coat. Cool completely.

DO AHEAD *Can be made 2 hours ahead. Cover; let stand at room temperature.*

JUST before serving, mix in vinegar and season to taste with salt and pepper.

Rice salad with sugar snap peas, mint, and lime

6 SERVINGS *Asparagus, zucchini, or English peas are also delicious in this springtime salad, if there are no sugar snaps on hand.*

- 2 cups water
- 1 teaspoon salt
- 1⅓ cups blue rose rice

- 2 cups sugar snap peas
- ½ cup chopped fresh mint leaves
- ½ cup chopped green onions
- 3 tablespoons olive oil
- 2 tablespoons fresh lime juice
- 2 tablespoons julienned peeled fresh ginger
- 1 teaspoon sugar

BRING 2 cups water and 1 teaspoon salt to boil in heavy medium saucepan. Add rice; reduce heat to low, cover, and simmer until tender, about 15 minutes. Remove from heat. Let stand 5 minutes. Fluff rice with fork, transfer to large bowl, and cool.

COOK snap peas in large saucepan of boiling salted water until crisp-tender, about 1 minute; drain. Rinse peas under cold water to cool; drain.

ADD sugar snap peas and all remaining ingredients to rice; toss to coat. Season with salt and pepper.

Orzo, feta, and tomato salad with marjoram vinaigrette

8 SERVINGS *Orzo is small pasta that works especially well in salads: Its rice-like shape makes for easy blending and tossing with chopped ingredients.*

1	**pound orzo**
¼	**cup fresh lemon juice**
6	**teaspoons finely chopped fresh marjoram, divided**
4	**teaspoons Dijon mustard**
1	**teaspoon finely grated lemon peel**
½	**cup olive oil**
1½	**cups crumbled feta cheese**
3	**green onions, thinly sliced**
1	**cup pitted Kalamata olives, quartered**
24	**ounces cherry tomatoes, halved**

COOK orzo in pot of boiling salted water until just tender but still firm to bite, stirring occasionally. Drain. Rinse under cold water to cool. Drain well. Transfer to large bowl.

WHISK lemon juice, 5 teaspoons marjoram, mustard, and lemon peel in small bowl. Whisk in olive oil. Set aside 2 tablespoons vinaigrette. Add remaining vinaigrette, cheese, green onions, and olives to orzo; toss to coat. Season to taste with salt and pepper. Cover and let stand 2 hours to allow flavors to develop.

DO AHEAD *Can be made 1 day ahead. Cover and refrigerate salad and reserved vinaigrette separately.*

TOSS tomatoes with reserved vinaigrette. Season to taste with salt and pepper. Mix tomatoes into orzo. Sprinkle orzo with remaining 1 teaspoon marjoram.

sandwiches, burgers, and pizzas

SANDWICHES

Pancetta, Mizuna, and Tomato Sandwiches with Green Garlic Aioli

The Best BLTs

Tomato and Cucumber Sandwiches with Garlic-Anchovy Butter

Watercress Sandwiches with Jalapeño-Lemon Butter

Goat Cheese and Watercress Tea Sandwiches

Feta, Garbanzo Bean, and Eggplant Pita Sandwiches

Greek Salad Pita Sandwiches

Chicken Salad Sandwiches with Blue Cheese

Tuscan-Style Grilled Chicken Sandwiches

Mexican-Style Chicken Sandwiches

Chicken and Mustard Green Sandwiches

Ciabatta Deli Sandwiches with Peperoncini and Artichoke Relish

Western Club Sandwiches

Smoked Turkey Sandwiches with Orange-Cranberry Sauce

Smoked Turkey Wraps with Fresh Mango and Curried Mayonnaise

Warm Black Bean and Vegetable Wraps

Open-Face Lobster Salad Sandwiches

Smoked Salmon and Cucumber Sandwiches

Enlightened Tuna Sandwiches

Pan Bagnat

Fried Egg Sandwiches with Pancetta and Arugula

Curried Egg Salad Sandwiches

Grilled Ham and Gouda Sandwiches with Frisée and Caramelized Onions

Grilled Blue Cheese Sandwiches with Walnuts and Watercress

Grilled Asiago and Prosciutto Sandwiches with Basil and Heirloom Tomato

Open-Face Wild Mushroom and Fontina Sandwiches

Portobello Mushroom Sandwiches with Tahini Sauce

Pork Sandwiches with Bourbon-Barbecue Sauce and Coleslaw

Toasted Almond and Pecorino Sandwiches

Spiced Lamb in Pita Bread

Croque-Monsieur

Meatless Monte Cristo Sandwiches

Turkey Sausage and Vegetable Frittata Sandwiches

Grilled Turkey, Bacon, Radicchio, and Blue Cheese Sandwiches

Grilled Steak and Bell Pepper Sandwiches with Chimichurri Sauce

Open-Face Ham, Cheddar, and Apple Butter Sandwiches

Pepper-Crusted Beef, Bacon, and Arugula Sandwiches with Spicy Mustard

Horseradish-Spiked Roast Beef and Arugula Sandwiches

Grouper Sandwiches with Wasabi Coleslaw

Open-Face Crab and Artichoke Melts

Oyster Po'boys

Mini Grilled Tuna, Prosciutto, and Lemon Sandwiches

Cal-Asian Seared Tuna Sandwiches

Italian Sausage Meatball Heroes

BURGERS

Grilled Mustard-Dill Burgers

Cheddar Cheese-Stuffed Burgers

Sun-Dried Tomato Burgers with Balsamic-Glazed Onions

Mustard Seed–Crusted Burgers with Horseradish Slaw

Beef and Gorgonzola Burgers

Grilled Burgers with Argentinean Parsley Sauce

Turkey and Fresh Tarragon Cheeseburgers

Spicy Turkey Burgers

Open-Face Turkey Burgers with Gruyère, Mushrooms, and Arugula Salad

Spicy Turkey Sloppy Joes

Minted Lamb Burgers with Feta and Hummus

Salmon Burgers with Dill Tartar Sauce

Tuna Burgers Niçoise

Portobello Burgers and Spinach Salad with Red Pepper Mayonnaise

PIZZAS

White Four-Cheese Pizza with Basil and Garlic

Bell Pepper, Red Onion, and Goat Cheese Pizza with Thyme

Radicchio, Fontina, and Goat Cheese Pizza

Tomato-Mozzarella Pizza with Phyllo Crust

Fast Deep-Dish Pepperoni Pizza

Goat Cheese and Asparagus Pizza

Artichoke and Feta Cheese Pizza

Potato, Sage, and Rosemary Pizza

Ricotta, Pesto, and Smoked Salmon Pizza

Scampi and Two-Cheese Pizza

Fisherman's Pizza Bianca

Tarragon Pizza Bianca

Lavash Vegetarian Pizza

Onion and Bacon Tart

Pizza with Caramelized Onions, Blue Cheese, and Mushrooms

Manchu Spiced Garlic Chicken Pizzettas

Wild Mushroom Pizza with Garlic Confit and Bacon

Duck Sausage Pizza with Green Onions and Tomato

Sausage, Red Onion, and Wild Mushroom Pizzas

Garlicky Eggplant, Tomato, and Fresh Basil Pizzas

Pronto Turkey Sausage and Tapenade Pizzas

Santa Fe Pizza

Ciabatta Pizza with Gorgonzola, Walnut Pesto, and Pears

Double-Cheese and Prosciutto Calzone

Cabbage, Bacon, and Cheese Calzones

Three-Cheese Spinach Calzones

Spinach and Feta Turnovers

Grilled Chorizo, Goat Cheese, and Watercress Pita Pizzas

Grilled Pizzas with Tomato, Mozzarella, and Basil

tool kit In sandwiches and burgers, the primary ingredients tend to take the spotlight—but flavorful spreads and toppings play a delicious role in tying the whole package together, transforming even a simple sandwich or basic burger into something special.

MAYO MAKEOVERS

Mix purchased mayonnaise with minced garlic and olive oil to make an impromptu aioli for BLTs and burgers. Add a Spanish accent by softening saffron threads in a bit of water and stirring them into the aioli for a delicious spread on turkey, ham, or sausage and bell pepper sandwiches. Stir prepared horseradish or crumbled blue cheese (or both) into mayonnaise to make a classic pairing for roast beef sandwiches.

TOP THAT

Toss sliced red onions with vinegar before piling them on your burger—the vinegar cuts the sharp flavor of the raw onions and adds a little zip. Blend chopped olives, roasted bell peppers, and fresh parsley in a little vinaigrette, and spoon the mixture over deli meats in your favorite sub sandwich. Or finely chop drained rinsed *giardiniera* (pickled Italian vegetables sold in jars) in a food processor for a tasty low-fat addition to sandwiches and burgers.

PESTO POWER

Classic pesto is usually made with olive oil, fresh basil, and pine nuts—but you can use whatever herbs and nuts you have on hand. A combination of basil, cilantro, or parsley with pine nuts, walnuts, or pecans packs a punch on all kinds of sandwiches.

SANDWICHES

Pancetta, mizuna, and tomato sandwiches with green garlic aioli

MAKES 6 *Meet the PMT: Pancetta (Italian bacon) stands in for the bacon, and mizuna (a delicate Asian salad green) replaces plain old lettuce. And the mayo? It's been dressed up with green garlic—young garlic that has a mild, subtle flavor.*

¼ cup extra-virgin olive oil

2 tablespoons chopped green garlic or 1 regular garlic clove, blanched 2 minutes

¼ teaspoon fleur de sel or coarse kosher salt

¾ cup mayonnaise, divided

2 teaspoons fresh lemon juice

2 3-ounce packages thinly sliced pancetta (Italian bacon; about 30 slices)

12 ½-inch-thick slices brioche or egg bread, lightly toasted

1 large bunch mizuna or arugula, torn into 2-inch pieces

3 beefsteak tomatoes, cut into ¼-inch-thick rounds

BLEND olive oil, garlic, and fleur de sel in mini processor until garlic is minced. Add 2 tablespoons mayonnaise and blend well. Transfer to small bowl; whisk in remaining mayonnaise and lemon juice. Season to taste with pepper.

DO AHEAD *Can be made 1 day ahead. Cover; chill.*

PREHEAT oven to 450°F. Arrange pancetta slices in single layer on 2 large rimmed baking sheets. Bake until crisp, about 10 minutes. Transfer to paper towels to drain.

PLACE all toasted bread slices on work surface. Spread each with aioli. Divide mizuna among 6 slices; top with tomatoes, then pancetta. Top with remaining 6 bread slices, aioli side down. Cut each sandwich in half.

MARKET TIP Look for mizuna at farmers' markets and Asian markets. Green garlic, which resembles baby leeks with long green tops and small white bulbs sometimes tinged with pink, is available at some farmers' markets.

The best BLTs

MAKES 6 *To make these sandwiches extra-special, use colorful heirloom tomatoes (such as Green Zebra, Gold Medal Yellow, or Cherokee Purple) instead of regular red tomatoes.*

2½ **cups (lightly packed) fresh basil leaves (about 2½ ounces)**
 1 **cup mayonnaise**
 ¼ **cup (½ stick) butter, room temperature**

 1 **pound thick-cut bacon slices**

12 **½-inch-thick slices country white bread**
 3 **large tomatoes, cut into ¼-inch-thick rounds**
 2 **ripe avocadoes, halved, pitted, peeled, sliced**
 1 **red onion, thinly sliced**
 6 **lettuce leaves**

MIX basil, mayonnaise, and butter in processor until basil is finely chopped and mixture is well blended. Season to taste with salt and pepper.

DO AHEAD *Can be made 1 day ahead. Cover and chill.*

COOK bacon in heavy large skillet over medium-high heat until brown and crisp. Transfer to paper towels to drain.

ARRANGE bread slices on work surface. Spread each with mayonnaise mixture. Top 6 slices with tomatoes; sprinkle with salt and pepper. Top tomatoes with avocado, then with bacon, onion, and lettuce. Place remaining bread slices atop lettuce, mayonnaise side down. Cut sandwiches in half.

Tomato and cucumber sandwiches with garlic-anchovy butter

MAKES 4 *A compound butter—softened butter mixed with flavorful ingredients—is a cook's best friend. Here it adds zip to summer's fresh veggies. Make double the amount of butter and freeze half. It would be delicious over grilled steaks, chops, or burgers.*

 ¼ **cup (½ stick) butter, room temperature**
 1 **large garlic clove, minced**
 1 **anchovy fillet, chopped**
 ¼ **teaspoon hot pepper sauce**
 1 **tablespoon minced fresh Italian parsley**

 1 **10×8-inch focaccia or ciabatta bread, cut into 4 equal pieces, each split horizontally**
 4 **medium tomatoes, thinly sliced into rounds**
24 **thin slices unpeeled English hothouse cucumber**
16 **thin red onion slices**
 4 **heads of baby lettuce (such as oakleaf) or 4 curly lettuce leaves**

COMBINE butter, garlic, anchovy, and hot pepper sauce in medium bowl. Using back of fork, mash until mixture is almost smooth. Season to taste with salt and pepper. Mix in parsley.

PREHEAT oven to 325°F. Arrange bread pieces, cut side down, directly on oven rack. Bake until bread is slightly crusty, about 5 minutes. Arrange bread, cut side up, on work surface; spread with garlic-anchovy butter. Arrange tomatoes, cucumber, and onion on bottom halves of bread. Top with lettuce, then bread tops. Press to compact slightly. Cut sandwiches diagonally in half.

Watercress sandwiches with jalapeño-lemon butter

4 SERVINGS *Make these into tea sandwiches by trimming off the crusts and cutting each sandwich into four triangles.*

6 tablespoons (¾ stick) butter, room temperature
1½ tablespoons fresh lemon juice
1½ tablespoons minced seeded jalapeño chile
1½ teaspoons (packed) finely grated lemon peel

8 thin slices whole wheat bread
or other whole grain bread
1 large bunch watercress (about 6 ounces),
tough ends trimmed

COMBINE first 4 ingredients in small bowl; stir to blend. Season butter mixture with salt and pepper.

ARRANGE bread slices on work surface. Spread jalapeño-lemon butter on each. Top 4 slices generously with watercress. Cover with remaining 4 bread slices, buttered side down, pressing lightly to adhere. Cut sandwiches in half and serve immediately.

Goat cheese and watercress tea sandwiches

8 SERVINGS *Serve with Earl Grey tea or (if you're in the mood for something a little stronger) a glass of dry Sherry.*

2 5½-ounce logs soft fresh goat cheese,
room temperature
½ cup chopped watercress leaves,
plus whole sprigs for garnish
16 thin slices cinnamon-raisin, date, or whole
wheat sandwich bread, crusts trimmed
5 tablespoons (about) unsalted butter,
room temperature

¾ cup pecans, toasted, finely chopped

COMBINE cheese and chopped watercress in medium bowl; stir to blend. Season to taste with salt and pepper. Arrange 8 bread slices on work surface. Spread cheese mixture evenly over. Top with remaining bread. Butter sides of sandwiches. Cut sandwiches diagonally in half.

PLACE pecans on plate. Dip buttered sides into pecans. Arrange sandwiches on platter. Garnish with watercress sprigs.

DO AHEAD *Can be made 2 hours ahead. Cover sandwiches tightly; chill.*

The almost-instant tea party

1. Choose two or three sandwiches to prepare. Assemble them two hours before the party, place on a platter, then cover with damp paper towels and plastic wrap and refrigerate.

2. Stop by your favorite bakery and pick up an assortment of scones, brownies, tartlets, and other sweet treats.

3. Buy a selection of teas: Earl Grey, English breakfast, a fruit tea, and a green or white tea will give guests plenty to choose from. Put out pots of hot water, pitchers of milk, lemon wedges, and bowls of brown and white sugar cubes so guests can help themselves.

Feta, garbanzo bean, and eggplant pita sandwiches

MAKES 6 HALVES *The sandwich filling would also make a delicious side dish. Try it with grilled lamb.*

- 2 tablespoons olive oil
- 1 pound Japanese eggplants, unpeeled, cut into ¾-inch cubes
- 1½ cups chopped onion
- 1 15- to 16-ounce can garbanzo beans (chickpeas), drained, ½ cup juices reserved
- 1 tablespoon ground cumin
- 1 tablespoon fresh lemon juice
- 4 tablespoons chopped fresh mint, divided
- 5 tablespoons crumbled feta cheese, divided
- 3 6-inch-diameter pita breads, warmed in oven or toasted

HEAT oil in large nonstick skillet over medium-high heat. Add eggplant cubes and onion; sauté until soft and beginning to brown, about 9 minutes. Stir in garbanzo beans, cumin, and lemon juice. Sauté until heated through and flavors blend, adding reserved garbanzo bean liquid by tablespoonfuls to moisten if mixture is dry, about 4 minutes. Stir in 3 tablespoons mint and 3 tablespoons feta cheese. Season filling generously with salt and pepper.

CUT pita breads crosswise in half and gently pull open. Spoon in eggplant filling. Sprinkle filling with remaining mint and feta.

Greek salad pita sandwiches

MAKES 6 *Two of Greece's most delicious exports—feta cheese and Kalamata olives—give this sandwich its Mediterranean flavor. Feta is a tangy goat or sheep's milk cheese that is cured in a salty brine, then pressed into square cakes. Kalamata olives, which are named after the Greek city of Kalamata, have a rich, fruity flavor and a dark eggplant color. They are sold packed in olive oil, brine, or vinegar.*

- ¼ cup extra-virgin olive oil
- 1 tablespoon fresh lemon juice
- 2 tablespoons chopped pitted Kalamata olives
- 1 tablespoon chopped fresh oregano
- 3 cups (loosely packed) thinly sliced romaine lettuce
- 2 cups diced seeded plum tomatoes (about 8)
- 1 cucumber, peeled, halved, seeded, cut into ¼-inch cubes
- 1 cup crumbled feta cheese (about 4 ounces)
- 6 6-inch-diameter pita breads, top 1½ inches trimmed

WHISK first 4 ingredients in large bowl to blend; season dressing to taste with salt and pepper. Add next 4 ingredients and toss to combine. Carefully open pita breads at cut end. Fill each with salad.

Chicken salad sandwiches with blue cheese

MAKES 6 *If you don't have any leftover cooked chicken, pick up a roast chicken at the supermarket. For a slightly different twist, mix some chopped toasted pecans and dried cranberries into the chicken salad.*

2 cups chopped cooked chicken
⅔ cup chopped celery
⅓ cup mayonnaise
⅓ cup thinly sliced green onion
2 teaspoons fresh lemon juice

6 soft rolls (such as kaiser), split horizontally
6 ounces creamy blue cheese

COMBINE first 5 ingredients in medium bowl; toss to blend. Season filling to taste with salt and pepper.

ARRANGE roll bottoms on work surface; spread with cheese. Top each with chicken filling. Cover with roll tops and press to adhere.

Tuscan-style grilled chicken sandwiches

MAKES 2 *The pesto mayo soaks into the nooks and crannies of the bread. Ciabatta ("slipper" in Italian) got its name from its long flat shape. You can also use focaccia, which is similar.*

¼ cup mayonnaise
4 teaspoons prepared pesto
2 skinless boneless chicken breast halves
Olive oil

2 4×4-inch squares ciabatta or focaccia, each cut horizontally in half
4 thin slices fresh mozzarella cheese
2 canned artichoke hearts, drained, thinly sliced
1 plum tomato, thinly sliced
1 cup mixed baby greens

PREPARE barbecue (medium-high heat). Combine mayonnaise and pesto in small bowl; whisk to blend. Brush chicken lightly with oil; sprinkle with salt and pepper. Grill chicken until just cooked through, about 5 minutes per side. Transfer chicken to cutting board; cool slightly. Cut chicken on sharp diagonal into ½-inch-thick slices.

ARRANGE bread, cut sides up, on work surface. Spread each with pesto mayonnaise. Layer chicken, mozzarella, artichokes, tomato, and greens onto bottom halves. Top with bread tops, mayonnaise side down.

Mexican-style chicken sandwiches

MAKES 4 *Skinless, boneless chicken breasts get dressed up with lime mayo, cumin-scented black beans, tomato, and avocado.*

⅔ cup mayonnaise
2 tablespoons fresh lime juice
1½ teaspoons grated lime peel

1 15- to 16-ounce can black beans, drained, 2 tablespoons liquid reserved
1½ teaspoons ground cumin
4 French rolls, split horizontally, lightly toasted

4 skinless boneless chicken breast halves
¾ teaspoon cayenne pepper
1 tablespoon olive oil
4 ¼-inch-thick slices hot pepper Monterey Jack cheese

2 medium tomatoes, sliced
1 large avocado, halved, pitted, peeled, sliced

WHISK mayonnaise, lime juice, and lime peel in small bowl to blend; season dressing to taste with salt and pepper.

STIR beans and cumin in small skillet over medium heat until heated through, about 5 minutes. Remove from heat. Add reserved bean liquid. Using fork, mash beans in skillet into coarse paste. Season to taste with salt and pepper. Arrange French roll bottoms on plates. Spread with bean mixture.

SPRINKLE chicken with cayenne and salt. Heat oil in heavy large skillet over medium-high heat. Add chicken to skillet and sauté until just cooked through, about 4 minutes per side. Top chicken with cheese slices. Cover skillet, reduce heat to low, and cook until cheese melts, about 1 minute.

PLACE chicken on bean mixture. Top with tomato, then avocado. Spread lime mayonnaise generously on cut side of each roll top; press onto sandwiches, mayo side down.

Chicken and mustard green sandwiches

MAKES 2; CAN BE DOUBLED *A slightly sweet mayonnaise and mango chutney spread balances the bitter greens. If you can't find mustard greens, kale or collard greens would make a good substitute. Or for something with a little less bite, try spinach.*

5 tablespoons mayonnaise
¼ cup mango chutney (such as Major Grey)
1 baguette, ends trimmed, halved lengthwise, then crosswise

1 tablespoon butter
2 skinless boneless chicken breast halves
1 bunch mustard greens or other bitter greens, stemmed

PREHEAT broiler. Mix mayonnaise and chutney in small bowl. Spread some of mixture on cut sides of bread. Broil, cut sides up, until golden, about 2 minutes. Place bread on work surface, broiled sides up.

MELT butter in heavy large skillet over medium heat. Sprinkle chicken with salt and pepper. Add to skillet and sauté until just cooked through, about 5 minutes per side. Transfer to plate. Add greens to same skillet; sprinkle with salt and pepper. Stir until wilted, about 1½ minutes. Divide greens between bread bottoms. Thinly slice chicken and arrange over greens. Spread with any remaining mayonnaise mixture. Top with bread.

Ciabatta deli sandwiches with peperoncini and artichoke relish

MAKES 2 *Most of the ingredients for this sandwich—marinated artichoke hearts, peperoncini, ciabatta rolls, provolone cheese, great deli meats—can be found at an Italian market. Chili-garlic sauce is available in the Asian foods section of many supermarkets and at Asian markets.*

- 1 6- to 7-ounce jar marinated artichoke hearts, drained, coarsely chopped
- ¼ cup (packed) sliced peperoncini plus 5 teaspoons juice from jar
- 3 tablespoons chopped white onion
- 2 tablespoons drained capers
- 2 tablespoons chopped fresh oregano
- 2 teaspoons chili-garlic sauce

- 2 ciabatta rolls, halved horizontally
- 4 ounces sliced provolone cheese
- 6 ounces assorted sliced Italian deli meats (such as soppressata, prosciutto, and salami)
- 1½ cups (packed) fresh arugula

COMBINE artichoke hearts, peperoncini with 5 teaspoons juice from jar, onion, capers, oregano, and chili-garlic sauce in small bowl; toss to blend. Season relish to taste with pepper.

ARRANGE roll bottoms, cut side up, on work surface; spread artichoke mixture over. Layer each with provolone cheese, then deli meats and arugula. Cover with roll tops. Cut each sandwich diagonally in half.

Western club sandwiches

MAKES 2; CAN BE DOUBLED *Make this a meal: Serve the sandwiches with a chilled black bean and rice salad and chocolate-cinnamon brownies.*

- ⅓ cup mayonnaise
- 2 tablespoons chopped fresh cilantro
- 1 to 2 tablespoons minced drained pickled jalapeño chiles

- 6 slices firm whole grain bread
- 6 ounces thinly sliced smoked turkey
- 4 thin slices red onion
- 1 ripe avocado, halved, pitted, peeled, sliced
- 1 cup radish sprouts or alfalfa sprouts

STIR mayonnaise, cilantro, and jalapeños in small bowl to blend. Season dressing to taste with salt.

PLACE 2 bread slices on plates. Spread each with ¼ of dressing. Top with turkey, onion, a second bread slice, remaining dressing, avocado slices, and sprouts. Place third bread slice atop each sandwich; press to compact slightly. Cut sandwiches into quarters. Insert extra-long toothpick into each quarter to hold together, if desired.

Smoked turkey sandwiches with orange-cranberry sauce

MAKES 4 *Turkey with cranberry sauce is a classic combo, but this sandwich would also be delicious made with slices of roast chicken.*

- 1 medium sweet onion (such as Maui or Vidalia), thinly sliced
- 3 tablespoons apple cider vinegar
- 2 tablespoons chopped fresh dill
- 2 teaspoons sugar
- ¾ cup canned whole-berry cranberry sauce
- 1½ teaspoons finely grated orange peel

- 8 slices whole grain bread, toasted
- 8 ounces thinly sliced smoked turkey breast
- 1 bunch watercress, thick stems trimmed

STIR onion, vinegar, dill, and sugar in medium bowl to blend. Season with salt and pepper. Stir cranberry sauce and orange peel in small bowl to blend.

PLACE all bread slices on work surface; spread cranberry mixture over. Top 4 bread slices with onion mixture, then turkey and watercress. Top with remaining 4 bread slices, cranberry side down; press lightly to adhere.

Smoked turkey wraps with fresh mango and curried mayonnaise

MAKES 4 *Lavash (also spelled* lahvosh *or* lavosh*) is a large thin Middle Eastern flatbread available at some supermarkets and at Middle Eastern markets. If you can't find lavash, use large, burrito-size flour tortillas instead. A ripe mango or avocado will yield slightly when squeezed.*

- 2 teaspoons curry powder
- ½ cup mayonnaise
- 2 teaspoons fresh lemon juice

- 2 lavash, each cut in half crosswise to make total of four 12×12-inch squares
- 8 ounces thinly sliced smoked turkey
- 4 cups thinly sliced romaine lettuce
- 2 cups thinly sliced seeded peeled English hothouse cucumber
- 1 mango, peeled, pitted, chopped (about 1 cup)
- ½ cup fresh cilantro leaves
- ½ avocado, halved, pitted, peeled, thinly sliced

STIR curry powder in heavy small skillet over medium-low heat until fragrant, about 2 minutes. Transfer curry powder to small bowl. Stir in mayonnaise and lemon juice. Season with salt and pepper.

PLACE 1 lavash square on work surface; spread 2 tablespoons curried mayonnaise over. Place ¼ of turkey in center of lavash. Top turkey with 1 cup lettuce, ½ cup cucumber, ¼ of mango, and ¼ of cilantro, then ¼ of avocado slices. Fold sides of lavash over ends of filling, then roll up like burrito, enclosing filling completely. Repeat process for remaining 3 wraps.

DO AHEAD *Can be made 2 hours ahead. Wrap tightly with plastic wrap and refrigerate.*

CUT wraps in half crosswise.

Warm black bean and vegetable wraps

MAKES 4 *To give the veggies a smoky flavor, brush them with olive oil and toss them on the grill for a few minutes instead of sautéing. Feel free to use both red and yellow peppers, if you like. Serve the wraps with your favorite purchased salsa and sour cream.*

1½ tablespoons olive oil

2 large garlic cloves, minced

2 cups diced red or yellow bell peppers

1 cup ½-inch cubes zucchini

1 cup ½-inch cubes peeled seeded butternut squash

1 cup chopped red onion

2 teaspoons ground cumin

1 15- to 16-ounce can black beans, drained

1 cup (packed) grated hot pepper Monterey Jack cheese

4 9- to 10-inch-diameter flour tortillas (burrito size)

4 tablespoons chopped fresh cilantro, divided

HEAT olive oil in heavy large skillet over medium-high heat. Add garlic and stir 30 seconds. Add all vegetables and sauté until crisp-tender, about 8 minutes. Mix in cumin and sauté until vegetables are tender, about 2 minutes longer. Season with salt and pepper. Place beans in large bowl; mash coarsely with fork. Mix in vegetables, then cheese.

PREHEAT oven to 350°F. Place tortillas on work surface. Spoon ¼ of filling down the center of each; sprinkle filling on each with 1 tablespoon cilantro. Roll up tortillas, enclosing filling. Arrange wraps, seam side down, on baking sheet. Cover wraps with foil. Bake until filling is just heated through, about 10 minutes. Cut each into 2 or 3 sections.

Open-face lobster salad sandwiches

2 SERVINGS; CAN BE DOUBLED *To complete the New England clam shack effect, serve this sandwich with lemonade and potato chips—and blueberry pie for dessert.*

¼ cup mayonnaise

¼ cup finely chopped celery

1 teaspoon fresh lemon juice

½ teaspoon grated lemon peel

3 tablespoons chopped fresh chives, divided

1 11- to 12-ounce frozen lobster tail, thawed

4 slices egg bread, toasted

COMBINE first 4 ingredients and 2 tablespoons chives in medium bowl; stir to blend. Cook lobster tail in medium pot of boiling salted water until just opaque in center, about 8 minutes. Drain; cool. Remove meat from shell. Dice lobster; fold into mayonnaise mixture. Season with salt and pepper.

SPOON salad atop bread slices. Sprinkle with remaining 1 tablespoon chives.

Smoked salmon and cucumber sandwiches

2 SERVINGS *Danish pumpernickel is a dense, approximately 4-inch-square, light-colored bread available in the refrigerated deli section of most supermarkets.*

- 2 tablespoons (¼ stick) unsalted butter, room temperature
- 1 teaspoon minced fresh dill
- ¾ teaspoon Dijon mustard

- 3 slices thin Danish pumpernickel bread
- 12 thin slices English hothouse cucumber
- 3 ounces thinly sliced smoked salmon or lox
  Fresh dill sprigs

STIR first 3 ingredients in small bowl to blend.

ARRANGE bread on work surface; spread with butter mixture. Top with cucumber slices, then salmon. Sprinkle with pepper. Cut each sandwich into 4 triangles. Top triangles with dill sprigs.

Enlightened tuna sandwiches

MAKES 2 *A mixture of nonfat yogurt and low-fat mayonnaise lightens up this version of the all-American classic. Lots of vegetables (cucumber, red onion, bell peppers, and romaine lettuce) add color, freshness, and flavor.*

- 3 tablespoons plain nonfat yogurt
- 3 tablespoons low-fat mayonnaise
- 1½ tablespoons fresh lemon juice
- 1 6½-ounce can white tuna packed in water, drained
- ⅓ cup diced unpeeled English hothouse cucumber
- ⅓ cup diced red onion
- ¼ cup finely chopped red bell pepper

- 4 thin slices whole wheat bread, toasted
  Romaine lettuce leaves

STIR first 3 ingredients in medium bowl to blend. Add next 4 ingredients and stir with fork to break up tuna. Season salad to taste with salt and pepper.

PLACE 1 bread slice on each plate. Cover each with lettuce, half of tuna salad, and 1 bread slice. Cut sandwiches in half on diagonal.

A moveable feast Taking your sandwiches to the park or the beach? Here's how to keep them fresh and delicious.

— To prevent the filling from falling out, wrap sandwiches tightly in foil or plastic wrap, then place in resealable plastic bags.

— Hate soggy bread? Choose sturdy varieties like ciabatta, focaccia, and crusty French bread that can withstand mayo and other wet toppings.

— Layer tomato slices between lettuce, cheese, or meat to prevent the juices from soaking into the bread.

— Pack mayonnaise-based fillings (tuna, egg, or chicken salad) in separate containers and assemble the sandwiches just before serving.

Pan bagnat

4 SERVINGS *Pan bagnat ("soaked bread") is a popular sandwich in southern France. The interior of a loaf of bread is hollowed out, brushed with olive oil, and filled with goodies (tuna, olives, and other vegetables, in this case). The sandwich is then wrapped and pressed so the juices can soak into the bread. Because it is made ahead,* pan bagnat *makes a great picnic sandwich. Serve with chilled rosé and imagine yourself in the French countryside.*

1   1-pound loaf unsliced French bread (about 14 inches long)
¼   cup extra-virgin olive oil
⅓   cup fresh basil leaves, plus whole sprigs for garnish
2   6-ounce cans tuna packed in olive oil, undrained
2   large plum tomatoes, diced
⅔   cup coarsely chopped pitted assorted brine-cured olives
½   cup chopped sweet onion (such as Vidalia or Maui)
2   tablespoons fresh lemon juice

CUT bread in half lengthwise. Pull out most of bread, leaving ¾-inch-thick shell. Brush inside of both halves with olive oil. Line bottom half with basil leaves in single layer.

COMBINE undrained tuna, tomatoes, olives, onion, and lemon juice in medium bowl; stir to blend. Season to taste with salt and pepper. Spoon salad evenly into bottom bread shell. Cover with top of bread. Wrap loaf tightly with plastic. Place in shallow baking pan; top with another baking pan. Fill top pan with heavy cans to weigh down. Let stand 20 minutes.

REMOVE top pan and weights. Unwrap *pan bagnat* and cut crosswise into 1½-inch-thick sections. Place on platter and garnish with basil sprigs.

WASTE NOT... Use the bread that you pulled from the inside of the loaf to make fresh breadcrumbs for another dish.

Fried egg sandwiches with pancetta and arugula

MAKES 2 *The pancetta and Parmesan add salt, so the eggs and arugula probably won't need any additional seasoning.*

4   ½-inch-thick slices egg bread or sourdough bread (each about 4×4 inches)
     Butter
2   ounces thinly sliced pancetta (Italian bacon)
2   large eggs
1   ounce Parmesan cheese, shaved into strips with vegetable peeler (about ⅓ cup)
2   ounces arugula (about 2 cups lightly packed)

TOAST bread; butter lightly. Heat heavy large nonstick skillet over medium heat. Add pancetta and cook until crisp. Transfer to paper towels to drain. Crack eggs and drop carefully into drippings in skillet to keep yolks whole. Cook until edges are opaque and whites are nearly set, about 3 minutes. Carefully turn eggs over. Cook until whites are set, about 1 minute. Transfer each egg to slice of toast. Top each with cheese and pancetta. Add arugula to same skillet. Toss until beginning to wilt, about 30 seconds. Divide arugula between sandwiches. Top with remaining toast.

Curried egg salad sandwiches

MAKES 6 *If you want a little more kick in your egg salad, use some chopped jalapeño chile instead of curry powder.*

- 12   **hard-boiled eggs, peeled, halved**
- ¼   **cup dried currants**
- 1   **large green onion, finely chopped**
- 2   **tablespoons minced fresh cilantro**
- ½   **cup plus additional mayonnaise**
- 2¾   **teaspoons curry powder**
- 1   **small cucumber, peeled, cut lengthwise in half, seeded**
- 12   **slices firm white sandwich bread or country white bread, toasted**

SCOOP egg yolks into large bowl; mash well with fork. Finely chop egg whites; add to yolks. Mix in currants, green onion, and cilantro. Mix ½ cup mayonnaise and curry powder in small bowl; stir into egg mixture. Mix in more mayonnaise by tablespoonfuls to moisten, if desired. Season to taste with salt and pepper.

DO AHEAD *Can be made 3 hours ahead. Cover; chill.*

THINLY slice cucumber crosswise into half-rounds. Place slices on paper towels to drain. Arrange bread on work surface; spread with mayonnaise. Top 6 slices with egg salad and cucumber slices, then second bread slice. Cut sandwiches in half.

How to boil an egg For perfect hard-boiled eggs, start with large eggs that are more than 1 week old—fresh eggs are harder to shell. Place in single layer in saucepan, cover with 1½ inches of cold water, and add 1 tablespoon salt. Cover pan partially and bring water to boil. Immediately reduce heat to low; simmer 30 seconds. Remove from heat, cover, and let stand 15 minutes. Drain eggs. Shake pan to crack shells. Transfer eggs to bowl, cover with cold water, and cool, changing water frequently, before peeling.

Grilled ham and gouda sandwiches with frisée and caramelized onions

MAKES 2 *Instead of white bread, try pumpernickel. Accompany with a lager-style beer.*

1 tablespoon extra-virgin olive oil

1 large onion, thinly sliced

   Butter, room temperature

4 ⅓-inch-thick slices country white bread or sourdough bread

4 ounces thinly sliced smoked ham, divided

3 ounces Gouda cheese, thinly sliced, divided

2 large handfuls frisée, torn into bite-size pieces (about 1 cup), divided

HEAT oil in large nonstick skillet over medium heat. Add onion; sauté 5 minutes. Reduce heat to medium-low; cover and cook until onion is very tender and golden, stirring frequently, about 25 minutes longer. Season with salt and pepper. Cool slightly.

BUTTER 2 bread slices; place, buttered side down, on work surface. Divide onion, ham, cheese, and frisée between prepared bread slices. Top each sandwich with another bread slice; butter top slices.

HEAT medium nonstick skillet over medium heat. Add sandwiches and cook until bread is golden brown and cheese melts, pressing occasionally with spatula, about 4 minutes per side. Transfer sandwiches to plates and cut in half diagonally.

Grilled blue cheese sandwiches with walnuts and watercress

MAKES 8 *Assemble the sandwiches a couple of hours ahead, then grill when your guests arrive. For a more casual look, leave the crusts on the bread.*

16 slices whole wheat bread, trimmed to crustless 3-inch squares

1 cup crumbled blue cheese (about 4 ounces)

½ cup walnuts, toasted, finely chopped

16 small watercress sprigs

6 tablespoons (¾ stick) butter, divided

ARRANGE 8 bread squares on work surface. Divide cheese and walnuts equally among squares. Top each with 2 watercress sprigs. Sprinkle with pepper and gently press remaining bread squares over, making 8 sandwiches total.

DO AHEAD *Sandwiches can be prepared 2 hours ahead. Cover and chill.*

MELT 3 tablespoons butter on large nonstick griddle or in large skillet over medium heat. Place 4 sandwiches on griddle and cook until golden brown and cheese melts, about 3 minutes per side. Transfer to cutting board. Repeat with remaining 3 tablespoons butter and 4 sandwiches. Cut sandwiches diagonally in half. Transfer to plates.

Grilled Asiago and prosciutto sandwiches with basil and heirloom tomato

MAKES 2 *Young Asiago cheese adds a slight tang to this deluxe version of the classic BLT. Avoid using an aged Asiago. It will overpower the rest of the flavors. Asiago cheese is available at some supermarkets and at specialty foods stores and Italian markets.*

Butter, room temperature

4   7×3½-inch slices country white bread or sourdough bread (each cut from loaf on deep diagonal and about ⅓-inch-thick)

4   thin slices prosciutto

8   large fresh basil leaves

8   ¼-inch-thick slices young Asiago cheese or drained fresh mozzarella cheese

¼   teaspoon dried crushed red pepper

2   tablespoons olive oil

6   ⅓-inch-thick slices heirloom tomato (from about 1 large)

PREHEAT oven to 400°F. Lightly butter 1 side of each bread slice. Place 2 bread slices, buttered side down, on work surface. Top each with 2 prosciutto slices, then 4 basil leaves and 4 cheese slices. Sprinkle with salt and crushed red pepper. Top with remaining 2 bread slices, buttered side up. Heat olive oil in heavy large ovenproof skillet over medium-high heat. Add sandwiches to skillet, buttered slice on top. Cook until golden on bottom, about 4 minutes. Turn sandwiches over, transfer skillet to oven, and bake until bread is golden and cheese melts, about 5 minutes.

TRANSFER sandwiches to plates. Carefully lift off top bread slices from sandwiches and insert 3 tomato slices into each; re-cover with bread tops.

Open-face wild mushroom and Fontina sandwiches

MAKES 4 *For an easy appetizer, cut the broiled cheese bread into smaller pieces, then top with the mushroom mixture.*

1   pound assorted fresh wild mushrooms (such as stemmed shiitake, chanterelles, and porcini)

5   tablespoons olive oil

1   teaspoon minced fresh rosemary

2   medium shallots, minced

1   teaspoon minced fresh thyme

¼   cup Marsala

4   ½- to ¾-inch-thick center-cut slices country French bread

1½   cups (packed) coarsely grated imported Italian Fontina cheese (about 6 ounces)

2   tablespoons minced fresh parsley

CUT all mushrooms lengthwise into ½-inch-thick slices. Heat olive oil in large nonstick skillet over medium-high heat. Add rosemary and stir 10 seconds, then add mushrooms. Sprinkle with salt and pepper. Sauté until mushrooms begin to brown, about 10 minutes. Add shallots and thyme; stir 2 minutes. Add Marsala and boil until evaporated, about 30 seconds. Remove from heat. Season mushrooms to taste with salt and pepper.

DO AHEAD *Can be prepared 2 hours ahead. Let stand at room temperature. Rewarm before using.*

PREHEAT broiler. Place bread slices on baking sheet; broil until lightly toasted, about 2 minutes per side. Leave bread on sheet; top with cheese, covering completely. Broil until cheese melts, about 2 minutes. Place toasts on plates. Mix parsley into mushrooms. Spoon mushrooms onto toasts.

Portobello mushroom sandwiches with tahini sauce

MAKES 6 *Tahini(sesame seed paste) is available at some supermarkets, Middle Eastern markets, and natural foods stores. Look for Creole or Cajun season-ing in the spice section of the supermarket.*

12	slices country whole wheat bread
⅔	cup purchased ranch dressing
¼	cup tahini (sesame seed paste)
¼	cup whole milk
¼	cup vegetable oil
1¼	pounds large portobello mushrooms (about 4), stemmed, cut into ⅓-inch-thick slices
1	large onion, thinly sliced
2	teaspoons Creole or Cajun seasoning
12	thin tomato slices
6	thin slices Swiss cheese
	Red leaf lettuce leaves

PREHEAT broiler. Place bread in single layer on baking sheet. Broil until toasted, about 1 minute per side. Transfer 6 slices to plates. Whisk ranch dressing, tahini, and milk in medium bowl to blend.

HEAT oil in heavy large skillet over medium-high heat. Add mushrooms and onion; sauté until ten-der, about 10 minutes. Add seasoning; cook 2 min-utes to blend flavors.

DIVIDE mushroom-onion mixture among bread slices on plates. Top each with 1 tablespoon tahini sauce, 2 tomato slices, 1 slice cheese, and lettuce. Top sandwiches with second bread slice.

Pork sandwiches with bourbon-barbecue sauce and coleslaw

MAKES 2; CAN BE DOUBLED *Here's a quick and easy version of the pulled pork sandwich, which is a staple of Carolina barbecue. Be sure to use soft rolls so the barbecue sauce and the juices from the coleslaw can soak into the bread.*

8	ounces boneless pork loin chops, cut crosswise into ¼-inch-thick strips
2	tablespoons olive oil
1	large onion, thinly sliced
3	tablespoons bourbon
⅓	cup purchased tomato-based barbecue sauce
2	large sandwich buns or kaiser rolls, split horizontally
½	cup purchased coleslaw

SPRINKLE pork strips with salt and pepper. Heat oil in heavy large skillet over medium-high heat. Add pork and sauté until just cooked through, about 2 minutes. Using slotted spoon, transfer pork to plate. Add onion to same skillet. Sauté until golden brown, about 7 minutes; remove from heat. Add bourbon to skillet and stir, scraping up browned bits. Add barbecue sauce and return to medium heat. Simmer until sauce thickens, stirring often, about 3 minutes. Add pork to sauce; heat 1 minute.

ARRANGE bun bottoms on plates. Top with pork and sauce, then coleslaw and bun tops.

Toasted almond and pecorino sandwiches

MAKES 6 *The flavorful almond-sage spread would also be great on a grilled chicken sandwich.*

- 3 **cups whole unblanched almonds (about 1 pound), toasted, cooled**
- ½ **cup plus 2 tablespoons olive oil**
- 3 **tablespoons fresh lemon juice**
- 1 **tablespoon finely grated lemon peel**
- 1 **tablespoon chopped fresh sage**
- ½ **teaspoon salt**
- ¼ **teaspoon ground black pepper**
- 12 **½-inch-thick slices country white bread (each about 3½×5½ inches)**
- 1 **10- to 12-ounce wedge pecorino cheese, cut into very thin slices**
  Additional olive oil (for brushing)

COARSELY chop nuts in processor. Add next 6 ingredients. Blend until mixture forms coarse paste.

DO AHEAD *Can be made 3 days ahead. Cover and chill. Let stand at room temperature 1 hour before using.*

ARRANGE 6 bread slices on work surface; spread with almond paste. Top with cheese. Sprinkle with pepper. Cover with remaining bread slices. Brush tops with oil.

HEAT 2 large nonstick skillets over medium-high heat. Add 3 sandwiches, oiled side down, to each skillet. Cook until bread is crusty on bottom, about 6 minutes. Brush tops with oil. Turn sandwiches over. Cook until brown and crusty on bottom, pressing to compact, about 6 minutes. Transfer to plates and cut in half.

HOW TO TOAST NUTS Toasting nuts makes them crunchier and more flavorful—and it couldn't be easier. Place the almonds in single layer on a rimmed baking sheet and bake in a 350°F oven until fragrant and golden, stirring occasionally, about 10 minutes. You can also toast nuts in a large skillet over medium-high heat: Stir or shake the pan until the nuts are fragrant and golden, about 5 minutes.

Spiced lamb in pita bread

2 SERVINGS; CAN BE DOUBLED *Top the lamb burgers with a quick version of the cooling Indian condiment known as* raita: *Mix plain yogurt with chopped cucumbers and tomatoes.*

- 10 **ounces ground lamb**
- ½ **cup chopped onion**
- 3 **tablespoons chopped fresh mint**
- 1 **teaspoon dried oregano**
- ½ **teaspoon ground cumin**
- ½ **teaspoon salt**
- ½ **teaspoon ground black pepper**
- ¼ **teaspoon ground cinnamon**
- 2 **warm 5- to 6-inch pita breads, each cut crosswise in half**

COMBINE lamb and next 7 ingredients in medium bowl; blend well. Shape lamb mixture into four ¼-inch-thick patties. Heat heavy large skillet over medium-high heat. Add lamb patties and sauté until brown and just cooked through, about 3 minutes per side. Gently open each pita bread half; fill each with lamb patty.

Croque-monsieur

MAKES 2; CAN BE DOUBLED *In this take on the Parisian grilled ham and cheese (the name literally means "Mister Crunch"), the sandwich is topped with a rich béchamel sauce. Serve this for brunch with a salad of bitter greens (perhaps a mix of endive, arugula, and frisée).*

3	tablespoons butter, room temperature, divided
2	tablespoons all purpose flour
1	cup whole milk
	Pinch of ground nutmeg
1	Turkish bay leaf
4	slices firm white sandwich bread
4	ounces thinly sliced Black Forest ham
4	ounces sliced Gruyère cheese
¼	cup (packed) grated Gruyère cheese
2	teaspoons chopped fresh chives

MELT 2 tablespoons butter in heavy small saucepan over medium heat. Add flour and stir 1 minute. Gradually whisk in milk. Add nutmeg and bay leaf. Increase heat to medium-high and cook until sauce thickens and boils, whisking constantly, about 2 minutes. Season to taste with salt and pepper. Discard bay leaf.

PREHEAT broiler. Place 2 bread slices on work surface. Top each with ham, sliced cheese, and remaining bread. Heat heavy large skillet over low heat. Coat sandwiches with remaining 1 tablespoon butter. Add sandwiches to skillet and sauté until bread is deep golden brown, about 2 minutes per side. Transfer to small baking sheet. Spoon sauce, then grated cheese over sandwiches. Broil until cheese begins to brown, about 2 minutes. Transfer to plates; sprinkle with chives.

Meatless Monte Cristo sandwiches

2 SERVINGS; CAN BE DOUBLED *A Monte Cristo is a luxurious grilled sandwich traditionally made with turkey, ham, or chicken, but you won't miss the meat in this vegetarian version.*

6	slices egg bread
4	teaspoons (about) Dijon mustard
4	ounces sliced Swiss cheese
1	large tomato, thinly sliced
2	large eggs
2	tablespoons water
1½	tablespoons chopped fresh sage
2	tablespoons (¼ stick) butter

ARRANGE bread slices on work surface. Spread each with mustard. Top 3 slices with cheese and tomato; sprinkle with salt and pepper. Top with remaining bread slices, mustard side down, forming 3 sandwiches.

WHISK eggs, 2 tablespoons water, and sage in medium shallow bowl to blend. Melt butter in heavy large skillet over medium-low heat. Dip both sides of each sandwich into egg mixture and place in skillet. Cook until cheese melts and sandwiches are golden, about 4 minutes per side. Transfer sandwiches to work surface and cut each diagonally in half. Transfer 3 halves to each of 2 plates.

Turkey sausage and vegetable frittata sandwiches

6 SERVINGS *The frittata makes a great sandwich, but it's also delicious on its own. Cut it into wedges and serve with a salad for brunch. Save the insides of the bread to make breadcrumbs for another dish.*

1   10- to 12-inch unsliced round French bread

3   tablespoons olive oil, divided

½   pound spicy Italian turkey sausages, casings removed

1   onion, chopped

2   zucchini, trimmed, diced

1   green bell pepper, diced

1   large tomato, seeded, diced

3   garlic cloves, chopped

¼   cup chopped fresh basil

10   large eggs

⅓   cup freshly grated Parmesan cheese

CUT bread horizontally in half. Cut or pull out soft insides, leaving ½-inch-thick shells. Brush inside of bread shells with 1 tablespoon olive oil.

CRUMBLE sausages into large nonstick broilerproof skillet. Sauté over medium heat until brown, about 5 minutes. Transfer sausages to bowl. Add onion, zucchini, bell pepper, tomato, and garlic to drippings in skillet. Sauté until vegetables are tender and juices evaporate, about 9 minutes. Mix in basil. Cool briefly.

PREHEAT broiler. Beat eggs in large bowl to blend; sprinkle with salt and pepper. Stir in sausages, then vegetable mixture. Heat remaining 2 tablespoons oil in same skillet over medium heat. Pour in egg mixture. Cover and cook until eggs are almost set, occasionally lifting edges to allow uncooked portion to flow underneath, about 7 minutes.

SPRINKLE top of frittata with cheese. Broil until eggs are set in center and top is golden brown, about 3 minutes. Run spatula around edge of skillet to loosen frittata and slide into bottom shell of bread, pressing to fit. Press top half of bread over. Cut into wedges and serve or wrap in foil and let stand at room temperature up to 1 hour.

Grilled turkey, bacon, radicchio, and blue cheese sandwiches

MAKES 2 *Thanksgiving leftovers never had it so good. If you don't have any leftover roasted turkey, substitute turkey from the deli counter, slices of roasted chicken, or even a hamburger patty.*

6   slices applewood-smoked bacon

¼   cup mayonnaise

¼   cup crumbled Maytag blue cheese or other mild blue cheese

4   ½-inch-thick slices country white bread (about 5×3 inches)

4   leaves radicchio

6   ounces thinly sliced cooked turkey

4   teaspoons butter, room temperature, divided

COOK bacon in large skillet over medium heat until crisp. Transfer to paper towels to drain. Pour off fat from skillet; reserve skillet.

MASH mayonnaise and blue cheese in small bowl to coarse puree; season to taste with pepper. Place bread on work surface. Spread cheese mayo over all bread slices. Divide bacon, radicchio, and turkey between 2 bread slices. Top sandwiches with remaining bread, cheese side down. Melt 2 teaspoons butter in reserved skillet over medium heat. Place sandwiches in skillet. Spread remaining 2 teaspoons butter on top slices of bread. Cover sandwiches with lid that is slightly smaller than skillet, pressing lightly to compact. Cook sandwiches until lightly browned, about 4 minutes per side. Transfer to plates and cut in half.

Grilled steak and bell pepper sandwiches with chimichurri sauce

MAKES 4 *Chimichurri is an Argentinean herb sauce. It's fresh and bright—with a bit of heat thanks to a little crushed red pepper.*

- 1 cup (packed) fresh Italian parsley
- 1 cup (packed) fresh cilantro
- 3 tablespoons white wine vinegar
- 2 tablespoons chopped fresh oregano
- 2 garlic cloves, peeled
- ½ teaspoon dried crushed red pepper
- ⅔ cup plus ¼ cup olive oil
- 2 large bell peppers (preferably 1 red and 1 yellow), seeded, cut into ¾-inch-wide strips
- 2 12-ounce rib-eye steaks (each ¾ to 1 inch thick)
- 4 sourdough demi-baguettes or four 6-inch-long pieces of baguette, halved horizontally

PREPARE barbecue (medium-high heat). Combine parsley and next 5 ingredients in processor; add ⅔ cup oil and process until almost smooth. Season chimichurri to taste with salt and pepper.

BRUSH pepper strips, steaks, and cut side of bread with remaining ¼ cup oil. Sprinkle peppers and steaks with salt and pepper. Grill peppers until tender, about 5 minutes per side; transfer to baking sheet. Grill steaks to desired doneness, about 4 minutes per side for medium-rare; transfer to same sheet. Grill bread, cut side down, until beginning to brown, about 2 minutes. Place bread bottoms on plates.

THINLY slice steaks; divide among bread bottoms. Spoon chimichurri over steak (about ¼ cup per sandwich), then top with peppers and bread tops.

THREE MORE TO TRY The *chimichurri* sauce would also be great with grilled chicken or burgers. For a delicious side dish, roast potato wedges in a 400°F oven until almost tender, about 25 minutes. Toss with some *chimichurri* and roast another 10 minutes until tender.

Open-face ham, cheddar, and apple butter sandwiches

MAKES 6 *Despite its name, apple butter contains no butter. It's a spread made by slowly cooking apples, cider, sugar, and spice until the mixture is as thick as jam.*

- 3 ciabatta rolls, halved horizontally, or six ½-inch-thick slices country white bread
- 2 tablespoons olive oil
- 6 tablespoons purchased apple butter
- 4 tablespoons Dijon mustard
- 1¼ pounds Black Forest ham, thinly sliced
- 12 ounces extra-sharp white cheddar cheese, thinly sliced
- 1 bunch fresh chives, chopped

PREHEAT broiler. Brush cut side of ciabatta rolls with oil. Place rolls, cut side up, on baking sheet. Broil until rolls begin to brown around edges, about 2 minutes. Transfer sheet with rolls to work surface. Spread apple butter and mustard on each roll half. Top with ham, then cheese. Broil until cheese melts and begins to brown in spots, about 2 minutes. Transfer to plates. Sprinkle with chives.

Pepper-crusted beef, bacon, and arugula sandwiches with spicy mustard

MAKES 6 *The steaks need to marinate for at least 30 minutes, so plan accordingly.*

3 8-ounce beef tenderloin steaks
3 tablespoons coarsely cracked black pepper
6 tablespoons mayonnaise
2 tablespoons spicy Dijon mustard
1 tablespoon prepared white horseradish

12 mushrooms, thinly sliced
6 tablespoons fresh lemon juice
Olive oil
1 pound sliced bacon

6 3- to 4-inch-diameter kaiser, egg, or crusty rolls, cut in half horizontally, toasted if desired
3 cups (packed) baby arugula (about 3 ounces)

COAT steaks all over with pepper. Mix mayonnaise, mustard, and horseradish in small bowl for dressing. Cover steaks and dressing separately and refrigerate at least 30 minutes and up to 1 day.

TOSS mushrooms and lemon juice in medium bowl to coat; sprinkle lightly with salt. Brush heavy large skillet generously with oil and heat over medium-high heat. Sprinkle steaks with salt. Add to skillet and cook to desired doneness, about 5 minutes per side for medium-rare. Transfer steaks to plate; let stand 15 minutes. Add bacon to same skillet and cook over medium-high heat until brown and crisp. Using tongs, transfer bacon to paper towels to drain.

PLACE roll bottoms on plates; spread with dressing. Slice steaks thinly and divide among rolls. Top with bacon, mushrooms, arugula, and roll tops.

Horseradish-spiked roast beef and arugula sandwiches

MAKES 2; CAN BE DOUBLED *Pair the sandwiches with tomato wedges tossed with a little red wine vinaigrette. Use any leftover horseradish cream to top baked potatoes.*

4½ tablespoons sour cream
1½ tablespoons prepared white horseradish
1½ teaspoons chopped fresh thyme

2 ciabatta or large crusty rolls, cut in half horizontally
8 ounces thinly sliced cooked roast beef
4 thin sweet onion slices (preferably Vidalia or Maui)
2 arugula bunches, stems trimmed

STIR sour cream, horseradish, and thyme in small bowl to blend. Season dressing to taste with salt and pepper. Let stand 5 minutes or cover and refrigerate up to 3 hours.

ARRANGE rolls, cut sides up, on work surface; spread with dressing. Arrange half of roast beef on roll bottoms. Sprinkle beef with salt and pepper. Top with onion slices, then arugula and roll tops, dressing side down. Press lightly to compact.

Grouper sandwiches with wasabi coleslaw

MAKES 4 *The fried fish sandwich gets an Asian make-over. Running short on time? Use a cabbage slaw mix instead of cutting up the cabbage yourself. Look for panko and rice vinegar in the Asian foods section of the supermarket and at Asian markets. Wasabi mayonnaise can be found in the supermarket's condiment aisle, or you can make it yourself by mixing ¼ cup mayonnaise with 1½ teaspoons wasabi paste (green Asian horseradish paste sold in tubes or at the sushi counter).*

2 cups thinly sliced red cabbage

¼ cup wasabi mayonnaise

2 tablespoons unseasoned rice vinegar

4 5-ounce grouper fillets or other firm white fish (such as mahi-mahi)

½ cup panko (Japanese breadcrumbs) or fresh breadcrumbs made from crustless French bread

3 tablespoons vegetable oil

4 sesame-seed sandwich buns, split, toasted
   Lemon wedges

TOSS cabbage, wasabi mayonnaise, and vinegar in medium bowl to blend; season to taste with salt and pepper. Let coleslaw stand 15 minutes. Sprinkle fish fillets on both sides with salt and pepper. Place panko in shallow dish. Dredge fish in panko, turning to coat evenly.

HEAT oil in heavy large nonstick skillet over medium-high heat. Add fish and sauté until golden brown and just opaque in center, about 4 minutes per side. Place 1 bun bottom on each of 4 plates. Top each with fish. Squeeze lemon over fish, then spoon slaw over. Cover with bun tops.

Open-face crab and artichoke melts

MAKES 8 *The crab salad can be made in the morning, then baked and broiled just before serving.*

2 cups freshly grated Parmesan cheese (about 6 ounces)

1½ cups mayonnaise

1⅓ cups chopped onion (about 1 medium)

12 ounces fresh crabmeat, picked over, patted dry

1 13- to 14-ounce can quartered artichoke hearts in water, drained, chopped

½ cup plus 2 tablespoons chopped fresh Italian parsley

8 ¾-inch-thick slices sourdough bread (each about 5×3 inches)

8 plum tomatoes, sliced

8 ounces Monterey Jack cheese, thinly sliced

COMBINE first 5 ingredients and ½ cup parsley in large bowl; stir to blend. Transfer crab mixture to 8×8×2-inch glass baking dish.

DO AHEAD *Can be prepared 6 hours ahead. Cover and refrigerate.*

PREHEAT oven to 400°F. Bake crab mixture uncovered until bubbling and heated through, about 25 minutes.

PREHEAT broiler. Place bread in single layer on large baking sheet. Divide hot crab mixture among bread slices (using generous ½ cup each). Top with tomato slices, then cheese. Broil sandwiches until cheese melts, watching carefully to avoid burning, about 2 minutes. Transfer to plates and sprinkle with remaining 2 tablespoons parsley.

Oyster po'boys

MAKES 2 *Americans have no shortage of names for giant sandwiches—submarines, heroes, hoagies, grinders, and, in Louisiana, po'boys. The classic po'boy is stuffed with fried seafood, like the oysters in this recipe.*

¼ cup mayonnaise

2 teaspoons fresh lemon juice

1 teaspoon minced lemon peel

2 long French rolls, split horizontally, lightly toasted

Vegetable oil (for frying)

⅓ cup yellow cornmeal

¼ teaspoon cayenne pepper

1 8-ounce can oysters, drained, cut into 1-inch pieces

1 cup shredded iceberg lettuce

STIR mayonnaise, lemon juice, and lemon peel in small bowl to blend. Season to taste with salt and pepper. Pull out some bread from bottom half of each roll to form shallow pocket. Spread mayonnaise in pockets.

POUR oil into medium skillet to depth of ¼ inch. Heat 5 minutes over medium heat. Blend cornmeal and cayenne in small bowl; sprinkle with salt and pepper. Roll oysters in cornmeal mixture to coat. Fry oysters until golden brown, about 2 minutes per side. Transfer oysters to paper towel to drain.

ARRANGE oysters in bottom halves of rolls. Top with shredded lettuce and roll tops.

Mini grilled tuna, prosciutto, and lemon sandwiches

MAKES 15 *These little grilled sandwiches are perfect party fare. Serve with beer or a dry Fumé Blanc.*

1 6-ounce can albacore tuna, drained

5 tablespoons mayonnaise

2 tablespoons minced onion

2 tablespoons minced dill pickle

½ teaspoon Dijon mustard

30 ½-inch-thick slices sourdough baguette (cut from one 22- to 24-inch-long baguette)

4 ounces chilled Fontina or mozzarella cheese, cut into 1/16-inch-thick slices

5 very thin slices prosciutto, each cut crosswise into thirds

15 paper-thin lemon slices (cut from 2 to 3 lemons)

5 tablespoons (about) butter, room temperature, divided

COMBINE first 5 ingredients in medium bowl; stir to blend. Season to taste with salt and pepper.

ARRANGE 15 bread slices on work surface. Top with half of cheese, trimming cheese to fit. Cover each with 1 piece of prosciutto, 1 lemon slice, 1 tablespoon tuna mixture, and remaining cheese, trimming cheese to fit again. Top each with 1 remaining bread slice. Generously spread both sides of sandwiches with butter.

DO AHEAD *Sandwiches can be prepared 2 hours ahead. Cover and chill.*

MELT 2 tablespoons butter in heavy large skillet over medium-high heat. Working in batches, add sandwiches to skillet and sauté until cheese melts and bread is golden brown, adding more butter as necessary, about 1 minute per side. Transfer sandwiches to platter.

Cal-Asian seared tuna sandwiches

MAKES 4 *Cooking the tuna quickly over high heat locks in the juices, keeping the fish tender and moist.*

- ½ cup mayonnaise
- 3 tablespoons finely chopped green onions
- 2 teaspoons minced peeled fresh ginger
- 1 teaspoon soy sauce
- 1 teaspoon Asian sesame oil
- 8 ½-inch-thick slices country white bread
- ½ medium unpeeled English hothouse cucumber, thinly sliced
- 8 radishes, thinly sliced
- 1 ripe avocado, halved, pitted, peeled, sliced

- 4 ¾-inch-thick tuna steaks (each about 5 ounces)
- 1 tablespoon vegetable oil

COMBINE first 5 ingredients in small bowl; stir to blend. Arrange all bread slices on work surface. Spread with mayonnaise mixture. Top 4 bread slices with cucumber, radishes, then avocado. Sprinkle with salt and pepper.

SPRINKLE tuna with salt and pepper. Heat vegetable oil in heavy large skillet over medium-high heat. Add tuna and cook to desired doneness, about 2 minutes per side for medium-rare.

PLACE tuna on sandwiches. Top with remaining bread slices, mayonnaise side down. Transfer sandwiches to plates and cut in half.

Italian sausage meatball heroes

MAKES 4 *Fresh marinara sauce is the key to these hearty sandwiches. Look for it in the refrigerated section of the supermarket, near the cheese and fresh pasta. Serve with a cold beer (and pass the remote control).*

- 1 pound spicy or sweet Italian sausages, casings removed
- 1 23- to 24-ounce container purchased fresh marinara sauce, divided
- ½ cup freshly grated Parmesan cheese (about 1½ ounces)
- ⅓ cup chopped fresh Italian parsley, divided
- ⅓ cup chopped fresh basil, divided

- 4 5- to 6-inch-long pieces baguette, split horizontally
- 1 cup (packed) coarsely grated whole-milk mozzarella cheese (about 4 ounces)

PREHEAT oven to 400°F. Mix sausages, ½ cup marinara, Parmesan, 2 tablespoons parsley, and 2 tablespoons basil in large bowl. Using wet hands, shape mixture into 8 meatballs. Bring 2 tablespoons parsley, 2 tablespoons basil, remaining marinara, and meatballs to boil in large skillet. Cover, reduce heat, and simmer until meatballs are cooked through, turning often, about 20 minutes.

PLACE baguette bottoms on baking sheet; spread each with about 2 tablespoons sauce from skillet. Cut meatballs in half in skillet; overlap 4 halves on each baguette bottom. Spoon remaining sauce over meatballs, then sprinkle mozzarella over. Bake until cheese melts, about 5 minutes. Sprinkle with remaining parsley and basil. Cover with baguette tops and serve immediately.

BURGERS

Grilled mustard-dill burgers

MAKES 2; CAN BE DOUBLED *Mixing sour cream, Dijon mustard, and dill into the ground beef gives the hamburger patties a fresh tang.*

> 3 tablespoons sour cream
> 3 tablespoons Dijon mustard
> 1½ tablespoons chopped fresh dill
> 10 ounces lean ground beef
>
> 2 hamburger buns, split
> 2 tomato slices
> 2 Bibb lettuce leaves

PREPARE barbecue (medium-high heat). Combine first 3 ingredients in medium bowl; stir to blend. Transfer 3 tablespoons sauce to small bowl and reserve. Add meat to remaining sauce in medium bowl and mix gently. Divide meat mixture into 2 equal portions. Flatten each to ½-inch-thick patty; sprinkle on both sides with salt and pepper.

GRILL cut sides of buns until toasted, about 1 minute. Transfer to work surface, cut side up. Grill patties to desired doneness, about 4 minutes per side for medium. Spread bottom half of buns with reserved sauce. Top each with burger, tomato, lettuce, and bun top.

Burgers 101

— For the juiciest burgers, start with ground beef that contains 20 percent fat.

— For tender burgers, don't overwork the meat. Mix in seasonings gently, form into patties, and stop.

— Because burgers will shrink in diameter as they cook, make the patties larger than the buns or bread you plan to use.

— Burgers naturally puff up in the center as they cook. If you prefer a flatter patty, gently press your fingers or a small glass into the center of an *uncooked* burger, forming a slight indention.

— Resist the temptation to squish the burgers with a spatula while they cook. You'll push out all the delicious juices.

— Before you put the burgers on the grill or in the pan, prepare the buns and any condiments or toppings. That way, the burgers can be assembled quickly and served hot, when they're at their best.

Cheddar cheese-stuffed burgers

MAKES 2; CAN BE DOUBLED *Who says the cheese has to be on the outside of a burger? Here, grated cheddar is stuffed inside the ground beef before the burgers hit the grill. English muffins make a fun alternative to regular buns.*

10 ounces ground sirloin or lean ground beef
⅓ cup finely chopped red onion
¼ cup chopped fresh parsley
2 teaspoons Worcestershire sauce
¼ teaspoon salt
¼ teaspoon pepper
½ cup (packed) coarsely grated sharp cheddar cheese (about 2 ounces)

2 large (about 4-inch-diameter) English muffins, split horizontally

PREPARE barbecue (medium-high heat). Combine first 6 ingredients in medium bowl; blend well. Divide meat mixture into 2 equal portions. Shape each into ball. Poke deep hole in each ball and fill each with half of cheese. Mold meat around cheese to enclose. Flatten each filled burger to ¾-inch-thick patty.

GRILL muffin halves until beginning to color, about 1 minute per side; transfer to work surface, cut side up. Grill burgers to desired doneness, about 5 minutes per side for medium. Place burgers on muffin bottoms. Cover with tops.

BEYOND THE BUN This recipe uses large English muffins instead of hamburger buns, but there's no need to stop there. Focaccia, ciabatta, pita bread, dinner rolls, and even thick slices of rustic bread would be great alternatives to the traditional bun.

Sun-dried tomato burgers with balsamic-glazed onions

MAKES 8 *For juicy, flavorful burgers, ground chuck is one of the best choices.*

3 pounds ground beef
1⅓ cups chopped drained oil-packed sun-dried tomatoes, 6 tablespoons oil reserved, divided
½ cup grated onion
¼ cup chopped fresh basil
2 teaspoons ground cumin
1½ teaspoons salt
¾ teaspoon ground black pepper

3 onions, halved, thinly sliced
¼ cup balsamic vinegar

8 hamburger buns, split, toasted

LINE large baking sheet with parchment paper. Combine beef, tomatoes, 2 tablespoons reserved tomato oil, and next 5 ingredients in large bowl; blend well. Shape mixture into eight ¾-inch-thick patties. Transfer patties to prepared baking sheet. Cover with plastic wrap and refrigerate at least 1 hour.

DO AHEAD *Can be made 4 hours ahead. Keep chilled.*

HEAT remaining 4 tablespoons reserved tomato oil in heavy large skillet over medium-high heat. Add onions and sauté until soft and starting to brown, about 10 minutes. Add vinegar; sprinkle with salt and pepper. Sauté until onions are deep brown, stirring occasionally, about 10 minutes. Remove from heat.

DO AHEAD *Can be prepared 4 hours ahead. Let stand at room temperature. Place skillet at edge of grill and rewarm onions before serving.*

PREPARE barbecue (medium-high heat). Grill burgers until cooked to desired doneness, about 5 minutes per side for medium. Place 1 burger on bottom half of each bun. Top with onions and bun tops.

Mustard seed–crusted burgers with horseradish slaw

MAKES 4 *To make the topping a true slaw, use a purchased cabbage slaw mix instead of sliced iceberg lettuce. Make this burger deluxe by adding sliced onion and tomato and a few strips of crispy bacon.*

½ cup mayonnaise

½ cup sour cream

3 tablespoons prepared white horseradish

1⅓ pounds ground beef

¼ cup yellow mustard seeds (about 2 ounces), coarsely crushed

1 tablespoon vegetable oil

4 kaiser rolls, halved horizontally

3 cups (about 6 ounces) thinly sliced iceberg lettuce

WHISK mayonnaise, sour cream, and horseradish in medium bowl to blend for dressing. Season to taste with salt and pepper.

SHAPE beef into four ½-inch-thick burgers; sprinkle both sides with salt and pepper. Spread mustard seeds on small plate. Press both sides of burgers firmly into mustard seeds to coat.

HEAT oil in heavy large skillet over medium-high heat. Add burgers and sauté to desired doneness, about 3 minutes per side for medium. Arrange roll bottoms on each of 4 plates. Transfer burgers to roll bottoms. Stir lettuce into dressing; mound atop hamburgers. Cover with roll tops.

GRIND IT UP To crush the mustard seeds, use a mortar and pestle, or place the seeds in a heavy-duty resealable plastic bag and crush with a mallet or the bottom of a heavy pan.

Beef and Gorgonzola burgers

MAKES 2; CAN BE DOUBLED *In this take on the classic beef and blue cheese combo, Gorgonzola is stuffed inside the burgers. To prevent the cheese from leaking out, be sure to securely seal the edges of the hamburger patties.*

12 ounces ground chuck

2 ounces Gorgonzola cheese or other blue cheese

Vegetable oil

4 ½-inch-thick slices country white bread

2 large tomato slices

4 thin slices red onion

½ bunch arugula

SHAPE beef into four 3-inch-diameter patties. Form cheese into two 1½-inch rounds; place cheese atop two beef patties. Top each with another beef patty, sealing at edges. Sprinkle burgers with pepper.

PREPARE barbecue (medium-high heat) or preheat broiler. Brush barbecue rack with oil. Grill bread slices until lightly toasted, about 1 minute per side; place on plates. Grill burgers to desired doneness, about 4 minutes per side for medium. Place burgers on 2 bread slices. Top with tomato, onion, arugula, and another bread slice.

Grilled burgers with Argentinean parsley sauce

MAKES 2; CAN BE DOUBLED *The sauce is inspired by* chimichurri, *the fresh and tangy condiment that's popular in Argentina. Since these are "bunless" burgers, toss some sliced parboiled potatoes on the grill and brush with a little sauce to serve alongside.*

3	tablespoons chopped fresh parsley
2	tablespoons olive oil
1	tablespoon red wine vinegar
1	large garlic clove, chopped
1	teaspoon chopped fresh oregano
½	teaspoon cayenne pepper, divided
12	ounces lean ground beef
½	teaspoon salt

PREPARE barbecue (medium-high heat). Whisk parsley, oil, vinegar, garlic, oregano, and ¼ teaspoon cayenne in small bowl to blend. Season sauce to taste with salt.

COMBINE beef, salt, and remaining ¼ teaspoon cayenne in medium bowl; blend well. Shape beef into two 1-inch-thick patties. Grill burgers until cooked to desired doneness, about 5 minutes per side for medium.

TRANSFER to plates. Spoon sauce over.

Turkey and fresh tarragon cheeseburgers

MAKES 2; CAN BE DOUBLED *Here's a simple recipe for a moist, flavorful turkey burger—the rest is up to you. Serve it on a bun or on a plate with a salad alongside. Top with your favorite cheese (cheddar or Gruyère would be delicious) and anything else you like (tomato slices, pickles, mayo, or mustard).*

⅔	cup fresh sourdough breadcrumbs, made from 1 large crustless slice
2	tablespoons minced shallots
4	teaspoons olive oil
1	tablespoon minced fresh tarragon
¼	teaspoon (generous) salt
¼	teaspoon freshly ground black pepper
10	ounces ground turkey
	Olive oil
	Sliced Gouda or other cheese
	Red onion slices

MIX first 6 ingredients in medium bowl. Add ground turkey and blend gently. Shape mixture into two ½-inch-thick patties.

POUR thin layer of oil into heavy medium skillet; heat over medium heat. Add patties, cover, and sauté until just cooked through, about 3 minutes per side. Top each patty with cheese; cover skillet and cook just until cheese melts, about 1 minute. Transfer to plates. Top with onion slices.

Spicy turkey burgers

MAKES 4 *Ground turkey gets a hit of flavor from salsa, shallots, cilantro, and cumin, and heat from the chipotle sauce. If you prefer cheeseburgers, just before the burgers are finished, top with slices of pepper Jack cheese and cover the pan until the cheese melts. To continue the Tex-Mex theme, serve with chilled Mexican beer, such as Bohemia.*

1¼	pounds ground turkey
1	cup mild salsa, divided
½	cup finely chopped shallots
¼	cup chopped fresh cilantro
4	tablespoons vegetable oil, divided
1	tablespoon chipotle-flavored hot sauce
1	teaspoon ground cumin
1	teaspoon salt
½	teaspoon ground black pepper
4	crusty rolls, halved horizontally, toasted if desired
4	lettuce leaves

MIX ground turkey, ½ cup salsa, shallots, cilantro, 3 tablespoons oil, and next 4 ingredients in large bowl. Shape turkey mixture into four 3½- to 4-inch-diameter patties.

HEAT remaining 1 tablespoon oil in large nonstick skillet over medium-high heat. Add burgers; sauté until brown, about 3 minutes per side. Reduce heat to low. Sauté until burgers are cooked through, turning occasionally, about 4 minutes longer.

ARRANGE roll bottoms on 4 plates. Place lettuce, then burgers on roll bottoms. Top each burger with 2 tablespoons of remaining salsa, then roll tops.

Open-face turkey burgers with Gruyère, mushrooms, and arugula salad

MAKES 2 *Any kind of mushroom—or a mix of several different kinds—would be great with this burger.*

10	ounces ground turkey
3	tablespoons olive oil, divided
½	teaspoon (scant) salt
¼	teaspoon ground black pepper
2	slices country white bread, toasted Mayonnaise
8	ounces mushrooms, sliced
2	shallots, sliced
1	large garlic clove, chopped
2	thin slices Gruyère cheese
1	teaspoon white wine vinegar
1	cup thinly sliced arugula

MIX turkey, 1 teaspoon oil, salt, and pepper in medium bowl. Shape into two ½-inch-thick patties. Place 1 toasted bread slice on each of 2 plates; spread each with mayonnaise.

HEAT 2 tablespoons oil in large nonstick skillet over medium-high heat. Add mushrooms, shallots, and garlic; sauté 2 minutes, then push to side of skillet. Add turkey patties to other side of skillet. Cook until brown on bottom, about 4 minutes. Turn patties over; top with cheese. Cook until patties are cooked through, cheese melts, and mushrooms are brown, stirring mushrooms often, about 4 minutes. Season mushrooms to taste with salt and pepper.

MEANWHILE, whisk vinegar and remaining 2 teaspoons oil in small bowl; mix in arugula. Sprinkle with salt and pepper.

SPOON mushrooms onto bread; top with patties and arugula salad.

Spicy turkey sloppy joes

MAKES 6 *This all-American sandwich has been around for more than 70 years. And there's a reason it persists: It's delicious. The messy treat gets a lighter spin here, with ground turkey and a topping of greens.*

3	tablespoons olive oil
1½	pounds ground turkey
1	large green bell pepper, chopped
4	large garlic cloves, chopped
3	tablespoons chili powder
1¼	cups ale or beer
¾	cup chili sauce or ketchup
1	4-ounce can diced green chiles
2	tablespoons Worcestershire sauce
1	cup finely chopped green onions
6	sourdough rolls, split, toasted
2	cups thinly sliced romaine lettuce or packaged garden salad mix

HEAT oil in heavy large pot over medium-high heat. Add turkey, green pepper, and garlic and sauté until turkey is no longer pink, breaking up meat with back of fork, about 10 minutes. Mix in chili powder; stir 1 minute. Add next 4 ingredients. Reduce heat to medium-low and simmer until mixture thickens, stirring often, about 15 minutes. Mix in green onions; season to taste with salt and pepper.

ARRANGE roll bottoms on plates. Spoon sloppy joe mixture over; top with lettuce and roll tops.

Minted lamb burgers with feta and hummus

MAKES 4 *Lamb's classic partner, mint, is incorporated into the burger. To enjoy these at their juicy best, cook only until medium-rare.*

1½	pounds ground lamb
½	cup minced fresh mint
2	garlic cloves, pressed
1	tablespoon paprika
1	teaspoon salt
½	teaspoon cayenne pepper
¼	teaspoon ground cinnamon
1	tablespoon olive oil
1	7- to 8-ounce block feta cheese, sliced thinly
4	kaiser rolls, split, lightly toasted
8	onion slices
4	romaine lettuce leaves
	Purchased hummus

COMBINE first 7 ingredients in medium bowl; blend gently. Shape mixture into four 4-inch-diameter patties. Heat oil in heavy large skillet over medium-high heat. Add patties to skillet; cook until bottoms are well browned, about 3 minutes. Turn patties over and top each with feta cheese. Continue cooking to desired doneness, about 3 minutes longer for medium-rare.

PLACE roll bottoms on plates. Top each with 1 onion slice, burger, lettuce leaf, another onion slice, then hummus. Press on roll tops.

Salmon burgers with dill tartar sauce

MAKES 2 *Chilling the salmon patties for at least an hour makes them easier to handle.*

10 ounces skinless salmon fillet, cut into 1-inch pieces
3 tablespoons plus ½ cup purchased tartar sauce
2 tablespoons chopped fresh dill, divided
¼ teaspoon salt
¼ teaspoon ground black pepper

1 teaspoon (packed) finely grated lemon peel
2 sesame seed rolls, split
Red onion slices
4 Bibb lettuce leaves

PLACE salmon pieces, 3 tablespoons tartar sauce, 1 tablespoon dill, salt, and pepper in processor. Blend using on/off turns until coarsely ground. Shape mixture into two ½-inch-thick patties.

DO AHEAD *Can be made 6 hours ahead. Cover and refrigerate.*

PREPARE barbecue (medium-high heat). Whisk ½ cup tartar sauce, remaining 1 tablespoon dill, and lemon peel in medium bowl to blend. Grill rolls until toasted, about 1 minute per side. Transfer to 2 plates and spread bottom halves generously with sauce. Grill patties until just opaque in center, about 2 minutes per side. Place burgers atop sauce on rolls. Top each with onion slices, 2 lettuce leaves, and top half of roll. Serve, passing remaining sauce separately.

Tuna burgers Niçoise

MAKES 4 *A handheld version of the classic French salad. Serve with glasses of rosé.*

1 10-ounce russet potato, pierced several times with fork
½ cup mayonnaise, divided
5 teaspoons Dijon mustard
½ teaspoon salt
¼ teaspoon pepper
½ cup finely chopped fresh basil, divided
¼ cup diced pitted Kalamata olives
4 teaspoons chopped capers
1 pound skinless boneless fresh tuna steaks, finely chopped

Nonstick vegetable oil spray

4 3-inch-long pieces French bread, each cut horizontally in thirds, centers discarded
4 tomato slices

COOK potato in microwave until tender, about 5 minutes per side. Peel potato; mash enough to measure ¼ cup (packed).

PLACE ¼ cup mashed potato in bowl. Mix in ¼ cup mayonnaise, mustard, salt, and pepper, then ¼ cup basil, olives, and capers. Add tuna and combine gently. Shape into four 1-inch-thick patties. Mix remaining ¼ cup mayonnaise and ¼ cup basil in small bowl.

PREPARE barbecue (medium-high heat). Spray both sides of burgers with nonstick spray; grill until just opaque in center, about 4 minutes per side.

SPREAD basil mayonnaise on bread bottoms. Top with burgers, tomatoes, and bread tops.

Portobello burgers and spinach salad with red pepper mayonnaise

MAKES 4 *Portobello mushrooms are the steak of the vegetable kingdom. And they are "meaty" enough to make a substantial burger.*

½   **cup chopped drained roasted red peppers from jar**

¼   **cup mayonnaise**

1   **garlic clove, chopped**

⅛   **teaspoon cayenne pepper**

    Nonstick vegetable oil spray

4   **large portobello mushrooms, stems removed**

4   **½-inch-thick red onion slices**

4   **½-inch-thick crusty country bread slices (each about 5×3 inches)**

2   **tablespoons unseasoned rice vinegar**

4   **cups (packed) baby spinach leaves (about 4 ounces)**

BLEND first 4 ingredients in processor until smooth. Season mayonnaise to taste with salt and pepper.

SPRAY grill with nonstick spray and prepare barbecue (medium heat). Spray mushrooms and onion slices with nonstick spray; sprinkle with salt and pepper. Grill mushrooms, onion, and bread until vegetables are tender and bread is golden, turning often, about 12 minutes for vegetables and 5 minutes for bread.

MEANWHILE, transfer 2 tablespoons red pepper mayonnaise to large bowl; whisk in vinegar. Add spinach and toss to coat. Divide salad among 4 plates. Place 1 bread slice on each salad. Top bread with 1 mushroom, 1 onion slice, and 2 tablespoons red pepper mayonnaise.

A world of burgers Give the classic ground beef patty an international flavor with these easy additions.

ITALIAN: Brush radicchio wedges with a little olive oil and balsamic vinegar; grill until slightly wilted. Chop coarsely and place atop burgers, along with some Parmesan cheese shavings and a few fresh basil leaves.

SPANISH: Toss some red bell peppers onto the grill; cook until tender. While the peppers are cooking, mix some chopped garlic and a little hot smoked paprika into mayonnaise.

FRENCH: Top burgers with garlic mayo (also known as aioli) and Roquefort cheese.

ASIAN: Brush shiitake mushrooms with a little soy sauce; grill until tender. Add mushrooms to burger, along with mayo that's been mixed with wasabi, sesame oil, and chopped fresh cilantro.

PIZZAS

White four-cheese pizza with basil and garlic

MAKES 32 PIECES *White pizza (sometimes called* pizza bianca*) is basically pizza without the tomato sauce. Instead of cutting the pizza into small appetizer squares, you could slice it into larger pieces and serve with a salad for lunch.*

- 3 **tablespoons extra-virgin olive oil, divided**
- 1 **garlic clove, minced**

- 1 **13.8-ounce tube refrigerated pizza dough**
  All purpose flour
- 6 **ounces fresh mozzarella cheese,
  cut into ¼- to ⅓-inch cubes**
- 3 **ounces soft fresh goat cheese, crumbled**
- ½ **cup part-skim ricotta cheese**
- 3 **tablespoons freshly grated Parmesan cheese**
- 3 **tablespoons thinly sliced fresh basil**

POSITION rack in center of oven and preheat to 450°F. Brush 13×9×2-inch metal baking pan with 1 tablespoon oil. Mix remaining 2 tablespoons oil and garlic in small bowl.

ROLL out pizza dough on lightly floured work surface to 14×10-inch rectangle. Transfer dough to prepared pan, pushing dough slightly up sides. Brush dough with some of garlic oil. Top with mozzarella cheese and goat cheese, leaving ½-inch plain border. Crumble ricotta cheese over, then sprinkle with Parmesan cheese.

BAKE pizza until crust is golden brown and cheeses melt, about 18 minutes. Drizzle remaining garlic oil over. Let stand 3 minutes.

DO AHEAD *Can be made 4 hours ahead. Let stand at room temperature. Rewarm in 350°F oven until heated through, about 10 minutes, before serving.*

CUT pizza crosswise into 8 strips, then cut each strip crosswise into 4 pieces. Sprinkle with basil. Transfer to platter and serve hot.

Bell pepper, red onion, and goat cheese pizza with thyme

2 TO 4 SERVINGS *Using a purchased, prebaked crust cuts down on both prep time and cooking time.*

- ¼ **cup olive oil**
- 1 **large red onion, thinly sliced**
- 6 **large garlic cloves, thinly sliced**
- ½ **large red bell pepper, thinly sliced**
- ½ **large yellow or green bell pepper, thinly sliced**
- ¼ **teaspoon dried crushed red pepper**

- 1 **14-ounce purchased fully baked pizza crust**
- 5 **ounces soft goat cheese, crumbled**
- 1 **tablespoon fresh thyme leaves**

PREHEAT oven to 450°F. Heat oil in heavy large skillet over medium-low heat. Add onion and garlic; sauté until very soft, about 20 minutes. Add bell peppers; sauté 5 minutes. Mix in crushed red pepper. Sprinkle with salt and pepper.

PLACE crust on large baking sheet; brush with some oil from skillet. Top with onion-pepper mixture. Sprinkle with cheese and thyme. Bake until crust is crisp and topping is heated through, about 12 minutes. Cut into wedges.

Radicchio, Fontina, and goat cheese pizza

6 SERVINGS *For a meatier version, sprinkle some chopped pancetta (Italian bacon) over this pie before it goes in the oven. If the goat cheese is very cold, it will be easier to crumble.*

1½ **tablespoons olive oil**

2 **large garlic cloves, finely chopped**

3 **cups ½-inch-wide strips radicchio (about 4 ounces)**

1¼ **cups (packed) coarsely grated Fontina cheese (about 5 ounces)**

1 **cup thinly sliced fresh fennel (from 1 medium bulb)**

½ **cup sliced drained roasted red peppers from jar**

1 **10-ounce purchased fully baked thin pizza crust**

⅔ **cup crumbled soft fresh goat cheese (about 3 ounces)**

Parmesan cheese shavings (optional)

POSITION rack in center of oven and preheat to 425°F. Whisk oil and garlic in large bowl to blend. Add radicchio, Fontina, fennel, and roasted peppers and toss to coat; sprinkle with salt and pepper. Place crust on rimless baking sheet. Mound radicchio mixture on crust, leaving ¾-inch plain border. Top with crumbled goat cheese. Bake pizza until crust is crisp and topping is heated through, about 13 minutes. Sprinkle with Parmesan shavings, if desired. Cut pizza into wedges and serve.

Pizza perfection A few tips on making the perfect pie:

— To start shaping the dough, hold a disk of dough vertically and let gravity pull it down. Turn the dough slowly like a wheel, letting it stretch out to a more uniform round.

— Use a lightly floured rolling pin to roll the pizza dough to its designated shape and size. Fresh yeasted pizza dough is often very elastic, so it tends to spring back and resist rolling. If this happens, let the dough rest for a few minutes and then roll again or pull and stretch the dough gently with your hands.

— Check the pizza while it bakes. If it's cooking unevenly, rotate the pan.

— The pizza is done when the toppings are sizzling and the crust is crisp and deep golden brown. Near the end of the baking time, lift up a corner of the crust with a spatula to make sure the bottom is fully cooked.

— A pizza wheel can drag the toppings as it cuts. To make sure toppings stay put, use a large chef's knife instead.

— If you're not a fan of cold pizza, reheat leftovers in a 300°F oven until just warm. Don't use the microwave to reheat pizza. It will make the dough dry and tough.

Tomato-mozzarella pizza with phyllo crust

MAKES 15 PIECES *In this recipe, crispy phyllo dough takes the place of a traditional crust. Cut into smaller pieces and serve as an appetizer or slice into larger squares to serve as an entrée.*

- 6 tablespoons (¾ stick) butter, melted
- 8 sheets fresh phyllo pastry or frozen, thawed (each about 18×13 inches)
- 8 tablespoons grated Parmesan cheese, divided
- 1¾ cups (packed) coarsely grated mozzarella cheese (about 6 ounces)
- 1 medium onion, thinly sliced
- 1½ pounds plum tomatoes, sliced into rounds
- 1 tablespoon chopped fresh oregano
- 1 teaspoon chopped fresh thyme

PREHEAT oven to 375°F. Brush 15×10×1-inch baking sheet with butter. Place 1 phyllo sheet in prepared pan (edges of phyllo may go up sides). Brush phyllo with butter; sprinkle with 1 tablespoon Parmesan cheese. Repeat layering with remaining phyllo, butter, and Parmesan cheese. Top with even layers of mozzarella cheese and onion, then tomatoes. Sprinkle with oregano and thyme.

BAKE pizza until crust is crisp and golden brown at edges, cheeses melt, and tomatoes are tender, about 30 minutes. Let stand 5 minutes. Cut pizza into squares and serve hot.

Fast deep-dish pepperoni pizza

8 SERVINGS *Serve this hearty pizza with a fork and knife. Instead of using only mozzarella, try a blend of Fontina, mozzarella, and Parmesan.*

- 2 28-ounce cans plum tomatoes, drained
- 2 tablespoons chopped fresh parsley
- 2 large garlic cloves, pressed
- 1½ teaspoons dried oregano, crumbled
- 1 teaspoon dried basil
- 3 teaspoons olive oil, divided
  Cornmeal
- 1 1-pound loaf frozen bread dough, thawed
- 1 pound coarsely grated mozzarella cheese (about 4 cups packed)
- 7 ounces thinly sliced pepperoni
- ½ cup freshly grated Parmesan cheese

PREHEAT oven to 425°F. Coarsely chop tomatoes. Place in strainer and drain well. Combine tomatoes, parsley, garlic, oregano, and basil in medium bowl. Brush 12-inch-diameter deep-dish pizza pan with 1 teaspoon oil; sprinkle with cornmeal. Roll bread dough out on lightly floured surface to 13-inch round. Transfer dough to prepared pan, pressing 1 inch up pan sides. Spread dough with 1 cup tomato mixture. Sprinkle half of mozzarella over. Top with half of pepperoni and remaining tomato mixture, then remaining mozzarella and pepperoni. Sprinkle with Parmesan. Drizzle with remaining 2 teaspoons oil.

BAKE pizza until cheese bubbles and begins to brown and crust is golden brown, about 40 minutes.

CHEFS' CHOICE Many chefs swear by the full, rich flavor of Italian San Marzano plum tomatoes grown in the San Marzano valley of Campania (the home of pizza). These tomatoes are tart and firm with very few seeds. They are available canned at some supermarkets and specialty foods stores.

Goat cheese and asparagus pizza

2 SERVINGS; CAN BE DOUBLED *To trim asparagus, bend the stalk. It will naturally break between the tender top and the woody bottom.*

- 6 asparagus spears, trimmed, halved lengthwise, cut into 1½-inch pieces
- 3 tablespoons extra-virgin olive oil
- 1 13.8-ounce tube refrigerated pizza dough
- 1 14.5-ounce can diced tomatoes with Italian seasonings, drained
- 1 5.5-ounce log soft fresh goat cheese
- 3 tablespoons chopped fresh marjoram
- ¼ teaspoon dried crushed red pepper

PREHEAT oven to 400°F. Toss asparagus and oil in medium bowl to coat. Unroll pizza dough on large baking sheet, forming 12×8-inch rectangle. Spoon tomatoes over dough, leaving ¾-inch plain border. Scatter asparagus with oil over tomatoes.

BAKE pizza 7 minutes. Remove from oven. Crumble goat cheese over pizza. Sprinkle with marjoram and crushed red pepper. Bake until crust is crisp and golden around edges, about 9 minutes longer.

GOING GREEN Make this a green party: Start with small bowls of green pea soup sprinkled with chives, serve the pizza with an arugula and endive salad, and finish with pistachio gelato.

Artichoke and feta cheese pizza

2 SERVINGS; CAN BE DOUBLED *The mint is sprinkled on the pizza just before serving to preserve its fresh sweetness (and to keep its bright green color).*

- 1 6.5-ounce jar marinated artichoke hearts, drained, 2 tablespoons marinade reserved
- 1 tablespoon cornmeal
- 1 13.8-ounce tube refrigerated pizza dough
- 6 ounces plum tomatoes, thinly sliced into rounds
- 1 cup crumbled herb-seasoned feta cheese (about 4 ounces)
- ½ medium sweet onion (such as Vidalia or Maui), thinly sliced
- 2 tablespoons thinly sliced fresh mint

PREHEAT oven to 425°F. Cut artichokes into ½-inch pieces. Sprinkle large baking sheet with cornmeal. Unroll pizza dough on prepared sheet. Stretch and press dough to 11-inch square; brush with 1 tablespoon reserved marinade. Top dough with artichokes, tomatoes, feta cheese, and onion. Drizzle with remaining 1 tablespoon marinade.

BAKE pizza until crust is crisp and golden, about 15 minutes. Transfer to platter. Sprinkle with mint. Cut pizza into 4 squares.

Potato, sage, and rosemary pizza

4 MAIN-COURSE SERVINGS *The potatoes are sautéed briefly before being put on the pizza to make sure they'll be tender when the pizza is finished baking.*

3   tablespoons extra-virgin olive oil

12 ounces unpeeled small Yukon Gold
    potatoes, sliced into very thin rounds

1   13.8-ounce tube refrigerated pizza dough

2   teaspoons chopped fresh rosemary

2   teaspoons chopped fresh sage

2   garlic cloves, chopped

¼   teaspoon dried crushed red pepper

1   cup (packed) grated whole-milk
    mozzarella cheese (about 4 ounces)

½   cup freshly grated Parmesan cheese

PREHEAT oven to 400°F. Heat oil in heavy large skillet over medium heat. Add potato slices in single layer. Sauté until just tender, about 5 minutes. Cool briefly.

UNROLL dough on large rimmed baking sheet. Scatter potato slices over dough, leaving ¾-inch plain border. Sprinkle with rosemary, sage, garlic, and crushed red pepper. Sprinkle with cheeses to cover pizza.

BAKE pizza until crust is crisp and cheeses melt, about 20 minutes. Using metal spatula, loosen crust from sheet. Slide out onto platter or board.

GO FOR THE GOLD Yukon Gold potatoes have a thin skin and a light yellow interior. They have a buttery flavor, making them especially good when mashed.

Ricotta, pesto, and smoked salmon pizza

4 SERVINGS *You can use a purchased fully baked pizza crust with equally good results. Toss any leftover pesto with pasta for a quick dinner or spread it on toasted bread rounds for an instant appetizer.*

1   refrigerated pie crust (half of
    15-ounce package)

½   cup ricotta cheese

3   tablespoons purchased pesto

3   tablespoons pine nuts

3   ounces thinly sliced smoked salmon,
    cut into 1-inch pieces
    Fresh basil leaves

PREHEAT oven to 400°F. Lay pie crust in center of large baking sheet. Fold in ½ inch of crust edge. Stand up double edge and crimp decoratively, forming upright rim. Blend cheese and pesto in small bowl. Spread cheese mixture over crust. Sprinkle with pine nuts. Bake pizza until crust is cooked through and golden, about 18 minutes.

ARRANGE salmon pieces over pizza. Garnish with basil leaves.

Scampi and two-cheese pizza

4 SERVINGS *Shrimp sautéed with a little butter, garlic, and wine (a dish known as "shrimp scampi") tops this pizza. To keep the crust crisp, it's broiled before adding the shrimp, vegetables, and cheese toppings.*

1	14-ounce purchased fully baked pizza crust
5	tablespoons olive oil, divided
1	large garlic clove, minced
10	ounces uncooked large shrimp, peeled, deveined
2	tablespoons dry white wine
1	tablespoon chopped fresh parsley
2	tomatoes (about 10 ounces), seeded, chopped
2	green onions, chopped
½	cup (packed) shredded mozzarella cheese
¼	cup freshly grated Parmesan cheese

PREHEAT broiler. Brush crust with 1 tablespoon oil. Broil oiled side until browning in spots, about 1 minute. Turn crust over, brush with 1 tablespoon oil, and broil until beginning to crisp, about 1 minute. Transfer crust to large baking sheet, right side up.

PREHEAT oven to 425°F. Heat 1 tablespoon oil in heavy large skillet over medium-high heat. Add garlic and stir 30 seconds. Add shrimp and sauté 1 minute. Add wine and parsley and sauté until shrimp are almost opaque in center, about 1 minute. Using slotted spoon, transfer shrimp to plate. Boil juices in skillet 30 seconds; pour over shrimp.

MIX tomatoes and green onions in medium bowl. Stir in remaining 2 tablespoons oil; sprinkle with salt and pepper. Spoon vegetable mixture over crust. Top with shrimp and any juices. Sprinkle cheeses over.

BAKE pizza until cheeses melt and topping is heated through, about 7 minutes. Cut into wedges.

Fisherman's pizza bianca

2 SERVINGS; CAN BE DOUBLED *Clam pizza comes from New Haven, Connecticut, where the folks at Frank Pepe Pizzeria Napoletana claim to have invented this unusual pie. At Pepe's the pizza is made with fresh littleneck clams, but our version makes things easier by using canned clams.*

	All purpose flour
1	13.8-ounce tube refrigerated pizza dough
2	6.5-ounce cans chopped clams, well drained
1	tablespoon chopped garlic
½	teaspoon dried crushed red pepper
½	cup chopped fresh Italian parsley
⅓	cup grated Parmesan cheese
2	tablespoons extra-virgin olive oil

PREHEAT oven to 425°F. Lightly sprinkle large baking sheet with flour. Unfold dough on prepared sheet. Stretch dough to 13×10-inch rectangle. Sprinkle clams, garlic, crushed red pepper, then parsley and cheese over dough, leaving 1-inch plain border. Drizzle oil over.

BAKE pizza until crust is golden brown and crisp, about 12 minutes. Transfer pizza to work surface. Cut into squares and serve hot.

Tarragon pizza bianca

8 APPETIZER SERVINGS *Because Brie is a soft cheese, it's tricky to remove the rind or cut the wedge into small pieces. To make the job easier, place the Brie in the freezer for 15 minutes.*

- 6 tablespoons extra-virgin olive oil
- 2 13.8-ounce tubes refrigerated pizza dough
- 4 teaspoons chopped fresh tarragon
- 1⅓ cups (packed) grated whole-milk mozzarella cheese
- 1 medium fennel bulb, trimmed, very thinly sliced
- 1 small zucchini, very thinly sliced
- 1 small yellow crookneck squash, very thinly sliced
- 2 tablespoons minced shallot
- 4 ounces Brie, rind removed, cheese cut into ½-inch cubes

POSITION rack in bottom third of oven and preheat to 425°F. Brush large baking sheet with some of oil. Unroll dough onto floured surface. Cut each rectangle in half crosswise. Stretch each half to 8-inch square; transfer to prepared sheet. Brush 1 tablespoon oil over each; sprinkle each with 1 teaspoon tarragon. Top with mozzarella and vegetables. Drizzle with remaining oil. Sprinkle with shallot, salt, and pepper, then Brie.

BAKE pizzas until crusts are crisp and cheese is bubbling, about 14 minutes. Cut each into 6 pieces.

Lavash vegetarian pizza

6 SERVINGS *Lavash, a Middle Eastern flatbread, comes in large soft sheets and hard cracker-like varieties. Use soft lavash for this recipe. If you can't find it, use very large flour tortillas instead.*

- 1 soft lavash bread (about 18×12 inches)
- 3 tablespoons olive oil, divided
- ½ cup chopped pitted Kalamata olives
- 1 cup (packed) coarsely grated Monterey Jack cheese (about 4 ounces)
- 1¾ cups crumbled feta cheese (about 7 ounces)
- 1½ cups sliced mushrooms
- ½ cup diced red onion
- 1 cup diced green bell pepper
- 1 cup diced seeded plum tomatoes

PREHEAT broiler. Place lavash on large baking sheet; brush with 1½ tablespoons oil. Broil until lavash just begins to crisp, about 1 minute.

REDUCE oven temperature to 450°F. Turn lavash over on baking sheet so broiled side is down. Brush with remaining 1½ tablespoons oil. Spread with olives; sprinkle with cheeses, then mushrooms, onion, bell pepper, and tomatoes. Sprinkle with salt and pepper. Bake until pizza is heated through and cheeses melt, about 10 minutes. Cut into squares.

Onion and bacon tart

6 SERVINGS *Sautéing the onions in bacon drippings gives them a nice smoky flavor. Serve the pizza-tart, conveniently made with refrigerated pizza dough, with a semi-dry Riesling.*

  8 bacon slices, chopped
  5 cups sliced onions (about 3 large)

  ½ cup sour cream
  1 large egg
  1 teaspoon salt
  ½ teaspoon ground black pepper
     Pinch of ground nutmeg

  1 13.8-ounce tube refrigerated pizza dough
  ¼ teaspoon caraway seeds

PREHEAT oven to 375°F. Sauté bacon in heavy large skillet over medium heat until beginning to crisp. Drain all but 1 tablespoon bacon drippings from skillet. Add onions to skillet; sauté until very tender but not brown, about 20 minutes. Cool.

WHISK sour cream, egg, salt, pepper, and nutmeg in large bowl to blend. Stir in cooled onion mixture.

ROLL pizza dough out on lightly floured surface to 13×10-inch rectangle. Transfer to large baking sheet. Spread onion mixture over dough, leaving ½-inch plain border. Sprinkle with caraway seeds.

BAKE tart until custard is set and crust is brown around edges and on bottom, about 25 minutes.

Pizza with caramelized onions, blue cheese, and mushrooms

MAKES 1 LARGE PIZZA *Caramelizing onions breaks down and browns their natural sugars, making the onions softer and slightly sweet.*

  2½ tablespoons olive oil, divided
  2 large onions, thinly sliced (about 5 cups)
  2 teaspoons golden brown sugar

  8 ounces fresh shiitake mushrooms, stemmed, caps sliced

  1 14-ounce purchased fully baked pizza crust
  2 cups crumbled blue cheese (about 8 ounces)
  1 tablespoon chopped fresh thyme

HEAT 1 tablespoon oil in large nonstick skillet over medium heat. Add onions and sauté until tender, about 10 minutes. Sprinkle sugar over onions. Reduce heat to medium-low; sauté until onions are golden brown, about 20 minutes.

HEAT remaining 1½ tablespoons oil in large skillet over high heat. Add mushrooms; sprinkle with salt and pepper. Sauté mushrooms until tender and golden, about 8 minutes.

DO AHEAD *Onions and mushrooms can be prepared 1 day ahead. Cover separately and refrigerate.*

PREHEAT oven to 450°F. Place pizza crust on large baking sheet. Sprinkle blue cheese and thyme over. Top with onions, then mushrooms. Bake pizza until crust is crisp and topping is heated through, about 15 minutes. Cool in pan 5 minutes. Cut into wedges.

Manchu spiced garlic chicken pizzettas

MAKES 4 *Each pizzetta is perfect for one person. Look for the hot chili sauces in the Asian foods section of some supermarkets and at Asian markets.*

¼ cup plus 2 tablespoons olive oil

2 large onions, thinly sliced

3 tablespoons golden brown sugar

1½ tablespoons apple cider vinegar

5 garlic cloves, finely chopped, divided

1 pound skinless boneless chicken thighs, cut into ¾-inch pieces

2 tablespoons hot chili sauce or paste (such as sriracha, sambal oelek, or chili-garlic sauce)

6 tablespoons chopped fresh cilantro, divided

2 13.8-ounce tubes refrigerated pizza dough

2 cups (packed) coarsely grated mozzarella cheese (about 8 ounces)

3 large plum tomatoes, seeded, chopped

HEAT ¼ cup oil in heavy large skillet over high heat. Add onions; sauté 5 minutes. Reduce heat to medium-low; sauté until onions are dark brown, about 25 minutes. Add sugar, vinegar, and 2 garlic cloves; stir until sauce thickens and onions are glazed, about 2 minutes. Season to taste with salt and pepper. Cool.

SPRINKLE chicken with salt. Heat 2 tablespoons oil in another heavy large skillet over medium-high heat. Add chicken; sauté 2 minutes. Add remaining 3 garlic cloves; sauté 2 minutes. Add chili sauce; stir 1 minute. Remove chicken from heat. Stir in 3 tablespoons cilantro.

PREHEAT oven to 425°F. Sprinkle 2 large baking sheets with flour. Unroll dough from 1 tube; trim to 12×8-inch rectangle. Cut crosswise in half, forming two 6×8-inch rectangles; transfer to prepared sheet. Repeat with remaining dough. Bake crusts until light brown, about 8 minutes.

SPRINKLE cheese, tomatoes, onions, chicken, and remaining 3 tablespoons cilantro over crusts. Bake until topping is heated through and cheese melts, about 5 minutes.

Wild mushroom pizza with garlic confit and bacon

4 SERVINGS *Slow-cooking the garlic softens its bite. Any mixture of mushrooms would work well.*

- 3 bacon slices, cut crosswise into ½-inch pieces
- ½ cup peeled halved large garlic cloves (about 16)
- 2 tablespoons olive oil
- 12 ounces assorted fresh wild mushrooms (such as crimini, portobello, and stemmed shiitake), thinly sliced
- ½ red bell pepper, cut into matchstick-size strips
- 1 10-ounce purchased fully baked thin pizza crust
- 1 cup (packed) mixed shredded Italian cheeses (about 4 ounces)

COOK bacon in large skillet over medium heat until brown and crisp. Using slotted spoon, transfer bacon to paper towels to drain. Pour off drippings from skillet; add garlic and oil. Cover and cook over low heat until garlic is soft and golden, stirring occasionally, about 15 minutes. Add mushrooms and bell pepper; cover and cook over high heat until vegetables are tender, stirring often, about 5 minutes. Sprinkle with salt and pepper.

DO AHEAD *Can be made 8 hours ahead; chill bacon and vegetables separately.*

PREHEAT oven to 450°F. Place pizza crust on large baking sheet. Sprinkle cheeses, then vegetable mixture and bacon over crust. Bake until crust is crisp and topping is heated through, about 15 minutes. Let stand 2 minutes. Cut into wedges.

Duck sausage pizza with green onions and tomato

4 SERVINGS *If you can't find duck sausage, use chicken or turkey sausage instead.*

- 1 tablespoon extra-virgin olive oil
- 2 garlic cloves, minced
- ⅛ teaspoon dried crushed red pepper
- 1 10-ounce purchased fully baked thin pizza crust
- 1½ cups (packed) coarsely grated mozzarella cheese (about 6 ounces)
- ½ cup chopped tomato
- 1 tablespoon chopped fresh oregano
- 2 fully-cooked smoked duck, chicken, or turkey sausages, sliced into thin rounds
- ⅓ cup finely chopped green onions
- ½ cup freshly grated Parmesan cheese (about 1½ ounces)

POSITION rack in center of oven and preheat to 450°F. Mix oil, garlic, and crushed red pepper in small bowl. Place crust on large baking sheet. Sprinkle mozzarella cheese over, leaving 1-inch plain border. Top with tomato, then oregano, sausages, green onions, and Parmesan cheese. Drizzle garlic-oil mixture over.

BAKE pizza until crust is crisp and brown and cheeses melt, about 12 minutes. Cut into wedges.

Sausage, red onion, and wild mushroom pizzas

MAKES 2 *Look for the fresh pizza dough at markets like Trader Joe's or thaw a one-pound loaf of frozen bread dough.*

- 1 16-ounce ball purchased fresh pizza dough, room temperature
- ⅔ cup finely grated Parmesan cheese, divided
- 2¼ teaspoons finely chopped fresh rosemary, divided
- ½ teaspoon dried crushed red pepper, divided
  Coarse kosher salt

- 1½ tablespoons olive oil, divided
- 2½ hot Italian sausages, casings removed
- 1 small red onion, thinly sliced
- 7 ounces assorted fresh wild mushrooms (such as stemmed shiitake, oyster, and chanterelle), thickly sliced
- 1¾ cups (packed) coarsely grated whole-milk mozzarella cheese (about 7 ounces), divided

POSITION 1 rack in top third and 1 rack in bottom third of oven and preheat to 450°F. Lightly flour 2 large baking sheets. Divide dough in half. Press and stretch each piece out on lightly floured surface to 5-inch round. Sprinkle each with ⅓ cup Parmesan, ¾ teaspoon rosemary, and ¼ teaspoon crushed red pepper; sprinkle with coarse kosher salt. Roll each piece of dough out to 10-inch round, pressing in seasonings. Transfer dough rounds to prepared baking sheets.

HEAT 1 tablespoon oil in large nonstick skillet over medium-high heat. Add sausages. Sauté until brown, breaking into ½-inch pieces with back of spoon, about 5 minutes. Using slotted spoon, transfer sausages to bowl. Add onion to skillet. Sauté until crisp-tender, about 2 minutes; transfer to plate. Add remaining ½ tablespoon oil to skillet. Add mushrooms and remaining ¾ teaspoon rosemary; sprinkle with salt and pepper. Sauté until brown, about 5 minutes. Leaving ½-inch plain border, top each dough round with ¾ cup mozzarella, then onion, sausages, and mushrooms.

BAKE pizzas until crust bottoms are crisp and brown, reversing sheets after 10 minutes, about 20 minutes total. Using large spatula, transfer pizzas to work surface. Sprinkle each pizza with 2 tablespoons mozzarella.

Garlicky eggplant, tomato, and fresh basil pizzas

8 SERVINGS *Japanese eggplants are smaller, thinner, and sweeter than regular eggplants. They do not need to be salted before cooking. Look for them in the produce section of some supermarkets and at Asian markets. While you're shopping, keep in mind that they come in a range of colors, including purple, pink, green, and white.*

  4 medium Japanese eggplants, thinly sliced lengthwise
  ¼ cup olive oil

  3 cups (packed) coarsely grated mozzarella cheese (about 12 ounces)
  2 14-ounce purchased fully baked pizza crusts
  1½ pounds plum tomatoes, halved, seeded, chopped
  6 ounces chilled fresh soft goat cheese, coarsely crumbled
  15 large garlic cloves, very thinly sliced
  1½ cups thinly sliced fresh basil leaves (about 2 bunches)

PREHEAT broiler. Brush both sides of eggplant slices with oil. Arrange on large baking sheet; sprinkle with salt and pepper. Broil until eggplant is tender and begins to brown, turning occasionally, about 6 minutes. Cool.

POSITION 1 rack in top third and 1 rack in bottom third of oven and preheat to 475°F. Place large baking sheet on each rack to heat.

SPRINKLE 1 cup mozzarella cheese over each crust. Top each with eggplant, tomatoes, goat cheese, garlic, and basil. Sprinkle remaining mozzarella cheese over. Transfer pizzas to hot baking sheets in oven.

BAKE pizzas until cheeses melt and crusts are brown and crisp, reversing sheets after 6 minutes, about 12 minutes total. Let stand 10 minutes. Cut into wedges.

Pronto turkey sausage and tapenade pizzas

MAKES 2 *If you can't find tapenade (a chopped olive mixture that usually includes capers and anchovies), coarsely chop pitted Kalamata olives in a processor.*

  2 tablespoons olive oil
  4 small leeks (white parts only), sliced crosswise (about 3 cups)
  2 large red bell peppers, thinly sliced, halved crosswise
  ¼ teaspoon dried crushed red pepper
  12 ounces turkey Italian sausages, casings removed

  2 14-ounce purchased fully baked pizza crusts
  ½ cup tapenade
  6 cups (packed) coarsely grated mozzarella cheese (about 1½ pounds)
  ⅔ cup chopped fresh basil

PREHEAT oven to 450°F. Heat oil in heavy large skillet over medium-high heat. Add leeks and bell peppers and sauté until just tender, about 8 minutes. Add crushed red pepper and stir 30 seconds. Transfer to plate. Add sausages to same skillet and sauté until no longer pink, breaking up with fork, about 4 minutes. Transfer to another plate.

PLACE crusts on large baking sheets. Spread ¼ cup tapenade over each. Top each with cheese, sausages, and vegetables. Bake until crusts are crisp and cheese melts, about 15 minutes. Sprinkle each with basil.

Santa Fe pizza

6 SERVINGS *Serve each slice topped with chopped avo-cado and a dollop of sour cream.*

1 10-ounce purchased fully baked thin pizza crust

1¾ cups (packed) coarsely grated sharp cheddar cheese (about 7 ounces), divided

2 cups roast chicken strips

½ teaspoon ground cumin

½ cup thinly sliced red onion

6 tablespoons frozen corn kernels, thawed, drained, divided

6 tablespoons chopped fresh cilantro, divided

2 large jalapeño chiles, seeded, coarsely chopped

⅔ cup drained purchased refrigerated fresh salsa

POSITION rack in center of oven and preheat to 425°F. Place crust on large baking sheet. Sprinkle 1 cup cheese, chicken strips, and cumin over crust, leaving ¾-inch plain border. Top with onion, 4 tablespoons corn, 4 tablespoons cilantro, remaining ¾ cup cheese, jalapeños, and remaining 2 table-spoons corn. Bake pizza until crust is crisp and top-ping is heated through, about 13 minutes. Top with salsa and remaining 2 tablespoons cilantro.

Ciabatta pizza with Gorgonzola, walnut pesto, and pears

12 APPETIZER OR 6 MAIN-COURSE SERVINGS *A chopped walnut pesto is the foundation of this sophisticated fall pizza. When cut into squares, it makes a terrific appetizer. Ciabatta bread can be found at many su-permarkets and bakeries.*

2 cups walnuts (about 8 ounces)

1 cup olive oil

¼ cup honey

2 tablespoons chopped fresh thyme

1 loaf ciabatta bread (about 1⅓ pounds), halved horizontally

10 ounces thinly sliced Havarti cheese

6 ounces thinly sliced prosciutto, cut crosswise into strips

2 pears, halved, cored, thinly sliced

⅔ cup crumbled Gorgonzola cheese

2 cups arugula

PREHEAT oven to 450°F. Toast nuts on baking sheet until brown, about 5 minutes. Transfer hot nuts to processor. Add oil, honey, and thyme; blend until nuts are finely chopped. Season pesto to taste with salt and pepper. Maintain oven temperature.

PLACE bread halves, cut side up, on baking sheet. Spread half of pesto over each. Top with Havarti. Bake until bubbly and golden, about 12 minutes. Top with prosciutto, then pears and Gorgonzola. Sprinkle with pepper and top with arugula.

Double-cheese and prosciutto calzone

4 SERVINGS *Calzones are sometimes called stuffed pizzas because the toppings are inside, not on top of, the crust. For a lower-calorie, lower-fat version, use part-skim mozzarella.*

2	cups (packed) coarsely grated mozzarella cheese (about 8 ounces)
1	cup crumbled soft fresh goat cheese (about 4 ounces)
2	ounces thin prosciutto slices, chopped
2½	teaspoons chopped fresh thyme
1	garlic clove, pressed
1	13.8-ounce tube refrigerated pizza dough
	Extra-virgin olive oil

POSITION rack in center of oven; preheat to 425°F. Toss first 5 ingredients in medium bowl. Unroll dough into rectangle on large rimmed baking sheet. Mound filling in strip on 1 long half of dough, leaving 1-inch plain border on sides. Sprinkle with pepper. Fold other half of dough over. Crimp edges to seal; fold corners under to form half-circle. Bake calzone until puffed and brown, about 18 minutes. Brush with oil. Transfer to platter and cut calzone into 4 pieces.

THE WORD ON PROSCIUTTO Italian prosciutto is air-dried, salt-cured, seasoned ham. Because the meat has been pressed, it is firmer and denser than typical American ham. You can find prosciutto packaged in very thin slices in the refrigerated deli section of some supermarkets, at specialty foods stores, and at Italian markets. It's delicious on pizzas, in sandwiches, and wrapped around slices of melon for an appetizer or a snack.

Cabbage, bacon, and cheese calzones

MAKES 2; CAN BE DOUBLED *Brushing a little egg wash (egg yolk beaten with water) on the edge of the dough helps tightly seal the calzone.*

4	slices thick-cut bacon, coarsely chopped
½	medium onion, thinly sliced
¼	small cabbage, thinly sliced
¼	teaspoon dried crushed red pepper, divided
1	tablespoon balsamic vinegar
2	teaspoons chopped fresh thyme
1½	pounds frozen bread dough, thawed
2¼	cups (packed) coarsely grated Fontina cheese (about 9 ounces)
2	tablespoons soft fresh goat cheese
1	large egg yolk beaten with 1 tablespoon water (for egg wash)
	Olive oil

PREHEAT oven to 450°F. Cook bacon in heavy large skillet over medium heat until fat begins to render, stirring frequently, about 3 minutes. Add onion, cabbage, and ⅛ teaspoon crushed red pepper. Sauté until cabbage is tender, stirring occasionally, about 12 minutes. Mix in vinegar and thyme; season to taste with salt and pepper. Cool.

KNEAD dough until smooth. Divide into 2 pieces. Roll each piece out on lightly floured surface to 11-inch round. Spread Fontina, cabbage mixture, and goat cheese over half of each round, leaving ½-inch plain border. Brush dough edge around filling with egg wash. Fold other half of dough over. Seal edges with fork. Transfer calzones to large baking sheet.

BRUSH calzones with oil; sprinkle with ground black pepper and remaining crushed red pepper. Bake until golden brown, about 13 minutes.

Three-cheese spinach calzones

MAKES 2; CAN BE DOUBLED *If you're having trouble getting the dough into an 11-inch square, let it rest for a few minutes. After the dough relaxes, you should be able to roll or pull it into the desired size and shape.*

- 1 10-ounce package frozen chopped spinach, thawed, squeezed very dry
- 3 green onions, chopped
- ½ cup part-skim ricotta cheese
- ½ cup crumbled Gorgonzola or other blue cheese (about 2 ounces)
- 1 cup (packed) coarsely grated Fontina cheese (about 4 ounces)

- 1 13.8-ounce tube refrigerated pizza dough

PREHEAT oven to 425°F. Mix first 5 ingredients in medium bowl to blend. Sprinkle filling with salt and pepper.

LIGHTLY sprinkle large baking sheet with flour. Unfold dough on prepared sheet. Stretch and press dough to 11-inch square; cut in half diagonally, forming 2 triangles. Place half of filling in center of each triangle. Fold 1 side of each triangle over filling and press edges to seal, forming 2 triangular calzones. Cut 3 small slits in tops to allow steam to escape.

BAKE calzones until filling is heated through and crusts are golden brown, about 15 minutes; serve calzones hot.

Spinach and feta turnovers

MAKES 2; CAN BE DOUBLED *To avoid a watery filling, squeeze as much liquid as possible out of the spinach.*

- 2 large eggs
- 1 10-ounce package frozen chopped spinach, thawed, squeezed very dry
- ¾ cup crumbled feta cheese (about 3 ounces)
- 2 tablespoons chopped fresh mint
- 2 garlic cloves, chopped
- ¼ teaspoon freshly ground black pepper

- 1 13.8-ounce tube refrigerated pizza dough

PREHEAT oven to 425°F. Whisk eggs in large bowl to blend. Transfer 1 tablespoon beaten eggs to small bowl and reserve for glaze. Mix spinach, cheese, mint, garlic, and pepper into remaining eggs in large bowl.

UNFOLD dough on lightly floured work surface. Stretch and press dough to 11-inch square. Cut dough into 4 equal squares. Spoon ¼ of spinach filling (about ⅓ cup) into center of each dough square. Fold 1 corner of each square over filling to opposite corner, forming triangle. Press dough edges with fork to seal. Cut 3 small slits in top of each turnover to allow steam to escape. Brush tops with reserved egg glaze.

BAKE turnovers until filling is cooked through and tops are golden brown, about 15 minutes. Serve warm.

Grilled chorizo, goat cheese, and watercress pita pizzas

MAKES 8 *The goat cheese will soften, but will not melt, as the pizzas cook. At the supermarket, look for a package of yellow, orange, and red mini sweet peppers.*

14 ounces fresh pork or beef chorizo
   sausages, casings removed
4 cups (packed) watercress tops, divided
8 ounces soft fresh goat cheese, crumbled

8 5- to 6-inch-diameter pita breads
   Olive oil
3 mini sweet peppers (1 yellow, 1 orange,
   and 1 red), cut into thin rings

PREPARE barbecue (medium heat). Sauté chorizo in large skillet over medium-high heat until cooked through, breaking up with spoon, about 8 minutes. Transfer chorizo to sieve set over bowl and drain. Mix 2½ cups watercress and goat cheese in medium bowl.

LIGHTLY brush 1 side of each pita bread with oil. Grill, oiled side down, until bottom is just crisp, about 2 minutes. Transfer to work surface, grilled side up. Cover each pita bread with cheese mixture, chorizo, and several sweet pepper rings, dividing equally.

RETURN pizzas to barbecue. Cover and grill until goat cheese softens, about 2 minutes. Transfer pizzas to platter. Top each with more watercress.

TEST-KITCHEN TIPS

For a vegetarian version of this pizza, use soy chorizo, available at some supermarkets and at specialty and natural foods stores. Follow the same cooking directions, but do not drain.

Goat cheese is much easier to crumble if it is very cold.

Grilled pizzas with tomato, mozzarella, and basil

2 SERVINGS *Dinner is served—without even turning on the oven. While you're grilling the pizzas, cut up a few peaches or pears and grill for a few minutes. Serve the grilled fruit for dessert with vanilla ice cream or sweetened mascarpone cheese (Italian cream cheese).*

2½ tablespoons olive oil, divided
 1 cup diced seeded tomatoes (about 4)
1½ cups (packed) coarsely grated
   mozzarella cheese (about 6 ounces)
 ½ cup thinly sliced green onions
 ½ cup thinly sliced fresh basil
 2 tablespoons balsamic vinegar
 2 large garlic cloves, minced

 1 13.8-ounce tube refrigerated pizza dough
 ¼ cup freshly grated Parmesan cheese

COMBINE 2 tablespoons oil and next 6 ingredients in medium bowl; toss to blend. Let tomato mixture stand at least 15 minutes and up to 30 minutes.

PREPARE barbecue (medium-high heat). Brush grill rack with remaining ½ tablespoon oil. Unroll dough onto work surface; stretch and press dough to 12-inch square. Cut into 4 equal squares. Transfer squares to barbecue. Cover and grill until bottoms are brown, about 4 minutes. Turn squares over on grill and immediately top each with tomato mixture, leaving ½-inch plain border. Cover and grill until pizza bottoms are brown and cheese is melted, about 4 minutes. Sprinkle pizzas with Parmesan.

Sweet on pizza Pizza for dessert? Why not? Brush plain dough with a little cream, sprinkle with sugar, bake until golden, and cool. Then it's time to get creative with the toppings.

— Spread some sweetened cream cheese on the crust. Top with fresh fruit (try a mix of raspberries, blackberries, and sliced strawberries). To make the fruit glisten, brush with a little melted red currant jelly.

— For a cross between dessert and a cheese course, spread mascarpone cheese (Italian cream cheese) over the crust. Top with thin slices of fresh fig. Sprinkle with crumbled blue cheese, chopped fresh mint, and black pepper. Drizzle with honey.

— Top the crust with chocolate-hazelnut spread (such as Nutella). Sprinkle with a mix of white and semisweet chocolate chips and coarsely chopped almonds. Place back in the oven until the chocolate chips melt.

pastaandrice

PASTA 200   RICE 229

PASTA

Linguine with Spicy Tomato and Clam Sauce

Linguine with Steamed Cockles in Saffron-Tarragon Sauce

Spicy Asian-Style Noodles with Clams

Perciatelli with Shrimp and Garlic Breadcrumbs

Fettuccine with Mussels and Cream

Pasta with Anchovies, Currants, Fennel, and Pine Nuts

Spaghetti with Olive Oil, Garlic, and Anchovies

Pasta with Chicken, Curly Endive, and Blue Cheese

Linguine with Chicken and Spicy Pesto Sauce

Pasta with Beans and Beef

Spaghetti with Turkey-Pesto Meatballs

Rigatoni with Cheese and Italian Sausage

Baked Rigatoni with Ham, Tomatoes, and Feta Cheese

Castellane Pasta with Sausage, Peppers, Cherry Tomatoes, and Marjoram

Farfalle with Sausage, Tomatoes, and Cream

Farfalle with Bitter Greens and Sausage

Perciatelli with Prosciutto, Wilted Radicchio, Blue Cheese, and Dried Figs

Linguine with Pancetta and Sautéed Cherry Tomatoes

Antipasto Pasta

Fettuccine Quattro Formaggi

Fettuccine with Cream, Basil, and Pecorino Romano Cheese

Linguine with Winter Pesto

Pasta with Pesto, Beans, and Potatoes

Orecchiette with Turnip Greens

Spaghetti alla Carbonara di Zucchine

Pasta with Pecorino Romano and Black Pepper

Pasta with Three Peas

Linguine Avgolemono with Artichoke Hearts and Green Beans

Spaghettini with Spicy Escarole and Pecorino Romano

Campanelle Pasta with Burrata Cheese, Spinach, Lemon, and Toasted Almonds

Spaghetti with Tomatoes, Arugula, Capers, and Olives

Linguine with Pears and Gorgonzola Cheese

Farfalle with Wilted Frisée and Burst Tomatoes

Orecchiette with Garbanzos, Tomatoes, Feta, and Mint

Fettuccine with Asparagus, Morels, and Tarragon

Tagliatelle with Shredded Beets, Sour Cream, and Parsley

Fusilli with Eggplant, Pine Nuts, Currants, and Capers

Linguine with Red Peppers, Green Onions, and Pine Nuts

Pasta with Grilled Vegetables and Feta

Tortellini with Mushroom Carbonara Sauce

Cheese Tortellini with Pesto Cream Sauce

Cheese Ravioli with Old-Fashioned Meat Sauce

Nacho Macaroni and Cheese

Wisconsin Mac and Cheese

One-Step Lasagna with Sausage and Basil

Noodles with Poppy Seeds and Peas

Szechuan Sesame Noodles

Brown Butter Caraway Noodles

Orzo with Peas, Dill, and Pancetta

Carrot Orzo

Orzo with Tomatoes, Feta, and Green Onions

Orzo Pilaf with Mushrooms, Leeks, and Sun-Dried Tomatoes

Greek Pasta Salad with Shrimp and Olives

Lemon Pasta Salad with Tomatoes and Feta

Couscous with Dried Apricots and Pistachios

Saffron Couscous with Fresh Peas and Chives

Toasted Israeli Couscous with Pine Nuts and Parsley

RICE

Florida Jambalaya

One-Hour Shrimp Paella

Celery Root Risotto and Pesto

Risotto with Zucchini and Parmesan

Red Beet Risotto with Mustard Greens and Goat Cheese

Porcini Risotto

Crayfish-Corn Risotto

Red Chard Risotto

Feta and Mint Rice

Rice Pilaf with Basil and Pine Nuts

Rice, Raisin, and Herb Pilaf

Classic Red Rice

Aromatic Yellow Rice

Jasmine Rice with Garlic, Ginger, and Cilantro

Pesto Rice Timbales

West Indian Rice and Beans

Fried Rice with Shiitake Mushrooms and Sugar Snap Peas

Brown and Wild Rice with Sausage and Fennel

Brown Rice Salad with Mango Chutney Dressing

Coconut Basmati Rice

tool kit There are dozens of great pasta dishes in this chapter—and there are hundreds more waiting in your pantry, fridge, and freezer. Pasta is one of the easiest dishes to improvise: Start by looking at the ingredients you have on hand (since you have them on hand, presumably you like them already), and think about which flavor combinations would taste good tossed with pasta. *[Note: See "How to Cook Pasta" on page 219 for tips on achieving perfectly cooked, al dente pasta.]*

Another recipe-creation trick: Select one or more vegetables, a cheese or two, and a meat; and imagine them in different combinations paired with pasta. For instance, say you have asparagus, spinach, prosciutto, and Parmesan cheese. Lightly stir-fry the asparagus in some olive oil, then add the prosciutto; toss with the pasta, spinach, and cheese just until the spinach wilts, mixing in a ladleful of pasta cooking liquid for added moisture.

If you really want to go all out, add ingredients that lend a lot of flavor with little effort—such as fresh garlic, herbs (fresh or dried), dried crushed red pepper, olives, capers, anchovies, lemon zest, dry white wine, or jarred roasted bell peppers. These ingredients can be sautéed right along with the vegetables—or for an uncooked sauce, omit the wine and toss these ingredients with freshly cooked pasta in a large bowl and serve warm or at room temperature.

And remember: Pastas don't always have to include Italian flavors; you can borrow ingredients from other cuisines. Create a pasta with Latin flavors, for example, by using frozen corn kernels, canned black beans, fresh cilantro, chili powder, hot pepper Monterey Jack cheese, and shredded roast chicken. Or stir-fry some carrots, snow peas, minced ginger, and garlic, then toss them with spaghetti, a little coconut milk, green onions, Asian sesame oil, and soy sauce for an Asian-style pasta. It all adds up to a world of delicious no-fuss pastas.

PASTA

Linguine with spicy tomato and clam sauce

2 SERVINGS; CAN BE DOUBLED *This pasta is as delicious with mussels as it is with clams. You can prepare the sauce early in the day, then return the sauce to a simmer before adding the clams. Offer a simple green salad with the pasta. Finish the meal with pears and an Italian cheese.*

- 4 tablespoons olive oil, divided
- ½ red onion, chopped
- 3 garlic cloves, minced
- ¼ teaspoon dried crushed red pepper
- 1 28-ounce can chopped tomatoes, drained
- 2 tablespoons chopped fresh marjoram, divided
- 2 tablespoons chopped fresh Italian parsley, divided
- 1 pound littleneck or Manila clams, scrubbed
- 8 ounces linguine

HEAT 3 tablespoons oil in heavy large saucepan over medium heat. Add onion and sauté until tender, about 5 minutes. Add garlic and sauté until soft, about 4 minutes. Add crushed red pepper; stir 20 seconds. Mix in tomatoes and simmer until sauce thickens, stirring frequently, about 5 minutes. Season to taste with salt and pepper. Stir in 1 tablespoon marjoram and 1 tablespoon parsley. Add clams to sauce. Cover and cook until clams open, about 5 minutes (discard any clams that do not open).

MEANWHILE, cook linguine in large pot of boiling salted water until just tender but still firm to bite, stirring occasionally. Drain. Transfer to large bowl. Add remaining 1 tablespoon oil and toss to coat. Pour clams and sauce over. Sprinkle with remaining marjoram and parsley.

Linguine with steamed cockles in saffron-tarragon sauce

2 SERVINGS *Cockles are small heart-shaped bivalves; if you can't find them, substitute small Manila or littleneck clams. Saffron is expensive, but a little goes a long way in flavoring and coloring food. To preserve saffron's pungency, store it in an airtight container in the freezer.*

- 10 ounces linguine
- 2 tablespoons (¼ stick) butter
- ¼ cup chopped shallots
- 3 garlic cloves, minced
- 1 cup dry white wine
- 2 tablespoons chopped fresh tarragon, divided
- ¼ teaspoon (scant) saffron threads
- 2 pounds cockles or small Manila clams, scrubbed
- 2 tablespoons whipping cream

COOK linguine in large pot of boiling salted water until just tender but still firm to bite, stirring occasionally. Drain.

MEANWHILE, melt butter in heavy large skillet over medium heat. Add shallots and garlic; sauté 2 minutes. Add wine, 1 tablespoon tarragon, and saffron. Increase heat to high; bring to boil. Add cockles; cover and cook until cockles open, about 3 minutes (discard any cockles that do not open). Using tongs, transfer cockles to bowl. Stir cream into sauce in skillet. Season to taste with salt and pepper. Add pasta to skillet and toss. Divide pasta and sauce between 2 bowls and sprinkle with remaining 1 tablespoon tarragon. Top with cockles.

Spicy Asian-style noodles with clams

4 SERVINGS *For best results, use clams that are two inches or smaller in size. When cooking clams and other mollusks, be sure to discard any that do not open and those that open only slightly. Vermicelli is a very thin pasta; angel hair pasta will work, too.*

2	tablespoons Asian sesame oil, divided
1	red bell pepper, thinly sliced
½	cup chopped onion
6	garlic cloves, chopped
1	tablespoon minced peeled fresh ginger
1	teaspoon dried crushed red pepper
1	cup water
3	tablespoons unseasoned rice vinegar
2	tablespoons soy sauce
24	clams, scrubbed
8	ounces vermicelli pasta
½	cup chopped fresh cilantro

HEAT 1 tablespoon oil in large pot over medium-high heat. Add bell pepper, onion, garlic, ginger, and crushed red pepper. Sauté until bell pepper begins to soften, about 2 minutes. Add 1 cup water, vinegar, and soy sauce; bring to boil. Add clams. Cover pot and cook until clams open, about 10 minutes (discard any clams that do not open).

MEANWHILE, cook pasta in another large pot of boiling salted water until just tender but still firm to bite, stirring occasionally. Drain. Return to same pot; toss with remaining 1 tablespoon oil. Divide pasta among shallow bowls. Spoon clams and sauce over pasta. Sprinkle with cilantro.

FRESH BREADCRUMBS To make breadcrumbs, cut fresh French bread into chunks, then blend in a food processor until coarsely or finely ground, depending on recipe.

Perciatelli with shrimp and garlic breadcrumbs

4 TO 6 SERVINGS *Perciatelli is a long hollow pasta. If you can't find it, spaghetti or linguine makes an excellent substitution. To cut down on labor, buy shrimp that have already been peeled and deveined. Some markets sell bags of flash-frozen cleaned and shelled shrimp—keep a bag on hand in the freezer. Thaw them by putting the bag in the refrigerator overnight, or in a bowl of cold water on the counter for 45 minutes to an hour.*

8	tablespoons olive oil, divided
2	cups coarsely ground fresh breadcrumbs made from French bread
8	garlic cloves, minced, divided
12	ounces perciatelli (long hollow pasta) or spaghetti
1¼	pounds uncooked large shrimp, peeled, deveined
½	cup chopped fresh Italian parsley, divided
6	tablespoons drained capers
4	teaspoons finely grated lemon peel

HEAT 3 tablespoons oil in large nonstick skillet over medium heat. Add breadcrumbs and half of garlic; sauté until crumbs are golden and crisp, about 10 minutes. Transfer to medium bowl.

COOK pasta in large pot of boiling salted water until just tender but still firm to bite, stirring occasionally. Drain, reserving 1 cup pasta cooking liquid. Return pasta to pot.

SPRINKLE shrimp with salt and pepper. Heat remaining 5 tablespoons oil in same skillet over medium-high heat. Add shrimp and remaining garlic to skillet; sauté until shrimp are just opaque in center, about 3 minutes. Stir in ¼ cup parsley, capers, and lemon peel. Add shrimp mixture and ½ cup reserved pasta cooking liquid to pasta. Mix in 1 cup garlic breadcrumbs, adding more pasta cooking liquid if dry. Season to taste with salt and pepper. Transfer to bowl. Sprinkle with remaining garlic breadcrumbs and parsley.

Fettuccine with mussels and cream

2 SERVINGS; CAN BE DOUBLED *Fennel seed and orange peel lend unique flavors to this recipe. To debeard mussels, locate any hair-like fibers protruding from the mussel at the base of the shell, hold fibers tightly, and pull gently but firmly toward the top of the mussel. Discard the beard.*

- 2 tablespoons (¼ stick) butter
- 4 green onions, sliced, dark green tops reserved separately
- 2 3-inch-long orange peel strips
- ⅛ teaspoon fennel seeds
- 2 pounds mussels, scrubbed, debearded
- ½ cup heavy whipping cream

- 8 ounces fettuccine or linguine

MELT butter in heavy large saucepan over medium heat. Add white and light green parts of green onions and sauté 2 minutes. Add orange peel and fennel seeds, then mussels. Cover and cook until mussels open, about 5 minutes (discard any mussels that do not open). Transfer mussels to bowl; cover with foil to keep warm. Add cream and any liquid accumulated in mussel bowl to saucepan; boil until slightly thickened, about 2 minutes. Season to taste with salt and pepper.

MEANWHILE, cook pasta in large pot of boiling salted water until just tender but still firm to bite, stirring occasionally. Drain. Transfer to large bowl. Top with mussels, then sauce, discarding orange peel. Sprinkle with reserved green onion tops.

> **TOASTED CRUMBS** Make fresh breadcrumbs (see page 201), then toast them on a rimmed baking sheet in a 350°F oven until golden, stirring occasionally, about 10 minutes.

Pasta with anchovies, currants, fennel, and pine nuts

4 SERVINGS *This dish is a variation on the traditional Sicilian pasta made with sardines. Chopped raisins can replace the currants in a pinch. If you're running short on time, panko (dried Japanese breadcrumbs) can be used instead of fresh breadcrumbs.*

- ½ cup extra-virgin olive oil
- 8 anchovy fillets
- 1 large onion, very thinly sliced
- 1 large fresh fennel bulb, trimmed, halved, very thinly sliced
- ¼ teaspoon dried crushed red pepper
- 2 plum tomatoes, chopped
- ¼ cup pine nuts
- ¼ cup dried currants

- ¾ pound perciatelli (long hollow pasta) or linguine
- ¼ teaspoon saffron threads
- 1 cup fresh breadcrumbs, toasted

HEAT oil in large skillet over medium heat. Add anchovies; mash with back of fork. Add onion, fennel, and crushed red pepper; sauté until vegetables are tender, about 5 minutes. Add tomatoes, pine nuts, and currants. Reduce heat to low and sauté 5 minutes to blend flavors. Season to taste with salt and pepper.

MEANWHILE, cook pasta in large pot of boiling salted water until just tender but still firm to bite, stirring occasionally. Drain, reserving 1 cup pasta cooking liquid. Add saffron to reserved liquid and stir to dissolve. Return pasta and saffron liquid to pot. Add tomato mixture; toss over low heat until sauce coats pasta. Mix in breadcrumbs and transfer to bowl.

Spaghetti with olive oil, garlic, and anchovies

2 SERVINGS; CAN BE DOUBLED *This pasta makes excellent use of pantry ingredients. If your refrigerator is really empty, you can substitute one teaspoon of dried oregano for the fresh parsley—add it to the skillet along with the anchovies.*

¼ cup olive oil

4 garlic cloves, minced

1 2-ounce can anchovy fillets, drained, chopped

8 ounces spaghetti

1 teaspoon fresh lemon juice
  Chopped fresh Italian parsley
  Freshly grated Parmesan cheese (optional)

HEAT oil in heavy small skillet over low heat. Add garlic and sauté 2 minutes. Add chopped anchovies and sauté until garlic just begins to color, about 3 minutes.

MEANWHILE, cook spaghetti in large pot of boiling salted water until just tender but still firm to bite, stirring occasionally. Drain. Return spaghetti to pot. Add oil mixture and lemon juice and toss to coat. Season to taste with pepper. Divide between plates. Sprinkle generously with parsley. Serve, passing Parmesan separately if desired.

Pasta with chicken, curly endive, and blue cheese

6 SERVINGS *Many markets sell skinless, boneless chicken or turkey breast meat cut into strips. Purchase about 1½ pounds of these strips to cut down on prep time. Gorgonzola cheese would work here in place of the Maytag blue.*

1 pound gnocchi-shaped pasta (such as cavatelli) or shell pasta

3 tablespoons olive oil

1 large red onion, halved, sliced crosswise

4 skinless boneless chicken breast halves, cut crosswise into ⅓- to ½-inch-thick slices

4 teaspoons chopped fresh rosemary

1 large head of curly endive, trimmed, very coarsely chopped (about 12 cups)

1½ cups crumbled blue cheese (such as Maytag; about 9 ounces)

¾ cup coarsely chopped toasted walnuts (optional)

COOK pasta in large pot of boiling salted water until just tender but still firm to bite, stirring occasionally.

MEANWHILE, heat oil in heavy large deep skillet over medium-high heat. Add onion; sauté until slightly softened, about 4 minutes. Sprinkle chicken with salt and pepper; add to skillet along with rosemary and sauté until chicken is almost cooked through, about 4 minutes. Add endive; toss until slightly wilted and chicken is cooked through, about 1 minute.

DRAIN pasta, reserving ¾ cup pasta cooking liquid. Return pasta to pot. Add chicken mixture, blue cheese, and enough pasta cooking liquid to moisten; toss to blend. Season to taste with salt and pepper. Transfer to large bowl; sprinkle with walnuts, if desired.

203

Linguine with chicken and spicy pesto sauce

4 SERVINGS *Purchased traditional pesto, made with basil and pine nuts, is blended with Southwestern flavors like cilantro, pecans, and jalapeño chile in this main-dish pasta. Continue the Southwest theme by adding a pinch of ground cumin to your favorite vinaigrette to toss with a green salad.*

 2 tablespoons olive oil

 1 pound skinless boneless chicken breast halves, cut crosswise into ⅓-inch-wide strips

 3 green onions, thinly sliced

 ⅓ cup chopped fresh cilantro plus additional for garnish

 ⅓ cup chopped pecans, toasted

 3 garlic cloves, minced

 2 teaspoons (or more) minced seeded jalapeño chile

 ½ cup purchased pesto

 12 ounces linguine

Freshly grated Parmesan cheese

HEAT oil in heavy large skillet over medium-high heat. Sprinkle chicken with salt and pepper. Add chicken to skillet and sauté until cooked through and beginning to brown, about 3 minutes. Using slotted spoon, transfer chicken to bowl. Add green onions, ⅓ cup cilantro, pecans, garlic, and 2 teaspoons jalapeño to same skillet. Sauté 2 minutes. Mix in pesto, chicken, and any accumulated juices, adding more jalapeño if desired. Remove sauce from heat.

MEANWHILE, cook linguine in large pot of boiling salted water until just tender but still firm to bite, stirring occasionally. Drain, reserving ¼ cup pasta cooking liquid.

BRING sauce to simmer. Add linguine and reserved pasta cooking liquid to sauce and toss to coat. Season to taste with salt and pepper. Transfer to large bowl. Sprinkle with additional cilantro. Serve, passing Parmesan separately.

Pasta with beans and beef

6 SERVINGS *This hearty main dish pasta is like an extra-thick soup. You can make it a day ahead—just reheat and add some more broth as the pasta and beans will continue to absorb liquid. To serve the pasta, ladle it into bowls. A sprinkle of freshly grated Parmesan is a nice finishing touch.*

 3 tablespoons olive oil

 2 cups chopped onions

 2 garlic cloves, chopped

 1 pound ground chuck or lean ground beef

 ¾ teaspoon dried crushed red pepper

 6½ to 7½ cups beef broth

 1 15- to 16-ounce can kidney beans, drained

 1 8-ounce can tomato sauce

 1 pound small shell pasta or elbow macaroni

HEAT oil in heavy large pot over medium-high heat. Add onions and garlic; sauté 5 minutes. Add meat and crushed red pepper. Sauté until meat is no longer pink, breaking up large pieces, about 5 minutes. Add 6½ cups broth, beans, and tomato sauce; bring to boil. Mix in pasta. Reduce heat to medium. Simmer uncovered until pasta is just tender but still firm to bite, stirring often and adding remaining broth by ¼ cupfuls if mixture is too thick, about 12 minutes. Season to taste with salt and pepper.

Spaghetti with turkey-pesto meatballs

2 SERVINGS; CAN BE DOUBLED *This updated version of spaghetti and meatballs still goes well with the usual accompaniments: green salad, garlic bread, and red wine. The sauce can be made up to a day ahead to cut down on last-minute preparation; just reheat it and serve with freshly cooked pasta.*

- 2 cups purchased chunky tomato pasta sauce
- 8 ounces ground turkey
- ¾ cup fresh breadcrumbs made from crustless Italian or French bread
- 2½ tablespoons purchased pesto
- 1 egg white
- ¼ teaspoon salt

- 8 ounces spaghetti

SPREAD 1 cup pasta sauce over bottom of heavy medium skillet. Mix turkey, breadcrumbs, pesto, egg white, and salt in medium bowl. Using moistened hands, form mixture into 8 meatballs. Place meatballs in single layer in sauce. Spoon remaining sauce over. Bring to simmer. Cover; reduce heat to medium-low and simmer until meatballs are cooked through, stirring occasionally, about 20 minutes.

MEANWHILE, cook spaghetti in large pot of boiling salted water until just tender but still firm to bite, stirring occasionally.

DRAIN pasta; divide between bowls. Top with meatballs and sauce.

Rigatoni with cheese and Italian sausage

2 SERVINGS *Marinara sauce is a classic Italian sauce made with tomatoes, garlic, onions, and basil or oregano. There are several varieties of marinara sauce on the market, some in jars and some in the refrigerated section. Look for one that's nice and chunky, with plenty of herbs, garlic, and onions for flavor. A little sugar is fine, but it shouldn't be high on the ingredient list.*

- 8 ounces rigatoni

- 4 ounces hot Italian sausage, casings removed
- 2 garlic cloves, thinly sliced
- 1½ cups prepared marinara sauce
- ½ teaspoon dried crushed red pepper
- ¼ cup grated mozzarella cheese
- 2 tablespoons grated Parmesan cheese
- 1 tablespoon chopped fresh Italian parsley
  Extra-virgin olive oil

COOK rigatoni in large pot of boiling salted water until just tender but still firm to bite, stirring occasionally. Drain.

MEANWHILE, preheat broiler. Sauté sausage in heavy large saucepan over medium-high heat until no longer pink, breaking up with back of fork. Add garlic; stir 2 minutes. Drain off excess drippings in pan and return to medium-high heat. Stir in marinara sauce and crushed red pepper, then pasta. Season to taste with salt and pepper. Transfer to 8×8×2-inch broilerproof baking dish. Sprinkle mozzarella and Parmesan over. Place in broiler until cheeses melt and begin to brown, watching closely to prevent burning, about 1½ minutes. Sprinkle rigatoni with parsley and drizzle with olive oil.

Baked rigatoni with ham, tomatoes, and feta cheese

6 SERVINGS *This rich, comforting pasta is a wonderful midweek meal. You can put it together in minutes, and the recipe is very forgiving: Try diced leftover chicken in place of the ham; roasted red peppers or sun-dried tomatoes in place of the fresh tomatoes; or stir in some chopped fresh herbs, such as thyme, basil, or parsley, instead of the dried thyme.*

12	ounces rigatoni
1½	cups diced ham (about 8 ounces)
4	large plum tomatoes, chopped
1	cup crumbled feta cheese
1	cup (packed) grated mozzarella cheese (about 4 ounces)
1½	teaspoons dried thyme
1	cup heavy whipping cream

PREHEAT oven to 375°F. Butter 13×9×2-inch glass baking dish. Cook rigatoni in large pot of boiling salted water until just tender but still firm to bite, stirring occasionally. Drain. Place in prepared baking dish. Mix in ham, tomatoes, cheeses, and thyme. Pour cream over. Sprinkle with salt and pepper and toss to blend. Cover with foil.

BAKE pasta 15 minutes. Uncover and stir to coat pasta evenly with melted cheeses. Cover again. Bake until heated through, about 30 minutes longer.

Castellane pasta with sausage, peppers, cherry tomatoes, and marjoram

4 TO 6 SERVINGS *Castellane are long, oval shells—they catch the goat cheese nicely. Feel free to use medium-size shell pasta instead of the castellane and oregano in place of the marjoram. Goat cheese crumbles easily when it's cold from the refrigerator; crumble it and keep it chilled until ready to use.*

1	tablespoon extra-virgin olive oil
1	pound hot Italian sausages, casings removed
2	red bell peppers, chopped (about 2 cups)
1	large onion, chopped (about 2 cups)
2½	teaspoons chopped fresh marjoram
2	12-ounce packages cherry tomatoes
12	ounces castellane (long oval shells) or fusilli (spiral-shaped pasta)
5	ounces crumbled goat cheese (about 1 cup)

HEAT oil in large nonstick skillet over medium-high heat. Add sausages; sauté until browned, breaking up with back of fork, about 5 minutes. Add peppers and onion; sauté until soft and onion is golden brown, about 13 minutes. Stir in marjoram, then tomatoes. Simmer until tomatoes soften and release their juices, crushing with back of fork, about 5 minutes. Season to taste with salt and pepper.

MEANWHILE, cook pasta in large pot of boiling salted water until just tender but still firm to bite, stirring occasionally. Drain.

RETURN pasta to pot. Add sausage mixture and goat cheese; stir to blend. Transfer pasta to plates.

Farfalle with sausage, tomatoes, and cream

6 SERVINGS *What we call bow ties, the Italians call butterflies (farfalle). The sauce can be made ahead and left at room temperature for an hour while you finish your dinner preparations. Reserving some of the pasta cooking water and adding it by small amounts to the farfalle ensures a moist and creamy pasta dish.*

- 2 tablespoons olive oil
- 1 pound sweet Italian sausages, casings removed
- ½ teaspoon dried crushed red pepper
- 1 cup chopped onion
- 3 garlic cloves, minced
- 1 28-ounce can crushed tomatoes with added puree
- ½ cup heavy whipping cream
- 1 pound farfalle (bow-tie pasta)
- ½ cup (packed) chopped fresh basil
  Freshly grated Pecorino Romano cheese

HEAT oil in heavy large skillet over medium-high heat. Add sausages and crushed red pepper. Sauté until sausages are no longer pink, breaking into chunks with fork, about 5 minutes. Add onion and garlic; sauté 3 minutes. Add tomatoes and cream. Reduce heat to low; simmer until mixture thickens, about 3 minutes. Season with salt and pepper.

MEANWHILE, cook farfalle in large pot of boiling salted water until just tender but still firm to bite, stirring occasionally. Drain, reserving 1 cup pasta cooking liquid. Return pasta to same pot.

ADD sausage mixture to pasta; toss over medium heat, adding reserved pasta cooking liquid by ¼ cupfuls if dry. Transfer pasta to serving dish. Sprinkle with basil. Serve, passing cheese separately.

Farfalle with bitter greens and sausage

2 SERVINGS; CAN BE DOUBLED *Bags of prewashed, precut bitter greens, such as mustard or turnip greens, are available at many markets and are a great time-saver. Some markets offer a "Southern Blend" that usually contains mustard, turnip, collard greens, and kale, which can be used here. The recipe can be doubled—just use a large, deep skillet or a large pot.*

- 1 tablespoon olive oil
- 1 large onion, chopped
- 3 hot Italian sausages, casings removed
- 2 garlic cloves, minced
- 1 large bunch mustard greens, stems trimmed, cut crosswise into 2-inch pieces (about 4 cups)
- ⅓ cup heavy whipping cream
- 8 ounces farfalle (bow-tie pasta)
- ½ cup freshly grated Pecorino Romano cheese plus additional for serving

HEAT oil in heavy skillet over medium heat. Add onion and sauté until soft, about 8 minutes. Add sausages and garlic; sauté until sausages are no longer pink, breaking up with back of fork. Add greens and stir until just wilted, about 3 minutes. Add cream and boil until slightly thickened, about 2 minutes.

MEANWHILE, cook farfalle in large pot of boiling salted water until just tender but still firm to bite, stirring occasionally. Drain. Return pasta to pot. Mix in sauce and ½ cup cheese. Season to taste with salt and pepper. Serve, passing additional cheese separately.

Perciatelli with prosciutto, wilted radicchio, blue cheese, and dried figs

2 SERVINGS *This rich pasta is perfect for a special occasion—its sweet, salty, and bitter tastes blend beautifully. Arugula and linguine can replace the radicchio and perciatelli. Save some of the pasta cooking liquid to moisten the pasta, as blue cheese varies in creaminess. Accompany this pasta with a salad of thinly sliced fennel sprinkled with sea salt and drizzled with extra-virgin olive oil and lemon juice.*

 8 ounces perciatelli (long hollow pasta) or linguine

 3 tablespoons olive oil

 4 cups (packed) thinly sliced radicchio (about 6 ounces)

 4 ounces thinly sliced prosciutto, cut crosswise into ½-inch-wide strips

 ¾ cup sliced stemmed dried black Mission figs (about 4 ounces)

 ¾ cup crumbled blue cheese (such as Maytag; about 4 ounces), divided

 ¼ cup chopped fresh Italian parsley, divided

COOK pasta in large pot of boiling salted water until just tender but still firm to bite, stirring occasionally. Drain. Return to pot.

HEAT oil in large nonstick skillet over medium-high heat. Add radicchio, prosciutto, and figs; sauté until radicchio is just wilted, about 2 minutes. Add mixture to pasta. Add half of blue cheese and half of parsley. Season pasta lightly with salt and generously with pepper; toss gently. Divide pasta between 2 plates. Sprinkle with remaining blue cheese and parsley.

Linguine with pancetta and sautéed cherry tomatoes

4 SERVINGS *Pancetta is Italian bacon cured with salt and such spices as cinnamon and cloves. You can find it at an Italian market or at a deli, where it comes in a large sausage-like roll, which is then thinly sliced. Some supermarkets carry thinly sliced pancetta in the deli section; it comes in vacuum-sealed packages. If you can't find it, bacon is also delicious in this recipe.*

 12 ounces linguine

 ¼ cup olive oil

 6 garlic cloves, chopped

 4 ounces sliced pancetta or bacon, chopped

 ¼ teaspoon dried crushed red pepper

 1½ pounds cherry tomatoes

 1¼ cups grated Pecorino Romano or Parmesan cheese, divided

 ½ cup chopped fresh basil, divided

COOK linguine in pot of boiling salted water until tender but still firm to bite, stirring occasionally. Drain, reserving 1 cup pasta cooking liquid. Return pasta to pot.

MEANWHILE, heat oil in heavy large skillet over medium-high heat. Add garlic; stir 30 seconds. Add pancetta and crushed red pepper; sauté until pancetta is crisp, about 4 minutes. Add tomatoes; sauté until soft, about 4 minutes.

TRANSFER tomato mixture to pot with pasta. Add ¾ cup cheese and ⅓ cup basil. Toss over medium heat until cheese melts and sauce coats pasta, adding pasta cooking liquid by ¼ cupfuls if dry. Season to taste with salt and pepper. Transfer to bowl. Sprinkle with remaining basil. Serve, passing remaining cheese separately.

Antipasto pasta

4 SERVINGS *Asiago, an Italian cow's milk cheese with a rich nutty flavor, can be found at some supermarkets, specialty foods stores, and Italian markets. If you're in a hurry, omit the sautéed mushrooms.*

12 ounces linguine

3 tablespoons olive oil

4 large (5-inch-diameter) portobello mushrooms, stemmed, dark gills removed, caps sliced ¼ inch thick

6 ounces ⅛-inch-thick slices Genoa salami, cut into thin strips

1 cup sliced vegetables and 6 tablespoons marinade from 16-ounce jar antipasto salad with olives

2 cups grated Asiago cheese, divided

2 cups chopped fresh basil, divided

COOK linguine in large pot of boiling salted water until just tender but still firm to bite, stirring occasionally. Drain, reserving ½ cup pasta cooking liquid.

HEAT oil in same pot over medium-high heat. Add mushrooms; sauté until tender and brown, about 6 minutes. Add salami; toss 30 seconds. Add pasta, ½ cup pasta cooking liquid, sliced vegetables, reserved marinade, and 1½ cups cheese; toss until liquid thickens and coats pasta, about 3 minutes. Mix in 1½ cups basil. Season to taste with pepper. Transfer to bowl. Sprinkle with remaining ½ cup basil. Serve, passing remaining ½ cup cheese separately.

Fettuccine quattro formaggi

8 SERVINGS *Except for the Parmesan cheese, which is pretty much a requirement, this ultra-cheesy cousin of fettuccine Alfredo can be made with any number of four-cheese combinations. The recipe calls for spinach fettuccine, which adds flavor and color, but regular or whole wheat fettuccine works well, too.*

1 pound spinach fettuccine

1½ cups heavy whipping cream

¾ cup crumbled Gorgonzola cheese

⅔ cup grated provolone cheese

½ cup crumbled soft fresh goat cheese

¼ cup (½ stick) butter

½ teaspoon dried crushed red pepper

¼ teaspoon ground nutmeg

¾ cup freshly grated Parmesan cheese

¼ cup pine nuts, toasted

COOK fettuccine in large pot of boiling salted water until just tender but still firm to bite, stirring occasionally.

MEANWHILE, combine cream and next 6 ingredients in heavy large saucepan. Whisk over medium heat until mixture simmers and is smooth.

DRAIN pasta; return to same pot. Add cream sauce and Parmesan to pasta; toss to coat. Season to taste with salt and pepper. Transfer to large bowl. Sprinkle with pine nuts.

Fettuccine with cream, basil, and Pecorino Romano cheese

2 SERVINGS; CAN BE DOUBLED *Green onions and basil add freshness to the sauce, which is quick enough to make while the pasta cooks. Italian parsley would also be good in this recipe. Serve this with sliced tomatoes drizzled with balsamic vinegar.*

- 4 thick-cut bacon slices, chopped
- 4 green onions, chopped
- ½ cup heavy whipping cream
- ½ cup freshly grated Pecorino Romano or Parmesan cheese plus additional for serving
- ⅓ cup chopped fresh basil

- 8 ounces fettuccine

COOK bacon in heavy medium skillet over medium heat until bacon begins to brown. Add green onions and stir until slightly softened, about 1 minute. Add cream and simmer until sauce begins to thicken, about 1 minute. Mix in ½ cup cheese and basil.

MEANWHILE, cook fettuccine in large pot of boiling salted water until just tender but still firm to bite, stirring occasionally. Drain. Return pasta to pot. Add sauce and stir to coat. Season to taste with salt and pepper. Serve, passing additional cheese separately.

Linguine with winter pesto

4 FIRST-COURSE OR 2 MAIN-COURSE SERVINGS *This parsley-based pesto is a nice alternative to the classic basil recipe. You can make the pesto ahead and store it in the refrigerator. Pouring a thin layer of olive oil over the surface of the pesto keeps it green. Try the pesto spooned over goat cheese with baguette slices for a tasty appetizer.*

- 2½ cups lightly packed fresh Italian parsley leaves
- ¾ cup olive oil
- ½ cup pine nuts, toasted plus ⅓ cup chopped toasted pine nuts for garnish
- 2 teaspoons fresh thyme leaves
- 1 teaspoon minced fresh rosemary
- 1 garlic clove, peeled
- ⅓ cup freshly grated Parmesan cheese

- 12 ounces linguine

COMBINE parsley, oil, ½ cup pine nuts, thyme, rosemary, and garlic in processor and blend to coarse puree. Blend in cheese using on/off turns. Season to taste with salt and pepper.

DO AHEAD *Can be made 2 days ahead. Transfer pesto to jar. Pour enough oil over pesto to cover completely. Cover and chill. Pour off extra oil before using.*

COOK linguine in large pot of boiling salted water until just tender but still firm to bite, stirring occasionally. Drain. Return pasta to pot. Add pesto sauce and toss to coat. Transfer to large bowl. Garnish with chopped pine nuts.

Pasta with pesto, beans, and potatoes

4 TO 6 SERVINGS *Liguria is the region in Italy that hugs the Mediterranean and borders France—this is the quintessential pasta dish of that region. Enjoy it with green beans in fall and with fava beans in spring. You can find fava beans at some Middle Eastern markets, specialty markets, and farmers' markets. Middle Eastern markets also sell frozen double-peeled fava beans, which can be thawed and used in place of the fresh, as can frozen thawed lima beans, to cut down on prep time.*

6½ ounces fresh basil, stemmed (about 6 cups)
⅓ cup freshly grated Parmesan cheese
2 tablespoons pine nuts
2 garlic cloves, peeled
¼ cup extra-virgin olive oil

3 medium red-skinned potatoes, peeled, cut crosswise into ¼-inch-thick slices
12 ounces fresh fava beans, shelled, halved, or 6 ounces thin green beans, trimmed
14 ounces fettuccine

1 tablespoon butter

PUREE first 5 ingredients in processor. Transfer pesto to bowl; season to taste with salt and pepper.

DO AHEAD *Can be made 1 day ahead. Press plastic wrap onto pesto surface and chill.*

COOK potatoes in large pot of boiling salted water until just tender, about 5 minutes. Using slotted spoon, transfer potatoes to large bowl. Add beans to same pot and boil until tender, about 3 minutes. Using slotted spoon, transfer beans to bowl with potatoes. Cook linguine in same pot until just tender but still firm to bite, stirring occasionally. Drain, reserving ⅓ cup pasta cooking liquid. Add pasta to potatoes and beans.

WHISK enough reserved pasta cooking liquid into pesto to moisten. Add pesto and butter to pasta. Season to taste with salt and pepper. Toss to coat.

Orecchiette with turnip greens

4 SERVINGS *Orecchiette are little ear-shaped pasta from the Apulia region of Italy. The simple turnip green topping, flavored with anchovies, garlic, and chile, is also an Apulian specialty. To cut down on prep time, you can substitute 10 ounces of frozen chopped spinach, thawed and squeezed dry, for the fresh turnip greens, or add two 6-ounce bags of fresh spinach to the cooked pasta and stir just until wilted.*

1 pound fresh turnip greens, trimmed, coarsely chopped

5 tablespoons extra-virgin olive oil
8 anchovy fillets
1 jalapeño chile, halved, seeded
1 garlic clove, thinly sliced crosswise
1 bay leaf

12 ounces orecchiette (little ear-shaped pasta) or shells

COOK greens in pot of boiling salted water until wilted, about 2 minutes. Using sieve or slotted spoon, transfer greens to strainer; drain well. Reserve cooking liquid in pot. Squeeze greens dry.

HEAT oil in heavy large skillet over medium-high heat. Add anchovies, jalapeño, garlic, and bay leaf; sauté until garlic is golden, mashing anchovies with back of spoon, about 3 minutes. Add greens and sauté 2 minutes. Discard jalapeño and bay leaf.

RETURN reserved cooking liquid to boil. Add orecchiette and cook until just tender but still firm to bite, stirring occasionally. Drain; return pasta to pot. Add greens to pasta and stir to coat. Season to taste with salt and pepper. Transfer to bowl.

Spaghetti alla carbonara di zucchine

4 TO 6 SERVINGS *Spaghetti carbonara is a Roman classic, traditionally made with eggs and pancetta or bacon. Here, golden brown zucchini slices stand in for the pancetta—making it a hearty vegetarian dish. Make sure to toss the noodles with the beaten eggs and cheese as soon as the hot pasta is drained, so that there will be enough heat to cook the eggs.*

- 5 tablespoons extra-virgin olive oil
- 1 garlic clove, peeled
- 1 pound medium zucchini, trimmed, cut into ¼-inch thick rounds (about 3½ cups)

- 2 large eggs, room temperature
- ¾ cup freshly grated Parmesan cheese
- 12 ounces spaghetti

- 6 large fresh basil leaves, torn into pieces, divided

HEAT oil in heavy large skillet over medium heat. Add garlic and sauté until pale golden, about 1 minute. Add zucchini and sauté until beginning to color, about 15 minutes. Remove from heat; discard garlic clove.

MEANWHILE, whisk eggs and Parmesan in large bowl to blend. Cook spaghetti in large pot of boiling salted water until just tender but still firm to bite, stirring occasionally. Drain pasta; add to egg mixture and toss to coat (heat from pasta will cook eggs).

ADD zucchini mixture and half of basil to pasta; stir gently to blend. Season to taste with salt and pepper. Sprinkle with remaining basil.

Pasta with Pecorino Romano and black pepper

2 SERVINGS *Based on the Italian dish cacio e pepe (cheese and pepper), this simple but delicious pasta deserves to be made with the very best ingredients: imported Pecorino Romano, top-quality pasta, and fragrant peppercorns. Although untraditional, the addition of arugula adds color and freshness.*

- 6 ounces penne or bucatini (hollow spaghetti-like pasta)
- 3 tablespoons extra-virgin olive oil
- 1 cup (packed) fresh arugula, torn into pieces
- ⅓ cup (packed) freshly grated Pecorino Romano cheese
  Freshly ground black pepper

FILL large serving bowl with hot water to heat bowl; let stand while cooking pasta. Cook pasta in large pot of boiling salted water until just tender but still firm to bite, stirring occasionally. Drain pasta, reserving ½ cup pasta cooking liquid. Pour out and discard hot water from serving bowl. Immediately add drained pasta and oil to bowl, then arugula and cheese, and toss to coat. If dry, add some of reserved pasta cooking liquid by tablespoonfuls. Season to taste with salt and freshly ground black pepper. Divide between plates.

Pasta with three peas

4 SERVINGS *Pea tendrils (called* dau miu *in Chinese cooking) taste like a cross between peas and spinach. You can find the tendrils at some farmers' markets and Asian markets. Pea sprouts, an immature version of the tendrils, are available at some supermarkets and specialty and natural foods stores; they make a good substitute for the tendrils, as do readily available watercress and baby spinach leaves.*

12　ounces orecchiette (little ear-shaped pasta)

8　ounces bacon, chopped
8　shallots, trimmed, quartered
2　cups sugar snap peas (about 8 ounces)
4　cups (4½ ounces) pea tendrils
1　cup frozen petite peas, thawed
⅓　cup thinly sliced fresh mint
1　cup shaved Parmesan cheese plus additional for serving

COOK orecchiette in large pot of boiling salted water until just tender but still firm to bite, stirring occasionally. Drain, reserving 1 cup pasta cooking liquid. Transfer pasta to large bowl.

MEANWHILE, sauté bacon in heavy large skillet over high heat until crisp, about 5 minutes. Using slotted spoon, transfer bacon to paper towels. Add shallots to skillet; sauté over medium-high heat until golden brown, pressing with spoon to separate layers, about 5 minutes. Add snap peas; stir until bright green and crisp-tender, about 1 minute. Add pea tendrils and petite peas, stirring just until tendrils wilt, about 1 minute. Add pea mixture, bacon, mint, and enough reserved pasta cooking liquid to moisten pasta. Stir in 1 cup cheese. Serve, passing additional cheese separately.

Linguine avgolemono with artichoke hearts and green beans

4 SERVINGS Avgolemono *is the name for both a tangy Greek sauce and soup made with lemon juice, egg yolks, and chicken broth. Here, the lemon and egg yolks combine with pasta and veggies for a tart twist on linguine carbonara. Sugar snap peas would be a tasty spring replacement for the green beans.*

3　large egg yolks
¼　cup fresh lemon juice
½　cup heavy whipping cream

12　ounces frozen artichoke hearts
8　ounces green beans, trimmed, cut on diagonal into 2-inch-long pieces
12　ounces linguine

¾　cup freshly grated Parmesan cheese plus additional for serving
¼　cup chopped fresh Italian parsley

PLACE yolks in medium bowl. Gradually whisk in lemon juice, then cream.

COOK artichoke hearts and green beans in large pot of boiling salted water until crisp-tender, about 5 minutes. Using sieve, transfer vegetables from pot to large skillet. Return water to boil. Add linguine; boil until just tender but still firm to bite, stirring occasionally. Drain pasta, reserving 1½ cups pasta cooking liquid.

ADD pasta to skillet with vegetables. Whisk ¾ cup pasta cooking liquid into yolk mixture. Add yolk mixture, ¾ cup cheese, and parsley to skillet. Toss over medium heat just until sauce thickens and coats pasta, about 4 minutes, adding more pasta cooking liquid by tablespoonfuls if dry. Season to taste with salt and pepper. Serve, passing additional cheese separately.

Spaghettini with spicy escarole and Pecorino Romano

4 TO 6 SERVINGS *Escarole is a member of the endive family. It has a slightly nutty, mildly bitter flavor that is delicious in this simple yet versatile pasta dish. Serve the pasta as an entrée or as a first course before roasted chicken or beef.*

4 tablespoons extra-virgin olive oil, divided

3 anchovy fillets, chopped

¼ teaspoon dried crushed red pepper

2 garlic cloves, minced

1½ pounds escarole (about 1 large head), cut into 1- to 2-inch strips

1 cup water

1 pound spaghettini
Freshly grated Pecorino Romano cheese

HEAT 2 tablespoons oil in heavy large saucepan over medium heat. Add anchovies and crushed red pepper; stir 1 minute. Add garlic; stir 30 seconds. Stir in escarole. Add 1 cup water, cover pan, and reduce heat to low. Cook until escarole is tender, about 5 minutes. Season to taste with salt and pepper.

MEANWHILE, cook spaghettini in large pot of boiling salted water until just tender but still firm to bite, stirring occasionally. Drain pasta, reserving 1 cup pasta cooking liquid. Return pasta to same pot. Add escarole mixture to pasta and stir over low heat to combine, adding pasta cooking liquid by tablespoonfuls to moisten if necessary. Stir in remaining 2 tablespoons oil. Divide pasta among shallow bowls and sprinkle with cheese.

CLEAN GREENS To clean greens, cut the leaves into 1-inch pieces and place them in a large basin of cold water (any dirt will sink to the bottom). Pull the greens out a handful at a time and dry them in a salad spinner.

Campanelle pasta with burrata cheese, spinach, lemon, and toasted almonds

6 SERVINGS *Burrata is a luscious Italian cheese made by mixing cream and unspun mozzarella curds together (for a texture similar to ricotta); the mixture is then inserted into a ball of fresh mozzarella. It can be found in some supermarkets, specialty foods stores, and at Italian markets. Substitute regular fresh mozzarella if you can't find burrata.*

1 pound campanelle (trumpet-shaped pasta) or fusilli (spiral-shaped pasta)

2 tablespoons (¼ stick) butter

⅓ cup olive oil

2 garlic cloves, minced

¼ cup fresh lemon juice

1 teaspoon finely grated lemon peel

1 6-ounce package baby spinach

¾ cup sliced almonds, toasted

1 pound burrata cheese, cut into 1-inch chunks

COOK pasta in large pot of boiling salted water until just tender but still firm to bite, stirring occasionally.

MEANWHILE, melt butter with oil in heavy large skillet over medium heat. Add garlic; sauté until soft, about 2 minutes. Add lemon juice and peel.

DRAIN pasta; transfer to large bowl. Place spinach and almonds atop hot pasta. Pour hot lemon mixture over. Toss until spinach is wilted, about 1 minute. Divide pasta among plates. Top with burrata cheese and sprinkle with salt and pepper.

THE PEEL STORY To grate lemon peel: Hold the lemon steady in one hand on the work surface. Using a Microplane or other razor-sharp zester, scrape the sharp side down across the top of the lemon just until you reach the bitter white layer (the pith). Turn the lemon and continue.

Spaghetti with tomatoes, arugula, capers, and olives

4 SERVINGS *This is one of those great pasta dishes where the pasta is tossed with uncooked ingredients in a large bowl. The recipe is a perfect opportunity to improvise. Try adding chopped jarred roasted peppers or chopped anchovies. Or replace the olives with a few tablespoons of tapenade. Serve the dish, passing additional olive oil separately.*

- 6 plum tomatoes, halved, juiced, seeded, chopped
- ⅓ cup halved pitted Kalamata olives
- ⅓ cup (packed) chopped arugula
- ⅓ cup olive oil
- 3 tablespoons capers, drained
- 3 garlic cloves, pressed
- ¾ teaspoon dried crushed red pepper

- 1 pound spaghetti

MIX first 7 ingredients in large bowl; season to taste with salt and pepper. Let stand 30 minutes at room temperature for flavors to develop.

COOK spaghetti in large pot of boiling salted water until just tender but still firm to bite, stirring occasionally. Drain. Return pasta to pot; add tomato mixture and toss. Season to taste with salt and pepper. Transfer to large bowl.

DO AHEAD *Can be made 1 day ahead. Cover and chill. Bring to room temperature before serving.*

Linguine with pears and Gorgonzola cheese

4 SERVINGS *Pears and Gorgonzola cheese are a classic combination in Italy. If desired, you can add diced roast chicken or ham to the sauce, which can be made up to two hours ahead. Reserve a little pasta cooking liquid to thin the sauce if necessary after tossing it with the pasta.*

- ¼ cup (½ stick) butter
- 4 firm pears (about 2 pounds), peeled, cored, cut into ⅓-inch-thick strips
- 1 tablespoon chopped fresh rosemary
- 1 cup low-salt chicken broth
- 4 ounces Gorgonzola cheese, crumbled (about 1 cup)
- ¾ cup freshly grated Parmesan cheese, divided
- ½ cup heavy whipping cream

- 12 ounces linguine
- ⅓ cup chopped pecans

MELT butter in heavy large skillet over medium-high heat. Add pears; sauté until tender and beginning to brown but not soft, about 8 minutes. Using slotted spoon, carefully transfer pears to bowl. Add rosemary to skillet and stir until fragrant, about 1 minute. Add broth, Gorgonzola cheese, ½ cup Parmesan, and cream. Simmer until sauce thickens enough to coat spoon, whisking occasionally, about 6 minutes. Return pears and any accumulated juices to sauce.

DO AHEAD *Sauce can be made 2 hours ahead. Let stand at room temperature. Bring to simmer before continuing.*

COOK linguine in large pot of boiling salted water until just tender but still firm to bite, stirring occasionally. Drain; return pasta to pot. Add sauce and pecans to pasta; toss over medium-low heat until sauce coats pasta, about 3 minutes. Season to taste with salt and pepper. Transfer to large bowl. Sprinkle with remaining ¼ cup Parmesan cheese.

Farfalle with wilted frisée and burst tomatoes

4 TO 6 SERVINGS *When choosing frisée, look for small, compact heads and store in the refrigerator for up to one week. Use the tender, lighter-colored inner leaves and the center of the head. The tomatoes in this pasta literally burst when cooked over high heat—just make sure that you don't overcook the tomatoes and turn them to sauce.*

    3 tablespoons extra-virgin olive oil
 1½ pints cherry tomatoes
    2 garlic cloves, minced
    1 teaspoon finely grated lemon peel
  ¼ teaspoon dried crushed red pepper
    2 large heads of frisée (about 1 pound), coarsely chopped

  12 ounces farfalle (bow-tie pasta)

  ¼ cup (½ stick) butter, cut into ½-inch pieces
  ½ cup freshly grated Parmesan cheese

HEAT oil in heavy large skillet over medium-high heat. Add tomatoes and cook until tomatoes begin to burst, stirring frequently, about 8 minutes. Add garlic, lemon peel, and crushed red pepper; sauté 2 minutes longer. Add frisée in batches and sauté until wilted, about 3 minutes total. Season to taste with salt and pepper.

MEANWHILE, cook farfalle in large pot of boiling salted water until just tender but still firm to bite, stirring occasionally. Drain, reserving 1 cup pasta cooking liquid.

ADD pasta to skillet with tomato-frisée mixture. Stir in butter. Add reserved pasta cooking liquid by ¼ cupfuls if dry. Divide pasta among shallow bowls. Serve, passing cheese separately.

Orecchiette with garbanzos, tomatoes, feta, and mint

6 TO 8 SERVINGS *Italy meets Greece in this pasta, which pairs well with grilled lamb or chicken. Golden Grape tomatoes are sweet orange-colored cherry tomatoes; they are available at many supermarkets, but the sweetest come from farmers' markets. Serve the pasta hot or at room temperature.*

    1 pound orecchiette (little ear-shaped pasta)
    1 pound Golden Grape or cherry tomatoes (scant 4 cups), halved
    7 tablespoons extra-virgin olive oil, divided
  ⅓ cup chopped fresh mint plus sprigs for garnish
  ⅓ cup thinly sliced green onions
  ¼ cup chopped fresh cilantro plus sprigs for garnish
    2 garlic cloves, minced

    1 15- to 16-ounce can garbanzo beans (chickpeas), well drained
    6 ounces feta cheese, coarsely crumbled (about 1½ cups)

COOK orecchiette in large pot of boiling salted water until just tender but still firm to bite, stirring occasionally. Drain.

MEANWHILE, combine tomatoes, 6 tablespoons olive oil, chopped mint, green onions, chopped cilantro, and garlic in large bowl. Season to taste with salt.

HEAT remaining 1 tablespoon olive oil in medium skillet over medium-high heat. Add garbanzo beans and sauté until lightly browned, about 5 minutes. Add garbanzo beans and pasta to tomato mixture in bowl; toss to coat. Add feta and toss briefly. Season to taste with salt and pepper. Garnish with mint and cilantro sprigs. Serve warm or let stand at room temperature up to 2 hours.

DO AHEAD *Can be made 1 day ahead. Cover and chill. Bring to room temperature before serving.*

Fettuccine with asparagus, morels, and tarragon

4 SERVINGS *A morel is a dark brown wild mushroom with a cone-shaped cap that looks like a miniature sponge. When cooked, it has a slightly smoky, nutty, and earthy flavor. Fresh, uncultivated morels are in season from April to June, which is when asparagus is at its peak, so it's best to enjoy this rich pasta in the spring. If you can't find fresh morels, dried will do.*

8	ounces fresh morel mushrooms, halved if large, or 1 ounce dried morels
3	tablespoons butter
1	cup (packed) sliced shallots
1	pound asparagus, trimmed, cut into 1½-inch lengths
1¼	cups vegetable broth (if using fresh morels)
⅔	cup heavy whipping cream
2½	tablespoons chopped fresh tarragon, divided
12	ounces fettuccine
1	cup grated Parmesan cheese, divided

IF using dried morels, place in 2-cup measuring cup and pour enough hot water over to reach 2-cup mark. Let soak until soft, pushing down occasionally if morels rise to top, about 20 minutes. Drain, reserving soaking liquid; add enough water to measure 1¼ cups if needed. Cut large morels in half.

MELT butter in heavy large skillet over medium-high heat. Add shallots and fresh or reconstituted morels; sauté until shallots are tender, about 6 minutes. Add asparagus and broth (if using fresh morels) or reserved soaking liquid (if using dried morels). Bring to boil, cover, and cook 2 minutes. Stir in cream and 2 tablespoons chopped tarragon. Simmer uncovered until sauce thickens slightly, about 4 minutes. Season sauce to taste with salt and pepper.

MEANWHILE, cook fettuccine in large pot of boiling salted water until just tender but still firm to bite, stirring occasionally. Drain pasta and return to pot. Add ½ cup Parmesan cheese and sauce; toss. Transfer to bowl; sprinkle with remaining ½ tablespoon tarragon. Serve with remaining Parmesan.

Tagliatelle with shredded beets, sour cream, and parsley

6 FIRST-COURSE OR 4 MAIN-COURSE SERVINGS *Sour cream and beets are inseparable in Eastern European cooking, and here is a fresh new way to enjoy them together. Using latex gloves (sold at drugstores) helps protect your hands from beet stains.*

1	tablespoon butter
2	tablespoons olive oil
2	garlic cloves, minced
3	cups (packed) coarsely grated peeled uncooked beets (about 3 large)
½	teaspoon cayenne pepper
2	tablespoons fresh lemon juice
12	ounces tagliatelle or fettuccine
1	8-ounce container sour cream
6	tablespoons chopped fresh Italian parsley, divided

MELT butter with oil in large nonstick skillet over medium heat. Add garlic; stir until pale golden, about 1 minute. Add beets and cayenne; reduce heat to medium-low and sauté just until beets are tender, about 12 minutes. Stir in lemon juice.

MEANWHILE, cook pasta in large pot of boiling salted water until just tender but still firm to bite, stirring occasionally.

DRAIN pasta and return to pot. Stir in sour cream and 4 tablespoons parsley, then beet mixture. Season to taste with salt and pepper. Transfer pasta to bowl. Sprinkle with remaining 2 tablespoons chopped parsley.

Fusilli with eggplant, pine nuts, currants, and capers

8 FIRST-COURSE OR 6 MAIN-COURSE SERVINGS *This hearty vegetarian pasta hails from Tuscany. Don't skip the first step of salting the eggplant slices—this draws out the excess moisture so that the eggplant will absorb less oil and stay firm when cooked.*

2 16-ounce eggplants, cut crosswise into ½-inch-thick slices

2 tablespoons olive oil
1 medium onion, chopped
4 garlic cloves, minced
¾ cup pine nuts, toasted
¾ cup dried currants
½ cup drained capers
2 14½-ounce cans diced tomatoes in juice

1 pound fusilli (spiral-shaped pasta)
1 cup freshly grated Pecorino Romano cheese, divided
½ cup chopped fresh basil

PLACE eggplant slices on large rimmed baking sheet. Sprinkle with salt. Let stand 20 minutes. Turn eggplant slices over. Sprinkle with salt. Let stand 20 minutes longer. Rinse eggplant. Drain; pat dry with paper towels. Cut eggplant into ½-inch cubes. Set aside.

HEAT oil in heavy large skillet over medium-high heat. Add onion and sauté until golden, about 4 minutes. Add garlic; sauté 1 minute. Add eggplant; sauté until tender, about 10 minutes. Stir in pine nuts, currants, and capers; sauté 1 minute. Add tomatoes with juices; bring to simmer. Season to taste with salt and pepper.

MEANWHILE, cook fusilli in large pot of boiling salted water until just tender but still firm to bite, stirring occasionally. Drain. Return pasta to pot. Add eggplant mixture, ¼ cup cheese, and basil. Toss to combine. Transfer to large bowl. Serve, passing remaining cheese separately.

Linguine with red peppers, green onions, and pine nuts

2 SERVINGS; CAN BE DOUBLED *Because pine nuts burn easily, it's a good idea to toast them on the stovetop where you can keep an eye on them. Stir the pine nuts constantly in a heavy medium, dry skillet over medium heat until golden, about five minutes. Transfer the pine nuts immediately to a small bowl—the hot skillet could continue to brown the pine nuts.*

1 tablespoon olive oil
2 red bell peppers, cut into strips
6 green onions, thinly sliced
⅔ cup heavy whipping cream
½ cup dry white wine
¼ cup freshly grated Parmesan cheese

9 ounces fresh linguine

¼ cup pine nuts, toasted

HEAT oil in heavy large skillet over medium-high heat. Add peppers; sauté until crisp-tender, about 4 minutes. Add green onions and sauté 2 minutes. Transfer vegetable mixture to bowl. Add cream and wine to same skillet and simmer until mixture thickens slightly, about 3 minutes. Mix in cheese and all but 1 cup vegetable mixture; simmer 2 minutes to blend flavors. Season to taste with salt and pepper.

MEANWHILE, cook linguine in large pot of boiling salted water until just tender but still firm to bite, stirring occasionally. Drain, reserving ½ cup pasta cooking liquid.

RETURN pasta to pot. Add sauce and toss to coat over medium heat, adding reserved pasta cooking liquid by tablespoonfuls to moisten, if desired. Mound pasta on plates. Garnish with reserved 1 cup vegetables. Sprinkle with pine nuts.

Pasta with grilled vegetables and feta

6 SERVINGS *Using jarred marinated feta cheese cubes cuts down on prep time in this quick summer pasta. If you're unable to find the jars of feta, you can still make the pasta with 4 ounces cubed feta (about 1 cup), ⅓ cup extra-virgin olive oil, 1 teaspoon Italian seasoning, and 1 minced garlic clove. You'll need either wooden or thin metal skewers to grill the cherry tomatoes; if using wooden skewers, first soak them in water for 30 minutes.*

1 10½-ounce jar feta cheese cubes in oil with herbs and spices

3 bell peppers (1 yellow, 1 orange, and 1 red), cut into ¾-inch-thick strips

1 large red onion, halved through root end, cut into ¾-inch-thick wedges with some root left intact

1 12-ounce package cherry tomatoes

2 tablespoons chopped fresh oregano, divided

1 pound castellane (long oval shells) or penne

PREPARE barbecue (medium-high heat). Drain all marinade from feta cheese into large bowl. Add bell pepper strips, onion wedges, and cherry tomatoes to marinade in bowl; sprinkle with salt and pepper and toss to coat. Thread cherry tomatoes on skewers. Grill all vegetables until tender and slightly charred, about 15 minutes for onion wedges, 10 minutes for bell pepper strips, and 5 minutes for cherry tomatoes. Return vegetables to same bowl. Sprinkle with 1½ tablespoons chopped oregano; toss to blend.

MEANWHILE, cook pasta in large pot of boiling salted water until just tender but still firm to bite, stirring occasionally. Drain.

ADD pasta and feta cheese to bowl with grilled vegetables; toss to coat. Season to taste with salt and pepper. Sprinkle with remaining ½ table-spoon oregano.

How to cook pasta Cook pasta in plenty of rapidly boiling, salted water (about 3 to 4 quarts per pound of dried pasta). As long as you use enough water, the pasta won't get sticky—it's not necessary to add oil to the boiling water.

— Follow the cooking time directions on the package, and test periodically for doneness by biting the pasta. It's done when it is just tender, but your teeth still meet some resistance.

— Drain pasta as soon as it is cooked and toss immediately with sauce. Or, if desired, cook the pasta halfway, then remove the pasta to a strainer, keeping the cooking liquid boiling in the pot. When ready to toss with sauce, return pasta to the *same* boiling liquid and finish cooking until just tender (it will just take a couple of minutes), then drain and toss with sauce.

— When draining pasta, save some of the pasta cooking water—this water can play an important role in adding moisture and creaminess to the pasta dish. The starch in the water creates a creamy, more cohesive sauce and helps the sauce cling to the pasta.

— When making a hot or warm pasta dish, don't rinse the pasta under running water—you'll remove a thin starchy layer that picks up flavor from sauces.

Tortellini with mushroom carbonara sauce

6 SERVINGS *Although delicious on simple cheese tortellini, this sauce would also be wonderful on penne or ziti. Some markets sell sliced crimini (also called baby bella) mushrooms in six- to eight-ounce packages as well as pre-chopped onions, which will cut down on the slicing and chopping.*

- 1 **pound fresh tortellini**

- 12 **bacon slices, coarsely chopped**
- 1 **pound crimini mushrooms, sliced**
- 2 **cups chopped onions**
- 4 **garlic cloves, minced**
- ½ **teaspoon dried sage leaves**
- 4 **large egg yolks**
- 1 **cup heavy whipping cream**
- ⅔ **cup freshly grated Parmesan cheese, divided**

COOK pasta in pot of boiling salted water until just tender but still firm to bite, stirring occasionally. Drain, reserving 1 cup pasta cooking liquid.

SAUTÉ bacon in heavy large skillet over medium-high heat until crisp and brown. Using slotted spoon, transfer bacon to paper towels to drain. Pour off all but 3 tablespoons drippings from skillet. Add mushrooms, onions, garlic, and sage to skillet. Sauté over medium-high heat until mushrooms are tender, about 8 minutes. Add ½ cup reserved pasta cooking liquid to skillet. Bring to boil over medium-high heat. Whisk egg yolks and cream in small bowl to blend. Add cream mixture, tortellini, and ⅓ cup Parmesan cheese to mushroom mixture. Toss until sauce thickens and coats tortellini, adding more pasta cooking liquid by tablespoonfuls to thin sauce, if desired, about 3 minutes. Season to taste with salt and pepper. Transfer pasta to serving bowl and sprinkle with remaining ⅓ cup Parmesan.

Cheese tortellini with pesto cream sauce

4 APPETIZER OR 2 MAIN-COURSE SERVINGS *You can also make this appetizer or rich entrée with farfalle (bow-tie) pasta. Packaged prewashed and pre-trimmed baby spinach leaves work well in the sauce.*

- 3 **tablespoons butter**
- ½ **cup sliced mushrooms**
- 6 **garlic cloves, minced**
- 2 **cups (packed) fresh spinach leaves**
- 1 **cup heavy whipping cream**
- ¼ **cup chopped drained oil-packed sun-dried tomatoes**

- 1 **9-ounce package fresh cheese tortellini**

- ½ **cup freshly grated Parmesan cheese**
- ¼ **cup chopped fresh basil**
- 3 **tablespoons pine nuts, toasted**

MELT butter in heavy large skillet over medium heat. Add mushrooms and garlic; sauté until mushrooms are tender, about 5 minutes. Add spinach; stir until wilted. Add cream and sun-dried tomatoes and boil until thickened to sauce consistency, stirring occasionally, about 6 minutes.

MEANWHILE, cook tortellini in large pot of boiling salted water until just tender but still firm to bite, stirring occasionally. Drain.

ADD tortellini and Parmesan to sauce in skillet and stir over medium heat until heated through. Season to taste with salt and pepper. Mix in basil and pine nuts. Transfer to bowl.

Cheese ravioli with old-fashioned meat sauce

4 SERVINGS; CAN BE DOUBLED *This sauce also tastes great on spaghetti. Serve it with freshly grated Parmesan or Pecorino Romano cheese.*

- 1 **28-ounce can Italian-style tomatoes in juice**
- 1 **tablespoon olive oil**
- 1 **medium onion, chopped**
- 12 **ounces extra-lean ground beef**
- 2 **garlic cloves, chopped**
- 2 **cups canned tomato puree**
- 1 **teaspoon dried basil**
- 1 **teaspoon dried oregano**
- ⅛ **teaspoon dried crushed red pepper**

- 1½ **pounds cheese ravioli**

PUREE tomatoes with juice in processor. Heat oil in heavy medium saucepan over medium heat. Add onion; sauté until tender, about 8 minutes. Add ground beef and garlic; sauté until meat is no longer pink, breaking up with fork, about 5 minutes. Add pureed tomatoes with juice, canned tomato puree, basil, oregano, and crushed red pepper to saucepan. Simmer 30 minutes, stirring occasionally. Season sauce to taste with salt and pepper.

COOK ravioli in large pot of boiling salted water until just tender but still firm to bite, stirring occasionally. Drain; return ravioli to pot. Add enough sauce to coat; stir to blend. Transfer to bowl.

Nacho macaroni and cheese

6 TO 8 SERVINGS *This Southwestern twist on mac 'n' cheese can be made in about 30 minutes. If you like things on the spicy side, you can add one teaspoon minced canned chipotle chiles in adobo to the macaroni along with the cheese sauce. To add a fresh touch, sprinkle with some chopped cilantro.*

- 2 **cups small elbow macaroni**

- ½ **cup bottled thick and chunky salsa verde (medium heat)**
- 1 **cup (packed) fresh cilantro leaves**
- 3 **cups (packed) coarsely grated sharp cheddar cheese (12 ounces), divided**
- 4 **teaspoons all purpose flour**

- 1 **cup whole milk**
- ¾ **cup heavy whipping cream**
- ¼ **teaspoon (scant) ground cloves**

- 1 **cup large corn chips**

PREHEAT oven to 425°F. Cook macaroni in large saucepan of boiling salted water until just tender but still firm to bite, stirring occasionally, about 6 minutes. Drain.

MEANWHILE, blend salsa and cilantro in processor. Toss 2 cups cheddar cheese and flour in medium bowl to coat.

BRING milk, cream, and cloves to simmer in large saucepan over medium-high heat. Add cheese mixture. Whisk until sauce is smooth, about 1 minute. Mix in macaroni; season to taste with pepper.

SPREAD half of macaroni mixture in 11×7-inch baking dish. Drop half of salsa mixture over in dollops. Sprinkle with ½ cup cheese. Top with remaining macaroni mixture and salsa mixture. Sprinkle chips over. Top with remaining ½ cup cheese. Bake until heated through, about 10 minutes.

Wisconsin mac and cheese

2 SERVINGS; CAN BE DOUBLED *You'll never again need to reach for boxed or frozen macaroni and cheese when you see how simple it is to make the comfort-food favorite from scratch. This version uses low-fat milk, vegetable broth, and whole wheat bread for the crunchy topping, so you can feel good about serving it to kids and adults alike.*

1⅓   **cups small elbow macaroni**

  1   **slice whole wheat bread**
  2   **tablespoons (¼ stick) butter**
  2   **tablespoons all purpose flour**
  ¾   **cup low-fat milk**
  ¾   **cup vegetable broth**
  2   **green onions, thinly sliced**
1½   **cups (packed) grated sharp cheddar cheese (about 6 ounces)**

COOK macaroni in medium saucepan of boiling salted water until just tender but still firm to bite, stirring occasionally. Drain.

MEANWHILE, grind bread in processor to fine crumbs; transfer to small bowl. Melt butter in medium saucepan. Mix ½ tablespoon butter into crumbs. Add flour to remaining butter; whisk over medium heat 2 minutes. Gradually whisk in milk and broth. Bring to boil, whisking constantly. Add green onions. Whisk 2 minutes longer. Remove from heat. Add cheese; stir until melted.

PREHEAT broiler. Mix macaroni into sauce. Season to taste with salt and pepper. Spoon into broilerproof 9-inch pie dish. Sprinkle crumbs over. Broil until crumbs brown, about 2 minutes.

One-step lasagna with sausage and basil

6 TO 8 SERVINGS *If you've been looking for a quick, delicious lasagna, here it is. There is no need to boil the noodles before assembling this hearty casserole. Simply layer the noodles (not the precooked variety) with purchased sauce, cheese, and meat. If you prefer the dish on the spicy side, use hot Italian sausage; otherwise, use the sweet variety. Because lasagna freezes beautifully, this is a perfect make-ahead recipe. After baking, cool, chill, then wrap tightly with foil and freeze up to one month.*

12   **ounces lean ground beef**
  8   **ounces Italian sausages, casings removed**

  1   **26-ounce jar thick spaghetti or marinara sauce**
1½   **cups water**
  ½   **cup chopped fresh basil**
  1   **1-pound box lasagna noodles, divided**
  1   **15-ounce container part-skim ricotta cheese, divided**
  1   **pound mozzarella cheese, coarsely grated, divided**
  1   **cup freshly grated Parmesan cheese, divided**

PREHEAT oven to 350°F. Sauté beef and sausages in heavy large skillet over medium-high heat until cooked through, breaking up meats with back of fork, about 4 minutes. Transfer to bowl.

COMBINE spaghetti sauce, 1½ cups water, and basil in large bowl. Spread 1½ cups sauce mixture in bottom of 13×9×2-inch glass baking dish. Arrange ⅓ of noodles, slightly overlapping if necessary, atop sauce. Spread half of ricotta over noodles. Sprinkle with half of mozzarella cheese, half of meat mixture, and ¼ cup Parmesan cheese. Top with 1½ cups sauce. Repeat layering with noodles, ricotta, mozzarella, meat mixture, and ¼ cup Parmesan cheese. Arrange remaining noodles over. Spoon remaining sauce over, covering completely. Sprinkle with remaining ½ cup Parmesan. Cover tightly with heavy-duty foil. Place on baking sheet.

BAKE until noodles are tender and lasagna is heated through, about 1 hour. Uncover; let stand 15 minutes.

DO AHEAD *Can be made 1 day ahead. Chill until cold, then cover with foil and keep chilled. Rewarm covered in 350°F oven about 45 minutes.*

Noodles with poppy seeds and peas

4 SIDE-DISH SERVINGS *The tiny dried blue or white seeds of poppy plants have a pleasant, nutty flavor. Here, they blend nicely with the sweet peas in this side-dish pasta. Serve the noodles with a creamy main course.*

- 8 ounces fettuccine or egg noodles
- 1 10-ounce package frozen peas
- 2 tablespoons (¼ stick) butter
- 2 teaspoons poppy seeds

COOK pasta in large pot of boiling salted water until almost tender, stirring occasionally. Add peas and cook until peas and fettuccine are just tender, about 2 minutes. Drain. Return noodle mixture to pot. Add butter and poppy seeds and toss to coat. Season with salt and pepper. Transfer to bowl.

Szechuan sesame noodles

6 SIDE-DISH SERVINGS *Bottled teriyaki and chili-garlic sauces make an instant seasoning for these spicy noodles. Find the sauces, along with the sesame oil and noodles, in the Asian foods section of the supermarket. For added crunch, add a few snow peas and sliced red bell pepper to the mix. To turn this side dish into a main course, you can toss in some cooked shredded chicken or thinly sliced roast pork.*

- 8 ounces thin dried Asian noodles or linguine
- 4 tablespoons Asian sesame oil, divided
- 3 tablespoons chopped peanuts

- 2 tablespoons minced peeled fresh ginger
- 3 garlic cloves, minced
- 6 tablespoons bottled teriyaki sauce
- 2 tablespoons fresh lime juice
- 1 teaspoon chili-garlic sauce
- 1½ cups thinly sliced green or red onions

COOK noodles in large pot of boiling salted water until just tender but still firm to bite, stirring occasionally. Drain; return noodles to pot. Mix in 1 tablespoon oil and peanuts.

HEAT remaining 3 tablespoons oil in heavy small skillet over medium-low heat. Add ginger and garlic; stir 10 seconds. Add teriyaki sauce, lime juice, and chili-garlic sauce; simmer 30 seconds. Mix sauce and onions into noodles. Season to taste with salt and pepper. Serve warm or at room temperature.

Brown butter caraway noodles

6 SIDE-DISH SERVINGS *The process of browning butter—cooking it slowly and browning the milk solids without burning them—adds an incredible depth of flavor to this super simple side dish. The noodles would be the perfect accompaniment to chicken, fish, or veal in a creamy dill sauce.*

6 **tablespoons (¾ stick) butter**
2 **teaspoons caraway seeds**

12 **ounces fettuccine**

MELT butter in small saucepan over medium heat. When butter foams, add caraway seeds. Reduce heat to low and cook until butter is light brown, stirring often, about 5 minutes. Remove from heat.

COOK fettuccine in large pot of boiling salted water until just tender but still firm to bite, stirring occasionally. Drain. Return pasta to pot. Add brown butter; stir over low heat until coated, about 3 minutes. Season to taste with salt and pepper. Transfer to bowl.

Orzo with peas, dill, and pancetta

6 SIDE-DISH SERVINGS *This flavorful low-fat and low-calorie side dish can be prepared from start to finish in less than half an hour. Serve it warm or at room temperature with grilled trout, or pack it for a picnic along with tuna sandwiches. Although the orzo (rice-shaped pasta) is great with dill, it's good with tarragon, too.*

½ **pound orzo**
3 **ounces pancetta (Italian bacon), chopped (about ½ cup)**
½ **cup chopped shallots (about 4)**
1 **cup shelled fresh peas or frozen petite peas, thawed**
5 **tablespoons chopped fresh dill, divided**
1 **cup low-salt chicken broth**
1 **tablespoon Sherry wine vinegar**

COOK orzo in large saucepan of boiling salted water until just tender but still firm to bite, stirring occasionally. Drain.

MEANWHILE, sauté pancetta and shallots in heavy large skillet over medium-high heat until brown, about 4 minutes. Add peas and 4 tablespoons dill; stir to coat. Add chicken broth and boil until reduced by half, about 4 minutes. Add vinegar; boil 1 minute. Add orzo to skillet; stir to coat. Season to taste with salt and pepper. Transfer to medium bowl; sprinkle with remaining 1 tablespoon dill. Serve warm or at room temperature.

Carrot orzo

4 SERVINGS *Orzo is rice-shaped pasta, and when cooked with a measured amount of liquid, not boiled in a large amount of water and drained, it resembles risotto. Chopping already-peeled baby carrots in the food processor makes the preparation a breeze. Serve the orzo with lamb chops or chicken breasts.*

6	ounces peeled baby carrots (about 1¼ cups; from 16-ounce package)
2	tablespoons (¼ stick) butter
1	cup orzo (about 8 ounces)
1½	cups water
1¼	cups low-salt chicken broth
1	garlic clove, minced
¼	cup freshly grated Parmesan cheese
2	tablespoons chopped green onions
1	teaspoon minced fresh rosemary

PLACE carrots in processor. Using on/off turns, finely chop carrots. Melt butter in heavy medium saucepan over medium heat. Add orzo and carrots; sauté until orzo is golden, about 5 minutes. Add 1½ cups water, broth, and garlic; cook uncovered over medium heat until all liquid is absorbed, stirring frequently, about 10 minutes. Stir in Parmesan cheese, green onions, and rosemary. Season to taste with salt and pepper.

Orzo with tomatoes, feta, and green onions

8 SERVINGS *Lemon, honey, and feta cheese add a Greek flavor to this side dish. Teardrop or grape tomatoes are smaller than cherry tomatoes and are available at some supermarkets, farmers' markets, and specialty foods stores. Serve this at room temperature with grilled lamb.*

¼	cup red wine vinegar
2	tablespoons fresh lemon juice
1	teaspoon honey
½	cup olive oil
6	cups chicken broth
1	pound orzo
2	cups red and yellow teardrop or grape tomatoes, halved
1	7-ounce package feta cheese, cut into ½-inch cubes (about 1½ cups)
1	cup chopped fresh basil
1	cup chopped green onions
½	cup pine nuts, toasted

WHISK vinegar, lemon juice, and honey in small bowl. Gradually whisk in oil. Season vinaigrette to taste with salt and pepper.

BRING broth to boil in heavy large saucepan. Stir in orzo, reduce heat to medium, and cover partially; boil until just tender but still firm to bite, stirring occasionally. Drain. Transfer to large wide bowl, tossing frequently until cool.

MIX tomatoes, feta, basil, and green onions into orzo. Add vinaigrette; toss to coat. Season to taste with salt and pepper.

DO AHEAD *Can be made 2 hours ahead. Let stand at room temperature.*

ADD pine nuts; toss. Serve at room temperature.

225

Orzo pilaf with mushrooms, leeks, and sun-dried tomatoes

8 SERVINGS *Remove the gills from the portobello mushrooms to keep the pilaf pretty and prevent the color from turning too dark. If you want a milder mushroom flavor, use regular button mushrooms; for a stronger flavor, use wild mushrooms such as shiitake or oyster mushrooms.*

    Nonstick vegetable oil spray

1½ cups low-salt chicken broth

⅓ cup chopped sun-dried tomatoes (not packed in oil)

1⅓ cups orzo

1 tablespoon olive oil

12 ounces portobello mushrooms, stemmed, diced

3 cups sliced leeks (white and pale green parts only)

3 garlic cloves, chopped

¼ cup chopped fresh basil

2 tablespoons balsamic vinegar

PREHEAT oven to 350°F. Spray 8×8×2-inch glass baking dish with nonstick spray. Bring broth and tomatoes just to boil in small saucepan. Remove from heat; let stand 10 minutes.

MEANWHILE, cook orzo in medium saucepan of boiling salted water until just tender but still firm to bite, stirring occasionally. Drain.

HEAT oil in large nonstick skillet over medium heat. Add mushrooms, leeks, and garlic. Cover skillet and cook until vegetables are tender, stirring occasionally, about 12 minutes. Remove from heat. Mix in tomato-broth mixture, cooked orzo, basil, and vinegar. Season to taste with salt and pepper. Transfer to prepared dish; cover with foil.

BAKE pilaf until heated through, about 40 minutes. Serve hot.

PREPARING LEEKS Slice off and discard the dark green end of the leek. Leaving the root end intact, cut the leek in half lengthwise. Rinse the leek under running water, removing any dirt from between the layers. Using a sharp knife, slice the leek halves crosswise. Or slice the leek first, then place the slices in a large bowl of water and separate the leaves; let the sediment fall to the bottom of the bowl.

Greek pasta salad with shrimp and olives

6 SERVINGS *To make this a vegetarian salad, omit the shrimp. A tablespoon of freshly chopped oregano can be substituted for the thyme.*

12 ounces linguine

12 ounces cooked bay shrimp

12 ounces tomatoes, chopped

6 green onions, chopped

1 large red bell pepper, chopped

1 cup crumbled feta cheese (about 4 ounces)

3 garlic cloves, chopped

½ cup chopped pitted Kalamata olives

½ cup olive oil

¼ cup fresh lemon juice

1 tablespoon chopped fresh thyme

COOK linguine in large pot of boiling salted water until just tender but still firm to bite, stirring occasionally. Drain; cool. Transfer to large bowl.

ADD all remaining ingredients to pasta and toss to blend. Season salad to taste with salt and pepper.

DO AHEAD *Can be made 1 hour ahead. Let stand at room temperature.*

Lemon pasta salad with tomatoes and feta

8 SIDE-DISH SERVINGS *Garnish this pretty summer pasta with lots of lemon wedges and serve with grilled fish for dinner—or add chunks of cooked chicken to the mix and turn it into a simple lunch. Pack any leftovers in single-serving containers to take to work or school.*

7	tablespoons extra-virgin olive oil
4	tablespoons fresh lemon juice
3	tablespoons whole grain mustard
2	garlic cloves, minced
2	teaspoons finely grated lemon peel

12	ounces penne
2	cups small cherry tomatoes, halved
1½	cups chopped red bell peppers
1½	cups crumbled feta cheese (about 6 ounces)
1	cup chopped green onions

WHISK first 5 ingredients in small bowl to blend. Season dressing to taste with salt and pepper.

COOK penne in large pot of boiling salted water until just tender but still firm to bite, stirring occasionally. Drain. Rinse pasta with cold water to cool quickly and drain again. Transfer pasta to large bowl. Add tomatoes, bell peppers, feta cheese, and green onions. Pour dressing over and toss to coat. Season to taste with salt and pepper.

Couscous with dried apricots and pistachios

10 SERVINGS *Similar to pasta, couscous is a granular form of semolina. It's a staple in North Africa, where it is traditionally served with stewed meats. Packaged couscous is available at most large supermarkets and at Middle Eastern markets.*

3	cups water
4½	tablespoons extra-virgin olive oil
2	teaspoons salt
1½	10-ounce boxes couscous (about 2¼ cups)
1¼	cups (about 7 ounces) dried apricots, thinly sliced
2¼	teaspoons ground cinnamon
½	teaspoon ground allspice

1½	cups (about 4 ounces) unsalted pistachios, toasted, chopped
¾	cup chopped green onions
6	tablespoons thinly sliced fresh basil

COMBINE 3 cups water, oil, and salt in medium saucepan; bring to boil. Combine couscous, apricots, cinnamon, and allspice in large bowl. Add boiling liquid. Cover immediately; let stand until water is absorbed, about 5 minutes. Uncover; fluff with fork. Cool.

DO AHEAD *Can be made 6 hours ahead. Cover and chill. Bring to room temperature before continuing.*

MIX pistachios, green onions, and basil into couscous. Season to taste with salt and pepper.

Saffron couscous with fresh peas and chives

4 SERVINGS *A pinch of saffron threads adds an earthy bittersweet perfume and a rich golden-yellow color to this side dish. While fresh English peas and snipped chives add elegance, thawed frozen peas and minced green onion are excellent—and readily available—replacements.*

    1   14-ounce can low-salt chicken broth
 1½   cups shelled fresh peas or frozen peas
    2   tablespoons (¼ stick) butter
        Pinch of saffron threads
 1¼   cups couscous
   ¼   cup chopped fresh chives

BRING broth to simmer in medium saucepan. Add peas and cook just until tender, about 2 minutes. Using slotted spoon, transfer peas to bowl. Add butter and saffron threads to broth and bring to boil. Remove from heat. Add couscous; stir to blend. Cover tightly and let stand until liquid is absorbed and couscous is tender, about 5 minutes. Fluff couscous with fork. Gently mix in chives and peas. Season to taste with salt and pepper. Transfer couscous to bowl.

Toasted Israeli couscous with pine nuts and parsley

8 SERVINGS *Israeli couscous (sometimes called pearl or toasted couscous or toasted Israeli pasta) is a larger, round version of the North African favorite. You can find it at Middle Eastern and kosher markets, at some specialty foods stores, and online at amazon. com. It has a toasted, slightly nutty flavor and a nice chewy texture.*

    5   tablespoons butter, divided
   ⅔   cup pine nuts (about 3½ ounces)

   ⅔   cup finely chopped shallots
    3   cups (16 ounces) toasted Israeli couscous
    2   fresh or dried bay leaves
    1   cinnamon stick
 3¾   cups low-salt chicken broth
    1   teaspoon salt
   ½   cup minced fresh Italian parsley

MELT 1 tablespoon butter in heavy large saucepan over medium-low heat. Add pine nuts and stir until nuts are golden brown, about 8 minutes. Transfer to small bowl.

MELT remaining 4 tablespoons butter in same pan over medium heat. Add shallots and sauté until golden, about 10 minutes. Add couscous, bay leaves, and cinnamon stick; sauté until couscous browns slightly, stirring frequently, about 5 minutes. Add broth and salt and bring to boil. Reduce heat to low; cover and simmer until couscous is tender and liquid is absorbed, about 10 minutes. Stir in parsley and pine nuts. Season to taste with pepper. Discard bay leaves and cinnamon stick. Transfer couscous to serving dish.

RICE

Florida jambalaya

4 SERVINGS *Jambalaya is a hallmark of Creole cookery—it's a versatile dish that combines cooked rice with a variety of ingredients including tomatoes, onion, green peppers, and almost any kind of meat, poultry, or shellfish. The addition of fresh cilantro gives this version a Latin touch. Buy already peeled and deveined shrimp to save time.*

- 3 tablespoons butter
- ½ cup chopped onion
- 3 garlic cloves, chopped
- 8 ounces fully cooked smoked sausage (such as kielbasa), cut into ½-inch pieces
- 1 cup long-grain white rice
- 2 medium potatoes, peeled, cut into ½-inch cubes
- 2¼ cups chicken broth
- ½ cup dry white wine
- 1 4-ounce jar sliced pimientos with juices
- ½ teaspoon turmeric
  Cayenne pepper
- 8 ounces uncooked large shrimp, peeled, deveined
- ½ cup chopped fresh cilantro plus additional sprigs for garnish

MELT butter in heavy large saucepan over medium heat. Add onion and garlic and sauté until just soft, about 5 minutes. Add sausage; sauté until beginning to brown, about 5 minutes. Add rice and stir to coat with pan juices. Mix in potatoes, broth, wine, pimientos with juices, and turmeric. Sprinkle with salt, pepper, and cayenne. Bring to boil; stir well. Reduce heat to medium-low, cover and cook until rice and potatoes are tender and liquid is absorbed, about 20 minutes. Mix in shrimp and chopped cilantro. Cover and cook until shrimp are just cooked through, about 4 minutes. Season to taste with more salt, pepper, and cayenne, if desired.

MOUND jambalaya on large platter. Garnish with cilantro sprigs.

One-hour shrimp paella

4 SERVINGS *Paella is the delicious but usually time-consuming and labor-intensive rice dish from Valencia, Spain. This speedy version is low in fat and calories yet high in flavor. To make it in even less time, buy already chopped onions and bell peppers; they're available at many supermarkets.*

1	tablespoon olive oil
8	ounces ½-inch cubes smoked ham (about 1¾ cups)
2	cups chopped onions
1	cup chopped red bell pepper
¼	teaspoon (generous) saffron threads, crumbled
¼	teaspoon hot Spanish or Hungarian paprika
3¼	cups (or more) low-salt chicken broth, divided
1½	cups arborio rice or medium-grain white rice
1	pound uncooked large shrimp, peeled, deveined
½	cup pimiento-stuffed green olives, halved

HEAT oil in heavy large skillet over medium-high heat. Add smoked ham, onions, and bell pepper; sauté until golden brown, about 8 minutes. Stir in saffron and paprika, then 3 cups broth and rice. Bring to boil. Sprinkle with salt and pepper. Reduce heat to low, cover, and simmer until rice is almost tender, about 15 minutes. Nestle shrimp into rice, top with olives, and drizzle with ¼ cup (or more) broth to moisten. Cover and cook until shrimp are just opaque in center, about 6 minutes. Season to taste with more salt and pepper.

Celery root risotto and pesto

4 FIRST-COURSE OR 2 MAIN-COURSE SERVINGS *The knobby, brown vegetable sometimes called "celeriac" or "celery knob" has strong celery and parsley flavors. The emerald green pesto in this dish is made from the celery root leaves.*

2	medium celery roots (celeriac) with leafy tops
¼	cup olive oil
3	tablespoons butter
1½	cups chopped leek (white and pale green parts only)
¾	cup arborio or medium-grain white rice
3	cups (about) low-salt chicken broth
1	cup freshly grated Parmesan cheese, divided

PLACE 1½ cups (packed) celery root leaves and oil in mini processor. Blend until leaves are minced. Season pesto to taste with salt and pepper.

PEEL celery roots. Cut into ⅓-inch-thick slices. Cut slices into enough ⅓-inch cubes to measure 2 cups.

MELT butter in heavy large saucepan over medium-low heat. Stir in celery root cubes and leek. Cover and cook until celery root is tender but not brown, stirring often, about 10 minutes. Mix in rice; stir 1 minute. Add broth; increase heat and bring to boil. Reduce heat and simmer until rice is tender and risotto is creamy, stirring occasionally, about 20 minutes. Mix in ¾ cup cheese. Season risotto to taste with salt and pepper.

DIVIDE risotto between bowls; swirl some pesto on top. Serve, passing remaining cheese and pesto separately.

GETTING TO THE ROOT Using a large sharp knife, trim away the rough, brown outer layer of the celery root. Keep the peeled celery root in acidulated water (cool water with a little lemon juice added) to prevent browning.

Risotto with zucchini and Parmesan

4 SIDE-DISH OR 2 MAIN-COURSE SERVINGS *Short-grain arborio rice is best for creating the creamy texture desired in risotto. Find it at many supermarkets and at Italian markets. Medium-grain white rice can be substituted quite successfully. This can be enjoyed as a main course or as a side dish.*

- 3 tablespoons butter, divided
- 2 medium zucchini, cut into ⅜×1-inch sticks
- 3 cups (about) low-salt chicken broth
- 1 large onion, chopped
- ¾ cup arborio rice or medium-grain white rice
- ⅔ cup freshly grated Parmesan cheese

MELT 1 tablespoon butter in heavy medium saucepan over medium-high heat. Add zucchini and sauté until beginning to soften, about 3 minutes. Transfer to bowl; reserve saucepan (do not clean).

BRING broth to simmer in small saucepan. Reduce heat to low; cover to keep warm. Melt remaining 2 tablespoons butter in reserved saucepan over medium-low heat. Add onion and sauté until tender, about 6 minutes. Add rice and stir until opaque, about 2 minutes. Add ½ cup broth. Adjust heat so liquid simmers slowly and cook rice until broth is absorbed, stirring occasionally. Continue adding broth ½ cup at a time until rice is just tender and creamy, stirring occasionally, about 25 minutes. Add zucchini and stir until heated through. Mix in cheese. Season to taste with salt and pepper.

Red beet risotto with mustard greens and goat cheese

6 FIRST-COURSE SERVINGS *This ruby-hued risotto makes a gorgeous one-pot meal; when made with vegetable broth, it's a great vegetarian main course. If you purchase a bunch of beets with abundant crisp leaves, use the thoroughly cleaned beet tops in place of the mustard greens. Shaved Parmesan is also good here if you're not a fan of goat cheese.*

- ¼ cup (½ stick) butter
- 2 2½- to 3-inch-diameter beets, peeled, cut into ½-inch cubes
- 1½ cups chopped white onion
- 1 cup arborio rice or medium-grain white rice
- 3 cups low-salt chicken broth or vegetable broth
- 1 tablespoon balsamic vinegar
- 1½ cups chopped mustard greens
- 1 5½-ounce package chilled soft fresh goat cheese, coarsely crumbled

MELT butter in heavy large saucepan over medium heat. Add beets and onion. Cover and cook until onion is soft, about 8 minutes. Mix in rice. Add broth and vinegar. Increase heat and bring to boil. Reduce heat to medium-low. Simmer uncovered until rice and beets are just tender and risotto is creamy, stirring occasionally, about 15 minutes. Season to taste with salt and pepper. Spoon into shallow bowls. Sprinkle with greens and cheese.

Porcini risotto

4 SERVINGS *Wild porcini mushrooms, also called cèpes in France, have a pungent, earthy, and yeast-bread–like flavor. The large caramel-brown mushrooms are harvested in pine and oak forests in Europe and North America in the fall. Porcini dry and reconstitute beautifully, so their rich flavor can be enjoyed year-round.*

1½ ounces dried porcini mushrooms
1½ cups hot water

3 tablespoons butter
1 large onion, coarsely chopped
1½ cups arborio rice or medium-grain white rice
3½ to 4 cups low-salt chicken broth
¼ cup Cognac or brandy
  Freshly grated Parmesan cheese

PLACE porcini in medium bowl; pour 1½ cups hot water over. Let stand until mushrooms are soft, about 30 minutes. Strain, reserving soaking liquid. Coarsely chop porcini.

MELT butter in heavy large saucepan over medium heat. Add onion. Cover and cook until golden, stirring occasionally, about 15 minutes. Add rice, porcini, 1 cup reserved porcini soaking liquid (leaving any sediment behind), 3½ cups broth, and Cognac. Bring to boil. Reduce heat to medium-low; simmer uncovered until rice is tender and mixture is creamy, stirring occasionally and adding more broth by ¼ cupfuls if dry, about 20 minutes. Season to taste with salt and pepper. Transfer risotto to bowl. Serve, passing cheese separately.

Crayfish-corn risotto

4 TO 6 FIRST-COURSE SERVINGS *It's important to serve risotto as soon as it finishes cooking—if it is allowed to sit, it will become stiff and starchy. If you can't find the uncooked crayfish tails, shrimp make a good substitute. Garnish with fresh chopped parsley.*

¼ cup corn oil
¾ cup chopped onion
4 garlic cloves, minced
1 cup arborio rice or medium-grain white rice
3 tablespoons tomato paste
1 cup dry Sherry
3 cups low-salt chicken broth, divided
⅔ cup corn kernels cut from 1 ear of corn
½ pound peeled uncooked crayfish tails or medium peeled deveined uncooked shrimp
¼ cup freshly grated Parmesan cheese
2 tablespoons (¼ stick) butter

HEAT oil in heavy large saucepan over medium heat. Add onion and garlic; sauté until tender but not brown, about 4 minutes. Add rice and stir until translucent at edges, about 2 minutes. Add tomato paste and stir 1 minute. Add Sherry and cook until reduced by half and rice mixture thickens, stirring occasionally, about 3 minutes. Add 2 cups broth, 1 cup at a time, cooking until almost all liquid is absorbed between additions and stirring frequently, about 13 minutes total. Add remaining 1 cup broth. Cook until rice is tender, stirring often, about 3 minutes. Add corn and crayfish; cook until almost all liquid is absorbed, rice is creamy and tender, and crayfish is cooked through, about 3 minutes longer. Stir in cheese and butter. Season risotto to taste with salt and pepper.

Red chard risotto

6 SERVINGS *Any variety of Swiss chard can be used in this risotto, including the white-ribbed variety or the multicolored Bright Lights. To prepare chard, remove the tough center rib and chop the leaves. Wash coarsely chopped chard in a salad spinner.*

- 4½ to 5 cups low-salt chicken broth
- 2 tablespoons olive oil
- 1 medium onion, chopped
- 1½ cups arborio rice or medium-grain white rice
- 4 cups (packed) coarsely chopped red Swiss chard leaves (about 1 bunch)
- ½ cup dry white wine
- ½ cup freshly grated Parmesan cheese plus additional for serving

BRING broth to simmer in medium saucepan. Cover and keep warm. Heat oil in heavy large pot over medium heat. Add onion and sauté until translucent, about 5 minutes. Add rice and chard and stir until chard begins to wilt, about 3 minutes. Add wine and simmer until absorbed, stirring occasionally, about 2 minutes. Add 4½ cups hot broth. Simmer until rice is just tender and risotto is creamy, stirring frequently and adding remaining ½ cup broth by ¼ cupfuls if mixture is dry, about 20 minutes. Mix in ½ cup Parmesan cheese. Season to taste with salt and pepper. Transfer risotto to medium bowl. Serve, passing additional Parmesan separately.

Feta and mint rice

2 SERVINGS; CAN BE DOUBLED *This easy dish is very adaptable. Fresh basil, cilantro, oregano, or marjoram can be used instead of the mint. For a light meal, top with a few shrimp sautéed in olive oil.*

- 2 tablespoons olive oil
- ½ small onion, chopped
- 1 cup long-grain rice
- 1 14-ounce can low-salt chicken broth
- ½ cup crumbled feta cheese
- 3 tablespoons minced fresh mint

HEAT oil in heavy medium saucepan over medium heat. Add onion and sauté until translucent, about 5 minutes. Add rice and stir 1 minute. Add broth. Bring to boil. Reduce heat to low; cover and cook until broth is absorbed and rice is tender, about 20 minutes. Fluff rice with fork. Stir in feta and mint. Season to taste with salt and pepper.

Rice pilaf with basil and pine nuts

2 SERVINGS; CAN BE DOUBLED *This dish begins by first browning the rice in oil before cooking it in stock; the cooking of the grains keeps them separate. Pilafs often contain chopped cooked vegetables, meats, seafood, poultry, dried fruit, or nuts. If you add some diced cooked chicken to this version, it can be served as a main dish.*

- 1 14-ounce can low-salt chicken broth
- 1½ tablespoons olive oil
- ½ large onion, chopped
- 1 cup long-grain rice
- ⅓ cup chopped fresh basil
- ¼ cup pine nuts, toasted

BRING broth to simmer in small saucepan. Reduce heat to low and keep warm. Meanwhile, heat oil in heavy medium saucepan over medium heat. Add onion and sauté until translucent, about 6 minutes. Add rice and stir 1 minute. Add broth and bring to boil. Reduce heat to low. Cover and cook until broth is absorbed and rice is tender, about 20 minutes. Stir basil and pine nuts into rice. Season to taste with salt and pepper.

Rice, raisin, and herb pilaf

6 SERVINGS *This versatile pilaf can be enjoyed any number of ways: Serve on a bed of baby spinach with a healthy crumble of feta cheese over the top as a main course; serve it as a side dish with barbecued leg of lamb or lamb chops; or even use it to fill grape leaves for dolmades.*

- ¼ cup olive oil
- 2½ cups chopped onions
- 1 cup long-grain white rice
- 1½ cups low-salt chicken broth
- ½ cup golden raisins
- 2 tablespoons fresh lemon juice
- ⅛ teaspoon ground allspice
- ½ cup pine nuts, toasted
- 1 tablespoon chopped fresh mint
- 1 tablespoon chopped fresh dill

HEAT oil in large saucepan over medium heat. Add onions and sauté 10 minutes. Mix in rice, then broth, raisins, lemon juice, and allspice. Bring to boil. Reduce heat to medium-low, cover, and cook until rice is tender and broth is absorbed, about 20 minutes. Mix in pine nuts, mint, and dill. Season to taste with salt and pepper.

Classic red rice

4 TO 6 SERVINGS *In Mexico, this popular rice dish is usually made with vine-ripened tomatoes. For best results, use good-quality canned tomatoes, or in the summer, shop for tomatoes at a farmers' market if you don't grow your own. Simple grilled meats or tomato-sauced main dishes pair perfectly with this.*

- 1   14½-ounce can peeled whole tomatoes in juice, drained
- 3   tablespoons chopped white onion
- 2   garlic cloves, peeled

- ¼   cup corn oil
- 1   cup medium-grain white rice
- 1   cup hot water
- 1   medium carrot, peeled, cut into ⅓-inch pieces
- ⅓   cup shelled fresh peas or frozen
- ⅓   cup fresh corn kernels or frozen
- 6   fresh cilantro sprigs
- 2   to 3 serrano chiles, halved lengthwise
- 1   teaspoon salt

PUREE tomatoes, onion, and garlic in blender until smooth.

HEAT oil in heavy medium saucepan over medium-high heat. Add rice; stir until rice is pale golden, about 1 minute. Stir in pureed tomato mixture, then 1 cup hot water and all remaining ingredients. Bring to boil. Reduce heat to low, cover, and cook until almost all liquid is absorbed, about 12 minutes. Uncover and cook until rice is tender and all liquid is absorbed, about 10 minutes longer. Remove rice from heat, cover, and let stand 5 minutes. Discard cilantro sprigs and chiles. Fluff rice with fork.

Aromatic yellow rice

6 SERVINGS *All over Southeast Asia, the color yellow is associated with gods, royalty, and feasts, and any celebration is likely to have a large dish of yellow rice like this at the center of the table. Fresh and frozen kaffir or Thai lime leaves are available at Asian markets.*

- 2   tablespoons peanut oil
- 3   large shallots, chopped
- 2   cups jasmine rice or other long-grain white rice, rinsed, drained
- 1   teaspoon turmeric
- 1   teaspoon ground coriander
- 1   cinnamon stick
- 1   teaspoon salt
- ½   teaspoon ground cumin
- 3½   cups low-salt chicken broth
- 3   fresh or frozen kaffir lime leaves

HEAT oil in heavy saucepan over medium heat. Add shallots and stir 3 minutes. Add rice and next 5 ingredients; stir 2 minutes. Add broth and lime leaves and bring to boil. Reduce heat to low; cover and cook until liquid is absorbed and rice is tender, about 20 minutes. Remove from heat. Let stand, covered, 5 minutes. Discard cinnamon stick and lime leaves. Transfer rice to bowl.

ANY LIME AT ALL If kaffir lime leaves are unavailable, use 1 tablespoon fresh lime juice plus ½ teaspoon grated lime peel for each lime leaf.

Jasmine rice with garlic, ginger, and cilantro

8 SERVINGS *Jasmine rice is aromatic rice from Thailand that has a slight nutty flavor and fragrance. It's available at many supermarkets, specialty foods stores, and at Asian markets. Or use basmati rice from India, which is comparable.*

  3 **cups jasmine rice**
  3 **tablespoons vegetable oil**
  ⅓ **cup finely chopped peeled fresh ginger**
  3 **garlic cloves, minced**
4½ **cups low-salt chicken broth**
  ¾ **teaspoon salt**
  1 **large bunch fresh cilantro, 2 inches of bottom stems trimmed and discarded, tops and remaining stems coarsely chopped**

PLACE rice in large sieve; rinse under cold running water until water runs clear. Drain. Heat oil in heavy large saucepan over medium-high heat. Add ginger and garlic; stir until fragrant, about 30 seconds. Add rice and stir 3 minutes. Stir in broth and salt. Sprinkle cilantro over. Bring to boil. Reduce heat to medium-low; cover and cook until rice is tender, about 18 minutes. Remove from heat; let stand covered 10 minutes. Fluff rice with fork. Transfer to bowl.

Pesto rice timbales

6 SERVINGS *A timbale is a fun, old-school way of presenting rice in a neatly molded serving. You can dispense with the custard cups and soufflé dishes and simply present this pesto-flavored rice in a serving dish with the extra bell pepper sprinkled over the top as a garnish.*

  2 **cups lightly packed fresh basil leaves plus sprigs for garnish**
  1 **tablespoon water**
  2 **teaspoons vegetable oil**
  1 **cup long-grain white rice**
  1 **medium onion, finely chopped**
  1 **garlic clove, minced**
  1 **medium red bell pepper, diced**
1¾ **cups low-salt chicken broth**
  ½ **teaspoon dried oregano**
  ¼ **cup finely chopped fresh parsley**

PUREE 2 cups basil and 1 tablespoon water in processor. Heat oil in heavy medium saucepan over medium heat. Add rice and sauté until golden, about 4 minutes. Add onion and garlic; sauté 1 minute. Add all but 3 tablespoons red bell pepper to rice. Add broth and oregano; bring to boil, stirring occasionally. Reduce heat to low; cover and cook until rice is tender and liquid is absorbed, about 15 minutes. Remove from heat. Let stand covered 10 minutes. Mix in basil puree and parsley. Season to taste with salt and pepper.

SPRINKLE ½ tablespoon red bell pepper mixture into each of six ½-cup custard cups or soufflé dishes. Pack each with rice. Unmold onto dinner plates. Garnish with basil sprigs.

West Indian rice and beans

2 SERVINGS; CAN BE DOUBLED *Suitable accompaniments to this Caribbean-influenced, risotto-like vegetarian main course are crusty bread and an avocado and orange salad with a cilantro vinaigrette. Coconut milk lends richness and a slight sweetness—find it in the Asian foods section of the supermarket and at Indian, Southeast Asian, and Latin markets.*

2½ cups (about) vegetable broth, divided
  1 15- to 16-ounce can kidney beans, drained
  1 cup canned unsweetened regular
    or light coconut milk
  1 tablespoon minced seeded jalapeño chile
  1 teaspoon dried thyme
  ¼ teaspoon ground allspice
  ¾ cup medium-grain white rice

  1 cup thinly sliced green onions, divided

COMBINE 2 cups broth, beans, coconut milk, jalapeño chile, thyme, and allspice in heavy large saucepan. Bring to boil over medium-high heat. Stir in rice. Reduce heat to medium-low and simmer uncovered until most of liquid is absorbed and rice is almost tender, stirring often, about 20 minutes.

MIX ¾ cup green onions into rice. Continue to simmer until rice is very tender and mixture is creamy, adding more broth by ¼ cupfuls if mixture seems dry and stirring often, about 5 minutes longer. Season to taste with salt and pepper. Transfer to serving bowl. Sprinkle with remaining ¼ cup green onions.

Fried rice with shiitake mushrooms and sugar snap peas

6 TO 8 SIDE-DISH SERVINGS *You can make this vegetarian main course in less than a half an hour, especially if you already have leftover cooked rice on hand (or the rice can be cooked, then quick-chilled in the freezer while you prepare the remaining ingredients). If you like your fried rice on the spicy side, add one to two teaspoons of bottled Asian chili-garlic sauce when adding the rice. Oyster sauce is available in the Asian foods section of some supermarkets and at Asian markets.*

  5 tablespoons vegetable oil, divided
 12 ounces fresh shiitake mushrooms,
    stems removed, caps sliced
  1 8-ounce package trimmed fresh
    sugar snap peas, halved diagonally
  4 garlic cloves, minced
  2 tablespoons minced peeled fresh ginger
1¾ cups thinly sliced green onions (about 6 large)
  3 cups cooked long-grain white rice, cooled
  3 tablespoons soy sauce plus
    additional for serving
  2 tablespoons oyster sauce
  3 large eggs, beaten to blend

HEAT 3 tablespoons oil in large nonstick skillet over medium-high heat. Add mushrooms and sugar snap peas and sauté until mushrooms are tender, about 7 minutes. Add 1 tablespoon oil to skillet, then add garlic and ginger; sauté 3 minutes. Add green onions; stir 1 minute. Stir in rice, 3 tablespoons soy sauce, and oyster sauce and sauté until rice is coated and heated through, about 4 minutes. Using wooden spoon, push rice mixture to 1 side of skillet. Add remaining 1 tablespoon oil to empty part of skillet, then pour in beaten eggs and stir with wooden spoon just until eggs are cooked through, breaking up into small pieces, about 1 minute. Mix eggs into rice mixture. Season to taste with salt and pepper. Transfer fried rice to bowl. Serve, passing additional soy sauce.

237

Brown and wild rice with sausage and fennel

6 SIDE-DISH OR 2 MAIN-COURSE SERVINGS *Wild rice is wild, but it isn't rice: It's the seed of a marsh grass native to the Great Lakes and now farmed around the U.S. It has a rich flavor and firm, chewy texture. Chopped fennel seeds amp up the slight licorice flavor in the fresh fennel and in the fennel-flavored sweet Italian sausage. Serve this as a casual main course, as a side dish with roast chicken or duck, or as stuffing with turkey.*

2	**cups water**
½	**cup wild rice**
8	**ounces sweet Italian sausage, casings removed**
3	**tablespoons olive oil, divided**
1	**12-ounce fresh fennel bulb, trimmed, diced**
1	**large red bell pepper, diced**
¼	**teaspoon chopped fennel seeds**
2	**large leeks (white and pale green parts only), chopped**
3	**garlic cloves, minced**
1⅓	**cups long-grain brown rice**
2	**14-ounce cans low-salt chicken broth**

SIMMER 2 cups water and wild rice in small saucepan 20 minutes. Drain.

HEAT heavy large saucepan over medium-high heat. Add sausage and sauté until cooked through, breaking up with fork, about 4 minutes. Using slotted spoon, transfer sausage to large bowl.

ADD 2 tablespoons oil to same saucepan. Add fennel, bell pepper, and fennel seeds; sauté until vegetables are tender, about 10 minutes. Transfer to bowl with sausage. Heat remaining 1 tablespoon oil in same saucepan. Add leeks and garlic; sauté until tender and golden, about 8 minutes. Add brown rice and stir 1 minute. Mix in broth and wild rice; bring to boil. Reduce heat to low. Cover and simmer until rice is tender and liquid is absorbed, about 40 minutes. Add hot rice to sausage mixture and toss well. Season to taste with salt and pepper.

DO AHEAD *Can be made 1 day ahead. Cover and chill. Rewarm over medium heat before serving.*

Brown rice salad with mango chutney dressing

8 SERVINGS *Brown rice is rice that still has its bran coating—which is both high in fiber and flavorful. But it can go bad more quickly, so don't keep packages longer than six months. Brown rice also takes longer to cook (about 35 to 45 minutes total) than regular white long-grain rice.*

- 2 cups long-grain brown rice
- 1 cup mango chutney (such as Major Grey)
- ¼ cup olive oil
- 2 large unpeeled Granny Smith apples, cored, cut into ⅓-inch cubes
- 2 cups thinly sliced celery
- 1 cup golden raisins
- ¼ cup finely chopped fresh mint
- ¼ cup chopped toasted slivered almonds

COOK rice in large pot of boiling salted water until just tender but still firm to bite, about 40 minutes. Drain well. Transfer to large bowl and cool.

WHISK chutney and oil in small bowl to blend for dressing. Add apples, celery, raisins, mint, and almonds to rice. Toss to combine. Add dressing; toss. Season to taste with salt and pepper.

DO AHEAD *Can be made 2 hours ahead. Let stand at room temperature.*

Coconut basmati rice

6 SERVINGS *Basmati is a wonderfully aromatic rice that has long been grown in the Himalayas. It has a long grain, a nut-like flavor, and a fine texture. It's available at many supermarkets and at Indian and Middle Eastern markets. Canned coconut milk is sold at many supermarkets and at Indian, Southeast Asian, and Latin markets.*

- 2 cups water
- 1½ cups canned unsweetened coconut milk
- 2 teaspoons (packed) golden brown sugar
- 1 teaspoon salt
- 2 cups basmati rice (about 13 ounces), well rinsed, drained
- ½ cup sweetened flaked coconut, lightly toasted

COMBINE 2 cups water, coconut milk, sugar, and salt in heavy large saucepan. Bring to simmer, then stir in rice. Cover, leaving slight opening for steam to escape. Reduce heat to medium-low and simmer 12 minutes. Cover tightly, remove from heat, and let stand 10 minutes. Transfer rice to bowl; sprinkle with toasted coconut.

chicken and more poultry

CHICKEN

Rosemary Chicken and Summer Squash Brochettes

Spicy Grilled Chicken and Green Onions

Grilled Lemon and Rosemary Chicken

Hoisin Chicken Skewers

Apple-Glazed Barbecued Chicken

Chicken Tikka Kebabs

Grilled Chicken with Olive Puree

Achiote-Grilled Chicken

Grilled Spicy-Citrus Chicken Thighs with Corn and Green Onions

Barbecued Chicken Thighs with Brown Sugar-Hickory Sauce

Bourbon-Molasses Chicken Drumsticks

Spice-Rubbed Chicken and Vegetable Tacos with Chipotle Cream

Green Mountain Maple Barbecued Chicken

Chicken Under a Brick with Fresh Herb and Garlic Sauce

Cilantro-Lime Chicken Fajitas with Grilled Onions

Grilled Chicken with Salsa Verde

Mojito-Marinated Chicken Breasts

Grilled Chicken with Chimichurri Sauce

Lemony Chicken Milanese with Arugula Salad

Chicken Piccata

Pecan- and Panko-Crusted Chicken Breasts

Achiote Chicken with Tangerine Sauce

Chicken with Bell Peppers, Smoked Ham, and Paprika

Sautéed Chicken with Parsnip, Apple, and Sherry Pan Sauce

Chicken Breasts with Wild Mushrooms, Marjoram, and Marsala

Chicken Breasts with Pistachio-Cilantro Pesto

Chicken with Green Olives, Orange, and Sherry

Braised Chicken with Green Peppers and Tomatoes

Orange and Ginger Chicken

Chicken Paillards with Tomato, Basil, and Roasted-Corn Relish

Sautéed Chicken Paillards with Muscat Sauce

Chicken with Asiago, Prosciutto, and Sage

Cinnamon Chicken with Couscous and Dried Fruit

Sautéed Chicken with Tomato-Saffron Vinaigrette on Frisée

Sautéed Chicken with Tomatoes, Olives, and Feta

Chicken Sauté with Green Olive Topping

Layered Chicken Enchiladas with Salsa Verde

Chicken Schnitzel with Anchovy-Chive Butter Sauce

Chicken Sauté with Wilted Endive and Brussels Sprouts

Wasabi-Crusted Chicken Breasts

Skillet Chicken and Vegetables

Dijon Chicken

Chicken with Mustard Cream on Watercress

Chicken Curry with Dried Apricots

Poached Chicken with Green Herb Sauce

Chicken Breasts with Prosciutto and Sage

Smothered Chicken with Creamy Mushroom Gravy

Roast Moroccan-Spiced Chicken

Roast Chicken with Artichokes and Gremolata Butter

Lemon-Oregano Roast Chicken and Potatoes

Chicken Roasted on Leeks and Sage Sprigs

Greek-Style Roast Chicken

Oven-Fried Deviled Drumsticks

Spicy Oven-Fried Chicken

Chicken with Tarragon Vinegar Sauce

Chicken Breasts with Sun-Dried Tomato and Garlic Crust

Chicken in Lemongrass Sauce

Chicken Baked with Fresh Tarragon Pesto

Chicken Breasts with Spicy Peanut Sauce

Roquefort-Lemon Roast Chicken

Sautéed Chicken with Garlic and Rosemary

Walnut-Coated Chicken with Pomegranate Sauce

Chicken Thighs with Creole Mustard-Orange Sauce

Chicken with Indian-Spiced Tomato Sauce

Chicken, Asparagus, and Broccoli Stir-Fry

Chicken Cutlets Véronique

Chicken, Red Pepper, and Green Bean Stir-Fry

Chicken and Mushroom Enchiladas

Tunisian Chicken with Raisins and Lemon

Chicken Breasts with Goat Cheese and Rosemary Stuffing

Chicken with Carrots, Prunes, and Rice

Malaysian Chicken Curry with Sweet and Spicy Peppers

Chicken Cacciatore with Marsala and Capers

Roast Chicken with Cumin, Paprika, and Allspice

Chicken-Cheddar Quesadillas with Tomato and Corn Salsa

Chicken with Cranberry-Mustard Sauce

Chinese-Style Chicken in Lettuce Cups

Oaxacan Chicken Mole

TURKEY

Chipotle-Seasoned Turkey Enchiladas

Turkey Chilaquiles

Turkey, Mushroom, and Barley Risotto

Turkey-Cheese Burritos with Salsa and Cilantro

Turkey Tonnato

Turkey Cutlets Piccata

Turkey Cutlets with Paprika Cream Sauce

Chipotle Turkey Cutlets with Charred Corn Salsa

GAME HENS AND DUCK

Grilled Cornish Game Hens with Garlic-Citrus Marinade

Cornish Game Hens with Blackberry Sauce

Cornish Game Hen with Curried Plum Glaze

Roast Cornish Game Hens with Orange-Teriyaki Sauce

Cornish Game Hens with Honey-Ginger Glaze

Cornish Game Hens with Maple-Mustard Glaze

Cornish Game Hen with Raspberry-Red Wine Sauce

Sautéed Duck Breasts with Wild Mushrooms

Duck Breast with Crème Fraîche and Roasted Grapes

tool kit Chicken breasts are *the* go-to ingredient for weeknight cooking. Boneless breasts are naturally tender and quick-cooking, provide a canvas for every kind of seasoning and flavoring, and, when the skin is removed, are very low in fat. What's not to love? But because they're so lean, chicken breasts can easily dry out and become tough when overcooked. So keep in mind the following guidelines.

THINK FAST: Quick-cooking methods, such as pan-frying, grilling, broiling, sautéing, and stir-frying, prevent the meat from becoming dry. In just minutes, these methods turn chicken breasts golden brown on the outside and opaque and firm throughout.

WATCH THE TIME: As a general guideline, pan-frying or grilling an average-size boneless chicken breast over medium-high heat takes about six minutes on each side to become cooked through but remain moist and juicy. That is, after about 12 minutes total, the thickest part of the breast should reach an internal temperature of 160°F, the meat should no longer be pink, and the juices should run clear when the meat is pierced with a fork.

Chicken breasts with the bone will take about twice as long to cook through.

MAKE IT UNIFORM: To help cook the meat quickly and evenly, use a meat mallet or rolling pin to pound the chicken breasts between sheets of plastic wrap or waxed paper and create a uniform thickness.

CUT ACROSS: When stir-frying and sautéing, cut chicken breasts across the grain into strips. This will prevent the meat from shrinking, shriveling, and becoming tough.

DON'T REMOVE THE SKIN: While grilling and broiling, keep the skin on to prevent the meat from drying out—then remove it, if desired, after the chicken is cooked.

BRINE: If you brine chicken breasts in a saltwater solution (about ¼ cup of salt to 3 cups of water) for 30 to 60 minutes, the meat will turn out juicier and more flavorful.

SIMMER DOWN: When poaching chicken breasts or adding chicken pieces to soups or stews, watch the time and be sure the liquids are simmering very gently—a roaring boil will toughen the meat quickly and dry it out.

SOAK WITH FLAVOR: Marinades aren't necessary to tenderize chicken breasts, but they do add much-needed flavor.

243

CHICKEN

Rosemary chicken and summer squash brochettes

2 SERVINGS; CAN BE DOUBLED Brochette *is French for "skewer." If pattypan squash aren't available, cut regular zucchini or yellow crookneck squash cross-wise into pieces that are the same size as the chicken. This preparation uses metal skewers for grilling; to make appetizer servings, thread one piece each of chicken and squash onto woody rosemary sprigs—they add flavor and look beautiful.*

- 2 tablespoons extra-virgin olive oil
- 1 tablespoon fresh lemon juice
- 1 tablespoon chopped fresh rosemary or 1½ teaspoons dried
- 2 garlic cloves, minced
- 1 teaspoon finely grated lemon peel
- 2 skinless boneless chicken breast halves, each cut into 6 pieces
- 3 large pattypan squash, quartered

PREPARE barbecue (medium-high heat). Whisk first 5 ingredients in medium bowl. Add chicken and squash; toss to coat. Let stand 10 minutes; toss occasionally.

ALTERNATE 3 chicken pieces with 3 squash pieces on each of 4 metal skewers. Sprinkle generously with salt and pepper. Grill until chicken is cooked through and squash is just tender, turning often, about 10 minutes.

FREEZE AND SLICE Use fresh or frozen boneless, skinless chicken breasts for this recipe. If using frozen breasts, quickly thaw them in a bowl of cold water and cut into pieces while still partially frozen—it's easier than cutting them when completely thawed.

Spicy grilled chicken and green onions

2 SERVINGS; CAN BE DOUBLED *Some of the marinade is set aside and used as a sauce for the chicken, making this recipe especially quick and easy.*

- 2 tablespoons vegetable oil
- 1 tablespoon hot pepper sauce
- 2 teaspoons honey
- 1 teaspoon paprika
- 7 green onions, divided
- 2 skinless boneless chicken breast halves

PREPARE barbecue (medium-high heat). Whisk oil, hot sauce, honey, and paprika in 9-inch-diameter glass pie dish to blend. Mince 1 green onion; mix into marinade. Transfer 2 tablespoons marinade to small bowl and reserve. Add chicken to marinade in pie dish and turn to coat. Let stand 10 minutes, turning occasionally.

SPRINKLE chicken and remaining whole green onions with salt. Grill chicken and whole onions until chicken is cooked through and onions soften, turning occasionally, about 10 minutes. Transfer chicken and onions to plates. Drizzle with reserved 2 tablespoons marinade.

Grilled lemon and rosemary chicken

4 SERVINGS *Grilling lemon softens the acidity in exchange for a rich roasted flavor. Place slices around the edge of the grill, where the heat is less intense, so they don't burn.*

- 4 large skinless boneless chicken breast halves
- ¾ cup bottled Italian-style dressing, divided
- 1½ tablespoons chopped fresh rosemary

- 1 lemon, cut crosswise into ⅛-inch-thick rounds

PREPARE barbecue (medium-high heat). Using meat mallet or rolling pin, pound chicken between sheets of plastic wrap to ¼- to ½-inch thickness. Place chicken in glass baking dish. Pour ½ cup dressing over chicken. Sprinkle with rosemary; turn to coat. Let marinate at least 10 minutes and up to 2 hours.

REMOVE chicken from marinade and place on grill rack. Dip lemon rounds into remaining ¼ cup dressing and place on edge of rack. Grill chicken and lemon until chicken is cooked through and lemon rounds are slightly charred, turning occasionally, about 5 minutes total. Transfer chicken to plates. Top with lemon rounds.

Hoisin chicken skewers

2 SERVINGS; CAN BE DOUBLED *Hoisin sauce is a thick, sweet, and spicy mixture made from soybeans, garlic, chiles, and various spices. It's available in the Asian foods section of most supermarkets. You'll need metal skewers for grilling the chicken.*

- ¼ cup hoisin sauce
- 1 tablespoon minced peeled fresh ginger
- 1 tablespoon Asian sesame oil
- 1 tablespoon unseasoned rice vinegar
- 2 skinless boneless chicken breast halves, cut into 1-inch pieces
- 1 tablespoon sesame seeds

PREPARE barbecue (medium-high heat). Whisk first 4 ingredients in medium bowl to blend. Transfer 2 tablespoons sauce to small bowl for glaze; reserve. Mix chicken into remaining sauce; let stand 10 minutes. Thread chicken onto 4 metal skewers, spacing pieces ½ inch apart. Sprinkle lightly with salt and pepper. Grill chicken until cooked through and slightly charred, brushing with reserved glaze and turning often, about 8 minutes. Sprinkle with sesame seeds.

MAKE IT YOUR OWN Many prepared sauces like hoisin sauce can be greatly improved by adding a few flavorful ingredients, such as the fresh ginger, sesame oil, and rice vinegar added here.

Apple-glazed barbecued chicken

4 SERVINGS *Sweet barbecue sauces and glazes can burn quickly because of the sugar they contain. Be sure the chicken pieces are almost cooked through before brushing them with the glaze, then allow just a few minutes for the glaze to caramelize slightly. Ask your butcher to cut the chicken for you, or use four leg-thigh pieces.*

¾ cup frozen apple juice concentrate, thawed
¼ cup (packed) golden brown sugar
¼ cup ketchup
1 tablespoon apple cider vinegar
1 teaspoon dried thyme
⅛ teaspoon hot pepper sauce

1 3-pound chicken, cut into 4 pieces
Vegetable oil (for brushing)

COMBINE first 6 ingredients in heavy small saucepan. Stir over medium heat until sugar dissolves.

PREPARE barbecue (medium-high heat). Brush chicken with oil. Sprinkle generously with salt and pepper. Grill chicken until almost cooked through, turning occasionally, about 20 minutes. Brush with apple glaze and continue grilling until chicken is tender and cooked through, frequently brushing with glaze and turning occasionally, about 10 minutes longer.

Chicken tikka kebabs

6 SERVINGS *Tikka is an Indian dish featuring chunks of meat cooked on skewers. Yogurt, a staple of Indian cuisine, forms the base for this marinade. Marinating the chicken in the lemon juice and salt mixture helps flavor the meat and make it juicier. If time is tight, sprinkle the chicken with salt, then marinate it in the yogurt mixture for 20 minutes before grilling.*

2 pounds skinless boneless chicken breast halves, cut into 1-inch pieces
¼ cup fresh lemon juice
½ teaspoon salt

¼ cup plain yogurt
4 garlic cloves, minced
1½ tablespoons ground coriander
2 teaspoons ground cumin
1 teaspoon ground turmeric
⅛ teaspoon ground ginger
Pinch of dried crushed red pepper

12 6- to 8-inch wooden skewers, soaked in water 30 minutes
2 tablespoons (¼ stick) butter, melted

COMBINE chicken, lemon juice, and salt in medium bowl; let stand 30 minutes.

MIX yogurt, garlic, coriander, cumin, turmeric, ginger, and crushed red pepper in small bowl. Add to chicken and stir until chicken is well coated with spice mixture. Cover and refrigerate chicken at least 3 hours or overnight.

PREPARE barbecue (medium-high heat). Thread chicken on skewers, dividing equally. Brush chicken with melted butter. Sprinkle with salt. Grill kebabs until just cooked through, turning frequently, about 7 minutes.

Grilled chicken with olive puree

6 SERVINGS *If you prefer, you can use* olivada *instead of pureeing the Kalamata olives with oil. Olivada is a simple olive spread, sometimes called black olive cream, that blends Italian black olives, olive oil, and black pepper. It is available at some supermarkets and at specialty foods stores and Italian markets. For a last-minute meal, skip the marinating time.*

1⅓   cups pitted Kalamata olives or
      9 tablespoons olivada

3   tablespoons (or more) olive oil, divided

6   large boneless chicken breast halves with skin

1½   teaspoons minced fresh rosemary
      or ½ teaspoon dried

PUREE olives with 2 tablespoons olive oil in processor. Gently slide hand under skin of chicken breasts to loosen, forming pocket and keeping skin attached. Spread 1½ tablespoons olive puree under skin of each chicken breast. Fasten skin with toothpicks to hold olive filling in place. Brush chicken with 1 tablespoon olive oil and sprinkle with rosemary. Place chicken in shallow dish. Cover and refrigerate at least 3 hours or overnight.

PREPARE barbecue (medium-high heat). Sprinkle chicken with salt and pepper. Grill until golden and cooked through, turning frequently and brushing with more olive oil if necessary to prevent sticking, about 20 minutes.

Achiote-grilled chicken

12 SERVINGS *Achiote paste—a blend of ground achiote seeds (also called annatto seeds), vinegar, salt, and spices including oregano, cumin, pepper, and cloves—comes from the Yucatán region of Mexico and gives this chicken a bright orange color and earthy flavor. It's formed into small bricks and sold at Latin markets.*

⅓   cup (about 4 ounces) achiote paste

6   garlic cloves, peeled

3   tablespoons olive oil

3   tablespoons fresh lime juice

3   large fresh oregano sprigs

2   tablespoons water

2   teaspoons coarse kosher salt

2   teaspoons freshly ground black pepper

12   chicken thighs

12   chicken drumsticks

BLEND first 8 ingredients in processor to form paste. Place chicken in 15×10×2-inch glass baking dish. Coat chicken with paste; cover and refrigerate at least 30 minutes or overnight.

Prepare barbecue (medium heat). Sprinkle chicken with additional salt and pepper. Grill chicken until brown, about 2 minutes per side. Cover barbecue; continue to grill chicken until cooked through, turning and moving to coolest part of grill if necessary to prevent burning, about 25 minutes longer.

MORE FOR TOMORROW This recipe makes enough to serve 12, so you might have more than you need for a weeknight family meal, but leftovers are great the next day in salads, sandwiches, soft tacos, or quesadillas.

Grilled spicy-citrus chicken thighs with corn and green onions

8 SERVINGS *Although the chicken and vegetables marinate for up to four hours, this recipe is a cinch to put together as a simple main course for guests. Using resealable bags makes it easy to marinate all sides of the chicken and vegetables in a single turn, and also simplifies cleanup.*

 1 cup fresh lime juice
⅔ cup fresh orange juice
 ½ cup olive oil
 ½ cup chopped fresh cilantro
 4 garlic cloves, chopped
 2 teaspoons hot pepper sauce
 2 teaspoons dried crushed red pepper
16 large boneless chicken thighs with skin
16 green onions
 8 ears of corn, husked

WHISK first 7 ingredients in medium bowl. Season marinade with salt and pepper. Place chicken in large resealable plastic bag. Place green onions and corn in extra-large resealable plastic bag. Divide marinade equally between bags; seal bags, turning to coat contents. Chill chicken, corn, and green onions in bags at least 1 hour and up to 4 hours, turning bags occasionally.

PREPARE barbecue (medium heat). Remove chicken and vegetables from bags; discard marinade. Grill chicken until charred and juices run clear when pierced with knife, turning occasionally and rearranging on grill for even cooking, about 20 minutes. Grill green onions and corn until charred on all sides, about 6 minutes for green onions and 13 minutes for corn. Transfer chicken, green onions, and corn to platter.

GRILL MASTERY Grills usually have "hot spots" and cooler areas. Begin by grilling chicken and vegetables on the hot spots, then move them to the cooler areas to continue cooking evenly.

Barbecued chicken thighs with brown sugar-hickory sauce

6 SERVINGS *Blending purchased sauces with fresh garlic, lemon juice, and other spices creates this quick and easy barbecue sauce that's great on both chicken and ribs. You can use chicken breasts, but chicken thighs work best because they remain tender and succulent even after they're cooked through.*

 ½ cup soy sauce
 ½ cup ketchup
 ½ cup bottled chili sauce
 ½ cup bottled hickory-flavor barbecue sauce
 ½ cup (packed) golden brown sugar
 6 tablespoons fresh lemon juice
 3 garlic cloves, crushed
 2 teaspoons onion powder
 1 teaspoon hot pepper sauce
 ½ teaspoon dry mustard

   Nonstick vegetable oil spray
12 chicken thighs with skin and bones

BRING first 10 ingredients to boil in medium saucepan, whisking to blend. Reduce heat to low; simmer 10 minutes.

DO AHEAD *Can be made 1 week ahead. Cover and chill.*

SPRAY grill rack with nonstick spray. Prepare barbecue (medium-high heat). Sprinkle chicken with salt and pepper. Place chicken, skin side down, on grill; cook until skin browns, about 8 minutes. Turn chicken over and continue grilling until cooked through, about 8 minutes longer. Transfer 1 cup barbecue sauce to small dish. Brush skin side of chicken with sauce from dish; turn skin side down and cook 2 minutes. Brush chicken with more sauce; turn skin side up and grill 2 minutes. Arrange chicken on platter. Serve, passing remaining sauce separately.

Bourbon-molasses chicken drumsticks

4 SERVINGS *It might seem strange to cook the small amount of sauce for this recipe in a large saucepan, but the size is important: The large capacity and high sides of the saucepan help contain the fumes of the bourbon and prevent the mixture from igniting.*

- ¼ cup (½ stick) butter
- 1 cup minced onion
- 1 cup ketchup
- ¼ cup mild-flavored (light) molasses
- 2 tablespoons (packed) brown sugar
- 1½ tablespoons Worcestershire sauce
- 2 teaspoons yellow mustard
- ¼ teaspoon ground black pepper
- ¼ teaspoon chili powder
- ¼ cup bourbon

- 12 chicken drumsticks

MELT butter in large saucepan over medium heat. Add onion; sauté until soft, about 6 minutes. Add next 7 ingredients. Reduce heat to medium-low; simmer until sauce thickens, about 15 minutes. Stir in bourbon; cook until heated through, about 3 minutes. Season to taste with salt.

DO AHEAD *Can be made 1 day ahead. Cover and chill.*

PREPARE barbecue (medium heat). Sprinkle chicken generously with salt and pepper. Grill until skin is crisp and chicken is cooked through, turning to cook all sides, about 25 minutes. Transfer ½ cup barbecue sauce to small bowl; reserve. Brush chicken with remaining sauce and cook until glaze forms, about 3 minutes longer. Transfer chicken to platter and serve, passing remaining sauce separately.

ALCOHOL SAFETY When adding liquor to a saucepan on the stove, take the following precautions to prevent the alcohol from igniting: Remove the pan from the heat when adding the alcohol, and premeasure the amount needed in a measuring cup away from the stove—never pour alcohol directly from the bottle into a saucepan set over an open flame.

Spice-rubbed chicken and vegetable tacos with chipotle cream

6 SERVINGS *This is a wonderful party dish: It comes together quickly and tastes amazing. Chipotle chiles canned in a spicy tomato sauce called adobo are available at some supermarkets, and at specialty foods stores and Latin markets. Smoked paprika is available at some supermarkets and at specialty foods stores. Serve the tacos with a cilantro slaw: Toss purchased coleslaw mix with equal parts canola oil and lime juice and add chopped cilantro.*

1½	cups sour cream
1	tablespoon chopped canned chipotle chiles (about 2)
2	tablespoons (packed) golden brown sugar
1	tablespoon smoked paprika
2¼	teaspoons chili powder
2	teaspoons garlic powder
1½	teaspoons coarse kosher salt
2	small zucchini, quartered lengthwise
1	red bell pepper, seeded, cut lengthwise into ¾-inch-thick strips
2	tablespoons canola oil
1	pound skinless boneless chicken breast halves, each halved horizontally
12	5- to 6-inch-diameter corn tortillas, warmed

PREPARE barbecue (medium heat). Whisk sour cream and chipotle chiles in small bowl; season with salt. Whisk brown sugar and next 4 ingredients in another small bowl to blend for spice rub.

PLACE zucchini and bell pepper on rimmed baking sheet. Drizzle with canola oil; toss to coat. Sprinkle spice rub over both sides of vegetables and chicken.

PLACE chicken and vegetables on barbecue. Grill until vegetables are tender and browned in spots and chicken is cooked through, turning occasionally, about 5 minutes. Transfer to work surface; cut chicken crosswise into ½-inch-thick strips. Cut vegetables crosswise into ¾-inch pieces. Place chicken and vegetables in large bowl; toss to blend.

PLACE chicken and vegetables, chipotle cream, and tortillas on table. Allow guests to assemble their own soft tacos.

THERE'S THE RUB This spice rub is a kind of "instant" alternative to a marinade, adding a burst of flavor very quickly. If you don't have time to make the rub here, try one of the spice blends available in supermarkets; look for those that don't contain a lot of salt or monosodium glutamate.

Green mountain maple barbecued chicken

2 SERVINGS; CAN BE DOUBLED *Maple syrup gives this sauce authentic Vermont flavor. Flash-frozen skinless, boneless chicken thighs are available in bags in the freezer section of most supermarkets. Keep a bag on hand for a quick barbecue any night of the week.*

- 3 tablespoons pure maple syrup
- 3 tablespoons bottled chili sauce
- 1 tablespoon apple cider vinegar
- 2 teaspoons country-style Dijon mustard
- 4 skinless boneless chicken thighs
- 1 tablespoon vegetable oil

PREPARE barbecue (medium-high heat). Stir first 4 ingredients in small saucepan until well blended. Brush chicken with oil; sprinkle with salt and pepper. Grill chicken until cooked through, turning occasionally and brushing generously with sauce during last 5 minutes, about 18 minutes total.

DEFROSTING DEMYSTIFIED For defrosting chicken quickly, nothing beats the microwave. If you don't have a defrost setting on your microwave, use low power and check the chicken often to make sure it hasn't started cooking. Or put the chicken in a resealable plastic bag and place the bag in a sink full of cold water.

Chicken under a brick with fresh herb and garlic sauce

8 SERVINGS *Cooking under a brick, a technique that dates back to Etruscan times, flattens the chicken and helps it cook faster. If bricks are not available, arrange the chicken breasts close together on the grill. Set a large baking sheet over all of them, and weigh down the sheet with heavy items such as a cast-iron skillet.*

- 12 garlic cloves, peeled, divided
- 1½ cups (packed) fresh Italian parsley sprig tops
- ⅓ cup white balsamic vinegar
- ¼ cup (packed) fresh mint leaves
- ¼ cup (packed) fresh basil leaves
- 1 teaspoon dried oregano
- ¼ teaspoon dried crushed red pepper
- 1 cup olive oil

- 8 large boneless chicken breast halves with skin

   Nonstick vegetable oil spray
- 8 bricks, each wrapped in foil

COOK 8 garlic cloves in boiling water 2 minutes. Drain garlic. Place in processor and cool. Add remaining 4 garlic cloves and next 6 ingredients. With machine running, gradually add oil, blending until thick sauce forms. Season to taste with salt.

DO AHEAD *Can be made 2 days ahead. Transfer to bowl; cover and chill.*

PLACE chicken in large resealable plastic bag. Add ½ cup herb-garlic sauce and turn to coat evenly. Chill at least 30 minutes and up to 4 hours, turning bag occasionally.

SPRAY grill rack with nonstick spray and prepare barbecue (medium-high heat). Place chicken, skin side down, on grill. Top each piece with 1 foil-wrapped brick. Grill until skin is golden brown and crisp, about 5 minutes. Remove bricks. Turn chicken over; grill until cooked through, about 5 minutes. Arrange chicken on platter. Spoon some sauce over. Serve, passing remaining sauce separately.

Cilantro-lime chicken fajitas with grilled onions

6 SERVINGS *Traditionally, fajitas are made by sauté-ing strips of marinated skirt steak in a hot cast-iron skillet. This grilled chicken version is just as easy and—because the already-tender chicken needs to marinate for flavor only while the grill gets hot (not for 24 hours, as with skirt steak)—it's even quicker.*

1¼ cups coarsely chopped fresh cilantro
¾ cup olive oil
5 tablespoons fresh lime juice
2½ teaspoons ground cumin
1¼ teaspoons ancho chile powder

6 skinless boneless chicken breast halves
3 large poblano chiles, halved, seeded, cut into ¾-inch-wide strips
3 large yellow bell peppers, cut into ¾-inch-wide strips
2 red onions, peeled, sliced into ½-inch rounds
12 8-inch-diameter flour tortillas

Purchased salsas, guacamole, sour cream (optional)

PREPARE barbecue (medium heat). Puree first 5 ingredients in processor. Season marinade to taste with salt and pepper.

PLACE chicken in 13×9×2-inch glass baking dish. Pour ⅓ cup marinade over; turn to coat. Arrange poblano chiles, bell peppers, and onions on large rimmed baking sheet. Pour ½ cup marinade over; turn to coat. Sprinkle chicken and vegetables with salt and pepper. Reserve remaining marinade.

GRILL chicken until cooked through, about 7 minutes per side. Grill vegetables until tender, turning frequently, about 15 minutes for onions and 12 minutes for poblano chiles and bell peppers. Grill tortillas until charred, about 1 minute per side. Transfer chicken to work surface; slice crosswise into strips. Fill tortillas with chicken and vegetables; drizzle with reserved marinade. Serve with salsas, guacamole, and sour cream, if desired.

HOT, FRESH TORTILLAS One of the best ways to keep tortillas hot after they come off the grill is to place them in a terra cotta or plastic tortilla warmer. You can find them at Latin markets and cookware stores. (They can even double as pancake warmers.) The tortillas can also be stacked and wrapped tightly in foil.

Grilled chicken with salsa verde

8 SERVINGS *This "green sauce" isn't the familiar Mexican salsa made with tomatillos. Rather, this fresh Italian sauce, similar to chimichurri, is made with parsley, olive oil, garlic, lemon juice, anchovies, and capers. It makes a delicious topping for grilled lamb, beef, fish, or chicken, and can even be used as a spread for deli sandwiches.*

3	cups (loosely packed) fresh Italian parsley leaves (from about 1 very large bunch)
3	green onions, sliced
3	tablespoons fresh lemon juice
3	garlic cloves, peeled
2	drained canned anchovy fillets
1	tablespoon drained capers
1	tablespoon Dijon mustard
1½	teaspoons finely grated lemon peel
½	cup plus 2 tablespoons extra-virgin olive oil
8	skinless boneless chicken breast halves

COMBINE first 8 ingredients and ½ cup oil in processor. Using on/off turns, process until coarse paste forms. Season to taste with salt and pepper.

DO AHEAD *Can be made 1 day ahead. Cover; chill.*

PREPARE barbecue (medium-high heat). Brush chicken with remaining 2 tablespoons oil. Sprinkle with salt and pepper. Grill chicken until cooked through, about 7 minutes per side. Transfer chicken to plates. Serve, passing sauce separately.

Mojito-marinated chicken breasts

6 SERVINGS *The popular rum, mint, and lime cocktail from Cuba was the inspiration for this entrée. Look for the mint syrup in the coffee and tea aisle at the supermarket. If it is unavailable, you can make one by stirring ¼ cup each of sugar and water in a small saucepan over medium heat until the sugar dissolves; mix in 2 tablespoons chopped mint and cool.*

¾	cup fresh lime juice
½	cup plus 2 tablespoons light rum
½	cup finely chopped fresh mint plus whole sprigs for garnish
6	tablespoons mint syrup
1	tablespoon vegetable oil
1	tablespoon coarse kosher salt
6	chicken breast halves with skin and bones
3	large limes, quartered lengthwise

WHISK lime juice, ½ cup rum, chopped mint, mint syrup, oil, and salt in bowl. Place chicken in resealable plastic bag. Pour marinade over; seal bag. Turn bag to distribute marinade. Chill at least 1 hour and up to 4 hours, turning bag twice.

PLACE lime quarters in shallow bowl. Pour remaining 2 tablespoons rum over, tossing to coat. Let stand at room temperature.

PREPARE barbecue (medium heat). Grill chicken until cooked through, about 15 minutes per side. Transfer to platter.

GRILL limes until soft and slightly charred, about 5 minutes. Garnish platter with mint sprigs. Squeeze grilled limes over chicken.

Grilled chicken with chimichurri sauce

6 SERVINGS *This garlicky parsley sauce from Argentina is great spooned over grilled chicken, beef, or pork. In this version, a touch of cilantro is added, but other fresh herbs, such as oregano and basil, make good alternatives. If you don't have a food processor, puree the ingredients in a blender, or mince the herbs and garlic by hand and stir everything together in a bowl.*

1	cup (packed) fresh Italian parsley
½	cup olive oil
⅓	cup red wine vinegar
¼	cup (packed) fresh cilantro
2	garlic cloves, peeled
¾	teaspoon dried crushed red pepper
½	teaspoon ground cumin
½	teaspoon salt
6	skinless boneless chicken breast halves

PUREE first 8 ingredients in processor. Transfer 2 tablespoons sauce to small bowl; transfer remaining sauce to separate bowl.

DO AHEAD *Sauce can be made 2 hours ahead. Cover and let stand at room temperature.*

PREPARE barbecue (medium-high heat). Brush chicken with 2 tablespoons sauce. Sprinkle with salt and pepper. Grill chicken until cooked through, about 7 minutes per side. Transfer chicken to plates. Serve, passing remaining sauce separately.

Lemony chicken milanese with arugula salad

4 SERVINGS *Panko is a type of coarse breadcrumb typically used in Japanese cooking to coat fried foods; it creates a wonderfully crunchy coating for the chicken breasts in this Italian-style entrée. Look for panko in the Asian foods section of the supermarket. Pork chops or veal cutlets would also work well in this recipe.*

4	skinless boneless chicken breast halves
2	large eggs
1¼	cups panko (Japanese breadcrumbs)
2	tablespoons chopped fresh parsley
2	teaspoons chopped fresh oregano
1	teaspoon coarse kosher salt
¾	teaspoon ground black pepper
4	tablespoons olive oil, divided
2	tablespoons fresh lemon juice
2	cups (packed) baby arugula leaves (about 2 ounces)

USING meat mallet or rolling pin, pound chicken between sheets of plastic wrap to ½-inch thickness. Whisk eggs in medium bowl to blend. Mix panko, parsley, oregano, salt, and pepper on plate. Dip chicken into beaten eggs; turn to coat. Dredge in breadcrumb mixture, coating completely.

HEAT 3 tablespoons oil in large nonstick skillet over medium heat. Add chicken and sauté until golden brown and cooked through, about 5 minutes per side. Transfer chicken to plates; sprinkle with lemon juice. Toss arugula with remaining 1 tablespoon oil in medium bowl to coat; sprinkle with salt and pepper. Mound salad atop chicken.

TALKING TURKEY Turkey cutlets would also work well in this dish and in the Chicken Piccata. Just skip the step of flattening with a mallet.

Chicken piccata

2 SERVINGS *Classic Italian veal piccata—in which veal scallops are sautéed with lemon juice, white wine, parsley, and vinegar—goes weeknight by substituting chicken breasts flattened with a mallet for fast cooking.*

2 6- to 8-ounce skinless boneless
   chicken breast halves

¼ cup fresh Italian parsley leaves

3 teaspoons olive oil, divided

1½ teaspoons plus 2 tablespoons minced shallot

½ teaspoon plus 2 tablespoons fresh lemon juice

4½ teaspoons drained capers, divided

2 garlic cloves, minced

⅓ cup dry white wine

1 tablespoon butter

1½ teaspoons minced fresh Italian parsley

USING meat mallet or rolling pin, pound chicken breasts between sheets of plastic wrap to ⅓- to ½-inch thickness.

TOSS parsley in small bowl with 1½ teaspoons oil, 1½ teaspoons shallot, ½ teaspoon lemon juice, and 1½ teaspoons capers. Season parsley-caper mixture to taste with salt and pepper.

HEAT remaining 1½ teaspoons oil in heavy large nonstick skillet over high heat. Sprinkle chicken with salt and pepper. Add to skillet and sauté until just cooked through and golden brown, about 3 minutes per side. Transfer to platter and cover with foil to keep warm. Reduce heat to medium-high. Add remaining 2 tablespoons shallot and garlic to same skillet and sauté until tender, about 1 minute. Add wine and remaining 2 tablespoons lemon juice and simmer 1 minute. Whisk in remaining 3 teaspoons capers, butter, and minced parsley. Stir any juices from chicken into sauce; season to taste with salt and pepper. Pour sauce over chicken. Sprinkle chicken with parsley-caper mixture.

Pecan- and panko-crusted chicken breasts

4 SERVINGS *Because this chicken is browned in a skillet, then finished in a hot oven, be sure to use an ovenproof skillet—a cast-iron skillet or a sauté pan with metal handles will work best. This two-step pan-roasting method allows the chicken to cook through evenly without burning the delicate pecan coating. Panko can be found in the Asian foods section of the supermarket.*

4 skinless boneless chicken breast halves

1 cup panko (Japanese breadcrumbs)

1 cup finely chopped pecans

6 tablespoons (¾ stick) butter, divided

¼ cup minced shallots

¾ cup low-salt chicken broth

2 tablespoons chopped fresh parsley

PREHEAT oven to 400°F. Sprinkle chicken with salt and pepper. Mix panko and pecans on plate. Melt 4 tablespoons butter in heavy large ovenproof skillet over medium-high heat. Remove skillet from heat; brush some of melted butter onto chicken, then coat chicken with panko mixture. Place skillet over medium heat. Add chicken and sauté until brown on bottom, about 2 minutes. Turn chicken over. Place skillet in oven. Bake until chicken is cooked through, about 18 minutes. Transfer chicken to platter.

USING slotted spoon, remove any crumbs from skillet. Add remaining 2 tablespoons butter and shallots; sauté over medium-high heat 1 minute. Add broth and simmer until slightly reduced, about 1 minute. Mix in parsley. Season sauce to taste with salt and pepper; drizzle over chicken.

Achiote chicken with tangerine sauce

4 SERVINGS *Marinating the chicken for 4 hours in this spicy Mexican paste will result in intensely flavored chicken; if time is limited, a quick 20-minute dousing will suffice. The warm spices of cinnamon and cumin pair well with the vibrant flavor of tangerine. As an alternative, try orange peel and juice instead of tangerine. Achiote paste is available at Latin markets.*

> 2　tablespoons achiote paste
> 1　tablespoon honey
> 1　tablespoon red wine vinegar
> 1　tablespoon finely grated tangerine peel
> 2　garlic cloves, peeled
> 1　teaspoon cumin seeds
> ½　teaspoon ground cinnamon
> 4　skinless boneless chicken breast halves
>
> 1　tablespoon olive oil
> 1　cup fresh tangerine juice, divided
> 　　Chopped fresh cilantro

BLEND first 7 ingredients in processor to form paste. Place chicken in 8-inch square baking dish. Spread marinade over, turning to coat. Cover; refrigerate at least 2 hours and up to 4 hours.

HEAT oil in large nonstick skillet over medium-high heat. Sprinkle chicken with salt. Add chicken to skillet; cook until brown, about 2 minutes per side. Add ½ cup juice to skillet. Cover, reduce heat to medium, and simmer until chicken is cooked through, turning once, about 5 minutes. Transfer chicken to plates. Add remaining ½ cup juice to skillet; boil until thickened, about 2 minutes. Season sauce to taste with salt and pepper; spoon over chicken. Sprinkle with cilantro.

Chicken with bell peppers, smoked ham, and paprika

4 SERVINGS *The combination of red bell peppers, ham, and smoked paprika add classic Basque flavors to this comforting stewed chicken. Ask the butcher to cut a whole chicken into eight pieces, or buy a prepackaged cut-up chicken. Serve the stew with rice or crusty bread (or both) to soak up all the juices. Smoked paprika is available at some supermarkets and at specialty foods stores.*

> 1　tablespoon olive oil
> 1　3- to 3½-pound chicken, cut into 8 pieces
> 2　large red bell peppers, cut into strips (about 4 cups)
> 2　medium onions, halved, cut lengthwise into strips (about 3 cups)
> 2　cups diced smoked ham steak (such as Nueske's; about 11 ounces)
> 1　teaspoon smoked paprika or hot paprika, divided
> 1½　cups low-salt chicken broth
> ¼　cup chopped fresh Italian parsley

HEAT oil in heavy wide pot over medium-high heat. Sprinkle chicken with salt and pepper; add to pot. Cook until browned, about 6 minutes per side. Transfer chicken to bowl. Increase heat to high. Add next 3 ingredients and ½ teaspoon paprika to drippings in pot; sauté until vegetables are soft and light brown, about 8 minutes. Return chicken to pot; add broth. Sprinkle chicken with remaining ½ teaspoon paprika. Bring to boil. Reduce heat, cover, and simmer 10 minutes. Uncover; simmer until chicken is tender, about 10 minutes longer. Season with salt and pepper. Sprinkle parsley over.

SKIN, NO SKIN The chicken skin adds wonderful flavor and body to the cooking liquids in this stew. If you prefer to eat the chicken without the skin, just remove it after the chicken is cooked.

Sautéed chicken with parsnip, apple, and Sherry pan sauce

4 SERVINGS *After the chicken has been sautéed, the bottom of the skillet is left with caramelized browned bits. These intensely flavored bits are valuable "ingredients" for making the rich, flavorful pan sauce that accompanies the chicken. They scrape up easily when the Sherry is added to the hot skillet—a technique known as deglazing.*

- 4 tablespoons olive oil, divided
- 1 large parsnip, peeled, trimmed, cut into ½-inch pieces
- 1 large Granny Smith apple, peeled, cored, cut into ½-inch pieces
- 2 teaspoons chopped fresh thyme plus whole sprigs for garnish
- 4 6- to 8-ounce skinless boneless chicken breast halves, pounded to ½-inch thickness
- 1 cup dry Sherry
- 2 tablespoons (¼ stick) butter

HEAT 2 tablespoons oil in heavy large skillet over medium-high heat. Add parsnip; sauté until beginning to brown, about 2 minutes. Add apple and chopped thyme; cook until parsnip and apple are tender, about 6 minutes. Transfer parsnip mixture to plate.

SPRINKLE chicken with salt and pepper. Heat remaining 2 tablespoons oil in same skillet over medium-high heat. Add 2 chicken breasts; sauté until cooked through and golden, about 3 minutes per side. Transfer chicken to platter; tent with foil to keep warm. Repeat with remaining 2 chicken breasts.

ADD Sherry to same skillet. Stir over medium-high heat, scraping up browned bits. Add parsnip mixture and cook until liquid is reduced by half, about 2 minutes. Remove from heat and stir in butter. Season sauce to taste with salt and pepper. Spoon over chicken; garnish with thyme sprigs.

Chicken breasts with wild mushrooms, marjoram, and Marsala

4 SERVINGS *As the cream sauce simmers, excess water from the broth and cream evaporates and the sauce reduces (in fact, the resulting sauce is called a "reduction"). In the process, the flavors become more concentrated and the level of salt in the sauce intensifies; using a low-salt chicken broth helps ensure the sauce will not become too salty. Fresh oregano, rosemary, or thyme make great substitutes for the marjoram.*

- 4 large skinless boneless chicken breast halves
- 6 teaspoons chopped fresh marjoram, divided
- 2 tablespoons (¼ stick) butter, divided
- 2 tablespoons olive oil, divided
- 12 ounces assorted fresh wild mushrooms (such as oyster, stemmed shiitake, and baby bella), thickly sliced
- 1 cup sliced shallots (about 5)
- ¾ cup low-salt chicken broth
- ½ cup heavy whipping cream
- 3 tablespoons dry Marsala

SPRINKLE chicken with salt and pepper, then 2 teaspoons marjoram. Melt 1 tablespoon butter with 1 tablespoon oil in large nonstick skillet over medium-high heat. Add chicken to skillet and sauté until just cooked through, about 7 minutes per side. Transfer chicken to plate; tent with foil to keep warm. Melt remaining 1 tablespoon butter with 1 tablespoon oil in same skillet. Add mushrooms, shallots, and 2 teaspoons marjoram. Sauté until mushrooms are brown and tender, about 6 minutes. Season to taste with salt and pepper. Transfer to bowl.

COMBINE broth, cream, Marsala, and remaining 2 teaspoons marjoram in same skillet; boil until thickened and reduced to ½ cup, about 5 minutes. Season sauce to taste with salt and pepper.

DIVIDE mushrooms among 4 plates. Top with chicken. Spoon sauce over.

Chicken breasts with pistachio-cilantro pesto

4 SERVINGS *Serve the chicken with rice pilaf or purchased tabbouleh for dinner. Slice any leftover chicken into strips and tuck them into pita pockets with diced cucumber, tomato, and romaine lettuce for lunch the next day.*

- 1 cup unsalted raw pistachios
- 2 cups (packed) fresh cilantro leaves
- 4 teaspoons fresh lemon juice, divided
- 1 garlic clove, chopped
- 1 teaspoon ground cardamom
- ¾ teaspoon salt
- ½ cup plus 5 tablespoons olive oil, divided

- 4 large chicken breast halves with skin and bones

PREHEAT oven to 400°F. Toast pistachios on baking sheet until golden, about 7 minutes. Transfer to processor. Maintain oven temperature. Add cilantro leaves, 3 teaspoons lemon juice, garlic, cardamom, and salt to processor. Using on/off turns, process until coarse paste forms. With machine running, gradually add ½ cup olive oil. Season pesto to taste with pepper.

USING fingers, gently loosen skin from 1 side of each chicken breast, forming pocket. Spread 1 tablespoon pesto evenly under skin of each. Sprinkle chicken generously with salt and pepper.

HEAT 1 tablespoon olive oil in heavy large ovenproof skillet over medium-high heat. Add chicken, skin side down. Cook until skin is dark golden, about 5 minutes. Turn chicken over and transfer skillet to oven. Roast chicken until cooked through, about 25 minutes.

PLACE ½ cup remaining pesto into small bowl. Whisk in remaining 4 tablespoons olive oil and remaining 1 teaspoon lemon juice. Drizzle pesto sauce over chicken.

Chicken with green olives, orange, and Sherry

4 SERVINGS *Browning the chicken is an important flavor-enhancing step in this braise, so be sure to use a skillet wide enough to fit the chicken pieces without crowding them. Allowing some room between the pieces will help them brown instead of steam.*

- 2 tablespoons olive oil
- 1 4¾-pound chicken, cut into 8 pieces
- 1 cup sliced shallots (about 3 large)
- 2 garlic cloves, minced
- 1 cup medium Sherry
- 1 cup low-salt chicken broth
- 1 orange, halved lengthwise, each half cut into 5 wedges
- ⅓ cup brine-cured green olives (such as picholine)

- 1 tablespoon honey

PREHEAT oven to 425°F. Heat oil in large ovenproof skillet over high heat. Sprinkle chicken with salt and pepper. Add chicken to skillet; cook until skin is crisp and brown, about 6 minutes per side. Transfer chicken to plate. Reduce heat to medium-high. Drain all but 2 tablespoons drippings from skillet. Add shallots; stir until soft and beginning to brown, about 2 minutes. Add garlic; stir 30 seconds. Add Sherry; boil until reduced by half, scraping up browned bits, about 3 minutes. Add chicken broth; bring to boil. Return chicken, skin side up, to skillet. Place orange wedges and olives among chicken pieces. Transfer to oven and braise uncovered until chicken is cooked through, about 20 minutes.

TRANSFER chicken to platter. Bring sauce to boil over high heat. Stir in honey; boil until thickened, about 5 minutes. Season to taste with salt and pepper. Pour sauce, oranges, and olives over chicken.

Fettuccine with Asparagus, Morels, and Tarragon

Wisconsin Mac and Cheese

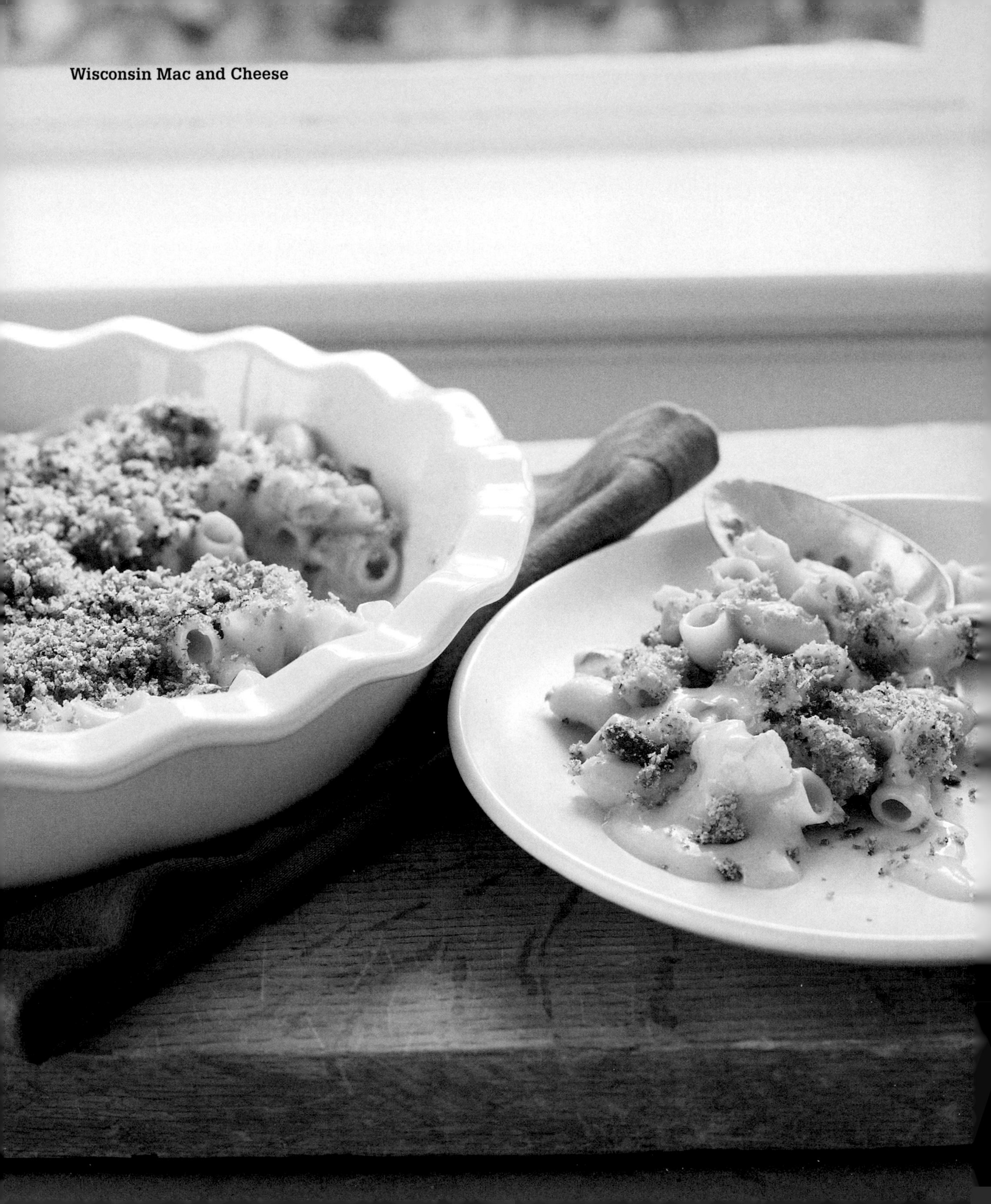

Spicy Oven-Fried Chicken

Lemon-Oregano Roast Chicken and Potatoes

Radicchio and Haricot Vert
Salad with Candied Walnuts

Turkey Chilaquiles

Strawberry and Peach Sangria

Spiced Winter Squash with Fennel

Braised chicken with green peppers and tomatoes

6 SERVINGS *Chicken thighs remain tender even after cooked through, so they work better in braises than chicken breasts, which can become dry if overcooked.*

4 tablespoons (about) extra-virgin olive oil, divided

2¼ pounds skinless boneless chicken thighs (about 12)

1 large onion, minced

3 garlic cloves, minced

2 tablespoons minced fresh Italian parsley

2 green bell peppers, cut into 1-inch squares

6 whole tomatoes from 28-ounce can, drained, chopped

1 cup dry white wine

HEAT 2 tablespoons oil in heavy large skillet over medium-high heat. Sprinkle chicken with salt and pepper. Working in batches, cook chicken until golden brown, about 4 minutes total, adding more oil as necessary. Transfer chicken to platter (reserve skillet).

ADD onion, garlic, and parsley to same skillet; sauté until onion is soft, scraping up browned bits, about 4 minutes. Add bell peppers, tomatoes, and wine; return chicken to skillet. Cover; simmer over medium-low heat 30 minutes. Uncover; cook until chicken is tender and sauce is reduced, about 15 minutes. Season to taste with salt and pepper.

In praise of braising Braising is a simple technique in which meat is browned first, then covered partially with a cooking liquid and simmered very gently, usually in a tightly covered pan, until the meat is tender. While this technique takes a bit longer than a quick stir-fry or sauté, it requires minimal attention, freeing up your time to prepare a side dish or set the table.

Orange and ginger chicken

4 SERVINGS *Flouring the chicken serves a few purposes in this recipe: It acts as a barrier between the oil and the chicken, it creates a crunchy coating and a juicy interior, and it helps thicken the sauce. To give the sauce a spicy kick, add some dried crushed red pepper along with the orange juice and peel.*

 4 **boneless chicken breast halves with skin**
    All purpose flour
 2 **tablespoons (¼ stick) butter**
 1 **tablespoon olive oil**
 4 **teaspoons minced peeled fresh ginger**
 2 **tablespoons (packed) brown sugar**
 1 **teaspoon dry mustard**
 2 **cups orange juice**
 2 **teaspoons finely grated orange peel**
 ¾ **cup thinly sliced green onions**

SPRINKLE chicken with salt and pepper; dust with flour. Melt butter with oil in large skillet over medium-high heat. Add chicken; sauté until brown, about 3 minutes per side. Transfer chicken to plate. Add ginger to skillet; stir 1 minute. Add brown sugar and mustard and stir to blend into drippings. Add orange juice and orange peel. Simmer until sauce is slightly reduced, stirring occasionally, about 8 minutes. Return chicken and any juices to skillet. Simmer 3 minutes. Turn chicken over and add green onions. Simmer until chicken is cooked through and sauce is thick enough to coat spoon, about 3 minutes longer. Season sauce to taste with salt and pepper. Transfer chicken and sauce to platter.

Chicken paillards with tomato, basil, and roasted-corn relish

4 SERVINGS *Paillards are simply thin slices of meat, usually veal or beef, that are quickly grilled or sautéed. Here, chicken breasts are pounded into thin paillards.*

Relish

 3   **tablespoons extra-virgin olive oil, divided**
 1½ **cups fresh corn kernels**
 12 **ounces cherry tomatoes, halved**
 ¼   **cup chopped green onions**
 3   **tablespoons finely sliced fresh basil**

Chicken

 4   **large skinless boneless chicken breast halves, tenderloins removed**
     All purpose flour
 1½ **tablespoons butter**
 1½ **tablespoons extra-virgin olive oil**

FOR RELISH: Preheat oven to 375°F. Brush rimmed baking sheet with 1 teaspoon oil. Toss corn and 2 teaspoons oil on prepared sheet. Roast until corn begins to brown, stirring occasionally, about 18 minutes. Transfer to bowl. Mix in tomatoes, green onions, basil, and remaining 2 tablespoons oil; season with salt and pepper.

FOR CHICKEN: Using meat mallet or rolling pin, pound chicken between sheets of plastic wrap to ½-inch thickness. Pat chicken dry. Sprinkle with salt and pepper, then dust with flour to coat. Melt butter with oil in heavy large skillet over medium-high heat. Add chicken to skillet and sauté until cooked through, about 5 minutes per side. Transfer to plates and top with relish.

TENDERLOIN TIP The tenderloin (also called a chicken tender) is the long strip of meat on the underside of the chicken breast that is easily removed with a gentle pull. Although it is very tender, removing it from the breasts helps create an even thickness when the breasts are pounded. Save the tenderloins for quick stir-fries or satays.

Sautéed chicken paillards with Muscat sauce

4 SERVINGS *Fresh Muscat grapes—in season from August to October—have a musky flavor and sweet floral aroma, but other grapes work nicely, too. Use a dry, fruity white wine, such as Gewürztraminer or Riesling, to make the sauce. Because the chicken breasts are pounded into very thin paillards, they will cook quickly—so have all the ingredients ready before the skillet is even hot.*

- 4 large skinless boneless chicken breast halves, tenderloin removed
- ¼ cup all purpose flour
- 4 tablespoons (½ stick) butter, divided
- 1 tablespoon minced shallot
- 1 cup red Muscat grapes or other red grapes, halved, seeded
- ¼ cup dry fruity white wine
- 1 tablespoon heavy whipping cream
- 1 tablespoon chopped fresh tarragon

USING meat mallet or rolling pin, pound chicken between sheets of plastic wrap to ¼-inch thickness. Place flour in dish. Sprinkle chicken with salt and pepper. Dredge in flour to coat. Melt 2 tablespoons butter in very large skillet over medium-high heat. Add chicken; sauté until cooked through, about 2 minutes per side. Transfer to platter; tent with foil. Melt remaining butter in same skillet over medium-high heat. Add shallot and grapes; sauté 2 minutes. Add wine; bring to boil. Add cream; bring to simmer. Stir in tarragon. Season sauce to taste with salt and pepper. Spoon over chicken.

Chicken with Asiago, prosciutto, and sage

4 SERVINGS *This version of saltimbocca, a Roman specialty, substitutes chicken for veal. After the chicken is browned in the skillet, it should still be a bit underdone, as it will continue cooking in the oven. Reserve all the pan drippings in the skillet to make the flavorful pan sauce. If Asiago cheese is not available, use a sharp provolone cheese.*

4	small skinless boneless chicken breast halves
	All purpose flour
6	tablespoons (¾ stick) butter, divided
½	cup finely grated Asiago cheese
8	thin prosciutto slices, folded over crosswise
⅔	cup dry white wine
2	teaspoons minced fresh sage plus 4 whole leaves for garnish

PREHEAT oven to 375°F. Using meat mallet or rolling pin, pound chicken between sheets of plastic wrap to ¼-inch thickness. Sprinkle chicken with salt and pepper. Coat both sides with flour, shaking off excess. Melt 4 tablespoons butter in very large skillet over medium-high heat. Add chicken and sauté until brown, turning once, about 5 minutes. Transfer chicken to rimmed baking sheet; reserve skillet. Sprinkle 2 tablespoons cheese over each chicken breast. Top each with 2 prosciutto slices. Bake chicken until cooked through, about 5 minutes.

MEANWHILE, add wine, minced sage, and remaining 2 tablespoons butter to skillet. Boil until sauce is reduced to ⅓ cup, scraping up browned bits, about 4 minutes.

TRANSFER chicken breasts to platter. Garnish each with sage leaf, drizzle pan sauce over, and serve.

Cinnamon chicken with couscous and dried fruit

4 SERVINGS *Classic North African flavors—cinnamon, mint, and dried fruit—play off each other beautifully in this exotic, one-skillet meal. Look for whole chicken legs that include both the thigh and drumstick and ask the butcher to cut them into separate pieces. If whole chicken legs are unavailable, use eight thighs instead.*

4	whole chicken legs (about 3 pounds), cut into leg and thigh pieces
2	teaspoons ground cinnamon, divided
1	teaspoon ground ginger, divided
1	tablespoon olive oil
1	cup chopped onion
¾	cup chopped assorted dried fruit (such as currants, apricots, and prunes)
1	14-ounce can low-salt chicken broth
1	cup couscous
2	teaspoons finely chopped fresh mint, divided

PREHEAT oven to 375°F. Sprinkle chicken with salt, pepper, 1 teaspoon cinnamon, and ½ teaspoon ginger. Heat oil in large ovenproof skillet over medium-high heat. Add chicken pieces, skin side down, and cook until skin is brown, about 8 minutes. Turn chicken over and transfer skillet to oven. Roast chicken until thermometer inserted into thickest part of thigh registers 175°F, about 15 minutes. Transfer chicken to plate; tent with foil.

ADD onion to drippings in same skillet; sauté onion over medium-high heat until beginning to brown, about 5 minutes. Add dried fruit and remaining 1 teaspoon cinnamon and ½ teaspoon ginger; stir to coat. Add broth; bring to boil. Remove skillet from heat; stir in couscous and 1 teaspoon mint. Cover and let stand 5 minutes. Season couscous to taste with salt and pepper.

MOUND couscous on platter; place chicken atop couscous. Sprinkle with remaining 1 teaspoon mint.

Sautéed chicken with tomato-saffron vinaigrette on frisée

4 SERVINGS *White balsamic vinegar is milder than traditional balsamic vinegar and is almost colorless, so it doesn't interfere with the subtle flavor or bright yellow color of the saffron in this vinaigrette. And because white balsamic is also less acidic, not as much oil is needed to balance the flavors. You'll find it alongside other vinegars at some supermarkets and most specialty foods stores. If it is unavailable, use unseasoned rice vinegar, which is also mild.*

- 3 tablespoons white balsamic vinegar or unseasoned rice vinegar
- 1½ teaspoons hot paprika, divided
- ⅛ teaspoon crumbled saffron threads
- 4 tablespoons extra-virgin olive oil, divided
- ½ cup minced shallots
- 2 tablespoons chopped fresh thyme, divided
- 1 1-pint basket cherry tomatoes, halved

- 4 skinless boneless chicken breast halves
- 1 head of frisée, torn apart

MIX vinegar, ½ teaspoon paprika, and saffron in medium bowl. Mix in 3 tablespoons oil, shallots, and 1 tablespoon thyme. Stir in tomatoes. Season to taste with salt and pepper.

HEAT remaining 1 tablespoon oil in large nonstick skillet over medium-high heat. Sprinkle chicken with remaining 1 teaspoon paprika, 1 tablespoon thyme, salt, and pepper. Add chicken to skillet; sauté until cooked through, turning often, about 12 minutes. Transfer chicken to work surface. Divide frisée among plates. Slice chicken; fan atop frisée. Spoon vinaigrette over chicken.

Sautéed chicken with tomatoes, olives, and feta

6 SERVINGS *Scoring the top of the chicken breasts creates more surface area, allowing the marinade to penetrate deeper into the meat.*

- 6 skinless boneless chicken breast halves
- ½ cup plus 2 tablespoons olive oil
- ⅓ cup fresh lemon juice
- 8 teaspoons chopped fresh oregano, divided
- 2 garlic cloves, pressed
- 30 pitted Kalamata olives, cut lengthwise into slivers
- 16 grape tomatoes, stemmed, quartered lengthwise
- ½ cup crumbled feta cheese

USING meat mallet or rolling pin, pound chicken between sheets of plastic wrap to ⅓-inch thickness. Score top of chicken breasts with sharp knife; place in large glass baking dish. Whisk ½ cup oil, lemon juice, 6 teaspoons oregano, and garlic in small bowl to blend. Season dressing to taste with salt and pepper. Chill 3 tablespoons dressing for tomatoes. Pour remaining dressing over chicken; turn chicken to coat. Cover; refrigerate at least 1 hour and up to 6 hours, turning occasionally.

TOSS olives, tomatoes, feta, remaining 2 teaspoons oregano, and reserved dressing in medium bowl. Heat remaining 2 tablespoons olive oil in heavy large skillet over medium-high heat. Working in batches, add chicken and sauté until cooked through, about 3 minutes per side. Transfer to platter; season to taste with salt and pepper. Spoon tomato mixture over chicken.

Chicken sauté with green olive topping

4 SERVINGS *Cumin, cayenne pepper, and salt make a flavorful rub for these chicken breasts. If you're having guests for dinner, season the chicken and prepare the olive topping ahead of time and keep them refrigerated; cook the chicken and finish the sauce just before serving. Serve with orzo and green beans sautéed with almonds.*

2 garlic cloves, peeled

½ cup drained pimiento-stuffed green olives (about 2½ ounces)

½ cup (packed) whole fresh parsley sprigs

1 teaspoon minced lemon peel

1 tablespoon fresh lemon juice

4 skinless boneless chicken breast halves (about 5 ounces each), flattened to ½-inch thickness

1½ tablespoons ground cumin

1 teaspoon cayenne pepper

3 tablespoons olive oil

USING on/off turns, coarsely chop garlic in processor. Add olives, parsley, and lemon peel; blend until finely chopped. Mix in lemon juice.

SPRINKLE chicken on both sides with cumin, cayenne, and salt. Heat oil in heavy very large skillet over medium-high heat. Add chicken and sauté until browned and just cooked through, about 3 minutes per side. Transfer chicken to plates.

ADD olive topping to drippings in skillet; cook over medium-high heat until warm, about 1 minute. Spoon topping over chicken.

Layered chicken enchiladas with salsa verde

8 SERVINGS *Using purchased roast chicken makes quick work of these easy enchiladas. And because the chicken and cheese are layered between corn tortillas (instead of rolled), prep time is reduced even more. The casserole can be assembled a day ahead and refrigerated, but it will need to bake about 10 minutes longer. Serve with black beans, rice, and extra salsa, if desired. This makes enough for eight, but any leftovers will keep for up to three days in the fridge, and are easily reheated in the microwave.*

2 16-ounce jars salsa verde (tomatillo salsa)

2 cups sliced green onions

2 cups (packed) very coarsely chopped fresh cilantro

14 5- to 6-inch-diameter corn tortillas

1 purchased roast chicken, meat torn into strips (about 4 cups)

1 pound whole-milk mozzarella cheese or Monterey Jack cheese, grated

1 cup heavy whipping cream

PREHEAT oven to 425°F. Combine salsa, green onions, and cilantro in processor. Using on/off turns, blend until onions and cilantro are finely chopped.

OVERLAP 7 tortillas in bottom of 13×9×2-inch oval or rectangular baking dish. Top tortillas with half of chicken strips and half of cheese. Pour half of salsa evenly over. Top with remaining tortillas, chicken strips, and cheese. Pour remaining salsa over, then cream. Bake until bubbling, about 30 minutes. Cool casserole 10 minutes.

Chicken schnitzel with anchovy-chive butter sauce

4 SERVINGS *Schnitzel is the German word for a cutlet that is dipped in egg, then coated with breadcrumbs and pan-fried. If anchovies rolled with capers aren't available, substitute a two-ounce can of anchovies plus one teaspoon of capers. Serve the schnitzel with such traditional accompaniments as potato pancakes, chunky applesauce, and red-cabbage slaw.*

- 4 skinless boneless chicken breast halves
- 1 cup panko (Japanese breadcrumbs) or unseasoned breadcrumbs
- 2 teaspoons paprika
- 1 large egg

- 3 tablespoons unsalted butter, divided
- 1 2-ounce can anchovies rolled with capers
- ½ cup dry white wine
- 2 tablespoons chopped chives, divided

  Lemon wedges

USING meat mallet or rolling pin, pound chicken between sheets of plastic wrap to ¾-inch thickness. Mix panko and paprika in shallow dish. Beat egg in small dish to blend. Sprinkle chicken with salt and pepper. Dip chicken into beaten egg, then into panko mixture, coating completely.

MELT 2 tablespoons butter in large skillet over medium-high heat. Add chicken and cook until brown, crisp, and cooked through, turning once, about 4 minutes per side. Transfer chicken to platter. Add remaining 1 tablespoon butter and anchovies with capers to skillet. Cook over medium heat until mixture turns brown, mashing anchovies to blend into butter, about 1 minute. Add wine; simmer until slightly reduced, stirring occasionally, about 2 minutes. Stir in 1½ tablespoons chives.

SPOON anchovy-chive sauce over chicken and sprinkle with remaining ½ tablespoon chives. Serve with lemon wedges.

Chicken sauté with wilted endive and brussels sprouts

2 SERVINGS *Browning the butter before the Belgian endive and brussels sprouts are added gives them a rich, nutty flavor. It only takes a minute but makes a world of difference in the overall flavor of this entrée. Look for heads of Belgian endive that have tightly packed leaves with pale, yellow-green tips.*

- 2 skinless boneless chicken breast halves
- 2 teaspoons chopped assorted fresh herbs (such as tarragon and chives), divided

- 4 tablespoons (½ stick) butter, divided
- 5 large brussels sprouts, quartered
- 2 large heads of Belgian endive, quartered lengthwise
- ¼ cup low-salt chicken broth
- 2 teaspoons white balsamic vinegar

USING meat mallet or rolling pin, pound chicken between sheets of plastic wrap to ½-inch thickness. Sprinkle chicken with 1 teaspoon chopped fresh herbs, salt, and pepper.

MELT 2 tablespoons butter in large nonstick skillet over medium-high heat. Add chicken and sauté until cooked through, about 3 minutes per side. Transfer chicken to plate and tent with foil. Add remaining 2 tablespoons butter to same skillet and cook until brown, about 1 minute. Add brussels sprouts and endive and sauté until golden, adding broth to moisten, about 3 minutes. Add vinegar; toss to coat. Season to taste with salt and pepper. Mix in remaining 1 teaspoon herbs. Divide vegetables between plates. Top with chicken and serve.

Wasabi-crusted chicken breasts

4 SERVINGS *Wasabi powder (horseradish powder), which can be found in the spice aisle or Asian foods section of most supermarkets, gives the breadcrumb coating a spicy kick. Over time, wasabi powder can become bitter, so buy fresh powder every 18 months. Continue the Asian theme by serving the chicken with steamed rice enlivened with sliced green onions and a few drops of Asian sesame oil. Add a salad of mixed baby greens tossed with ginger vinaigrette.*

1¼ cups panko (Japanese breadcrumbs)
     or fresh breadcrumbs made from
     crustless French bread

4 teaspoons wasabi powder
    (horseradish powder)

½ teaspoon salt

¼ teaspoon pepper

2 eggs, beaten to blend

4 skinless boneless chicken breast halves,
    flattened to ⅓-inch thickness

4 tablespoons peanut oil, divided

3 tablespoons teriyaki sauce

3 tablespoons sake

3 tablespoons low-salt chicken broth

3 green onions, thinly sliced

COMBINE panko, wasabi powder, salt, and pepper in large shallow dish. Place eggs in pie dish. Dip chicken into beaten eggs, then into panko mixture, turning to coat completely.

HEAT 2 tablespoons peanut oil in heavy large skillet over medium-high heat. Sauté 2 chicken breasts until golden and cooked through, about 3 minutes per side. Transfer to platter. Repeat with remaining oil and chicken.

ADD teriyaki sauce, sake, and chicken broth to skillet; bring to boil, scraping up browned bits. Drizzle sauce over chicken. Sprinkle with sliced green onions and serve.

Skillet chicken and vegetables

4 SERVINGS *Here's a simple but hearty skillet stew that's ready in a hurry. To easily remove the skin from small boiling onions, first submerge them in a saucepan of boiling water for 30 seconds. One tablespoon of flour may seem like a small amount, but it is just enough to form a delicious, gravy-like sauce.*

4 chicken thighs with skin and bones

1 tablespoon paprika

2 tablespoons vegetable oil

¾ pound small red-skinned potatoes, halved

8 boiling onions, peeled, or 8 peeled
    1½-inch-thick onion wedges

2 large carrots, peeled, cut into 1-inch pieces

1 tablespoon all purpose flour

1 cup low-salt chicken broth

½ cup dry white wine
   Chopped fresh parsley

SPRINKLE chicken on all sides with paprika, salt, and pepper. Heat oil in heavy large skillet over medium-high heat. Add chicken and sauté until brown, about 3 minutes per side. Transfer chicken to plate. Add potatoes, onions, and carrots to skillet and stir 2 minutes. Sprinkle vegetables with flour and stir to coat. Gradually stir in broth and wine; bring to boil, stirring frequently. Return chicken and any juices to skillet; bring to boil. Reduce heat to medium-low, cover, and simmer until chicken is cooked through, about 30 minutes. Season to taste with salt and pepper. Sprinkle with parsley.

MIX IT UP This simple stew can be altered in many different ways. Try adding other winter vegetables, such as peeled baby turnips and parsnips. Throw in a few sprigs of fresh thyme—you don't even need to perform the tedious removal of tiny leaves from the stems. By the time the stew is ready, the leaves will have fallen off and you can discard the stems.

Dijon chicken

6 TO 8 SERVINGS *This stew is great for entertaining, as it can be prepared in advance and reheated. In fact, making it ahead actually improves the mustard flavor. Do a little multitasking to minimize prep time, such as chopping the onions, leeks, and garlic while browning the chicken, and chopping the thyme while the onion-leek mixture cooks. Browning the chicken until it is a dark caramel color is an important step, as this process adds both color and flavor. Serve with French bread to soak up all the delicious sauce.*

- 1 **tablespoon olive oil**
- 1 **5½-pound chicken, cut into 8 pieces (2 breasts, 2 wings, 2 legs, and 2 thighs), each breast cut crosswise into 3 pieces**
- 3 **large leeks (white and pale green parts only), sliced**
- 2 **medium onions, chopped**
- 6 **garlic cloves, minced**
- ¼ **cup plus 2 teaspoons chopped fresh thyme**
- 2 **cups Sauvignon Blanc or other dry white wine**
- ¾ **cup Dijon mustard**
- 2 **cups low-salt chicken broth**
- ⅓ **cup heavy whipping cream**

HEAT oil in large wide pot over medium heat. Sprinkle chicken with salt and pepper. Working in 2 batches, cook chicken until brown, turning frequently, about 12 minutes per batch. Transfer chicken to bowl. Add leeks and onions to same pot and sauté until tender and beginning to turn golden, about 12 minutes. Add garlic and ¼ cup thyme and sauté 2 minutes. Stir in wine and mustard to blend. Bring to simmer. Stir in broth. Return chicken to pot, arranging legs, thighs, and wings on bottom and breast pieces on top. Bring to simmer. Reduce heat to low, cover, and simmer very gently until breast pieces are just cooked through, about 15 minutes. Transfer breast pieces to bowl.

CONTINUE simmering until remaining chicken pieces are cooked through and tender, about 15 minutes longer. Transfer remaining chicken to bowl with breast pieces.

BOIL cooking liquids until mixture thickens slightly and is reduced to about 4 cups, stirring often, about 12 minutes. Whisk in cream; season sauce to taste with salt and pepper. Return chicken to pot.

DO AHEAD *Can be made up to 2 days ahead. Cool slightly. Refrigerate uncovered until cold, then cover and keep chilled.*

SIMMER gently until chicken is heated through. Sprinkle with remaining 2 teaspoons thyme and serve.

SIMPLE CHICKEN Ask your butcher to cut up the chicken for you, or purchase a cut-up large chicken (known as best of fryer). "Best of fryer" refers to a package that contains two legs, thighs, breasts, and wings. To ensure best quality and consistency in serving sizes, look for a label stating that all the pieces come from the same chicken.

Chicken with mustard cream on watercress

2 SERVINGS *The peppery taste of watercress is a tasty contrast to the rich honey-mustard cream sauce; mixed baby salad greens make a good alternative to the watercress.*

1 bunch watercress, stems trimmed
2 skinless boneless chicken breast halves

1 tablespoon butter
⅓ cup low-salt chicken broth
¼ cup heavy whipping cream
2½ tablespoons honey-Dijon mustard

DIVIDE watercress between 2 plates. Using meat mallet or rolling pin, pound chicken between sheets of plastic wrap to ½-inch thickness. Sprinkle chicken with salt and pepper.

MELT butter in heavy medium skillet over medium heat. Add chicken; sauté until cooked through, about 4 minutes per side. Place chicken atop watercress. Add broth, cream, and mustard to skillet. Boil until sauce thickens, whisking often, about 2 minutes. Season sauce to taste with salt and pepper. Spoon sauce over chicken.

Chicken curry with dried apricots

4 SERVINGS *Indian and Thai flavors marry beautifully in this single-dish chicken dinner. Thai curry pastes are available in red, green, and yellow blends; the red version used here is made from red chiles, lemongrass, and additional herbs and spices. A little adds a lot of flavor and heat, so use cautiously. Red curry paste, coconut milk, and mango chutney can be found in the Asian foods section of most supermarkets, and at Asian markets.*

2 tablespoons vegetable oil
½ cup chopped shallots
1 tablespoon Thai red curry paste
1 tablespoon minced peeled fresh ginger
1 pound chicken tenders

2 14-ounce cans unsweetened coconut milk
½ cup dried apricots, quartered
2 tablespoons mango chutney
   (such as Major Grey)
¾ cup chopped fresh cilantro, divided
   Freshly steamed white rice

HEAT oil in heavy large skillet over medium heat. Add shallots and sauté until golden brown, about 5 minutes. Mix in red curry paste and ginger and cook 1 minute. Add chicken and sauté until cooked through, about 6 minutes. Using tongs, transfer chicken to bowl.

ADD coconut milk and apricots to skillet and boil until mixture is reduced to 2¼ cups, about 10 minutes. Mix in mango chutney and ½ cup cilantro. Return chicken to skillet. Season to taste with salt and pepper. Stir to heat through. Sprinkle with remaining ¼ cup cilantro. Serve over rice.

Poached chicken with green herb sauce

2 SERVINGS; CAN BE DOUBLED *This is a great do-ahead meal for a hot summer night. Cutting the chicken breasts crosswise (against the grain) shortens the fibers and creates tender pieces of meat.*

- 1 cup fresh parsley leaves
- 2 tablespoons (packed) chopped fresh tarragon
- 1 garlic clove, peeled
- 1 teaspoon Dijon mustard
- ½ cup mayonnaise

- 2 skinless boneless chicken breast halves

  Fresh parsley or tarragon sprigs (optional)

FINELY chop parsley, tarragon, and garlic with mustard in processor. Add mayonnaise and process until almost smooth, occasionally scraping down sides of bowl. Season sauce to taste with salt and pepper. Transfer sauce to small bowl; cover and refrigerate.

DO AHEAD *Can be made 1 day ahead.*

SPRINKLE chicken with salt and pepper. Place in heavy medium skillet. Pour enough cold water over to barely cover. Bring water to simmer over medium heat and poach chicken until just cooked through, about 10 minutes. Transfer chicken to plate and refrigerate until cool, about 10 minutes. Cut chicken crosswise into ¼-inch-thick slices.

DO AHEAD *Can be made 4 hours ahead and refrigerated. Let stand 1 hour at room temperature before serving.*

FAN chicken slices on plates. Spoon sauce over chicken. Garnish with parsley sprigs, if desired.

MOIST HEAT, DELICIOUS FLAVOR

Poaching is a simple, moist-heat cooking method in which chicken, fish, or meat is submerged in gently simmering water or a flavorful broth. It is a good technique to use when counting calories, as no oil is required. The key to poaching is to keep the cooking liquid at a *very gentle* simmer. Never add meat—especially lean chicken breasts—to liquids that are boiling or even simmering vigorously, as the high heat will toughen the meat and dry it out.

Chicken breasts with prosciutto and sage

2 SERVINGS; CAN BE DOUBLED *Using bone-in chicken breasts helps keep them moist as they simmer in the cooking liquid. If you prefer boneless, cut the cooking time in half. Use a dry white wine, such as Pinot Grigio, Sauvignon Blanc, or Chardonnay, in the cooking liquid. To prevent the sauce from evaporating, be sure to cover the skillet while the mixture simmers.*

2	chicken breast halves with skin and bones
2	tablespoons olive oil
½	cup finely chopped onion
¼	cup finely chopped carrot
¼	cup finely chopped celery
½	cup dry white wine
¼	cup (packed) slivered prosciutto (about 1½ ounces)
1½	tablespoons chopped fresh sage or 1½ teaspoons dried

SPRINKLE chicken with salt and pepper. Heat oil in heavy medium skillet over medium-high heat. Add chicken and sauté until brown, about 3 minutes per side. Transfer chicken to plate. Add onion, carrot, and celery to skillet; sauté until vegetables begin to brown, about 5 minutes. Return chicken and any juices to skillet; add wine, prosciutto, and sage. Bring to boil. Reduce heat to medium-low. Cover; simmer until chicken is cooked through, about 6 minutes per side. Serve chicken with sauce.

Smothered chicken with creamy mushroom gravy

4 SERVINGS *White mushrooms work well in this recipe—they are very economical and are sometimes available sliced, which is a nice time-saver. Look for pure-white caps that are tightly closed around the stems. Mixing in other types of mushrooms, such as crimini, shiitake, and oyster, creates an interesting mélange. Be sure to trim the tough shiitake stems.*

⅓	cup all purpose flour
1½	teaspoons dried thyme, divided
½	teaspoon ground allspice
4	large skinless boneless chicken breast halves
¼	cup (½ stick) butter
1	pound mushrooms, thinly sliced
1	small onion, chopped
1	cup heavy whipping cream
1	cup low-salt chicken broth

BLEND flour, ½ teaspoon thyme, and allspice in small bowl. Set aside 1 tablespoon flour mixture. Sprinkle chicken with salt and pepper, then enough remaining flour mixture to coat.

MELT butter in heavy large skillet over medium-high heat. Add chicken to skillet. Sauté until brown, about 4 minutes per side. Transfer chicken to plate. Add mushrooms, onion, and remaining 1 teaspoon thyme to skillet. Sauté until mushrooms are brown, about 5 minutes. Mix in reserved 1 tablespoon flour mixture; cook 1 minute. Add cream and broth and bring to boil, stirring occasionally. Return chicken and any juices to skillet. Reduce heat to medium-low; simmer uncovered until chicken is cooked through and gravy thickens slightly, about 5 minutes. Season to taste with salt and pepper.

Roast Moroccan-spiced chicken

2 SERVINGS; CAN BE DOUBLED *The wonderful Moroccan flavors and aromas of this dish can be created with spices that are probably already in your kitchen cupboard.*

1 3½-pound chicken
4 garlic cloves, flattened
1 lemon, halved
½ teaspoon ground cumin
½ teaspoon ground coriander
½ teaspoon paprika
½ teaspoon freshly ground black pepper
¼ teaspoon cinnamon
¼ teaspoon cayenne pepper
½ teaspoon salt

3 tablespoons olive oil

PREHEAT oven to 400°F. Pat chicken dry. Rub all over with garlic cloves; place garlic in cavity. Squeeze lemon into small bowl; place both lemon halves in cavity. Brush chicken with half of lemon juice. Combine all spices and salt in small bowl; rub chicken inside and out with spice mixture. Tie chicken legs together.

HEAT oil in heavy large ovenproof skillet over high heat. Remove from heat. Add chicken, breast side up, to skillet. Add remaining lemon juice to skillet. Baste chicken with pan juices. Transfer skillet to oven. Bake until juices run clear when chicken is pierced in thickest part of thigh, basting occasionally, about 1 hour. Discard string. Serve chicken hot, cold, or at room temperature.

SPICES OF LIFE Sniff the spices in your cupboard before cooking with them: If they smell musty or faint, it's time to replace them. Ground spices fade in taste and color after a few months; whole spices will keep for up to a year. Storing them in airtight containers and in a cool area away from direct sunlight helps keep them fresh.

Great roast chicken If you know the basics, a roast chicken is one of the easiest things you can make—once you have it ready to go, the oven does the rest of the work.

— Cook with adequate heat: Hot and fast is usually the best way to roast a chicken. This promotes even cooking and browning, i.e., crisp skin and succulent breast and thigh meat.

— Coat the skin with oil or butter before roasting; this promotes the coveted golden, crisp appearance that everyone loves.

— Use a roomy roasting pan with a rack, a heavy rimmed baking sheet, or a large ovenproof skillet with enough room for air to circulate around the bird. A heavy pan conducts heat more efficiently.

— Use a meat thermometer; it takes the guesswork out of testing for doneness.

— Let the chicken rest for 10 to 15 minutes before carving.

Roast chicken with artichokes and gremolata butter

4 SERVINGS *A seasoned butter inspired by the fragrant garnish for osso bucco adds great flavor to a simple roast chicken. Frozen artichoke hearts taste just as good as the fresh ones in many preparations—and require no prep at all. Serve the chicken with orzo, creamy polenta, or bread to soak up the juices.*

- 5 **tablespoons butter, room temperature**
- ¼ **cup chopped fresh Italian parsley**
- 1 **tablespoon finely grated lemon peel**
- 3 **garlic cloves, pressed**

- 1 **5-pound chicken, rinsed, patted dry**

- 2 **8-ounce packages frozen artichoke hearts, thawed**
- 2 **tablespoons fresh lemon juice**

PREHEAT oven to 425°F. Mix first 4 ingredients in small bowl to blend; season with salt and pepper.

PLACE chicken on large rimmed baking sheet. Starting at neck end, gently slide hand under breast skin to loosen. Spread 2 tablespoons seasoned butter on meat under loosened skin and 1 tablespoon over outside of chicken; sprinkle skin all over with salt and pepper. Transfer to oven; roast 45 minutes.

ARRANGE artichokes on baking sheet around chicken; baste with drippings. Continue roasting until thermometer inserted into thickest part of thigh registers 180°F, about 25 minutes longer. Spoon artichokes around edge of platter. Tilt chicken over baking sheet, allowing juices to empty onto sheet. Place chicken on platter; brush with 1 tablespoon seasoned butter. Scrape pan juices and any browned bits into sauceboat; mix in remaining seasoned butter and lemon juice. Serve with chicken and artichokes.

SAVORY BUTTER Flavored (or compound) butters add instant flavor to a roast bird, sautéed chicken breasts, or steamed vegetables. They're also great for scrambling eggs. Mix any variety of herbs and spices into softened butter (you can soften it in the microwave at low power in 10-second intervals). The butter will keep for a few days in the fridge, or a few months in the freezer.

Roasters vs. fryers What's the difference between a roaster and a broiler/fryer? Broiler/fryers are younger chickens, generally weighing between three and four and a half pounds; roasters are larger, about five to seven pounds. Of course, you can roast, fry, or grill both roasters and broiler/fryers but, true to their name, roasters do make the better roast chicken. Why? Their relatively larger size and higher fat content is just right for cooking evenly in the oven, meaning that skin and white and dark meat are optimally done at the same time. Because roasters are somewhat older, their meat is also more flavorful.

Lemon-oregano roast chicken and potatoes

4 SERVINGS *Don't worry about crowding the potatoes around the edges of the pan—they will bake up with deliciously crisp edges. Use any thin-skinned, waxy potatoes like red-skinned or white-skinned (they don't need to be peeled, and they retain their shape when cooked).*

6	tablespoons olive oil, divided
3	large garlic cloves, minced
3	teaspoons dried oregano, divided
2¼	pounds red-skinned potatoes, each cut lengthwise into 6 wedges
1	4-pound chicken, cut into 8 pieces
3	tablespoons fresh lemon juice

PREHEAT oven to 400°F. Brush large rimmed baking sheet with 2 tablespoons oil. Combine remaining 4 tablespoons oil, garlic, and 1½ teaspoons oregano in bowl. Add potatoes and toss to coat. Sprinkle potatoes with salt and pepper. Sprinkle chicken with remaining 1½ teaspoons oregano, then salt and pepper. Arrange chicken, skin side up, in single layer in center of prepared baking sheet. Arrange potatoes around chicken. Drizzle chicken with lemon juice and any remaining oil mixture from bowl of potatoes.

ROAST chicken and potatoes until chicken is cooked through and potatoes are tender, about 1 hour 10 minutes.

Chicken roasted on leeks and sage sprigs

4 SERVINGS *A whole chicken roasts atop a bed of leeks, infusing the chicken with flavor while roasting the leeks to perfection. You can keep fresh sage in the fridge, sealed in a plastic bag, for up to four days.*

1	4-pound chicken
¼	cup balsamic vinegar
2	tablespoons olive oil
2	tablespoons chopped fresh sage plus 2 large sprigs
2	teaspoons chopped fresh rosemary
2	garlic cloves, minced
5	leeks, trimmed (white and pale green parts only), halved lengthwise
½	cup low-salt chicken broth

PREHEAT oven to 400°F. Place chicken, vinegar, oil, chopped sage, rosemary, and garlic in large bowl; turn chicken several times to coat.

ARRANGE leeks and sage sprigs in bottom of 13×9×2-inch metal baking pan. Place chicken with herb and vinegar mixture atop leeks. Sprinkle chicken with salt and pepper. Pour broth around chicken. Roast until juices run clear when thigh is pierced, about 45 minutes. Place chicken and leeks on platter. Serve, passing pan juices separately.

Greek-style roast chicken

4 SERVINGS *Serve this super-easy entrée with warmed pita bread or roast potatoes, and a Greek salad or blanched green beans sautéed with chopped tomato.*

1   3¾-pound chicken, quartered
3   tablespoons fresh lemon juice
2   large garlic cloves, minced
2   tablespoons chopped fresh oregano
    or 1 tablespoon dried, crumbled

PREHEAT oven to 400°F. Arrange chicken, skin side up, on small rimmed baking sheet. Sprinkle chicken all over with lemon juice, garlic, and oregano, then salt and pepper. Roast until chicken is tender and thermometer inserted into thickest part of thigh registers 180°F, about 45 minutes. Serve with pan juices.

Oven-fried deviled drumsticks

2 SERVINGS *Everyday condiments and seasoned breadcrumbs create a crisp, flavorful coating without frying. Serve the drumsticks with potato salad or oven fries (which could roast alongside).*

    Nonstick vegetable oil spray
¼   cup mayonnaise
¼   cup coarse-grained mustard
2   teaspoons Worcestershire sauce
¾   cup dry Italian-style breadcrumbs
1   green onion, finely chopped
4   large chicken drumsticks (about 1 pound)

PREHEAT oven to 425°F. Spray small baking sheet with nonstick spray. Whisk mayonnaise, mustard, and Worcestershire sauce in medium bowl to blend. Whisk breadcrumbs and green onion in another medium bowl to blend. Dip each drumstick in mayonnaise mixture; turn to coat. Place each drumstick in crumb mixture; turn to coat. Transfer to prepared sheet. Bake drumsticks until brown and cooked through, about 25 minutes.

Spicy oven-fried chicken

6 SERVINGS *This delectable baked chicken would be excellent straight from the oven for dinner. Or take it on a picnic, as it's also great at room temperature.*

1¼	cups buttermilk
2	tablespoons Dijon mustard
4	garlic cloves, pressed
2	teaspoons salt, divided
1½	teaspoons cayenne pepper, divided
12	chicken pieces with skin and bones (4 breasts, 4 thighs, and 4 drumsticks)
1	cup unseasoned dry breadcrumbs
⅓	cup freshly grated Parmesan cheese
¼	cup all purpose flour
2	teaspoons dried thyme
½	teaspoon paprika
3	tablespoons unsalted butter, melted

WHISK buttermilk, mustard, garlic, 1 teaspoon salt, and 1 teaspoon cayenne in large bowl. Add chicken and turn to coat. Cover and chill at least 3 hours or overnight, turning chicken occasionally.

PLACE 1 rack on each of 2 large rimmed baking sheets. Mix breadcrumbs, cheese, flour, thyme, paprika, remaining 1 teaspoon salt, and ½ teaspoon cayenne in medium bowl. Remove chicken from buttermilk mixture, allowing excess to drip off. Working in batches, add chicken to breadcrumb mixture; turn to coat. Arrange chicken pieces, skin side up, on racks. Let stand 30 minutes at room temperature.

PREHEAT oven to 425°F. Drizzle butter over chicken; bake until crisp, brown, and cooked through, about 50 minutes. Serve warm or at room temperature.

Chicken with tarragon vinegar sauce

2 SERVINGS; CAN BE DOUBLED *You can make this classic French bistro dish in a flash. There's a cooking lesson in it, too: Layering a flavor is a fast and easy way to maximize its impact. In this recipe, freshly chopped tarragon adds an anise-like punch on top of purchased tarragon-infused vinegar.*

2	tablespoons (¼ stick) butter
2	chicken breast halves with skin and bones
3	shallots, chopped
½	cup tarragon vinegar
1	cup low-salt chicken broth
1½	tablespoons chopped fresh tarragon

MELT butter in heavy medium skillet over medium-high heat. Sprinkle chicken with salt and pepper. Add to skillet and sauté until golden, about 4 minutes per side. Transfer chicken to plate. Add shallots to skillet; sauté 30 seconds. Add vinegar; boil until reduced to glaze, stirring occasionally, about 2 minutes. Add broth. Return chicken, skin side up, to skillet. Reduce heat to medium-low, cover, and simmer until cooked through, about 12 minutes.

USING tongs, transfer chicken to plates. Add tarragon to skillet. Increase heat to medium-high; boil uncovered until sauce is slightly thickened, about 2 minutes. Season to taste with salt and pepper; spoon over chicken.

GOLDEN BROWN Browning adds depth of flavor—as well as an appealing golden color—to meats. To get a nice sear on chicken breasts or cutlets, pat chicken dry and sprinkle with seasonings. Keep the heat high enough, make sure there's sufficient oil or butter in the pan, and avoid lifting to check the underside for browning too soon.

Chicken breasts with sun-dried tomato and garlic crust

4 SERVINGS *Here one ingredient does double-duty: Oil from a jar of sun-dried tomatoes is used for sautéing the chicken, while the tomatoes are processed with garlic and fresh breadcrumbs for the topping. Orzo with chopped fresh herbs and lemon zest would make a nice side.*

- 2 **cups fresh breadcrumbs made from crustless French bread**
- ½ **cup drained oil-packed sun-dried tomatoes, 3½ tablespoons oil from jar reserved, divided**
- 2 **large garlic cloves, peeled**
- 4 **large chicken breast halves with skin and bones**

PREHEAT oven to 375°F. Combine breadcrumbs, tomatoes, 2 tablespoons reserved oil, and garlic in processor. Using on/off turns, process until tomatoes are coarsely chopped. Season topping to taste with salt and pepper. Sprinkle chicken with salt and pepper. Heat remaining 1½ tablespoons reserved oil in heavy large skillet over medium-high heat. Add chicken, skin side down, and cook until skin is crisp and golden, about 5 minutes.

TRANSFER chicken, skin side up, to rimmed baking sheet. Spoon breadcrumb topping atop chicken, pressing to adhere. Bake until chicken is cooked through, about 30 minutes.

BETTER BREADCRUMBS To make fresh breadcrumbs, remove the crust from bread and cut the bread into cubes. Working in batches, blend in a food processor to crumbs. For dry breadcrumbs, bake them on a sheet in a 200°F oven until just dry but not browned, about 10 minutes.

Chicken in lemongrass sauce

4 TO 6 SERVINGS *Lemongrass is available at many supermarkets and at Asian markets. Use the bottom three inches only. Remove a few reedy outer layers, then trim off the tough end and chop. If fresh lemongrass is not available, substitute grated lemon peel, which adds a similar citrusy brightness. Fish sauce and oyster sauce are available in the Asian foods section of many supermarkets. You can also order them from kalustyans.com. Serve this dish with aromatic jasmine rice.*

- 12 **ounces green Chinese long beans or green beans, trimmed, cut into 1½-inch pieces**
- 2 **tablespoons peanut oil**
- 1½ **pounds skinless boneless chicken breast halves, cut crosswise into ½-inch-wide strips**
- 1 **medium onion, sliced**
- 4 **garlic cloves, minced**
- ⅓ **cup minced lemongrass or 3 tablespoons finely grated lemon peel**
- 3 **tablespoons fish sauce (such as nam pla or nuoc nam)**
- 3 **tablespoons sugar**
- 1 **teaspoon turmeric**
- ½ **cup low-salt chicken broth**
- 2 **tablespoons oyster sauce**

COOK beans in large saucepan of boiling salted water until crisp-tender, about 2 minutes. Drain.

HEAT oil in heavy large skillet over high heat. Add chicken, onion, and garlic; stir-fry until chicken is partially cooked, about 4 minutes. Add lemongrass and next 3 ingredients; stir 2 minutes. Add cooked beans, broth, and oyster sauce; reduce heat and simmer until sauce thickens and chicken is cooked through, tossing occasionally, about 4 minutes longer. Season to taste with salt and pepper.

Chicken baked with fresh tarragon pesto

4 SERVINGS *Basil pesto is the classic, but you can create any number of variations using fresh herbs, nuts, and seasonings. This one can be made in minutes in the processor.*

   4   green onions, cut into 1-inch pieces
   ½   cup (packed) fresh Italian parsley leaves
   ¼   cup fresh tarragon leaves or basil leaves
   2   tablespoons walnut pieces
   4   large garlic cloves, peeled
 1½   teaspoons finely grated lemon peel
   ⅓   cup olive oil

   1   3½-pound chicken, cut into quarters

PREHEAT oven to 450°F. Finely mince first 6 ingredients in processor. With machine running, add oil through feed tube and process to coarse paste. Season pesto to taste with salt and pepper.

OIL large baking dish. Pat chicken dry; sprinkle with salt and pepper. Spread pesto over chicken, coating all sides. Arrange chicken, skin side up, in prepared dish. Bake chicken until tender, basting once, about 30 minutes.

Chicken breasts with spicy peanut sauce

2 SERVINGS *Simply marinate the chicken breasts in soy sauce and fresh ginger for 20 minutes, roast 15 minutes more, and top with a creamy pan sauce. Look for the chili-garlic paste in the Asian foods section of the supermarket. Serve with steamed rice on the side.*

   2   boneless chicken breast halves with skin
   3   tablespoons soy sauce, divided
   1   tablespoon vegetable oil
 2½   teaspoons minced peeled fresh ginger, divided

   6   tablespoons chunky peanut butter (do not use freshly ground or old-fashioned style)
   ½   cup low-salt chicken broth
   1   tablespoon (packed) golden brown sugar
   1   teaspoon chili-garlic paste

   2   green onions, thinly sliced

PLACE chicken in small baking pan. Add 2 tablespoons soy sauce, oil, and 1 teaspoon ginger. Turn chicken several times to coat. Let stand 20 minutes at room temperature.

PREHEAT over to 450°F. Roast chicken until just cooked through, about 15 minutes.

MEANWHILE, combine peanut butter, broth, sugar, chili-garlic paste, remaining 1 tablespoon soy sauce, and 1½ teaspoons ginger in heavy small saucepan. Simmer until smooth and slightly thickened, whisking frequently, about 2 minutes.

ARRANGE chicken on plates. Spoon sauce over and sprinkle with green onions.

Roquefort-lemon roast chicken

6 SERVINGS *Roquefort is a legendary French blue cheese made from ewe's milk. Gorgonzola or Maytag blue would be fine substitutes here. Just add crusty French bread and a leafy green salad.*

¼ cup all purpose flour
1 tablespoon minced fresh rosemary
1 teaspoon salt
¼ teaspoon freshly ground black pepper
6 chicken breast halves with skin and bones
3 tablespoons butter
⅔ cup sour cream
½ cup crumbled Roquefort cheese (about 2 ounces)
2 tablespoons fresh lemon juice
1 green onion, thinly sliced
2 teaspoons finely grated lemon peel

PREHEAT oven to 350°F. Stir first 4 ingredients in shallow dish to blend. Dredge chicken in flour mixture; shake off excess. Melt butter in heavy large skillet over medium-high heat. Add chicken and sauté until golden brown, about 3 minutes per side. Transfer chicken, skin side up, to baking dish. Combine sour cream and all remaining ingredients in small bowl; stir to blend. Spread over chicken. Bake until topping is golden and chicken is just cooked through, about 30 minutes.

Sautéed chicken with garlic and rosemary

4 SERVINGS *Succulent chicken thighs are finished with a savory pan sauce in this Parisian bistro-style dish.*

2 pounds chicken thighs with skin and bones
2 tablespoons olive oil
3 large garlic cloves, minced
2 tablespoons chopped fresh rosemary
1 cup low-salt chicken broth
2 tablespoons red wine vinegar

SPRINKLE chicken with salt and pepper. Heat oil in heavy large skillet over high heat. Add chicken to skillet and sauté until brown, about 5 minutes per side. Reduce heat to medium-low, cover, and cook until chicken is tender and cooked through, about 15 minutes. Transfer chicken to bowl. Discard all but 2 tablespoons drippings from skillet; add garlic and rosemary. Sauté until fragrant, about 1 minute. Add broth and vinegar. Boil until sauce is reduced to ½ cup, scraping up browned bits, about 7 minutes. Season sauce to taste with salt and pepper. Return chicken and any juices to skillet. Simmer over low heat until chicken is heated through, about 5 minutes.

Walnut-coated chicken with pomegranate sauce

4 SERVINGS *The rich flavors of* fesenjan, *a traditional Persian stew made with walnuts and pomegranate, are combined in a quick-cooking weeknight meal. Turkey cutlets would also be delicious in this. Look for fresh pomegranate juice in the refrigerated juice section of the supermarket. Pomegranate molasses, a sweet-tart, syrupy reduction of the juice, is available in the ethnic foods section of some supermarkets and at Middle Eastern markets, or online at kalustyans.com.*

- ¾ **cup chopped walnuts (about 3 ounces)**
- ½ **cup all purpose flour**
- 1 **egg, beaten to blend**
- 4 **skinless boneless chicken breast halves**
- 3 **tablespoons butter, divided**

- ¼ **cup dry white wine**
- 1 **shallot, chopped**
- ½ **cup low-salt chicken broth**
- ½ **cup pure pomegranate juice**
- 1½ **teaspoons pomegranate molasses**
- 1 **teaspoon honey**

BLEND walnuts and flour in processor until nuts are finely chopped; transfer to plate. Place egg in shallow bowl. Using meat mallet or rolling pin, pound chicken between sheets of plastic wrap to ¼-inch thickness. Dip chicken into beaten egg, then into walnut mixture to coat. Melt 2 tablespoons butter in large nonstick skillet over medium-high heat. Add chicken and sauté until brown and cooked through, about 3 minutes per side. Transfer to plate; tent loosely with foil to keep warm.

BOIL wine and shallot in heavy small saucepan until most of wine evaporates, about 2 minutes. Add broth, pomegranate juice, pomegranate molasses, and honey. Boil until reduced to ¾ cup, about 5 minutes. Whisk in remaining 1 tablespoon butter. Season sauce to taste with salt and pepper. Spoon sauce over chicken and serve.

DO IT YOURSELF Make your own pomegranate molasses by boiling 2 cups of fresh pomegranate juice in a heavy small saucepan until reduced to a thick syrup, about ⅓ cup. Stir it often to prevent burning; it should take about 20 minutes. Leftover molasses keeps a month or more in the fridge, and makes a wonderful marinade for meats. It's also delicious in sauces and salad dressings.

279

Chicken thighs with Creole mustard-orange sauce

2 SERVINGS; CAN BE DOUBLED *Creole mustard is a coarse-grained mustard made with garlic and other spices to give it a New Orleans-style kick. Zatarain's brand Creole mustard is widely available, but any whole grain mustard works well as a substitute. Cornbread or corn muffins would be great on the side.*

- 4 **small skinless boneless chicken thighs (about 12 ounces)**
- 1½ **tablespoons olive oil**
- ¾ **cup orange juice**
- ¾ **cup low-salt chicken broth**
- ¼ **cup Creole or whole grain Dijon mustard**
- 1 **tablespoon honey**
- 1 **teaspoon hot pepper sauce**

SPRINKLE chicken on both sides with salt and pepper. Heat oil in heavy medium skillet over medium-high heat. Add chicken and sauté until brown, about 6 minutes per side. Add orange juice and broth to skillet. Simmer until chicken is cooked through, about 5 minutes. Transfer chicken to plate. Add mustard, honey, and hot pepper sauce to skillet. Increase heat and boil until sauce thickens enough to coat spoon, whisking occasionally, about 7 minutes. Return chicken to skillet. Simmer until heated through, about 1 minute. Transfer chicken to plates; spoon sauce over.

Chicken with Indian-spiced tomato sauce

4 SERVINGS *If you like chicken* tikka masala, *you'll love this curry-in-a-hurry that has a similarly creamy tomato-based sauce. Serve it with steamed basmati, a fragrant and nutty Indian rice, or another long-grain rice. Whole cumin seeds add complexity to many Indian and Mexican dishes; toasting or sautéing them releases their fragrance and warm, earthy flavor.*

- 4 **skinless boneless chicken breast halves, cut into 2-inch pieces**
- ¼ **cup fresh lemon juice**
- ½ **teaspoon turmeric**

- 2 **tablespoons vegetable oil**
- 1 **large onion, chopped**
- 1 **tablespoon minced peeled fresh ginger**
- ½ **teaspoon cumin seeds**
- 1 **14.5-ounce can diced tomatoes in juice**
- 1¼ **teaspoons chili powder**
- 2 **tablespoons sour cream**

COMBINE chicken, lemon juice, and turmeric in medium bowl; toss to coat. Marinate 30 minutes.

HEAT oil in large skillet over medium heat. Add onion, ginger, and cumin seeds; sauté until onion is tender, about 5 minutes. Add chicken with marinade; sauté until most of marinade evaporates, about 3 minutes. Add tomatoes with juice and chili powder. Simmer uncovered until chicken is cooked through and sauce thickens, about 10 minutes; season to taste with salt and pepper. Remove from heat. Mix in sour cream.

Chicken, asparagus, and broccoli stir-fry

4 SERVINGS *This stir-fry has lots of flavor and requires minimal slicing and dicing. For a variation, try making it with shrimp instead of chicken. Serve steamed rice on the side. Look for sesame oil, hoisin sauce, and oyster sauce in the Asian foods section of the supermarket.*

- 2 tablespoons Asian sesame oil, divided
- 2 garlic cloves, chopped
- 2 cups 1½-inch pieces asparagus, from trimmed stalks
- 2 cups small broccoli florets
- 6 tablespoons low-salt chicken broth, divided
- 1¼ pounds skinless boneless chicken breast halves, thinly sliced crosswise
- 4 large green onions, chopped
- 3 tablespoons hoisin sauce
- 1 tablespoon oyster sauce

HEAT 1 tablespoon oil in large nonstick skillet over medium-high heat. Add garlic and stir 30 seconds. Add asparagus, broccoli, and 4 tablespoons broth. Cover and cook until vegetables are crisp-tender, about 3 minutes. Transfer vegetables to bowl.

ADD remaining 1 tablespoon oil to same skillet. Sprinkle chicken with salt and pepper; add chicken and green onions to skillet. Stir-fry until chicken is just cooked through, about 3 minutes. Mix in hoisin sauce, oyster sauce, vegetables, and remaining 2 tablespoons broth. Toss until heated through and evenly coated with sauce, about 1 minute. Season to taste with salt and pepper.

Chicken cutlets véronique

2 SERVINGS *Here's a simplified version of the elegant French entrée that combines tender chicken and fresh seedless grapes. You can make the sauce more substantial by sautéing sliced mushrooms with the shallots. Serve with couscous or crusty French bread, plus buttered carrots or green beans.*

- 2 skinless boneless chicken breast halves
- 3 teaspoons chopped fresh tarragon, divided
- 2 tablespoons (¼ stick) butter
- 1 shallot, chopped
- ⅔ cup small green and/or red seedless grapes
- ½ cup dry white wine
- ½ cup heavy whipping cream

USING meat mallet or rolling pin, pound chicken between sheets of plastic wrap to ½-inch thickness. Sprinkle chicken with 1 teaspoon tarragon, then salt and pepper. Melt butter in heavy medium skillet over medium-high heat. Add chicken; sauté until brown and cooked through, about 3 minutes per side. Transfer to plates.

ADD shallot and remaining 2 teaspoons tarragon to drippings in skillet. Sauté over medium-high heat until shallot begins to soften, about 2 minutes. Add grapes, wine, and cream. Boil until sauce thickens enough to coat spoon, about 5 minutes. Season sauce to taste with salt and pepper. Spoon sauce over chicken.

Chicken, red pepper, and green bean stir-fry

2 SERVINGS *This is just one of countless recipes that make perfect use of frozen chicken breasts. Defrost a skinless, boneless chicken breast quickly in the microwave or overnight in the fridge, then add fresh green beans, slices of sweet red pepper, and Asian pantry seasonings for a weeknight dinner in minutes. Serve with rice pilaf or Asian-style noodles like rice vermicelli, soba, ramen, or udon. Rice vinegar and sesame oil can be found in the Asian foods section of the supermarket.*

4 ounces green beans, trimmed

3 tablespoons Asian sesame oil, divided

1 8-ounce skinless boneless chicken breast, cut crosswise into strips

1 red bell pepper, very thinly sliced

1 tablespoon minced peeled fresh ginger

2 large garlic cloves, minced

3 tablespoons soy sauce

2 tablespoons unseasoned rice vinegar

COOK beans in pot of boiling salted water until crisp-tender, about 3 minutes. Drain.

HEAT 2 tablespoons oil in heavy medium skillet over medium-high heat. Sprinkle chicken with salt and pepper. Add to skillet; stir-fry until just cooked through, about 2 minutes. Transfer chicken to plate. Add remaining 1 tablespoon oil to same skillet. Add bell pepper, ginger, and garlic; stir-fry 2 minutes. Return chicken to skillet; add beans. Stir in soy sauce and vinegar. Toss until sauce thickens slightly, about 2 minutes. Season to taste with salt and pepper.

BRIGHT GREEN BEANS It's easy to over-cook green beans when blanching, so keep a close eye on them, and remove them from the boiling water while they are still bright green and just crisp-tender. Cook them in generously salted water, which helps to set their color.

Chicken and mushroom enchiladas

4 SERVINGS *For convenience, pick up cooked chicken, either whole or in pieces, from the supermarket. Use Monterey Jack cheese instead of cheddar, if you like, or a combination of cheeses.*

2	tablespoons corn oil plus more for brushing
¾	pound mushrooms, sliced
1	10-ounce can enchilada sauce
8	8-inch-diameter flour tortillas
½	cup sour cream
2	cups diced cooked chicken
1	7-ounce can diced mild green chiles
2	cups (packed) coarsely grated sharp cheddar cheese (about 8 ounces)

BRUSH 13×9×2-inch glass baking dish with oil. Heat 2 tablespoons oil in heavy large skillet over high heat. Add mushrooms; sprinkle with salt and pepper. Sauté until golden, about 10 minutes.

POUR enchilada sauce into shallow bowl. Dip 1 tortilla into sauce; place on piece of waxed paper. Spread 1 tablespoon sour cream across center of tortilla. Top with ¼ cup chicken, 3 tablespoons mushrooms, then 1 tablespoon chiles and ¼ cup cheese. Fold bottom half of tortilla over filling and roll up to enclose completely. Place enchilada, seam side down, in prepared dish. Repeat dipping and filling with remaining tortillas, sour cream, chicken, mushrooms, chiles, and cheese. Spoon remaining enchilada sauce evenly over.

DO AHEAD *Can be prepared 2 hours ahead. Let stand at room temperature.*

PREHEAT oven to 350°F. Bake until enchiladas are heated through and sauce is bubbling, about 30 minutes.

Tunisian chicken with raisins and lemon

4 SERVINGS *Sweet-sour fruit and meat combinations like this are typical of the cooking of North Africa. If you want to put a more savory spin on this dish, use pitted olives instead of the raisins.*

1	3½-pound chicken, cut into 8 pieces
2	tablespoons olive oil
2	large russet potatoes (about 1¼ pounds), peeled, cut into 1½-inch chunks
2	garlic cloves, minced
1½	teaspoons turmeric
1	large lemon, peel and white pith cut away, very thinly sliced into rounds
½	cup raisins
3½	cups (about) low-salt chicken broth
2	tablespoons fresh lemon juice

ARRANGE chicken in single layer in heavy large pot. Drizzle oil over. Tuck potatoes between chicken pieces. Sprinkle with garlic and turmeric, then salt and pepper. Lay lemon slices over. Sprinkle with raisins. Pour enough broth to barely cover chicken. Bring to boil over high heat. Cover and boil 10 minutes. Uncover, reduce heat to medium, and simmer until chicken is just cooked through and potatoes are tender, about 20 minutes. Transfer chicken and potatoes to platter. Tent with foil to keep warm. Add lemon juice to pot. Boil cooking liquid until thickened to light sauce consistency and reduced by half, about 7 minutes. Season with salt and pepper. Spoon sauce over chicken.

Chicken breasts with goat cheese and rosemary stuffing

2 SERVINGS *You'll need skin-on breast halves for this recipe; an herbed goat-cheese filling is stuffed under the skin before the chicken bakes. Choose any soft fresh goat cheese (packaged in logs and often labeled* chèvre*), but don't use packaged crumbled goat cheese.*

- 2 **teaspoons butter, divided**
- 2 **tablespoons chopped shallots**
- ¾ **teaspoon chopped fresh rosemary or ½ teaspoon dried**
- 3 **ounces soft fresh goat cheese**
- ½ **teaspoon crushed black peppercorns**
- 2 **large chicken breast halves with skin and bones**

MELT 1 teaspoon butter in heavy small skillet over medium-low heat. Add shallots and rosemary and sauté until shallots are tender, about 4 minutes. Remove from heat and cool to lukewarm. Mix in goat cheese and pepper. Season to taste with salt. Using fingertips, loosen skin of chicken breasts, leaving skin attached on 1 long side and forming pocket. Spread half of cheese filling over meat under skin of each breast. Pull skin over filling and secure with toothpick. Rub remaining 1 teaspoon butter over skin, dividing equally.

DO AHEAD *Can be prepared 1 day ahead. Cover; chill.*

PREHEAT oven to 425°F. Arrange chicken on small rimmed baking sheet. Roast uncovered until brown and cooked through, about 25 minutes.

Chicken with carrots, prunes, and rice

6 SERVINGS *This North African–spiced one-pot meal bakes for an hour, but it's a snap to assemble. Grating the carrots in a processor cuts the prep time even more. Don't skip the prunes; they add just a touch of mellow sweetness (they're dried plums, after all) that harmonizes deliciously with the chicken and other ingredients.*

- 1 **3¾- to 4-pound chicken, cut into 6 pieces**
- 3 **tablespoons olive oil**
- 1 **large onion, chopped**
- 1 **pound large carrots, peeled, coarsely grated**
- 2 **cups long-grain white rice (about 13 ounces)**
- 12 **ounces pitted prunes**
  Paprika
- 6 **cups boiling low-salt chicken broth**

PREHEAT oven to 350°F. Sprinkle chicken with salt and pepper. Heat oil in heavy large ovenproof pot over medium-high heat. Add chicken to pot and sauté until brown, about 4 minutes per side. Transfer chicken to bowl. Add onion to same pot and sauté until golden, about 5 minutes. Remove pot from heat. Spread ⅓ of carrots over onion, then ⅓ of rice, ⅓ of prunes, and half of chicken. Sprinkle with paprika, salt, and pepper. Repeat layering with ⅓ each of carrots, rice, and prunes, then remaining chicken. Sprinkle with paprika, salt, and pepper. Layer with remaining carrots, rice, and prunes. Pour boiling broth over. Cover pot and place in oven. Bake until chicken and rice are cooked through, about 1 hour.

Malaysian chicken curry with sweet and spicy peppers

4 SERVINGS *Coconut milk thickens the curry and adds richness. You'll find it in the Asian foods section of most supermarkets and at Asian markets; shake it well before you open it to combine the thick coconut cream on top with the milk. Serve the curry with steamed white rice.*

3	tablespoons vegetable oil
1	3- to 3½-pound chicken, cut into 8 pieces
½	cup minced shallots (about 3)
4	teaspoons curry powder
1	medium tomato, finely chopped
½	cup canned unsweetened coconut milk
2	teaspoons paprika
2	medium red bell peppers, chopped
3	jalapeño chiles, seeded, sliced
2	teaspoons fresh lemon juice

HEAT oil in heavy large skillet over medium-high heat. Sprinkle chicken with salt and pepper. Add chicken to skillet and sauté until golden on all sides, about 12 minutes. Transfer chicken to plate. Discard all but 1 tablespoon drippings from skillet. Add shallots and sauté until slightly softened, about 3 minutes. Add curry powder and stir until aromatic, about 30 seconds. Add tomato, coconut milk, and paprika; bring to boil. Return chicken to skillet. Reduce heat to medium-low, cover, and simmer until chicken is tender, turning chicken and scraping bottom of skillet occasionally, about 20 minutes.

ADD bell peppers, jalapeño chiles, and lemon juice to skillet. Cover and simmer until peppers are slightly softened, about 5 minutes longer. Arrange chicken on platter. Tilt skillet and spoon off fat from top of sauce. Season to taste with salt. Spoon sauce over chicken.

How to degrease pan juices You can remove the fat from pan juices by spooning it off if it's a small amount in a skillet. For a large amount, it's much easier to use a fat separator (sold at cookware stores), which looks like a measuring cup with a spout that pours from the bottom. When you fill it with the juices, the fat naturally rises to the top; as you pour the juices back into the pan, the fat is left behind. Use this technique to degrease pan juices from a whole roast chicken, for example. Insert the handle of a wooden spoon into the cavity of the chicken and tilt the chicken to empty any juices into the pan, then pour the juices into the separator.

Chicken cacciatore with Marsala and capers

4 SERVINGS *Purchased marinara sauce and the addition of Marsala, herbs, and veggies make for a shortcut cacciatore with delicious fresh flavor. If you prefer, use diced pitted Kalamata olives instead of capers. Serve with pasta, polenta, or plenty of country bread to soak up the sauce, and pass freshly grated Parmesan cheese.*

1	3½-pound chicken, cut into 6 pieces
6	tablespoons olive oil, divided
¾	pound mushrooms, halved
2	green bell peppers, diced
1	onion, chopped
4	garlic cloves, chopped
1½	teaspoons dried oregano
1	cup purchased marinara sauce
⅔	cup low-salt chicken broth
½	cup dry Marsala (preferably imported)
1½	tablespoons drained capers

SPRINKLE chicken with salt and pepper. Heat 3 tablespoons oil in heavy large skillet over medium-high heat. Add chicken and sauté until brown, about 4 minutes per side. Transfer chicken to plate. Pour off fat from skillet. Add remaining 3 tablespoons oil to skillet. Add mushrooms, bell peppers, onion, garlic, and oregano. Sauté until onion is tender, about 10 minutes. Mix in marinara sauce, broth, Marsala, and capers. Return chicken to skillet, spooning sauce over. Bring sauce to boil. Reduce heat to medium-low, cover, and simmer until chicken is tender, about 20 minutes.

USING tongs, transfer chicken to large platter. Boil sauce until slightly thickened, about 5 minutes; spoon off fat. Season sauce to taste with salt and pepper; spoon over chicken.

Roast chicken with cumin, paprika, and allspice

4 TO 6 SERVINGS *This whole chicken, seasoned with a fragrant Middle Eastern spice rub, roasts for a couple of hours, but just minutes are required to get it into the oven. Serve it with couscous blended with currants and toasted pine nuts, or add chunks of potato and peeled butternut squash to the roasting pan for the last 45 minutes or so.*

1	6- to 6½-pound chicken
2	tablespoons olive oil
1½	teaspoons ground cumin
1	teaspoon garlic powder
1	teaspoon onion powder
1	teaspoon ground allspice
1	teaspoon paprika
½	teaspoon salt
½	teaspoon ground black pepper
1	large lemon, halved

PREHEAT oven to 375°F. Rinse chicken; pat dry. Place chicken on rack in large roasting pan. Stir oil and next 7 ingredients in small bowl to form paste. Rub spice paste all over chicken. Roast chicken 1 hour. Squeeze juice from lemon halves over chicken; place lemon halves inside main cavity. Continue to roast until chicken is cooked through and thermometer inserted into thickest part of thigh registers 180°F, about 1 hour longer. Transfer to platter; let stand 15 minutes.

Chicken-cheddar quesadillas with tomato and corn salsa

4 MAIN-COURSE SERVINGS *For the best flavor, choose a fresh salsa from the deli or supermarket refrigerator case. If you have frozen boneless chicken breasts, they can be used in place of the tenders. Just thaw and slice crosswise on a slight diagonal into half-inch-thick strips. Serve the quesadillas with black beans topped with crumbled queso fresco or feta cheese, and a crisp green salad. These are nice as an appetizer, too, for up to eight people.*

1½ cups purchased medium-hot chunky salsa verde (tomatillo salsa)
 1 cup frozen corn kernels, thawed
 1 cup chopped red onion, divided
 ¼ cup plus 6 tablespoons chopped fresh cilantro

 1 pound chicken tenders
 2 teaspoons chili powder
 1 teaspoon ground cumin
 4 tablespoons olive oil, divided
 2 large garlic cloves, chopped
 3 cups (packed) coarsely grated sharp cheddar cheese (about 12 ounces)
 3 burrito-size flour tortillas (about 11 inches in diameter)

STIR salsa, corn, ¼ cup onion, and ¼ cup cilantro in small bowl to blend. Season salsa to taste with salt and pepper.

PLACE chicken in bowl; sprinkle with chili powder, cumin, salt, and pepper, tossing to coat evenly. Heat 2 tablespoons oil in heavy large skillet over medium-high heat. Add garlic and remaining ¾ cup onion and sauté 1 minute. Add chicken and sauté until just cooked through, about 5 minutes. Sprinkle ½ cup cheese over half of 1 tortilla. Top cheese with ⅓ of chicken mixture, 2 tablespoons cilantro, and another ½ cup cheese. Fold plain half of tortilla over filling. Repeat with remaining tortillas, cheese, chicken mixture, and cilantro.

HEAT 1 tablespoon oil in each of 2 heavy large skillets over medium-high heat. Place 2 quesadillas in 1 skillet and third in second skillet. Cook until brown and cheese melts, about 4 minutes per side. Transfer quesadillas to work surface and cut into wedges. Arrange on platter; serve with salsa.

Chicken with cranberry-mustard sauce

4 SERVINGS *This recipe proves you can cook up an elegant main dish using freezer and pantry ingredients. Frozen cranberry juice concentrate adds a delicious sweet-tart kick to the sauce.*

 4 large skinless boneless chicken breast halves
 1 teaspoon onion powder
 1 teaspoon dried thyme
 4 tablespoons (½ stick) butter, divided
 2 tablespoons all purpose flour
 ½ teaspoon dry mustard
1½ cups low-salt chicken broth
 ¾ cup frozen cranberry juice cocktail concentrate, thawed
 ¼ cup dried cranberries

SPRINKLE chicken on both sides with onion powder, thyme, salt, and pepper. Melt 2 tablespoons butter in heavy large skillet over medium-high heat. Add chicken and sauté until brown, about 5 minutes per side. Using tongs, transfer chicken to plate. Add remaining 2 tablespoons butter to same skillet and melt. Whisk in flour and mustard; cook 1 minute. Gradually whisk in broth, juice concentrate, and cranberries. Bring to boil, whisking occasionally. Boil until sauce thickens enough to coat spoon, about 6 minutes. Return chicken to skillet. Reduce heat to medium-low and simmer just until chicken is cooked through, about 5 minutes. Season sauce to taste with salt and pepper.

Chinese-style chicken in lettuce cups

2 MAIN-COURSE SERVINGS *Leaves of tender Boston lettuce (also called Bibb or butter lettuce) make the best "cups," or wrappers, for the filling. If you can't find ground chicken, use ground turkey instead. This also makes a great appetizer for up to six people. Just let everyone spoon the filling into a lettuce leaf, tuck in the edges, and wrap it up. Some nice additions would be roasted peanuts and chopped green onions.*

¾ **pound ground chicken**

¼ **cup chopped fresh basil**

2 **tablespoons soy sauce**

2 **tablespoons fresh lime juice**

2 **large garlic cloves, chopped**

1 **large jalapeño chile, chopped**

1 **teaspoon sugar**

1 **teaspoon chili-garlic sauce or hot pepper sauce**

1 **tablespoon Asian sesame oil or vegetable oil**
    Boston lettuce leaves

COMBINE first 8 ingredients in medium bowl and stir to blend well.

DO AHEAD *Can be made 1 day ahead. Cover and chill.*

HEAT oil in heavy medium skillet over high heat. Add chicken mixture. Sauté until cooked through, breaking up with back of fork, about 4 minutes. Transfer chicken mixture to bowl in center of platter. Arrange lettuce around edges and serve.

Oaxacan chicken mole

2 SERVINGS *This is an amazingly quick and easy version of the usually complex Mexican mole, famous for its rich, spicy flavor and hint of chocolate. Serve with rice and warm tortillas.*

2 **skinless boneless chicken breast halves**

3½ **teaspoons chili powder, divided**

1½ **tablespoons olive oil**

½ **teaspoon ground cumin**

¼ **teaspoon ground cinnamon**

1 **14- to 16-ounce can stewed tomatoes**

¼ **ounce unsweetened chocolate**

SPRINKLE chicken with 1 teaspoon chili powder, salt, and pepper. Heat oil in heavy medium skillet over medium-high heat. Add chicken; sauté until brown, about 2 minutes per side. Transfer chicken to plate. Add remaining 2½ teaspoons chili powder, cumin, and cinnamon to skillet; stir 15 seconds. Mix in tomatoes with juice and chocolate; simmer until sauce thickens, about 5 minutes. Return chicken to skillet; simmer until just cooked through and sauce thickens slightly, about 4 minutes. Season to taste with salt and pepper.

TURKEY

Chipotle-seasoned turkey enchiladas

6 SERVINGS *This is one of the best things you can do with your leftover Thanksgiving turkey. During the rest of the year, substitute any shredded meat you have on hand. Canned chipotle chiles and plum tomatoes add an extra-smoky spiciness and tang to purchased enchilada sauce. The enchiladas can easily be assembled ahead, refrigerated, and heated just before serving. Chipotle chiles canned in a spicy tomato sauce called* adobo *can be found in the Latin foods section of many supermarkets.*

3	tablespoons plus ½ cup vegetable oil
1¾	cups finely chopped onions, divided
1	28-ounce can or three 10-ounce cans enchilada sauce
5	plum tomatoes, finely chopped
1½	teaspoons finely chopped canned chipotle chiles
1	cup chopped fresh cilantro, divided
3	cups coarsely shredded cooked turkey
2	cups (packed) coarsely grated Monterey Jack cheese (about 8 ounces), divided
¾	cup sour cream
12	5- to 6-inch-diameter corn tortillas

HEAT 3 tablespoons oil in heavy large saucepan over medium heat. Add 1½ cups onions and sauté until tender, about 5 minutes. Add enchilada sauce, tomatoes, and chipotles. Cover; simmer 20 minutes, stirring often. Remove from heat. Stir in ½ cup cilantro. Season sauce to taste with salt and pepper.

STIR turkey, 1½ cups cheese, sour cream, remaining ¼ cup onions, and ½ cup cilantro in large bowl to blend. Season filling to taste with salt and pepper.

PREHEAT oven to 350°F. Heat ½ cup vegetable oil in medium skillet over medium heat. Add 1 tortilla and heat until pliable, about 20 seconds per side. Transfer to paper towels to drain. Repeat with remaining tortillas.

SPREAD ½ cup sauce over bottom of 13×9×2-inch glass baking dish. Spoon ¼ cup turkey mixture down center of each tortilla. Roll up tortillas. Arrange enchiladas, seam side down, in prepared dish. Spoon 2½ cups sauce over enchiladas. Sprinkle with remaining ½ cup cheese. Bake enchiladas until heated through, about 30 minutes.

REWARM remaining sauce in pan. Serve with enchiladas.

Turkey chilaquiles

4 TO 6 SERVINGS *This is a dinner version of the popular Mexican breakfast dish.* Crema mexicana *(a cultured cream similar to crème fraîche or sour cream) and crumbled* queso fresco *(a fresh white cheese) are available in the cheese and deli sections of many supermarkets and at Latin markets. Diced cooked chicken can be used instead of turkey.*

  2 **tablespoons vegetable oil**
1½ **cups chopped red onion, divided**
  2 **cups diced cooked turkey**
  1 **4-ounce can diced mild green chiles**
  3 **cups purchased medium-hot salsa with chipotles and garlic (from about two 16-ounce jars)**
  4 **cups unsalted tortilla chips**
  2 **cups crumbled queso fresco, cotija cheese, or feta cheese (about 8 ounces)**
  ¼ **cup chopped fresh cilantro**
     Crema mexicana or sour cream

PREHEAT oven to 450°F. Heat oil in heavy large ovenproof skillet. Add 1¼ cups onion; sauté until onion begins to soften, about 5 minutes. Add turkey and green chiles; sauté 3 minutes. Stir in salsa; simmer until heated through, about 3 minutes. Season with salt and pepper. Stir in chips. Sprinkle with cheese. Place skillet in oven; bake just until cheese melts, about 5 minutes. Sprinkle with remaining ¼ cup onion and cilantro; drizzle with crema mexicana.

Turkey, mushroom, and barley risotto

4 MAIN-COURSE SERVINGS *In place of the traditional arborio rice, pearl barley brings a delicious nuttiness to this risotto. Dried porcini mushrooms are available in the produce section of many supermarkets, and at specialty foods stores and Italian markets.*

  6 **cups (or more) low-salt chicken broth**
  1 **cup pearl barley**
  1 **ounce dried porcini mushrooms, broken in half if very large**

  2 **tablespoons (¼ stick) butter**
  1 **large (10- to 12-ounce) onion, chopped**
  1 **large Bosc pear, halved, cored, cut into ½-inch cubes**
  2 **cups diced cooked dark turkey meat**

  ⅓ **cup dry Marsala**
  ½ **cup chopped fresh Italian parsley, divided**

BRING 6 cups broth, barley, and mushrooms to boil in large saucepan. Cover; cook over medium-low heat until barley is just tender, stirring occasionally and adding more broth by ¼ cupfuls if barley becomes dry, about 35 minutes.

MEANWHILE, melt butter in large skillet over medium-high heat. Add onion; sprinkle lightly with salt and pepper. Sauté until golden brown, about 10 minutes. Add pear and sauté until just tender, about 5 minutes. Mix in turkey.

ADD barley mixture and Marsala to turkey mixture. Simmer until creamy, adding more broth if dry. Mix in half of parsley. Season to taste with pepper. Mound in bowl. Sprinkle with remaining parsley.

Turkey-cheese burritos with salsa and cilantro

6 SERVINGS *Turkey has a bold flavor that is a natural with Mexican food. Fresh fire-roasted salsa can be found in the refrigerated deli case at most supermarkets, but a good bottled fire-roasted salsa will do. You can substitute a blend of Monterey Jack and other cheeses for the Mexican four-cheese blend.*

- 3 tablespoons olive oil
- 2 red onions, sliced
- 2 bell peppers (preferably 1 red and 1 yellow), seeded, sliced
- 4 cups diced cooked turkey meat
- ¾ cup purchased fresh fire-roasted salsa
- 1 tablespoon ground cumin
- 1 8-ounce package grated Mexican four-cheese blend (about 2 cups)
- ¾ cup chopped fresh cilantro
- 6 burrito-size flour tortillas (about 11 inches in diameter)

PREHEAT oven to 300°F. Heat oil in large nonstick skillet over medium-high heat. Add onions and bell peppers; sauté until tender and golden, about 15 minutes. Add turkey, salsa, and cumin; stir until heated through, about 5 minutes. Stir in cheese and cilantro; season generously with salt and pepper. Remove from heat; cover to keep warm.

WORKING with 1 tortilla at a time, heat tortilla directly over gas flame (or in dry skillet over medium-high heat) until warm, softened, and browned in spots, about 30 seconds per side. Place tortilla on work surface. Spoon 1 cup warm turkey mixture down center of tortilla; fold sides in over ends of filling, then roll up tortilla to enclose filling. Place burrito, seam side down, on baking sheet and place in oven to keep warm. Repeat with remaining tortillas and filling.

Turkey tonnato

6 SERVINGS *This is based on a classic Italian dish, vitello tonnato, in which chilled slices of veal are topped with a pureed sauce of tuna, anchovies, capers, and lemon. You can make the sauce and chill it up to a day ahead. For the best flavor, buy good-quality turkey breast from the supermarket deli section and canned tuna packed in olive oil.*

- 2 6-ounce cans light tuna packed in olive oil, undrained
- ¼ cup mayonnaise
- ¼ cup low-salt chicken broth
- 5 anchovy fillets, 1 teaspoon oil from can reserved
- 2 tablespoons fresh lemon juice
- 1 tablespoon finely grated lemon peel
- 2 teaspoons plus ¼ cup drained capers

- 1 5- to 6-ounce package fresh baby spinach
- 2½ pounds roast turkey breast, cut into ⅓-inch-thick slices
- ⅓ cup chopped fresh parsley

BLEND tuna with oil, mayonnaise, broth, anchovies with oil, lemon juice, lemon peel, and 2 teaspoons capers in processor until smooth, about 2 minutes. Season sauce to taste with salt and pepper. Refrigerate until cold, at least 1 hour and up to 1 day.

ARRANGE spinach on platter. Arrange turkey slices atop spinach. Spoon sauce over turkey. Sprinkle with parsley and remaining ¼ cup capers.

Turkey cutlets piccata

2 SERVINGS *Lean, tasty, and inexpensive, turkey cutlets are a fine canvas for this piquant pan sauce.*

　　All purpose flour
¾　pound turkey cutlets or ⅜-inch-thick turkey breast slices

4　tablespoons (½ stick) butter, divided
1　tablespoon vegetable oil
2　tablespoons fresh lemon juice
1½　tablespoons dry white wine
1½　tablespoons minced fresh parsley
1　tablespoon drained capers

PLACE flour on plate. Sprinkle turkey with salt and pepper. Dredge turkey in flour; shake off excess.

MELT 1 tablespoon butter with oil in heavy medium skillet over medium-high heat. Add turkey and sauté until just cooked through, about 2 minutes per side. Divide turkey between 2 plates. Add remaining 3 tablespoons butter, lemon juice, wine, parsley, capers, and any turkey juice from plates to same skillet and bring to boil, scraping up browned bits. Season sauce to taste with salt and pepper; spoon over turkey.

CREATING CUTLETS If you don't find turkey cutlets at the market, purchase a turkey tenderloin and cut it crosswise on a slight diagonal into ½-inch-thick slices. Using a meat mallet or rolling pin, pound cutlets between sheets of plastic wrap to ¼- to ⅜-inch thickness.

Turkey cutlets with paprika cream sauce

2 SERVINGS *This is a fast and easy spin on Hungarian chicken* paprikás. *Serve the cutlets with buttered fettuccine or egg noodles; add poppy seeds and peas or parsley if you like.*

2　tablespoons (¼ stick) butter, divided
½　onion, chopped
1　teaspoon Hungarian sweet paprika
½　cup heavy whipping cream
1　teaspoon Dijon mustard
2　teaspoons minced fresh dill

¾　pound turkey cutlets
　　All purpose flour

MELT 1 tablespoon butter in heavy medium skillet over medium heat. Add onion and sauté until tender, about 8 minutes. Add paprika and stir 1 minute. Add cream. Simmer until sauce thickens slightly, about 1 minute. Mix in mustard and dill. Season sauce to taste with salt and pepper. Cover and set aside.

SPRINKLE turkey with salt and pepper. Dredge in flour; shake off excess. Melt remaining 1 tablespoon butter in heavy large skillet over medium-high heat. Add turkey and sauté until just cooked through, about 1 minute per side. Transfer to plates. Spoon sauce over turkey.

Chipotle turkey cutlets with charred corn salsa

4 SERVINGS *Cooking thawed frozen corn first in a dry skillet puts a smoky char on the kernels and adds roasted flavor in a flash. Look for chipotle chile powder in the spice section of the supermarket. Serve with warm tortillas and sautéed summer squash or a watercress salad with jicama and orange segments.*

1½ **cups frozen corn kernels, thawed**

1¼ **pounds turkey cutlets**
  2 **teaspoons chipotle chile powder**
  4 **tablespoons corn oil, divided**

  1 **medium green bell pepper, diced**
  1 **small red onion, diced**
  ¼ **cup chopped fresh cilantro**
  1 **tablespoon fresh lime juice**

CHAR corn in heavy medium nonstick skillet over medium-high heat, stirring often, about 4 minutes. Set aside.

SPRINKLE turkey on both sides with chipotle chile powder and salt. Heat 1 tablespoon oil in large skillet over medium-high heat. Add half of turkey and sauté until cooked through, about 1½ minutes per side. Transfer to plate. Repeat with 1 tablespoon oil and remaining turkey.

ADD remaining 2 tablespoons oil to drippings in skillet. Add bell pepper and onion; sauté 3 minutes. Increase heat to high and add charred corn. Sauté until pepper begins to brown, about 3 minutes longer. Stir in cilantro and lime juice. Season salsa to taste with salt and pepper; transfer to medium bowl. Return turkey to same skillet and reheat 1 minute. Transfer to plates. Spoon salsa over.

GAMEHENSANDDUCK

Grilled Cornish game hens with garlic-citrus marinade

4 SERVINGS *Preparing a game hen is as simple as roasting a chicken. Another bonus: Their diminutive size allows them to cook much faster. Let the hens marinate for 20 minutes, then just put them on the grill. Serve them with lemon and lime wedges.*

¼ cup olive oil

4 teaspoons chopped fresh thyme

3 garlic cloves, finely chopped

2 teaspoons finely grated lemon peel plus wedges for serving

2 teaspoons finely grated lime peel plus wedges for serving

1 teaspoon honey

½ teaspoon salt

½ teaspoon freshly ground black pepper

2 Cornish game hens (1¼ to 1½ pounds each), halved lengthwise

COMBINE oil, thyme, garlic, lemon peel, lime peel, honey, salt, and pepper in baking dish. Stir marinade to blend well. Place hen halves in marinade and turn to coat. Let marinate at least 20 minutes and up to 2 hours at room temperature, turning occasionally.

PREPARE barbecue (medium heat). Grill hen halves until just cooked through and skin is lightly charred, about 12 minutes per side.

We got game hens Cornish game hens have the same flavor as chicken (they're a cross between a Cornish gamecock and a white Plymouth Rock hen), and they have a higher percentage of white meat to dark meat than other birds.

Cornish game hens with blackberry sauce

6 SERVINGS *This dish has a European flair and a fancy result without the fuss—especially if you ask the butcher to halve and remove the backbones from the game hens for you. The Port-berry sauce can be made a day ahead. Serve these with a leafy green salad and mashed potatoes.*

4	tablespoons (½ stick) plus 1 teaspoon butter, melted, divided
¾	cup chopped onion
2½	tablespoons chopped fresh thyme, divided
1	cup tawny Port
1¾	cups fresh blackberries or frozen unsweetened blackberries, thawed
1½	cups low-salt chicken broth
1	teaspoon all purpose flour
3	1¾-pound Cornish game hens, halved lengthwise, backbones removed

HEAT 1 tablespoon butter in heavy large saucepan over medium-high heat. Add onion and ½ tablespoon thyme; sauté 5 minutes. Add Port and boil 4 minutes. Add blackberries and broth; boil until mixture is reduced to 1½ cups, stirring frequently, about 10 minutes. Strain into heavy medium saucepan, pressing on solids to release as much liquid and berry puree as possible. Discard solids.

MIX flour and 1 teaspoon melted butter in small bowl to smooth paste. Bring sauce to simmer. Gradually whisk in butter paste. Simmer until sauce thickens slightly, whisking until smooth, about 1 minute. Season to taste with salt and pepper.

DO AHEAD *Sauce can be made 1 day ahead. Cover and chill. Rewarm before using.*

PREHEAT oven to 425°F. Brush baking sheet with 1 tablespoon melted butter. Place hens, skin side up, on sheet; brush with remaining 2 tablespoons melted butter. Sprinkle with remaining 2 tablespoons thyme, then salt and pepper. Roast until cooked through, about 35 minutes. Serve hens with sauce.

Cornish game hen with curried plum glaze

2 SERVINGS *Believe it or not, just a few purchased condiments combine to create a gorgeous, sophisticated glaze for the hen. Serve with steamed basmati rice to complement the Indian flavors.*

1	1¾-pound Cornish game hen, halved lengthwise
⅓	cup plum jam
2	tablespoons mango chutney (such as Major Grey)
1	teaspoon curry powder
¼	cup low-salt chicken broth
1	lime, halved
	Chopped green onions
	Chopped roasted salted peanuts

PREHEAT oven to 400°F. Rinse hen halves and pat dry. Sprinkle with salt and pepper. Line rimmed baking sheet with foil. Arrange hen halves, skin side up, on prepared sheet. Combine jam, chutney, and curry powder in small saucepan. Stir over low heat until glaze comes to boil. Brush 2 tablespoons glaze over each hen half to coat generously. Add chicken broth to remaining glaze in pan and reserve for sauce.

BAKE hen halves until golden and tender, about 30 minutes. Transfer hens to plates. Squeeze juice from lime halves over each. Pour pan juices into reserved glaze mixture and bring to boil. Reduce heat and simmer to thicken slightly, about 3 minutes. Spoon sauce around hens. Sprinkle with green onions and peanuts.

Roast Cornish game hens with orange-teriyaki sauce

4 SERVINGS *Part of the marinade is mixed with chicken broth to cook up a quick and delicious pan sauce. Allow at least an hour's marinating time.*

- 1 **cup teriyaki baste and glaze**
- 1 **cup orange juice**
- 4 **green onions, finely chopped**
- 2 **tablespoons finely grated orange peel**
- 1 **tablespoon minced peeled fresh ginger**
- 4 **1- to 1¼-pound Cornish game hens**

- ⅔ **cup low-salt chicken broth**

WHISK first 5 ingredients in small saucepan to blend for marinade. Place hens in large resealable plastic bag. Add 1 cup marinade; seal bag. Let hens marinate 1 hour at room temperature or refrigerate up to 3 hours, turning bag occasionally. Reserve remaining marinade in pan.

PREHEAT oven to 400°F. Place rack on large rimmed baking sheet. Arrange hens on rack; drizzle with marinade from bag. Roast hens until cooked through and brown, basting occasionally with reserved marinade from pan, about 1 hour.

TRANSFER hens to platter. Scrape juices from baking sheet into pan; add broth. Bring sauce to boil. Season with salt and pepper; spoon over hens.

Cornish game hens with honey-ginger glaze

2 SERVINGS; CAN BE DOUBLED *These game hens are simply seasoned with herbs and glazed with a mixture of honey, white wine, and ginger. Brush a little of the glaze on acorn or butternut squash and roast them with the hens.*

- 2 **1½- to 1¾-pound Cornish game hens**
  Crumbled dried thyme
- 1 **small onion, halved**
- 2 **tablespoons (¼ stick) butter**

- 3 **tablespoons honey**
- 1 **tablespoon dry white wine**
- 2 **teaspoons ground ginger**

PREHEAT oven to 450°F. Line small baking sheet with foil. Place rack on sheet. Pat hens dry inside and out. Sprinkle cavities with salt, pepper, and thyme. Place onion half in cavity of each. Place hens on rack. Melt butter in heavy small saucepan. Brush some butter over hens. Sprinkle outside of hens with salt, pepper, and generous amount of dried thyme.

BAKE hens 15 minutes. Add honey, wine, and ginger to butter in pan and heat until thinned. Brush hens generously with glaze. Bake until hens are cooked through, basting occasionally with glaze and pan drippings, about 20 minutes.

Cornish game hens with maple-mustard glaze

2 SERVINGS *Wild rice and roasted winter squash, like butternut or kabocha, would be perfect with this. An easy way to test if the chicken is done is to pierce the thickest part of the thigh; if the juices run clear—with no pink—the hens are done.*

- 2 tablespoons pure maple syrup
- 1½ tablespoons butter
- 1 tablespoon Dijon mustard
- 1 teaspoon dried thyme, crumbled

- 2 1½-pound Cornish game hens

PREHEAT oven to 350°F. Combine first 4 ingredients in small saucepan for glaze. Cook over low heat until butter melts, whisking to blend.

PAT hens dry. Place on small baking sheet. Sprinkle with salt and pepper. Brush with glaze. Roast until hens are cooked through, brushing occasionally with glaze, about 1 hour.

Cornish game hen with raspberry-red wine sauce

2 SERVINGS *For a warming winter meal, serve soft polenta alongside.*

- 1 1½- to 1¾-pound Cornish game hen, halved
- 1 teaspoon dried thyme, crumbled
- 2 tablespoons olive oil

- 4 shallots, chopped
- 2 cups low-salt chicken broth
- ⅔ cup dry red wine
- ⅔ cup frozen unsweetened raspberries
- 2 teaspoons (or more) sugar
- ¼ teaspoon ground allspice

PREHEAT oven to 475°F. Sprinkle hen halves with thyme, salt, and pepper. Heat oil in heavy large skillet over medium-high heat. Add hen halves, skin side down, and cook until brown, about 6 minutes per side. Transfer hen halves to baking sheet (do not clean skillet). Roast until juices run clear when thigh is pierced, about 25 minutes.

MEANWHILE, pour off all but 2 tablespoons fat from skillet. Add shallots and sauté over medium heat until soft, about 3 minutes. Add broth, wine, raspberries, 2 teaspoons sugar, and allspice. Boil until sauce thickens enough to coat spoon, scraping up browned bits and crushing raspberries with back of fork, about 12 minutes. Strain wine sauce into small bowl. Season sauce to taste with salt and pepper, adding more sugar, if desired.

SERVE hen halves with sauce.

Sautéed duck breasts with wild mushrooms

4 SERVINGS *Sophisticated ingredients like duck and fresh wild mushrooms need little embellishment. Choose any assortment of mushrooms you like, and wipe clean with a damp towel or by brushing gently. Scoring the duck skin allows the fat to render more efficiently, and makes the skin nice and crisp.*

4 **8-ounce boneless duck breast halves with skin**

1¼ **pounds assorted fresh wild mushrooms (such as oyster, baby portobello, and stemmed shiitake), sliced (about 9 cups)**

1 **cup thinly sliced shallots (about 4 large)**

½ **cup dry red wine**

PREHEAT oven to 300°F. Using sharp knife, cut on diagonal to score skin of duck breasts, creating ¾-inch-wide diamond pattern (do not cut through to meat); pat dry. Sprinkle duck with salt and pepper. Heat heavy large skillet over high heat. Add duck, skin side down. Sauté until skin is deep golden brown, about 8 minutes. Turn duck over; sauté about 3 minutes longer for medium-rare. Transfer duck to rimmed baking sheet and place in oven to keep warm.

POUR off all but 2 tablespoons drippings from skillet. Reduce heat to medium-high. Add mushrooms and shallots, sprinkle with salt and pepper, and sauté until mushrooms are tender, about 8 minutes. Add wine and stir until juices thicken, scraping up browned bits, about 1 minute.

PLACE 1 duck breast on each plate. Spoon mushrooms over duck breasts.

Finding duck breast Look for duck breast in the frozen foods or fresh poultry section of well-stocked supermarkets or specialty foods stores; smoked duck breast can be found in the deli section. Or order both from Grimaud Farms (800-466-9955; grimaud.com) or D'Artagnan (800-327-8246; dartagnan.com). If you find large duck breasts (12 to 14 ounces), you can divide one of them into two half-breasts for the servings called for in the recipe.

Duck breast with crème fraîche and roasted grapes

6 SERVINGS *Both rustic and luxurious, this is a truly fresh rendition of a decadent dinner party main course. Sautéed duck breast is drizzled with crème fraîche and topped with oven-roasted purple grapes. Juniper is a traditional seasoning for meats and game and the dominant flavor in gin. Look for dried juniper berries in the spice section of the supermarket. For ease, prep the duck ahead of time and let it season in the fridge overnight before cooking.*

6	6- to 8-ounce duck breasts (thawed if frozen)
1	tablespoon dried juniper berries, crushed in resealable plastic bag using flat side of mallet
1	tablespoon fresh thyme leaves
½	pound purple seedless grapes, separated into small clusters
½	tablespoon olive oil Coarse kosher salt
3	cups (packed) baby arugula (about 3 ounces)
¼	cup crème fraîche or sour cream, stirred to loosen

USING sharp knife, cut on diagonal to score skin of duck breast, creating ¾-inch-wide diamond pattern (do not cut through to meat). Sprinkle crushed juniper berries and thyme over both sides of duck breasts; press to adhere. Place on rimmed baking sheet, cover with plastic wrap, and chill at least 4 hours.

DO AHEAD *Can be made 1 day ahead. Keep chilled.*

PREHEAT oven to 500°F. Combine grapes and oil in large bowl; toss to coat. Place in single layer on baking sheet. Sprinkle with kosher salt and pepper. Roast until grape skins are slightly crisp but grapes are still soft and juicy inside, about 14 minutes. Cool on sheet.

SPRINKLE both sides of duck with kosher salt and pepper. Heat heavy large skillet over medium heat. Add duck, skin side down; cook until almost all fat is rendered, about 7 minutes. Increase heat to medium-high and cook until skin is brown and crisp, about 4 minutes. Turn duck over and cook about 3 minutes longer for medium-rare. Transfer to cutting board; let rest 5 minutes.

DIVIDE arugula among plates. Thinly slice duck breasts crosswise and arrange 1 breast atop arugula on each plate. Drizzle crème fraîche over. Garnish with grapes.

COOKS LIKE CHICKEN Cooking a duck breast is no more difficult than preparing a chicken. Duck has richer flavor than chicken and instantly injects a note of special occasion to a meal. Of the three domesticated types available, Muscovy is especially meaty and lean—as lean as a skinless chicken breast.

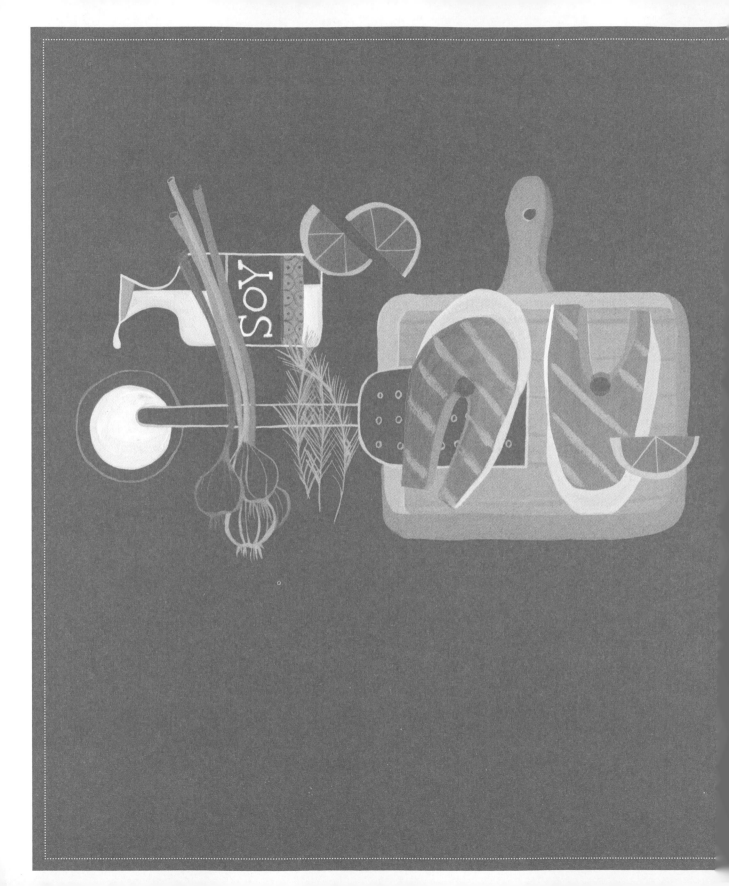

salmonand morefish

SALMON

Salmon with Chile-Mango Salsa

Grilled Salmon with
Tomato-Olive Salsa

Salmon with Pineapple Salsa
and Spicy Chile Sauce

Grilled Salmon Steaks with
Lime-Pepper Butter

Fennel-and-Dill-Rubbed
Grilled Salmon

Salmon and Halibut Kebabs
with Spicy Lemon Marinade

Grilled Salmon Cakes with
Lemon Mayonnaise

Maple-Soy–Glazed Salmon

Crunchy Wasabi
Salmon with Lime

Spicy Salmon with
Tomatoes and Star Anise

Salmon with Mustard and
Brown Sugar Glaze

Plank-Roasted Wild Salmon with
White Nectarine-Serrano Salsa

Pepper-and-Coriander–
Coated Salmon Fillets

Herb-Crusted Salmon on Greens

Seared Salmon on Baby Spinach

Red Curry–Roasted Salmon
with Green Beans, Red Bell
Pepper, Mint, and Basil

Salmon with Roasted Asparagus
and Lemon-Caper Sauce

Salmon with Pistachio-
Basil Butter

Poached Salmon with
Green Goddess Dressing

Salmon with Parsley Cream Sauce

Salmon Wellington

STRIPED BASS

Striped Bass with Swiss
Chard, Chestnuts, and
Pomegranate Vinaigrette

Striped Bass with Garlic-Herb Oil

Striped Bass with Moroccan Salsa

Striped Bass with Roasted
Tomatoes and Green Beans

Ginger-Miso Striped Bass in
Shiitake Mushroom Broth

HALIBUT

Roasted Halibut and Green Beans
with Asian Cilantro Sauce

Halibut with Capers,
Tomatoes, and Olives

Prosciutto-Roasted Halibut
with Fresh Thyme

Baked Halibut with Orzo,
Spinach, and Cherry Tomatoes

Grilled Halibut with
Pesto and Arugula

Classic Pesto

Grilled Halibut with Lemon-
Basil Vinaigrette

Cajun-Style Blackened Halibut

Halibut Pot Pie with
Mashed Potato Crust

Chili-Seasoned Fish Sticks

Grilled Fish Tostadas with
Pineapple-Jicama Salsa

TUNA AND MORE

Grilled Tuna with Herbed Aioli

Fresh Tuna Tacos

Oil-Poached Tuna with
Escarole and Lima Beans

Asian Seared Tuna Pepper Steaks

Rosemary-and-Orange-
Marinated Tuna Kebabs

Seared Tuna on Fettuccine with
Green Olives and Arugula

Sautéed Black Cod with
Shallot-Lemon Vinaigrette
and Fresh Herb Salad

Miso-Glazed Black Cod
on Sunflower Sprouts

Roasted Cod on Saffron
Mashed Potatoes

Beer-Batter Fish

Pumpkin-Seed-Crusted Trout
with Cabbage-Cilantro Salad

Trout with Tropical Fruit
Salsa and Mixed Greens

Whole Baked Trout
with Mushrooms

Crispy Trout with
Wilted Watercress

Grilled Swordfish with
Mint-Cucumber Salsa

Swordfish with Tomato,
Cucumber, and Radish Relish

Swordfish with Salmoriglio Sauce

Broiled Swordfish with
Marmalade-Ginger Glaze

Swordfish with Grapefruit-
and-Rosemary Butter Sauce

Pan-Roasted Swordfish Steaks
with Mixed-Peppercorn Butter

Swordfish with Balsamic
Brown Butter Sauce

Mahi-Mahi with Blood Orange,
Avocado, and Red Onion Salsa

Grilled Mahi-Mahi with
Lime-Ginger Vinaigrette

Mahi-Mahi with
Macadamia Nut Crust

Steamed Tilapia with Ginger,
Lime, and Cilantro

Baked Tilapia with Fennel-
Scented Tomato Sauce

Fish and Vegetables with
Pesto Baked in Foil Packets

Sole Piccata with
Grapes and Capers

Fried Catfish with Chive-
Ginger Sauce

tool kit Salmon, striped bass, halibut, tuna—these and all the other delicious fish in this chapter are perfect for creating no-fuss meals, especially when you know a few helpful tricks for expert shopping and preparation.

— When at the market, find out what fish were delivered that day. A good fishmonger will show off the freshest catch.

— Fresh fish is available nearly every day at reputable markets—but keep in mind that fish is not usually delivered on Sundays.

— Make the fish counter your last stop at the market, then head straight home and refrigerate the fish before unpacking any other groceries. You can even ask the fishmonger to wrap the fish up with a small amount of crushed ice.

— Use fillets rather than the whole fish. Since fillets come without the head and bones, they're pan-ready, and easy to serve and eat. Note that in BON APPÉTIT recipes, fish fillets are always skinless unless the recipe specifies "with skin." For smaller fish, such as trout and tilapia, fillets are sides of fish that taper at one end, and come cleaned, boned, and sometimes skinned. For large fish, like salmon, mahi-mahi, or halibut, these sides are commonly cut into single-serving rectangular fillets.

— When using fillets from the larger fish, ask for center-cut fillets, which are cut from the center toward the head end of the fish and have a uniform thickness, so they'll cook more evenly. Tail-end fillets are thinner at one end, which can result in uneven cooking—but they are great cut into pieces and used in fish stews and chowder.

— Ask the fishmonger to remove any bones before wrapping up the fish.

TOP-OF-THE-LINE SUBSTITUTIONS

If you're not able to find the fish you need, look for fish fillets that have the same thickness called for in the recipe, as this will affect the cooking time. Next, tell the fishmonger how you're planning to cook the fish—he or she should know what fish are best grilled, broiled, fried, or baked. Then look for fish that have similar textures. Here are some good (and environmentally friendly) substitutions to try when your first choice is not available:

FIRST CHOICE: Wild Alaskan salmon

SUBSTITUTIONS: Troll-caught ahi (yellowfin or bigeye) tuna, farmed arctic char, farmed rainbow trout

FIRST CHOICE: Pacific halibut

SUBSTITUTIONS: Pacific Alaskan cod, U.S. mahi-mahi, Pacific flounder, sole

FIRST CHOICE: Troll-caught albacore tuna

SUBSTITUTIONS: U.S. mahi-mahi, troll-caught ahi (yellowfin or bigeye) tuna

FIRST CHOICE: U.S. farmed tilapia

SUBSTITUTIONS: Farmed or wild striped bass, U.S. farmed catfish, black sea bass

FIRST CHOICE: Pacific Alaskan cod

SUBSTITUTIONS: Wild Alaskan pollock, Pacific halibut, black sea bass

SALMON

Salmon with chile-mango salsa

2 SERVINGS; CAN BE DOUBLED *Serranos are thinner, hotter chiles than jalapeños. To give the salsa more heat, leave the seeds in or add another teaspoon of minced chile.*

1 large mango, peeled, pitted, diced
¼ cup chopped fresh cilantro
¼ cup chopped red onion
1 tablespoon fresh lime juice
2 teaspoons minced seeded serrano chile
1 teaspoon finely grated lime peel
1 garlic clove, minced
2 tablespoons olive oil, divided
2 6-ounce salmon fillets

PREPARE barbecue (medium-high heat). Combine first 7 ingredients in small bowl; mix in 1½ tablespoons oil. Season salsa to taste with salt and pepper. Brush salmon with remaining ½ tablespoon oil. Sprinkle with salt and pepper. Grill until just opaque in center, about 4 minutes per side. Transfer salmon to plates. Serve, passing salsa separately.

Grilled salmon with tomato-olive salsa

6 SERVINGS *Kalamata olives, basil, and capers give this salsa a distinctive Mediterranean flavor. Creamy polenta and grilled eggplant slices would round out the meal nicely.*

1½ cups diced seeded plum tomatoes (about 10 ounces)
6 tablespoons olive oil, divided
12 Kalamata olives or other brine-cured black olives, pitted, chopped
¼ cup chopped fresh basil
2 tablespoons drained capers
2 garlic cloves, minced
1 shallot, finely chopped

6 6-ounce salmon fillets

COMBINE tomatoes, 4 tablespoons oil, olives, basil, capers, garlic, and shallot in medium bowl; stir to blend. Season salsa to taste with salt and pepper. Refrigerate at least 15 minutes and up to 2 hours.

PREPARE barbecue (medium-high heat). Brush salmon with remaining 2 tablespoons oil; sprinkle with salt and pepper. Grill salmon until just opaque in center, about 4 minutes per side. Transfer salmon to plates. Top with salsa.

Salmon with pineapple salsa and spicy chile sauce

4 SERVINGS *Canned chipotle chiles are dried, smoked jalapeños in a spicy tomato sauce called adobo. Look for them in the Latin foods section of the supermarket and at specialty foods stores and Latin markets. Ginger preserves are available at some supermarkets, at specialty foods stores, and online at britishdelights. com and amazon.com. Use the leftover preserves on English muffins or as a glaze for roasted chicken.*

¼ cup mayonnaise

1¼ teaspoons chopped canned chipotle chiles in adobo sauce

1 cup diced cored fresh pineapple

2 tablespoons ginger preserves or orange marmalade

2 tablespoons chopped fresh cilantro

1 tablespoon fresh lime juice

1 teaspoon minced peeled fresh ginger

4 6-ounce salmon fillets with skin (each 1 to 1¼ inches thick)

2 tablespoons olive oil

MIX mayonnaise and chipotle chiles in small bowl. Mix pineapple, ginger preserves, cilantro, lime juice, and ginger in another small bowl for salsa. Season salsa to taste with salt and pepper.

BRUSH salmon with oil; sprinkle with salt and pepper. Heat heavy large skillet over medium-high heat. Add salmon and cook until just opaque in center, about 5 minutes per side. Transfer salmon to plates. Spoon chile mayonnaise over. Spoon pineapple salsa alongside.

Grilled salmon steaks with lime-pepper butter

4 SERVINGS *Don't leave the salmon steaks in the lime-juice marinade for much longer than 1 hour: The acid in the juice will begin to "cook" the salmon, resulting in tough and rubbery fish.*

4 9-ounce salmon steaks

½ cup (1 stick) butter, melted

¼ cup fresh lime juice

1 tablespoon freshly ground black pepper

Lime wedges

PLACE salmon in glass baking dish. Mix butter, lime juice, and pepper in small bowl. Pour lime butter over salmon. Let marinate 1 hour at room temperature. Prepare barbecue (medium-high heat) or preheat broiler. Grill or broil salmon until just opaque in center, brushing occasionally with lime butter marinade, about 4 minutes per side. Transfer salmon to plates. Serve with lime wedges.

Fennel-and-dill-rubbed grilled salmon

8 SERVINGS *A few clever tricks—such as using un-rimmed baking sheets to flip the fish—make it easy to grill a whole side of salmon. (Even simpler: Use a grill basket, available in cookware and barbecue stores.) Some markets carry a whole side of fish with skin, but you may have to special order it. Spanish smoked paprika, sometimes labeled Pimentón de La Vera picante (hot or spicy) or Pimentón de La Vera dulce (sweet), is available at specialty foods stores or order it online at tienda.com. Domestic smoked paprika (sweet only) is now available at many su-permarkets and can be used with good results.*

1	tablespoon fennel seeds
¼	cup plus 2 teaspoons (packed) golden brown sugar
3	tablespoons sweet or hot smoked Spanish paprika (Pimentón de La Vera)
1	tablespoon coarse kosher salt
2	teaspoons freshly ground black pepper
2	teaspoons dried dill
	Nonstick vegetable oil spray
1	3¾- to 4-pound side of salmon with skin (preferably wild salmon)
	Olive oil

FINELY grind fennel seeds in spice mill or coffee grinder. Transfer to small bowl. Mix in next 5 ingredients.

SPRAY grill rack with nonstick spray. Prepare barbecue (medium-high heat). Brush salmon lightly on both sides with olive oil. Rub spice mixture generously over flesh side of salmon. Place salmon, skin side up, on grill rack; cover and cook until fish is slightly firmer, about 8 minutes. Slide rimless baking sheet under salmon to turn salmon over without breaking. Place another rimless baking sheet atop salmon. Using both hands, firmly hold baking sheets together and invert salmon; slide salmon, flesh side up, off baking sheet and onto grill rack.

Cover and grill until just opaque in center, about 8 minutes longer. Using rimless baking sheet, remove salmon from grill. Gently slide salmon, flesh side up, onto platter.

Salmon and halibut kebabs with spicy lemon marinade

8 SERVINGS *Lemon and orange slices are grilled with salmon and halibut for colorful, spicy-tart kebabs. You'll need eight metal skewers for the grilling.*

4	large shallots, minced
¼	cup dry white wine
¼	cup fresh lemon juice
3	tablespoons olive oil
1	tablespoon chopped fresh thyme
2	teaspoons hot pepper sauce
1½	pounds salmon fillets, cut into 1½-inch cubes
1½	pounds halibut fillets, cut into 1½-inch cubes
2	lemons, cut into rounds
1	orange, quartered lengthwise, then sliced crosswise

WHISK first 6 ingredients in large bowl to blend. Season to taste with salt and pepper. Add salmon and halibut; toss gently to coat. Cover and chill at least 1 hour.

DO AHEAD *Can be made 4 hours ahead. Keep chilled.*

PREPARE barbecue (medium-high heat). Alternate 2 salmon pieces, 2 halibut pieces, 2 lemon slices, and 2 orange slices on each skewer. Grill fish until opaque in center, turning often, about 8 minutes. Transfer skewers to platter.

Grilled salmon cakes with lemon mayonnaise

MAKES 8 *These cakes are excellent as is, or on a bun with lettuce, tomato, and the lemony mayo. Panko is becoming increasingly popular outside of Japan because it's crisper than other breadcrumbs. It can be found in the Asian foods section of some supermarkets and at Asian markets.*

- 1 cup plus 1 tablespoon mayonnaise
- 6 green onions (2 minced, 4 cut into 4-inch lengths), divided
- 1 tablespoon fresh lemon juice
- 2 teaspoons finely grated lemon peel

- ¼ cup (packed) chopped fresh Italian parsley
- 1¼ pounds salmon fillets, cut into 1-inch cubes
- 2 tablespoons Dijon mustard
- ½ cup panko (Japanese breadcrumbs)
- ¾ teaspoon salt
- ¾ teaspoon ground black pepper
  Olive oil

WHISK 1 cup mayonnaise, 2 minced green onions, lemon juice, and grated lemon peel in small bowl to blend. Season lemon mayonnaise to taste with salt and pepper.

FINELY chop remaining 4 green onions and parsley in processor. Add salmon, mustard, and remaining 1 tablespoon mayonnaise. Using on/off turns, blend until salmon is coarsely chopped. Transfer salmon mixture to large bowl. Mix in breadcrumbs, salt, and pepper. With moistened hands and using about ⅓ cupful for each, shape salmon mixture into 8 patties, each about ½ inch thick. Brush both sides of salmon cakes with oil.

PREPARE barbecue (medium heat). Grill salmon cakes to desired doneness, about 3 minutes per side for medium. Divide patties among 4 plates. Serve, passing lemon mayonnaise separately.

Maple-soy–glazed salmon

4 SERVINGS *It takes only four ingredients to create a richly flavored entrée. Asian-Flavored Coleslaw with Rice Vinegar and Ginger on page 138 would round out the meal. Adobo sauce is the spicy tomato sauce that coats canned chipotle chiles. Look for chipotles in adobo at the supermarket, a specialty foods store, or a Latin market.*

- ⅓ cup pure maple syrup
- ¼ cup soy sauce
- 1 teaspoon adobo sauce from canned chipotle chiles
- 4 6-ounce salmon fillets

WHISK maple syrup, soy sauce, and adobo in pie dish to blend. Add salmon; turn to coat. Marinate 30 minutes, turning occasionally. Drain marinade into small saucepan.

HEAT heavy nonstick skillet over medium heat. Add salmon and cook until slightly charred outside and just opaque in center, about 3 minutes per side.

MEANWHILE, boil marinade until reduced to scant ¼ cup glaze, about 4 minutes.

PLACE 1 salmon fillet on each of 4 plates and drizzle with glaze.

Crunchy wasabi salmon with lime

4 SERVINGS *Wasabi peas are dried green peas coated with spicy wasabi powder. They're typically a snack food, but here the peas become a quick, crunchy crust for salmon. They're sold at some supermarkets and natural foods stores and at Asian markets.*

- ¾ cup wasabi peas (about 3 ounces)
- 4 8-ounce salmon fillets with skin (each about 1 inch to 1¼ inches thick)
- 1 tablespoon finely grated lime peel
- 2 tablespoons olive oil, divided

- 6 cups thinly sliced red cabbage (about ½ large head)
- 1 8-ounce package trimmed sugar snap peas

- 2 tablespoons fresh lime juice
  Lime wedges

PREHEAT oven to 400°F. Blend wasabi peas in processor until ground but with some coarsely crushed pieces. Lightly oil rimmed baking sheet. Arrange salmon fillets, skin side down, on prepared baking sheet. Sprinkle fish with salt. Press ground wasabi peas onto tops of salmon fillets to adhere, covering tops completely. Sprinkle grated lime peel over salmon; drizzle with 1 tablespoon oil. Roast salmon just until opaque in center, about 10 minutes.

MEANWHILE, heat remaining 1 tablespoon oil in large nonstick skillet over medium-high heat. Add cabbage and sugar snap peas; sauté until vegetables are crisp-tender, about 5 minutes. Season to taste with salt and pepper.

TRANSFER 1 salmon fillet to each of 4 plates. Drizzle with lime juice. Mound cabbage-snap pea mixture alongside. Garnish with lime wedges.

Spicy salmon with tomatoes and star anise

4 SERVINGS *Star anise (an integral ingredient in the Indian spice mixture garam masala and in Chinese five-spice powder) gives salmon a pungent, licorice flavor. The star-shaped pods are available in the spice aisle at some supermarkets and at Indian and Asian markets. Grind them in a spice mill or coffee grinder.*

- 1 tablespoon Asian sesame oil
- 4 6-ounce wild salmon fillets with skin

- 1 cup chopped red onion
- 2 teaspoons minced peeled fresh ginger
- ¾ teaspoon freshly ground star anise
- ¼ to ½ teaspoon dried crushed red pepper
- 4 plum tomatoes, seeded, chopped
- 2 tablespoons soy sauce
- 1½ tablespoons sugar

PREHEAT oven to 325°F. Heat oil in large nonstick skillet over medium heat. Add salmon, skin side down; cook 2 minutes. Cover skillet; cook salmon 2 minutes longer. Transfer salmon, skin side down, to baking sheet. Place in oven; cook until just opaque in center, about 8 minutes.

MEANWHILE, heat same skillet over medium heat. Add onion and next 3 ingredients; sauté until onion is golden, about 5 minutes. Stir in tomatoes, soy sauce, and sugar. Increase heat to medium-high and cook mixture until slightly thickened, stirring occasionally, about 3 minutes.

DIVIDE salmon among 4 plates and top with tomato sauce.

Salmon with mustard and brown sugar glaze

6 SERVINGS *The mustard-brown sugar glaze, which caramelizes as the fillet broils, gives the fish a deep, intense flavor. Serve with a spinach salad dressed with a simple vinaigrette.*

¾ **cup dry white wine**
¼ **cup (½ stick) butter, diced**
1½ **teaspoons Old Bay seasoning**
1 **2-pound center-cut salmon fillet**

⅓ **cup spicy brown mustard (such as Gulden's)**
¼ **cup (packed) golden brown sugar**

PREHEAT oven to 350°F. Boil wine, butter, and Old Bay seasoning in small saucepan 3 minutes. Sprinkle salmon on both sides with salt and pepper. Place on rimmed baking sheet; pour wine mixture over. Bake until salmon is just opaque in center, about 14 minutes. Remove from oven.

PREHEAT broiler. Mix mustard and sugar in small bowl to blend; spread over salmon to cover. Broil salmon until topping is brown and bubbling, about 3 minutes. Transfer salmon to platter.

Plank-roasted wild salmon with white nectarine-serrano salsa

4 SERVINGS *Look for cedar planks at kitchenware stores or at lumberyards (but be sure to buy those marked "untreated" and soak them for 30 minutes to one hour to prevent burning). A little vegetable oil rubbed on the plank will help keep the food from sticking. White nectarines make for a lovely salsa, but yellow nectarines or any peaches will also work.*

2 **firm but ripe white nectarines (about 12 ounces), halved, pitted, cut into ¼-inch pieces**
1 **serrano chile, seeded, minced**
1 **tablespoon minced fresh cilantro**
2 **teaspoons minced fresh mint**
2 **teaspoons fresh lime juice**
1 **teaspoon sugar**

1 **cedar plank (approximately 10×17 inches)**
4 **6-ounce wild salmon fillets with skin**

COMBINE first 6 ingredients in small bowl. Season salsa to taste with salt and pepper. Cover with plastic wrap and chill until cold.

DO AHEAD *Can be made 3 hours ahead. Keep chilled.*

PLACE cedar plank in oven; set oven at 250°F and let plank heat for 30 minutes. Sprinkle salmon with salt and pepper; place skin side down on heated cedar plank. Bake until salmon is just opaque in center, about 25 minutes. Transfer salmon to plates. Top with salsa.

Technique: planking Grilling fish on a cedar or alder plank gives food a subtly smoky, almost sweet flavor and an incredibly moist texture. These days, all kinds of foods are being cooked on the plank, from salmon, halibut, and shrimp to chicken, pizza, and apples. And planking has moved indoors. Plank-roasted salmon has the same great aroma—but none of the hassle—of food cooked on a grill.

Pepper-and-coriander–coated salmon fillets

6 SERVINGS *Simple pan-seared salmon gets a savory-sweet browned crust and a bright citrus topping.*

- 3 tablespoons chopped fresh Italian parsley
- 3 tablespoons finely grated orange peel
- ¼ cup coriander seeds (½ ounce), coarsely crushed
- 1 tablespoon (packed) dark brown sugar
- 2 teaspoons coarsely ground black pepper

- 6 6-ounce salmon fillets
- 1 tablespoon butter, divided
- 1 tablespoon canola oil, divided

MIX parsley and orange peel in small bowl. Mix coriander, brown sugar, and black pepper in medium bowl.

DO AHEAD *Can be made 8 hours ahead. Cover separately. Chill parsley mixture. Store spice mixture at room temperature.*

SPRINKLE salmon with salt. Coat salmon on all sides with spice mixture. Melt ½ tablespoon butter and ½ tablespoon oil in heavy large skillet over medium-high heat. Add 3 salmon fillets. Cook fish until crust is golden and center is just opaque, about 4 minutes per side. Transfer fish to platter. Tent with foil to keep warm. Wipe skillet. Repeat with remaining butter, oil, and salmon. Spoon parsley mixture atop salmon.

Herb-crusted salmon on greens

2 SERVINGS; CAN BE DOUBLED *If you double the recipe, you'll have enough for lunch the next day. Just refrigerate the salmon, the greens, and the dressing separately, and assemble the dish right before mealtime. (There's no need to reheat the salmon—it's delicious cold, too.)*

- 2 tablespoons fresh lime juice
- 1 teaspoon finely grated peeled fresh ginger
- 2 teaspoons Dijon mustard
- 6 tablespoons vegetable oil, divided

- 2 6- to 7-ounce salmon fillets
- 2½ tablespoons finely chopped fresh dill, divided
- 2½ tablespoons finely chopped fresh basil, divided
- 1 5-ounce bag mixed baby greens

WHISK lime juice, ginger, and mustard in small bowl. Slowly whisk in 4 tablespoons oil. Season dressing to taste with salt and pepper.

BRUSH salmon on both sides with 1 tablespoon oil; sprinkle with salt and pepper, then 1 tablespoon dill and 1 tablespoon basil. Press herbs to adhere. Heat remaining 1 tablespoon oil in large nonstick skillet over medium-high heat. Add salmon, herb side down; sauté 4 minutes. Turn over; sauté until salmon is just opaque in center, about 5 minutes.

TOSS greens with remaining herbs and some dressing. Divide between 2 plates. Top with salmon and remaining dressing.

Seared salmon on baby spinach

2 SERVINGS; CAN BE DOUBLED *This simple recipe yields a main course, a sauce, and a side, all in the same skillet. Complete the meal with buttered steamed squash.*

- 2 **7-ounce salmon fillets**
- 2 **tablespoons (¼ stick) butter, divided**

- 3 **large shallots, sliced, divided**
- 4½ **teaspoons chopped fresh tarragon, divided**
- 5 **cups (loosely packed) fresh baby spinach (about 3 ounces)**

- ⅓ **cup dry white wine**
- ¼ **cup heavy whipping cream**

SPRINKLE salmon with salt and pepper. Melt 1 tablespoon butter in medium skillet over medium-high heat. Add salmon; cook until just opaque in center, about 4 minutes per side. Transfer to plate.

MELT ½ tablespoon butter in same skillet. Add half of shallots and half of tarragon; sauté 30 seconds. Increase heat to high; add half of spinach and toss 30 seconds. Add remaining spinach; toss until wilted. Divide between plates.

MELT remaining ½ tablespoon butter in same skillet over medium-high heat. Add remaining shallots and tarragon; sauté 30 seconds. Add wine and cream and boil until sauce is thick enough to coat spoon, about 3 minutes. Season to taste with salt and pepper. Return salmon to skillet; simmer 1 minute. Arrange salmon with sauce atop spinach.

Red curry–roasted salmon with green beans, red bell pepper, mint, and basil

4 SERVINGS *Thai red curry paste is a concentrated mixture of chiles, lemongrass, and other Thai spices. You can find it in the Asian foods section of supermarkets and at Asian markets. This recipe would work equally well with any other fish fillets of the same thickness. Pass lime wedges alongside to squeeze over the fish.*

-   **Nonstick vegetable oil spray**
- 4 **6-ounce center-cut salmon fillets (each about 1½ inches thick)**
- 1 **tablespoon plus 1 teaspoon vegetable oil**
- 1 **tablespoon fresh lime juice**
- 2 **teaspoons Thai red curry paste**
- 8 **ounces green beans, trimmed**
- 1 **red bell pepper, cut into long strips**

- 1 **generous tablespoon thinly sliced fresh mint leaves**
- 1 **generous tablespoon thinly sliced fresh basil leaves**

PREHEAT oven to 400°F. Spray heavy, very large rimmed baking sheet with nonstick spray. Place fish on half of prepared baking sheet. Whisk 1 tablespoon oil, lime juice, and curry paste in small bowl to blend. Spread curry mixture over fish. Toss green beans and bell pepper in medium bowl with remaining 1 teaspoon oil. Arrange green beans and pepper on second half of baking sheet. Sprinkle with salt.

ROAST in oven until fish is just opaque in center and vegetables are crisp-tender, about 12 minutes. Transfer fish to plates. Toss vegetables and pan juices on baking sheet with basil and mint; transfer to plates.

Salmon with roasted asparagus and lemon-caper sauce

4 SERVINGS *Salmon and asparagus are frequent part-ners: Both epitomize spring and they both work well with rich sauces. Here, they're roasted together and share a zingy lemon-caper sauce.*

2 tablespoons fresh lemon juice

2 tablespoons minced red onion

1 tablespoon olive oil

1 tablespoon drained capers, chopped

1 teaspoon chopped fresh thyme

½ teaspoon finely grated lemon peel

1 1½-pound salmon fillet (1¼ to 1½ inches thick)

1 pound asparagus, trimmed

1 tablespoon extra-virgin olive oil

WHISK first 6 ingredients in small bowl to blend. Season sauce to taste with salt and pepper.

PREHEAT oven to 450°F. Cut three ½-inch-deep slits crosswise in top of salmon (as if dividing into 4 equal pieces but do not cut through). Arrange asparagus in single layer on rimmed baking sheet. Drizzle with oil and turn to coat. Sprinkle with salt and pepper. Place salmon atop asparagus; sprinkle with salt and pepper. Roast until salmon is just opaque in center, about 20 minutes.

TRANSFER asparagus and salmon to platter. Spoon sauce over salmon. Cut salmon into 4 equal pieces along slits.

Salmon with pistachio-basil butter

6 SERVINGS *A flavored butter elevates this salmon dish. Walnuts or pine nuts can be used in place of the pistachios.*

¼ cup shelled pistachios

10 large fresh basil leaves plus additional leaves for garnish

1 garlic clove, peeled

½ cup (1 stick) butter, room temperature

1 teaspoon fresh lime juice

6 6-ounce salmon fillets (each about 1½-inches thick)

½ cup dry white wine

FINELY chop pistachios, 10 basil leaves, and garlic in processor. Add butter and lime juice and process until well blended. Season to taste with salt and pepper. Transfer pistachio butter to small bowl. Cover and chill until cold.

DO AHEAD *Can be made 3 days ahead. Keep chilled.*

PREHEAT oven to 400°F. Butter 13×9×2-inch bak-ing dish. Place salmon fillets in dish in single layer. Pour wine over. Sprinkle salmon with salt and pep-per. Bake salmon until almost opaque on top, about 8 minutes. Place 2 tablespoons pistachio butter atop each salmon piece. Continue baking until salmon fillets are just opaque in center, about 5 minutes longer. Transfer salmon to plates. Garnish with additional basil leaves.

Poached salmon with green goddess dressing

6 SERVINGS *The classic creamy dressing, invented in the 1920s, is a perfect accompaniment to the salmon. It's also great for a mixed-greens or chicken salad.*

- 3 cups bottled clam juice
- 3 cups dry white wine
- 10 whole peppercorns
- 6 lemon slices
- ½ bunch fresh chives
- 6 6- to 7-ounce salmon fillets

- ½ cup mayonnaise
- ⅔ cup coarsely chopped fresh chives
- ½ cup sour cream
- 1 garlic clove, peeled
- 1 tablespoon tarragon white wine vinegar
- 1 teaspoon chopped fresh tarragon
- 1 teaspoon sugar
- 1 teaspoon Worcestershire sauce

COMBINE first 5 ingredients in large skillet; simmer over medium heat 5 minutes. Reduce heat to medium-low. Add salmon fillets, cover and simmer until just opaque in center, about 7 minutes. Transfer salmon to platter. Cover and chill until cold.

DO AHEAD *Can be made 1 day ahead; keep chilled.*

BLEND mayonnaise and all remaining ingredients in blender until smooth. Season dressing to taste with salt and pepper.

DO AHEAD *Can be made 1 day ahead. Cover and chill.*

TRANSFER salmon fillets to plates. Spoon dressing alongside.

Salmon with parsley cream sauce

4 SERVINGS *The cream sauce is rich, so serve the salmon with a couple of light sides, such as rice pilaf, a green salad, or roasted asparagus.*

- 1 cup dry white wine
- 3 tablespoons bottled clam juice
- 3 garlic cloves, minced
- 2 large shallots, minced
- 1 cup heavy whipping cream
- ½ cup plus 3 tablespoons chopped parsley

- 1 1½-pound salmon fillet with skin (about ¾ to 1 inch thick)
  Olive oil

- 1 tablespoon minced fresh tarragon
- 1 tablespoon minced chives or green onion

COMBINE first 4 ingredients in heavy small saucepan. Boil until mixture is reduced to ⅔ cup, about 6 minutes. Stir in cream and ½ cup parsley. Boil until mixture is reduced to 1½ cups, about 4 minutes. Transfer mixture to blender. Blend until parsley is finely minced. Return liquid to same saucepan and boil until sauce coats spoon, about 3 minutes.

PREHEAT broiler. Brush both sides of salmon with oil. Sprinkle with salt and pepper. Broil salmon, skin side up, 4 minutes. Turn salmon over; broil until salmon is opaque in center, about 3 minutes longer. Transfer to platter.

BRING sauce to simmer. Whisk in tarragon, chives, and remaining 3 tablespoons parsley. Season sauce to taste with salt and pepper. Pour sauce over salmon on platter.

Salmon Wellington

4 SERVINGS *Beef Wellington—filet mignon wrapped in puff pastry—gets a clever update here, with salmon taking the starring role.*

1 **17.3-ounce package frozen puff pastry (2 sheets), thawed**

4 **6-ounce salmon fillets (each about ¾ inch thick)**

6 **tablespoons minced shallots, divided**

4 **tablespoons plus 2 teaspoons chopped fresh tarragon**

1 **egg, beaten to blend (for glaze)**

½ **cup dry white wine**

½ **cup white wine vinegar**

½ **cup (1 stick) chilled butter, diced**

PREHEAT oven to 425°F. Roll out each pastry sheet on lightly floured surface to 12-inch square. Cut each in half, forming four 12×6-inch rectangles. Place 1 salmon fillet in center of each rectangle, about 3 inches in from and parallel to 1 short edge. Sprinkle each fillet with salt, pepper, 1 tablespoon shallots, and 1 tablespoon tarragon. Brush edges of rectangles with some of egg glaze. Fold long sides of pastry over fillets. Fold short edge of pastry over fillets and roll up pastry, enclosing fillets. Seal edges of pastry. Place pastries, seam side down, on baking sheet. Brush with egg glaze.

BAKE pastries until crust is golden brown, about 20 minutes. Remove from oven; let stand 10 minutes.

MEANWHILE, boil wine, vinegar, and remaining 2 tablespoons shallots in heavy small saucepan until mixture is reduced to 6 tablespoons, about 8 minutes. Remove pan from heat. Add butter 1 piece at a time, whisking until melted before adding next piece. Whisk in remaining 2 teaspoons tarragon. Season sauce to taste with salt and pepper.

CUT pastries into thirds. Place pastries on plates; spoon sauce alongside.

STRIPED BASS

Striped bass with Swiss chard, chestnuts, and pomegranate vinaigrette

4 SERVINGS *Pomegranate molasses is a tart, syrupy reduction made from pomegranate juice; it's sold at some supermarkets and Middle Eastern markets, and online at adrianascaravan.com. You can make your own by boiling 2 cups of pomegranate juice in a heavy small saucepan until reduced to a thick syrup, about ⅓ cup. Stir often to prevent burning; it should take about 20 minutes. Let it cool before using 3 tablespoons in the recipe.*

- 7 **tablespoons olive oil, divided**
- 4 **5-ounce striped bass fillets**
- 2 **cups (packed) thinly sliced Swiss chard**
- 1 **cup peeled roasted chestnuts from jar, chopped**
- ⅓ **cup dry white wine**
- ⅓ **cup bottled clam juice**
- 3 **tablespoons pomegranate molasses**
- 1 **tablespoon Sherry wine vinegar**
- 1 **teaspoon Dijon mustard**
- 1 **large shallot, minced**

HEAT 3 tablespoons oil in large nonstick skillet over medium-high heat. Sprinkle both sides of fish fillets with salt and pepper; add to skillet and cook until golden, about 3 minutes per side. Transfer fish to platter; tent with foil to keep warm. Add chard, chestnuts, wine, and clam juice to skillet; cook until chard is just wilted, about 3 minutes. Using slotted spoon, place chard mixture atop fish; tent with foil. Boil juices in skillet to reduce slightly, about 3 minutes. Remove skillet from heat; add pomegranate molasses, vinegar, mustard, and shallot. Slowly whisk in remaining 4 tablespoons oil. Season vinaigrette to taste with salt and pepper. Spoon over fish.

Striped bass with garlic-herb oil

2 SERVINGS; CAN BE DOUBLED *This super-easy herb-oil marinade is a great one to keep on hand: It's made with a few pantry staples and can be used with virtually any other type of fish or with chicken. Or just put some in a small bowl and use it as a dipping sauce for bread.*

- 6 tablespoons extra-virgin olive oil
- 3 large garlic cloves, flattened and peeled
- ⅛ teaspoon (generous) dried crushed red pepper
- 4 teaspoons fresh lemon juice
- 2 teaspoons chopped fresh marjoram

- 2 6-ounce striped bass fillets (each about ¾ inch thick)

  Chopped fresh Italian parsley

COMBINE oil and garlic in heavy small saucepan; cook over low heat until garlic begins to brown, about 1 minute. Discard garlic. Add crushed red pepper to oil and stir 30 seconds. Remove from heat. Add lemon juice and marjoram.

PLACE fish on large plate. Spoon oil over, turning to coat both sides. Let fish stand for 30 minutes.

PREHEAT broiler. Sprinkle fish with salt and pepper. Broil until just opaque in center, about 3 minutes per side. Sprinkle with parsley.

Striped bass with Moroccan salsa

6 SERVINGS *The salsa brings together the flavors of North Africa: peppers, cumin, cinnamon, raisins, and orange peel. It would also be a great accompaniment to roasted lamb.*

- 5 tablespoons olive oil, divided
- 1 teaspoon ground cumin
- ½ teaspoon ground cinnamon
- 2 7-ounce jars roasted red bell peppers, drained, coarsely chopped
- ½ cup chopped pitted Kalamata olives
- ½ cup chopped red onion
- ⅓ cup chopped fresh cilantro
- ¼ cup golden raisins
- 3 tablespoons fresh lemon juice
- 2 tablespoons (packed) chopped fresh mint
- 2 teaspoons finely grated orange peel
- ½ teaspoon (scant) cayenne pepper

- 6 6-ounce striped bass fillets

HEAT 1 tablespoon oil in heavy small skillet over medium heat. Add cumin and cinnamon; stir until fragrant, about 1 minute. Remove from heat. Mix in peppers, 2 tablespoons oil, olives, and next 7 ingredients. Season salsa to taste with salt and pepper.

DO AHEAD *Can be made 2 hours ahead. Cover and let stand at room temperature, tossing occasionally.*

PREHEAT broiler. Brush fish all over with remaining 2 tablespoons oil. Sprinkle with salt and pepper. Broil until fish is opaque in center, about 2 minutes per side. Transfer fish to plates. Spoon salsa over fish.

The lowdown on bass Striped bass is a large fish in the sea

bass family. It's an excellent alternative to Chilean sea bass (which is vulnerable to overfishing and illegal fishing methods). Striped bass has a similar firm, flaky texture and works well with a number of preparations, including frying and roasting. It's thinner than Chilean sea bass, so it will cook more quickly.

Striped bass with roasted tomatoes and green beans

4 SERVINGS *You can change this entrée from Indian to Southeast Asian by substituting ½ to 1 teaspoon Thai red curry paste (depending on spiciness preference) for the curry powder. Steamed white rice is a nice accompaniment to either version.*

Nonstick vegetable oil spray

1½ pounds plum tomatoes, each cut into 8 wedges

1 large onion, halved through root end, each half cut into thin wedges

2 garlic cloves, minced

1 tablespoon extra-virgin olive oil

8 ounces green beans, trimmed, cut diagonally into 2-inch pieces

2 teaspoons curry powder

2 teaspoons minced peeled fresh ginger

4 5- to 6-ounce striped bass fillets (each about ¾ to 1 inch thick)

PREHEAT oven to 400°F. Spray large rimmed baking sheet with nonstick spray. Combine tomatoes, onion, and garlic on prepared sheet. Drizzle with olive oil; toss to coat. Spread in even layer. Sprinkle vegetables generously with salt and pepper. Roast until onion begins to brown, stirring occasionally, about 35 minutes.

REMOVE baking sheet from oven; increase temperature to 450°F. Mix beans, curry powder, and ginger into tomato mixture; top with fish. Sprinkle fish with salt and pepper. Spoon some tomato mixture over fish. Roast until fish fillets are just opaque in center, about 7 minutes. Transfer fish to plates, spooning tomato mixture over.

Ginger-miso striped bass in shiitake mushroom broth

2 SERVINGS *Red miso—a savory paste made from fermented soybeans and sometimes labeled aka-miso—is available in the refrigerated Asian foods section of some supermarkets, at natural foods stores and Japanese markets, and online from asian-foodgrocer.com. Panko is sold in the Asian foods section of the supermarket and at Asian markets.*

2 cups water

4 tablespoons red miso (fermented soybean paste), divided

4 large shiitake mushrooms (about 4 ounces), stemmed, thinly sliced

3 green onions, dark and pale green part thinly sliced, white part minced

4 tablespoons vegetable oil, divided

1 tablespoon minced peeled fresh ginger

2 6-ounce striped bass fillets

¼ cup panko (Japanese breadcrumbs)

Chopped fresh cilantro

WHISK 2 cups water and 2 tablespoons red miso in medium saucepan. Add shiitake mushrooms and simmer over medium heat until mushrooms are soft, about 5 minutes. Stir in dark and pale green onion tops. Cover to keep warm and set aside.

MEANWHILE, mix remaining 2 tablespoons red miso, white part of green onions, 2 tablespoons oil, and ginger in small bowl. Sprinkle striped bass fillets with salt and pepper. Spread ginger mixture over 1 side of bass fillets, pressing to adhere. Sprinkle panko over coated side of fillets; press to adhere.

HEAT remaining 2 tablespoons oil in medium nonstick skillet over medium-high heat. Add fillets to skillet, coated side down, and sauté until brown and crisp, about 3 minutes. Turn fillets over and sauté until cooked through, about 3 minutes. Divide shiitake mushroom broth and shiitake mushrooms between 2 shallow bowls. Place 1 fish fillet in center of each bowl. Sprinkle cilantro over.

HALIBUT

Roasted halibut and green beans with Asian cilantro sauce

2 SERVINGS *The entrée and side dish roast together in the same spicy-tangy sauce. Serve with steamed rice to soak it all up. And be sure to use Asian sesame oil, which is darker and has a stronger, more toasted flavor than regular sesame oil.*

- 2 cups (loosely packed) fresh cilantro leaves (from 1 large bunch)
- 2 tablespoons fresh lemon juice
- 1 green onion, chopped
- 1 tablespoon minced peeled fresh ginger
- 2 teaspoons chopped jalapeño chile with seeds
- 5 tablespoons safflower oil, divided
- 2 teaspoons Asian sesame oil, divided
- 3 teaspoons soy sauce, divided

- 2 8-ounce halibut fillets (each about 1 inch thick)
- 4 ounces green beans
- 10 fresh oyster mushrooms or fresh stemmed shiitake mushrooms

PREHEAT oven to 450°F. Place first 5 ingredients, 3 tablespoons safflower oil, 1 teaspoon sesame oil, and 1 teaspoon soy sauce in processor; puree. Season sauce to taste with salt.

PLACE fish fillets, green beans, and mushrooms in single layer on rimmed baking sheet. Whisk remaining 2 tablespoons safflower oil, 1 teaspoon sesame oil, and 2 teaspoons soy sauce in bowl to blend. Pour over fish, green beans, and mushrooms; toss green beans and mushrooms to coat. Sprinkle with salt and pepper. Roast until fish is opaque in center and green beans are crisp-tender, about 8 minutes. Divide fish, vegetables, and cilantro sauce between plates.

Halibut with capers, tomatoes, and olives

4 SERVINGS *Serve the fish and sauce over couscous, orzo, or a rice pilaf.*

- 4 6- to 7-ounce halibut fillets
  All purpose flour
- 4 tablespoons olive oil, divided
- 2 large shallots, chopped
- ¼ teaspoon dried crushed red pepper
- 4 plum tomatoes, seeded, chopped
- ½ cup chopped pitted Kalamata olives
- ½ cup chopped fresh basil, divided
- 1 tablespoon drained capers
- ⅓ cup bottled clam juice
- ¼ cup dry white wine

SPRINKLE fish with salt and pepper. Dredge in flour. Heat 2 tablespoons oil in heavy large skillet over medium-high heat. Add fish and cook until lightly browned and just opaque in center, about 4 minutes per side. Transfer fish to platter. Heat remaining 2 tablespoons oil in same skillet. Add shallots and crushed red pepper; sauté 1 minute. Mix in tomatoes, olives, ¼ cup basil, and capers. Add clam juice and wine. Boil until sauce thickens slightly, about 4 minutes. Mix in remaining ¼ cup basil. Season sauce to taste with salt and pepper. Spoon sauce over fish.

Prosciutto-roasted halibut with fresh thyme

2 SERVINGS *Prosciutto adds a salty richness to pan-seared halibut, and wrapped around the fish it helps to keep the halibut moist. Place the fish packets seam side down in the skillet so that they won't fall apart. Thinly sliced Smithfield or Serrano ham can be used in place of prosciutto.*

- 2   **5-ounce halibut fillets**
- 3   **teaspoons chopped fresh thyme, divided**
- 4   **thin slices prosciutto**

- 2   **teaspoons olive oil**

- 2   **tablespoons chopped shallot**
- ¼   **cup dry white wine**
- 1   **tablespoon butter**

PREHEAT oven to 400°F. Sprinkle fish fillets with salt and pepper. Sprinkle 1 teaspoon thyme atop each fish fillet. Place 2 slices prosciutto on work surface, overlapping slightly. Place 1 fish fillet crosswise in center of prosciutto; fold prosciutto over fish fillet. Repeat with remaining prosciutto and fish fillet.

HEAT oil in medium ovenproof skillet over medium-high heat. Add prosciutto-wrapped fish, seam side down. Cook until prosciutto is brown, about 1 minute per side. Transfer skillet to oven and roast fish until cooked through, about 6 minutes. Transfer fish to plates.

ADD shallot to same skillet; sauté over medium-high heat until beginning to brown, about 1 minute. Add wine and remaining 1 teaspoon thyme. Simmer until sauce is slightly reduced, about 1 minute. Whisk in butter. Drizzle sauce over fish.

WRAP IT UP When placing the prosciutto on the work surface prior to wrapping the halibut, slightly overlap the prosciutto slices along their longer sides. After folding the slices over each fillet, press the packets lightly to make sure the prosciutto adheres.

Baked halibut with orzo, spinach, and cherry tomatoes

2 SERVINGS *Here's a complete meal from just seven ingredients. For more Mediterranean flavor, add sliced Kalamata olives and toasted pine nuts to the pasta.*

- 4   **tablespoons extra-virgin olive oil, divided**
- 2   **tablespoons fresh lemon juice**
- 2   **6- to 7-ounce halibut fillets**

- 1   **cup orzo (rice-shaped pasta)**
- 1   **garlic clove, minced**
- 4   **cups (packed) fresh baby spinach**
- 1   **cup halved cherry tomatoes**

PREHEAT oven to 425°F. Whisk 2 tablespoons oil and lemon juice in small bowl; season dressing to taste with salt and pepper. Place halibut on rimmed baking sheet; sprinkle with salt and pepper. Drizzle lightly with some of dressing. Bake until just opaque in center, about 12 minutes.

MEANWHILE, cook pasta in large saucepan of boiling salted water until just tender but still firm to bite; drain. Add remaining 2 tablespoons oil and garlic to same saucepan; sauté over medium heat 1 minute. Add drained pasta, spinach, and tomatoes; stir to coat. Season to taste with salt and pepper. Remove from heat. Cover and let stand 1 minute (spinach will wilt). Divide pasta between 2 plates. Top with halibut and remaining dressing.

Grilled halibut with pesto and arugula

4 SERVINGS *The pesto is spread on the halibut fillets after they're cooked so the sauce keeps its fresh flavor.*

    4 8-ounce halibut fillets
    6 tablespoons extra-virgin olive oil, divided
    ½ cup Classic Pesto (see recipe)
       or purchased pesto
    1 tablespoon fresh lemon juice
    3 cups arugula leaves

PREPARE barbecue (medium-high heat). Brush each halibut fillet with 1 tablespoon oil. Sprinkle with salt and pepper. Grill until just opaque in center, about 4 minutes per side. Spread each fillet with thin layer of pesto, dividing equally.

WHISK lemon juice and remaining 2 tablespoons oil in medium bowl to blend. Add arugula; toss to coat. Divide arugula among 4 plates; top with grilled halibut.

Classic pesto

MAKES ABOUT 1 CUP *Here's a very traditional version of the versatile Italian sauce, prepared in a blender to create a smoother puree. Use any leftover pesto as a sauce for pasta, a spread for sandwiches, or as a dip for pita chips. If you don't have Pecorino Sardo cheese, you can double the amount of Parmesan instead (½ cup total).*

    4 cups fresh basil leaves (from
       about 3 large bunches)
    ½ cup olive oil
    ⅓ cup pine nuts
    2 garlic cloves, peeled
    ¼ cup freshly grated Parmesan cheese
    ¼ cup freshly grated Pecorino Sardo cheese

COMBINE first 4 ingredients in blender. Blend until paste forms, stopping often to push down basil. Add both cheeses; blend until smooth. Transfer to small bowl. Season to taste with salt.

DO AHEAD *Can be made 1 day ahead. Top with ½ inch olive oil; cover and chill.*

Grilled halibut with lemon-basil vinaigrette

4 SERVINGS *Try this tangy vinaigrette on grilled shrimp or grilled salmon. A simple, creamy risotto and a fresh green salad would round out the meal.*

    5 tablespoons fresh lemon juice
    ¼ cup extra-virgin olive oil
    4 garlic cloves, crushed
    1 teaspoon finely grated lemon peel
    6 tablespoons thinly sliced fresh basil, divided
    4 teaspoons drained capers

    4 5- to 6-ounce halibut steaks
       (each about ¾ inch thick)

WHISK lemon juice, oil, garlic, and lemon peel in small bowl to blend. Stir in 4 tablespoons basil and capers. Season vinaigrette to taste with salt and pepper.

PREPARE barbecue (medium-high heat) or preheat broiler. Sprinkle halibut steaks with salt and pepper. Brush fish with 1 tablespoon vinaigrette, dividing equally. Grill or broil halibut steaks until just cooked through, about 4 minutes per side. Transfer fish to plates. Rewhisk remaining vinaigrette; pour over fish. Garnish fish with remaining 2 tablespoons basil.

Cajun-style blackened halibut

4 SERVINGS *Blackening is a cooking technique made famous by New Orleans chef Paul Prudhomme. The fish (or meat) is rubbed with a Cajun spice mixture and is cooked in a red-hot skillet (preferably cast-iron), giving the food a dark, extra-crisp crust. Salmon or the more traditional redfish can be substituted for halibut. Blackened fish is delicious on Caesar salad.*

1	teaspoon salt
1	teaspoon minced fresh thyme
½	teaspoon dried oregano
½	teaspoon cayenne pepper
½	teaspoon sweet paprika
½	teaspoon ground black pepper
½	teaspoon fennel seeds, crushed
4	6-ounce halibut fillets
2	tablespoons olive oil, divided
4	teaspoons butter

PREHEAT oven to 400°F. Mix first 7 ingredients in small bowl. Place fish fillets on rimmed baking sheet. Brush on both sides with 1 tablespoon oil. Sprinkle top of each fillet with spice mixture.

HEAT heavy large skillet (preferably cast-iron) over high heat until very hot. Add remaining 1 tablespoon oil; swirl to coat. Place fish fillets, seasoned side down, in skillet. Cook until very brown on bottom, 1 minute. Return fillets, brown side up, to baking sheet. Place in oven and bake until just opaque in center, about 8 minutes. Transfer fish to plates. Top each fish fillet with 1 teaspoon butter.

Halibut pot pie with mashed potato crust

4 SERVINGS *Here's the perfect use for leftover mashed potatoes. Before spooning them over the filling, rewarm the mashed potatoes in the microwave (adding more milk if they seem too thick). Salmon or mahi-mahi can be used in place of the halibut.*

2	tablespoons (¼ stick) butter
1	large fennel bulb, trimmed, halved, thinly sliced crosswise (about 3 cups)
½	cup sliced shallots (about 2 medium)
2	tablespoons all purpose flour
1½	cups vegetable broth
1½	pounds halibut fillets, cut into 1-inch cubes
1	6-ounce package fresh baby spinach
3½	cups warm mashed potatoes

PREHEAT broiler. Melt butter in heavy large saucepan over medium heat. Add fennel and shallots. Cover and cook until tender, stirring occasionally, about 8 minutes. Sprinkle with flour, salt, and pepper. Sauté 2 minutes. Add broth; bring to boil, stirring often. Add fish and spinach. Cover; simmer over medium heat until fish is almost cooked through, about 4 minutes.

TRANSFER fish mixture to 11×7×2-inch baking dish. Spoon mashed potatoes over, covering completely. Broil until filling bubbles at edges and potatoes are brown in spots, about 4 minutes.

Chili-seasoned fish sticks

2 SERVINGS; CAN BE DOUBLED *These spicy, breaded fish sticks are baked, not fried. For a more delicate crust, substitute* panko *(Japanese breadcrumbs) for the flour and cornmeal.*

    Nonstick vegetable oil spray
 6 tablespoons all purpose flour
 3 tablespoons yellow cornmeal
1¾ teaspoons chili powder
 ⅓ cup mayonnaise
 2 tablespoons fresh lemon juice
12 ounces firm white fish fillets (such as halibut),
    cut crosswise into ¾-inch-wide strips

POSITION rack in top third of oven and preheat to 500°F. Spray small rimmed baking sheet with nonstick spray. Whisk flour, cornmeal, and chili powder in shallow dish to blend. Mix mayonnaise and lemon juice in another shallow dish. Sprinkle fish on all sides with salt and pepper. Dip fish into mayonnaise mixture, then into flour mixture to coat completely. Arrange fish on prepared sheet. Bake until coating is crisp and golden and fish is cooked through, about 10 minutes.

Grilled fish tostadas with pineapple-jicama salsa

4 SERVINGS *Grilled, spiced corn tortillas are topped with grilled halibut and zucchini and a fresh, tropical salsa. The salsa is also great with chicken or grilled shrimp.*

1½ cups diced peeled pineapple
 1 cup diced peeled jicama
 ½ cup diced red onion
 ¼ cup chopped fresh cilantro
 ¼ cup fresh lime juice
 2 serrano chiles, seeded, chopped

 ¼ cup olive oil
 2 teaspoons chili powder
 3 small zucchini (about 10 ounces),
    each cut lengthwise into 5 slices
 1 pound halibut fillets
 4 5- to 6-inch corn tortillas

PREPARE barbecue (medium-high heat). Mix first 6 ingredients in medium bowl. Season salsa to taste with salt and pepper.

WHISK oil and chili powder in small bowl. Arrange zucchini, fish, and tortillas in single layer on large baking sheet. Brush chili oil on both sides of zucchini, fish, and tortillas. Sprinkle zucchini and fish with salt and pepper. Grill until fish is cooked through and zucchini is tender, about 3 minutes per side. Grill tortillas until charred, about 2 minutes per side. Divide zucchini among tortillas. Cut fish into strips and place atop zucchini. Top tostadas with salsa.

TUNAANDMORE

Grilled tuna with herbed aioli

4 SERVINGS *The herb-filled aioli features mayonnaise enhanced with some of the same marinade that flavors the fish. Chopped fresh tarragon can be used in place of dried. This combination of flavors would also work well with grilled salmon.*

- ¼ cup olive oil
- 2 tablespoons red wine vinegar
- 2 tablespoons chopped fresh basil
- 2 teaspoons chopped fresh thyme
- 2 teaspoons dried tarragon
- 2 garlic cloves, minced
- ⅓ cup mayonnaise
- 4 7-ounce tuna steaks (each about 1 inch thick)

WHISK first 6 ingredients in 11×7×2-inch glass baking dish for marinade. Place mayonnaise in small bowl. Whisk in 1½ tablespoons marinade to make aioli. Set aioli aside.

SPRINKLE fish with salt and pepper. Place fish in marinade in dish, turning to coat. Let marinate 1 hour at room temperature, turning fish occasionally.

OIL grill rack. Prepare barbecue (medium-high heat). Grill fish to desired doneness, about 2 minutes per side for medium-rare. Top fish with aioli.

Fresh tuna tacos

MAKES 4 *Serve with shredded lettuce or cabbage,* pico de gallo, *and sliced avocado. For a more authentic, Baja-style taco, use soft corn tortillas instead of the taco shells. Chipotle chiles canned in spicy adobo sauce are available in the Latin foods section of the supermarket and at Latin markets.*

- ⅓ cup sour cream
- ¼ cup chopped red onion
- 3 tablespoons chopped fresh cilantro
- 1 teaspoon minced canned chipotle chiles
- 1 8-ounce ahi tuna steak, cut into ¾-inch pieces
- 1 tablespoon taco seasoning mix
- 1 tablespoon vegetable oil
- 4 taco shells

MIX first 4 ingredients in small bowl. Place tuna in medium bowl; sprinkle with taco seasoning and toss. Heat oil in heavy medium skillet over medium-high heat. Add tuna; sauté to desired doneness, about 2 minutes for medium-rare. Reduce heat to medium-low. Stir in sour cream mixture. Cook just until heated through, stirring frequently, about 2 minutes (do not boil or sauce may curdle).

HEAT taco shells in microwave 20 seconds. Fill taco shells with tuna mixture.

Oil-poached tuna with escarole and lima beans

2 SERVINGS *Poaching fish in olive oil is a popular restaurant technique: The oil creates a seal that keeps all the moisture in the fish. It's a surprisingly easy—and healthy—way to cook. The resulting dish is low in calories and fat, and high in fiber. Escarole is a type of endive; it has broad, slightly curved pale green leaves and a nice mildly bitter flavor. The leafy green is available year-round at most supermarkets, but is best in season from summer to early fall.*

1 lemon, thinly sliced
1 10-ounce albacore tuna fillet, cut into ⅓-inch-thick slices
  Olive oil (for poaching)

1 large green onion, thinly sliced
4 cups coarsely chopped escarole
1 8½-ounce can baby lima beans, drained
4 tablespoons chopped fresh parsley, divided
1 tablespoon white balsamic vinegar

LINE heavy medium skillet with lemon slices. Sprinkle tuna with salt and pepper and place atop lemon. Add just enough olive oil to cover tuna. Poach tuna over medium-low heat until almost cooked through, about 3 minutes. Using slotted spoon, transfer tuna to plate. Discard lemon slices.

DISCARD all but 1 tablespoon oil from skillet. Add green onion to skillet and sauté over medium-high heat 1 minute. Add escarole, lima beans, and 3 tablespoons parsley; sauté until escarole begins to wilt, about 1 minute. Sprinkle with vinegar. Season to taste with salt and pepper.

DIVIDE escarole-bean mixture between 2 plates and top with tuna slices. Sprinkle with remaining 1 tablespoon parsley.

NOT TOO HOT Keep the temperature of the olive oil very low when cooking the tuna—if there are any bubbles in the oil, you're boiling the fish, not poaching it, and it will end up tough and dry.

Asian seared tuna pepper steaks

4 SERVINGS *A spicy pepper coating and Asian sauce give the steaks an intense flavor. Oven-roasted sweet potatoes would be great alongside.*

4 6- to 7-ounce ahi tuna steaks (each about 1 inch thick)
1 tablespoon coarsely cracked black pepper
2 teaspoons Asian sesame oil
2 tablespoons soy sauce
¼ cup dry Sherry
2 tablespoons chopped green onion tops

SPRINKLE tuna steaks on both sides with salt, then sprinkle with coarsely cracked black pepper, pressing gently to adhere. Heat oil in large nonstick skillet over high heat. Add tuna steaks and sear until brown outside but still pink in center, about 2 minutes per side. Transfer tuna steaks to platter; tent loosely with foil to keep warm. Add soy sauce, then Sherry to same skillet. Reduce heat and simmer until sauce is slightly reduced, scraping up any browned bits, about 1 minute. Spoon sauce over tuna steaks. Sprinkle with green onion tops.

Rosemary-and-orange-marinated tuna kebabs

4 SERVINGS *Two grilling favorites—tuna and kebabs—are combined for a lovely summer main course. You'll need eight 8- to 10-inch skewers for grilling; if using wooden skewers, first soak them in water for 30 minutes. Serve the kebabs with potato salad.*

1½   **pounds tuna steaks, cut into sixteen 1- to 1¼-inch cubes**
1   **tablespoon olive oil**
2   **garlic cloves, minced**
1¾   **teaspoons finely grated orange peel**
1½   **teaspoons minced fresh rosemary**

1   **large orange, peel and pith removed, cut into 8 pieces**
8   **cherry tomatoes**

PREPARE barbecue (medium-high heat) or preheat broiler. Toss first 5 ingredients in bowl. Sprinkle with salt and pepper.

THREAD 2 pieces of tuna alternately with 1 orange piece and 1 cherry tomato on each skewer. Rub any remaining seasonings from bowl over kebabs.

GRILL or broil tuna kebabs to desired doneness, turning kebabs often, about 4 to 5 minutes total for medium-rare.

EVEN EASIER Cut the orange into ½-inch-thick slices (without removing the peel and pith), and cut the slices into quarters.

Seared tuna on fettuccine with green olives and arugula

4 SERVINGS *Green olive bruschetta spread is typically a mixture of chopped olives and sun-dried tomatoes, herbs, and oil. Here it's used as the base for a pasta sauce. You can find it near the jarred olives and pasta sauces or in the refrigerated deli section of the supermarket. You can also use the more common black olive bruschetta spread.*

12   **ounces fettuccine**
1   **cup green olive bruschetta spread from jar (about 8 ounces)**
6   **tablespoons olive oil, divided**
4   **teaspoons finely grated lemon peel, divided**
4   **teaspoons fresh lemon juice**
1   **5-ounce package baby arugula**

2   **12-ounce tuna steaks (each about 1 inch thick)**
4   **teaspoons chopped fresh marjoram**

COOK pasta in large pot of boiling salted water until just tender but still firm to bite, stirring occasionally. Drain, reserving ½ cup pasta cooking liquid. Return pasta to pot. Add olive bruschetta spread, 3 tablespoons oil, 2 teaspoons lemon peel, lemon juice, and enough pasta cooking liquid to coat. Season to taste with salt and generous amount of pepper. Mix in arugula, which will wilt slightly.

MEANWHILE, brush each tuna steak with 1 tablespoon oil; sprinkle with salt and pepper. Sprinkle both sides of steaks with marjoram and remaining 2 teaspoons lemon peel; press gently to adhere.

HEAT remaining 1 tablespoon oil in large nonstick skillet over high heat. Add tuna; sear until crusty and brown outside but still pink inside, about 1½ minutes per side. Transfer tuna to work surface; slice thinly. Divide pasta among plates; top with tuna slices.

Sautéed black cod with shallot-lemon vinaigrette and fresh herb salad

4 SERVINGS *An herb-and-edible-flower salad and Sherry wine vinegar bring sophisticated flavor to this unpretentious dish. Edible flowers can be found at some supermarkets and at farmers' markets. Use only those flowers that have been grown without pesticides. Other meaty fish fillets, such as tuna, swordfish, or halibut, can stand in for the cod.*

- 7 tablespoons olive oil, divided
- ⅓ cup minced shallots
- 2 tablespoons fresh lemon juice
- 1 tablespoon Sherry wine vinegar
- 2 teaspoons finely grated lemon peel
- 6 cups assorted fresh herb leaves (such as Italian parsley, basil, and dill) and edible flowers
- 4 6- to 7-ounce black cod fillets with skin

WHISK 6 tablespoons oil and next 4 ingredients in small bowl. Season vinaigrette to taste with salt and pepper. Place herb and edible flower mixture in large bowl.

HEAT remaining 1 tablespoon oil in large nonstick skillet over medium-high heat. Sprinkle fish with salt and pepper. Add fish to skillet and cook until just opaque in center, about 4 minutes per side. Arrange fish fillets on plates. Spoon 1 tablespoon vinaigrette over each. Toss herb salad with remaining vinaigrette. Serve salad with fish.

COD IN BLACK AND WHITE Black cod isn't actually a cod: This luxurious fish is also known as sablefish. It has an incredibly buttery taste and texture, and is impressive for entertaining.

Miso-glazed black cod on sunflower sprouts

4 SERVINGS *White miso (also known as shiro miso) is a delicately flavored Japanese bean paste. Mirin is a sweet, golden rice wine. Look for both in the Asian foods section of the supermarket, at a natural foods store, or at an Asian market. If you can't find sunflower sprouts, use a couple of handfuls of bean sprouts instead.*

- ⅓ cup white miso (fermented soybean paste)
- ¼ cup plus 1 teaspoon mirin (sweet Japanese rice wine)
- 3 tablespoons unseasoned rice vinegar, divided
- 2 tablespoons minced peeled fresh ginger
- 4 teaspoons Asian sesame oil, divided
- 4 6-ounce black cod fillets
- ½ cup chopped green onions, divided
- 5 ounces sunflower sprouts

WHISK miso, ¼ cup mirin, 2 tablespoons vinegar, ginger, and 2 teaspoons oil in small bowl to blend. Place fish in 8×8×2-inch glass baking dish. Pour miso mixture over; turn to coat. Let stand 30 minutes at room temperature.

PREHEAT broiler. Line baking sheet with foil; brush with 1 teaspoon oil. Place fish on foil; pour marinade over fish. Broil until fish is cooked through and brown in spots, about 6 minutes.

MEANWHILE, mix remaining 1 teaspoon mirin, 1 tablespoon vinegar, 1 teaspoon oil, and ¼ cup green onions in medium bowl. Add sunflower sprouts; toss to coat. Divide salad among 4 plates; top with fish and sprinkle with remaining green onions.

Roasted cod on saffron mashed potatoes

4 SERVINGS *Here's a great new take on fish and saffron. Instead of being mixed into a sauce or used to season rice, the saffron deliciously flavors the mashed potatoes. When you're shopping for the fish, look for Pacific cod. It has the same mild, flaky white flesh as its Atlantic cousin, but unlike Atlantic cod, it's still plentiful and ecologically friendly.*

 2 pounds russet potatoes, peeled, cut into 1½-inch pieces
 ½ cup heavy whipping cream
 ¼ teaspoon crushed saffron threads

 4 6-ounce cod or striped bass fillets (each about ¾ inch thick)
 3 tablespoons olive oil, divided

 1½ teaspoons balsamic vinegar
 1 cup (packed) arugula
 ½ cup mixed fresh herbs (such as basil, dill, and tarragon)

PREHEAT oven to 400°F. Cook potatoes in large saucepan of boiling salted water until tender, about 20 minutes. Drain well. Return potatoes to saucepan and mash. Add cream and saffron; mix to blend. Season to taste with salt and pepper. Cover to keep warm.

MEANWHILE, sprinkle cod with salt and pepper. Heat 2 tablespoons oil in large ovenproof nonstick skillet over high heat. Add cod; cook 2 minutes. Turn cod over. Transfer skillet to oven; bake until cod is opaque in center, about 6 minutes.

MIX vinegar and remaining 1 tablespoon oil in medium bowl. Add arugula and herbs and toss to coat. Season salad to taste with salt and pepper.

MOUND mashed potatoes on 4 plates. Top with fish, then with salad.

Beer-batter fish

4 SERVINGS *Dark beer gives the crispy fish a malty flavor. Make sure the oil is hot enough before you add the battered fish sticks so they don't absorb too much of the oil.*

 1 cup all purpose flour plus additional flour
 1 12-ounce bottle or can porter (a type of dark brown beer)
 1 teaspoon onion powder

 1½ pounds cod or other white fish fillets (such as halibut), cut crosswise into 1-inch-wide strips
    Vegetable oil (for deep-frying)

PLACE 1 cup flour in medium bowl. Gradually whisk in enough beer (1 to 1¼ cups) to form medium-thick smooth batter. Whisk in onion powder.

DO AHEAD *Batter can be made 1 hour ahead. Let stand at room temperature.*

SPRINKLE fish with salt and pepper. Dust with additional flour. Pour enough oil into large saucepan to reach depth of 1½ inches. Heat oil to 375°F. Working in batches, dip fish into batter, coating completely but allowing excess batter to drip back into bowl. Add fish to oil; fry fish until cooked through and batter is deep golden brown, turning occasionally, about 4 minutes. Transfer fish to paper towels to drain. Arrange fish on platter.

Pumpkin-seed-crusted trout with cabbage-cilantro salad

2 SERVINGS *Cilantro, pumpkin seeds, and chili powder give this whole, pan-seared trout a Southwestern flair. Serve with Mexican rice.*

- 3 cups shredded green cabbage
- 1½ cups fresh cilantro leaves, divided
- 3 tablespoons fresh lime juice

- ½ cup natural unsalted shelled pumpkin seeds (pepitas)
- 1 teaspoon chili powder
- 2 whole boneless butterflied trout
- 1 egg, beaten to blend

- 2 tablespoons olive oil

TOSS cabbage, 1 cup cilantro, and lime juice in medium bowl. Season salad to taste with salt and pepper.

COARSELY chop pumpkin seeds in processor (pieces will vary in size). Add remaining ½ cup cilantro and process 10 seconds. Turn mixture out onto plate; mix in chili powder. Brush flesh side of each trout with egg, coating generously. Sprinkle trout with salt and pepper. Sprinkle half of pumpkin seed mixture over flesh side of each trout; press firmly to adhere.

HEAT 1 tablespoon oil in each of 2 large nonstick skillets over medium-high heat. Add 1 trout to each skillet, skin side down. Cook 2 minutes. Turn trout over and cook until browned on bottom and opaque in center, about 2 minutes. Transfer trout to plates; top with cabbage salad.

Trout with tropical fruit salsa and mixed greens

4 SERVINGS *The spicy-sweet vinaigrette dresses both the salsa and the salad. Tilapia can be used as an alternative to the trout.*

- 6 tablespoons vegetable oil, divided
- ¼ cup fresh lime juice
- 1 tablespoon dark brown sugar
- 2 teaspoons minced peeled fresh ginger
- 4⅛ teaspoons Creole seasoning, divided
- 1 cup diced peeled cored pineapple
- 1 cup diced peeled pitted mango
- ½ cup diced red bell pepper
- ½ cup diced red onion
- 6 cups mixed baby greens

- 4 5- to 6-ounce golden trout fillets with skin

WHISK 4 tablespoons oil, lime juice, brown sugar, ginger, and ⅛ teaspoon Creole seasoning in small bowl to blend. Season vinaigrette to taste with salt and pepper. Combine pineapple, mango, bell pepper, and onion in large bowl. Add half of vinaigrette; toss to coat. Season salsa to taste with salt and pepper. Toss greens in medium bowl with remaining vinaigrette.

BRUSH trout fillets with 1 tablespoon oil. Sprinkle with remaining 4 teaspoons Creole seasoning, about ½ teaspoon per side, then salt and pepper. Heat remaining 1 tablespoon oil in large nonstick skillet over medium-high heat. Add trout fillets and cook until just opaque in center and browned, about 2 minutes per side.

DIVIDE greens among 4 plates. Place trout fillets and salsa alongside.

Whole baked trout with mushrooms

4 SERVINGS *The mushroom stuffing keeps the fish moist as it bakes. Serve with an herbed rice pilaf.*

- 7 tablespoons butter, divided, plus additional for buttering baking sheet
- 3 tablespoons vegetable oil
- 12 ounces assorted fresh wild mushrooms (such as portobello, crimini, and stemmed shiitake), sliced (about 6 cups)
- 1½ cups chopped onion
- 3 tablespoons chopped fresh parsley
- 1½ teaspoons dried thyme
- 3 ounces sliced prosciutto, chopped

- 4 12-ounce whole boneless trout
- 2 tablespoons fresh lemon juice

MELT 3 tablespoons butter with oil in heavy large skillet over medium-high heat. Add mushrooms, onion, parsley, and thyme; sauté until mushrooms brown and all liquid evaporates, about 12 minutes. Remove from heat. Stir in prosciutto. Season filling to taste with salt and pepper. Cool.

DO AHEAD *Can be made 1 day ahead. Cover and chill.*

PREHEAT oven to 350°F. Butter large baking sheet. Open each fish flat on work surface. Drizzle with lemon juice. Sprinkle with salt and pepper. Spoon filling over 1 side of each fish, dividing equally. Fold second side over, enclosing filling. Place stuffed fish on prepared sheet. Melt remaining 4 tablespoons butter; brush over outside of fish.

BAKE fish until just opaque in center, about 20 minutes. Transfer to platter.

Crispy trout with wilted watercress

4 SERVINGS *This simply seasoned dish can be paired with a rich side, such as creamy mashed potatoes or risotto. Pass lemon wedges to squeeze over fish.*

- ⅓ cup yellow cornmeal
- 1 teaspoon finely grated lemon peel
- 1 teaspoon salt
- ¾ teaspoon coarsely ground pepper
- 4 boneless trout fillet halves

- 1 tablespoon butter
- 2 tablespoons olive oil, divided

- 1 tablespoon lemon juice
- 1 bunch watercress, trimmed

COMBINE first 4 ingredients in shallow dish. Moisten trout with cold water and dip into cornmeal mixture, turning to coat.

MELT butter with 1 tablespoon oil in large nonstick skillet over medium-high heat. Add trout, skin side down, and cook until coating is brown, about 3 minutes. Turn trout over; cook just until opaque in center, about 2 minutes. Transfer trout to platter (do not clean skillet).

ADD remaining 1 tablespoon oil and lemon juice to same skillet, stirring to scrape up browned bits. Add watercress and cook until barely wilted, tossing with pan drippings, about 30 seconds. Season to taste with salt and pepper. Top trout fillets with watercress.

Grilled swordfish with mint-cucumber salsa

2 SERVINGS; CAN BE DOUBLED *Grill some crusty bread and thick zucchini slices, too, for a complete meal. If you use an English hothouse cucumber, you won't need to seed it.*

- ¾ cup diced seeded peeled cucumber
- 6 tablespoons chopped red onion
- 3 tablespoons chopped fresh mint
- 1 tablespoon white wine vinegar
- 2½ teaspoons olive oil, divided
- 1½ teaspoons sugar

- 2 6- to 7-ounce swordfish steaks (each about 1 inch thick)

MIX cucumber, onion, mint, vinegar, 1½ teaspoons oil, and sugar in medium bowl. Season salsa to taste with salt and pepper.

DO AHEAD *Can be made 2 hours ahead. Let stand at room temperature.*

PREPARE barbecue (medium-high heat) or preheat broiler. Brush swordfish with remaining 1 teaspoon oil; sprinkle with salt and pepper. Grill or broil swordfish until just opaque in center, about 4 minutes per side. Place swordfish on plates. Top with mint-cucumber salsa.

Swordfish with tomato, cucumber, and radish relish

2 SERVINGS; CAN BE DOUBLED *Try the summery relish on roast chicken as well. The swordfish steaks can also be grilled.*

- 2 6- to 7-ounce swordfish steaks
- 4 tablespoons olive oil, divided
- 1 tablespoon plus 2 teaspoons fresh lemon juice

- 2 tomatoes, seeded, diced
- ⅔ cup diced pickling cucumber or English hothouse cucumber
- 5 radishes, diced
- 3 tablespoons chopped fresh cilantro

BRUSH swordfish steaks on both sides with 1 tablespoon oil. Drizzle fish with 1 tablespoon lemon juice. Let stand while preparing relish.

COMBINE tomatoes, cucumber, radishes, cilantro, remaining 3 tablespoons oil, and remaining 2 teaspoons lemon juice in small bowl. Season relish to taste with salt and pepper.

PREHEAT broiler. Sprinkle fish with salt and pepper. Broil until just opaque in center, about 4 minutes per side. Transfer fish to plates. Spoon some of relish over each fish steak; spoon remainder alongside.

Swordfish with salmoriglio sauce

6 SERVINGS Salmoriglio *is a Sicilian sauce made from olive oil, lemon juice, garlic, and herbs. Here it works as both glaze and sauce for grilled swordfish.*

- ½ cup extra-virgin olive oil
- ¼ cup fresh lemon juice
- 2 tablespoons hot water
- 6 tablespoons chopped fresh parsley
- 2 garlic cloves, minced
- 1 tablespoon dried oregano

- 6 6-ounce swordfish fillets (each about 1 inch thick)

PREPARE barbecue (medium-high heat) or pre-heat broiler. Whisk oil in top of double boiler over simmering water until heated through. Gradually whisk in lemon juice, then 2 tablespoons hot water. Add parsley, garlic, and oregano; cook 5 minutes to blend flavors, whisking frequently. Season sauce to taste with salt and pepper. Remove sauce from over simmering water.

LIGHTLY brush swordfish on both sides with sauce. Sprinkle with salt and pepper. Grill or broil fish until just opaque in center, about 4 minutes per side. Transfer to platter. Spoon remaining sauce over.

Broiled swordfish with marmalade-ginger glaze

2 SERVINGS; CAN BE DOUBLED *Bump up the ginger quotient in the sweet-tart glaze by substituting ginger preserves for the orange marmalade.*

- 2 8-ounce swordfish steaks (each about 1½ inches thick)
  Soy sauce
  Asian sesame oil

- 6 tablespoons strained fresh orange juice
- 6 tablespoons strained fresh lemon juice
- 2 tablespoons orange marmalade
- 2 teaspoons minced peeled fresh ginger
- ¼ cup vegetable oil

  Orange slices

BRUSH both sides of swordfish with soy sauce and sesame oil. Sprinkle with pepper. Let stand while preparing glaze.

BOIL orange juice, lemon juice, marmalade, and ginger in small saucepan until reduced to 4 table-spoons, stirring often, about 6 minutes. Cool slight-ly. Mix in vegetable oil.

PREHEAT broiler. Line broiler pan with foil. Place fish on prepared pan. Brush with half of glaze; broil 3 minutes. Turn fish over; brush with remaining glaze and broil until just opaque in center, about 5 minutes. Transfer fish to plates. Garnish with orange slices.

Swordfish with grapefruit-and-rosemary butter sauce

2 SERVINGS; CAN BE DOUBLED *Fresh grapefruit juice gives the pan sauce a sweet-tart citrus flavor. This sauce would also be a good accompaniment to pan-fried chicken.*

- 2 6-ounce swordfish steaks (each about 1 to 1¼ inches thick)
- 3 tablespoons butter, divided

- 2 shallots, minced
- 2 teaspoons chopped fresh rosemary plus additional sprigs for garnish
- ¾ cup fresh grapefruit juice

SPRINKLE fish with salt and pepper. Melt 1 tablespoon butter in heavy medium skillet over medium heat. Add fish and cook until just opaque in center, about 4 minutes per side. Transfer fish to platter. Tent with foil to keep warm.

ADD shallots and rosemary to same skillet; stir over medium heat until shallots soften slightly, about 2 minutes. Add grapefruit juice and any accumulated juices from fish platter. Boil until sauce is syrupy, scraping up any browned bits, about 5 minutes. Remove from heat and swirl in remaining 2 tablespoons butter, 1 tablespoon at a time. Season sauce to taste with salt and pepper. Spoon over fish. Garnish with rosemary sprigs.

Pan-roasted swordfish steaks with mixed-peppercorn butter

4 SERVINGS *A peppercorn medley (often labeled peppercorn mélange) contains black, green, pink, red, and white peppercorns. To make prep work easier, it often comes packaged in a pepper grinder.*

- ¼ cup (½ stick) butter, room temperature
- 2 teaspoons chopped fresh parsley
- 1 garlic clove, minced
- ½ teaspoon ground mixed peppercorns, plus more for sprinkling
- ½ teaspoon finely grated lemon peel

- 1 tablespoon olive oil
- 4 6-ounce swordfish fillets (each about 1 inch thick)

PREHEAT oven to 400°F. Mix butter, parsley, garlic, ½ teaspoon peppercorns, and lemon peel in small bowl to blend. Season to taste with salt.

HEAT oil in heavy large ovenproof skillet over medium-high heat. Sprinkle swordfish with salt and ground peppercorns. Add swordfish to skillet. Cook until browned, about 3 minutes. Turn swordfish over and transfer to oven. Roast until just opaque in center, about 8 minutes longer. Transfer swordfish to plates. Add seasoned butter to same skillet. Cook over medium-high heat, scraping up browned bits, until melted and bubbling. Pour butter sauce over swordfish.

Swordfish with balsamic brown butter sauce

6 SERVINGS *For a sweeter, richer flavor, use a good-quality aged balsamic vinegar. Serve with crusty bread to soak up the sauce.*

- ½ cup (1 stick) unsalted butter
- 3 tablespoons balsamic vinegar
- 1 tablespoon honey
- 1 tablespoon Dijon mustard

- 6 6-ounce swordfish steaks (each about ¾ inch thick)
  Olive oil
- 2 tablespoons drained capers

SIMMER butter in heavy medium saucepan over medium heat until deep golden brown, swirling pan occasionally, about 6 minutes. Remove from heat. Whisk in vinegar, honey, and mustard. Season sauce to taste with salt and pepper.

BRUSH fish with oil; sprinkle with salt and pepper. Heat heavy large skillet over medium-high heat. Add 3 swordfish steaks. Cook just until opaque in center, about 4 minutes per side. Transfer to plates; tent loosely with foil to keep warm. Repeat with remaining fish. Whisk sauce over low heat to re-warm if necessary. Spoon sauce over fish. Sprinkle with capers.

Mahi-mahi with blood orange, avocado, and red onion salsa

2 SERVINGS *This low-fat dish is brilliantly colored with red or pink oranges, green avocados, and deep-purple onions. Because they're more mature, red jalapeños are hotter than the green ones.*

- 1 blood orange, Cara Cara orange, or regular orange
- ½ cup ⅓-inch cubes avocado
- ⅓ cup chopped red onion
- 2 teaspoons minced red jalapeño chile
- 2 teaspoons fresh lime juice

- 2 teaspoons olive oil
- 2 6-ounce mahi-mahi fillets

USING small sharp knife, cut peel and white pith from orange. Working over small bowl, cut between membranes to release segments. Add avocado, onion, jalapeño, and lime juice to oranges in bowl; stir gently to blend. Season salsa to taste with salt.

HEAT oil in heavy medium skillet over medium-high heat. Sprinkle fish with salt and pepper. Add fish to skillet and sauté until brown and cooked through, about 5 minutes per side.

PLACE 1 fish fillet on each of 2 plates. Spoon salsa atop fish.

ORANGE OF A DIFFERENT COLOR The red-fleshed blood oranges are more tart-sweet and pink-fleshed Cara Caras are less acidic than typical navel oranges. You can find them both in the winter months at some supermarkets and at farmers' markets, or at melissas.com.

Grilled mahi-mahi with lime-ginger vinaigrette

4 SERVINGS *Lemongrass is one of the most important ingredients in Southeast Asian cooking. Here, the stalk gives exotic flavor to a light main course. You can find fresh lemongrass at some supermarkets and at Asian markets.*

½ cup canola oil or vegetable oil

½ cup chopped fresh lemongrass (from bottom 4 inches of 2 stalks)

3 tablespoons chopped peeled fresh ginger

2 tablespoons fresh lime juice

2 teaspoons finely grated lime peel

4 7- to 8-ounce mahi-mahi fillets (each about ¾ inch thick)

COOK oil, lemongrass, and ginger in small saucepan over low heat 15 minutes to develop flavor. Cool completely. Strain ginger oil into small bowl.

WHISK ¼ cup ginger oil, lime juice, and lime peel in medium bowl to blend. Season vinaigrette to taste with salt and pepper.

PREPARE barbecue (medium-high heat). Brush remaining ginger oil over fish. Sprinkle with salt and pepper. Grill until fish is just cooked through, about 3 minutes per side. Transfer fish to plates and drizzle with vinaigrette.

Mahi-mahi with macadamia nut crust

2 SERVINGS *A crust of chopped macadamia nuts gives a rich, buttery flavor to the fish fillets. Panko (Japanese breadcrumbs) can be found in the Asian foods section of most supermarkets and at Asian markets.*

2 5-ounce mahi-mahi fillets (each about 1 inch thick)

½ cup fresh lime juice

⅓ cup panko (Japanese breadcrumbs)

¼ cup chopped macadamia nuts

1 teaspoon minced fresh cilantro

4 tablespoons (½ stick) butter, melted, divided

PLACE mahi-mahi in shallow dish. Pour lime juice over. Marinate 1 hour at room temperature, turning fish occasionally.

PREHEAT oven to 350°F. Combine panko, nuts, and cilantro in small bowl. Mix in 2 tablespoons melted butter. Season with salt and generously with pepper. Pour remaining 2 tablespoons butter into shallow baking dish. Remove mahi-mahi from marinade and place in baking dish, turning to coat with butter; sprinkle fish with salt and pepper. Spoon panko mixture atop fish fillets, pressing gently to adhere. Bake until fish is opaque in center, about 10 minutes. Transfer to plates.

INTRODUCING: TILAPIA Tilapia is a small freshwater fish that's currently farmed all over the world. U.S.-farmed tilapia has very little negative impact on the environment because it's raised in re-circulating pools. Tilapia has a firm, flaky texture and sweet mild flavor. It's a good alternative to overfished red snapper.

Steamed tilapia with ginger, lime, and cilantro

2 SERVINGS *This low-fat, low-calorie dish is high in flavor. Look for fish sauce in the Asian foods section of the supermarket or specialty foods store, or at an Asian market.*

 5 tablespoons chopped fresh cilantro, divided
 ¼ cup bottled clam juice
 2 tablespoons fresh lime juice
 2 tablespoons chopped green onion
 1 tablespoon grated peeled fresh ginger
 1 tablespoon soy sauce
 1 tablespoon Asian sesame oil
 1 teaspoon fish sauce (such as nam pla or nuoc nam)

 4 4- to 5-ounce tilapia fillets or two 6-to 7-ounce halibut fillets

MIX 3 tablespoons cilantro and next 7 ingredients in small bowl to blend. Set aside. Pour enough water into large pot to reach depth of 1 inch. Add steamer rack or basket. Top with 9-inch-diameter glass pie dish. Bring water to boil.

PLACE fish in pie dish. Pour cilantro sauce over. Sprinkle with salt and pepper. Cover pot; steam fish just until opaque in center, about 4 to 5 minutes for tilapia and 8 minutes for halibut. Serve with sauce; garnish with remaining 2 tablespoons cilantro.

Baked tilapia with fennel-scented tomato sauce

2 SERVINGS; CAN BE DOUBLED *If you don't have an orange on hand, use lemon peel. Serve with crusty bread to catch all the juices.*

 2 tablespoons olive oil, divided
 ½ large onion, sliced
 1 28-ounce can Italian-style plum tomatoes, drained
 ¼ cup dry white wine
 2 2½x1-inch pieces orange peel (orange part only)
 ¼ teaspoon fennel seeds
 ⅛ teaspoon dried crushed red pepper

 4 4- to 5-ounce tilapia fillets or other firm fish fillets

PREHEAT oven to 400°F. Heat 1 tablespoon oil in heavy medium skillet over medium heat. Add onion and sauté until tender, about 8 minutes. Add tomatoes, wine, orange peel, fennel seeds, and crushed red pepper. Boil gently until reduced to chunky sauce, breaking up tomatoes with spoon, about 12 minutes. Season to taste with salt and pepper.

DO AHEAD *Can be made 1 day ahead. Cover and chill. Rewarm before continuing.*

POUR remaining 1 tablespoon oil into small baking dish. Add fish and turn to coat with oil. Sprinkle with salt and pepper. Spoon warm tomato sauce over fish. Bake until fish is just opaque in center, about 6 to 7 minutes.

Fish and vegetables with pesto baked in foil packets

4 SERVINGS *On your next camping trip, bring along this recipe—the foil packets can easily be cooked on the grill. If you prefer to make your own pesto, the Classic Pesto on page 320 can be used instead of purchased pesto.*

⅔ cup purchased pesto

2 tablespoons fresh lemon juice

¼ teaspoon hot pepper sauce

4 5- to 6-ounce tilapia or black cod fillets

16 asparagus spears, each trimmed
to 4-inch length

3 large plum tomatoes, coarsely chopped

2 yellow crookneck squash,
thinly sliced on diagonal

PREHEAT oven to 350°F. Mix pesto, lemon juice, and hot pepper sauce in small bowl. Arrange four 12×12-inch pieces of heavy-duty foil on work surface. Place 1 fish fillet in center of each. Sprinkle fish lightly with salt and pepper. Spread each fillet with 1 tablespoon pesto mixture. Top each fillet with asparagus, tomatoes, and squash, then dollop with remaining pesto mixture. Fold sides of foil over fish and vegetables, covering completely; seal packets closed.

TRANSFER foil packets to large rimmed baking sheet. Bake until fish is just opaque in center and vegetables are crisp-tender, about 20 minutes.

Sole piccata with grapes and capers

4 SERVINGS *Piccata has come to mean the lemon-caper sauce that was traditionally used with veal, but which is equally delicious with chicken or sole. Here, the pan sauce has a bit of sweetness, thanks to the grapes and grape juice.*

2 tablespoons olive oil

4 5- to 6-ounce Dover sole or petrale sole fillets
All purpose flour

½ cup seedless red grapes, cut in half

¼ cup white grape juice

¼ cup dry white wine

2 tablespoons (¼ stick) butter

1 tablespoon drained capers

1 tablespoon chopped fresh parsley

HEAT oil in large nonstick skillet over medium-high heat. Sprinkle fish with salt and pepper; dust both sides with flour. Add to skillet; cook until browned and just opaque in center, about 2 minutes per side. Transfer fish to platter. Add grapes, grape juice, wine, and butter to same skillet. Bring mixture to boil, whisking up any browned bits. Add capers and parsley. Simmer sauce until slightly thickened, about 3 minutes. Season to taste with salt and pepper. Spoon sauce over fish.

Fried catfish with chive-ginger sauce

2 SERVINGS *Serve with steamed rice to soak up the Asian-flavored sauce. Rainbow trout fillets would be a good substitute for the catfish.*

2½ tablespoons seasoned rice vinegar

1½ tablespoons light soy sauce

1 tablespoon fresh lime juice

1 teaspoon finely grated peeled fresh ginger

1 garlic clove, pressed

1 teaspoon (packed) golden brown sugar

4 tablespoons chopped fresh chives, divided, plus additional whole chives for garnish

2 6- to 7-ounce catfish fillets
    All purpose flour

    Peanut oil (for frying)

WHISK first 6 ingredients in small bowl to blend. Mix in 3 tablespoons chopped chives.

DO AHEAD *Can be made 1 day ahead. Cover and chill.*

PRESS remaining 1 tablespoon chopped chives onto both sides of fish. Sprinkle fish with salt and pepper. Dredge fish lightly in flour.

POUR enough oil into heavy large skillet to reach depth of ¼ inch; heat oil over medium-high heat. Add fish fillets to skillet and cook until crisp outside and just opaque in center, about 3 minutes per side. Transfer catfish to paper towels to drain. Place catfish on plates. Pour sauce over. Garnish catfish with whole chives.

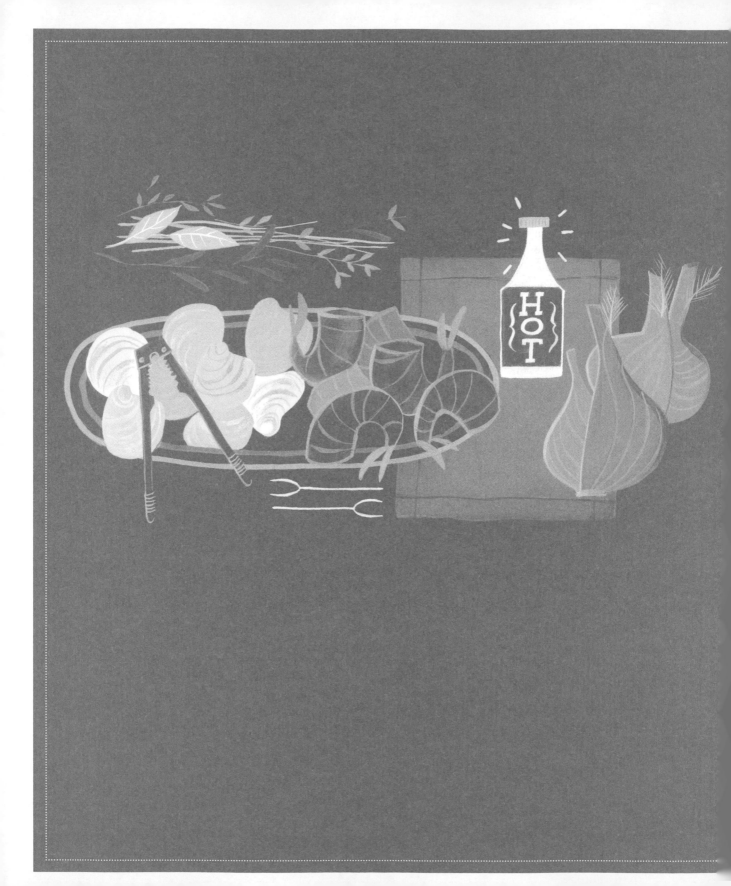

shrimpand moreshellfish

SHRIMP

Grilled Shrimp with
Pineapple Salsa

Jerked Shrimp with Melon Salsa

Grilled Shrimp with
Cucumber-Kiwi Salsa

Grilled Brined Shrimp
with Garlic Oil

Grilled Shrimp with Ponzu Sauce

Shrimp and Vegetable Brochettes

Mixed Seafood Grill with
Paprika-Lemon Dressing

Shrimp with Spicy
Southeast Asian Pesto

Shrimp with Ginger-Herb Butter

Sautéed Shrimp with
Lemon-Garlic Butter

Andouille Sausage and Shrimp
with Creole Mustard Sauce

Moroccan Shrimp and
Red Onion Sauté

Pan-Roasted Sizzling Shrimp

Shrimp with Shallot-Tarragon
Sauce on Wilted Spinach

Soy-Sake Shrimp with
Ginger Aioli

Shrimp with Fennel,
Dill, and Feta

Shrimp Palermo

Indian Curried Shrimp

Garlic-Roasted Shrimp with Red
Peppers and Smoked Paprika

Szechuan Shrimp with Peppers

Broiled Shrimp with
Mustard and Tarragon

Shrimp with Romesco Sauce

Sautéed Shrimp with
Grits and Lime Butter

Singapore Shrimp Stir-Fry

SCALLOPS

Pan-Seared Sea Scallops on
Red Onion Marmalade

Seared Scallops with Fresh
Fennel Salad and Kumquat-
Tarragon Vinaigrette

Tarragon Scallop Gratins

Sautéed Sea Scallops with
Lemon-Dill Sauce

Sautéed Scallops with Shiitake
Mushrooms and Broccoli

Scallops with Hazelnuts and
Brown Butter Vinaigrette

Seared Coriander Scallops
with Bok Choy and Hoisin

Sautéed Scallops with
Cherry Tomatoes, Green
Onions, and Parsley

Spicy Stir-Fried Brown Rice
with Broccolini and Scallops

Grilled Skewered Scallops
and Apricots with Honey-
Mustard Dressing

CLAMS AND MUSSELS

Portuguese Clams with
Linguiça and Tomatoes

Steamed Spicy Garlic
Clams with Pasta

Mussels with Pernod and Cream

LOBSTER AND CRAB

Steamed Lobster with
Lemon-Herb Butter

Roasted Lobster Tails with
Shallots, Parsley, and Lemon

Grilled Surf-and-Turf with
Spicy Garlic-Shallot Butter

Spicy Oven-Roasted Orange-
Scented Dungeness Crab

Crab and Avocado Tostadas

Cayenne-Spiked Crab Cakes

Asian-Style Crab and
Shrimp Cakes

tool kit Shrimp, lobsters, scallops, clams, and mussels are all very tender and quick-cooking, which make them ideal for spontaneous meals. But they're touchy, too—overcook them, and those succulent morsels turn tough and rubbery. So it's best to know a little bit about each of them before you throw them on the grill, in the pot, or on the stove.

SHRIMP AND LOBSTER

Most of the shrimp recipes in this chapter call for **large peeled and deveined shrimp.** If large shrimp are unavailable, your next best choice is jumbo or extra-large shrimp. Peeling and deveining shrimp takes some time, but you can buy shrimp that are already peeled and deveined. Most upscale markets sell them this way, but if they don't, ask the fishmonger to peel them for you (give advance notice for this request). They may cost a bit more than shrimp with their shells on, but they'll save you time and mess. You can also buy bags of frozen shrimp, which are both convenient and of the same good quality as most shrimp sold in markets, which are often frozen and thawed anyway.

Bay shrimp (also known as miniature shrimp; they come about 100 to the pound) are almost always sold already cooked, and are especially good in salads or mixed-seafood dishes.

Even a luxurious **lobster** dinner can be fast and easy, particularly when you use convenient frozen uncooked lobster tails. Cooking a whole live lobster makes for the freshest meal imaginable and is surprisingly easy to do. Both shrimp and lobster "tell" you when they're done cooking: The shells turn from gray to pink or bright red. ➡

SCALLOPS

Pan-seared scallops make an impressive main course and couldn't be easier. For a quick meal, use **sea scallops,** which are about three times the size of bay scallops. Although many markets sell scallops that already have the side muscle removed, it's important to check each one for a small strip along the side and gently remove it; when cooked, the muscle gets very tough. Pat the scallops dry so they'll brown rather than steam. Sprinkle them with salt and pepper, add them to a hot sauté pan with some butter, and cook until they're dark golden brown and caramelized on the outside, by which time they will be just done in the center. Then transfer them to a warm plate and deglaze all the tasty pan drippings to create an easy sauce right in the same pan. Here are some quick sauces to spoon over the scallops:

— Set the seared scallops over a bed of mixed baby greens, then deglaze the pan with balsamic vinegar and spoon the sauce over the scallops and salad.
— Add some fresh lemon juice or dry white wine and capers to the pan, then whisk in a knob of butter and some parsley.
— Simmer some cream in the pan with a little Dijon mustard, curry paste, or smoked paprika until slightly thickened.

Bay scallops, on the other hand, are best when lightly sautéed and mixed into pastas, rice dishes, chowders, stews, and stir-fries, where they can be enjoyed in every bite.

MUSSELS AND CLAMS

Mussels and clams get a bad rap for being sandy and gritty. Look for those that are farmed rather than wild. Not only are they environmentally friendly options, but they are also grit-free. While mussels and clams are interchangeable in most recipes, clam shells are heavier than mussel shells, so you'll need to consider this weight difference when substituting one for the other.

The fuzzy little protrusion between the straight-sided mussel shells is called the beard. Grasp the beard and pull it off *just before cooking* the mussels— don't remove the beards too far in advance since removing them can kill the mussels, which should be alive before cooking.

Mussels and clams let you know when they're done cooking: Their tightly closed shells begin to open. Discard any that haven't opened by the end of the cooking time; they're no good.

SHRIMP

Grilled shrimp with pineapple salsa

6 SERVINGS *The salsa would also be delicious with two peeled, seeded mangoes cut into wedges in place of the pineapple. Have six metal skewers on hand— you'll thread the shrimp onto them for grilling.*

> Nonstick vegetable oil spray
> 4 tablespoons olive oil, divided
> 4 tablespoons fresh lime juice, divided
> 36 uncooked large shrimp, peeled, deveined
> ½ large pineapple, peeled, cut into ½-inch-thick slices, cored
> ¾ cup chopped red onion
> ¼ cup chopped fresh cilantro
> 2 tablespoons chopped seeded jalapeño chile

SPRAY grill rack with nonstick spray; prepare barbecue (medium-high heat). Whisk 2 tablespoons oil and 2 tablespoons lime juice in small bowl to blend; add shrimp and toss to coat. Let marinate 15 minutes, tossing occasionally.

MEANWHILE, sprinkle pineapple slices with salt and pepper. Grill pineapple until just tender, about 4 minutes per side. Transfer to work surface; cut pineapple into ½-inch pieces. Place in bowl; mix in onion, cilantro, jalapeño, remaining 2 tablespoons oil and remaining 2 tablespoons lime juice. Season salsa with salt and pepper.

THREAD shrimp on 6 metal skewers. Sprinkle shrimp with salt and pepper.

GRILL shrimp until just opaque in center, about 5 minutes. Serve with salsa.

Make it quick Be sure not to marinate fish or seafood too long in anything containing acid, such as citrus juice or vinegar. One hour should be plenty; any longer and the raw seafood will become opaque and firm, and no longer suitable for cooking. In fact, this longer marinating technique is the secret behind the delicious South American appetizer called *ceviche*, in which raw fish and seafood are "cooked" in citrus juice.

Jerked shrimp with melon salsa

2 SERVINGS *Jerk seasoning, a blend of hot chiles, herbs, and spices, originated in Jamaica. Packaged jerk seasoning is now available in the spice section of most supermarkets and at specialty foods stores. You'll also need metal skewers for grilling the shrimp. Serve this with steamed rice and a green salad.*

12 uncooked large shrimp, peeled, deveined

3 tablespoons olive oil

4 teaspoons fresh lime juice, divided

2 teaspoons jerk or Caribbean-style
 seasoning blend

¾ cup diced peeled seeded cantaloupe melon

¾ cup diced peeled seeded honeydew melon

¼ cup chopped fresh cilantro

¼ cup diced red onion

PREPARE barbecue (medium heat). Toss shrimp, oil, 2 teaspoons lime juice, and jerk seasoning blend in medium bowl. Let marinate 10 minutes.

MEANWHILE, toss cantaloupe, honeydew, cilantro, red onion, and remaining 2 teaspoons lime juice in medium bowl. Season salsa with salt and pepper.

THREAD shrimp onto metal skewers. Grill until just opaque in center, about 5 minutes, turning once. Serve, passing salsa separately.

Grilled shrimp with cucumber-kiwi salsa

6 SERVINGS *This colorful salsa is also a delicious topping for grilled scallops. You can peel the cucumber or leave it unpeeled, as you prefer.*

4½ teaspoons fresh lime juice

1½ teaspoons chopped seeded jalapeño chile

1 teaspoon minced peeled fresh ginger

½ teaspoon finely grated lime peel

1 cup chopped peeled kiwi (about ½ pound)

1 cup chopped seeded cucumber

¼ cup thinly sliced green onions

1 tablespoon chopped fresh mint

2 pounds uncooked large shrimp,
 peeled, deveined

2 tablespoons olive oil

WHISK first 4 ingredients in medium bowl to blend. Add kiwi, cucumber, green onions, and mint; toss to coat. Season salsa to taste with salt and pepper.

DO AHEAD *Can be made 4 hours ahead. Cover; chill.*

PREPARE barbecue (medium-high heat). Place shrimp and oil in large bowl. Sprinkle with salt and pepper; toss to coat.

GRILL shrimp until just opaque in center, about 2 minutes per side. Serve with salsa.

Grilled brined shrimp with garlic oil

8 APPETIZER SERVINGS OR 4 MAIN-COURSE SERVINGS
This brine, or saltwater mixture, not only infuses the shrimp with the flavors of the lemon, wine, and herbs, but also ensures that the shrimp will be juicy and tender once they are grilled. Ciabatta is a rustic, chewy bread and is available at many supermarkets and bakeries.

8 cups ice water, divided
⅓ cup coarse kosher salt
1 cup dry white wine
6 bay leaves, divided
2 lemons; 1 chopped, 1 cut into wedges
½ teaspoon whole black peppercorns
2 pounds uncooked large shrimp with shells

¾ cup extra-virgin olive oil
4 garlic cloves, chopped

1 ciabatta bread, sliced

STIR 1 cup water and kosher salt in small saucepan over high heat until salt dissolves, about 5 minutes. Transfer salt water to large bowl. Stir in wine, 2 bay leaves, chopped lemon, peppercorns, and remaining 7 cups ice water. Add shrimp. Chill at least 15 minutes and up to ½ hour.

MEANWHILE, prepare barbecue (medium-high heat). Whisk oil and garlic in small bowl to blend.

DRAIN shrimp, rinse, and drain well. Using kitchen scissors, cut shells down center of back side and devein, leaving shells intact. Grill shrimp in shells until charred and just opaque, 3 to 4 minutes per side. Grill bread until beginning to brown, about 2 minutes per side.

TRANSFER shrimp to another large bowl. Add half of garlic oil and toss to coat. Mound shrimp on platter. Garnish with remaining 4 bay leaves and lemon wedges. Serve with grilled bread and remaining garlic oil.

BRINE MAGIC Brining, or soaking in a saltwater solution that can contain sugar, herbs, and spices, is a wonderful method for adding flavor and moisture to meats and seafood. It's simple osmosis—the saltier water soaks through the membranes of the protein until a more balanced level is reached. The result is a savory, succulent dish.

Grilled shrimp with ponzu sauce

2 SERVINGS *Ponzu is a citrus- and soy-sauce-based dipping sauce popular at many Japanese restaurants. Mirin can be found in the Asian foods section of many supermarkets and at Asian markets. Try substituting sake for the mirin, or lime juice for the lemon juice.*

3 tablespoons soy sauce
3 tablespoons mirin (sweet Japanese rice wine)
3 tablespoons fresh lemon juice
2 tablespoons olive oil
1 tablespoon chopped peeled fresh ginger
1 teaspoon finely grated lemon peel
10 uncooked extra-large shrimp, peeled, deveined

2 cups thinly sliced bok choy or Napa cabbage

PREPARE barbecue (medium-high heat). Whisk first 6 ingredients in small bowl. Add shrimp and toss to coat; let marinate 10 minutes.

DRAIN marinade into small saucepan and boil 1 minute; set aside. Grill shrimp until just opaque in center, turning occasionally, about 4 minutes.

DIVIDE bok choy between 2 plates and drizzle with some of warm marinade. Top with shrimp. Serve, passing remaining marinade separately, if desired.

Shrimp and vegetable brochettes

2 SERVINGS *Substitute metal skewers for the wooden skewers, if you like. They are available in many fun decorative styles and have the extra time-saving bonus of not requiring any soaking.*

  5 **tablespoons olive oil**

2½ **tablespoons fresh lemon juice**

  1 **tablespoon Dijon mustard**

  ¾ **teaspoon finely grated lemon peel**

12 **uncooked large shrimp, peeled, deveined**

  4 **10- to 12-inch-long wooden skewers, soaked in water 30 minutes**

  1 **medium zucchini, trimmed, cut into ½-inch-thick rounds**

  1 **red bell pepper, cut into 1½-inch squares**

  6 **green onions, trimmed**

PREPARE barbecue (medium-high heat). Whisk first 4 ingredients in small bowl. Season marinade to taste with salt and pepper. Add shrimp to marinade; toss to coat. Marinate shrimp 10 minutes. Strain marinade into saucepan and bring to boil; remove from heat. Thread 6 shrimp on each of 2 skewers. Alternate zucchini and bell pepper on 2 remaining skewers. Brush vegetable skewers and green onions with some of marinade; sprinkle with salt and pepper.

GRILL vegetable skewers, shrimp skewers, and green onions until just cooked through, turning occasionally and basting with marinade, about 12 minutes for vegetables, 4 minutes for shrimp, and 3 minutes for green onions. Remove skewers and green onions from grill.

Mixed seafood grill with paprika-lemon dressing

6 SERVINGS *Serve with grilled pita breads and an heirloom tomato salad. Cleaned squid is available in the frozen seafood section of many supermarkets.*

  7 **tablespoons olive oil, divided**

  ¼ **cup fresh lemon juice plus lemon wedges for garnish**

  2 **tablespoons chopped fresh Italian parsley**

  3 **garlic cloves, sliced thinly**

  2 **teaspoons paprika**

     Nonstick vegetable oil spray

  2 **pounds 1-inch-thick firm white fish fillets (such as halibut), cut crosswise into 2-inch-wide strips**

  2 **pounds uncooked large shrimp, peeled, deveined, tails left intact**

  2 **pounds cleaned fresh or thawed frozen squid, each body cut open on 1 long side and scored lightly (tentacles reserved for another use)**

WHISK 4 tablespoons oil, lemon juice, parsley, garlic, and paprika in small bowl. Season dressing with salt and pepper.

DO AHEAD *Cover and chill up to 6 hours. Bring to room temperature before using.*

SPRAY grill rack with nonstick spray. Prepare barbecue (medium-high heat). Arrange seafood on baking sheets. Drizzle with remaining 3 tablespoons oil and turn to coat; sprinkle with salt and pepper. Transfer seafood to grill. Cook until just opaque in center, about 4 minutes per side for fish, 2 minutes per side for shrimp, and 30 seconds per side for squid. Arrange on platter. Spoon dressing over. Garnish with lemon wedges.

Shrimp with spicy Southeast Asian pesto

6 SERVINGS *Some of the Asian pesto is smeared under the shell before the shrimp is grilled, keeping both the flavors and all of the juices from dripping away.*

2½ tablespoons peanut oil

6 garlic cloves, finely chopped

2 tablespoons finely chopped seeded jalapeño chiles

2 tablespoons finely chopped fresh basil

2 tablespoons finely chopped peeled fresh ginger

2 teaspoons sake

2 teaspoons salt

1 teaspoon Asian sesame oil

½ teaspoon freshly ground pepper

1½ pounds uncooked large shrimp with shells

MIX first 9 ingredients in blender until paste forms.

DO AHEAD *Can be made 1 day ahead. Cover and chill.*

USING small sharp knife or scissors, cut each shrimp shell along back. Remove vein, keeping shell intact. Pat dry. Spoon ½ teaspoon paste mixture under each shrimp shell. Cover and chill 1 hour.

PREPARE barbecue (high heat). Grill shrimp until just opaque in center, about 3 minutes per side.

Shrimp with ginger-herb butter

4 SERVINGS *This can be the centerpiece of an easy Asian-inspired meal: Start with some purchased avocado rolls from the sushi counter at your supermarket. Serve the shrimp with braised baby bok choy and steamed rice. Green tea ice cream and almond cookies would make a nice finish.*

6 tablespoons (¾ stick) butter, room temperature

¼ cup (packed) chopped fresh cilantro

3 garlic cloves, minced

2 tablespoons chopped fresh chives

2 teaspoons minced peeled fresh ginger

2 teaspoons Asian sesame oil

24 uncooked large shrimp, peeled, deveined

  Lime wedges

MIX first 6 ingredients in small bowl to blend; season to taste with salt and pepper. Brush 13×9×2-inch metal pan with some of seasoned butter. Arrange shrimp in single layer in prepared pan; sprinkle lightly with salt and pepper. Spread remaining seasoned butter over shrimp, dividing equally.

DO AHEAD *Can be prepared 1 day ahead. Cover and chill. Let stand at room temperature 30 minutes before continuing.*

PREHEAT broiler. Broil shrimp just until opaque in center, about 2 minutes. Transfer shrimp to plates. Spoon butter from pan over shrimp. Serve with lime wedges.

Sautéed shrimp with lemon-garlic butter

4 SERVINGS *Whisking the butter into the garlic-wine reduction one piece at a time over low heat ensures that the sauce will stay emulsified. If the mixture begins to look broken, or curdled, remove the skillet from the heat and continue whisking in the butter. A splash of cream can also help to hold the sauce together. Serve the shrimp with orzo with fresh herbs and steamed asparagus.*

- ½ cup dry white wine
- 8 garlic cloves, minced
- 2 tablespoons white wine vinegar
- ½ cup (1 stick) chilled butter, cut into ½-inch pieces
- 2 tablespoons fresh lemon juice

- 2 tablespoons olive oil
- 1½ pounds uncooked large shrimp, peeled, deveined
- 2 tablespoons finely grated lemon peel
- 1 tablespoon chopped fresh chives

BOIL wine, garlic, and vinegar in small saucepan until mixture is reduced to ¼ cup, about 4 minutes. Reduce heat to low. Whisk in butter, 1 piece at a time, allowing butter to melt before adding more. Remove from heat. Whisk in lemon juice. Season with salt and pepper. Cover and keep warm.

HEAT oil in large nonstick skillet over high heat. Sprinkle shrimp with salt and pepper. Add shrimp to skillet and sauté until just opaque in center, about 3 minutes. Transfer shrimp to plates. Drizzle lemon-garlic butter over. Sprinkle with lemon peel and chives.

Andouille sausage and shrimp with Creole mustard sauce

4 TO 6 SERVINGS *Creole or Cajun seasoning can be found in the spice section of many supermarkets and at specialty foods stores. If you'd like to tame the heat in this recipe (or pump it up), reduce (or increase) the seasoning and mustard to your liking.*

- 1 pound uncooked large shrimp, peeled, deveined
- 1 tablespoon Creole or Cajun seasoning
- 2 tablespoons vegetable oil, divided
- 1 pound andouille sausage, cut crosswise on diagonal into ¾-inch-thick pieces
- 1 large onion, halved, thinly sliced
- 1 large red bell pepper, cut into ⅓-inch-wide strips
- 1 tablespoon chopped fresh thyme
- 1 cup low-salt chicken broth
- 5 tablespoons Creole mustard (such as Zatarain's)
- 2 teaspoons red wine vinegar

TOSS shrimp with Creole seasoning in medium bowl to coat. Heat 1 tablespoon oil in heavy large skillet over high heat. Add sausage pieces, cut side down. Cook until browned on both sides, about 5 minutes. Transfer sausage to bowl. Add shrimp to skillet; cook until browned and just opaque in center, turning once, about 3 minutes. Transfer to bowl with sausage. Add remaining 1 tablespoon oil, onion, bell pepper, and thyme to skillet. Sauté until vegetables are beginning to soften, about 5 minutes. Add broth, mustard, and vinegar. Stir until sauce thickens, about 2 minutes. Return sausage and shrimp to skillet. Simmer until heated through, stirring occasionally, about 1 minute. Season with salt and pepper.

Moroccan shrimp and red onion sauté

2 SERVINGS *Moroccan flavors (coriander, cumin, ginger, cinnamon) meet Southeast Asian heat in this sauté. Hot chili sauce, such as* sriracha, *can be found in the Asian foods section of many supermarkets and at Asian markets. Or use your favorite hot pepper sauce. Serve with couscous.*

- 1 teaspoon whole coriander seeds
- ¾ teaspoon cardamom seeds
- ¾ teaspoon cumin seeds
- 3 tablespoons olive oil
- 1 tablespoon minced peeled fresh ginger
- 2 teaspoons hot chili sauce
- ¾ teaspoon ground cinnamon
- ½ teaspoon honey
- 12 uncooked large shrimp, peeled, deveined, tails left intact
- 1 red onion, halved, peeled, each half cut into 4 wedges through root end

    Fresh cilantro leaves (optional)

TOAST coriander seeds, cardamom seeds, and cumin seeds in small skillet over medium-high heat until fragrant, shaking skillet, about 1 minute. Coarsely grind spices in mortar and pestle or spice grinder. Transfer to large bowl; mix in oil, ginger, chili sauce, cinnamon, and honey. Season with salt and pepper. Add shrimp and onion; toss to coat.

HEAT large nonstick skillet over medium-high heat. Add onion; cook until blackened in spots, turning occasionally, about 5 minutes. Move onion wedges to side of pan. Add shrimp and marinade; sauté until shrimp are just cooked through, about 3 minutes. Transfer shrimp and onion to plates. Top with cilantro, if desired.

Pan-roasted sizzling shrimp

2 SERVINGS *Three different kinds of sweet and hot peppers are combined in this pretty shrimp dish: a red bell pepper for color and sweetness, a green Anaheim chile pepper with a mild amount of heat, and spicy jalapeño for a bit of punch.*

- 2 tablespoons olive oil
- 12 uncooked large shrimp, peeled, deveined
- 1 red bell pepper, seeded, cut into thin strips
- 1 fresh Anaheim chile, seeded, cut into thin strips
- ½ jalapeño chile, cut lengthwise, seeded, cut into thin strips
- ½ small onion, cut into thin strips (about 1 cup)
- 1 garlic clove, minced
- ½ teaspoon ground cumin
    Chopped fresh cilantro

HEAT oil in heavy large skillet over high heat. Add shrimp; sauté until outside is pink but center is still translucent, about 2 minutes. Add bell pepper, both chiles, and onion; sauté until peppers begin to brown and shrimp are opaque in center, about 3 minutes. Add garlic and cumin; stir to coat. Season to taste with salt and pepper. Sprinkle with cilantro.

Shrimp with shallot-tarragon sauce on wilted spinach

2 SERVINGS *For a simple variation, try using escarole or chopped Swiss chard leaves instead of spinach.*

10	uncooked large shrimp, peeled, deveined
¼	cup chopped fresh Italian parsley
3	tablespoons olive oil, divided
2	tablespoons fresh lemon juice, divided
5	teaspoons chopped fresh tarragon, divided
2	teaspoons minced peeled fresh ginger, divided
½	cup finely chopped shallots (about 2 large)
2	tablespoons (¼ stick) butter
2	tablespoons heavy whipping cream
1	6-ounce package fresh baby spinach

TOSS shrimp, parsley, 1 tablespoon oil, 1 tablespoon lemon juice, 3 teaspoons tarragon, and 1 teaspoon ginger in medium bowl. Sprinkle mixture with salt and pepper.

HEAT 1 tablespoon oil in large nonstick skillet over medium heat. Add shallots; sauté 5 minutes. Add shrimp mixture; sauté until shrimp are almost cooked through, about 3 minutes. Add butter and cream; bring just to simmer. Add remaining 1 teaspoon ginger. Season with salt and pepper. Set shrimp aside.

HEAT remaining 1 tablespoon oil in another large nonstick skillet over high heat. Add spinach and remaining 1 tablespoon lemon juice; sprinkle with salt and pepper. Toss until just wilted, about 25 seconds. Mound spinach in center of plates; surround with shrimp and sauce. Sprinkle shrimp with remaining 2 teaspoons tarragon.

Soy-sake shrimp with ginger aioli

6 FIRST-COURSE OR 4 MAIN-COURSE SERVINGS
Traditionally, aioli is garlic mayonnaise, but here the garlic is replaced with fresh ginger. The result is a dipping sauce with a bright twist.

½	cup soy sauce
2	green onions, chopped
6	tablespoons olive oil, divided
2	tablespoons unseasoned rice vinegar
2	tablespoons sake
1	tablespoon golden brown sugar
3	garlic cloves, chopped
24	uncooked large shrimp, peeled, deveined
1	cup mayonnaise
1	tablespoon chopped peeled fresh ginger
	Cooked white rice

WHISK soy sauce, green onions, 4 tablespoons oil, vinegar, sake, brown sugar, and garlic in 13×9×2-inch glass baking dish. Add shrimp and toss to coat. Chill at least 30 minutes and up to 1 hour, turning shrimp occasionally.

BLEND mayonnaise and ginger in food processor until smooth. Transfer ginger aioli to small bowl and chill.

DRAIN marinade from shrimp into small saucepan and bring to boil; remove from heat. Whisk 2 tablespoons boiled marinade into ginger aioli; reserve remaining boiled marinade.

HEAT remaining 2 tablespoons oil in heavy large skillet over medium-high heat. Add shrimp; sauté until just opaque in center, about 4 minutes. Mound rice in center of plates. Arrange shrimp around rice; drizzle with ginger aioli. Serve, passing remaining marinade separately.

Shrimp with fennel, dill, and feta

4 SERVINGS *The full-flavored oil from sun-dried tomatoes is put to good use in this Greek-inspired dish. Serve with an orzo salad.*

- ½ cup sliced oil-packed sun-dried tomatoes, 2 tablespoons oil reserved
- 2 medium fennel bulbs, trimmed, halved, thinly sliced crosswise (about 3½ cups)
- 2 garlic cloves, minced
- 1⅓ pounds uncooked large shrimp, peeled, deveined, tails left intact
- 2 tablespoons chopped fresh dill
- ⅔ cup crumbled feta cheese

HEAT 2 tablespoons oil from sun-dried tomatoes in large nonstick skillet over medium-high heat. Add fennel; sauté 3 minutes. Add sun-dried tomatoes and garlic and stir 1 minute. Sprinkle shrimp with salt and pepper. Add shrimp to skillet and cook until just opaque in center, about 1 minute per side. Season to taste with salt and pepper. Sprinkle with dill, then feta.

Shrimp Palermo

2 SERVINGS *Named after the city in Sicily, this dish brings together fennel and oranges, two classic Sicilian ingredients, in a most delicious way.*

- 1½ tablespoons olive oil
- 1½ cups sliced fennel bulb plus chopped fronds for garnish
- ½ pound uncooked large shrimp, peeled, deveined
- 3 large garlic cloves, minced
- ⅓ cup dry vermouth
- 3 tablespoons fresh orange juice
- 1 teaspoon finely grated orange peel

HEAT oil in heavy medium skillet over medium heat. Add sliced fennel; sauté until beginning to soften and color, about 5 minutes. Add shrimp and garlic; sauté 1 minute. Cover skillet; cook until shrimp are just pink, about 2 minutes. Add vermouth, orange juice, and orange peel to skillet. Increase heat to medium-high; cook uncovered until sauce is slightly reduced and shrimp are opaque in center, stirring often, about 3 minutes longer. Season to taste with salt and pepper. Transfer shrimp to plates; top with sauce. Sprinkle with fennel fronds.

FENNEL FRONDS Fennel bulbs purchased at farmers' markets are generally sold untrimmed, giving you plenty of airy anise-scented fronds to chop up for garnishes. If you are purchasing fennel at the supermarket, where the bulbs are usually trimmed, look for bulbs with the most fronds still attached.

Indian curried shrimp

2 SERVINGS *A truly fast and easy curry that's also rich with flavor. Serve this over aromatic jasmine rice. Unsweetened coconut milk can be found at some supermarkets, natural foods stores, and at Southeast Asian and Indian markets.*

1 tablespoon olive oil
1 small onion, chopped
1 tablespoon minced peeled fresh ginger
1 tablespoon curry powder
1 14-ounce can unsweetened coconut milk
8 uncooked large shrimp, peeled, deveined
2 tablespoons chopped fresh cilantro

HEAT oil in heavy large skillet over medium-high heat. Add onion; sauté until soft, about 4 minutes. Add ginger and curry powder; sauté 1 minute. Stir in coconut milk. Simmer 2 minutes. Add shrimp and simmer until just opaque in center, about 3 minutes. Stir in cilantro. Season with salt and pepper.

Garlic-roasted shrimp with red peppers and smoked paprika

8 SERVINGS *Sweet (not spicy) smoked paprika is sometimes labeled Pimentón Dulce or Pimentón de La Vera Dulce, and can be found at some supermarkets and specialty foods stores, and online at tienda.com.*

Nonstick vegetable oil spray
3 pounds uncooked jumbo shrimp, peeled, deveined, tails left intact
3 red bell peppers, cut into 1½-inch triangles
6 tablespoons olive oil
6 garlic cloves, minced
2½ tablespoons sweet smoked paprika
1 teaspoon cayenne pepper

1½ tablespoons chopped fresh oregano
½ cup dry Sherry

SPRAY two 13×9×2-inch metal baking pans with nonstick spray. Mix shrimp, peppers, oil, garlic, smoked paprika, and cayenne in large bowl to coat. Divide mixture between prepared pans, arranging shrimp in single layer. Sprinkle with salt and pepper.

DO AHEAD *Can be prepared 8 hours ahead. Cover and chill.*

PREHEAT oven to 400°F. Roast shrimp and peppers 10 minutes. Turn shrimp; sprinkle with oregano. Roast until shrimp are just opaque in center, about 7 minutes longer. Transfer shrimp and peppers to platter. Place pans over 2 burners on medium heat. Add half of Sherry to each; boil until sauce is reduced by half, scraping up browned bits, about 2 minutes. Drizzle sauce over shrimp and serve warm or at room temperature.

Szechuan shrimp with peppers

4 SERVINGS *Chili-garlic sauce can be found in the Asian foods section of many supermarkets and at Asian markets. Serve over steamed rice.*

- 1 **pound uncooked large shrimp, peeled, deveined**
- 2 **tablespoons dry Sherry**
- 1½ **tablespoons minced peeled fresh ginger**
- 2 **garlic cloves, minced**
- ½ **teaspoon dried crushed red pepper**

- ½ **cup low-salt chicken broth**
- 2 **teaspoons cornstarch**
- 1½ **tablespoons soy sauce**
- 1 **tablespoon chili-garlic sauce**
- 1 **teaspoon sugar**

- 1 **tablespoon peanut oil**
- 1 **red bell pepper, cut into 1-inch diamonds**
- 6 **green onions, cut into ½-inch pieces**

COMBINE first 5 ingredients in large bowl; toss to coat. Cover; let stand at room temperature 30 minutes.

COMBINE broth and cornstarch in small bowl; stir to dissolve cornstarch. Combine soy sauce, chili-garlic sauce, and sugar in another small bowl.

HEAT peanut oil in wok or heavy large skillet over medium-high heat. Add bell pepper and stir-fry until slightly softened, about 4 minutes. Add shrimp mixture; stir-fry 2 minutes. Add green onions; stir-fry until shrimp are pink, 30 seconds. Mix in soy sauce mixture. Add cornstarch mixture. Cook until shrimp are just opaque in center and sauce thickens, about 1 minute.

Broiled shrimp with mustard and tarragon

8 FIRST-COURSE SERVINGS *These would also be delicious grilled. Serve as an appetizer with toothpicks on the side. Look for toothpicks (or "party picks") with fun motifs on the ends.*

- ⅓ **cup Dijon mustard**
- 3 **tablespoons olive oil**
- 1 **green onion, minced**
- 1½ **tablespoons minced fresh tarragon**
- 1½ **pounds uncooked large shrimp, peeled, deveined**

- 8 **wooden skewers, soaked in water 30 minutes**

WHISK first 4 ingredients in medium bowl to blend. Add shrimp; toss to coat. Chill at least 1 hour and up to 3 hours.

PREHEAT broiler. Line baking sheet with foil. Thread shrimp onto skewers. Sprinkle with salt and pepper. Broil shrimp until cooked through, about 2 minutes per side.

REMOVE shrimp from skewers. Arrange on platter. Serve with toothpicks.

Shrimp with romesco sauce

2 SERVINGS *Romesco sauce, a classic sauce from the Catalonia region of Spain, is also delicious served with grilled fish or chicken. Or spread some on grilled baguette slices for an appetizer or a side dish. For a smoky twist, replace the cayenne pepper with hot smoked paprika. Serve the shrimp with saffron rice and a mixed-greens salad.*

> 2 tablespoons slivered almonds
> 1 thin slice French bread (about 4×3×¼ inches)
> 1 large garlic clove
> 1 7-ounce jar roasted red peppers, drained
> 3 tablespoons olive oil, divided
> 1 tablespoon Sherry wine vinegar
> ¼ teaspoon cayenne pepper
>
> 16 uncooked large shrimp, peeled, deveined

STIR almonds in heavy small skillet over medium heat until golden, about 3 minutes. Transfer almonds to processor. Place bread in same skillet and cook until lightly toasted, about 1 minute per side. Tear bread into pieces and add to processor. With machine running, drop garlic through feed tube and process until almonds and garlic are finely chopped. Add red peppers, 2 tablespoons oil, vinegar, and cayenne; process until mixture is consistency of thick mayonnaise, scraping down sides of bowl occasionally.

DO AHEAD *Can be made 1 day ahead. Cover and chill. Bring to room temperature before serving.*

PREPARE barbecue (medium-high heat). Toss shrimp with remaining 1 tablespoon oil in medium bowl. Sprinkle with salt and pepper. Grill until shrimp are just opaque in center, about 2 minutes per side.

DIVIDE shrimp between plates. Spoon romesco sauce over.

Sautéed shrimp with grits and lime butter

2 SERVINGS *This southern comfort food would be delicious served with fried okra.*

> 2½ cups low-salt chicken broth
>   4 tablespoons (½ stick) butter, divided
>   ¾ cup quick-cooking white grits
>   3 tablespoons cream cheese
>   2 tablespoons half and half
>   ½ cup chopped green onions
>
>   1 pound uncooked medium shrimp, peeled, deveined
>   2 tablespoons fresh lime juice

COMBINE broth and 1 tablespoon butter in heavy medium saucepan and bring to boil. Stir in grits. Reduce heat to medium-low; cover and simmer 5 minutes, stirring occasionally. Mix cream cheese and half and half into grits. Cover and simmer mixture until almost all liquid has evaporated and grits are tender, stirring frequently, about 7 minutes. Stir in green onions. Remove grits from heat. Season to taste with salt and pepper.

MELT remaining 3 tablespoons butter in heavy large skillet over medium-high heat. Add shrimp and sauté until shrimp are just cooked through, about 3 minutes. Stir in lime juice. Remove skillet from heat. Season with salt and pepper. Spoon grits onto center of plate. Top with shrimp and drizzle with lime butter from skillet.

KEEP IT LOW-SALT Always use low-salt broth for cooking—it's easier to add a little salt later than to take it out!

Singapore shrimp stir-fry

4 SERVINGS *Thai oil can be found at Southeast Asian markets. Unsweetened coconut milk, ginger or spicy soy sauce, and Thai red curry paste or Thai green curry paste can be found in the Asian foods section of some supermarkets or at Southeast Asian markets.*

¼ cup Thai oil or other flavored cooking oil

20 ounces uncooked medium shrimp, peeled, deveined

1 16-ounce package mixed stir-fry vegetables (including snow peas, carrots, onion, and celery; about 6 cups)

1⅓ cups canned unsweetened coconut milk

¼ cup ginger-flavored or spicy soy sauce

2 teaspoons Thai red or green curry paste
Chopped green onions for garnish

HEAT oil in wok or heavy large skillet over high heat. Add shrimp and stir-fry until just cooked through, about 2 minutes. Using slotted spoon, transfer shrimp to plate. Add vegetables to wok and stir-fry 2 minutes. Add coconut milk, soy sauce, and curry paste. Boil until sauce is slightly thickened, stirring frequently, about 2 minutes. Return shrimp and any accumulated juices to wok. Stir 30 seconds; season with salt and pepper. Transfer to bowl; sprinkle with green onions.

SCALLOPS

Pan-seared sea scallops on red onion marmalade

4 MAIN-COURSE OR 8 FIRST-COURSE SERVINGS *Great for a party, this can be made in less than half an hour. Serve with soft polenta and steamed broccoli rabe. The red onion marmalade would be delicious with grilled chicken or steak or as an accompaniment for cheese.*

16 large sea scallops, side muscles removed

5 tablespoons olive oil, divided

1 tablespoon finely grated lemon peel

1 tablespoon minced peeled fresh ginger

3 medium red onions, thinly sliced

⅓ cup dry red wine

¼ cup red wine vinegar

2 tablespoons (packed) golden brown sugar
Chopped fresh chives

PREHEAT oven to 250°F. Toss scallops, 2 tablespoons oil, lemon peel, and ginger in medium bowl. Heat large nonstick skillet over medium-high heat. Sprinkle scallops with salt and pepper. Add scallops to skillet. Cook until brown and just opaque in center, about 2 minutes per side. Transfer scallops to small baking sheet; place in oven to keep warm.

ADD remaining 3 tablespoons oil to drippings in same skillet; place over high heat. Add onions; sprinkle with salt and pepper. Cover and cook until brown, stirring occasionally, about 10 minutes. Add wine, vinegar, and brown sugar. Cook until onion marmalade is thick, stirring often, about 2 minutes. Season with salt and pepper. Spoon marmalade onto plates. Top with scallops and any juices. Sprinkle with chives.

Seared scallops with fresh fennel salad and kumquat-tarragon vinaigrette

8 FIRST-COURSE SERVINGS *Kumquats are small, orange citrus fruits about the size of a large olive with a tangy, tart flavor. In this recipe, they are pureed, peel and all, in the dressing, bringing both flavor and body to the vinaigrette. Serve for brunch with blood orange Mimosas.*

  1 **cup plus 2 tablespoons olive oil**
10 **kumquats, stemmed, quartered, seeded**
  3 **tablespoons chopped fresh tarragon**
¼ **cup white wine vinegar**
  2 **tablespoons frozen orange juice concentrate**
  1 **tablespoon Dijon mustard**

  3 **medium fennel bulbs, thinly sliced (about 5 cups)**
  1 **medium head of radicchio, quartered, thinly sliced (about 4 cups)**
  4 **green onions, thinly sliced (about ¾ cup)**

24 **large sea scallops, side muscles removed**
  2 **tablespoons butter, divided**

PUREE oil, kumquats, and tarragon in processor. Add vinegar, orange juice concentrate, and mustard; process until just combined. Season vinaigrette with salt and pepper.

DO AHEAD *Can be made 1 day ahead. Cover and chill. Bring vinaigrette to room temperature before continuing.*

COMBINE fennel, radicchio, and green onions in large bowl. Add ¾ cup vinaigrette; toss to combine. Season salad with salt and pepper.

SPRINKLE scallops with salt and pepper. Melt 1 tablespoon butter in heavy large nonstick skillet over high heat. Add 12 scallops and cook until golden on both sides and just opaque in center, about 2 minutes per side. Transfer sautéed scallops to large plate, then tent with foil to keep warm. Repeat with remaining butter and scallops.

DIVIDE salad among 8 plates. Place 3 scallops on top of each. Drizzle scallops with remaining vinaigrette.

Tarragon scallop gratins

2 SERVINGS *If you like, combine everything except the breadcrumbs up to one hour ahead. Top with the breadcrumbs just before baking.*

  8 **ounces bay scallops, side muscles removed**
  2 **tablespoons olive oil**
  2 **tablespoons dry white wine or dry vermouth**
  1 **large shallot, chopped**
  1 **tablespoon chopped fresh tarragon**
⅓ **cup fresh white breadcrumbs**

PREHEAT oven to 450°F. Combine first 5 ingredients in medium bowl. Season with salt and pepper. Toss to coat. Divide mixture between 2 small gratin dishes. Sprinkle breadcrumbs over each.

BAKE until scallops are just opaque in center and breadcrumbs are golden, about 15 minutes.

Sautéed sea scallops with lemon-dill sauce

2 SERVINGS *This would also be great with orange peel replacing the lemon peel and basil in place of the dill.*

¼ cup all purpose flour
½ pound sea scallops, side muscles removed
5 tablespoons butter, divided

½ cup dry white wine
1 tablespoon chopped fresh dill plus 2 sprigs for garnish
1 teaspoon finely grated lemon peel
   Lemon wedges

SEASON flour with salt and pepper. Dredge scallops in flour mixture. Shake off excess. Melt 2 tablespoons butter in heavy medium skillet over high heat. Add scallops and cook until browned on both sides and just opaque in center, about 2 minutes per side. Using tongs, transfer scallops to plate; cover with foil.

ADD wine to same skillet. Bring to boil, scraping up browned bits. Boil until reduced to 3 tablespoons, about 3 minutes. Add dill and lemon peel. Reduce heat to very low. Add remaining 3 tablespoons butter and whisk just until melted. Season sauce to taste with salt and pepper. Spoon sauce over scallops. Garnish with lemon wedges and dill sprigs.

Sautéed scallops with shiitake mushrooms and broccoli

2 SERVINGS *Always remove the stems from shiitake mushrooms. Unlike the tender caps, the stems are very tough and rubbery when cooked. Serve this dish with steamed rice.*

1 ounce dried shiitake mushrooms
1 pound broccoli, trimmed, cut into florets

¼ cup (½ stick) butter
¾ pound sea scallops, side muscles removed, halved crosswise
1 bunch green onions, sliced
1½ tablespoons fresh lemon juice
2 tablespoons toasted pine nuts

PLACE mushrooms in small bowl. Add boiling water to cover. Let stand until softened, about 20 minutes. Drain, reserving 3 tablespoons soaking liquid. Squeeze out any liquid from mushrooms. Cut off stems and discard. Cut mushroom caps into quarters. Blanch broccoli in large pot of boiling salted water until just crisp-tender. Run under cold water to cool; drain well.

DO AHEAD *Mushrooms and broccoli can be made 1 day ahead. Cover separately and chill.*

MELT butter in heavy large skillet over medium-high heat. Add mushrooms and sauté 1 minute. Add scallops and green onions and stir until scallops are almost cooked through, about 3 minutes. Add broccoli and stir until broccoli is heated through and scallops are just opaque in center, about 2 minutes. Add reserved shiitake soaking liquid and lemon juice. Season to taste with salt and pepper. Sprinkle with pine nuts.

Scallops with hazelnuts and brown butter vinaigrette

2 SERVINGS *Husked hazelnuts are available at many supermarkets. If they're unavailable, rub the toasted hazelnuts in a kitchen towel to release the husks.*

5 tablespoons unsalted butter

12 large sea scallops, side muscles removed

1½ teaspoons chopped fresh thyme, divided

⅓ cup chopped shallots

¼ cup husked hazelnuts, toasted, chopped

1 tablespoon white balsamic vinegar

1 small bunch watercress, thick stems trimmed

COOK butter in large nonstick skillet over medium heat until deep golden brown and most of foam subsides, stirring often, about 4 minutes. Transfer butter to bowl. Sprinkle scallops with salt, pepper, and ½ teaspoon thyme. Add to same skillet; cook until just opaque in center, about 2 minutes per side. Transfer to plate. Add shallots, hazelnuts, and remaining 1 teaspoon thyme to skillet; stir 30 seconds. Remove skillet from heat. Mix in brown butter and vinegar. Season vinaigrette with salt and pepper.

DIVIDE watercress between plates. Top with scallops; spoon vinaigrette over.

NUTTY BUTTER In France, butter that has been cooked until the milk solids begin to brown is called *beurre noisette* because it takes on the color of hazelnuts (*noisettes*). In this dish, the nutty flavor of the brown butter amplifies that of chopped toasted hazelnuts.

Seared coriander scallops with bok choy and hoisin

2 SERVINGS *Hoisin sauce, a thick mixture of ground soybeans, garlic, chiles, and spices, is used as a condiment and an ingredient in Chinese cooking. It can be found in the Asian foods section of many supermarkets and at Asian markets.*

¾ cup fresh orange juice

2 tablespoons hoisin sauce

2 teaspoons minced peeled fresh ginger

10 large sea scallops, side muscles removed

1 tablespoon coriander seeds, coarsely crushed

2 teaspoons Asian sesame oil

2 baby bok choy, each cut lengthwise into eighths

2 tablespoons water

WHISK orange juice, hoisin sauce, and ginger in small bowl. Pat scallops dry on paper towels; sprinkle with salt and pepper. Sprinkle coriander seeds over top of scallops, pressing to adhere.

HEAT oil in large nonstick skillet over high heat. Add scallops, coriander side down, and cook just until opaque in center, about 2 minutes per side. Transfer scallops to plate. Add bok choy and 2 tablespoons water to skillet; sauté until wilted, about 2 minutes. Sprinkle with salt and pepper. Using tongs, divide bok choy between 2 plates, then top with scallops. Add hoisin mixture to same skillet; boil until reduced to ⅓ cup, about 2 minutes. Drizzle sauce over scallops and bok choy.

Sautéed scallops with cherry tomatoes, green onions, and parsley

4 SERVINGS *Any kind of cherry tomato would work well in this recipe—you can even mix colors and shapes for a lively presentation. Sweet smoked paprika, sometimes labeled Pimentón Dulce or Pimentón de La Vera Dulce, can be found at some supermarkets, specialty foods stores, and online from tienda.com.*

1½	pounds large sea scallops, side muscles removed
	Fleur de sel or coarse kosher salt
4	tablespoons extra-virgin olive oil, divided
4	large green onions, chopped, white and green parts separated
1	12-ounce container cherry tomatoes or grape tomatoes
4	tablespoons coarsely chopped fresh Italian parsley, divided
3	tablespoons fresh lemon juice
½	teaspoon sweet smoked paprika or Hungarian sweet paprika

PAT scallops dry. Sprinkle with fleur de sel and pepper. Heat 2 tablespoons oil in large skillet over medium-high heat. Add scallops; cook until browned outside and just opaque in center, about 2 minutes per side. Transfer scallops to plate; cover to keep warm. Add 1 tablespoon oil to same skillet; add white parts of green onions and sauté until almost tender, about 1 minute. Add tomatoes and green parts of onions and sauté until tomatoes begin to burst and release juices, about 5 minutes. Stir in 3 tablespoons parsley, lemon juice, and paprika. Return scallops and any accumulated juices to skillet and stir just until heated through, about 1 minute. Season to taste with salt and pepper. Transfer scallop mixture to platter. Drizzle with remaining 1 tablespoon oil and sprinkle with remaining 1 tablespoon parsley.

Spicy stir-fried brown rice with broccolini and scallops

4 SERVINGS *Broccolini, sometimes called baby broccoli, is actually a cross between broccoli and Chinese kale. The stalks are tall and thin with broccoli-like florets at the top. This is a great recipe for using up any leftover cooked rice.*

8	ounces broccolini, cut into 1-inch pieces (about 3 cups)
1	tablespoon vegetable oil
1	cup diced red bell pepper
1	cup chopped green onions
1	tablespoon minced peeled fresh ginger
2	garlic cloves, minced
¼	teaspoon dried crushed red pepper
12	ounces bay scallops, side muscles removed
1½	cups brown basmati rice or other brown rice, cooked, drained, cooled
2	tablespoons soy sauce
2	teaspoons Asian sesame oil

COOK broccolini in large skillet of boiling salted water until crisp-tender, about 3 minutes. Drain. Dry skillet. Heat vegetable oil in same skillet over high heat. Add next 5 ingredients; stir 30 seconds. Push vegetables to side of skillet; add scallops to other side. Sprinkle with salt and pepper; stir-fry 1 minute. Stir vegetables into scallops. Add broccolini, rice, soy sauce, and sesame oil; stir-fry until heated through, about 2 minutes. Season to taste with salt and pepper.

Grilled skewered scallops and apricots with honey-mustard dressing

4 SERVINGS *Slicing the scallops in half horizontally helps them to cook quickly—in just the same amount of time it takes for the apricots to soften and char slightly. You'll need eight metal skewers for grilling the scallops and apricots.*

½ cup olive oil

¼ cup honey mustard

¼ cup fresh lemon juice

¼ cup chopped fresh chives

8 fresh apricots, pitted, quartered

12 large sea scallops, side muscles removed, halved horizontally

6 cups baby romaine salad mix (about 3½ ounces)

PREPARE barbecue (medium-high heat). Whisk first 4 ingredients in medium bowl. Season dressing with salt and pepper. Transfer ¼ cup dressing to another medium bowl; set aside for salad.

ALTERNATELY thread 4 apricot quarters and 3 scallop halves onto each of 8 metal skewers; brush generously with remaining dressing. Sprinkle with salt and pepper. Grill until scallops are just opaque in center, occasionally brushing with more dressing, about 3 minutes per side.

ADD lettuce to bowl with reserved dressing and toss to coat. Season salad with salt and pepper. Divide salad among 4 plates. Top each with 2 scallop skewers; brush with any remaining dressing.

CLAMSANDMUSSELS

Portuguese clams with linguiça and tomatoes

6 SERVINGS *Linguiça is a thin pork Portuguese sausage made with garlic and spices. Use the smallest clams you can find for this dish; mussels would also work well.*

3 tablespoons olive oil

8 ounces linguiça, fully cooked chorizo, or kielbasa sausage, sliced

1 large onion, chopped

2 14½-ounce cans diced tomatoes with green pepper and garlic or Italian-style tomatoes

4 dozen littleneck or other small hard-shell clams, scrubbed

1 cup white wine

½ teaspoon (or more) hot pepper sauce

¼ cup chopped fresh cilantro, divided

HEAT oil in heavy large pot over medium-high heat. Add sausage and onion; cook until golden, stirring often, about 5 minutes. Stir in tomatoes with juice, then clams. Pour wine over. Bring to simmer. Cover pan and simmer until clams open, 5 to 10 minutes depending on size of clams (discard any that do not open). Using slotted spoon, divide clams among 6 shallow bowls. Bring broth to boil. Season with hot sauce and half of cilantro.

LADLE broth and sausage over clams. Sprinkle with remaining cilantro.

Steamed spicy garlic clams with pasta

6 SERVINGS *If you prefer, basil can replace the parsley. Serve with warm baguette slices to soak up any extra juices, and a simple, peppery arugula salad to complement the clams and pasta.*

    1 pound linguine
    6 pounds littleneck or other
       small clams, scrubbed
    ½ cup chopped fresh Italian parsley
    3 garlic cloves, chopped
    2 tablespoons extra-virgin olive oil
    ½ teaspoon dried crushed red pepper

COOK linguine in large pot of boiling salted water until just tender but still firm to bite, stirring occasionally. Drain.

MEANWHILE, cook clams, parsley, garlic, oil, and crushed red pepper in large covered pot until clams open, about 10 minutes (discard any clams that do not open). Season to taste with salt and pepper.

DIVIDE pasta among bowls. Divide clams and sauce atop pasta.

Mussels with Pernod and cream

2 SERVINGS *The anise flavor of Pernod, a liqueur from France, works beautifully with shellfish. Purchase mussels that are not chipped and are tightly shut. Remove them from any packaging (unless they are stored in a mesh bag) and store in a bowl in the refrigerator uncovered for up to one day.*

    1⅓ cups sliced leeks (white and
        pale green parts only)
    1¼ cups dry white wine
     ¼ cup diced red bell pepper
     2 pounds mussels, scrubbed, debearded
     ½ cup heavy whipping cream
     3 tablespoons Pernod or other anise liqueur
     3 tablespoons chopped fresh parsley

COMBINE leeks, wine, and bell pepper in large pot. Add mussels. Bring to boil over high heat. Cover pot and cook until mussels open, about 5 minutes. Using tongs, transfer mussels to medium bowl (discard any mussels that do not open). Add cream and Pernod to pot; boil until liquid is slightly reduced, about 4 minutes. Mix in parsley. Return mussels and any accumulated juices to pot. Simmer until mussels are warmed through, about 1 minute; season with salt and pepper. Divide mussels and broth between bowls.

LOBSTERANDCRAB

Steamed lobster with lemon-herb butter

6 SERVINGS *This is the pure lobster experience—and truly simple to prepare. Save this for a weekend or special occasion when you have time to savor the flavors. The freshest lobsters are those that are most lively when you purchase them. Store them in an open bag with a damp towel or cloth in the coldest part of the refrigerator up to 12 hours. The cold will calm them and make them less active before cooking. Add the lobsters headfirst to the boiling salted water.*

6 1¼- to 1½-pound live lobsters

1 cup (2 sticks) butter
2 teaspoons fresh lemon juice
2 teaspoons chopped fresh Italian parsley
2 teaspoons chopped fresh chives
2 teaspoons chopped fresh basil

Lemon wedges

COOK lobsters in 2 large pots of boiling salted water until shells are pink and lobsters are just cooked through, about 11 minutes.

MEANWHILE, melt butter in small saucepan. Add lemon juice and herbs. Season with salt and pepper.

SERVE lobsters with lemon wedges and warm herb butter on the side.

DIGGING IN Once the lobsters have cooked, remove them from the hot water with tongs and let them cool just enough so that you can handle them without burning your fingers. Place the lobsters on a work surface shell-side down, and using a heavy large knife, cut them in half lengthwise along the underside. Serve two halves to each person. For those who haven't eaten fresh lobster before, instruct them to twist off the claws and use nutcrackers to get at the meat inside the claws and tail. It's a matter of personal preference whether or not to eat the green tomalley; some people love it as a delicacy.

Roasted lobster tails with shallots, parsley, and lemon

2 SERVINGS *This presentation looks and tastes indulgent, but requires a minimum of effort—especially if you ask the fishmonger to cut the lobster tails in half lengthwise for you.*

- 2 tablespoons extra-virgin olive oil, divided
- 5 teaspoons minced shallots
- 2 teaspoons minced fresh Italian parsley
- ¼ teaspoon finely grated lemon peel
- 2 large frozen uncooked lobster tails, thawed, cut lengthwise in half
  Lemon wedges

PREHEAT oven to 450°F. Brush 13×9×2-inch metal baking pan with ½ tablespoon oil. Mix shallots, parsley, and lemon peel in small bowl. Arrange lobster tails, cut side up, in prepared baking pan; brush with remaining 1½ tablespoons oil. Sprinkle with salt and pepper, then shallot mixture. Roast until just opaque in center, about 15 minutes. Divide lobster halves between 2 plates. Pour any pan drippings over lobster. Serve with lemon wedges.

Grilled surf-and-turf with spicy garlic-shallot butter

6 SERVINGS *For those who want it all: The spicy garlic-shallot butter goes equally well with both the lobster tails and the steaks. Frozen lobster tails can be thawed overnight in the refrigerator.*

- ½ cup (1 stick) butter, room temperature
- ¼ cup olive oil
- 2 large shallots, quartered
- 4 large garlic cloves, halved
- 1 teaspoon salt
- 1 teaspoon cayenne pepper
- ½ teaspoon ground black pepper
- 6 8- to 10-ounce New York strip steaks (about ¾ inch thick)
- 3 10-ounce uncooked lobster tails, thawed if frozen, cut lengthwise in half

COMBINE first 7 ingredients in processor and blend until almost smooth. Spread 1 heaping teaspoon seasoned butter over each side of each steak and over cut side of each lobster half. Let steaks stand at room temperature 1 hour; chill lobsters 1 hour. Transfer remaining seasoned butter to small saucepan.

PREPARE barbecue (medium-high heat). Set pan with butter at edge of barbecue so that butter will melt and warm through. Grill steaks until cooked to desired doneness, about 4 minutes per side for medium-rare. Grill lobster, shell side down, for 5 minutes. Turn over and grill until meat is just opaque in center, about 3 minutes. Transfer steaks and lobster to plates. Serve with warm seasoned butter.

Spicy oven-roasted orange-scented dungeness crab

2 SERVINGS *Dispense with utensils and just eat this luscious crab with your hands. Serve with a crisp fruity white wine, such as an Albariño.*

- ¼ cup (½ stick) butter
- ¼ cup olive oil
- 2 tablespoons minced garlic
- 1 tablespoon minced shallot
- 1½ teaspoons dried crushed red pepper
- 2 large Dungeness crabs, cooked, cleaned, and cracked (about 4¼ pounds)
- 2 tablespoons chopped fresh thyme, divided
- 2 tablespoons chopped fresh parsley, divided

- ½ cup blood orange juice or regular orange juice
- 1 teaspoon finely grated blood orange peel or regular orange peel

PREHEAT oven to 500°F. Melt butter with oil in heavy large ovenproof skillet over medium-high heat. Stir in garlic, shallot, and crushed red pepper. Add crabs; sprinkle with salt and pepper. Sprinkle 1 tablespoon thyme and 1 tablespoon parsley over crabs. Stir to combine. Place skillet in oven and roast crabs until heated through, stirring once, about 12 minutes.

USING tongs, transfer crabs to platter. Add orange juice and peel to same skillet; boil until sauce is reduced by about half, about 5 minutes. Spoon sauce over crabs. Sprinkle with remaining 1 tablespoon thyme and 1 tablespoon parsley.

Crab and avocado tostadas

8 SERVINGS *Chipotle chiles are dried, smoked jalapeños that come canned in a spicy tomato sauce called adobo. Canned chipotle chiles in adobo and crema mexicana are available at some supermarkets, specialty foods stores, and Latin markets.*

- 1 cup crema mexicana or sour cream
- 1 teaspoon minced canned chipotle chiles

- ½ cup finely diced seeded tomatoes
- ¼ cup finely chopped white onion
- 3 tablespoons fresh lime juice
- 2 tablespoons minced fresh cilantro
- 1 jalapeño chile, seeded, minced
- 8 ounces Dungeness crabmeat
- 2 ripe avocados, peeled, seeded, diced
- 8 tostada shells
- 4 medium-size romaine lettuce leaves, thinly sliced crosswise

STIR crema and chipotles in small bowl to blend. Season to taste with salt.

COMBINE tomatoes, onion, lime juice, cilantro, and jalapeño in medium bowl. Fold in crabmeat and avocados. Season to taste with salt. Place tostada shells on plates and top with crab mixture, dividing equally. Sprinkle lettuce over tostadas. Drizzle with chipotle crema.

SAVE THE CHILES Only a small portion of the canned chipotles in adobo are used in this recipe. Instead of letting the leftovers turn into a science project in the back of your refrigerator, place one chile plus a little sauce in each compartment of a plastic ice cube tray. Transfer the frozen cubes to an airtight container and freeze for later use. Or puree the chiles in a blender or food processor before freezing.

Cayenne-spiked crab cakes

8 APPETIZER OR 4 MAIN-COURSE SERVINGS *Bread-crumbs give crab cakes their appealing crunch. Since it takes time for the breadcrumbs to adhere to the crab cakes, be sure to begin this recipe at least one hour ahead.*

¼ cup minced celery
¼ cup minced green onion
¼ cup mayonnaise
1 large egg
1 tablespoon dry mustard
¼ teaspoon salt
    Generous pinch of cayenne pepper
1 pound fresh crabmeat
2¾ cups (about) fresh breadcrumbs made from crustless French bread, divided

2 tablespoons (¼ stick) butter, divided
2 tablespoons olive oil, divided
    Lemon wedges

MIX first 7 ingredients in medium bowl. Fold in crab. Mix in enough breadcrumbs (about 2 cups) to form mixture that barely holds together. Spread remaining breadcrumbs on baking sheet.

SHAPE crab mixture into eight ¾-inch-thick patties. Coat crab cakes with remaining breadcrumbs, pressing to adhere. Cover with plastic wrap and refrigerate at least 1 hour.

DO AHEAD *Can be made 4 hours ahead; keep chilled.*

MELT 1 tablespoon butter with 1 tablespoon oil in large nonstick skillet over medium-high heat. Add 4 crab cakes; reduce heat to medium and cook until brown, about 4 minutes per side. Wipe skillet clean. Repeat with remaining butter, oil, and crab cakes. Transfer crab cakes to plates. Serve crab cakes immediately with lemon wedges.

USE THAT DAY-OLD BREAD Make breadcrumbs whenever you've got a day-old baguette left over. They can be frozen in an airtight container for later use. Just tear the bread into pieces and process until crumbs form.

Asian-style crab and shrimp cakes

2 SERVINGS *Fish sauce is a fermented sauce used in Thai and Vietnamese cooking and is available in the Asian foods section of many supermarkets and at Asian markets.*

¼ cup mayonnaise
2 tablespoons chopped fresh cilantro
1 tablespoon chopped peeled fresh ginger
2 teaspoons fish sauce (nam pla or nuoc nam) or soy sauce
6 ounces fresh crabmeat, drained, picked over, patted dry
3 ounces bay shrimp, chopped
1½ cups fresh breadcrumbs made from crustless French bread, divided

1½ tablespoons peanut oil

WHISK first 4 ingredients in medium bowl. Mix in crabmeat, shrimp, and ½ cup breadcrumbs. Season with pepper. Place remaining 1 cup breadcrumbs on plate. Drop ¼ of crab mixture into breadcrumbs; turn to coat. Shape into 2½-inch-diameter cake. Repeat coating and shaping with remaining crab mixture and crumbs, forming total of 4 cakes.

HEAT oil in heavy medium nonstick skillet over medium heat. Add cakes and sauté until crisp, about 5 minutes per side.

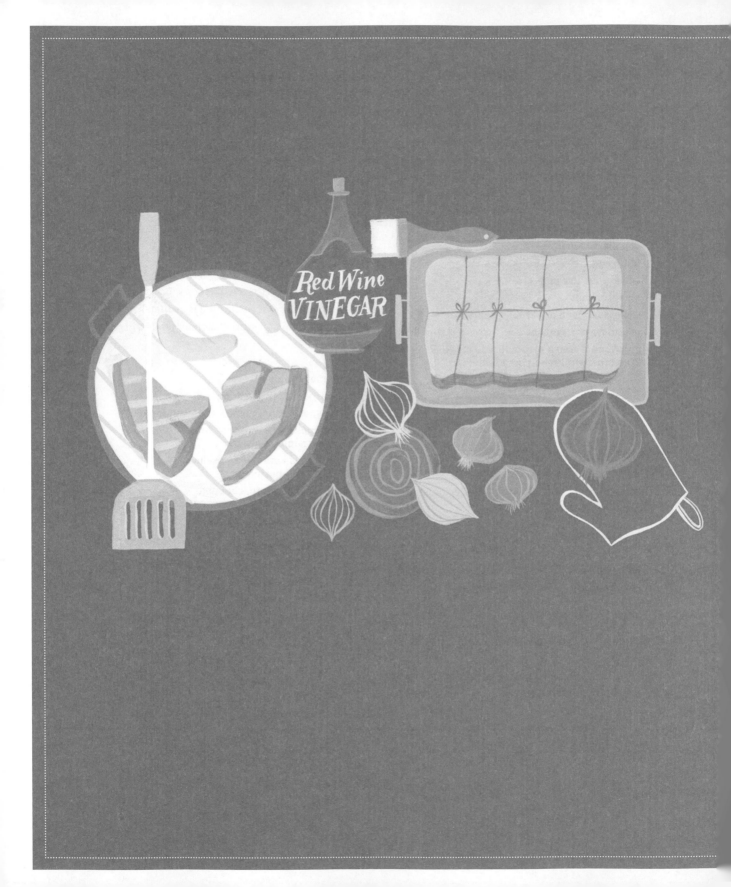

beef, pork, and lamb

BEEF

Grilled Steak with Fresh Garden Herbs

Grilled Rib-Eye Steaks with
Parsley-Garlic Butter

Grilled Steaks with Anchovy-Lemon Butter

Grilled Steaks with Arugula
and Shaved Parmesan

Chipotle-Rubbed Steaks with
Gorgonzola Toasts

Spiced Beef Tenderloin Steaks
with Spicy Mango Salsa

Grilled Porterhouse Topped with
Tarragon-Tomato Salad

Grilled Hoisin-Soy Steaks with
Shiitake and Bok Choy

Pepper-Crusted Steaks with
Worcestershire-Glazed Portobellos

Ginger-Soy Grilled Steak

Grilled Skirt Steak Tacos with Corn Relish

Grilled Korean-Style Short Ribs

Barbecued Beef Ribs with Hoisin-Chili Glaze

Beef Medallions with Cognac Sauce

Filet Mignon with Green
Peppercorn Cream Sauce

Hungarian-Style Beef with Bell
Peppers and Caraway

Sliced Filet Mignon with Fava Beans,
Radishes, and Mustard Dressing

Ancho-Rubbed Steaks with
Clementine-Red Onion Salsa

Porterhouse Steaks with Tapenade
and Balsamic Vinegar

Spice-Roasted Porterhouse Steaks

Skirt Steak with Poblano Rajas and Zucchini

Roast Beef Tenderloin with
Wasabi-Garlic Cream

Roast Beef Tenderloin with Sherry
Vinaigrette and Watercress

Flank Steak Salad with Roasted
Shallots and Goat Cheese

Harissa-Crusted Tri-Tip Roast

Beef Stroganoff

Sesame Beef and Asparagus Stir-Fry

Beef, Mushroom, and Broccoli Stir-Fry

Thai-Style Beef and Asparagus Curry

Cajun Meatloaf

Southwestern Blue Plate Special Meatloaf

Sausage and Bell Pepper Meatloaf

Meatballs with Parsley and Parmesan

South American picadillo

Corned Beef and Carrots with
Marmalade-Whiskey Glaze

Calf's Liver with Port Sauce

VEAL

Veal Cutlets with Mushrooms and Tomatoes

Classic Saltimbocca

Veal Scaloppine with Gorgonzola Sauce

Grilled Veal Chops and Radicchio
with Lemon-Caper Sauce

Grilled Veal Chops with Warm
Tomato-Olive Vinaigrette

Veal Chops with Creole Mustard Crust

Broiled Veal Chops with Mixed Peppercorns

Broiled Veal Chops with
Mustard-Sage Butter

PORK

Grilled Chipotle-Stuffed Pork Tenderloin

Grilled Asian Pork Chops
and Baby Bok Choy

Grilled Pork Chops with Chunky
Andouille Barbecue Sauce

Grilled Pork Tenderloin with
Fresh Cherry Chutney

Grilled Pork Satay

Pork Tenderloin with Rhubarb-
Currant Chutney

Pork Kebabs Marinated in Honey,
Rosemary, and Orange

Pork Rib Chops with Sautéed
Apples and Star Anise

Pork Chops with Cranberry,
Port, and Rosemary Sauce

Roast Pork Tenderloins with
Balsamic-Chestnut Glaze

Pork with Gorgonzola Sauce

Pork Medallions with Chili-Maple Sauce

Pork Cutlets with Maple,
Mustard, and Sage Sauce

Pork Cutlets with Figs and
Balsamic Vinegar

Pork and Sausage Sauté

Spiced Pork Tenderloin

Roast Pork Chops with Bacon
and Wilted Greens

Roast Pork Tenderloin with Kumquats,
Cranberries, and Apples

Salt- and Pepper-Crusted Pork

Spicy Pork and Kumquat Stir-Fry

Five-Spice Pork Stir-Fry with Soba Noodles

Jamaican Jerk Pork Tenderloin with
Black Beans and Yellow Rice

Asian-Style Pork Stir-Fry

Sweet and Spicy Chipotle-Glazed Ribs

Oven-Roasted Spareribs with Peach Glaze

Roasted Sausages, Apples, and
Cabbage with Caraway

Soft Tacos with Sausage and Feta

LAMB

Grilled Tandoori Lamb

Grilled Lamb Kebabs with
Coriander and Cumin

Hunan Lamb Chops

Lamb Chops with Spicy Peanut Sauce

Grilled Spiced Lamb Chops with
Cucumber-Mint Sauce

Grilled Lamb with Curried
Kumquat Chutney

Butterflied Leg of Lamb with
Thyme and Orange

Moroccan-Spiced Rack of Lamb
with Pomegranate Reduction

Roast Rack of Lamb with Hoisin-
Orange Glaze and Red Onions

Rosemary-Roasted Rack of Lamb
and Cherry Tomatoes

Honey-Roasted Lamb with
Arugula and Pine Nut Salad

Roast Lamb with Marionberry-Pecan Crust

Lamb Chops with Minted
Meyer Lemon Compote

Sautéed Lamb Chops with Béarnaise Butter

Lamb Chops with Herbed
Sweet Onion Compote

Lamb Chops with Artichokes and Rosemary

Lamb Tikka with Crispy Onions

Broiled Lamb Chops with
Rosemary-Mint Sauce

Lamb Shoulder Chops with
Tomatoes and Marjoram

Peppered Lamb with Pine Nut Sauce

Mint-Marinated Leg of Lamb

Tamarind-Honey Lamb Kebabs
on Mashed Yams

Cumin-and-Coffee-Roasted Leg of Lamb

Minced Lamb with Ginger,
Hoisin, and Green Onions

tool kit It might seem that there are hundreds of different cuts of meat, but in practical terms there are two: tender and tough. Understanding this simplifies things when it comes to figuring out how to cook meat. Tender cuts tend to come from the parts of the animal that get very little exercise—the short loin, sirloin, and rib sections. These include beef tenderloins, pork tenderloins, and racks of lamb. USE: dry-heat cooking methods (grilling, broiling, pan-frying, roasting, sautéing, stir-frying), which cook the meat quickly.

Tough cuts tend to come from the parts that get the most exercise and movement, such as the shoulders, legs, and cheeks. These include shanks, chuck roasts, and round or rump roasts. USE: moist-heat cooking methods (braising, stewing, pot-roasting), which tenderize the meat over a longer period until the meat is well-done and tender.

TENDER IS THE MEAT

For fast, easy, delicious dinners, these tender cuts of meat and suggested cooking methods are good ways to go.

BEEF

All steaks (rib-eye, New York, filet mignon, T-bone, porterhouse, skirt, and flank): grilled, pan-fried, stir-fried, broiled—and preferably not cooked beyond medium-rare

Tenderloin: grilled, roasted, sautéed

Ground beef: grilled, baked, pan-fried, broiled

VEAL

Cutlets: pan-fried, sautéed, broiled

Scaloppine: pan-fried, sautéed, broiled

Chops: grilled, roasted, broiled, pan-fried

PORK

Tenderloin: roasted, grilled, stir-fried, pan-fried

Chops: grilled, pan-fried, sautéed, broiled

Cutlets: stir-fried, pan-fried, sautéed, grilled

Ground pork/sausages: grilled, pan-fried, sautéed

LAMB

Butterflied leg of lamb: roasted, grilled, broiled

Rack of lamb: roasted

Chops: pan-fried, grilled, broiled, roasted, sautéed

Ground lamb/sausages: grilled, baked, pan-fried, roasted, sautéed

BEEF

Grilled steak with fresh garden herbs

4 SERVINGS *Depending on how much you want to spend, consider two types of steak for this recipe: Rib-eye is an expensive but very tender, boneless cut from the rib section. Skirt steak is a thinner, more affordable cut of beef. Whichever steak you use, any leftovers will make a great sandwich.*

¼ cup minced shallots (about 2 small)

3 tablespoons fresh lemon juice

1 tablespoon red wine vinegar

1 teaspoon Dijon mustard

¼ cup extra-virgin olive oil plus additional for brushing

¾ cup chopped assorted fresh herbs (such as parsley, tarragon, mint, basil, and cilantro)

4 8-ounce rib-eye steaks (each about 1 inch thick) or skirt steaks

WHISK first 4 ingredients in medium bowl to blend. Gradually whisk in ¼ cup oil, then herbs. Season dressing to taste with salt and pepper.

PREPARE barbecue (medium-high heat). Sprinkle steaks generously with salt and pepper; brush lightly with oil. Grill steaks until charred and cooked to desired doneness, about 5 minutes per side for medium-rare rib-eye or 3 minutes per side for medium-rare skirt steak. Transfer steaks to platter; let rest 5 minutes. Spoon herb dressing over steaks.

Grilled rib-eye steaks with parsley-garlic butter

6 SERVINGS *Beef topped with a pat of butter is a steakhouse classic. In this version, softened butter is mixed with parsley, chives, garlic, and Cognac. For a slightly different twist, try a shallot instead of garlic, and thyme in place of parsley.*

½ cup (1 stick) butter, room temperature

1 tablespoon finely chopped fresh parsley

1 tablespoon chopped fresh chives

1 garlic clove, pressed

2 teaspoons Cognac or brandy

3 1½-inch-thick rib-eye steaks (about 1 pound each)

PREPARE barbecue (medium-high heat). Stir first 5 ingredients in small bowl to blend. Season butter to taste with salt and pepper. Sprinkle steaks generously with salt and pepper. Grill steaks to desired doneness, about 6 minutes per side for medium-rare. Let rest 5 minutes. Cut each steak in half; transfer to plates. Top each with spoonful of seasoned butter.

Grilled steaks with anchovy-lemon butter

2 SERVINGS *To get the most juice out of a lemon (or any other citrus fruit), roll room-temperature fruit along the countertop with your palm before juicing. Be sure to grate the lemon peel first. A Microplane or other razor-sharp grater is very efficient for removing just the colored part of the peel.*

- 2 tablespoons (¼ stick) unsalted butter, room temperature
- 9 canned anchovy fillets, minced
- 1 tablespoon minced shallot
- 1 teaspoon fresh lemon juice
- ½ teaspoon finely grated lemon peel

- 2 7-ounce New York strip steaks (each about ¾ inch thick)

USING fork, mash first 5 ingredients in medium bowl until blended; season to taste with salt and pepper. Chill until ready to use, up to 1 day.

PREPARE barbecue (medium-high heat) or preheat broiler. Sprinkle steaks with salt and pepper. Grill or broil to desired doneness, about 5 minutes per side for medium-rare. Transfer to plates. Top with anchovy butter.

Better with butter Nothing finishes a steak like a pat of melting butter. Here are a few ideas for compound butters (butter with goodies mixed in). These will keep in the freezer for about a month, so you can make them in advance and have them on hand when you need them. Don't forget to season with salt and pepper to taste.

Soften some unsalted butter and mix in one of these combinations:
— Chopped fresh herbs and drained capers
— Chopped garlic, chopped Italian parsley, and finely grated lemon peel
— Chopped ginger, chopped green onion, and Asian sesame oil
— Grated Parmesan, blue, or flavored feta cheese and freshly ground black pepper
— Chopped Kalamata olives
— Chopped roasted red peppers and hot smoked paprika (Pimentón de La Vera)
— Chopped jalapeño chiles, chopped cilantro, and fresh lime juice

371

Grilled steaks with arugula and shaved Parmesan

4 SERVINGS *This recipe was inspired by* bistecca ai ferri *(grilled steak), a classic Italian dish that shows off thick, succulent steaks to their best advantage (T-bones would work well, too). The meat is coated with oil and garlic, then grilled and served on a bed of peppery arugula. The finishing touch? Shaved Parmesan cheese. A vegetable peeler makes it easy to produce the thin, curling strips of Parmesan.*

- 3 large garlic cloves, peeled
- 2 teaspoons plus 1 tablespoon extra-virgin olive oil
- 1 teaspoon freshly ground black pepper
- 2 1½-pound porterhouse steaks (each about 1½ inches thick)

- 6 cups (loosely packed) arugula (about 4 ounces)
 Parmesan cheese wedge
 Lemon wedges

BLEND garlic, 2 teaspoons oil, and pepper in mini processor (or mash on plate with back of fork) to form paste. Rub garlic paste over both sides of steaks. Let stand at room temperature 30 minutes or refrigerate up to 8 hours.

PREPARE barbecue (medium-high heat). Grill steaks to desired doneness, about 9 minutes per side for medium-rare. Transfer steaks to cutting board. Let rest 5 minutes. Cut steaks on slight angle into ¼-inch-thick slices.

ARRANGE arugula on platter. Top with steak slices. Pour any accumulated juices over steaks; sprinkle with salt. Drizzle remaining 1 tablespoon oil over steaks. Shave Parmesan cheese into strips over steaks. Serve with lemon wedges.

Chipotle-rubbed steaks with Gorgonzola toasts

4 SERVINGS *The meat gets a kick from crushed chipotle chile pepper and a smoky sweetness from Hungarian sweet paprika. Look for both ingredients in the supermarket's spice section. Ciabatta is a rustic, oval-shaped Italian bread and is available at many supermarkets and bakeries.*

- 4½ Turkish bay leaves
- 1½ tablespoons Hungarian sweet paprika
- 1½ teaspoons crushed chipotle chile pepper
- ¾ teaspoon cumin seeds
- 4 1-inch-thick T-bone or rib-eye steaks (about 1 pound each)

- 1 loaf ciabatta bread, halved horizontally, each half cut crosswise into eight 5×3-inch slices
 Olive oil
- 1 cup creamy Gorgonzola cheese
- 1 teaspoon chopped fresh thyme

PREPARE barbecue (medium-high heat). Finely grind bay leaves, paprika, chipotle, and cumin seeds in spice grinder. Reserve 1 teaspoon spice mixture; transfer remaining mixture to plate. Sprinkle steaks generously with salt and pepper. Press both sides of steaks into spice mixture on plate and rub to spread evenly.

GRILL steaks to desired doneness, about 5 minutes per side for medium-rare. Transfer steaks to plates; let rest 5 to 10 minutes.

BRUSH cut sides of bread with oil. Grill bread, cut side down, until slightly charred, about 1 minute. Spread Gorgonzola onto grilled side of each bread slice, then sprinkle with freshly ground black pepper and reserved spice mixture. Return bread, cheese side up, to grill. Grill until cheese begins to melt and bottom of bread is slightly charred, about 1 minute. Sprinkle bread with thyme; place 2 slices alongside steak on each plate.

Spiced beef tenderloin steaks with spicy mango salsa

6 SERVINGS *The sugar in the spice rub caramelizes as the meat cooks, forming a delicious brown crust.*

- ½ cup hot jalapeño jelly
- 3 tablespoons fresh lime juice
- 2½ cups chopped peeled pitted mango (from 2)
- 1¼ cups chopped red bell pepper
- ¾ cup chopped red onion
- ⅓ cup chopped fresh cilantro
- 1 jalapeño chile, minced

- 1 tablespoon ground cinnamon
- 1 tablespoon ground coriander
- 1 tablespoon sugar
- 1 tablespoon paprika
- 1½ teaspoons salt
- ½ teaspoon cayenne pepper
- 12 4-ounce beef tenderloin steaks (each about ½ inch thick)
  Olive oil

WHISK jelly and lime juice in large bowl to loosen. Mix in next 5 ingredients. ingredients. Season salsa to taste with salt and pepper.

DO AHEAD *Can be made 2 hours ahead. Cover; chill.*

PREPARE barbecue (medium-high heat). Mix cinnamon and next 5 ingredients in small bowl to blend for spice rub. Brush steaks all over with oil, then sprinkle each side with ½ teaspoon spice rub. Grill steaks to desired doneness, about 2 minutes per side for medium-rare. Place 2 steaks on each plate. Serve, passing salsa separately.

Grilled porterhouse topped with tarragon-tomato salad

2 SERVINGS *Make the tomato salad before you put the steak on the grill. As the salad sits, the flavors will meld and the salt will draw some of the juices out of the tomatoes.*

- 3 tablespoons extra-virgin olive oil
- 1 tablespoon balsamic vinegar
- 1 tablespoon chopped fresh tarragon
- 1 cup diced seeded beefsteak tomatoes
- 1 shallot, chopped
  Coarse kosher salt

- 1 1½-inch-thick porterhouse steak (about 1½ pounds)

PREPARE barbecue (medium-high heat). Whisk oil, vinegar, and tarragon in small bowl to blend. Mix in tomatoes and shallot. Season salad to taste with coarse salt and pepper. Let salad stand at room temperature.

SPRINKLE steak generously on both sides with coarse salt and pepper. Grill to desired doneness, about 6 minutes per side for medium-rare. Transfer to platter. Let rest 10 minutes.

SPOON salad over steak.

Grilled hoisin-soy steaks with shiitake and bok choy

2 SERVINGS; CAN BE DOUBLED *The perfect recipe for a hot summer evening—steaks, mushrooms, and bok choy all go on the grill together.*

4½ tablespoons mirin (sweet Japanese rice wine) or sweet Sherry

1½ teaspoons Chinese five-spice powder or 4 whole star anise, ground

3 tablespoons hoisin sauce

3 tablespoons toasted sesame seeds

3 tablespoons unseasoned rice vinegar

1½ tablespoons soy sauce

1½ tablespoons Asian sesame oil

2 10- to 12-ounce rib-eye steaks

4 large shiitake mushrooms, stemmed

2 baby bok choy, quartered lengthwise

PREPARE barbecue (medium-high heat). Combine mirin, five-spice powder, hoisin sauce, sesame seeds, vinegar, soy sauce, and oil in small saucepan; bring to boil, whisking to blend. Cool sauce.

PLACE steaks, mushrooms, and bok choy on small rimmed baking sheet. Sprinkle steaks with salt and pepper. Pour half of sauce over; turn to coat. Reserve remaining sauce in pan. Grill steaks, mushrooms, and bok choy until meat is medium-rare and vegetables are partially charred, turning occasionally, about 10 minutes for steaks, 8 minutes for mushrooms, and 5 minutes for bok choy. Slice steaks; divide between plates with mushrooms and bok choy. Bring remaining sauce in pan to simmer; drizzle over steaks and vegetables.

Flavors of the east If you can't find these ingredients in the Asian foods section of the supermarket, look for them at Asian markets.

— MIRIN: Sweet, golden Japanese rice wine.

— CHINESE FIVE-SPICE POWDER: Spice mix that often consists of cinnamon, cloves, fennel seeds, Szechuan peppercorns, and star anise. If you can't find five-spice powder, use star anise, a brown star-shaped seedpod native to China. Four whole star anise, finely ground, will equal 1½ teaspoons of five-spice powder.

— HOISIN SAUCE: Thick, reddish-brown sauce made of soybeans, garlic, chiles, and spices. The sweet-spicy condiment is sometimes labeled Peking sauce.

— UNSEASONED RICE VINEGAR: Asian vinegar that's milder and less acidic than apple cider, distilled white, or wine vinegars.

— ASIAN SESAME OIL: Oil that is dark caramel in color, with strong sesame flavor.

Pepper-crusted steaks with Worcestershire-glazed portobellos

4 TO 6 SERVINGS *Splurge on well-marbled Choice or Prime steaks for this recipe. Bringing the steaks to room temperature before grilling them will help the meat cook more evenly. Place the mushroom slices on the grill so that they sit crosswise across the grate—that way, they won't fall into the fire.*

- 4 14- to 16-ounce New York strip steaks (each 1 to 1¼ inches thick)
- 3 tablespoons whole black peppercorns, cracked with mallet in plastic bag
- 2 teaspoons coarse kosher salt
- ½ cup plus 2 tablespoons (1¼ sticks) butter, room temperature
- 4 teaspoons Worcestershire sauce
- 1½ teaspoons balsamic vinegar
- 1 pound large portobello mushrooms, stemmed, caps cut into ⅓-inch-thick slices

SPRINKLE steaks with cracked peppercorns and coarse salt. Let steaks stand at room temperature 30 minutes.

PREPARE barbecue (medium-high heat). Melt ½ cup butter in large skillet over medium heat. Stir in Worcestershire sauce and vinegar. Stir in mushrooms. Season to taste with salt. Remove from heat.

GRILL steaks until cooked to desired doneness, about 5 minutes per side for medium-rare. Transfer to plates. Top each steak with ½ tablespoon of remaining butter. Tent loosely with foil to keep warm. Grill mushrooms until soft and beginning to release juices, about 3 minutes per side. Divide mushrooms among steaks.

GRILL OF YOUR DREAMS Want picture-perfect grill marks? Place the steaks on the grill, pointing at ten o'clock. Halfway through cooking on one side, turn the steaks to two o'clock. Turn steaks over and repeat.

Ginger-soy grilled steak

4 TO 6 SERVINGS *A marinade of soy sauce, rice vinegar, sesame oil, ginger, and green onions gives this steak an Asian flavor. Look for rice vinegar in the Asian foods section of the supermarket. Asparagus stir-fried in a little sesame oil, garlic, and soy sauce would be great alongside.*

- 6 tablespoons soy sauce
- ¼ cup chopped onion
- ¼ cup unseasoned rice vinegar
- 2 tablespoons Asian sesame oil
- 1 tablespoon chopped peeled fresh ginger
- 1 cup chopped green onions (about 4 large)
- 1 1½-pound top sirloin steak (about 1 inch thick)

BLEND first 5 ingredients in processor until almost smooth; pour into 13×9×2-inch glass dish. Mix green onions into marinade. Add steak and turn to coat. Cover and refrigerate at least 1 hour and up to 1 day, turning steak occasionally.

PREPARE barbecue (medium-high heat) or preheat broiler. Pour marinade into small saucepan and bring to boil; transfer sauce to small bowl. Grill or broil steak to desired doneness, about 5 minutes per side for medium-rare. Transfer steak to cutting board; let rest 10 minutes. Cut steak crosswise on diagonal into thin slices. Serve steak with sauce.

Grilled skirt steak tacos with corn relish

4 SERVINGS *Grilling the corn and green onions gives the relish a smoky flavor. Look for spicy-smoky chipotle chile powder in the spice section of some supermarkets, or at specialty foods stores and Latin markets.*

  1 **pound skirt steak, cut into 4-inch lengths**
1½ **teaspoons chipotle chile powder, divided**
  3 **tablespoons olive oil, divided**
  2 **tablespoons fresh lime juice, divided**

  6 **green onions**
  2 **ears of corn, husked**
 ¼ **cup chopped fresh cilantro**
  1 **teaspoon finely grated lime peel**

  8 **5- to 6-inch-diameter corn tortillas**

PREPARE barbecue (medium-high heat). Sprinkle steak on both sides with salt and 1¼ teaspoons chile powder. Whisk 1½ tablespoons olive oil and 1 tablespoon lime juice in 11×7-inch glass dish. Add steak in single layer and turn to coat. Marinate 15 minutes.

MEANWHILE, brush green onions and corn with 1 tablespoon oil and sprinkle with salt and pepper. Grill vegetables until slightly charred, turning occasionally, about 2 minutes for green onions and 7 minutes for corn. Working over large bowl, cut corn from cob directly into bowl. Coarsely chop green onions and add to corn. Stir in cilantro, lime peel, and remaining ¼ teaspoon chile powder, ½ tablespoon oil, and 1 tablespoon lime juice. Season relish to taste with salt and pepper.

GRILL steak to desired doneness, about 2½ minutes per side for medium. Transfer to work surface; let rest 5 minutes.

PLACE tortillas at edge of grill to warm and soften, about 1 minute.

ARRANGE 2 warm tortillas on each plate. Thinly slice steak across grain. Divide steak and juices equally among tortillas. Spoon relish over each.

Grilled Korean-style short ribs

8 SERVINGS *Flanken ribs are cut thinly across (rather than between) the rib bones, so there are small ovals of bone in the strip of meat. Look for them at Korean markets, or ask your butcher to cut them for you. The ribs need to marinate overnight, so plan accordingly. If you can't find flanken ribs, the marinade would also be great on flank steak or chicken thighs.*

- 1 **cup soy sauce**
- ½ **cup mirin (sweet Japanese rice wine) or sweet Sherry**
- ½ **cup (packed) dark brown sugar**
- ¼ **cup unseasoned rice vinegar**
- ¼ **cup Asian sesame oil**
- ¼ **cup minced garlic (about 15 cloves)**
- 2 **large green onions, chopped**
- 5 **pounds Korean-style short ribs (beef chuck flanken, cut ⅓ to ½ inch thick across bones; about 20 pieces)**

COMBINE first 7 ingredients in medium bowl; whisk to blend well. Pour into heavy jumbo resealable plastic bag. Add ribs; seal bag. Turn bag over several times to coat ribs evenly. Refrigerate at least 2 hours or overnight, turning bag occasionally.

PREPARE barbecue (medium-high heat). Drain ribs; discard marinade. Working in batches, grill ribs until browned and cooked to medium-rare, about 3 minutes per side. Mound ribs on platter.

KOREAN BARBECUE AT HOME Want to make this meal even more authentic? Serve the ribs (called *kalbi kui* in Korean) with kimchi, a spicy pickled cabbage available in the refrigerated foods section of some supermarkets and at Korean markets. To turn it into a real party, put out a bowl of cooked short-grain rice (known as sticky rice) and plates of green or red lettuce leaves. Have guests spoon some rice on the lettuce, top with a little kimchi, pieces of meat, and soybean paste or Asian pear sauce, and roll up.

Barbecued beef ribs with hoisin-chili glaze

2 SERVINGS *Beef back ribs are from the prime rib, which makes them exceedingly tender—and big. Before cooking, slide a knife under the tough membrane (if there is one) on the meaty side of each rib and remove it. Look for hoisin sauce in the Asian foods section of the supermarket.*

- ½ cup chili sauce
- ¼ cup hoisin sauce
- 3 tablespoons (packed) golden brown sugar
- ¼ teaspoon ground ginger

- 6 beef back ribs (about 2 pounds)

COMBINE first 4 ingredients in heavy small saucepan. Stir over low heat until sugar dissolves.

DO AHEAD *Can be made 3 days ahead. Cover and chill.*

PREPARE barbecue (medium-high heat) or preheat broiler. (If broiling, line broiler pan with foil.) Sprinkle ribs with salt and pepper. Cook until brown, about 6 minutes per side. Brush 1 side with sauce and cook, sauce side down, until sauce bubbles and begins to brown, about 1 minute. Turn and repeat on second side.

Beef medallions with Cognac sauce

2 SERVINGS *Serve the steaks with smashed Yukon Gold potatoes and glasses of Cabernet Sauvignon.*

- 2 tablespoons (¼ stick) unsalted butter, divided
- ¼ cup chopped shallots
- 1 teaspoon (packed) dark brown sugar
- 1 cup low-salt chicken broth
- ½ cup beef broth
- ½ cup Cognac or brandy
- ¼ cup heavy whipping cream

- 2 4- to 5-ounce beef tenderloin steaks (each about 1 inch thick)

MELT 1 tablespoon butter in heavy medium saucepan over medium heat. Add shallots and sauté until tender, about 4 minutes. Add brown sugar; stir 1 minute. Add chicken broth, beef broth, and Cognac. Simmer until sauce is reduced to ½ cup, about 20 minutes. Whisk in cream.

DO AHEAD *Can be made 1 day ahead. Cover; chill.*

SPRINKLE steaks with salt and pepper. Melt remaining 1 tablespoon butter in heavy medium skillet over medium-high heat. Add steaks; cook to desired doneness, about 5 minutes per side for medium-rare. Transfer steaks to plates. Add sauce to skillet; bring to boil, scraping up browned bits. Season to taste with salt and pepper. Slice steaks; fan slices on plates. Top with sauce.

Filet mignon with green peppercorn cream sauce

4 SERVINGS *The green peppercorns called for—young peppercorns preserved in brine—add a tangy flavor to the sauce. Look for them in the supermarket near the olives and capers. Filet mignon steaks come from the small, tapered end of the tenderloin.*

1¾ cups beef broth

3 tablespoons butter

4 6- to 8-ounce filet mignon steaks (each about 1 inch thick)

¼ cup chopped shallots

1 cup heavy whipping cream

3 tablespoons Cognac or brandy

2 tablespoons drained green peppercorns in brine

BOIL broth in small saucepan until reduced to ¾ cup, about 7 minutes.

MEANWHILE, melt butter in large skillet over medium-high heat. Sprinkle steaks with salt and pepper. Add steaks to skillet and sauté to desired doneness, about 4 minutes per side for medium-rare. Transfer steaks to plate; tent loosely with foil to keep warm (do not clean skillet).

ADD shallots to same skillet and sauté 2 minutes. Remove from heat. Add reduced broth, cream, Cognac, and peppercorns. Boil until sauce thickens and coats spoon, about 6 minutes. Season sauce to taste with salt and pepper. Arrange steaks on plates. Spoon sauce over.

Hungarian-style beef with bell peppers and caraway

4 SERVINGS *This combination of ingredients—beef, paprika, caraway seeds, bell peppers, and tomato—is reminiscent of Hungarian goulash but much quicker to prepare. Serve with mashed potatoes or buttered egg noodles.*

1 1- to 1¼-pound rib-eye steak, trimmed, cut crosswise into ⅓-inch strips

1 tablespoon Hungarian sweet paprika

3 tablespoons olive oil, divided

4 garlic cloves, thinly sliced

½ teaspoon caraway seeds

3 bell peppers (preferably mixed colors), cut into ½-inch strips

⅓ cup beef broth

2 tablespoons tomato paste

1 teaspoon balsamic vinegar

TOSS beef with paprika, salt, and pepper in large bowl to coat. Heat 2 tablespoons oil in large non-stick skillet over high heat. Add garlic and caraway seeds; stir 30 seconds. Add bell peppers; toss 1 minute. Add broth. Cover; cook until peppers are crisp-tender, about 4 minutes. Using tongs, transfer peppers to bowl. Add remaining 1 tablespoon oil and beef to same skillet; sauté until beef is no longer pink on the outside, about 2 minutes. Mix in tomato paste and vinegar. Return half of peppers to skillet. Toss until beef is cooked to medium-rare, about 3 minutes longer. Season to taste with salt and pepper. Transfer to platter; top with remaining bell peppers.

Sliced filet mignon with fava beans, radishes, and mustard dressing

4 SERVINGS *For a gorgeous presentation, use a mix of regular radishes and, if you can find them, watermelon radishes, which have white or green skin and a bright pink interior. They are available at some supermarkets and natural foods stores, and at farmers' markets in late spring and early summer. In a pinch, frozen, shelled soybeans (edamame) or baby limas can stand in for the favas.*

    3   tablespoons apple cider vinegar
    2   teaspoons country-style Dijon mustard
    5   tablespoons extra-virgin olive oil, divided

    2   cups fresh fava beans (from about
         2 pounds pods) or frozen double-
         peeled fava beans, thawed
   10   medium radishes, very thinly sliced
    ¼   cup chopped assorted fresh herbs (such
         as tarragon, basil, thyme, and parsley)

    1   tablespoon butter
    4   6- to 7-ounce filet mignon steaks
         (each about ¾ inch thick)

    ⅓   cup crumbled feta cheese
         (preferably goat's-milk feta)

WHISK vinegar and mustard in small bowl. Gradually whisk in 4 tablespoons oil. Season dressing to taste with salt and pepper.

DO AHEAD *Dressing can be made 1 day ahead. Cover and chill.*

COOK fava beans in large pot of boiling salted water until tender, about 2 minutes. Transfer beans to bowl of ice water to cool quickly. Drain (and peel if using fresh). Transfer to paper towels to dry. Place beans, radishes, herbs, and dressing in medium bowl; toss to coat. Season with salt and pepper. Let salad stand at room temperature at least 20 minutes and up to 1 hour.

MELT butter with remaining 1 tablespoon oil in heavy large skillet over high heat. Sprinkle steaks with salt and pepper. Add steaks to skillet and cook to desired doneness, about 4 minutes per side for medium-rare. Transfer to cutting board; let rest 10 minutes. Cut each steak into 3 slices.

DIVIDE bean salad among plates. Arrange sliced steak atop salads and sprinkle cheese over.

SHELL GAME Fava beans need to be peeled twice, but it's easy to do. First, break open each pod and pop out the beans. Because the tender part of the bean is still encased in a tough shell, there's one more step. Boil the beans for about two minutes (at this point the shells will have started to split open), cool quickly in a bowl of ice water, and drain. The shells will slip off easily.

Ancho-rubbed steaks with clementine-red onion salsa

2 SERVINGS *The spicy steaks are balanced by the sweetness of the salsa. Members of the mandarin orange family, clementines have thin, easily peeled skins and tangy, red-orange fruit. They are widely available during the winter months, but can be hard to find (or poor quality) at other times of the year. If unavailable, substitute tangerines or regular oranges.*

1	cup diced peeled clementines
½	cup chopped red onion
¼	cup chopped fresh cilantro
2½	tablespoons olive oil, divided
2	teaspoons white wine vinegar
2½	teaspoons ancho chile powder or chili powder
⅛	teaspoon cayenne pepper
2	¾-inch-thick New York strip steaks

MIX clementines, red onion, cilantro, 1½ tablespoons oil, and vinegar in small bowl. Season salsa to taste with salt and pepper.

COMBINE chile powder and cayenne in small bowl. Sprinkle both sides of steaks with chile mixture, then salt. Heat remaining 1 tablespoon oil in heavy medium skillet over medium-high heat. Cook steaks to desired doneness, about 3 minutes per side for medium-rare. Serve steaks with salsa.

Porterhouse steaks with tapenade and balsamic vinegar

6 SERVINGS *Your butcher may have to cut these extra-thick steaks for you. In this recipe, the steaks are paired with tapenade, a paste made of olives, olive oil, capers, anchovies, lemon juice, and seasonings. It can be found at some supermarkets, specialty foods stores, and Italian markets. Or make something similar yourself: Blend pitted Kalamata olives and seasonings to coarse paste in the processor.*

¾	cup purchased tapenade or black olive paste
4	teaspoons chopped fresh rosemary
2	2-inch-thick porterhouse steaks (about 2 pounds each)
	Coarsely cracked black pepper
4	teaspoons olive oil
4	tablespoons balsamic vinegar

PREHEAT oven to 400°F. Mix tapenade and rosemary in small bowl to blend. Sprinkle steaks with salt and generous amount of pepper.

DIVIDE oil between 2 heavy medium ovenproof skillets set over high heat. Add 1 steak to each skillet and cook until browned, about 3 minutes per side. Spread half of tapenade mixture over each steak. Transfer skillets with steaks to oven. Roast until thermometer inserted into center of steaks registers 125°F for medium-rare, about 20 minutes. Transfer steaks to platter. Pour 2 tablespoons vinegar into each skillet. Cook over medium heat until pan juices are slightly reduced, scraping up browned bits, about 1 minute. Drizzle pan juices over steaks.

Spice-roasted porterhouse steaks

6 SERVINGS *The spice rub would also be delicious on a whole chicken, rack of lamb, or pork roast. Toasting the coriander seeds intensifies their flavor and adds smokiness. Ask the butcher to cut the steaks to 2-inch thicknesses. To check the internal temperature, insert the stem of an instant-read thermometer into the center of the larger meat portion from the side, not the top, of the steak.*

- 2 **tablespoons coriander seeds**
- 2 **tablespoons whole black peppercorns**
- 3 **tablespoons chopped fresh thyme**
- 3 **tablespoons chopped fresh rosemary**
- 4 **teaspoons coarse kosher salt**

- 2 **2-inch-thick porterhouse steaks**
  Extra-virgin olive oil

TOAST coriander seeds in heavy small skillet over medium heat until aromatic, about 2 minutes. Transfer to mortar or spice mill. Add peppercorns and crush or grind to coarse pieces. Transfer crushed spices to small bowl; mix in thyme, rosemary, and 4 teaspoons coarse salt. Store airtight for up to 3 days in refrigerator.

PLACE steaks on heavy rimmed baking sheet. Brush both sides with oil, then rub 1½ tablespoons spice mixture into each side of each steak. Let stand 30 minutes.

PREHEAT oven to 450°F. Roast steaks until thermometer inserted into center registers 125°F for rare, about 25 minutes. Transfer steaks to cutting board and let rest 10 minutes. Cut whole pieces of meat off bones and slice. Transfer slices to plates.

The grind If you don't already own a mortar and pestle, it's worth the small investment (usually less than $30). The tool, made up of a bowl-shaped base and a small, baseball-bat-shaped tool used for grinding, has been around for centuries. Some cooks say a mortar and pestle releases the flavor of spices better than a food processor or spice grinder and gives you more control over the grind consistency. Choose a sturdy, deep mortar (to keep the ingredients from popping out) and pestle made from nonporous material (granite and marble are good choices).

Skirt steak with poblano rajas and zucchini

4 SERVINGS Rajas *are roasted chile strips cooked with onion and spices (*raja *means "slice" in Spanish). The chile and zucchini mixture, with or without the steak, would also be delicious as a taco, tamale, or burrito filling. Look for fresh green poblano chiles (often called pasillas) in the produce section and ancho chile powder in the spice section of some supermarkets, and at specialty foods stores and Latin markets.*

2   **large poblano chiles, roasted (see note)**

2   **12-ounce skirt steaks**
3   **tablespoons olive oil, divided**
2   **teaspoons ground cumin, divided**
1   **teaspoon ancho chile powder**

1   **cup diced yellow or green zucchini**
¾   **cup chopped green onions**
½   **cup heavy whipping cream**

2   **tablespoons chopped fresh cilantro**

PEEL, seed, and cut roasted chiles lengthwise into ½-inch-wide strips.

BRUSH steaks with 1 tablespoon oil. Mix 1 teaspoon cumin and ancho chile powder in small bowl. Rub spice mixture on both sides of steaks, then sprinkle with salt and pepper.

HEAT 1 tablespoon oil in large nonstick skillet over medium-high heat. Add poblano chiles, zucchini, and green onions; sauté until zucchini is tender, about 2 minutes. Stir in remaining 1 teaspoon cumin. Add cream; boil until slightly thickened, about 2 minutes. Season rajas to taste with salt and pepper.

HEAT remaining 1 tablespoon oil in another large nonstick skillet over medium-high heat. Add steaks to skillet and cook to desired doneness, about 4 minutes per side for medium-rare. Transfer to board; let rest 5 minutes. Thinly slice across grain.

TRANSFER steak slices to platter. Top with rajas and chopped cilantro.

ROASTING CHILES To roast a chile (or bell pepper), place directly over a gas flame, using tongs to turn occasionally, until the chile is blackened on all sides. Then enclose it in a paper bag for 10 to 15 minutes to allow the chile to steam, which loosens the skin. (If you don't have a gas stove, you can roast the chile in the broiler.) Remove the blackened skin with your fingers or the back of a knife. Don't hold under water to remove the skin because flavorful juices will be rinsed away.

Roast beef tenderloin with wasabi-garlic cream

6 SERVINGS *Wasabi, the green Japanese horseradish paste used here, gives the sauce its heat. It is available in tubes in the Asian foods section of the supermarket or in small containers at sushi counters. For a different version, try Thai green curry paste in place of the wasabi (start with half a teaspoon and then add more to taste); finish the sauce by stirring in a little chopped fresh cilantro.*

- 1½ **cups heavy whipping cream**
- 2 **large garlic cloves, pressed**
- 1 **tablespoon wasabi paste (horseradish paste)**

- 1 **2¾- to 3-pound beef tenderloin**
- 2 **tablespoons olive oil**
- 1 **tablespoon coarse kosher salt**
- 1 **tablespoon sugar**

PREHEAT oven to 425°F. Cook cream and garlic in medium saucepan over medium-high heat until reduced to 1 cup, stirring frequently, about 15 minutes. Whisk in wasabi; cook 1 minute longer. Remove sauce from heat. Season to taste with salt.

PLACE beef on large rimmed baking sheet. Brush all over with oil. Mix coarse salt and sugar in small bowl; sprinkle all over top and sides of beef. Roast beef until thermometer inserted into center registers 125°F to 130°F for medium-rare (internal temperature will rise 5 to 10 degrees). Transfer to platter and let rest 15 minutes. Sprinkle with pepper. Reheat sauce. Cut beef into ½-inch-thick slices; serve with sauce.

> **KEEP IT STRAIGHT** Make sure all of the beef's thin, tough membrane (called silver skin) has been removed. If it is left on, the meat may curl as it cooks.

Roast beef tenderloin with sherry vinaigrette and watercress

6 SERVINGS *If you use the less-expensive tail end of the tenderloin, just tuck the tail under to create a roast of even thickness. Round out the meal with roasted new potatoes, green beans, and crusty bread.*

- 6 **tablespoons olive oil, divided**
- 1 **2¼-pound beef tenderloin roast (preferably from thick end or center)**
- 1½ **teaspoons coarse kosher salt**
- 2 **teaspoons coarsely ground mixed peppercorns**

- ¼ **cup Sherry wine vinegar**
- 1 **tablespoon whole grain Dijon mustard**
- ¼ **cup chopped shallots**

- 1 **large bunch watercress, thick stems trimmed**

PREHEAT oven to 500°F. Rub 1 tablespoon oil all over beef, then rub in coarse salt and peppercorns. Place beef on small rimmed baking sheet. Roast 10 minutes. Reduce heat to 450°F and roast until thermometer inserted into thickest part of meat registers 125°F for medium-rare, about 15 minutes longer. Let meat rest 15 minutes (internal temperature will rise 5 to 10 degrees).

MEANWHILE, whisk remaining 5 tablespoons oil, vinegar, and mustard in small bowl to blend. Stir in shallots and season vinaigrette to taste with salt and pepper.

ARRANGE watercress on small platter. Cut meat into ½-inch-thick slices; overlap slices atop watercress. Drizzle any accumulated juices over meat. Spoon half of vinaigrette down center of meat and over watercress. Serve, passing remaining vinaigrette separately.

Flank steak salad with roasted shallots and goat cheese

4 SERVINGS *This steak would also be great grilled. Roasting the shallots softens their bite and makes them slightly sweet.*

- 1 cup olive oil
- 5 tablespoons red wine vinegar
- 2 tablespoons fresh thyme leaves
- 2 large garlic cloves, peeled
- 1 1½-pound flank steak

- 18 large shallots, peeled, halved through root end

- 8 cups mixed salad greens (about 8 ounces)
- 1 cup crumbled chilled soft fresh goat cheese (about 4 ounces)

BLEND oil, vinegar, thyme, and garlic in blender until garlic is chopped; season dressing to taste with salt and pepper. Place steak in 13×9×2-inch glass baking dish. Add ⅓ cup dressing; turn to coat. Cover and chill 30 minutes.

DO AHEAD *Can be made 4 hours ahead; chill steak and dressing. Bring dressing to room temperature before using.*

MEANWHILE, preheat oven to 450°F. Toss shallots and 2 tablespoons dressing on rimmed baking sheet to coat. Roast shallots until brown and tender, stirring occasionally, about 20 minutes.

PREHEAT broiler. Place steak, with marinade still clinging, on broiler pan. Broil steak to desired doneness, about 4 minutes per side for medium-rare. Transfer to board; let rest 5 minutes. Slice thinly across grain on slight diagonal.

PLACE greens and roasted shallots in large bowl; toss with enough dressing to coat. Mound salad on large platter; surround with steak slices. Sprinkle goat cheese over. Serve, passing remaining dressing separately.

Harissa-crusted tri-tip roast

4 TO 6 SERVINGS *To save time, you can buy prepared harissa (a hot North African chili sauce) at some specialty foods stores and Middle Eastern markets. Sambal oelek (a fiery mixture of chiles, brown sugar, and salt) is available in the Asian foods section of most supermarkets and at Asian markets.*

- 1¾ teaspoons caraway seeds
- ¼ cup extra-virgin olive oil
- 6 garlic cloves, peeled
- ¼ cup chili paste (such as sambal oelek)
- 2 tablespoons tomato sauce
- 1½ teaspoons ground cumin
- 1¼ teaspoons chili powder

- 1 1¾- to 2-pound tri-tip beef roast, most of fat layer trimmed

PREHEAT oven to 400°F. Toast caraway seeds in small nonstick skillet over medium heat until seeds darken and begin to smoke, stirring often, about 5 minutes. Add oil and garlic. Cover; remove from heat. Let stand 1 minute. Pour caraway mixture into processor. Add chili paste, tomato sauce, cumin, and chili powder and blend until garlic cloves are pureed. Season harissa to taste with salt.

SPRINKLE beef all over with salt and pepper. Place beef, fat side down, on rack on rimmed baking sheet. Spread with half of harissa. Turn beef over; spread remaining harissa over top and sides. Roast beef until thermometer inserted into center registers 125°F for medium-rare, about 35 minutes. Let rest 10 minutes. Slice and serve.

WHAT'S IN A NAME? Tri-tip roast, which is popular on the West Coast, is cut from the bottom of the sirloin. It gets its name from its triangular shape. You may also see it labeled bottom sirloin roast, triangle roast, or Santa Maria steak.

Beef stroganoff

4 SERVINGS *The classic Russian dish-turned-classic American comfort food is now easier to make than ever. Use whatever combination of available wild mushrooms you like; regular button mushrooms would be fine, too.*

1½ pounds well-trimmed beef tenderloin, cut into 2×1×½-inch strips

8 tablespoons (1 stick) butter, divided

½ cup finely chopped shallots

4 garlic cloves, minced

1 pound assorted fresh wild mushrooms (such as stemmed shiitake, oyster, and crimini), thickly sliced

1 cup beef broth

1 cup heavy whipping cream

2 tablespoons brandy

4 tablespoons chopped fresh Italian parsley, divided

12 ounces wide egg noodles

SPRINKLE beef with salt and pepper. Melt 1 tablespoon butter in heavy large nonstick skillet over high heat. Add half of beef in single layer. Cook just until brown, about 1 minute per side. Transfer to bowl. Repeat with 1 tablespoon butter and remaining beef.

MELT 2 tablespoons butter in same skillet over medium-high heat. Add shallots and garlic. Sauté until tender, scraping up browned bits, about 2 minutes. Add mushrooms. Sprinkle with pepper and sauté until mushrooms brown and juices evaporate, about 4 minutes. Add broth, cream, and brandy. Simmer until thickened to sauce consistency, about 5 minutes. Add beef and any juices. Simmer over medium-low heat until beef is heated through but still medium-rare, about 2 minutes. Stir in 2 tablespoons parsley. Season with salt and pepper.

MEANWHILE, cook noodles in large pot of boiling salted water until tender, about 8 minutes. Drain. Transfer hot noodles to bowl. Add remaining 4 tablespoons butter and 2 tablespoons parsley and toss to coat. Season with salt and pepper. Divide noodles among plates. Top with beef and sauce.

Sesame beef and asparagus stir-fry

2 SERVINGS *This dish cooks in less than ten minutes, so it's important to have all of your ingredients prepped before you start cooking. Steam some rice ahead of time to serve with the stir-fry. Look for hoisin sauce and sesame oil in the Asian foods section of many supermarkets and at Asian markets. Slicing the sirloin across the grain creates shorter fibers, which makes the meat seem more tender.*

1½ tablespoons toasted sesame seeds

10 ounces top sirloin, thinly sliced across grain

2 tablespoons vegetable oil

¾ cup sliced red onion

8 ounces slender asparagus spears, trimmed, cut into 1½-inch pieces (about 2 cups)

⅓ cup water

2 tablespoons hoisin sauce

2 teaspoons Asian sesame oil

SPREAD sesame seeds on large plate. Sprinkle beef slices with salt and pepper, then coat with sesame seeds.

HEAT vegetable oil in heavy large skillet over high heat. Add onion; stir-fry 1 minute. Add asparagus; stir-fry until crisp-tender, about 2 minutes. Add beef; stir-fry until brown, about 2 minutes. Reduce heat to medium. Add ⅓ cup water and hoisin sauce. Cook until sauce is bubbling and coats beef and vegetables, tossing often, about 2 minutes. Stir in sesame oil. Season to taste with salt and pepper.

Seared Coriander Scallops with Bok Choy and Hoisin

Sautéed Shrimp with Lemon-Garlic Butter

Mahi-Mahi with Blood Orange, Avocado, and Red Onion Salsa

Grilled Porterhouse Topped with Tarragon-Tomato Salad
Zucchini, Red Onion, and Two-Cheese Flatbread

Sweet and Spicy Chipotle-Glazed Ribs

Polenta with Green Chiles and Cheese

Salmon wi
Pistachio-Basil But
Brussels Sprouts w
Lemon P

Beef, mushroom, and broccoli stir-fry

2 SERVINGS *In this recipe, you'll notice two uses for cornstarch—to coat the beef and keep its juices intact, and to thicken the sauce. Asian sesame oil and oyster sauce can be found in the Asian foods section of the supermarket. Rice is great alongside.*

½   **pound flank steak, cut crosswise into ⅛- to ¼-inch-thick slices, then into 3-inch pieces**

4½   **tablespoons plus ½ cup low-salt chicken broth, divided**

3   **tablespoons vegetable oil, divided**

2½   **tablespoons cornstarch, divided**

2   **tablespoons soy sauce, divided**

2   **tablespoons dry white wine**

2   **tablespoons Asian sesame oil**

1   **tablespoon oyster sauce**

2   **teaspoons minced peeled fresh ginger**

2   **cups broccoli florets**

8   **ounces mushrooms, sliced**

COMBINE beef, 1½ tablespoons broth, 1 tablespoon vegetable oil, 1 tablespoon cornstarch, and 1 tablespoon soy sauce in medium bowl and stir to coat. Refrigerate 30 minutes. Combine 3 tablespoons broth, wine, sesame oil, oyster sauce, and remaining 1½ tablespoons cornstarch and 1 tablespoon soy sauce in small bowl for sauce, stirring to dissolve cornstarch completely.

HEAT 1 tablespoon vegetable oil in heavy large skillet over high heat. Add beef with marinade and stir-fry until no longer pink, about 1½ minutes. Transfer to platter. Add remaining 1 tablespoon vegetable oil to skillet and heat over high heat. Add ginger; stir 30 seconds. Add broccoli and stir-fry until dark green, about 1 minute. Add remaining ½ cup broth. Cover, reduce heat, and simmer 2 minutes. Add mushrooms, cover, and cook until broccoli is crisp-tender, about 2 minutes. Return beef and juices to skillet. Stir sauce, add to wok, and toss until sauce thickens, about 30 seconds. Transfer mixture to platter.

Thai-style beef and asparagus curry

4 SERVINGS *In this intensely flavored dish, the heat from the Thai red curry paste is tempered by a little unsweetened coconut milk. Look for both ingredients in the Asian foods section of the supermarket and at Asian markets. Serve the curry over steamed jasmine rice. Round out the meal with mango sorbet.*

1   **pound top sirloin, cut crosswise into thin strips**

2   **teaspoons Thai red curry paste**

4   **tablespoons Asian stir-fry oil or peanut oil, divided**

12   **ounces asparagus spears, trimmed, cut into 1½-inch lengths**

1½   **cups canned unsweetened coconut milk**

⅓   **cup chopped fresh basil**
    Lime wedges

PLACE beef and curry paste in medium bowl. Stir to coat beef thoroughly.

DO AHEAD *Can be made 8 hours ahead. Cover; chill.*

HEAT 2 tablespoons oil in large skillet over high heat. Add asparagus and sauté until crisp-tender and beginning to char slightly, about 3 minutes. Using slotted spoon, transfer asparagus to bowl.

ADD remaining 2 tablespoons oil to same skillet. Add curry-coated beef in single layer. Cook over high heat without stirring until bottom of beef begins to brown, about 2 minutes. Add coconut milk and cook, stirring often, until sauce is bubbling and slightly reduced, about 2 minutes. Return asparagus to skillet and heat through. Stir in basil. Squeeze lime wedges over mixture.

Cajun meatloaf

2 TO 4 SERVINGS *Meatloaf was a staple on diner menus and dinner tables throughout the 20th century. It was particularly popular in the 1940s, when ground beef was a bargain and meat was rationed. This version of the classic dish has some spice and heat, thanks to cumin and a little cayenne pepper.*

 2   tablespoons (¼ stick) butter
 ½   large onion, chopped
 ½   green bell pepper, chopped
 1   teaspoon salt
 ¾   teaspoon cayenne pepper
 1   teaspoon ground cumin

 1   pound lean ground beef
 1   egg, beaten to blend
 ½   cup fine dry breadcrumbs
 ½   cup ketchup, divided

PREHEAT oven to 375°F. Melt butter in heavy medium skillet over medium-low heat. Add next 5 ingredients and sauté until vegetables are tender, about 10 minutes; sprinkle generously with pepper.

COMBINE meat, egg, breadcrumbs, and ¼ cup ketchup in medium bowl; blend well. Mix in sautéed vegetables. Form mixture into loaf 1¾ inches high and 5 inches wide in 11×7×2-inch glass baking dish. Bake 20 minutes. Spread top with remaining ¼ cup ketchup and bake until cooked through, about 40 minutes longer.

Southwestern blue plate special meatloaf

2 SERVINGS *In this recipe, crushed corn chips stand in for breadcrumbs or cracker crumbs. If you want to stay true to the recipe title, serve the meatloaf with mashed potatoes and gravy, green beans, and apple pie à la mode for dessert.*

 6   ounces ground pork
 6   ounces ground beef
 ½   cup finely crushed corn chips
 ½   cup thinly sliced green onions
 ½   cup chili sauce, divided
 1   large egg
 1¼   teaspoons chili powder
 ¾   teaspoon salt
 ½   teaspoon freshly ground black pepper

COMBINE pork, beef, corn chips, green onions, ¼ cup chili sauce, egg, chili powder, salt, and pepper in medium bowl; blend well. Divide mixture in half. Shape each half into ¾-inch-high oval and place halves, side by side, in 8×8×2-inch baking pan. Spread remaining ¼ cup chili sauce over loaves, dividing equally.

DO AHEAD *Can be made 8 hours ahead. Cover; chill.*

PREHEAT oven to 450°F. Bake meatloaves uncovered until cooked through and juices run clear when center is pierced with small sharp knife, about 20 minutes.

Sausage and bell pepper meatloaf

6 TO 8 SERVINGS *For a great sandwich, slice any leftover meatloaf and place on the bottom half of a lightly toasted ciabatta roll. Top with thinly sliced mozzarella or provolone cheese. Place the open-face sandwich under the broiler until the cheese melts. Cover with roll top and serve with chili sauce.*

- 1   **15-ounce can tomato sauce, divided**
- 2   **large eggs**
- 1½ **teaspoons dried sage, divided**
- 1   **teaspoon salt**
- ¾   **teaspoon coarsely ground black pepper, divided**
- 1¼ **pounds lean ground beef**
- 1   **12-ounce roll breakfast sausage**
- 1½ **cups chopped onion**
- 1½ **cups chopped green bell pepper**
- ½   **cup finely crushed crackers (such as Ritz)**
- 2   **large garlic cloves, minced**

PREHEAT oven to 350°F. Whisk ½ cup tomato sauce, eggs, 1 teaspoon sage, salt, and ½ teaspoon pepper in large bowl. Add ground beef, sausage, onion, bell pepper, cracker crumbs, and garlic; blend well. Pack mixture into 9×5×3-inch metal loaf pan. Mix remaining tomato sauce, ½ teaspoon sage, and ¼ teaspoon pepper in small bowl; pour over meatloaf.

BAKE meatloaf until thermometer inserted into center registers 160°F, about 1 hour 10 minutes.

Mastering meatloaf

— Before you start, leave the meat out on the counter for a few minutes. It will be easier to mix at room temperature.

— With hamburgers, the rule is not to overwork the meat. Not so with meatloaf. For a compact, flavorful meatloaf, you need to make sure the meat is seasoned throughout and the binder (e.g., breadcrumbs or crushed crackers) is evenly distributed. That means a bit of kneading with your hands until all ingredients are thoroughly mixed.

— For a perfectly cooked meatloaf, use a meat thermometer. Insert the thermometer into the center of the loaf. All meatloaves will be ready at 160°F.

— For maximum moistness, let the meatloaf rest in the pan for a few minutes before slicing into it.

Meatballs with parsley and Parmesan

MAKES ABOUT 44 *These meatballs are great with spaghetti and tomato sauce, as an hors d'oeuvre with a marinara dip, or in a submarine sandwich. To make fresh breadcrumbs, cut the crust off of a thick slice of French bread and process until crumbs form.*

  4 **large eggs**
  ½ **cup fresh breadcrumbs made
      from crustless French bread**
  6 **tablespoons grated Parmesan cheese**
  3 **tablespoons olive oil plus more for frying**
  ¼ **cup chopped fresh parsley**
  3 **large garlic cloves, minced**
  2 **teaspoons salt**
  1 **teaspoon freshly ground black pepper**
  2 **pounds lean ground beef**

STIR eggs, breadcrumbs, cheese, 3 tablespoons oil, parsley, garlic, 2 teaspoons salt, and 1 teaspoon pepper in large bowl to blend. Add ground beef and mix thoroughly. With moistened hands, form mixture into 1½-inch-diameter meatballs.

POUR enough oil into heavy large skillet to coat bottom; heat over medium-low heat. Working in batches, add meatballs and fry until brown and cooked through, turning frequently and adding more oil as needed, about 15 minutes per batch. Transfer to plate.

South American picadillo

4 SERVINGS *Picadillo is a popular dish in many Spanish-speaking countries. It is typically made with ground meat, tomatoes, garlic, and onions, but it's seasoned a little differently in every country—you might find capers, green olives, or raisins in the dish. Serve this version with rice, black beans, and a side of warm corn tortillas.*

  2 **tablespoons olive oil**
  2 **cups chopped onions**
  2 **cups chopped red bell peppers**
  4 **large garlic cloves, minced**
  2 **pounds lean ground beef**
  1 **tablespoon ground cumin**
  ½ **teaspoon cayenne pepper**
  2 **cups canned crushed tomatoes
      with added puree**
  1 **14.5-ounce can beef broth**
  1 **cup frozen peas**
  ¼ **cup drained capers**

HEAT oil in large pot over medium-high heat. Add onions, bell peppers, and garlic; sauté 5 minutes. Add beef, cumin, and cayenne; sauté until beef is brown, breaking up with back of fork, about 8 minutes. Add crushed tomatoes, broth, peas, and capers. Simmer until picadillo is thick, stirring occasionally, about 20 minutes. Season to taste with salt and pepper.

Corned beef and carrots with marmalade-whiskey glaze

6 SERVINGS *St. Patrick's Day falls on a weeknight? No problem. This zesty glaze comes together in just a few minutes, and the corned beef and carrots cook in just over half an hour. Buy the corned beef in the supermarket deli section or at a local delicatessen. Steam wedges of cabbage and toss with butter to serve on the side.*

	Nonstick vegetable oil spray
1	cup sweet orange marmalade
½	cup Irish whiskey
⅛	teaspoon ground nutmeg
1	tablespoon Dijon mustard plus more for serving
1	2- to 2¼-pound piece lean fully cooked corned beef
12	carrots, peeled, halved lengthwise
	Fresh parsley sprigs

PREHEAT oven to 425°F. Coat large rimmed baking sheet with nonstick spray. Boil next 3 ingredients in saucepan until reduced to generous ¾ cup, stirring often, about 7 minutes. Mix in 1 tablespoon mustard for glaze.

GENEROUSLY brush corned beef all over with some of glaze; place in center of prepared sheet. Toss carrots and ¼ cup glaze in large bowl to coat; place around beef. Sprinkle carrots with salt and pepper. Roast until carrots are tender and beef is golden, brushing occasionally with more glaze, about 35 minutes. Transfer to platter, garnish with parsley, and serve with mustard.

WHERE'S THE CORN? Corned beef gets its name from a form of curing known as "corning." When corned beef was made in earlier times, the meat was dry-cured with "corns," pellets of salt the size of corn kernels. Today, corned beef is brined instead of dry-cured, but the name remains.

Calf's liver with Port sauce

2 SERVINGS *Calf's liver is milder and more tender than beef liver. Ask your butcher to confirm that what you're buying is calf's liver, not "young beef liver," which will have a stronger flavor.*

    4 bacon slices, chopped
    ⅓ cup all purpose flour
    1 teaspoon salt
    1 teaspoon minced fresh thyme
    ¼ teaspoon freshly ground black pepper
    12 ounces calf's liver, sliced scant ½ inch thick
    1 small onion, chopped
    ¼ cup beef broth
    ¼ cup tawny or ruby Port
    2 tablespoons red wine vinegar

COOK bacon in heavy large skillet over medium-high heat until crisp. Transfer bacon to paper towels to drain. Pour off all but 2 tablespoons drippings from pan.

WHISK flour, salt, thyme, and pepper in shallow dish. Add liver and turn to coat; shake off excess. Heat drippings in skillet over medium-high heat. Add liver and cook until tender and brown on both sides, about 2½ minutes per side. Transfer liver to plates; tent loosely with foil to keep warm. Add onion to skillet and sauté until golden, about 5 minutes. Mix in broth, Port, and vinegar. Boil mixture until thick enough to coat spoon, about 2 minutes. Season sauce to taste with salt and pepper. Pour sauce over liver and sprinkle with bacon.

VEAL

Veal cutlets with mushrooms and tomatoes

4 SERVINGS *Any mushroom (or a mix of several different varieties) would be delicious in this dish. Three to try: crimini, portobello, and stemmed shiitake.*

- 4 tablespoons olive oil, divided
- 2 large garlic cloves, chopped
- ¾ teaspoon chopped fresh rosemary
- 12 ounces mushrooms, sliced
- 12 ounces plum tomatoes, seeded, chopped

- 1 pound thin veal cutlets
  All purpose flour
- 1 cup low-salt chicken broth
- ½ cup dry white wine

HEAT 2 tablespoons oil in heavy large saucepan over medium-high heat. Add garlic and rosemary; stir 30 seconds. Add mushrooms. Cover and cook 5 minutes, stirring occasionally. Uncover and sauté until mushrooms are golden brown, about 5 minutes longer. Add tomatoes and cook until softened, about 5 minutes. Remove from heat.

SPRINKLE veal with salt and pepper. Dust with flour. Heat 1 tablespoon oil in heavy large skillet over medium-high heat. Add half of veal. Sauté until brown and cooked through, about 2 minutes per side. Transfer veal to platter; tent with foil to keep warm. Repeat with remaining 1 tablespoon oil and veal. Add broth and wine to same skillet. Boil until reduced by half, scraping up browned bits, about 4 minutes. Add mushroom mixture and stir to blend. Season sauce to taste with salt and pepper; spoon sauce over veal.

Classic saltimbocca

6 SERVINGS *Saltimbocca is Italian for "jumps in the mouth," which implies that this traditional Roman dish is so tasty, it practically springs into your mouth. We won't argue: The combination of veal, sage, and prosciutto topped with a white-wine pan sauce is pretty tough to resist. Save time by having the butcher pound the scaloppine for you.*

- 1½ pounds veal scaloppine, pounded to ¼-inch thickness
- ¼ pound (about) thinly sliced prosciutto
- 1 large bunch fresh sage (with large leaves)
- 5 tablespoons (about) butter, divided

- 1 cup dry white wine

PREHEAT oven to 250°F. Sprinkle veal on both sides with salt and pepper. Top each piece with 1 prosciutto slice and 1 sage leaf. Reserve 1 tablespoon butter for sauce. Melt 1½ tablespoons of remaining butter in heavy large skillet over high heat until foaming. Working in batches and adding more butter as needed, add veal, prosciutto side down, in single layer. Sauté until brown, about 1 minute. Using spatula, carefully turn veal over, keeping sage leaf intact. Sauté until brown, about 1 minute longer. Transfer to rimmed baking sheet; keep warm in oven. Reserve skillet.

ADD wine to pan drippings in skillet; cook over high heat until sauce is reduced by ⅓, scraping up browned bits, about 2 minutes. Add any juices from baking sheet. Whisk in reserved 1 tablespoon butter. Season sauce to taste with salt and pepper. Transfer veal to platter and pour sauce over.

Veal scaloppine with Gorgonzola sauce

4 SERVINGS *Serve the veal over fettuccine or linguine with a green salad alongside. Chicken, turkey, or pork cutlets are good substitutes for the veal.*

1 cup beef broth
1 cup low-salt chicken broth

1 pound veal scaloppine
All purpose flour
3 tablespoons (about) olive oil, divided

1 cup heavy whipping cream
¾ cup chopped seeded plum tomatoes, divided
6 tablespoons chopped fresh basil, divided
1 tablespoon tomato paste
⅔ cup crumbled Gorgonzola cheese, divided

BOIL beef broth and chicken broth in medium saucepan until reduced to 1 cup, about 10 minutes. Remove from heat.

SPRINKLE veal with salt and pepper. Dredge veal in flour to coat; shake off excess. Heat 1 tablespoon oil in heavy large skillet over high heat. Working in batches, add veal and sauté until cooked through, about 2 minutes per side. Transfer veal to platter; tent with foil to keep warm. Repeat with remaining veal, adding more oil to skillet as needed.

ADD reduced broth mixture, cream, ½ cup chopped tomatoes, 4 tablespoons basil, and tomato paste to skillet. Simmer until reduced to sauce consistency, whisking frequently, about 5 minutes. Add ⅓ cup Gorgonzola; stir until melted.

POUR sauce over veal. Sprinkle with remaining ¼ cup chopped tomatoes, 2 tablespoons basil, and ⅓ cup Gorgonzola.

THE BLUES English Stilton, Spanish Cabrales, and American Maytag blue are other fabulous blue cheeses to use in place of the Gorgonzola.

Grilled veal chops and radicchio with lemon-caper sauce

2 SERVINGS *This sophisticated dish comes together in a flash. Make it an extra-special meal by adding an arugula salad, baby potatoes roasted with rosemary and thyme, and glasses of rosé Champagne.*

4 tablespoons extra-virgin olive oil, divided
1½ tablespoons white balsamic vinegar
1½ tablespoons drained capers
1½ tablespoons chopped fresh Italian parsley
1¼ teaspoons finely grated lemon peel
1 small garlic clove, minced

2 8- to 9-ounce veal rib chops
(each about ¾ inch thick)

6 radicchio leaves

WHISK 3 tablespoons oil and next 5 ingredients in small bowl to blend. Season sauce to taste with salt and pepper.

PREPARE barbecue (medium-high heat) or heat heavy large skillet over medium-high heat. Brush veal chops with remaining 1 tablespoon oil; sprinkle with salt and pepper. Place veal chops on grill or in skillet and cook to desired doneness, about 6 minutes per side for medium. Transfer to plates.

BRUSH radicchio lightly with some of sauce. Place leaves on grill or in batches in skillet and cook just until slightly wilted but not brown, pressing lightly to flatten, about 45 seconds to 1 minute per side.

DIVIDE radicchio between plates. Spoon sauce over veal and radicchio.

Grilled veal chops with warm tomato-olive vinaigrette

4 SERVINGS *When shopping for veal, look for meat that is white to pale pink with a smooth, fine-grained texture. Because veal doesn't contain much fat, it's important to keep an eye on the cooking time so the meat doesn't dry out.*

4   8-ounce veal rib chops
5   tablespoons extra-virgin olive oil, divided

1   large garlic clove, minced
1½   cups diced seeded plum tomatoes
½   cup coarsely chopped pitted Kalamata olives
½   cup thinly sliced fresh basil
1   tablespoon red wine vinegar

PREPARE barbecue (medium-high heat). Brush veal chops with 1 tablespoon oil; sprinkle with salt and pepper. Grill veal to desired doneness, about 4 minutes per side for medium. Transfer to plates.

MEANWHILE, combine remaining 4 tablespoons oil and garlic in small saucepan. Set at edge of grill to heat oil until garlic is fragrant, about 1 minute. Mix in tomatoes, olives, basil, and vinegar. Stir vinaigrette until heated through, about 2 minutes. Season to taste with salt and pepper; serve with chops.

Veal chops with Creole mustard crust

2 SERVINGS *Look for Creole mustard (whole grain mustard with a spicy kick) in the supermarket's condiment aisle. If you can't find Creole mustard, use whole grain Dijon mustard with a dash of hot pepper sauce.*

¼   cup Creole mustard
2   tablespoons mayonnaise
2   green onions, chopped, divided

2   8-ounce veal rib chops (each about 1 inch thick)
    Ground allspice
2   tablespoons olive oil
1   large garlic clove, minced
1   cup fresh breadcrumbs made from crustless French bread

POSITION rack in bottom third of oven; preheat to 450°F. Stir mustard, mayonnaise, and half of green onions in small bowl to blend.

SPRINKLE veal chops on both sides with salt, pepper, and allspice. Heat oil in heavy medium skillet over medium-high heat. Add veal; sauté until brown, about 2 minutes per side. Transfer veal to small rimmed baking sheet. Add garlic to drippings in skillet; stir 15 seconds. Add breadcrumbs; sauté until golden and crisp, about 1 minute.

SPREAD half of mustard mixture thickly atop each chop. Spoon crumbs atop mustard mixture. Bake until thermometer inserted horizontally into center of chops registers 135°F for medium-rare, about 7 minutes. Transfer to plates. Sprinkle with remaining green onions.

Broiled veal chops with mixed peppercorns

6 SERVINGS *Each peppercorn—black, green, pink, and white—adds a different flavor nuance to the chops. Jars of mixed peppercorns are available in the spice section of the supermarket.*

6   ¾-inch-thick veal loin chops (8 to 10 ounces each), trimmed
3   tablespoons olive oil
2   tablespoons coarsely ground mixed peppercorns
1   tablespoon minced fresh rosemary

PLACE veal chops in baking dish. Brush with oil, then sprinkle both sides with peppercorns and rosemary. Let stand at room temperature 1 hour.

DO AHEAD *Can be prepared 1 day ahead. Cover and refrigerate.*

PREHEAT broiler. Transfer veal chops to broiler pan. Sprinkle with salt. Broil veal to desired doneness, about 5 minutes per side for medium-rare. Transfer veal to plates. Pour any pan drippings over veal.

Broiled veal chops with mustard-sage butter

2 SERVINGS *Save some of the mustard-sage butter to mix with steamed brussels sprouts on the side, and serve the chops with linguine tossed with sautéed mushrooms.*

1½   tablespoons plus 2 teaspoons minced fresh sage
1   large garlic clove, minced
2   1½-inch-thick veal loin chops
2   teaspoons balsamic vinegar
1   tablespoon olive oil

3   tablespoons butter, room temperature
2   teaspoons Dijon mustard

RUB 1½ tablespoons sage and garlic onto both sides of veal; sprinkle with pepper. Drizzle vinegar over, then oil. Let stand at least 30 minutes and up to 2 hours.

MEANWHILE, combine butter, mustard, and remaining 2 teaspoons sage in small bowl. Season butter generously with pepper.

PREHEAT broiler. Broil veal until cooked to desired doneness, about 7 minutes per side for medium-rare. Transfer to plates. Top each chop with dollop of seasoned butter.

PORK

Grilled chipotle-stuffed pork tenderloin

4 SERVINGS *Serve this smoky-spicy dish with Spanish rice and grilled bell peppers drizzled with citrus vinaigrette.*

- 2 **15-ounce pork tenderloins**
- 2 **tablespoons finely chopped canned chipotle chiles in adobo sauce, 1 tablespoon sauce reserved**

- ⅓ **cup plain whole-milk yogurt**
- 1 **tablespoon olive oil plus more for brushing**
- 1 **tablespoon cumin seeds**

    Purchased guacamole

PREPARE barbecue (medium heat).

PLACE tenderloins on work surface. Starting at 1 long side, cut each horizontally to within ½ inch of opposite side. Open like book and sprinkle with salt. Spread 1 tablespoon chopped chiles down center of each tenderloin. Close tenderloins, pressing to adhere, and sprinkle with salt.

WHISK yogurt, 1 tablespoon oil, cumin, and reserved 1 tablespoon adobo sauce in small bowl to blend. Transfer tenderloins to plate and brush each heavily with some of yogurt sauce. Set tenderloins aside 15 minutes.

BRUSH grill rack with oil. Grill tenderloins, brushing occasionally with remaining yogurt sauce, until just cooked through and thermometer inserted into thickest part of meat registers 145°F, about 10 minutes per side. Transfer tenderloins to platter. Let stand 5 minutes, then cut crosswise into ½-inch-thick slices. Serve tenderloins with guacamole.

MORE FOR *MAÑANA* If you're cooking for only two, make both tenderloins anyway, then use the leftovers to make a *torta* (a Mexican sandwich): Place thin slices of the pork on a French roll and top with romaine lettuce, sliced tomatoes, onions, cilantro, and guacamole. You could even mix a little adobo sauce (from the can of chipotle chiles) into some mayonnaise and spread it over the bread.

Grilled Asian pork chops and baby bok choy

4 SERVINGS *The black bean garlic sauce used in the marinade for these pork chops is a Chinese staple made with salted, fermented black beans. Look for it in the Asian foods section of some supermarkets and at Asian markets.*

- ⅓ cup black bean garlic sauce
- 3 garlic cloves, minced
- 1½ tablespoons soy sauce
- 1½ tablespoons Asian sesame oil
- 1 tablespoon fresh lime juice
- 1 tablespoon finely chopped peeled fresh ginger
- 4 boneless center-cut pork chops (about 8 ounces each)

- 4 baby bok choy, halved lengthwise

- 2 tablespoons chopped fresh cilantro
- 4 lime wedges

PREPARE barbecue (medium-high heat). Whisk black bean sauce, garlic, soy sauce, oil, lime juice, and ginger in shallow dish. Measure 2 tablespoons marinade; set aside. Add pork to remaining marinade; let stand 20 minutes.

REMOVE pork from marinade; brush cut side of bok choy with reserved 2 tablespoons marinade. Grill pork until just cooked through and thermometer inserted into thickest part registers 145°F, about 5 minutes per side. Grill bok choy until softened and lightly charred, about 5 minutes total.

DIVIDE pork and bok choy among plates. Sprinkle with cilantro and garnish with lime wedges.

> **MORE TO TRY** Try mixing black bean garlic sauce into hoisin sauce for another quick marinade, or add it to a stir-fry for a jolt of flavor.

Grilled pork chops with chunky andouille barbecue sauce

6 SERVINGS *Pork rib chops are very lean and tender—perfect for grilling. They have a bit more fat than pork loin chops, which helps keep them moist, but if the ribs are not available, the loin chops make a good substitute. Be sure to take them off the grill as soon as they're cooked through: They'll become dry and tough the minute they're overcooked.*

- Nonstick vegetable oil spray
- 1½ cups diced andouille sausage (about 7 ounces)
- 1½ cups chopped onion
- 2 cups tomato sauce
- ¼ cup balsamic vinegar
- 1 tablespoon (packed) dark brown sugar
- 2 teaspoons chili powder plus more for sprinkling
- 1 teaspoon ground cumin plus more for sprinkling

- 6 1-inch-thick pork rib chops

SPRAY grill rack with nonstick spray and prepare barbecue (medium heat). Sauté sausage and onion in heavy large saucepan over medium-high heat until onion begins to brown, about 8 minutes. Add tomato sauce, vinegar, sugar, 2 teaspoons chili powder, and 1 teaspoon cumin. Bring to boil; remove from heat.

MEANWHILE, sprinkle pork chops on both sides with salt, then chili powder and cumin. Grill chops until cooked through but not dry, about 9 minutes per side.

SERVE chops with sauce.

Grilled pork tenderloin with fresh cherry chutney

4 SERVINGS *Chutney is a condiment made from fruit and accented with vinegar, sugar, and spices. This shortcut version mixes purchased cherry preserves with fresh cherries, and has a complex spicy, sweet, savory flavor that pairs well with the grilled pork. Serve any extra chutney as a spread for a grilled pork sandwich, or serve it with sharp cheddar cheese.*

¾ cup cherry preserves
3 tablespoons balsamic vinegar
¾ teaspoon ground allspice

1 tablespoon vegetable oil
⅔ cup chopped onion
2 cups fresh cherries, pitted
¼ teaspoon cayenne pepper

1 1¼-pound pork tenderloin

PREPARE barbecue (medium heat). Mix preserves, vinegar, and allspice in medium bowl. Set aside ¼ cup of preserves mixture for glaze; reserve remaining preserves mixture.

HEAT oil in large skillet over high heat. Add onion; sauté 1 minute. Add cherries, cayenne, and reserved preserves mixture. Boil chutney until thick, stirring often, about 8 minutes. Season to taste with salt. Set chutney aside.

SPRINKLE pork with salt and pepper; brush with some of glaze. Cook over hottest part of grill until brown. Move to coolest part and grill until thermometer inserted into thickest part of pork registers 145°F, turning often and brushing with glaze, about 25 minutes total. Transfer pork to platter. Let rest 10 minutes. Rewarm reserved chutney; serve with pork.

THE PITS If you don't have a cherry pitter, try this method: Place the flat side of a large knife on the cherry and press gently until it splits open, then pull out the pit—this is a technique you can also use to pit olives.

Grilled pork satay

2 SERVINGS; CAN BE DOUBLED *A popular snack sold by street vendors from Thailand to Indonesia, satay is made by pairing grilled skewered meats with a spicy peanut sauce. The sauce in this recipe doubles as the marinade—a real time-saver. Pork cutlets are used here, but pork scaloppine, chicken tenders, and beef tenderloin make good alternatives.*

3 tablespoons chunky peanut butter
2 tablespoons fresh lime juice
2 tablespoons low-sodium soy sauce
1 tablespoon minced peeled fresh ginger
2 garlic cloves, minced
¼ teaspoon (generous) dried crushed red pepper
8 to 10 ounces pork cutlets (about ¼ inch thick), cut into ½-inch-wide strips
4 8-inch wooden skewers, soaked in water 30 minutes

¼ cup thinly sliced green onions

PREPARE barbecue (medium-high heat). Whisk peanut butter, lime juice, soy sauce, ginger, garlic, and crushed red pepper in shallow baking dish until combined. Set aside 2 tablespoons sauce. Add pork strips to remaining sauce in baking dish and toss to coat completely. Thread pork strips onto skewers. Let stand 10 minutes.

GRILL until pork is slightly charred and cooked through, about 3 minutes per side. Brush with reserved 2 tablespoons sauce and cook 30 seconds. Transfer to platter. Sprinkle with green onions.

Pork tenderloin with rhubarb-currant chutney

6 SERVINGS *Make this recipe in the spring, when rhubarb is in season and at its peak. Rhubarb looks like a big, red celery stalk and has a tart flavor that pairs well with the sweet and spicy flavors here. It becomes very tender and falls apart easily when cooked, creating a nice texture in the chutney; the chutney would also complement grilled chicken or salmon.*

¾ cup (packed) dark brown sugar
⅓ cup apple cider vinegar
2 tablespoons water
1 tablespoon minced peeled fresh ginger
1½ teaspoons finely grated lemon peel
1 cinnamon stick
2 cups ½-inch pieces fresh rhubarb
½ cup dried currants

2 1-pound pork tenderloins
1 tablespoon vegetable oil

BRING first 6 ingredients to boil in heavy medium saucepan over high heat, stirring until sugar dissolves. Reduce heat to low and simmer 5 minutes. Increase heat to medium-high. Add rhubarb and currants; bring to boil. Reduce heat to low and simmer gently until rhubarb is tender, about 5 minutes. Season chutney to taste with salt.

DO AHEAD *Can be made 3 days ahead. Cool slightly. Cover and refrigerate. Rewarm before using.*

PREPARE barbecue (medium-high heat). Rub pork with oil and sprinkle with salt and pepper. Grill pork until thermometer inserted into thickest part registers 145°F, turning occasionally, about 20 minutes. Using tongs, transfer pork to cutting board; let pork rest 10 minutes. Cut into ½-inch-thick slices. Serve with chutney.

Pork kebabs marinated in honey, rosemary, and orange

6 SERVINGS *The marinade also makes a delicious glaze for the kebabs (it's boiled first, to destroy any harmful bacteria that may have been left behind by the pork). Because country-style pork ribs are well-marbled, they can stand the heat of the grill without drying out too quickly. You'll need 12 metal skewers for grilling the pork kebabs.*

2 tablespoons fresh rosemary leaves
4 2-inch-long strips orange peel
½ cup olive oil
6 tablespoons honey
6 tablespoons orange juice
3 tablespoons fresh lemon juice
2 garlic cloves, crushed
2 pounds boneless country-style pork ribs, trimmed, cut into 1-inch cubes

24 (about) bay leaves

COMBINE rosemary and orange peel in large bowl. Using wooden spoon, press down on mixture to release oils. Add olive oil, honey, orange juice, lemon juice, and garlic. Season with salt and pepper. Add pork, stirring to coat with marinade. Cover; chill at least 2 hours and up to 4 hours.

PREPARE barbecue (medium heat). Thread pork onto 12 metal skewers, sliding 1 bay leaf between every 2 or 3 cubes. Sprinkle pork with salt and pepper. Transfer marinade to heavy small saucepan; bring to boil, stirring frequently. Grill pork until cooked through, turning frequently and brushing occasionally with marinade, about 12 minutes. Arrange skewers on platter.

Pork rib chops with sautéed apples and star anise

2 SERVINGS *Pork and apples are a classic combination—and a little star anise in the caramelized apples adds a modern Asian twist. Look for these brown star-shaped seedpods in the spice section of the supermarket and at specialty foods stores and Asian markets.*

1 tablespoon vegetable oil
2 12-ounce pork rib chops

3 tablespoons butter, divided
1 tablespoon (packed) brown sugar
4 whole star anise
2 Fuji apples (about 1 pound), cored, sliced ½ inch thick
½ cup apple juice
2 teaspoons apple cider vinegar

HEAT oil in heavy large skillet over medium heat. Sprinkle pork with salt and pepper. Add pork to skillet; cook until brown on both sides and thermometer inserted horizontally into pork registers 140°F, about 7 minutes per side. Transfer to plates; tent with foil.

POUR off drippings from skillet. Add 2 tablespoons butter, brown sugar, and star anise to same skillet and stir over high heat until melted. Add apples; cook until brown and caramelized, stirring frequently, about 8 minutes. Spoon apples over pork. Add apple juice and vinegar to skillet; boil sauce until reduced to 2 tablespoons, about 3 minutes. Whisk in remaining 1 tablespoon butter; season to taste with salt and pepper. Drizzle sauce over apples and pork.

IT'S IN THE BONES Be sure to use chops—which have a curved rib bone attached and meat on one side—rather than boneless cutlets. The bone adds flavor and insulates the meat, keeping it from cooking too quickly.

Pork chops with cranberry, Port, and rosemary sauce

4 SERVINGS *This recipe would make delicious use of leftover Thanksgiving cranberry sauce, but it can be made any time of year with fresh, cooked, or canned cranberry sauce. The addition of Port gives the sauce a sophisticated flavor (no one needs to know the sauce came from a can).*

4 1-inch-thick pork rib chops
2¾ teaspoons minced fresh rosemary, divided
2 tablespoons (¼ stick) butter
¾ cup low-salt chicken broth
¾ cup tawny Port
1 cup cranberry sauce

SPRINKLE pork chops with salt, pepper, and 1 teaspoon rosemary. Cook butter in heavy large skillet over medium heat until beginning to brown. Add pork chops and cook until browned and cooked through, about 5 minutes per side. Transfer to platter; cover to keep warm. Add broth, Port, and remaining 1¾ teaspoons rosemary to same skillet; boil until liquid is slightly reduced, about 4 minutes. Add cranberry sauce; bring to boil, then reduce heat to medium and simmer until sauce is thickened, about 7 minutes. Season sauce to taste with salt and pepper. Spoon sauce over pork.

ANY PORT IN A STORM Tawny Port works best here for the nutty flavor it imparts, but ruby Port, dry Marsala, or Madeira would also taste good.

Roast pork tenderloins with balsamic-chestnut glaze

4 SERVINGS *When roasting this pork tenderloin, a very hot oven browns the outside of the meat: This not only makes it look delicious but also adds a rich, hearty flavor—and a little coating of Dijon mustard adds even more. Although the pork needs to marinate for at least an hour, it roasts in the oven without much supervision, freeing up your time to make the quick and easy pan sauce.*

¼ cup olive oil

¼ cup plus 3 tablespoons balsamic vinegar

2 12- to 16-ounce pork tenderloins

3 tablespoons Dijon mustard

2 tablespoons (¼ stick) butter

1½ cups peeled roasted chestnuts or jarred chestnuts, finely chopped

3 garlic cloves, chopped

1 tablespoon sugar

2 teaspoons chopped fresh sage

3 tablespoons water

COMBINE oil and ¼ cup vinegar in heavy large roasting pan. Add pork; turn to coat. Marinate pork 1 hour at room temperature or 2 hours in refrigerator. Transfer pork to large rimmed baking sheet; pat dry. Discard marinade in pan.

PREHEAT oven to 400°F. Spread mustard over top of pork, then sprinkle with salt and pepper. Roast pork until thermometer inserted into center registers 145°F, about 25 minutes. Remove pork from oven; let stand 10 minutes.

MEANWHILE, melt butter in heavy medium saucepan over medium heat. Stir in chestnuts, garlic, sugar, and sage; cook 2 minutes. Add remaining 3 tablespoons vinegar and 3 tablespoons water; bring to boil. Reduce heat to low and simmer until mixture thickens slightly, about 3 minutes. Season glaze to taste with salt and pepper.

SLICE pork into ½-inch-thick rounds. Transfer to platter. Drizzle with warm glaze.

Pork with Gorgonzola sauce

6 SERVINGS *Pork tenderloin is the leanest cut of pork, so it pairs well with this rich and creamy Gorgonzola sauce. Because the pork tenderloin is tender, it cooks quickly; because it is long, thin, and boneless, it is easy to carve and serve, making it a good choice for entertaining.*

Pork

- ¼ **cup Dijon mustard**
- 1 **tablespoon olive oil**
- 1 **tablespoon dried thyme**
- 2 **12-ounce pork tenderloins**

Gorgonzola Sauce

- 1 **tablespoon butter**
- 1 **tablespoon all purpose flour**
- 1 **cup heavy whipping cream**
- ¼ **cup dry white wine**
- ¼ **cup low-salt chicken broth**
- 1 **cup crumbled Gorgonzola cheese (about 4 ounces)**

FOR PORK: Oil large rimmed baking sheet. Whisk mustard, oil, and thyme in small bowl to blend. Sprinkle pork tenderloins with salt and pepper. Heat heavy large nonstick skillet over high heat. Add pork and sear until brown all over, turning occasionally, about 10 minutes. Transfer seared pork to prepared baking sheet. Spread mustard mixture over all sides of pork.

DO AHEAD *Can be prepared up to 2 hours ahead. Refrigerate pork uncovered.*

PREHEAT oven to 425°F. Roast pork until thermometer inserted into thickest part of meat registers 150°F, about 30 minutes. Remove from oven and let stand 5 minutes.

MEANWHILE, PREPARE GORGONZOLA SAUCE: Melt butter in heavy small saucepan over medium heat. Add flour and whisk 1 minute. Gradually whisk in cream, wine, and broth. Boil until mixture is thick enough to coat spoon, whisking frequently, about 1 minute. Add crumbled Gorgonzola cheese and whisk until cheese is melted and smooth and sauce is reduced to desired consistency, about 5 minutes.

SLICE pork and transfer to plates. Ladle some sauce over pork. Serve, passing additional sauce separately.

Pork medallions with chili-maple sauce

2 SERVINGS *Cutting the tenderloin crosswise into medallions shortens its long fibers, making this ultra-tender meat practically melt in your mouth. Pounding the medallions also tenderizes them, and creates more surface area to season, in this case with Chinese five-spice powder. You'll find this seasoning and the chili-garlic sauce in the Asian foods section of most supermarkets. Serve the pork with steamed white rice to soak up the sweet and spicy sauce.*

1   12-ounce pork tenderloin
½   teaspoon Chinese five-spice powder

1   tablespoon vegetable oil
¾   cup low-salt chicken broth
1½   tablespoons pure maple syrup
1   tablespoon chili-garlic sauce
1   green onion, chopped

CUT tenderloin crosswise into 6 slices. Using meat mallet or rolling pin, pound medallions between sheets of plastic wrap to ½-inch thickness. Sprinkle with salt, pepper, and five-spice powder.

HEAT oil in large skillet over high heat. Add pork; cook until brown and cooked through, about 3 minutes per side. Transfer to platter. Add next 3 ingredients to skillet. Boil until reduced to scant ¼ cup, about 2 minutes. Pour sauce over pork; sprinkle with green onion.

Pork cutlets with maple, mustard, and sage sauce

2 SERVINGS; CAN BE DOUBLED *When pan-frying these cutlets, you'll want to use a heavy skillet large enough to fit them all with space in between. If the meat is crowded, the temperature of the pan will be reduced and the meat will not brown properly.*

4   boneless pork loin chops
3   teaspoons minced fresh sage or
     1 teaspoon dried, divided

1   tablespoon butter
½   cup low-salt chicken broth
1   tablespoon pure maple syrup
1   tablespoon coarse-grained mustard

USING meat mallet or rolling pin, pound pork between sheets of plastic wrap to ⅓-inch thickness. Sprinkle with 1½ teaspoons fresh sage (or ½ teaspoon dried), salt, and generous amount of pepper.

MELT butter in heavy medium skillet over medium-high heat. Add pork and cook until brown on both sides and cooked through, about 1½ minutes per side. Transfer pork to plate, leaving drippings in skillet. Add broth, maple syrup, mustard, and remaining 1½ teaspoons fresh sage (or ½ teaspoon dried) to skillet. Boil until syrupy, scraping up browned bits, about 3 minutes. Reduce heat to low. Return pork and any juices to skillet and cook until just heated through, about 1 minute. Serve pork with sauce.

Pork cutlets with figs and balsamic vinegar

4 SERVINGS *Cooking the cutlets in two batches helps ensure that they brown evenly. Cook them just until they are brown on the outside and still pink in the center, as they will continue to cook through while in the oven. Use a rimmed baking sheet to catch all the juices from the pork; these juices give the sauce delicious pork flavor.*

8	⅓-inch-thick pork cutlets
1½	tablespoons olive oil
1	tablespoon butter
¼	cup minced shallots
3	tablespoons balsamic vinegar
1	cup low-salt chicken broth
6	fresh ripe figs, quartered
½	cup heavy whipping cream
1	tablespoon minced fresh parsley

PREHEAT oven to 200°F. Sprinkle pork with salt and pepper. Heat 1 tablespoon oil in heavy large skillet over medium-high heat. Add 4 pork cutlets and sauté until brown, about 2 minutes per side. Transfer pork to rimmed baking sheet. Add remaining ½ tablespoon oil to skillet. Repeat with remaining 4 pork cutlets. Transfer pork to oven to keep warm.

MELT butter in same skillet over medium-high heat. Add shallots and sauté until tender, about 2 minutes. Add 2 tablespoons vinegar. Simmer until vinegar evaporates, scraping up browned bits, about 1 minute. Add broth. Simmer until mixture is reduced by half, about 4 minutes. Add figs and cream. Simmer until sauce thickens slightly, about 4 minutes. Add remaining 1 tablespoon vinegar and any juices from pork. Simmer until sauce thickens enough to coat spoon, about 2 minutes longer. Season sauce to taste with salt and pepper.

ARRANGE pork on plates. Spoon sauce over and sprinkle with parsley.

Pan-frying 101 When pan-frying, the idea is to balance the amount of heat so that the outside of the meat browns in the same amount of time needed to cook the inside to the desired doneness, resulting in a nice crisp crust and moist interior. If the pan is too hot or if the cut of meat is too thick, the meat will brown before it is cooked through. If the pan is too cool, the meat won't brown enough by the time the center is done. The pan should be very hot before the butter or oil and cutlets are added. Listen to the sound of the pork: It should sizzle when it hits the pan. The dial on your stove will work as your "gas pedal" for the temperature as the meat cooks, and other visual cues will tell you if the temperature is correct. If the meat doesn't continue to sizzle as it cooks, turn the heat up. If you see smoke, turn the heat down.

Pork and sausage sauté

6 SERVINGS *This delicious regional specialty of Spain and Portugal, called* migas, *is a dish of sautéed meats served over fried bread. In this version, the pork tenderloin is cut into bite-size pieces and tossed with paprika. Linguiça is a seasoned, fully cooked smoked sausage used in many Portuguese and Brazilian dishes; kielbasa works, too.*

2 **pounds pork tenderloin, trimmed, cut into 1-inch cubes**

1 **tablespoon paprika**

8 **cups ¾-inch cubes crustless day-old French bread**

1 **cup (or more) boiling water**

½ **teaspoon salt**

¼ **teaspoon freshly ground black pepper**

4 **bacon slices, chopped**

8 **ounces fully cooked smoked sausage (such as linguiça or hot links), cut into ¾-inch pieces**

2 **garlic cloves, chopped**

¼ **cup olive oil**

PLACE pork in medium bowl. Add paprika; toss to coat. Cover; chill at least 4 hours or overnight.

PLACE bread cubes in large bowl. Add 1 cup boiling water. Using potato masher, crush mixture until bread reaches consistency of mashed potatoes, adding more boiling water if mixture is dry. Stir in ½ teaspoon salt and ¼ teaspoon pepper. Divide into 6 equal portions.

SAUTÉ bacon in large skillet over medium heat until golden, about 6 minutes. Add pork, sausage, and garlic. Sauté until pork is cooked through, about 15 minutes. Season to taste with salt and pepper.

HEAT oil in another large skillet over medium-high heat. Working in batches, add bread portions to oil, flattening to 4-inch rounds with wet spoon. Cook until brown, about 5 minutes per side. Place fried bread on plates. Top with meat.

Spiced pork tenderloin

2 SERVINGS; CAN BE DOUBLED *Use a heavy metal roasting pan, rather than a glass or ceramic baking dish, for this recipe: The pan comes out of the oven and is set over high heat on the stove to make the sauce; a glass or ceramic dish will shatter or crack from the direct heat. The sauce should be made in the roasting pan, as the pork leaves behind delicious pan drippings and browned bits that add great flavor to the sauce.*

1 **tablespoon olive oil**

1 **garlic clove, mashed**

¾ **teaspoon ground cumin**

¼ **teaspoon ground cinnamon**

¼ **teaspoon ground cloves**

1 **¾- to 1-pound pork tenderloin**

⅓ **cup low-salt chicken broth**

2 **tablespoons chopped fresh cilantro**

PREHEAT oven to 450°F. Blend first 5 ingredients in small bowl. Rub pork with spice mixture and sprinkle with salt and pepper. Place in 13×9×2-inch metal roasting pan. Roast until thermometer inserted into center of pork registers 145°F, about 20 minutes. Transfer pork to plate.

ADD broth to pan. Set pan directly over high heat and bring broth to boil, scraping up browned bits. Simmer until pan juices thicken slightly, about 3 minutes. Slice pork into rounds; place on plates. Top with pan juices and cilantro.

Roast pork chops with bacon and wilted greens

2 SERVINGS *Bags of assorted greens—washed, chopped, and ready to use—are available in the supermarket produce department. They give "fast food" new meaning, as they're also nutritional powerhouses, containing calcium, fiber, vitamins, and antioxidants.*

- 2   1½-inch-thick pork rib chops
- 3   tablespoons chopped fresh marjoram, divided
- ½   teaspoon ground allspice
- 2   tablespoons olive oil

- 2   thick-cut bacon slices, chopped
- 2   garlic cloves, pressed
- 8   cups (packed) wide strips assorted greens (such as mustard greens and red Swiss chard), stems discarded
- 5   teaspoons Sherry wine vinegar, divided
- ½   cup low-salt chicken broth
- 2   tablespoons Dijon mustard

PREHEAT oven to 475°F. Sprinkle both sides of pork with 2 tablespoons marjoram, allspice, and generous amount of salt and pepper. Heat oil in heavy large nonstick skillet over high heat. Add pork and brown well, including edges, turning with tongs, about 7 minutes. Transfer pork to small rimmed baking sheet; reserve skillet. Roast pork in oven until thermometer inserted into center of chops from side registers 145°F, about 9 minutes.

MEANWHILE, add bacon to oil in reserved skillet. Sauté over medium heat until brown, about 3 minutes. Mix in garlic. Add greens. Cook until just wilted, turning with tongs, about 3 minutes. Add 1 teaspoon vinegar; season to taste with salt and pepper. Using tongs, transfer greens to colander to drain, leaving some of bacon in skillet for sauce. Add broth, mustard, and remaining 4 teaspoons vinegar to skillet. Simmer until slightly thickened, about 4 minutes. Mix in remaining 1 tablespoon marjoram. Season to taste with salt and pepper.

MOUND greens on plates; top with pork. Spoon sauce alongside.

Roast pork tenderloin with kumquats, cranberries, and apples

6 SERVINGS *Sophisticated flavors make this an impressive dish for entertaining, yet it's easy to make. Because the rinds of the kumquats are edible, the fruit doesn't need to be peeled. Using an ovenproof skillet allows you to brown the pork on the stove, then roast it in the oven with all the other ingredients, saving you a little time on cleanup, too.*

- 2 1-pound pork tenderloins
- 2½ teaspoons chopped fresh rosemary, divided
- 2 tablespoons olive oil
- 4 large shallots, chopped
- ¾ cup diced dried apples
- ¼ pound kumquats, quartered, seeded
- ½ cup fresh cranberries or frozen, thawed
- 1½ cups low-salt chicken broth
- ½ cup dry white wine

PREHEAT oven to 375°F. Sprinkle pork with 2 teaspoons rosemary, salt, and pepper. Heat oil in large ovenproof skillet over medium-high heat. Add pork (cut to fit, if necessary) and brown on all sides, about 10 minutes. Transfer pork to plate. Add shallots to skillet and sauté 4 minutes. Add apples, kumquats, and cranberries; stir until heated through. Add broth, wine, and remaining ½ teaspoon rosemary. Boil 1 minute. Return pork and any juices to skillet, turning to coat with juices.

PLACE skillet in oven and roast pork until thermometer inserted into center registers 145°F, about 25 minutes. Transfer pork to platter; let stand 10 minutes. If thicker sauce is desired, boil juices in skillet until thick enough to coat spoon. Season sauce to taste with salt and pepper. Slice pork crosswise and spoon sauce over.

Salt- and pepper-crusted pork

2 SERVINGS; CAN BE DOUBLE OR TRIPLED *Rubs are great flavor enhancers for tender pork tenderloins. This one couldn't be any easier—you probably already have salt, pepper, and dried rosemary in your cupboard. While you're at it, make a little extra rub to have on hand for seasoning other meats, like steak and chicken, and oven-roasted potatoes. If doubling or tripling the recipe, brown the pork in batches in a skillet, then transfer to a rimmed baking sheet to finish cooking in the oven.*

- 2 teaspoons freshly ground black pepper
- 1 teaspoon salt
- 1 teaspoon dried rosemary, crumbled
- 1 large garlic clove, minced
- 1 12-ounce (about) pork tenderloin

- 1 tablespoon olive oil

COMBINE pepper, salt, rosemary, and garlic in small bowl. Rub over pork. Let pork stand 15 minutes.

PREHEAT oven to 400°F. Heat oil in heavy medium ovenproof skillet over high heat. Add pork and brown on all sides, about 6 minutes. Transfer skillet with pork to oven and roast until pork is cooked through, turning occasionally, about 20 minutes. Slice and serve.

SIMPLY THE BEST Because this rub is so simple, make sure that the ingredients are top quality. Instead of iodized table salt (which can have a slightly bitter flavor), use fine sea salt; and rather than waste time trying to extract flavor from previously ground black pepper, pull out that pepper mill or spice grinder for some freshly ground black pepper. These little upgrades will make a big difference in this rub—and in the rest of your cooking.

Spicy pork and kumquat stir-fry

4 SERVINGS *Because this stir-fry cooks so quickly—within five minutes—have all of the ingredients ready before you heat the pan, and line them up in the order they will be added to the pan. Hoisin sauce, oyster sauce, Chinese five-spice powder, and hot chili sesame oil are available in the Asian foods section of many supermarkets and at Asian markets.*

- 1 pound ½-inch-thick boneless pork loin chops (about 6), cut crosswise into ⅓-inch-wide strips
- 2 tablespoons hoisin sauce
- 1 tablespoon oyster sauce
- 1 tablespoon cornstarch
- 2 teaspoons Chinese five-spice powder
- 5 ounces kumquats, quartered lengthwise, seeded
- 1 tablespoon sugar

- 1½ tablespoons hot chili sesame oil
- 2 tablespoons minced peeled fresh ginger
- ½ cup low-salt chicken broth
- 1 teaspoon unseasoned rice vinegar

BLEND first 5 ingredients in medium bowl. Combine kumquats and sugar in small bowl. Let stand 30 minutes, stirring kumquat mixture occasionally.

HEAT oil in heavy large nonstick skillet over high heat. Add ginger and stir 1 minute. Add pork mixture and stir-fry until pork is just cooked through, separating pork strips, about 3 minutes. Add kumquat mixture, broth, and vinegar and stir until sauce boils and thickens, about 1 minute. Season to taste with salt and pepper.

Five-spice pork stir-fry with soba noodles

2 SERVINGS *Chinese five-spice powder is a mixture of Szechuan peppercorns, cinnamon, star anise, cloves, and fennel seeds, and is used in Chinese and Vietnamese cuisines. Japanese soba noodles contain buckwheat flour, which gives them their characteristic brown-gray color, and are boiled in salted water just like Italian pastas. Both of these ingredients can be found in the Asian foods section of most supermarkets. If soba noodles are not available, use rice noodles or spaghetti instead.*

- 1 6-ounce package soba noodles or other thin noodles
- ½ pound ⅓-inch-thick boneless center-cut pork chops, cut crosswise into thin strips
- 1 teaspoon Chinese five-spice powder
- 3 tablespoons peanut oil, divided
- 2 tablespoons soy sauce
- 1½ tablespoons unseasoned rice vinegar

- 1 cup thinly sliced green onions
- ¾ cup thinly sliced small radishes

COOK noodles in large pot of boiling salted water until almost tender but still firm to bite. Drain well, then return to pot.

MEANWHILE, sprinkle pork with salt, pepper, and five-spice powder. Heat 1 tablespoon oil in medium nonstick skillet over high heat. Add pork and stir-fry until cooked through, about 2 minutes. Add remaining 2 tablespoons oil, soy sauce, and vinegar; stir 30 seconds.

ADD pork, green onions, and radishes to noodles and toss. Season to taste with salt and pepper.

Jamaican jerk pork tenderloin with black beans and yellow rice

4 TO 6 SERVINGS *Jamaican jerk seasoning blends can include nearly a dozen different spices and flavorings (a hallmark of jerk seasonings), including allspice, cloves, ginger, mustard seed, fennel seed, thyme, paprika, garlic, and pepper. When using spice blends, look for those that do not contain salt or monosodium glutamate (MSG). While the pork roasts on the baking sheet in the oven, cook the rice and beans in the same skillet used to brown the pork.*

1   1¼-pound pork tenderloin

6   teaspoons salt-free Jamaican jerk seasoning (such as The Spice Hunter), divided

2   tablespoons olive oil, divided

1   large onion, finely chopped

1   cup basmati rice

¼   teaspoon turmeric

1½   cups low-salt chicken broth

¼   teaspoon (generous) salt

1   15-ounce can black beans, drained

3   tablespoons chopped fresh cilantro

SPRINKLE pork generously with salt and 5 teaspoons jerk seasoning, coating evenly. Let stand while preparing remaining ingredients.

PREHEAT oven to 350°F. Heat 1 tablespoon oil in heavy large skillet over medium-high heat. Add pork and cook until just browned on all sides, about 4 minutes. Transfer pork to rimmed baking sheet; reserve skillet. Roast pork in oven until instant-read meat thermometer inserted into thickest part registers 145°F, about 20 minutes. Let stand 5 minutes.

MEANWHILE, heat remaining 1 tablespoon oil in same skillet over medium-high heat. Add onion and sauté until tender, about 5 minutes. Add rice, turmeric, and remaining 1 teaspoon jerk seasoning and stir 1 minute. Add broth and generous ¼ teaspoon salt and bring to simmer. Reduce heat to low, cover tightly, and simmer without stirring until rice is tender and liquid is absorbed, about 15 minutes. Stir in beans and cilantro. Mound rice and beans on platter. Slice pork and arrange atop rice. Drizzle with any juices from pan and cutting board.

Asian-style pork stir-fry

4 SERVINGS *Peanut oil is the preferred oil for stir-frying because it can reach very high temperatures before it begins to burn or smoke—a requirement for this very high-heat cooking method. Safflower oil or soybean oil make good substitutes, as they, too, can get good and hot before burning.*

- 2 **tablespoons soy sauce**
- 2 **tablespoons honey**
- 1 **tablespoon minced peeled fresh ginger**
- ¼ **teaspoon dried crushed red pepper**
- 1 **12-ounce pork tenderloin, fat trimmed, halved lengthwise**

- 1 **pound green beans, trimmed**

- ⅓ **cup orange juice**
- 1 **teaspoon unseasoned rice vinegar**
- 1 **teaspoon cornstarch**
- 2 **teaspoons peanut oil**
- 1 **teaspoon finely grated orange peel**
- 1 **garlic clove, minced**

MIX first 4 ingredients in 13×9×2-inch glass baking dish. Add pork tenderloin halves and turn to coat. Cover and let stand at room temperature 1 hour or refrigerate up to 4 hours.

COOK green beans in large pot of boiling salted water until just crisp-tender. Drain.

HEAT large nonstick skillet over medium heat. Add pork, reserving marinade in dish. Cook until pork is deep brown and thermometer inserted into center of pork registers 145°F, turning often, about 9 minutes. Transfer to platter; let stand 10 minutes. Cut pork into ⅓-inch-thick slices. Wipe skillet clean.

WHISK orange juice, vinegar, cornstarch, and reserved marinade in small bowl. Heat oil in same skillet over high heat. Add green beans and sauté until beginning to brown, about 2 minutes. Add orange peel, garlic, pork slices, and orange-juice mixture. Stir until sauce boils, thickens slightly, and coats bean-pork mixture, about 1 minute. Season to taste with salt and pepper. Transfer to bowl.

Sweet and spicy chipotle-glazed ribs

2 SERVINGS; CAN BE DOUBLED OR TRIPLED *Look for meaty baby back pork ribs that aren't over-trimmed; the bones on top shouldn't show through. The baked ribs in this recipe are coated with a spicy, sweet, and smoky glaze; the sweetness comes from the red currant jelly and pomegranate molasses. You'll find pomegranate molasses at some supermarkets, specialty foods stores, and Middle Eastern markets. (Or boil 2 cups of pomegranate juice until reduced to a thick syrup, about ⅓ cup. It should take about 20 minutes; stir often to avoid burning.) Canned chipotle chile in adobo sauce are available in some supermarkets and at Latin markets.*

  1 **2-pound rack baby back pork ribs**

  ¼ **cup canned chipotle chiles**
  ¾ **cup red currant jelly**
  5 **tablespoons pomegranate molasses**
  ¼ **cup low-salt chicken broth**
  2 **tablespoons olive oil**
  ¼ **teaspoon ground allspice**

PREHEAT oven to 350°F. Line rimmed baking sheet with foil; place metal rack on sheet. Sprinkle ribs all over with salt and pepper; place ribs, meat side down, on rack.

PRESS chiles through sieve into heavy small saucepan; discard solids in sieve. Add all remaining ingredients to pan. Stir to blend over medium heat until sauce comes to boil. Season sauce to taste with salt. Transfer ½ cup sauce to bowl; reserve.

BRUSH ribs with 2 tablespoons sauce from pan. Turn ribs over; brush with 2 tablespoons sauce. Roast ribs until very tender, brushing with 2 tablespoons sauce every 15 minutes, about 1 hour 30 minutes. Cut rack into individual ribs. Serve with reserved sauce.

Oven-roasted spareribs with peach glaze

4 SERVINGS *Spareribs are larger and meatier than baby back ribs, and come from the side or belly area of the pig, whereas the baby back ribs come from the loin of the pig. Peach preserves, fresh lemon juice, and Dijon mustard form the sweet and tangy base for this glaze.*

  1 **cup peach preserves**
  ¼ **cup fresh lemon juice**
  ¼ **cup Dijon mustard**
  2 **teaspoons chili powder**
  ½ **teaspoon hot pepper sauce**
  ¼ **teaspoon salt**
  ¼ **teaspoon freshly ground black pepper**
  1 **3-pound rack pork spareribs**

PREHEAT oven to 350°F. Whisk first 7 ingredients in heavy small saucepan to blend for sauce. Place spareribs, meat side down, on large baking sheet. Sprinkle with salt and pepper; spread with ⅓ cup sauce. Turn ribs over. Sprinkle with salt and pepper; spread with ⅓ cup sauce. Roast ribs 45 minutes.

BRING remaining sauce in pan to boil. Brush 2 tablespoons sauce over ribs. Roast ribs until sauce forms sticky glaze, about 8 minutes. Cut rack into individual ribs; serve with sauce.

AMAZING GLAZE The chili powder and hot pepper sauce in the glaze can be swapped out to create lots of variations. For instance, use chopped fresh jalapeño chiles and a touch of allspice for a Jamaican twist; some fresh minced ginger, dry Sherry, and orange zest for an Asian-style glaze; or a splash of whiskey for a glaze with southern comfort.

Roasted sausages, apples, and cabbage with caraway

2 SERVINGS *Pick up any high-quality fully cooked German sausages such as bratwurst, knockwurst, and frankfurters. Because the sausages are already cooked, you need to roast them only until they are hot and browned. Serve this satisfying meal with coarse-grained mustard, a side of mashed potatoes, and ice-cold dark German beer.*

  3 tablespoons olive oil
  1 tablespoon chopped fresh thyme
  ½ teaspoon caraway seeds
  4 1-inch-thick wedges red onion
  2 1-inch-thick wedges red cabbage
  2 small apples (such as Pink Lady or Granny Smith), quartered, cored
  1½ teaspoons balsamic vinegar, divided
  3 assorted fully cooked smoked sausages

PREHEAT oven to 450°F. Mix oil, thyme, and caraway seeds in small bowl. Arrange onion, cabbage, and apples on heavy large baking sheet. Drizzle oil mixture over. Sprinkle generously with salt and pepper. Drizzle ¾ teaspoon vinegar over cabbage and onion. Roast 10 minutes. Add sausages to baking sheet; cook until sausages brown and cabbage is crisp-tender, turning once, about 15 minutes longer. Cut sausages diagonally in half. Transfer sausages, onion, cabbage, and apples to platter. Drizzle remaining ¾ teaspoon vinegar over cabbage and onion wedges.

Soft tacos with sausage and feta

MAKES 4 *When the casings are removed from sausage, the meat inside can be cooked like any ground meat. Here, the sausage meat is cooked with onion and cumin to make a kind of Mediterranean taco.*

  2 tablespoons olive oil
  2 hot Italian sausages (about 6½ ounces), casings removed
  1 small red onion, thinly sliced
  1 teaspoon ground cumin

  4 6-inch-diameter corn tortillas
  ⅓ cup crumbled feta cheese
  ½ cup chopped fresh cilantro
  1⅓ cups sliced romaine lettuce
      Purchased red or green salsa

HEAT oil in large nonstick skillet over medium-high heat. Add sausage and cook until brown, coarsely crumbling with back of spoon, about 4 minutes. Push sausage to side of skillet. Add onion and cumin to skillet; sauté until onion is golden and sausage is cooked through, about 8 minutes. Stir to combine.

CHAR tortillas over gas flame or electric burner until blackened in spots, turning with tongs. Wrap in foil; let stand 2 minutes. Fill each tortilla with sausage mixture, 1 generous tablespoon feta, 2 tablespoons cilantro, and ⅓ cup lettuce. Serve with salsa.

DON'T STOP THERE... There are plenty of other uses for hot Italian sausage meat: Form it into balls for a one-step version of spaghetti and meatballs, use it to stuff bell peppers, or shape it into patties and pan-fry to serve as burgers on dinner rolls.

LAMB

Grilled tandoori lamb

6 SERVINGS *This quick preparation creates the flavor that lamb gets from an Indian tandoor (clay oven). It takes only a few minutes of toasting for the spices to become aromatic, which makes a considerable difference in the flavor, so don't skip this important step. (Think of how different a piece of bread tastes after it is toasted—it takes on a whole new personality.)*

- 2 **tablespoons cumin seeds**
- 2 **teaspoons fennel seeds**
- 2 **teaspoons cardamom seeds**
- ½ **teaspoon whole black peppercorns**
- 1½ **teaspoons dried crushed red pepper**

- 6 **tablespoons olive oil**
- 2 **tablespoons minced peeled fresh ginger**
- 4 **garlic cloves, pressed**
- 1 **5¾-pound leg of lamb, boned, butterflied (about 4 pounds boned)**

  Nonstick vegetable oil spray

TOAST first 4 ingredients in heavy small skillet until aromatic, stirring constantly, about 2 minutes. Transfer to bowl; mix in crushed red pepper and cool. Finely grind mixture in spice grinder.

WHISK oil, ginger, and garlic in small bowl; whisk in spice mixture. Place lamb on rimmed baking sheet. Pour marinade over. Cover and refrigerate 3 hours.

SPRAY grill rack with nonstick spray; prepare barbecue (medium-high heat). Sprinkle lamb with salt and pepper. Grill lamb until instant-read thermometer inserted into thickest part of meat registers 125°F, about 25 minutes for medium-rare. Let lamb rest 5 minutes before slicing.

FRESHLY GROUND SPICES If you don't have a spice mill, a coffee grinder works just as well. To start and finish with a clean grinder, whirl some bread in the coffee grinder to absorb the residue, then toss the bread out and wipe the grinder clean.

Grilled lamb kebabs with coriander and cumin

2 SERVINGS; CAN BE DOUBLED *Lamb shoulder meat is great for kebabs—it's flavorful and inexpensive. When skewering the lamb, leave a little room between each piece, allowing the lamb pieces to brown on all sides and cook a bit more quickly. If unexpected dinner guests arrive, add some bell pepper pieces, cherry tomatoes, zucchini slices, or onion wedges to the skewers to serve more people.*

- 1½ tablespoons olive oil
- 2 teaspoons red wine vinegar
- 1 large garlic clove, minced
- ¾ teaspoon ground cumin
- ¾ teaspoon ground coriander
- ½ teaspoon cayenne pepper
- ¼ teaspoon salt
- 1⅓ to 1½ pounds lamb shoulder (round-bone) chops, trimmed, boned, cut into 1-inch pieces
- 4 8-inch wooden skewers, soaked in water 30 minutes

PREPARE barbecue (medium-high heat) or preheat broiler. Whisk first 7 ingredients in medium bowl to blend. Add lamb; toss to coat evenly. Let stand 5 minutes. Thread lamb onto skewers, leaving ½-inch space between pieces.

GRILL or broil lamb until crusty brown outside but still pink inside, turning occasionally, about 8 minutes. Arrange skewers on plates.

A TANGY FINISH Stick a lemon wedge on the end of each skewer before grilling—as the lemon cooks, the tartness mellows a bit—then squeeze the lemon over the grilled lamb.

Hunan lamb chops

4 SERVINGS *Szechuan-Hunan cuisine is well known for its hot and spicy flavors, dark-colored dishes, and use of chiles and garlic. These lamb chops have it all: lots of garlic, a little chili oil, and hoisin sauce (the latter two can be found in the Asian foods aisle of most supermarkets or at Asian markets). Serve the chops with a sesame noodle salad with chopped fresh cilantro, and cucumber slices tossed in rice wine vinaigrette.*

- ⅓ cup hoisin sauce
- 2 tablespoons soy sauce
- 2 tablespoons dry Sherry
- 2 teaspoons chili oil
- 1 tablespoon unseasoned rice vinegar
- 3 garlic cloves, finely chopped
- ½ cup thinly sliced green onions, divided
- 8 ½-inch-thick lamb shoulder (round-bone) chops (about 2 pounds total)

PREPARE barbecue (high heat). Whisk hoisin sauce, soy sauce, Sherry, chili oil, rice vinegar, and garlic to blend in shallow dish; mix in ⅓ cup green onions. Add lamb and turn to coat. Let lamb marinate 20 minutes.

BRUSH grill rack with oil. Grill lamb to desired doneness, about 3 minutes per side for medium-rare. Place 2 lamb chops on each plate. Sprinkle lamb with remaining green onions.

Lamb chops with spicy peanut sauce

4 SERVINGS *Lamb loin chops look like mini T-bone steaks. They are absolutely tender and delicious, and best suited for quick, dry-heat cooking methods, such as grilling, broiling, and pan-frying. Use chops that are at least ¾ inch thick so that they remain medium-rare, which is the best doneness for this cut.*

¾	cup purchased Asian peanut sauce
2	tablespoons soy sauce
1	tablespoon fresh lime juice
1	tablespoon grated peeled fresh ginger
8	¾- to 1-inch-thick lamb loin chops

PREPARE barbecue (medium-high heat). Whisk together first 4 ingredients in small saucepan. Brush about 5 tablespoons of sauce over both sides of chops. Reserve remaining sauce.

GRILL lamb to desired doneness, about 4 minutes per side for medium rare. Place 2 chops on each plate. Bring remaining sauce to simmer. Drizzle over lamb.

> **A SIMPLE SOLUTION** Adding a few flavorful ingredients to a purchased sauce or dressing is an easy way to create your own dish. The rule of thumb: Combine ingredients from the same cuisine. In this recipe, an Asian peanut sauce is improved with other robust Asian ingredients—ginger, soy sauce, and lime juice. Another example: Add fresh rosemary and minced garlic to a bottled balsamic vinaigrette.

Grilled spiced lamb chops with cucumber-mint sauce

4 SERVINGS *A cool and creamy raita—yogurt mixed with fresh mint and cucumber—is the perfect counterpoint to spicy Indian curry-coated lamb. Look for red curry paste in the Asian foods section of the supermarket; green curry paste would work, too. Steam basmati rice to go alongside.*

8	lamb loin chops (about 2½ pounds total)
2	to 3 tablespoons red curry paste
1	teaspoon cumin seeds
1	cup plain yogurt
1	cup diced seeded peeled cucumber
3	tablespoons chopped fresh mint

PREPARE barbecue (medium-high heat) or preheat broiler. Brush lamb on all sides with curry paste. Let stand 15 minutes.

TOAST cumin seeds in small skillet over medium heat 1 minute. Place seeds in resealable plastic bag; crush coarsely with rolling pin. Mix cumin, yogurt, cucumber, and mint in small bowl.

GRILL or broil lamb chops until charred outside and pink inside, about 3 minutes per side. Serve with cucumber-mint sauce on the side.

Grilled lamb with curried kumquat chutney

6 SERVINGS *This sweet-tart chutney is delicious alongside lamb or pork chops, atop goat cheese and crackers, or on biscuits with sliced ham. Reducing the liquids in the chutney helps concentrate the flavors and thicken it.*

- ½ cup sugar
- ¼ cup white wine vinegar
- 2 tablespoons chopped crystallized ginger
- 2 tablespoons dried cranberries
- 1 teaspoon curry powder
- 1⅓ cups thinly sliced seeded kumquats (6 to 7 ounces), divided
- 2 tablespoons chopped fresh cilantro

- 12 1-inch-thick lamb loin chops
  Olive oil

COOK first 5 ingredients and 1 cup kumquats in heavy small saucepan over medium heat until reduced to scant 1 cup, stirring occasionally, about 10 minutes. Transfer to small bowl. Chill until cold, then mix in remaining ⅓ cup kumquats and cilantro. Season chutney to taste with salt and pepper. Cool completely.

PREPARE barbecue (medium-high heat). Brush lamb with oil. Sprinkle with salt and pepper. Grill chops to desired doneness, about 4 minutes per side for medium-rare. Transfer lamb to plates. Serve with chutney.

Butterflied leg of lamb with thyme and orange

8 SERVINGS *If you find butterflied leg of lamb rolled up and tied with string or wrapped in netting, just remove the string or netting and unroll the lamb before preparing it.*

- 1½ tablespoons chopped fresh thyme
- 1½ tablespoons finely grated orange peel
- 3 garlic cloves, minced
- 1½ teaspoons coarse kosher salt
- 1½ teaspoons freshly ground black pepper
- 1 4-pound boneless leg of lamb, fat well trimmed
  Olive oil

COMBINE thyme, orange peel, garlic, salt, and pepper in small bowl. Open lamb on rimmed baking sheet. Using small sharp knife, make twelve ½-inch-deep slits on each side of lamb. Fill each slit with ½ teaspoon thyme mixture. Rub any remaining thyme mixture over both sides of lamb. Brush lamb lightly with olive oil.

DO AHEAD *Can be prepared ahead. Let stand 2 hours at room temperature or cover and refrigerate up to 1 day.*

PREPARE barbecue (medium-high heat). Grill lamb until brown and crusty and meat thermometer inserted into thickest part registers 125°F for medium-rare, about 8 minutes per side. Transfer lamb to platter. Let stand 15 minutes. Slice lamb thinly across grain.

Moroccan-spiced rack of lamb with pomegranate reduction

2 SERVINGS *Rack of lamb tastes and looks impressive but is very easy to cook. A heavy coating of Moroccan spices—cumin, coriander, cinnamon, paprika, and turmeric—is a perfect pairing with the robust flavors of lamb. Serve this with couscous (another Moroccan specialty) that's studded with toasted pine nuts and sprinkled with fresh mint. Pomegranate juice is available at many supermarkets and at natural foods stores and Middle Eastern markets.*

  1 **cup pomegranate juice**
  1 **cup low-salt chicken broth**
  1 **shallot, minced**
  1 **garlic clove, pressed**

  2 **teaspoons cumin seeds**
  2 **teaspoons coriander seeds**
 ½ **cinnamon stick**
  2 **teaspoons paprika**
 ¼ **teaspoon turmeric**

  1 **1½-pound rack of lamb, well-trimmed**
     Olive oil

  1 **tablespoon butter, room temperature**

COMBINE first 4 ingredients in heavy small saucepan. Simmer over medium heat until reduced to ⅓ cup, about 20 minutes. Remove sauce from heat. Cover and set aside.

MEANWHILE, preheat oven to 425°F. Toast cumin seeds, coriander seeds, and cinnamon in heavy small skillet over medium-high heat until aromatic, about 2 minutes. Cool slightly. Finely grind toasted spices in spice grinder or coffee grinder. Mix in paprika and turmeric.

PLACE lamb rack on heavy baking sheet. Brush lamb with olive oil. Sprinkle generously with salt and pepper. Sprinkle spices evenly over lamb.

ROAST lamb until instant-read meat thermometer inserted into thickest part of lamb registers 130°F to 135°F, about 28 minutes for medium-rare. Remove from oven and let stand 10 minutes.

BRING sauce to simmer. Remove from heat and whisk in butter. Season sauce to taste with salt and pepper. Cut lamb between bones into individual chops. Transfer to plates. Spoon sauce over lamb.

DRESS IT UP For a more elegant presentation of the lamb, ask the butcher to remove all the fat and meat from between and around the ends of the rib bones—a technique known as "frenching."

Roast rack of lamb with hoisin-orange glaze and red onions

4 SERVINGS *The addition of flavorful ingredients like ginger, hoisin sauce, chili-garlic sauce, and Chinese five-spice powder to frozen orange juice gives the glaze an Asian flavor. These ingredients can be found in the Asian foods section of many supermarkets and at Asian markets.*

    Olive oil
2 1⅓-pound racks of lamb, well trimmed
2 medium red onions, cut through root ends into ½-inch-thick wedges
½ cup hoisin sauce
¼ cup frozen orange juice concentrate
1½ tablespoons minced peeled fresh ginger
1 tablespoon chili-garlic sauce
¾ teaspoon Chinese five-spice powder or ground aniseed

PREHEAT oven to 450°F. Brush large rimmed baking sheet with olive oil. Place lamb racks in center of baking sheet. Arrange onion wedges around lamb. Brush lamb and onion wedges with olive oil. Whisk hoisin, orange juice concentrate, ginger, chili-garlic sauce, and five-spice powder in small bowl to blend. Brush hoisin glaze generously over lamb and onion wedges; sprinkle with salt and generous amount of pepper.

ROAST until instant-read thermometer inserted into lamb registers 125°F for medium-rare, about 25 minutes. Transfer lamb racks to plate. Continue roasting onion wedges until tender, about 5 minutes longer. Divide onion wedges among plates. Cut lamb racks into chops; place lamb atop onion wedges.

TIME SAVERS Ask the butcher to trim the excess fat from the lamb, and be sure to use a rimmed baking sheet to catch any glaze or juices from the lamb. For easy cleanup, line the baking sheet with foil.

Rosemary-roasted rack of lamb and cherry tomatoes

4 SERVINGS *This dazzling dish will impress guests— and it calls for just four ingredients. The trick is in using the same flavorings for both the meat and the tomatoes.*

1 2-pound rack of lamb (about 8 ribs)
3 tablespoons olive oil, divided
3 teaspoons chopped fresh rosemary, divided
2 12-ounce containers cherry tomatoes

PREHEAT oven to 425°F. Rub lamb with 1 tablespoon oil; sprinkle with 1½ teaspoons rosemary, then salt and pepper. Place on large rimmed baking sheet. Place remaining 2 tablespoons oil, 1½ teaspoons rosemary, and tomatoes in large bowl. Sprinkle with salt and pepper and toss to coat; scatter around lamb.

ROAST lamb and tomatoes until thermometer inserted into thickest part of lamb registers 125°F for medium-rare, about 30 minutes. Let rest 10 minutes. Cut lamb between bones into individual chops. Arrange on platter with tomatoes.

MIX ONCE, USE TWICE As a variation, blend together *herbes de Provence*, garlic, and oil, and use half of the mixture to coat a leg of lamb or prime rib; use the remainder to coat fingerling potatoes that roast alongside the meat.

Honey-roasted lamb with arugula and pine nut salad

4 FIRST-COURSE OR 2 MAIN-COURSE SERVINGS *Lamb chops are presented atop a salad inspired by the flavors of Sardinia, where honey is prized and thyme grows wild. In this recipe, the thyme infuses the honey mixture as it cooks.*

- 2 tablespoons honey
- 4 tablespoons extra-virgin olive oil, divided
- 2 fresh thyme sprigs
- 1 1½-pound rack of lamb, trimmed

- 2 tablespoons red wine vinegar
- 1 tablespoon water
- ¼ cup pine nuts, lightly toasted

- 6 cups arugula (about 4 ounces)

PREHEAT oven to 425°F. Combine honey, 1 tablespoon oil and thyme in heavy small saucepan. Stir over low heat until just warm. Remove from heat. Pour ⅔ of honey mixture into small bowl. Place lamb on rack set in roasting pan; brush with half of honey mixture from bowl. Roast lamb 12 minutes; brush with remaining honey mixture from bowl. Continue to roast until instant-read thermometer inserted into thickest part of meat registers 125°F for medium-rare, about 10 minutes. Transfer lamb to cutting board.

MEANWHILE, add vinegar, 1 tablespoon water, and remaining 3 tablespoons oil to honey mixture in saucepan. Stir over low heat until just warm. Mix in pine nuts; discard thyme sprigs. Season to taste with salt and pepper.

CUT lamb between ribs into individual chops. Divide arugula among plates. Top each serving with lamb chops. Drizzle warm dressing over.

Roast lamb with marionberry-pecan crust

4 SERVINGS *The pecan-and-fresh-breadcrumb topping on this rack of lamb adds a delicious textural contrast. For fresh breadcrumbs, grind pieces of crustless French bread in a food processor to form coarse crumbs. The marionberry-mustard glaze acts like glue to secure the breadcrumb coating.*

- 2 1¼-pound racks of lamb, well-trimmed
- 6 tablespoons marionberry jam or blackberry jam
- ¼ cup Dijon mustard
- ¾ cup finely chopped pecans
- 6 tablespoons minced fresh Italian parsley
- ¾ cup fresh breadcrumbs made from crustless French bread
- 4 tablespoons (½ stick) butter, melted

PREHEAT oven to 425°F. Sprinkle lamb with salt and pepper. Combine jam and mustard in small bowl; whisk to blend. Mix pecans, parsley, and breadcrumbs in another small bowl to blend. Spread half of mustard glaze over rounded side of each lamb rack. Pat half of breadcrumb mixture over mustard glaze on each. Drizzle each with 2 tablespoons melted butter. Transfer lamb to large rimmed baking sheet. Roast until breadcrumb topping is golden and thermometer inserted into lamb registers 130°F for medium-rare, about 30 minutes. Cut racks between bones into individual chops.

THE MARIONBERRY STORY Marionberries are a cross between the Chehalem and Olallieberry blackberry, and are named after Marion, Oregon, where they were developed. If you can't find marionberry jam, use blackberry.

Lamb chops with minted Meyer lemon compote

4 SERVINGS *Mint and lamb is a much-loved pairing—the strong, fresh flavor of mint brings out the best in lamb. Meyer lemons are not quite as tart as regular lemons, and they have a more fragrant aroma. But if Meyer lemons are not available, one regular lemon will do.*

¾ **cup dry white wine**
½ **cup sugar**
¼ **cup (packed) fresh mint leaves**

2 **Meyer lemons**
¼ **teaspoon coarse kosher salt**

8 **¾-inch-thick lamb rib or loin chops**
2 **tablespoons vegetable oil**

COMBINE wine, sugar, and mint in heavy small saucepan. Bring to boil, stirring until sugar dissolves. Remove from heat; let stand 30 minutes. Strain syrup into medium saucepan; discard mint.

USING vegetable peeler, remove peel from lemons in strips. Place strips in mini processor. Cut away all white pith from lemons; discard pith. Working on plate to catch juice, quarter lemons; remove seeds. Add lemons and juice to mini processor; using on/off turns, chop coarsely. Add lemon mixture to mint syrup. Boil until mixture is reduced to ⅔ cup, about 10 minutes. Stir in coarse salt. Cool.

SPRINKLE lamb with salt and pepper. Heat 1 tablespoon oil in each of 2 large skillets over medium-high heat. Add lamb; cook to desired doneness, about 2½ minutes per side for medium-rare. Serve lamb with compote.

Sautéed lamb chops with béarnaise butter

8 SERVINGS *A super-easy flavored butter mimics classic French béarnaise sauce (a rich butter-and-egg-yolk sauce with vinegar, wine, shallots, and tarragon). The butter tops the lamb chops while they're hot, causing the butter to melt temptingly. Stir some of the luxurious béarnaise butter into smashed potatoes to go with the lamb, or use it to dress up simple roast chicken, poached salmon, or steamed asparagus or broccolini.*

½ **cup chopped shallots**
½ **cup white wine vinegar**
3½ **tablespoons chopped fresh tarragon, divided**
3½ **tablespoons chopped fresh Italian parsley, divided**
¾ **cup plus 2 tablespoons (1¾ sticks) butter, room temperature**
½ **teaspoon finely grated lemon peel**

16 **1-inch-thick lamb rib chops (about 3¼ pounds total)**
2 **tablespoons olive oil**

PLACE shallots, vinegar, half of tarragon, and half of parsley in small saucepan. Simmer over medium-high heat until vinegar is reduced to 3 tablespoons, about 3 minutes. Strain into small bowl, pressing on solids to release any liquid. Discard solids; cool tarragon vinegar. Mix butter, lemon peel, and remaining tarragon and parsley in medium bowl to blend. Mix in cooled tarragon vinegar.

DO AHEAD *Can be made 3 days ahead. Cover and refrigerate. Bring to room temperature before using.*

SPRINKLE lamb chops with salt and pepper. Heat oil in heavy large skillet over medium-high heat. Working in 2 batches, sauté lamb chops until browned on both sides and cooked to medium-rare, about 2½ minutes per side. Transfer to platter and tent with foil to keep warm.

ARRANGE 2 chops on each plate. Top each chop with rounded teaspoonful béarnaise butter.

Lamb chops with herbed sweet onion compote

4 SERVINGS *This elegant dish is perfect for weeknight entertaining. There are many different kinds of herbed white wine vinegars to use in the compote; choose your favorite. Use Vidalia, Maui, Oso Sweet, Texas Sweet, Sweet Imperial, or Walla Walla onions, all of which are much sweeter than your standard brown, red, or white onions.*

¼   cup chopped fresh mint
1½   tablespoons chopped fresh oregano
2   garlic cloves, finely chopped
8   lamb loin chops (about 1½ pounds total)

2   tablespoons olive oil, divided
1   sweet onion (such as Vidalia), thinly sliced
2   tablespoons herbed white wine vinegar

MIX mint, oregano, and garlic in small bowl. Sprinkle lamb generously with salt and coarsely ground black pepper. Sprinkle 2 tablespoons herb mixture over lamb chops; press to adhere (reserve remaining herb mixture for compote).

HEAT 1 tablespoon oil in heavy large skillet over medium-high heat. Add lamb and cook to desired doneness, about 4 minutes per side for medium. Transfer lamb to platter (do not clean skillet). Tent lamb with foil. Reduce heat to medium. Add remaining 1 tablespoon oil to skillet. Add onion and sauté until beginning to soften, about 2 minutes. Add vinegar and reserved herb mixture; sauté 1 minute. Season compote to taste with salt and pepper. Spoon compote over lamb.

Lamb chops with artichokes and rosemary

4 SERVINGS *The use of frozen artichoke hearts means you can enjoy this dish year-round. They're perfect for this recipe, where they get to stew in a flavorful broth and become nice and tender.*

3   tablespoons olive oil, divided
3   garlic cloves, minced, divided
3½   teaspoons minced fresh rosemary, divided
2   teaspoons finely grated orange peel, divided
2   8-ounce packages frozen artichoke hearts, thawed
1½   cups low-salt chicken broth

8   1-inch-thick lamb loin chops

HEAT 2 tablespoons oil in large skillet over medium-high heat. Add 2 minced garlic cloves, 2 teaspoons rosemary, and ½ teaspoon orange peel; stir 30 seconds. Add artichoke hearts and broth; bring to boil. Cover; boil 5 minutes. Uncover; cook until sauce thickens, stirring occasionally, about 4 minutes. Remove from heat.

SPRINKLE lamb with remaining minced garlic clove and 1½ teaspoons rosemary, then salt and pepper. Heat remaining 1 tablespoon oil in another large skillet over medium-high heat. Add lamb; cook to desired doneness, about 4 minutes per side for medium-rare. Transfer lamb to platter.

SPOON off fat from skillet with lamb. Add artichoke mixture; boil 2 minutes, scraping up browned bits. Season with salt and pepper. Spoon artichoke mixture around lamb. Sprinkle with remaining 1½ teaspoons orange peel.

Lamb tikka with crispy onions

2 SERVINGS; CAN BE DOUBLED *Yogurt seasoned with fresh ginger and curry powder serves as the marinade for this Indian dish. Make sure the lamb and onion are about 5 inches from the heat source of your broiler—if lower, the meat and onions might not brown well; if too close, they'll char before cooked through.*

> Nonstick vegetable oil spray
>
> ⅓ cup plain low-fat yogurt
>
> 1 tablespoon minced peeled fresh ginger
>
> 1½ teaspoons curry powder
>
> 12 ounces trimmed boneless lamb sirloin chops, cut into 12 pieces
>
> 1 medium red onion, thinly sliced into rounds
>
> 2 teaspoons olive oil
>
> 2 8-inch wooden skewers, soaked in water 30 minutes
>
> Lemon wedges

PREHEAT broiler. Spray broiler pan with nonstick spray. Whisk yogurt, ginger, and curry powder in medium bowl to blend. Sprinkle lamb with salt and pepper. Stir lamb into yogurt mixture; let stand 5 minutes.

MEANWHILE, place onion rounds in shallow bowl. Sprinkle with salt and pepper. Drizzle with olive oil; toss to coat. Spread out onion in ½-inch-thick layer in broiler pan. Thread lamb pieces onto skewers. Arrange skewers alongside onion.

BROIL lamb and onion about 5 inches from heat source until lamb is brown outside but still pink inside and onion is lightly charred, turning occasionally, about 10 minutes. Transfer lamb and onion to plates. Serve with lemon wedges.

MAKE YOUR OWN CURRY Improvise with other spices, spice blends, and pastes to create your own curry flavor. Try mixing a tikka paste or other mild curry paste (found in the international foods section at some supermarkets) with fresh lemon juice, or garam masala with fresh garlic and cayenne pepper. If you don't have curry powder but do have lots of individual spices, such as cumin, coriander, turmeric, and cayenne pepper, make your own curry mix.

Broiled lamb chops with rosemary-mint sauce

2 SERVINGS; CAN BE DOUBLED *If you have a mortar and pestle, use it to crush the garlic with a little salt and pepper; the mortar and pestle really helps mash the garlic into a paste. When using a knife, the salt absorbs the garlic juices and helps prevent the garlic from sticking to the blade. Try this simple technique when making a vinaigrette or other sauces in which you want the garlic completely mashed.*

2   garlic cloves
1   teaspoon salt
1   teaspoon freshly ground black pepper
2   teaspoons olive oil
4   4-ounce lamb loin chops

3   tablespoons mint jelly
3   tablespoons white wine vinegar
1   teaspoon minced fresh rosemary
    or ½ teaspoon dried

CHOP garlic with salt and pepper on cutting board, then use flat side of knife blade to mash garlic mixture to paste. Scrape paste into small bowl; mix in olive oil. Rub garlic paste over both sides of lamb chops. Let lamb chops stand 10 minutes.

MEANWHILE, stir mint jelly, vinegar, and rosemary in small saucepan over high heat until jelly melts and mixture boils. Reduce heat to medium; cook until sauce thickens to syrup, about 2 minutes.

PREHEAT broiler. Broil lamb chops until well browned but still pink inside, about 4 minutes per side. Arrange lamb chops on plates. Spoon rosemary-mint sauce over.

Lamb shoulder chops with tomatoes and marjoram

2 SERVINGS; CAN BE DOUBLED *Braising is the best cooking method for lamb shoulder chops, since the simmering liquid tenderizes this rather tough cut. As the lamb braises, prepare a batch of mashed potatoes to soak up all the sauce.*

2   1½-inch-thick lamb shoulder (round-bone) chops (about 14 ounces total)
1   tablespoon olive oil
2   large garlic cloves, chopped
½   cup dry white wine
1   28-ounce can Italian plum tomatoes, drained, coarsely chopped
    Pinch of dried crushed red pepper

1½ tablespoons minced fresh marjoram

SPRINKLE lamb chops with salt and pepper. Heat oil in heavy large skillet over high heat. Add lamb and cook until brown, about 2½ minutes per side. Transfer to plate. Reduce heat to medium-low, add garlic, and cook until beginning to color, about 30 seconds. Add wine and bring to boil, scraping up browned bits. Add tomatoes and crushed red pepper. Return lamb to skillet. Cover and simmer until tender, turning occasionally, about 30 minutes.

TRANSFER lamb to plates and tent with foil to keep warm. Boil sauce until thickened, stirring occasionally and adding any accumulated juices from plates, about 8 minutes. Season to taste with salt and pepper. Spoon sauce over lamb chops. Sprinkle with marjoram.

Peppered lamb with pine nut sauce

4 SERVINGS *Try other herbs and seasonings in this basic sauce. Chopped rosemary or thyme would be good alternatives to the basil. Dropping a pressed garlic clove into the sauce as it simmers would lend a nice flavor, too. (Remove it before serving.) Serve this sauce with grilled steaks or pork chops.*

- 1 cup heavy whipping cream
- 3 ounces soft fresh goat cheese
- ¼ cup dried cranberries

    Coarsely ground black pepper
- 4 lamb shoulder (round-bone) chops (each about 8 ounces), trimmed
- 1 tablespoon butter

- ½ cup pine nuts, toasted
- 2 tablespoons thinly sliced fresh basil

WHISK cream, goat cheese, and cranberries in heavy small saucepan over medium-low heat until cheese melts. Simmer until sauce is reduced to 1¼ cups, stirring occasionally, about 8 minutes. Season to taste with salt and pepper. Cover and keep warm.

DO AHEAD *Can be made 2 hours ahead. Let stand at room temperature.*

PRESS coarsely ground pepper onto both sides of lamb. Sprinkle lamb with salt. Melt butter in heavy large skillet over medium heat. Add lamb to skillet; cook to desired doneness, about 4 minutes per side for medium-rare. Transfer lamb to plates.

ADD pine nuts to sauce and rewarm if necessary. Stir in basil. Pour sauce over lamb.

Mint-marinated leg of lamb

8 SERVINGS *As with any large piece of cooked meat, let the lamb sit for about 10 minutes before slicing to help keep the meat moist and juicy.*

- ½ cup olive oil
- ½ cup dry red wine
- ¼ cup (packed) minced fresh mint plus whole sprigs for garnish
- 4 large garlic cloves, minced
- 2 bay leaves, crumbled
- 1 5-pound leg of lamb, boned, butterflied

MIX first 5 ingredients in large glass baking dish. Season with generous amount of pepper. Add lamb; turn to coat. Cover and refrigerate at least 4 hours or overnight.

PREHEAT oven to 450°F. Drain lamb and transfer to large roasting pan. Season both sides with salt and generous amount of pepper. Arrange lamb, fat side down, in pan. Roast 15 minutes. Reduce oven temperature to 375°F and continue roasting until thermometer inserted into thickest part of lamb registers 125°F for medium-rare, about 20 minutes. Let rest 10 minutes. Cut into slices. Arrange on platter. Garnish with mint sprigs.

ON THE GRILL The lamb can also be grilled on a warm summer night. Prepare the barbecue (medium heat) and grill the lamb for about 15 minutes per side or until an instant-read thermometer inserted into the thickest part of the meat registers 125°F. Using a meat thermometer for large roasts like this is helpful whether grilling or oven-roasting.

Tamarind-honey lamb kebabs on mashed yams

4 SERVINGS *Tamarind concentrate is a dark, seedless paste that can be found at Middle Eastern, Indian, and some Asian markets and natural foods stores. It's tart and tangy, and balances the sweetness of the honey in this glaze. If it's unavailable, try this easy substitute: Whisk 2 chopped pitted Medjool dates with 2 tablespoons lime juice in a bowl until almost smooth. The chili-garlic sauce adds a slightly salty, spicy, and pungent flavor to the glaze, and can be found in the Asian foods section of many supermarkets and at some specialty foods stores and Asian markets. Ask your butcher to cube the lamb for you.*

⅔ cup honey

¼ cup chili-garlic sauce

3 tablespoons tamarind concentrate

1 teaspoon ground cumin

½ teaspoon ground cardamom

2¼ pounds yams (red-skinned sweet potatoes; about 3 medium)

¼ cup (½ stick) butter

20 1½-inch cubes boneless leg of lamb (about 2 pounds total)

4 metal skewers or wooden skewers, soaked in water 30 minutes

STIR first 5 ingredients in bowl to blend.

PIERCE yams with fork. Microwave on high until tender, about 12 minutes, turning once. Cut yams lengthwise in half; scoop flesh into microwave-safe bowl. Add butter; mash. Season to taste with salt and pepper.

MEANWHILE, preheat broiler. Line large rimmed baking sheet with foil; place rack on sheet. Transfer ½ cup tamarind glaze to large bowl. Add lamb; stir to coat. Let stand 5 to 10 minutes. Thread 5 pieces of lamb onto each of 4 skewers. Sprinkle with salt. Brush with some of remaining glaze. Broil lamb to desired doneness, occasionally brushing with glaze, about 3 minutes per side for medium-rare.

REWARM yams in microwave, about 2 minutes. Divide yams among plates; top yams with lamb skewers.

PIERCED YAMS Before the yams get a quick zap in the microwave, piercing them all over with a fork helps the water in the yams to evaporate as they cook, improving the texture.

Cumin-and-coffee-roasted leg of lamb

6 TO 8 SERVINGS *Five powerful ingredients create sensational flavor in this dish. Use instant espresso powder or coffee powder that will dissolve in the yogurt rather than freshly ground coffee beans, which will leave behind unappealing granules. Serve the lamb with Israeli couscous, which is larger and chewier than the common variety.*

¾ cup plain whole-milk yogurt
1 tablespoon ground cumin
1 tablespoon (packed) dark brown sugar
1 teaspoon instant espresso powder
⅛ teaspoon ground cloves
1 3¾-pound boneless leg of lamb, well-trimmed, butterflied

POSITION rack in top third of oven; preheat to 475°F. Stir yogurt, cumin, brown sugar, espresso powder, and cloves in small bowl until sugar dissolves. Place lamb, fat side up, on rimmed baking sheet. Sprinkle generously with salt and pepper. Spread ⅓ of yogurt mixture evenly over. Turn lamb over. Sprinkle generously with salt and pepper. Spread evenly with remaining yogurt mixture.

ROAST lamb until thermometer inserted into thickest part registers 125°F for medium-rare, about 25 minutes. Transfer to platter. Let rest 10 minutes. Slice thinly.

Minced lamb with ginger, hoisin, and green onions

4 SERVINGS *A tablespoon of cornstarch thickens the sauce in this quick stir-fry. Dissolve it in the orange juice to ensure that it gets distributed evenly in the sauce. Since the cornstarch will settle at the bottom of the juice, give it a quick stir before adding it to the stir-fry. Keep the lettuce leaves covered and chilled before using so that they stay cold and crisp. Hoisin sauce is available in the Asian section of some supermarkets and at Asian markets.*

2 tablespoons orange juice
1 tablespoon cornstarch
1 pound ground lamb
1 tablespoon Asian sesame oil
2 tablespoons minced peeled fresh ginger
1 tablespoon minced fresh garlic
1 tablespoon minced orange peel
1 bunch green onions, chopped
¼ cup hoisin sauce
   Butter lettuce leaves

COMBINE orange juice and cornstarch in small bowl. Sauté lamb in heavy large skillet over high heat until cooked through, breaking up with back of spoon, about 5 minutes. Pour lamb with juices into colander; drain. Heat oil in same skillet over high heat. Add ginger, garlic, and orange peel; stir-fry 30 seconds. Add green onions and stir-fry 1 minute. Add hoisin sauce and lamb to skillet; stir until blended. Add orange juice mixture; stir until thickened, about 1 minute. Spoon lamb mixture into lettuce leaves.

THE TASTE OF CITRUS A good way to add citrus flavor to dishes is by using the peel. As a nice alternative, substitute tangerine juice and peel for orange.

potatoes, grains, and beans

POTATOES

Parsley-Potato Pancakes

Herbed New Potatoes

Roasted Potatoes with Bay Leaves

Garlic and Olive Oil Smashed
Yukon Gold Potatoes

New Potato, Mustard Green,
and Wild Mushroom Sauté

Curried Potatoes

Chive and Garlic
Smashed Potatoes

Sour Cream-Horseradish
Mashed Potatoes

Fennel Mashed Potatoes

Mashed Potatoes with Green
Onions and Parmesan

Dill Mashed Potatoes with
Crème Fraîche and Caviar

Truffled Mashed Potatoes

Potato Gratin with Cream
and Fresh Herbs

Roquefort Potato Gratin

Scalloped Potatoes with
Gouda and Fennel

Creamy Potato-Parsnip Gratin

Bistro Oven Fries with
Parsley and Garlic

Honey-Glazed Oven-Roasted
Sweet Potato Wedges

Roasted Sweet Potatoes with
Crème Fraîche and Chives

Roasted Balsamic Sweet Potatoes

Sweet Potato Puree with
Brown Sugar and Sherry

GRAINS

Polenta with Green
Chiles and Cheese

Polenta with Bacon and Fontina

Skillet Polenta with
Tomatoes and Gorgonzola

Parmesan Grits

Creamy Baked Grits with
Sun-Dried Tomatoes

Bulgur with Root Vegetables

Lemon-Mint Tabbouleh

Spiced Carrot and
Zucchini Quinoa

Leek-Tomato Quinoa

BEANS

Lima Bean Puree

Spicy Black Beans with
Onion and Bacon

Rosemary and Lemon Pinto Beans

Garlicky Beans with
Feta And Mint

White Beans with
Tomatoes and Chiles

White Beans with Sage
and Olive Oil

"Soda Jerk" Beans

Sweet and Smoky Barbecue Beans

Lemon-Barley Pilaf

Spiced Lentils

Braised Lentils

tool kit It's a safe bet that most people believe mashed potatoes to be the highest and best use of the humble spud. Hot, fluffy potatoes with a pat of butter melting on top…it doesn't get better than that. Yet this simple creation can be surprisingly difficult to get right. Here's how to do it:

PICK THE RIGHT POTATOES—Use russets for light, airy mashed potatoes and Yukon Golds for creamier ones. Use red, white, and fingerling potatoes, which have a denser texture, for rustic, smashed potatoes (coarsely mashed potatoes, usually with the skins left on).

CHECK FOR SIZE—When cooking them whole, use potatoes that are the same size so they are all done cooking at the same time. If using pieces, cut the potatoes into large uniform chunks so they cook evenly.

COOK THEM RIGHT—Lower the potatoes into boiling salted water or cube and steam them until tender. Either method cooks them quickly enough to preserve nutrients.

TEST FOR DONENESS—A skewer or sharp knife should glide through the centers of the whole potatoes (or pieces) without resistance when they are tender enough to mash. Be sure to check the potatoes toward the end of the cooking time to ensure they do not overcook and start falling apart.

DRY, MASH, AND MIX—Drain the potatoes, then return them to the pot and stir over medium-low heat to cook off any excess water. Always mash the potatoes while they're steaming hot to get a smoother texture. Use a food mill or a potato ricer (which looks like an oversize garlic press) for super-smooth and creamy mashed potatoes. A potato masher creates chunky mashed potatoes that hold gravy well. Hand mixers, while not ideal, are okay for convenience, but avoid using a food processor or blender, which can make the potatoes pasty. For fluffier potatoes, mix in the butter first, then add warm milk to the desired consistency. ➡

431

KEEP THEM HOT—If eating the mashed potatoes within an hour, transfer them to a bowl, cover them with foil, and set the bowl over a saucepan of simmering water. If making them more than an hour in advance, transfer the potatoes to a bowl and cool. Then cover with plastic and refrigerate. Just before serving, reheat the potatoes in the microwave or in a saucepan over medium-low heat. Add more warm milk to adjust the consistency. Or keep them warm in a slow cooker, which also saves stovetop space and requires no attention.

DRESS THEM UP—Mashed potatoes work beautifully with all kinds of flavors and ingredients.

Add a few peeled whole garlic cloves to the potatoes as they boil. They'll become tender and creamy and will mash easily along with the potatoes.

Mix in chopped chipotle chiles (canned, in adobo sauce), shredded white cheddar cheese, and fresh cilantro.

Melt the butter with thyme or sage and cook until the butter becomes golden brown, then stir it into the potatoes.

Reserve some potato cooking liquid to quickly cook diced carrots, green beans, zucchini, and corn kernels just until they are crisp-tender, then add the vegetables to the mashed potatoes (a good way to get kids to eat their veggies).

Steep a few sprigs of herbs such as rosemary, thyme, basil, and bay leaves in the milk, then discard the sprigs before mixing the milk into the potatoes.

POTATOES

Parsley-potato pancakes

MAKES 6 *These are delicious alongside fried eggs or served with grilled fish. For a luxurious appetizer, serve the pancakes with a dollop of extra-rich crème fraîche instead of sour cream. Dress them up even more by adding a little spoonful of caviar. Keeping the oil temperature constant will ensure crisply browned pancakes, so fry them in small batches; crowding the pan will bring the temperature down.*

 1 12- to 13-ounce russet potato, peeled
 ⅓ cup minced fresh parsley
 ½ cup (about) vegetable oil
 Sour cream

USING hand grater, coarsely grate potato into large bowl. Add parsley and toss to blend. Divide mixture into 6 equal portions (about ⅓ cup each). Form each portion into ¾-inch-thick round, pressing firmly.

POUR oil into heavy large nonstick skillet to depth of ⅛ inch; heat over medium-high heat. Using spatula, carefully transfer 3 potato rounds to skillet.

FLATTEN each to 3½-inch round. Sprinkle with salt and pepper. Cook until pancakes are golden brown, crisp, and cooked through, pressing occasionally to compact, about 4 minutes per side. Transfer to paper towels to drain. Repeat with remaining potato rounds. Serve pancakes with sour cream.

DISK SENSE Using the large-holed grating disk of the food processor makes quick work of shredding or grating potatoes for potato pancakes.

Herbed new potatoes

8 SERVINGS *This super-quick sauté shows how fresh herbs brighten up a simple dish. Fingerling potatoes would also be terrific prepared this way; because they're so small, you may only need to halve them lengthwise before cooking.*

 3 pounds 1½-inch-diameter new potatoes, scrubbed, quartered
 2 tablespoons olive oil
 3 garlic cloves, minced
 6 tablespoons assorted chopped fresh herbs (such as parsley, dill, and chives)

STEAM potatoes until tender, about 10 minutes.

DO AHEAD *Can be made 2 hours ahead. Let stand at room temperature.*

HEAT oil in large skillet over medium-high heat. Add garlic and stir 30 seconds. Add potatoes and herbs; sprinkle lightly with salt and pepper. Sauté until potatoes are heated through and golden, about 8 minutes. Season to taste with more salt and pepper, if desired. Transfer to bowl.

WORKING WITH HERBS To prep fresh herbs for cooking, wash and dry or spin them in a salad spinner, then remove the leaves from the stems. For Italian or flat-leaf parsley, simply pinch off the leaves from the stems; for herbs with stockier stems, such as rosemary, oregano, and thyme, strip off the leaves by running your fingers down the stem from top to bottom.

433

Roasted potatoes with bay leaves

6 SERVINGS *Turkish bay leaves are smaller and rounder and have a softer, subtler fragrance than California bay leaves. They add depth of flavor to a simple infused oil that coats the potatoes as they roast.*

- 2 tablespoons extra-virgin olive oil
- 4 Turkish bay leaves
- 2 pounds small red-skinned potatoes

PREHEAT oven to 450°F. Combine oil and bay leaves in small skillet. Cook over medium heat just until warm. Remove from heat. Let stand at least 15 minutes and up to 1 hour to allow bay leaves to flavor oil.

TOSS potatoes with bay leaf oil on large rimmed baking sheet. Sprinkle with salt and pepper. Roast until potatoes are brown and tender, stirring occasionally, about 45 minutes. Discard bay leaves. Transfer potatoes to bowl.

Garlic and olive oil smashed Yukon Gold potatoes

4 SERVINGS *Yellow-fleshed Yukon Golds give smashed potatoes an extra-buttery flavor, and leaving the skins on adds a nice look and texture.*

- 2 pounds medium Yukon Gold potatoes, each cut into ½- to ¾-inch wedges
- 6 tablespoons olive oil, divided
- 5 large garlic cloves, peeled, halved
- 1 teaspoon chopped fresh thyme

STEAM potato wedges until very tender, about 15 minutes.

MEANWHILE, heat 5 tablespoons oil in large skillet over low heat. Add garlic; sauté until golden, about 6 minutes.

ADD potatoes and thyme to skillet. Using large fork, smash potatoes coarsely. Season to taste with salt and pepper. Transfer to bowl and drizzle with remaining 1 tablespoon oil.

New potato, mustard green, and wild mushroom sauté

2 SERVINGS; CAN BE DOUBLED OR TRIPLED *If mustard greens are not available, the outer dark green leaves from a head of escarole substitute beautifully; they have a milder flavor than mustard greens. You can use other wild mushrooms if preferred. Crimini (baby bellas) are easy to find and reasonably priced. Chanterelles, morels, and fresh porcini would be luxurious treats.*

2 medium red new potatoes, quartered

2 tablespoons (¼ stick) butter

4 ounces fresh oyster or stemmed shiitake mushrooms, halved

2 cups (tightly packed) thinly sliced mustard greens or escarole

STEAM potatoes until just tender. Cool potatoes slightly, then slice.

MELT butter in heavy large skillet over medium-high heat. Add potatoes and mushrooms. Sprinkle with salt and pepper. Sauté until mushrooms are tender and potatoes are heated through, about 2 minutes. Add greens and stir until wilted, about 1 minute.

Curried potatoes

4 SERVINGS *The Indian spice in these potatoes would complement tandoori roast chicken or grilled lamb chops or kebabs.*

1½ pounds white-skinned potatoes (about 4 medium)

3 tablespoons water

2 teaspoons curry powder

2 tablespoons vegetable oil

½ cup chopped shallots

COOK potatoes in large pot of boiling salted water until just tender, about 30 minutes. Cool potatoes slightly. Peel potatoes and cut into 1-inch cubes. Place in medium bowl. Add 3 tablespoons water and curry powder; toss to coat. Season to taste with salt.

HEAT oil in heavy large skillet over medium-high heat. Add shallots and potatoes. Sauté until potatoes are crusty and golden brown on all sides, stirring frequently, about 15 minutes.

Chive and garlic smashed potatoes

6 SERVINGS *Leaving the skins on the potatoes lends rustic appeal and lets them retain more nutrients—and makes this dish even easier to prepare.*

- 2 pounds small red-skinned potatoes, rinsed, cut into 1-inch pieces
- 10 tablespoons (1¼ sticks) butter
- 3 garlic cloves, minced
- ¾ cup chopped fresh chives (about 3 bunches)

COOK potatoes in large pot of boiling salted water until tender, about 18 minutes. Drain. Melt butter in same pot over medium heat. Add garlic and sauté until fragrant, about 30 seconds. Return potatoes to pot. Add chives. Smash potatoes coarsely. Season to taste with salt and pepper.

Sour cream–horseradish mashed potatoes

6 SERVINGS *The perfect accompaniment to corned beef and cabbage.*

- 2 pounds medium Yukon Gold or russet potatoes
- ¼ cup (½ stick) butter
- 1 cup sour cream
- ⅓ cup chopped fresh chives
- ¼ cup prepared white horseradish

COOK potatoes in large pot of boiling salted water until tender, about 20 minutes. Drain potatoes well; cool slightly.

PEEL, place in large bowl, and mash potatoes; return to same pot. Stir over medium heat until potatoes are dry, about 2 minutes. Stir butter into potatoes. Gradually mix in sour cream, then chives and horseradish. Season potatoes to taste with salt and pepper.

Fennel mashed potatoes

6 SERVINGS *Using fennel seeds along with fresh fennel really brings out the sweet anise flavor. Serve these potatoes with simply roasted salmon or chicken.*

- 2 **tablespoons (¼ stick) butter**
- 1 **fresh fennel bulb, trimmed, quartered, cored, thinly sliced crosswise**
- ½ **teaspoon fennel seeds, crushed in plastic bag**
- 2½ **pounds russet potatoes or Yukon Gold potatoes, peeled, cut into 2-inch pieces**
- 1 **cup (or more) half and half**

MELT butter in heavy large skillet over medium heat. Add sliced fennel and fennel seeds; stir to coat. Sprinkle with salt and pepper. Reduce heat to low, cover, and cook until fennel is tender but not brown, stirring often, about 20 minutes.

MEANWHILE, cook potatoes in large pot of boiling salted water until tender, about 15 minutes. Drain. Return potatoes to same pot. Stir over medium heat until potatoes are dry. Mash potatoes in pot.

ADD 1 cup half and half to fennel mixture and bring to simmer. Add fennel mixture to potatoes in 2 additions, stirring to combine. Season to taste with salt and pepper.

DO AHEAD *Can be made 2 hours ahead. Let stand at room temperature. Rewarm over medium heat, adding more half and half to moisten if dry.*

Mashed potatoes with green onions and Parmesan

2 SERVINGS; CAN BE DOUBLED OR TRIPLED *Most recipes that use green onions call for only the white and light green parts. In this recipe, we like using the deep green portions as well—they add vibrant color and flavor to the potatoes.*

- 2 **large russet potatoes (about 1¼ pounds), peeled, cut into chunks**
- 2 **tablespoons (¼ stick) butter, divided**
- 2 **tablespoons whole milk**
- 1 **bunch green onions (about 5), chopped**
- ⅔ **cup freshly grated Parmesan cheese**

COOK potatoes in large pot of boiling salted water until tender, about 15 minutes. Drain well. Return to pot and mash. Mix in 1½ tablespoons butter, then milk.

MELT remaining ½ tablespoon butter in heavy medium skillet over medium-high heat. Add green onions and sauté until wilted, about 1 minute. Add to potatoes. Add Parmesan and mix gently. Season to taste with salt and pepper.

Dill mashed potatoes with crème fraîche and caviar

6 TO 8 SERVINGS *Salmon roe looks (and tastes) fantastic, but there's a wonderful variety of other domestic caviar to choose from today. One of the best sources of sustainably farmed caviar is California-based Tsar Nicoulai (tsarnicoulai.com). Pair the potatoes with the first wild salmon of the year.*

3½   **pounds russet potatoes, peeled, cut into 2-inch pieces**
  1   **cup crème fraîche or sour cream**
  ¼   **cup (½ stick) butter, room temperature**
  3   **tablespoons (packed) finely chopped fresh dill**
  1   **4-ounce jar salmon caviar**

COOK potatoes in large pot of boiling salted water until very tender, about 25 minutes. Drain well. Return potatoes to same pot; mash over low heat until almost smooth. Add crème fraîche and butter; continue to mash until smooth and fluffy. Stir in dill. Season to taste with salt and pepper.

DO AHEAD *Potatoes can be made 2 hours ahead. Let stand at room temperature. Rewarm over low heat, stirring frequently.*

TOP potatoes with caviar.

Truffled mashed potatoes

4 SERVINGS *This decadent mash is luxurious enough to serve with lobster. Look for either black or white truffle oil in Italian markets, many specialty foods stores, and some supermarkets.*

  2   **pounds russet potatoes, peeled, cut into ¼-inch-thick slices**
  ⅓   **cup warm whole milk**
  ⅓   **cup crème fraîche or sour cream**
  2   **tablespoons chopped fresh chives**
1½   **teaspoons truffle oil**

COOK potatoes in large pot of boiling salted water until tender, about 10 minutes. Drain; return to same pot and mash potatoes. Stir in remaining ingredients. Season to taste with salt and pepper.

TRUFFLE OIL At a fraction of the price of fresh truffles, truffle oil adds an instant note of luxury to everyday fare such as pastas, risottos, eggs, and mashed potatoes. For the richest flavor, be sure to use truffle oil infused with real truffles. Because truffle oils will lose aroma over time, purchase a small bottle, store it in the refrigerator after opening, and don't let it sit around too long.

Potato gratin with cream and fresh herbs

8 SERVINGS *No careful layering required: Simply combine the potatoes with the other ingredients and bake for about an hour.*

- 3 tablespoons butter, room temperature, divided
- 3 pounds russet potatoes, peeled, cut into thin rounds
- 1¼ cups heavy whipping cream
- 1¼ cups whole milk
- ½ cup chopped fresh chives
- 2 teaspoons chopped fresh thyme
- 1 teaspoon salt
- ½ teaspoon freshly ground black pepper

PREHEAT oven to 400°F. Butter 8×8×2-inch glass baking dish with 1 tablespoon butter. Place potatoes, cream, milk, chives, thyme, salt, pepper, and remaining 2 tablespoons butter in large pot. Cover and bring mixture to boil over medium-high heat, stirring occasionally.

TRANSFER potato mixture to prepared dish, overlapping top layer of potatoes in pattern, if desired. Cover dish with foil. Bake 40 minutes. Uncover and continue to bake until potatoes are tender, sauce bubbles thickly, and top is brown, about 15 minutes. Let gratin stand 10 minutes before serving.

V-(ERY EASY) SLICING Most chefs use a special tool called a mandoline for making thin, uniform slices of potatoes and other vegetables. A V-slicer is a less-expensive, easier-to-use version—and that's what the BON APPÉTIT Test Kitchen uses. V-slicers are sold at cookware stores. You can also slice the potatoes using a heavy large chef's knife.

Roquefort potato gratin

12 SERVINGS *This deceptively simple gratin is a sophisticated partner for sautéed or grilled sausages, lamb, or steak. Gorgonzola or Maytag blue cheese can substitute for the French Roquefort.*

- 5¼ pounds russet potatoes, peeled, cut into ⅛-inch-thick slices
- 2 cups heavy whipping cream
- 5 ounces Roquefort cheese, crumbled (about 1¼ cups)
- ½ cup dry breadcrumbs
- ¼ cup (½ stick) butter, melted
- 1½ teaspoons chopped fresh rosemary

PREHEAT oven to 425°F. Butter 15×10×2-inch glass baking dish. Layer potatoes in prepared dish, sprinkling each layer lightly with salt and pepper. Bring cream to boil in heavy medium saucepan. Reduce heat to medium. Add cheese to cream; whisk until cheese melts. Pour cream mixture over potatoes. Cover dish with foil. Bake until potatoes are tender, about 1 hour.

PREHEAT broiler. Mix breadcrumbs, butter, and rosemary in small bowl to blend. Sprinkle over potatoes. Broil until crumb mixture is golden brown, watching closely to prevent burning, about 4 minutes. Let stand 10 minutes. Serve warm.

Scalloped potatoes with Gouda and fennel

6 SERVINGS *The mild anise flavor of cooked fennel goes particularly well with roast turkey or roast pork. If you prefer a different cheese, you can use Parrano, an aged Dutch cheese that tastes a bit like an aged Parmesan.*

 1 cup heavy whipping cream
 1 cup half and half
 1 medium fresh fennel bulb, trimmed, halved, thinly sliced
 1 teaspoon fennel seeds, crushed in plastic bag
 2 pounds russet potatoes, peeled
 2 cups (packed) coarsely grated Gouda cheese (about 8 ounces)

PREHEAT oven to 400°F. Generously butter 8×8×2-inch glass baking dish. Combine cream, half and half, sliced fennel, and fennel seeds in heavy large skillet. Thinly slice potatoes and add to skillet. Bring mixture to boil over high heat, stirring frequently to separate vegetable slices. Boil 5 minutes. Season generously with salt and pepper. Transfer half of potato mixture to prepared baking dish. Sprinkle half of Gouda over. Top with remaining potato mixture. Firmly press mixture down. Sprinkle remaining Gouda over. Cover dish tightly with foil. Bake until potatoes are tender, about 40 minutes. Uncover and bake until top is golden brown, about 10 minutes longer. Let stand 10 minutes.

Creamy potato-parsnip gratin

8 SERVINGS *The somewhat sweet flavor of parsnips harmonizes wonderfully with potatoes.*

 2⅓ pounds Yukon Gold potatoes, scrubbed, cut into ⅛-inch-thick rounds
 4 Turkish bay leaves
 1⅔ pounds large parsnips, peeled, cut into ⅛-inch-thick rounds
 2 cups heavy whipping cream
 2 cups half and half

PREHEAT oven to 450°F. Butter 13×9×2-inch glass baking dish. Arrange ⅓ of potatoes in even layer in dish. Top with bay leaves, then ½ of parsnips. Top with ⅓ of potatoes, remaining parsnips, then remaining potatoes, sprinkling each layer with salt and pepper. Pour cream and half and half over. Cover dish with foil. Bake until vegetables are tender, about 1 hour. Uncover and bake until sauce bubbles thickly and top is golden brown, about 20 minutes. Let stand 5 minutes.

Bistro oven fries with parsley and garlic

4 SERVINGS *Forget deep-frying. It's so much easier to toss potatoes with a small amount of canola oil and bake them in a very hot oven until brown and crisp. The "bistro" treatment is a sprinkling of chopped fresh herbs and seasonings.*

　　Nonstick vegetable oil spray
4 medium russet potatoes (about 1¾ pounds), scrubbed
2 tablespoons canola oil

¼ cup chopped fresh parsley
2 garlic cloves, minced
　　Coarse kosher salt

POSITION rack in center of oven and preheat to 425°F. Spray 2 large rimmed baking sheets with nonstick spray. Cut potatoes lengthwise into ⅓-inch-thick slices, then cut lengthwise into ⅓-inch-thick sticks. Pat potatoes dry with paper towels. Combine potatoes and oil in large bowl; toss to coat evenly. Spread potatoes in single layer on prepared sheets.

BAKE until potatoes are deep golden brown, turning and stirring potatoes frequently, about 40 minutes. Transfer potatoes to bowl. Toss with parsley, garlic, coarse kosher salt, and pepper.

Honey-glazed oven-roasted sweet potato wedges

6 SERVINGS *Brushing the potato wedges with honey subtly enhances their natural sweetness.*

5 long slender 10-ounce red-skinned sweet potatoes (yams)
¼ cup olive oil
　　Honey
　　Chopped fresh parsley

PREHEAT oven to 400°F. Peel yams, then quarter lengthwise. Place yams in large bowl. Drizzle with oil and sprinkle with salt and pepper; toss to coat. Arrange in single layer on rimmed baking sheet. Roast 45 minutes. Brush with honey. Roast until tender and beginning to brown in spots, about 15 minutes longer. Transfer to platter; sprinkle with parsley.

441

Roasted sweet potatoes with crème fraîche and chives

4 SERVINGS *A thoroughly modern take on the classic baked potato with sour cream. Fleur de sel is a refined French sea salt available at specialty foods stores and at some supermarkets.*

  4 **small to medium red-skinned sweet potatoes (yams), scrubbed**
1½ **tablespoons canola oil**
     Fleur de sel

     Crème fraîche or sour cream
     Chopped fresh chives

PREHEAT oven to 350°F. Place yams in large bowl. Add oil and toss to coat. Sprinkle generously with fleur de sel and freshly ground black pepper. Transfer yams to rimmed baking sheet; drizzle with any remaining oil from bowl.

ROAST yams until tender, about 45 minutes. Using sharp knife, slit yams lengthwise down center. Press ends in, forcing center of yam to open. Sprinkle yams with fleur de sel. Spoon in dollop of crème fraîche; sprinkle with chives and additional pepper.

Roasted balsamic sweet potatoes

6 SERVINGS *Balsamic vinegar is combined with brown sugar to make a sweet syrup with a tangy edge, which coats the potatoes before they're roasted. Try these with roast pork or baked ham.*

¼ **cup balsamic vinegar**
 1 **tablespoon (packed) golden brown sugar**
¼ **cup (½ stick) unsalted butter**
 1 **teaspoon coarse kosher salt**
 3 **large red-skinned sweet potatoes (yams), peeled, cut into 1¼-inch pieces**

PREHEAT oven to 400°F. Bring vinegar and brown sugar to boil in large skillet over medium heat, stirring until sugar dissolves. Reduce heat and simmer until vinegar syrup thickens slightly, about 2 minutes. Add butter and coarse kosher salt; stir until butter melts. Add yam pieces to skillet; toss to coat. Sprinkle yams with freshly ground black pepper. Spread yams evenly on rimmed baking sheet. Bake until yams are tender and golden, stirring occasionally, about 40 minutes. Transfer yams to large platter or bowl.

Sweet potato puree with brown sugar and Sherry

6 TO 8 SERVINGS *Think of this as a grown-up version of sweet potatoes with marshmallows. For the best flavor, avoid cooking Sherry, which has a high salt content. Instead, choose a Sherry that is also delicious to drink. Fino and Manzanilla Sherries are pale and delicately nutty; Amontillado and Oloroso Sherries are amber and sweeter. Any one of them would be lovely with the potatoes.*

- 2 **pounds medium-size red-skinned sweet potatoes (yams), scrubbed**
- 2 **pounds medium-size tan-skinned sweet potatoes, scrubbed**
- 10 **tablespoons (1¼ sticks) butter, room temperature**
- ¼ **cup (packed) golden brown sugar**
- 5 **tablespoons dry Sherry**

PREHEAT oven to 425°F. Pierce all sweet potatoes in several places with fork. Place on rimmed baking sheet. Bake until tender, about 55 minutes. Cool slightly.

CUT potatoes in half lengthwise. Using spoon, scoop potato pulp into large bowl. Add butter and brown sugar to potatoes. Using electric mixer, beat until smooth. Beat in Sherry. Season to taste with salt and pepper. Transfer to large saucepan.

DO AHEAD *Can be made 2 hours ahead. Let stand at room temperature.*

REWARM potatoes over medium-low heat, stirring often.

GRAINS

Polenta with green chiles and cheese

4 MAIN-COURSE OR 8 SIDE-DISH SERVINGS *This layered casserole makes a satisfying main or side dish. If it's the main event, add green beans and a tossed salad to the menu. On the side, it makes a great partner to lime-grilled chicken or carne asada. You can assemble and chill it a day before baking.*

- 2 **cups whole milk**
- 1 **cup water**
- ¾ **cup yellow cornmeal**
- 3 **garlic cloves, minced**
- 1 **teaspoon salt**
- ½ **cup freshly grated Parmesan cheese**

- 1 **7-ounce can whole green chiles, drained, divided**
- 1 **cup frozen corn kernels, thawed, divided**
- ⅔ **cup chopped fresh cilantro, divided**
- 2 **cups (packed) coarsely grated Monterey Jack cheese (about 8 ounces), divided**
- ½ **cup heavy whipping cream, divided**

BUTTER 8×8×2-inch glass baking dish. Combine first 5 ingredients in heavy medium saucepan. Bring to simmer over medium heat, whisking constantly. Cook until polenta is tender and thickens, stirring often, about 12 minutes. Season to taste with salt and pepper. Stir in Parmesan.

POUR half of polenta into prepared dish. Cover with half of chiles and half of corn. Sprinkle with half of cilantro and 1 cup Monterey Jack cheese. Drizzle with ¼ cup cream. Spoon remaining polenta evenly over. Top with remaining chiles, corn, cilantro, and cheese. Pour remaining ¼ cup cream over.

DO AHEAD *Can be made 1 day ahead. Cover and chill.*

PREHEAT oven to 400°F. Bake polenta uncovered until heated through, puffed, and golden brown, about 25 minutes (30 minutes if chilled).

Corn off the cob Cornmeal, polenta, grits—what's the difference? Cornmeal is made from ground dried corn kernels and comes in fine, medium, or coarse grinds. Polenta is coarse Italian cornmeal. The word *grits* originally had more to do with a grind of grain than the grain itself: Grits once were made from corn, oats, or rice. But the grits called for in these recipes are labeled "hominy grits," hominy being dried, hulled corn kernels. Quick-cooking grits are ground into smaller pieces to reduce cooking time.

Polenta with bacon and Fontina

6 SIDE-DISH SERVINGS *Polenta is available at Italian markets, natural foods stores, and some supermarkets. You can use regular yellow cornmeal instead—just cook the mixture for half the time.*

- ½ cup finely chopped bacon (about 4 ounces)
- ¼ cup chopped onion
- 1 garlic clove, minced
- 5 cups low-salt chicken broth
- 1 cup frozen corn kernels, thawed
- 1 cup polenta (coarse Italian cornmeal)
- 1 cup (packed) coarsely grated Fontina cheese (about 3 ounces)
- ¼ cup freshly grated Parmesan cheese
- 2 tablespoons chopped fresh parsley

SAUTÉ bacon in heavy large skillet over medium-high heat until brown and crisp. Using slotted spoon, transfer bacon to bowl. Add onion and garlic to drippings in skillet and sauté until golden brown, about 2 minutes. Add broth, corn, and bacon; bring to boil. Gradually add cornmeal, whisking constantly. Reduce heat to medium. Cook until polenta is soft and thick, stirring frequently, about 18 minutes. Add Fontina and Parmesan, stirring until melted, about 2 minutes. Stir in parsley. Season to taste with salt and pepper. Transfer to bowl and serve hot.

Skillet polenta with tomatoes and Gorgonzola

4 SERVINGS *Round out this vegetarian main course with steamed broccolini or sautéed zucchini, or a simple arugula salad dressed with lemon juice and olive oil.*

- 2 tablespoons extra-virgin olive oil, divided
- 4 cups water
- 1⅓ cups yellow cornmeal
- 1¼ teaspoons salt
- ½ cup slivered fresh basil leaves, divided
- 2 cups halved cherry tomatoes
- 2 garlic cloves, minced
- 1 cup crumbled Gorgonzola cheese (about 4 ounces)
- 1 cup (packed) coarsely grated mozzarella cheese (about 4 ounces)

PREHEAT oven to 450°F. Brush 12-inch-diameter ovenproof skillet with 1 tablespoon oil. Combine 4 cups water, cornmeal, and salt in heavy large saucepan. Bring to boil over medium-high heat, whisking constantly. Reduce heat to medium-low and cook until polenta is very thick and pulls away from sides of pan, whisking constantly, about 3 minutes. Whisk in remaining 1 tablespoon oil and ¼ cup basil.

TRANSFER polenta to prepared skillet; flatten to even thickness. Sprinkle with tomatoes and garlic, then Gorgonzola, mozzarella, and remaining ¼ cup basil. Bake until cheese topping is bubbling, about 15 minutes. Let stand 5 minutes. Cut polenta into wedges and serve from skillet.

NICE AND SMOOTH To prevent lumpiness in polenta and grits, stir or whisk constantly during the first few minutes of cooking as you pour the grains into the pan; then stir often as the mixture cooks.

Parmesan grits

4 SERVINGS *Simple, fast, and irresistible, these would make a great accompaniment to seasoned sautéed shrimp or blackened fish.*

    3 cups water
    1 cup whole milk
    1 cup quick-cooking grits
    1 teaspoon salt
    ½ cup freshly grated Parmesan cheese

BRING first 4 ingredients to boil in heavy large saucepan, whisking constantly. Reduce heat, cover, and simmer until grits are tender and creamy, stirring occasionally, about 10 minutes. Add cheese and whisk until melted. Season to taste with pepper.

Creamy baked grits with sun-dried tomatoes

6 SIDE-DISH SERVINGS *An updated version of a savory cheese grits casserole, this recipe features plenty of the traditional cream, but the new twist is crumbled goat cheese baked on top.*

    2¼ cups low-salt chicken broth
    2   tablespoons (¼ stick) butter
    1   garlic clove, chopped
    ½   cup quick-cooking grits
    ¾   cup heavy whipping cream, divided
    ½   cup diced drained oil-packed
        sun-dried tomatoes (about 2½ ounces)
    1   teaspoon chopped fresh thyme
    1   cup crumbled soft fresh goat cheese
        (about 4 ounces)

PREHEAT oven to 350°F. Generously butter 8×8×2-inch glass baking dish. Bring broth, 2 tablespoons butter, and garlic to boil in heavy medium saucepan. Gradually whisk in grits and return mixture to boil, whisking occasionally. Reduce heat to medium-low, cover, and simmer until grits are thick and almost all broth is absorbed, whisking often, about 8 minutes. Mix in ½ cup cream and simmer 5 minutes. Mix in remaining ¼ cup cream and simmer until very thick, whisking often, about 5 minutes longer. Stir in tomatoes and thyme. Season to taste with salt and pepper. Pour into prepared baking dish. Sprinkle goat cheese over. Bake until cheese softens, about 15 minutes.

Bulgur with root vegetables

8 SIDE-DISH SERVINGS *Bulgur (cracked wheat) is probably best known as the grain used in tabbouleh, the Middle Eastern salad that also includes parsley and tomatoes. Bulgur is available at natural foods stores and many supermarkets.* Look for herbes de Provence *in the spice section of supermarkets and at specialty foods stores, or use a combination of dried thyme, basil, savory, and fennel seeds. This dish would also make an excellent vegetarian main course for four people.*

- 2 tablespoons olive oil
- 4 cups ¾-inch pieces assorted peeled assorted root vegetables (such as carrots, turnips, celery root, and golden beets)
- 2 cups chopped onions
- 4 cups vegetable broth
- 1 rounded teaspoon herbes de Provence
- 1½ cups bulgur (about 8 ounces)
- 1 6-ounce package baby spinach leaves

HEAT oil in heavy large pot over high heat. Add root vegetables and onions; sauté until beginning to brown, about 10 minutes. Add broth and herbes de Provence; bring to boil. Mix in bulgur; cover pot and reduce heat to low. Simmer until bulgur is just tender and broth is absorbed, stirring occasionally, about 15 minutes. Add spinach; stir until wilted, about 1 minute. Season to taste with salt and pepper.

Lemon-mint tabbouleh

6 SERVINGS *If you have trouble finding plain bulgur (cracked wheat), use one cup of bulgur from two boxes of tabbouleh wheat salad mix (but don't use the seasoning packets). Look for bulgur and/or the mixes in the rice, grain, and pasta section of the supermarket; bulgur is also available at natural foods stores.*

- ¼ cup olive oil
- ¼ cup fresh lemon juice
- 3 large garlic cloves, minced
- 1 cup bulgur
- 1 cup boiling water
- 1 cup chopped seeded plum tomatoes
- ½ cup chopped fresh Italian parsley
- 2 large green onions, chopped
- 2 tablespoons chopped fresh mint

WHISK oil, lemon juice, and garlic in small bowl to blend; set dressing aside. Place bulgur in large bowl. Mix in 1 cup boiling water. Let stand until bulgur is tender and water is absorbed, about 15 minutes. Mix in tomatoes, parsley, green onions, and mint. Add dressing; toss to blend. Season tabbouleh to taste with salt and pepper. Let stand at least 30 minutes to blend flavors, stirring occasionally.

DO AHEAD *Can be made 1 day ahead. Cover and chill.*

Spiced carrot and zucchini quinoa

8 SERVINGS *Quinoa (KEEN-wah) is a high-protein grain native to South America. It's prepared like rice and has a fluffy texture and slightly nutty flavor when cooked. Unlike rice, though, it has a bitter-tasting coating and needs to be rinsed well before cooking. The seasonings in this recipe would complement a Moroccan-spiced tagine. You can make this a day ahead.*

4 cups water
2 cups quinoa (about 10 ounces), rinsed well, drained
2 tablespoons dried currants
½ teaspoon salt

¼ cup extra-virgin olive oil
2 medium carrots, peeled, cut into small cubes
2 medium zucchini, trimmed, cut into small cubes
1 teaspoon Hungarian sweet paprika
1 teaspoon ground cumin
½ teaspoon ground cinnamon

½ cup chopped fresh cilantro

COMBINE first 4 ingredients in heavy large saucepan. Bring to boil over medium-high heat, stirring occasionally. Reduce heat to medium-low, cover, and simmer until water is absorbed and quinoa is tender, about 20 minutes.

MEANWHILE, heat oil in heavy large skillet over medium heat. Add carrots; sauté until tender, about 5 minutes. Add zucchini; sauté until tender, about 3 minutes. Mix in paprika, cumin, and cinnamon.

ADD quinoa to skillet; toss to blend. Season to taste with salt and pepper.

DO AHEAD *Can be made 1 day ahead. Transfer to baking dish. Cover and chill. Rewarm, covered, in 350°F oven about 15 minutes.*

MIX in cilantro and serve.

Leek-tomato quinoa

MAKES ABOUT 2¾ CUPS *Try this topped with slices of grilled beef tenderloin.*

2 cups water
1½ cups quinoa (about 7½ ounces), rinsed well, drained

1 tablespoon butter
2 cups finely chopped leeks (white and pale green parts only)
¼ cup low-salt chicken broth
3 tablespoons olive oil
2 medium yellow tomatoes, seeded, chopped
3 tablespoons chopped green onions
3 tablespoons chopped fresh basil
1 tablespoon fresh lemon juice

COMBINE 2 cups water and quinoa in heavy medium saucepan; sprinkle generously with salt. Bring to boil. Reduce heat to medium-low; cover and simmer until quinoa is just tender and water is absorbed, about 20 minutes. Drain. Set aside.

DO AHEAD *Quinoa can be made 1 day ahead. Cool, then cover and chill.*

MELT butter in large nonstick skillet over medium heat. Add leeks; sauté until beginning to soften, about 5 minutes. Add broth. Cover; simmer until leeks are tender, about 5 minutes. Add quinoa and oil; stir until heated through, about 5 minutes. Stir in tomatoes, green onions, basil, and lemon juice. Season to taste with salt and pepper.

BEANS

Lima bean puree

8 SERVINGS *You can prepare this hours ahead and re-warm it just before serving. Try it with lamb seasoned with rosemary, mint, and garlic.*

- 6 **cups water**
- 3 **10-ounce packages frozen baby lima beans**
- 2 **garlic cloves, minced**
- 1 **large fresh rosemary sprig**
- 5 **tablespoons butter, room temperature**

COMBINE 6 cups water, beans, garlic, and rosemary sprig in large saucepan. Boil until beans are very soft, about 20 minutes. Drain, reserving cooking liquid. Discard rosemary sprig. Transfer bean mixture to processor. Add butter and puree until smooth, adding some of reserved cooking liquid by tablespoonfuls as needed to moisten if dry. Season to taste with salt and pepper.

DO AHEAD *Puree can be prepared 2 hours ahead. Let stand at room temperature. Rewarm over medium heat, stirring occasionally and adding more reserved cooking liquid if dry.*

Spicy black beans with onion and bacon

MAKES 4 CUPS *In this versatile, chili-style dish, canned black beans are spiced up with everyday pantry ingredients. The serving options are endless: Ladle the beans over rice and top with salsa, sour cream, chopped onion, and cilantro (to make it vegetarian, just omit the bacon and use some olive oil to sauté the onion and garlic); spoon the beans into bowls and serve with cornbread; use them to fill burritos; or serve alongside eggs over easy.*

- ¼ **pound bacon, chopped**
- 1 **large onion, chopped**
- 2 **large garlic cloves, chopped**
- 2 **15- to 16-ounce cans black beans, rinsed, drained**
- 1 **16-ounce can diced peeled tomatoes in juice**
- 1 **4-ounce can diced green chiles**
- 2½ **tablespoons chili powder**
- 2 **teaspoons dried oregano**
- ¼ **teaspoon cayenne pepper**

COOK bacon in heavy large saucepan over medium heat until brown and beginning to crisp. Add onion and garlic; sauté until onion is translucent, about 5 minutes. Add all remaining ingredients. Simmer until mixture is thick, stirring frequently, about 12 minutes. Season to taste with salt and pepper.

Rosemary and lemon pinto beans

4 SERVINGS *Pinto beans, usually found in Mexican and southwestern dishes, take on a different accent with Italian flavors and a dash of hot pepper sauce. Try these with grilled burgers, chicken, or fish. You can chill them overnight before serving.*

2   15- to 16-ounce cans pinto beans, rinsed, drained
¾   cup chopped onion
¼   cup extra-virgin olive oil
3   tablespoons red wine vinegar
1½   teaspoons minced fresh rosemary
1   garlic clove, minced
⅛   teaspoon hot pepper sauce

Fresh lemon juice

COMBINE first 7 ingredients in large bowl; toss to blend. Season to taste with salt and pepper.

DO AHEAD *Can be made 1 day ahead. Cover and chill. Let stand at room temperature 30 minutes before serving.*

MIX in lemon juice to taste.

Garlicky beans with feta and mint

4 SERVINGS *In an unusual preparation, garbanzo beans are roasted with garlic and olive oil until lightly browned and slightly crisp on the outside and creamy on the inside, then combined with crumbled feta and mint. These are particularly good with the Chicken Bouillabaisse on page 69.*

2   15- to 16-ounce cans garbanzo beans (chickpeas), rinsed, drained
3   tablespoons olive oil
2   garlic cloves, minced
⅛   teaspoon dried crushed red pepper
1   cup crumbled feta cheese (about 4 ounces)
½   cup chopped fresh mint

PREHEAT oven to 375°F. Combine first 4 ingredients in 11×7×2-inch glass baking dish. Sprinkle with salt and pepper; toss to blend. Bake until heated through and beans begin to crisp on top, about 15 minutes. Mix in cheese and mint.

Quick fixes with canned beans
Keeping a variety of canned beans in the pantry makes it fast and easy to create healthful, delicious snacks or meals.

— **WHITE BEANS WITH TOMATOES AND GARLIC:** Lightly sauté beans with olive oil, chopped garlic, and halved cherry tomatoes or diced tomatoes (even drained diced tomatoes from a can are excellent) until warm and fragrant. Stir in chopped fresh herbs and serve with grilled chicken or fish.

— **BEAN AND CHEESE QUESADILLA:** Combine a couple of spoonfuls of black beans, some chopped green onions, and shredded hot-pepper cheese in the middle of a corn tortilla; fold tortilla over and cook in nonstick pan over medium heat until cheese melts and tortilla is golden brown.

— **GREEK SALAD PITA:** Combine drained garbanzo beans with Greek salad ingredients: feta cheese, chopped tomatoes, onions, cucumbers, and olives. Dress with lemon juice and olive oil and spoon into pita bread.

White beans with tomatoes and chiles

4 SERVINGS *This side is a shortcut version of a traditional Tuscan bean dish. The beans are especially good with pork or lamb, but they also make a hearty meatless main course when tossed with pasta.*

- 1 tablespoon olive oil
- 2 tablespoons chopped pickled jalapeño chiles
- 1½ tablespoons chopped fresh sage or 2 teaspoons dried rubbed sage
- 3 garlic cloves, chopped
- 2 15-ounce cans cannellini (white kidney beans), drained
- 1¾ cups canned crushed tomatoes with added puree

HEAT oil in heavy medium saucepan over medium heat. Add pickled jalapeños, sage, and garlic. Sauté until garlic is tender but not brown, about 5 minutes. Add beans and tomatoes; simmer until mixture thickens and flavors blend, stirring occasionally, about 15 minutes. Season to taste with salt and pepper.

White beans with sage and olive oil

6 SERVINGS *This authentic Tuscan specialty (one of several regional recipes that feature white beans) requires very little active prep time, so it is truly easy to prepare.*

- 1 pound dried Great Northern beans
- 6 cups cold water
- ¼ cup extra-virgin olive oil plus more for serving
- 1½ tablespoons chopped fresh sage
- 1 large garlic clove, minced

PLACE beans in large saucepan. Add enough cold water to cover by 3 inches and bring to boil. Remove from heat; cover and soak 1 hour.

DRAIN beans and return to same pan. Add 6 cups cold water, ¼ cup oil, sage, and garlic. Bring to boil. Reduce heat to medium-low. Cover partially; simmer until beans are just tender, stirring occasionally, about 45 minutes. Season to taste with salt and pepper.

DO AHEAD *Can be made 1 day ahead. Cool. Cover and chill. Rewarm before continuing.*

USING slotted spoon, transfer beans to bowl. Drizzle with more oil.

"Soda jerk" beans

MAKES ABOUT 10 CUPS *Why "soda jerk"? Two different soft drinks lend just the right dose of sweetness. These are a perfect go-with at any backyard barbecue.*

- 4 15- to 16-ounce cans assorted beans (such as pork and beans, black beans, butter beans, and pinto beans), rinsed, drained
- 2 cups ½-inch cubes smoked ham
- 2 large bell peppers (preferably 1 red and 1 green), chopped
- 1 15- to 16-ounce can diced tomatoes in juice, drained
- 1 large onion, chopped
- ½ cup (packed) dark brown sugar
- ½ cup cola-flavored soda
- ½ cup lemon-lime soda
- 2 teaspoons curry powder
- 1 teaspoon garlic powder
- ¼ teaspoon cayenne pepper

PLACE all ingredients in heavy large pot. Bring to boil over medium-high heat, stirring until brown sugar dissolves. Reduce heat to medium and simmer uncovered until juices are thick, stirring gently and frequently to prevent burning, about 20 minutes. Season to taste with salt and pepper.

Sweet and smoky barbecue beans

6 SERVINGS *Add these to your favorite cookout fare or make them the centerpiece of a simple supper with a mixed-greens salad and warm cornbread.*

1   bacon slice

½   cup chopped onion
2   garlic cloves, minced
1   8-ounce can tomato sauce
1   cup water
¼   cup (packed) dark brown sugar
2   tablespoons robust (dark) molasses
2   tablespoons apple cider vinegar
¾   teaspoon dry mustard
1   15- to 16-ounce can red kidney beans, rinsed, drained
1   15- to 16-ounce can pinto beans, rinsed, drained
1   15-ounce can cannellini (white kidney beans), rinsed, drained

COOK bacon in large nonstick skillet over medium heat until crisp. Transfer to paper towel and drain. Crumble bacon and reserve.

HEAT drippings in same skillet over medium heat. Add onion and sauté until golden, about 5 minutes. Add garlic; stir 1 minute. Add tomato sauce, 1 cup water, brown sugar, molasses, vinegar, and dry mustard; bring to boil. Reduce heat and simmer 5 minutes, stirring often. Stir in all beans and bacon, and bring to boil. Reduce heat; simmer until flavors blend and mixture thickens slightly, stirring occasionally, about 10 minutes. Season to taste with salt and pepper.

Lemon-barley pilaf

4 SERVINGS *Pearl barley (so called because the outer bran has been removed and the grain polished like a pearl) has a pleasing al dente, or chewy, texture when cooked. Look for it in the grains and pasta section at natural foods stores and well-stocked supermarkets. Try this with fish or veal chops.*

1   tablespoon butter
1   small onion, finely chopped
¾   cup pearl barley
2   cups low-salt chicken broth
1   Turkish bay leaf

1   medium carrot, peeled, finely chopped
½   red bell pepper, finely chopped
1   teaspoon finely grated lemon peel

MELT butter in heavy medium saucepan over medium heat. Add onion; sprinkle with salt and pepper. Sauté until onion is beginning to soften, about 5 minutes. Add barley; cook 3 minutes, stirring constantly. Add broth and bay leaf; bring to boil. Reduce heat to low, stir once, and cover. Cook until barley is almost tender, about 25 minutes.

MIX in carrot and bell pepper; cover and cook until vegetables and barley are tender and broth is absorbed, about 6 minutes. Remove pilaf from heat. Stir to blend; cover and let stand 10 minutes. Discard bay leaf. Season to taste with salt and pepper. Stir in lemon peel.

Spiced lentils

6 SERVINGS *Known as* dal *in India, these lentils are often served over rice or topped with a cooling dollop of plain yogurt. While the lentils are cooking, slowly brown the onions, which will add a mellow sweetness and depth of flavor to the dish.*

  6 **cups water**
  2 **cups lentils, rinsed, drained**
  1 **tablespoon chopped peeled fresh ginger**
  1 **teaspoon salt**
  3 **tablespoons vegetable oil, divided**

  2 **cups finely chopped onions**
  1 **teaspoon chili powder**

     Curry powder
  ⅓ **cup chopped fresh cilantro**

BRING first 4 ingredients and 1 tablespoon oil to boil in large saucepan. Reduce heat to medium; simmer uncovered until lentils are tender, about 35 minutes.

MEANWHILE, heat remaining 2 tablespoons oil in heavy medium skillet over medium heat. Add onions and sauté until brown, about 18 minutes. Mix in chili powder; stir 1 minute.

STIR onion mixture into lentils. Season to taste with pepper. Transfer to bowl. Sprinkle with curry powder, then cilantro.

Braised lentils

4 SERVINGS *French green lentils are more delicately flavored than brown lentils, and they hold their shape well when cooked. Look for them at some supermarkets and at specialty foods stores. Try these alongside lamb shanks or chops, and drizzle each serving of lentils with extra-virgin olive oil.*

  3 **tablespoons extra-virgin olive oil**
  1 **cup finely chopped red onion**
  ⅔ **cup finely chopped carrot**
  ½ **cup finely chopped celery**
1¼ **cups dried French green lentils**
     (about 8 ounces)
  4 **cups low-salt chicken broth**

HEAT oil in heavy medium saucepan over medium-high heat. Add onion, carrot, and celery; sauté until slightly softened, about 5 minutes. Add lentils and stir 1 minute. Add broth and bring to boil. Reduce heat to medium-low; cover and simmer until lentils are just tender, stirring occasionally, about 35 minutes. Season to taste with salt and pepper.

vegetables

SPRING

Green Beans with Sweet-
and-Sour Red Onions

Green Beans with
Parsley and Mint

Green Beans with Walnuts
and Walnut Oil

Pancetta Green Beans

Sugar Snap Peas with
Toasted Sesame Seeds

Peas with Roasted
Onions and Mint

Sautéed Pea Tendrils

English Pea Puree

Spinach and Leek Gratin with
Roquefort Crumb Topping

Catalan Spinach

Pesto Creamed Spinach

Frisée and Morel Ragout
with Prosciutto

Wild Mushrooms with Shallots

Asparagus with Gremolata Butter

Roasted Green and
White Asparagus

Artichokes with Lemon-
Garlic Butter

Sautéed Baby Beets with
Haricots Verts and Lemon

Crunchy Chili Onion Rings

SUMMER

Marinated Broiled Onions

Grilled Corn with Sweet-
Savory Asian Glaze

Grilled Corn with Smoked
Paprika Butter

Skillet Corn on the Cob with
Parmesan and Cilantro

Summer Vegetable Skewers
with Cumin Butter

Fresh Corn Sauté with Tomatoes,
Squash, and Fried Okra

Andouille Succotash

Mexican Corn and Zucchini

Grilled Vegetables with Olive
and Sun-Dried Tomato Dressing

Grilled Vegetables
with Mint Raita

Grilled Zucchini

Baked Garden Tomatoes
with Cheese

Rosemary Broiled Tomatoes

Baked Eggplant Marinara

Spicy Eggplant and
Green Bean Curry

Grilled Japanese Eggplant with
Feta and Sun-Dried Tomatoes

Sautéed Swiss Chard

FALL/WINTER

Turnips and Peas with Ham

Roasted Parsnips

Pan-Fried Jerusalem Artichokes
in Lemon-Sage Butter

Rutabaga Puree with
Cardamom and Thyme

Brussels Sprouts with White
Beans and Pecorino

Brussels Sprout Chiffonade
with Poppy Seeds

Brussels Sprouts with Lemon Peel

Sweet-and-Sour Cabbage

Celery Root Puree

Sautéed Celery Root
with Swiss Chard

Spiced Winter Squash
with Fennel

Baked Squash with
Yogurt and Mint

Butternut Squash with
Onions and Pecans

Roasted Radicchio with
Balsamic Vinegar

YEAR-ROUND

Broccoli and Rapini with
Lemon and Shallots

Broccoli with Garlic and
Parmesan Cheese

Broccoli in Brown Butter

Cauliflower with Mustard-
Lemon Butter

Roasted Cauliflower with
Onions and Fennel

Thyme-Roasted Carrots

Sweet Maple Carrots

Glazed Carrots with
Molasses and Marjoram

Spiced Butter-Glazed Carrots

tool kit These days, the produce section of the supermarket is full of prepared vegetables that make it possible to get a delicious (and healthy) meal on the table with no peeling, seeding, or dicing required.

Look for prepared vegetables that would otherwise require time and muscle power to get ready—such as peeled and seeded butternut squash, cooked peeled beets, bags of cleaned spinach and other greens, shredded cabbage, peeled baby carrots, and broccoli and cauliflower florets.

Think beyond the label. Use the "vegetable crudités tray" of broccoli, cauliflower, and carrots for a stir-fry or a baked vegetable gratin. Sauté the medley of "stir-fry" vegetables with butter, garlic, and fresh thyme for a side dish with roast chicken. Roast the "fajita mélange" vegetables with quartered new potatoes for a hearty accompaniment to grilled steak, or sauté them and toss with cooked Italian sausage and pasta. If your supermarket has a salad bar, use it as a resource for prepared ingredients that can be used in recipes other than salads. Sliced celery, shredded carrots, and chopped onions are perfect for soups and sauces.

FREEZER-FRESH, CANNED CONVENIENCE

Using fresh seasonal vegetables is always preferable, but certain frozen vegetables—and even a few canned and jarred ones—are not only perfectly delicious (and nutritious because they retain vitamins), but they also come cleaned, peeled, seeded, trimmed, diced, roasted, or marinated.

— **FROM THE FREEZER:** artichoke hearts, brussels sprouts, corn kernels, green beans, lima beans, peas, spinach, vegetable medleys

— **IN THE CAN AND JAR:** artichoke hearts or bottoms, hominy, pumpkin puree, roasted peppers, tomatoes ➤

BEYOND STEAMED VEGETABLES

A few simple additions and methods can turn a vegetable side dish into the main attraction:

— Add flavor to vegetables by sautéing onions and garlic for a few minutes before adding the other vegetables to the pan. Dried crushed red pepper and fresh ginger are other aromatic ingredients that can liven up sautéed vegetables.

— Sauté vegetables in chicken broth for a lighter alternative to oil or butter. Add a slice of smoked ham to the broth for a subtle smoky flavor, or a sprig of fresh rosemary, then remove them before serving the vegetables.

— Roast vegetables to intensify and concentrate their flavors. Asparagus, potatoes, cauliflower, squash, portobello mushrooms, carrots, and fennel roast particularly well. Toss the vegetables with some sliced shallots, fresh thyme sprigs, and a little olive oil, then arrange them on a baking sheet, leaving enough room between the vegetables so they won't steam. Sprinkle with salt and roast in a 450°F oven until they're crisp-tender and slightly caramelized.

— Toss steamed vegetables with flavored butters, such as tarragon butter or garlic-parsley butter.

— Stir freshly grated Parmesan cheese into steamed, roasted, or sautéed veggies—its sharp, nutty, and slightly salty qualities enhance nearly every vegetable.

— Mix a handful of toasted nuts into sautéed vegetables just before serving.

— Grate some lemon peel over sautéed or roasted vegetables.

— Sprinkle roasted vegetables with chopped fresh herbs, like thyme, basil, oregano, cilantro, chives, or parsley.

— Toss steamed vegetables with a few drops of Asian sesame oil for an Asian twist.

SPRING

Green beans with sweet-and-sour red onions

6 SERVINGS *Oregano would be a great substitute for the marjoram in this recipe. Serve with pan-seared pork tenderloin and roasted yams.*

- 1 **pound slender green beans, trimmed**
- 3 **tablespoons butter**
- 1 **very large (14- to 16-ounce) red onion, peeled, halved lengthwise, sliced lengthwise**
- 1 **tablespoon chopped fresh marjoram**
- ½ **teaspoon dried crushed red pepper**
- ⅓ **cup red wine vinegar**
- 2 **tablespoons (packed) dark brown sugar**

STEAM beans until crisp-tender, about 5 minutes. Transfer to plate.

MELT butter in heavy large skillet over high heat. Add next 3 ingredients. Sauté until onion begins to soften, about 2 minutes. Add vinegar and sugar. Stir until sauce thickens, about 1½ minutes. Add beans; toss to coat and heat through, about 1 minute. Season to taste with salt and pepper. Mound in shallow bowl.

Green beans with parsley and mint

6 SERVINGS *Although the hard, flat end (the stem end) of green beans should always be trimmed, cutting off the wispy end (known as the tip) is a matter of preference. Serve this green bean dish with grilled lamb chops and an orzo salad.*

- 1½ **pounds green beans, trimmed**
- ¼ **cup extra-virgin olive oil**
- 3 **tablespoons minced fresh mint**
- 3 **tablespoons minced fresh parsley**
- 2 **tablespoons fresh lemon juice**
- 4 **teaspoons finely grated lemon peel**

COOK beans in large saucepan of boiling salted water until just tender, about 5 minutes. Drain. Transfer to bowl of ice water; cool. Drain well. Transfer beans to large bowl. Mix in oil, mint, and parsley. Season to taste with salt and pepper.

DO AHEAD *Can be made 1 hour ahead. Let stand at room temperature.*

JUST before serving, mix in lemon juice and lemon peel. Serve at room temperature.

Green beans with walnuts and walnut oil

8 SERVINGS *If walnut oil is unavailable, it's fine to substitute another type, such as almond or olive oil.*

2   pounds green beans, trimmed

2   tablespoons (¼ stick) butter
2   tablespoons walnut oil
1   cup chopped walnuts (about 3¾ ounces), toasted
2   tablespoons minced fresh parsley

COOK beans in large pot of boiling salted water until just tender, about 5 minutes. Drain. Rinse beans under cold water; drain well.

DO AHEAD *Can be made 4 hours ahead. Let stand at room temperature.*

MELT butter with oil in heavy large skillet over high heat. Add beans and cook until heated through, stirring often, about 4 minutes. Season to taste with salt and pepper. Add walnuts and parsley and toss to coat. Transfer to bowl.

Pancetta green beans

4 SERVINGS *Pancetta (Italian bacon) is sold in the deli case at most supermarkets and at Italian markets. Although both American bacon and pancetta are cured, American bacon is smoked, whereas pancetta is not. Prosciutto would be a fine substitute.*

12   ounces green beans, trimmed

3   ounces thinly sliced pancetta, coarsely chopped
1   tablespoon butter

COOK beans in large pot of boiling salted water until crisp-tender, about 4 minutes. Drain. Transfer to bowl of ice water; cool. Drain. Transfer beans to paper towels and pat dry.

DO AHEAD *Can be made 1 day ahead. Cover and chill.*

HEAT large skillet over medium heat. Add pancetta and sauté until crisp, about 3 minutes. Using slotted spoon, transfer to paper towels to drain. Increase heat to medium-high. Add butter to same skillet. Add beans and stir until heated through, about 4 minutes. Season to taste with salt and pepper. Stir in pancetta.

Blanched makes bright The word *blanched* can imply that something has had the color washed out. But when vegetables are blanched, their colors are enhanced. Blanched vegetables are cooked briefly in boiling salted water until they are just tender, then plunged into an ice bath or rinsed under cold running water to stop the cooking process. Not only do the colors become more vibrant, but you can also save time with this method. Store blanched vegetables wrapped in paper towels in airtight containers and chill for a few hours or up to two days before using. They'll be ready for a quick sauté or any other method that will just heat them through.

Sugar snap peas with toasted sesame seeds

6 SERVINGS *Toasted sesame seeds are available in the Asian foods section of many supermarkets and at Asian markets. If unavailable, toast white sesame seeds in a dry skillet over medium heat, stirring often, until light golden brown and fragrant.*

1 **pound sugar snap peas, stringed**
1 **teaspoon toasted sesame seeds**
1 **teaspoon Asian sesame oil**

STEAM sugar snap peas until crisp-tender, about 3 minutes. Transfer to bowl. Toss with sesame seeds and oil. Season to taste with salt.

Peas with roasted onions and mint

6 SERVINGS *The classic marriage of peas and mint is enhanced in this recipe with the addition of roasted onion rings.*

2 **medium onions, cut into ¼-inch-thick rounds, separated into rings**
1 **tablespoon olive oil**
½ **teaspoon coarse kosher salt**

3 **cups water**
4 **cups frozen petite peas**
¼ **cup finely chopped fresh mint**
½ **teaspoon freshly ground black pepper**
¼ **teaspoon sugar**

PREHEAT oven to 450°F. Combine onion rings, oil, and coarse salt in medium bowl; toss to coat. Spread onion rings in single layer on rimmed baking sheet. Roast until golden brown, stirring occasionally, about 20 minutes.

DO AHEAD *Can be made 1 day ahead. Cover and chill. Before continuing, rewarm in 350°F oven until heated through, about 10 minutes.*

BRING 3 cups water to boil. Add peas; simmer until tender, about 5 minutes. Drain. Return peas to saucepan. Mix in roasted onion rings, mint, pepper, and sugar. Transfer to bowl.

Sautéed pea tendrils

6 SERVINGS *Pea tendrils (sometimes labeled pea sprouts or pea shoots) are available in the spring at some supermarkets and farmers' markets, and at Asian markets.*

- 2 tablespoons olive oil
- 4 garlic cloves, crushed
- 2 tablespoons (¼ stick) butter
- 1 pound pea tendrils

HEAT oil in heavy large skillet over medium-high heat. Add garlic; cook until golden, about 2 minutes. Discard garlic. Add butter, then pea tendrils. Cover; cook just until wilted, stirring often, about 5 minutes for larger (older) pea tendrils or 2 to 3 minutes for young pea sprouts. Season to taste with salt and pepper.

SPROUTS, TENDRILS, SHOOTS Pea sprouts, pea tendrils, pea shoots—they are all different names for the same vegetable. Young pea sprouts are only a few inches long, and have a tiny cluster of small leaves at the top. Older sprouts have grown to be about a foot long, and have larger leaves and offshoots of spiraling tendrils. Often attached are delicious, pretty white flowers that taste like the freshest peas you've ever eaten. Though all can be eaten raw, young sprouts take only a minute or two to stir-fry (depending on how many you are cooking at a time), whereas the older ones can take up to five minutes.

English pea puree

6 SERVINGS *Mild-mannered English peas get a hit of Latin spice. Chiles de árbol are thin, red, very hot three-inch-long chiles. They are available at some supermarkets, and at specialty foods stores and Latin markets. Or substitute a pinch of dried crushed red pepper, eliminating the need to remove the chile before pureeing.*

- ½ cup extra-virgin olive oil
- 2 tablespoons (¼ stick) butter
- 1 whole dried chile de árbol
- 1 fresh mint sprig
- 1 garlic clove, minced
- 3 cups fresh or frozen peas
  Generous pinch of sugar

COOK oil, butter, chile, and mint in heavy medium saucepan over medium heat 2 minutes. Add garlic and stir 1 minute. Stir in peas and sugar; cook until peas are just tender, stirring occasionally, about 5 minutes. Discard chile and mint sprig. Transfer pea mixture to processor and puree until almost smooth (some texture should remain). Season puree to taste with salt and pepper.

DO AHEAD *Can be made 2 hours ahead. Let puree stand at room temperature. Rewarm in microwave on high about 2 minutes.*

SWEET PEA If using shelled fresh peas, be sure to cook them the same day they are purchased, for best flavor. The sugar in fresh peas quickly begins to turn to starch once the peas have been picked. Frozen peas are flash-frozen right after being picked and blanched, halting this starchy transformation and ensuring a sweet pea.

Spinach and leek gratin with Roquefort crumb topping

8 SERVINGS *Serve this ultimate creamed spinach with broiled strip steaks and roasted red potato wedges. To prevent the gratin from becoming watery, be sure to press out all of the liquid from the spinach before mixing it with the remaining ingredients.*

5	tablespoons butter, divided
3½	tablespoons horseradish Dijon mustard, divided
2⅓	cups fresh breadcrumbs made from crustless French bread
1	cup crumbled Roquefort cheese
3	9-ounce bags fresh spinach leaves
1	8-ounce leek, halved lengthwise, thinly sliced crosswise (about 3 cups)
¾	cup heavy whipping cream

PREHEAT oven to 400°F. Melt 3 tablespoons butter in medium skillet over medium-high heat. Mix in 2 tablespoons mustard, then breadcrumbs. Sauté breadcrumbs until golden, about 5 minutes. Cool briefly. Mix in cheese.

TOSS 1½ bags spinach in large nonstick pot over high heat until wilted, about 3 minutes. Transfer to sieve set over bowl. Repeat with remaining spinach. Press on spinach to drain.

MELT remaining 2 tablespoons butter in same pot over medium-high heat. Add leek and sauté 4 minutes. Add cream, remaining 1½ tablespoons mustard, and spinach. Toss until mixture is thick and blended, about 2 minutes. Season to taste with salt and pepper. Transfer to 11×7×2-inch baking dish. Top with breadcrumb mixture. Bake until bubbling, about 10 minutes.

TRULY GRIT-FREE Because leeks are grown in sandy soil, it is important to halve them lengthwise and rinse well between the layers to remove any dirt.

Catalan spinach

4 SERVINGS *This traditional dish is from Catalonia, in the northeastern part of Spain where Barcelona is located. Serve with shrimp sautéed with garlic in Spanish olive oil and a loaf of crusty bread for soaking up the flavorful juices.*

3	tablespoons olive oil, divided
1	medium Golden Delicious apple, peeled, cored, cut into ½-inch cubes
½	cup pine nuts
2	small shallots, finely chopped
½	cup raisins
2	9-ounce bags fresh spinach leaves

HEAT 1 tablespoon oil in heavy large pot over high heat. Add apple and sauté until golden brown around edges, about 3 minutes. Add pine nuts; sauté until pine nuts are lightly toasted, about 3 minutes. Add remaining 2 tablespoons oil to pot. Add shallots and raisins; stir to combine. Add spinach; cover and cook just until wilted, stirring occasionally, about 2 minutes. Season to taste with salt and pepper; transfer to bowl.

Pesto creamed spinach

2 SERVINGS; CAN BE DOUBLED OR TRIPLED *This twist on a classic steakhouse recipe can be pulled together in a matter of minutes. It would make a luxurious side for grilled steaks, chops, or chicken.*

- 1 **10-ounce package frozen chopped spinach, cooked according to package directions**
- 2 **tablespoons purchased pesto**
- ¼ **cup whipping cream**
- ⅓ **cup freshly grated Romano cheese (about 1½ ounces)**

DRAIN spinach and squeeze dry. Heat heavy medium skillet over medium heat. Add pesto, then spinach; stir until heated through. Add cream and stir until thickened slightly, about 2 minutes. Mix in cheese. Season to taste with pepper.

Frisée and morel ragout with prosciutto

4 TO 6 SERVINGS *When fresh morel mushrooms—with their trademark honeycomb-like caps—appear at the market, that's a sure sign spring has arrived. If you can't find morels, substitute your favorite fresh wild mushroom. Serve with pan-seared chicken breasts.*

- 3 **tablespoons butter**
- 7 **ounces small fresh morel mushrooms**
- ¼ **cup minced shallots (about 2)**
- ¾ **cup low-salt chicken broth**
- 2 **small heads of frisée (about 6 ounces), torn into 2-inch pieces**
- 1 **cup fresh sweet peas or frozen petite peas, thawed**
- ½ **cup crème fraîche or heavy whipping cream**
- 4 **thin prosciutto slices (about 1 ounce), cut into thin strips**
- 2 **teaspoons fresh lemon juice**

MELT butter in large skillet over medium-high heat. Add mushrooms and sauté, stirring frequently, until juices are released, about 3 minutes. Add shallots; sauté 1 minute. Add broth; bring to simmer. Cover skillet and simmer until mushrooms are tender, about 5 minutes. Add frisée and stir until just wilted. Add peas and crème fraîche; bring to simmer. Stir in prosciutto and lemon juice. Season with salt and pepper.

Wild mushrooms with shallots

6 SERVINGS *This would be ideal with fresh chanterelle mushrooms, which look like orange trumpets with thinly ridged stems. Be sure to rinse out any debris that may be stuck in the ridges and the top of the mushroom, then pat dry before using. If chanterelles are unavailable, any fresh wild mushroom—such as porcini, oyster, or morel—would also be delicious.*

- 2 tablespoons (¼ stick) butter
- 2 tablespoons olive oil
- 8 ounces fresh chanterelle mushrooms or other wild mushrooms, quartered if large
- 1 teaspoon minced shallot
- 1 garlic clove, minced

MELT butter with oil in heavy large skillet over medium-high heat. Add mushrooms; sauté until lightly browned, about 6 minutes. Add shallot and garlic; sauté 2 minutes longer. Season to taste with salt and pepper.

DO AHEAD *Can be made 2 hours ahead. Transfer to baking sheet. Cover loosely with foil and let stand at room temperature. Before serving, rewarm in 400°F oven until heated through, about 5 minutes.*

Asparagus with gremolata butter

6 SERVINGS *Gremolata is an Italian blend of garlic, parsley, and lemon peel traditionally sprinkled over the Italian veal dish osso buco. But why stop there? The combination is delicious mixed with butter and served with poultry or vegetables. Serve the asparagus for brunch with a delicate poached salmon, herb biscuits, and chilled Prosecco (sparkling wine).*

- 2 pounds asparagus, trimmed
- 2 tablespoons (¼ stick) butter
- 2 teaspoons finely grated lemon peel
- 1 garlic clove, minced
- 2 tablespoons fresh lemon juice
- 1 tablespoon chopped fresh Italian parsley

COOK asparagus in large pot of boiling salted water until just crisp-tender, about 4 minutes. Drain; rinse with cold water to cool quickly. Drain again.

DO AHEAD *Can be made 1 day ahead. Wrap in paper towels, cover, and chill.*

MELT butter in heavy large skillet over medium-high heat. Add lemon peel and garlic; stir 30 seconds. Add asparagus and toss to coat. Sprinkle lemon juice over. Sauté until asparagus is heated through and coated with butter sauce, about 3 minutes. Season asparagus to taste with salt and pepper. Transfer to platter. Sprinkle with parsley.

Roasted green and white asparagus

6 SERVINGS *White asparagus—the preferred variety in Northern Europe—is grown without direct sunlight, preventing photosynthesis (and, thus, any greening) from occurring. If you can't find white asparagus, use two pounds of green asparagus.*

- 4 tablespoons extra-virgin olive oil, divided
- 1 pound white asparagus, trimmed, peeled, cut on diagonal into 3-inch lengths
- 1 pound green asparagus, trimmed, cut on diagonal into 3-inch lengths
- ¼ cup finely chopped shallots
- ½ teaspoon finely grated lemon peel
- 1 tablespoon chopped fresh Italian parsley

PREHEAT oven to 450°F. Brush large rimmed baking sheet with 1 tablespoon olive oil. Arrange all asparagus on prepared baking sheet. Whisk remaining 3 tablespoons olive oil, shallots, and lemon peel in small bowl to blend; pour over asparagus and toss gently to coat. Spread asparagus in single layer. Sprinkle with salt and pepper. Roast until asparagus is tender, stirring occasionally, about 15 minutes.

DO AHEAD *Can be made 2 hours ahead. Let stand at room temperature. If desired, rewarm in 450°F oven 5 minutes before continuing.*

ADD parsley and toss gently. Season to taste with salt and pepper. Transfer to platter and serve warm or at room temperature.

Artichokes with lemon-garlic butter

4 SERVINGS *Artichokes served whole are about as impressive as any vegetable can be. Look for artichokes with firm, bright green leaves that are tightly packed; the artichokes should feel firm when squeezed.*

- 4 large artichokes
- ¼ cup olive oil
- 6 garlic cloves, minced
- 4 teaspoons minced fresh thyme
- ½ cup fresh lemon juice
- ½ cup (1 stick) butter, cut into ½-inch cubes

PLACE steamer rack in large pot. Fill pot with enough water to come just to bottom of rack. Cut stems and top 1½ inches from artichokes. Cut away first outside row of artichoke leaves. Using scissors, cut off pointed tips of leaves. Arrange artichokes on rack. Bring water to boil over high heat. Cover pot; steam artichokes until knife pierces base easily, adding more water if necessary, about 45 minutes.

MEANWHILE, heat oil in heavy medium saucepan over medium heat. Add garlic and thyme; cook 1 minute. Add lemon juice and butter; whisk until butter melts. Season to taste with salt and pepper. Serve artichokes warm with seasoned butter.

Sautéed baby beets with haricots verts and lemon

6 SERVINGS *Haricots verts are very delicate and slender stringless green beans. Regular green beans can be substituted, but will take a minute or two longer to cook.*

10 red or golden baby beets, trimmed, scrubbed
2 tablespoons olive oil

1½ pounds haricots verts, trimmed
¼ cup (½ stick) butter
2 tablespoons fresh lemon juice
1½ teaspoons finely grated lemon peel
½ cup fresh Italian parsley leaves

PREHEAT oven to 375°F. Toss beets with oil in roasting pan. Sprinkle with salt. Cover pan with foil. Bake until beets are tender, about 30 minutes. Uncover and let beets stand at room temperature 20 minutes. Cut beets into quarters (or halves if very small).

COOK haricots verts in large pot of boiling salted water until crisp-tender, about 4 minutes. Drain and transfer to bowl of ice water to cool. Drain and pat dry. Melt butter in large skillet over medium heat. Add lemon juice and lemon peel, then beets. Toss well. Stir in haricots verts and parsley; sauté until heated through, about 3 minutes. Season to taste with salt and pepper. Serve warm or at room temperature.

Crunchy chili onion rings

4 SERVINGS *Vidalia onions are sweet onions grown in Vidalia, Georgia. The soil there is unique because of its low sulfur content—the same seeds planted in different soil would not give you the flavor associated with this famous onion. Sweet Maui onions can be used instead, if desired. Serve with ice-cold beer.*

6 cups vegetable oil (for deep-frying)

1 1-pound Vidalia onion, peeled, cut into ⅓-inch-thick slices, separated into rings
3 cups buttermilk
2 cups all purpose flour
1 cup yellow cornmeal
3 tablespoons chili powder
2 tablespoons ground cumin
1 tablespoon salt
1 teaspoon cayenne pepper

Chopped fresh cilantro (optional)

POUR oil into heavy large deep skillet. Rest top of deep-fry thermometer against edge of skillet, submerging bulb end in oil. Heat oil over medium-high heat to 375°F.

MEANWHILE, combine onion rings and buttermilk in large bowl. Mix flour, cornmeal, chili powder, cumin, salt, and cayenne in another large bowl. Remove ⅓ of onion rings from buttermilk; add to flour mixture and toss well to coat.

ADD coated onion rings to oil; fry until golden brown, adjusting heat as needed to maintain oil temperature, about 3 minutes. Using tongs, transfer onion rings to paper towels to drain. Repeat with remaining onion rings in 2 more batches. Transfer onion rings to platter. Sprinkle with cilantro, if desired, and serve.

SUMMER

Marinated broiled onions

2 SERVINGS; CAN BE DOUBLED *Onions have a lot of sugars in them, despite their rather pungent flavor when raw. When onions are cooked until brown, or caramelized, the sugars come forth.*

- 1 large red onion, peeled, cut into ½-inch-thick slices
- 2 tablespoons extra-virgin olive oil, divided

- 1 teaspoon fresh lime juice
- ¼ teaspoon dried oregano, crumbled

PREHEAT broiler. Arrange onion slices on rimmed baking sheet. Brush both sides of onion with 1 tablespoon oil. Sprinkle generously with pepper. Broil until softened and beginning to char, about 7 minutes. Turn slices over, sprinkle with pepper, and broil until beginning to char, about 2 minutes.

TRANSFER onion to bowl. Separate into rings. Add remaining 1 tablespoon oil, lime juice, and oregano; toss to coat. Season to taste with salt. Cool to room temperature.

Grilled corn with sweet-savory Asian glaze

6 SERVINGS *Here is a recipe that is truly greater than the sum of its ingredients. Fish sauce is a salty fermented liquid used to flavor many Southeast Asian dishes. It is available at many supermarkets and some specialty foods stores, and at Asian markets.*

- 3 tablespoons fish sauce (such as nam pla or nuoc nam)
- 2 tablespoons water
- 1½ tablespoons (packed) golden brown sugar
- ½ teaspoon freshly ground black pepper
- 2 tablespoons (¼ stick) butter
- 2 tablespoons olive oil plus additional for brushing
- 1 tablespoon thinly sliced green onions (white part only; from about 3)

- 6 ears of corn, husked

STIR first 4 ingredients in small bowl until sugar dissolves. Melt butter with 2 tablespoons oil in small saucepan over medium heat. Add fish sauce mixture and green onions and simmer until sauce begins to thicken, about 2 minutes.

DO AHEAD *Butter sauce can be made 2 hours ahead. Let stand at room temperature.*

PREPARE barbecue (medium-high heat). Brush corn with oil. Grill corn until tender and charred in spots, turning often, about 13 minutes. Brush corn generously with butter sauce and serve, passing remaining sauce separately.

Grilled corn with smoked paprika butter

10 SERVINGS *Hot smoked Spanish paprika is sometimes labeled* Pimentón Picante *or* Pimentón de La Vera Picante. *It is available at specialty foods stores and from tienda.com. Serve the corn with grilled hamburgers and a green salad.*

  1 cup (2 sticks) butter, room temperature
  2 teaspoons hot smoked Spanish paprika
  1 garlic clove, chopped
  ½ teaspoon sugar
     Pinch of salt

20 ears of corn, husked

BLEND butter, paprika, garlic, sugar, and salt in processor until smooth. Wrap paprika butter in plastic, forming 1½-inch-diameter log. Refrigerate butter until firm, about 2 hours.

DO AHEAD *Can be made 1 day ahead. Keep chilled.*

PREPARE barbecue (medium-high heat). Working in batches, cook corn in large pot of boiling salted water until tender, about 5 minutes. Drain well. Grill corn until lightly browned in spots, turning occasionally, about 5 minutes. Serve corn hot with thick slices of paprika butter.

PINCH HITTER If hot smoked Spanish paprika is unavailable, substitute an equal amount of regular smoked paprika (available at many supermarkets) and add a pinch of cayenne pepper.

Skillet corn on the cob with Parmesan and cilantro

4 SERVINGS *Bring the barbecue inside—serve this corn with oven-roasted baby back ribs and coleslaw.*

  4 ears of corn, husked
  6 tablespoons olive oil, divided
  ⅓ cup grated Parmesan cheese
  1 garlic clove, minced
  1 tablespoon fresh lime juice
  1 teaspoon ground cumin
  ½ teaspoon hot pepper sauce
  ¼ cup chopped fresh cilantro

COOK corn in large pot of boiling salted water until tender, about 5 minutes. Drain.

WHISK 5 tablespoons oil, cheese, garlic, lime juice, cumin, and hot pepper sauce in medium bowl to blend. Season to taste with salt and pepper. Heat remaining 1 tablespoon oil in heavy large skillet over medium-high heat. Add corn and sauté until heated through, turning frequently, about 2 minutes. Brush corn with some of Parmesan mixture. Turn corn and brush with more cheese mixture. Cook until coating begins to color, about 3 minutes. Transfer corn to platter. Mix cilantro into any remaining Parmesan mixture and brush over corn.

Summer vegetable skewers with cumin butter

2 SERVINGS; CAN BE DOUBLED OR TRIPLED *For a smoky twist, replace the dried crushed red pepper with crushed chipotle chile pepper. The cilantro could also be replaced with parsley. You'll need four skewers to grill the vegetables; if using wooden skewers, first soak them in water for 30 minutes.*

1 small red bell pepper, cut into 1½-inch squares

1 small yellow bell pepper, cut into 1½-inch squares

2 small ears of corn, husked, cut into 1-inch-thick rounds

6 tablespoons (¾ stick) butter

⅜ teaspoon ground cumin

¼ teaspoon dried crushed red pepper

1½ tablespoons chopped fresh cilantro

PREPARE barbecue (medium heat). Arrange vegetables on 4 skewers, alternating and dividing equally. Place on rimmed baking sheet.

MELT butter with cumin and crushed red pepper in heavy small saucepan over medium heat. Season to taste with salt and pepper. Remove from heat and stir in cilantro.

BRUSH vegetables with some of butter mixture. Grill skewers until vegetables are just crisp-tender and beginning to char, turning and basting occasionally with cumin butter, about 15 minutes. Remove from grill. Brush with remaining butter.

CUTTING CORN COBS To cut an ear of corn into rounds, place it on a wood countertop or cutting board. Starting at one end and using a heavy, large knife, raise the knife several inches above the cob, then quickly and firmly cut off a one-inch-long section (if the knife does not go all the way through, twist the knife clockwise and the corn piece will break off). Twist the pointed end of a skewer firmly through the center of the cob, then push and slide the corn onto the skewer.

Fresh corn sauté with tomatoes, squash, and fried okra

4 TO 6 SERVINGS *Pattypan squash is short and squat and looks a little like a cartoon character's fancy hat. It comes in yellow and pale green; the smaller ones, as called for in this recipe, are sweeter and more tender than the larger ones.*

½ cup yellow cornmeal

¼ teaspoon (or more) cayenne pepper

12 okra pods, cut crosswise into ½-inch pieces

6 tablespoons olive oil, divided

2 cups fresh corn kernels (cut from about 3 ears of corn)

6 baby green pattypan squash, trimmed, each cut into 6 pieces

2 garlic cloves, chopped

1 12-ounce container cherry tomatoes, halved (2 cups)

2 tablespoons chopped fresh cilantro

2 green onions, chopped

MIX cornmeal and ¼ teaspoon cayenne in small bowl. Add okra and toss lightly to coat. Pour okra into sieve and shake off excess cornmeal. Heat 4 tablespoons oil in heavy large skillet over medium heat. Add okra and sauté until coating is golden brown, stirring occasionally, about 6 minutes. Using slotted spoon, transfer okra to paper towels to drain; sprinkle with salt and pepper. Wipe out skillet. Heat remaining 2 tablespoons oil in same skillet over medium heat. Add corn, squash, and garlic; sauté 2 minutes. Add tomatoes; cover and cook until squash is crisp-tender, about 5 minutes. Mix in okra, cilantro, and green onions. Remove from heat. Season to taste with salt, pepper, and more cayenne, if desired.

Andouille succotash

6 SERVINGS *Andouille sausage is a spicy smoked sausage used in Cajun cooking. It is traditionally added to gumbo and jambalaya, but here it is added to another southern favorite, succotash. Other spicy smoked sausages, such as linguiça or chorizo, would work well here.*

2 tablespoons (¼ stick) butter

¼ cup minced onion

2 cups frozen baby lima beans, thawed

2 cups frozen sweet corn kernels, thawed

6 ounces andouille sausage, thinly sliced into rounds

2 cups chopped seeded fresh tomatoes (about 3)

2 tablespoons chopped fresh parsley

2 teaspoons fresh lime juice

MELT butter in heavy large skillet over medium heat. Add onion; sauté until soft, about 5 minutes. Add lima beans, corn, and sausage; sprinkle with salt and pepper. Sauté until vegetables are cooked through, about 8 minutes. Add tomatoes and cook 3 minutes longer. Mix in parsley and lime juice. Season to taste with salt and pepper and serve.

SUCCOTASH Its name derived from the American Indian word for boiled corn kernels, succotash is a classic southern summer side dish. It always starts with lima beans and corn, and often has other ingredients added.

Mexican corn and zucchini

4 SERVINGS *Purchased salsa is added to this colorful side dish for a delicious punch of flavor. If desired, sprinkle a little extra chopped fresh cilantro over the dish before serving. This is great with fish tacos.*

- 3 tablespoons butter
- 1 10-ounce package frozen corn kernels, thawed
- 1 red bell pepper, chopped
- 1 cup chopped zucchini
- 2 green onions, chopped
- 1 jalapeño chile, seeded, chopped
- ½ cup purchased salsa
- 2 tablespoons chopped fresh cilantro

MELT butter in heavy large skillet over medium-high heat. Add corn, bell pepper, zucchini, green onions, and jalapeño; sauté until vegetables are tender, about 6 minutes. Mix in salsa and cilantro. Stir until heated through, about 1 minute. Season to taste with salt and pepper.

Grilled vegetables with olive and sun-dried tomato dressing

4 SERVINGS *Add grilled shrimp or chicken to this vegetable platter to turn it into a complete meal. Or sprinkle with crumbled feta cheese for a vegetarian main course.*

- 2 tablespoons vegetable oil plus additional for brushing
- 4 small zucchini, trimmed, cut lengthwise in half
- 2 red bell peppers, quartered
- 4 8-ounce yams (red-skinned sweet potatoes), peeled, each cut lengthwise into 6 wedges

- 3 tablespoons fresh lemon juice
- 2 tablespoons extra-virgin olive oil
- 1 tablespoon chopped Kalamata olives
- 2 oil-packed sun-dried tomato halves, drained, chopped

- 1 tablespoon finely grated orange peel
- 2 teaspoons chopped fresh rosemary

BRUSH grill rack with vegetable oil; prepare barbecue (medium-low heat). Place vegetables on rimmed baking sheet. Drizzle with 2 tablespoons vegetable oil. Sprinkle with salt and pepper; toss to coat. Grill vegetables until tender, turning often, about 10 minutes for zucchini, 12 minutes for bell peppers, and 30 minutes for yams.

MEANWHILE, whisk lemon juice and next 3 ingredients in large bowl. Season dressing to taste with salt and pepper.

ADD grilled vegetables to dressing; toss to coat. Divide vegetables among 4 plates. Sprinkle orange peel and rosemary over.

Grilled vegetables with mint raita

6 SERVINGS *Serve these kebabs with grilled lamb chops. Sliced mangos drizzled with fresh lime juice would be perfect for dessert.*

2 cups plain whole-milk yogurt
1 cup chopped fresh mint
2 teaspoons plus 1 tablespoon garam masala
¼ cup vegetable oil
2 red bell peppers, each cut into 6 wedges
3 large zucchini, each cut into 6 wedges
2 red onions, each cut into 6 wedges with some core still attached

Nonstick vegetable oil spray

MIX yogurt, mint, and 2 teaspoons garam masala in medium bowl. Season raita to taste with salt and pepper. Whisk oil and remaining 1 tablespoon garam masala in large bowl. Season marinade to taste with salt and pepper. Add peppers, zucchini, and onions to marinade; toss to coat.

SPRAY grill rack with nonstick spray; prepare barbecue (medium-high heat). Grill vegetables until slightly charred in spots, turning occasionally, about 8 minutes.

SERVE vegetables with mint raita.

A WORLD OF YOGURT The Greeks call their yogurt and cucumber salad *tzatziki,* while the similar Indian dish is called *raita.* Both are often flavored with mint, but this recipe takes a decidedly Indian turn with the addition of garam masala, a curry-like spice blend available at most supermarkets and at Indian markets.

Grilled zucchini

2 SERVINGS; CAN BE DOUBLED OR TRIPLED *Try this marinade with other vegetables, such as sliced red bell peppers or eggplant. Or marinate a little of each together for a colorful grilled vegetable side dish.*

3 tablespoons olive oil
2 garlic cloves, minced
2 teaspoons soy sauce
2 zucchini, trimmed, cut lengthwise into ½-inch-thick strips

COMBINE first 3 ingredients in glass baking dish. Add zucchini and turn to coat. Marinate 15 minutes, turning occasionally.

MEANWHILE, prepare barbecue (medium-high heat). Grill zucchini until browned and tender, about 4 minutes per side. Season to taste with salt and pepper. Transfer zucchini to plates.

Baked garden tomatoes with cheese

6 SERVINGS *This would be a wonderful side dish for roast beef or chicken. Or, for an appetizer, serve it with toasted baguette slices and allow guests to spoon the cheesy tomatoes over. Although the combination of the two cheeses is delicious, feel free to just use two cups of one cheese.*

- 2 tablespoons extra-virgin olive oil plus additional for brushing
- 3 garlic cloves, chopped
- 1 medium onion, chopped
- 1¾ pounds fresh vine-ripened or heirloom tomatoes, cut into ½-inch cubes
- 3 tablespoons chopped fresh chives
- 1 cup (packed) grated Parmesan cheese
- 1 cup (packed) grated Romano cheese

PREHEAT oven to 350°F. Brush 11×7×2-inch baking dish with oil. Heat 2 tablespoons oil in heavy large skillet over medium heat. Add garlic and sauté until aromatic, about 30 seconds. Add onion and sauté until soft, about 6 minutes. Add tomatoes, reduce heat to medium-low, and cook until beginning to soften, about 5 minutes. Mix in chives; season to taste with salt and pepper. Transfer tomato mixture to prepared baking dish; sprinkle both cheeses over. Bake until cheese melts and begins to turn golden, about 20 minutes.

MARKET TIP Although domestic Parmesan cheese is a good, economical choice, try Parmigiano-Reggiano—the real thing made in the Emilia-Romagna region of Italy—when the mood to splurge is upon you. Its intense flavor and smooth texture are worth the price.

Rosemary broiled tomatoes

4 SERVINGS *This colorful side dish or garnish would also be excellent made with fresh thyme instead of rosemary.*

- 2 ripe medium tomatoes, cored, halved crosswise
- 2 tablespoons (¼ stick) butter
- 1 garlic clove, minced
- ⅔ cup fresh breadcrumbs made from crustless French bread
- 1½ teaspoons minced fresh rosemary

BUTTER baking dish. Place tomato halves, cut side up, in prepared dish. Sprinkle tomatoes with salt and pepper.

MELT butter in heavy small skillet over medium-low heat. Add garlic; sauté 1 minute. Add breadcrumbs and rosemary; toss to coat. Spoon breadcrumbs evenly over tomatoes.

PREHEAT broiler. Set tomatoes 4 to 6 inches from heat source and broil until crumbs are brown and crisp and tomatoes are just warmed through. Transfer to platter.

Baked eggplant marinara

8 SERVINGS *Any leftovers would make a great sandwich, served hot in a crusty roll.*

8 ½-inch-thick center-cut eggplant
   rounds (from 2 small eggplants)
   All purpose flour
2 eggs
1½ cups fresh breadcrumbs made
   from crustless French bread
¾ cup freshly grated Parmesan cheese
   (about 2½ ounces)

4 tablespoons olive oil
1 cup ricotta cheese
1¼ cups purchased marinara sauce
¾ cup grated mozzarella cheese (about 3 ounces)

PREHEAT oven to 350°F. Lightly oil baking sheet. Sprinkle eggplant rounds with salt and pepper. Place flour in shallow bowl. Whisk eggs in another shallow bowl. Mix breadcrumbs and Parmesan cheese in a third shallow bowl. Coat eggplant rounds with flour, then eggs, then breadcrumb mixture, patting to adhere.

HEAT 2 tablespoons oil in heavy large skillet over medium-high heat. Add 4 eggplant rounds to skillet. Cook until golden brown, about 5 minutes per side; transfer to prepared sheet. Repeat with remaining oil and eggplant rounds. Spread 2 tablespoons ricotta cheese over each round. Top each with sauce and mozzarella cheese, dividing equally. Bake until rounds are heated through and cheese is melted, about 15 minutes.

Spicy eggplant and green bean curry

4 TO 6 SIDE-DISH SERVINGS *Thai green curry paste and unsweetened coconut milk can be found in the Asian foods section of many supermarkets and at Southeast Asian markets. Not having to peel the eggplant saves time; eggplant skin is completely edible and adds nice color and texture to this dish.*

5 tablespoons vegetable oil, divided
4 garlic cloves, chopped
1 tablespoon chopped peeled fresh ginger
1 14- to 16-ounce eggplant, cut
   into 2×½×½-inch sticks
8 ounces green beans, trimmed,
   cut into 2-inch pieces

1 tablespoon finely grated lime peel
1 teaspoon Thai green curry paste
1 cup canned unsweetened coconut milk
¼ cup chopped fresh cilantro
2 tablespoons chopped fresh mint

HEAT 4 tablespoons oil in heavy large skillet over medium-high heat. Add garlic and ginger; stir 30 seconds. Add eggplant and green beans. Cook until almost tender, stirring often, about 10 minutes. Cover and cook until completely tender, about 3 minutes longer. Transfer vegetables to bowl.

ADD remaining 1 tablespoon oil, lime peel, and curry paste to same skillet; stir 15 seconds. Add coconut milk; bring to boil, whisking until smooth. Return vegetables to skillet; toss until sauce thickens enough to coat vegetables, about 3 minutes. Season to taste with salt. Mix in cilantro and mint.

Grilled Japanese eggplant with feta and sun-dried tomatoes

12 SERVINGS *Salting the eggplant not only helps release the sometimes bitter juices from the eggplant, but also prevents the eggplant from acting like a sponge and soaking up too much oil when cooked.*

- 12 Japanese eggplants, stemmed, halved lengthwise
- 1 tablespoon salt

- ⅓ cup chopped drained oil-packed sun-dried tomatoes
- ¼ cup fresh lemon juice
- 2 tablespoons olive oil plus more for grilling
- 2 garlic cloves, minced
- 1 tablespoon chopped fresh Italian parsley
- 1 tablespoon chopped fresh mint
- 1 cup (packed) crumbled feta cheese

PLACE eggplant halves in large colander. Toss with 1 tablespoon salt. Let stand 30 minutes. Transfer to paper towels; pat dry.

MEANWHILE, stir tomatoes, lemon juice, 2 tablespoons oil, garlic, parsley, and mint in medium bowl. Mix in cheese. Season topping to taste with salt and pepper. Prepare barbecue (medium-high heat). Brush eggplant with oil. Grill until tender, about 3 minutes per side. Place eggplant, cut side up, on platter. Spoon feta topping over eggplant.

Sautéed Swiss chard

4 SERVINGS *Use rainbow or Bright Lights Swiss chard for a multicolored twist on this dish. Serve with pan-seared scallops and buttery mashed potatoes.*

- 1½ tablespoons butter
- 1½ tablespoons olive oil
- 2 garlic cloves, finely chopped
  Pinch of dried crushed red pepper
- 2 large bunches Swiss chard, stems trimmed, leaves cut crosswise into ½-inch-wide strips

MELT butter with oil in heavy large pot over medium-low heat. Add garlic and crushed red pepper. Sauté until aromatic, about 1 minute. Add chard; stir to coat. Cover; cook until tender, stirring occasionally, about 8 minutes. Season to taste with salt. Transfer to bowl.

SWISS CHARD STEMS The leaves of Swiss chard cook in a hurry, unlike the sturdy stems. But don't discard the delicious stems—they just need to be chopped and sautéed a little longer.

FALL/WINTER

Turnips and peas with ham

8 SERVINGS *Purchase turnips with the greens still attached, if you can, as the tops are the best indication of freshness. They should be green and show no signs of browning or wilting. The bulbs should not have any brown spots, and should feel firm and heavy for their size.*

- ¼ cup (½ stick) butter
- 2 pounds medium turnips, peeled, quartered, cut into thin wedges
- 3 cups frozen petite peas, thawed
- ¼ cup minced green onions
- 2 teaspoons minced fresh tarragon
- 2 ounces ham, chopped

MELT butter in heavy large skillet over medium heat. Add turnips and sauté until golden brown and tender, about 8 minutes. Season to taste with salt and pepper. Mix in peas, green onions, and tarragon and sauté just until heated through, about 3 minutes. Stir in ham. Season to taste with salt and pepper. Transfer to bowl.

Roasted parsnips

8 SERVINGS *Who knew that two ingredients could produce such a sweet side dish? If you'd like to add a third, replace half of the parsnips with carrots. Purchase parsnips that are less than 12 inches long; bigger ones tend to have very woody centers.*

- 8 large parsnips, peeled, quartered lengthwise, then quartered crosswise
- ¼ cup olive oil

PREHEAT oven to 425°F. Place parsnips on baking sheet. Drizzle oil over and toss to coat. Sprinkle with salt and pepper. Roast parsnips uncovered until tender, about 35 minutes.

Pan-fried Jerusalem artichokes in lemon-sage butter

4 TO 6 SERVINGS *Sometimes called sunchokes, Jerusalem artichokes are the tuberous roots of a variety of North American sunflower and resemble fresh ginger root in appearance. The sweet, mildly artichoke-flavored tubers are available at some supermarkets and farmers' markets.*

- 3 **tablespoons butter, divided**
- 2 **tablespoons olive oil**
- 1 **pound Jerusalem artichokes, scrubbed, cut crosswise into ¼-inch-thick rounds**
- 3 **tablespoons coarsely torn fresh sage leaves, divided**
- 2 **teaspoons fresh lemon juice**
- 2 **tablespoons chopped fresh Italian parsley**

MELT 1 tablespoon butter with olive oil in large nonstick skillet over medium-high heat. Add Jerusalem artichokes and half of sage. Sprinkle with salt and pepper. Sauté until Jerusalem artichokes are brown and just beginning to soften, turning frequently, about 10 minutes. Using slotted spoon, transfer Jerusalem artichokes to shallow serving bowl. Add remaining 2 tablespoons butter and sage to skillet; fry until sage darkens and begins to crisp, about 30 seconds. Add lemon juice; simmer 1 minute. Pour lemon-sage butter over Jerusalem artichokes in bowl, tossing to coat. Season to taste with salt and pepper. Sprinkle with parsley.

WHAT'S IN A NAME? The Italian word for sunflower, *girasole*, evolved into the word *Jerusalem* when this vegetable was introduced in Europe after being discovered in the Americas. At many supermarkets, however, you'll find Jerusalem artichokes labeled as sunchokes.

Rutabaga puree with cardamom and thyme

12 SERVINGS *Rutabagas look like colorful cousins of the turnip, with purple and yellow skin and pale orange flesh. Choose rutabagas that have smooth, unblemished skin and are heavy for their size. Store in plastic bags in the refrigerator for up to two weeks.*

- 6 **pounds rutabagas, peeled, cut into 1-inch cubes**
- 1 **teaspoon coarse kosher salt**
- 24 **whole green cardamom pods**
- ½ **cup crème fraîche or sour cream**
- 1 **tablespoon chopped fresh thyme Freshly ground white pepper**

PLACE rutabagas in large pot with enough cold water to cover by 1 inch. Add coarse kosher salt and cardamom pods; bring to boil. Reduce heat, cover partially, and simmer until rutabagas are tender, about 25 minutes.

DRAIN rutabagas; discard cardamom. Working in batches, puree rutabagas in processor. Return puree to pot. Cook over medium heat until dry, stirring, about 5 minutes. Mix in crème fraîche and thyme. Season to taste with salt and white pepper.

DO AHEAD *Can be made 1 day ahead. Spread puree in buttered baking dish. Cover; chill. Reheat in 350F° oven until heated through, about 25 minutes.*

CARDAMOM It is an expensive spice, but a little cardamom goes a long way. Cardamom is used extensively in Indian cooking, as well as in Scandinavian baking. Whole pods are available at many supermarkets and at Indian markets.

Brussels sprouts with white beans and pecorino

8 SERVINGS *Omit the cheese, if you like—the dish will still be delicious. Pecorino Toscano cheese is made in Tuscany, and is quite different from its sharp-flavored, aged Roman cousin, Pecorino Romano.*

- 8 tablespoons extra-virgin olive oil, divided
- 2 pounds brussels sprouts, trimmed, cut in half lengthwise
- 6 garlic cloves, chopped
- 1 cup low-salt chicken broth
- 1 15-ounce can cannellini (white kidney beans), drained
- 2 tablespoons (¼ stick) butter
- 1 cup (about 4 ounces) coarsely grated young pecorino (such as a young Pecorino Toscano)

HEAT 3 tablespoons oil in heavy large skillet over high heat until just beginning to smoke; add half of brussels sprouts. Cook until brown, stirring occasionally, about 5 minutes. Transfer to large bowl. Heat 3 tablespoons oil in same skillet. Add remaining brussels sprouts, reduce heat to medium-high, and cook until brown, stirring occasionally, about 5 minutes. Transfer brussels sprouts to same bowl.

ADD remaining 2 tablespoons oil to skillet; increase heat to high. Add garlic; sauté until brown, stirring constantly, about 1 minute. Add broth and brussels sprouts. Cook until brussels sprouts are crisp-tender, stirring frequently, about 3 minutes. Add beans and butter; stir until butter melts and broth is reduced to glaze, about 1 minute. Season to taste with salt and pepper. Stir in cheese.

Brussels sprout chiffonade with poppy seeds

8 SERVINGS *To shred the brussels sprouts quickly, use a V-slicer (available online and at kitchenware stores) or the thin slicing disk on the food processor. Be sure to push gently on the plunger to shred; pushing harder will make thicker slices.*

- 6 tablespoons (¾ stick) butter
- 1½ pounds brussels sprouts, halved, cut into ⅛- to ¼-inch-thick slices
- 1 tablespoon fresh lemon juice
- 1 tablespoon poppy seeds

MELT butter in heavy large skillet over medium-high heat. Add brussels sprouts and toss until just beginning to wilt, about 5 minutes. Add lemon juice and poppy seeds; toss to coat. Season to taste with salt and pepper.

Brussels sprouts with lemon peel

8 SERVINGS *Overcooking has given brussels sprouts a bad name over the years. When cooked just until tender, they are a beautiful vibrant green with a light sweet flavor.*

- ½ cup chopped fresh chives or green onions
- ¼ cup (½ stick) butter, cut into small pieces
- 1 tablespoon finely grated lemon peel
- 2 pounds brussels sprouts, halved

COMBINE chives, butter, and lemon peel in medium bowl. Cook brussels sprouts in large pot of boiling salted water until tender, about 8 minutes. Drain well. Return brussels sprouts to same pot. Rewarm over medium heat. Add butter mixture; stir until butter melts and coats sprouts. Season to taste with salt and pepper.

Sweet-and-sour cabbage

6 SERVINGS *A classic side dish for pork roast, this would also be delicious served with sausages or roast turkey.*

¼ cup (½ stick) unsalted butter
1 medium onion, thinly sliced
½ cup balsamic vinegar
3 tablespoons (packed) golden brown sugar
6 whole cloves
1 2-pound head of red cabbage, quartered, thinly sliced (about 10 cups)

MELT butter in heavy large pot over medium heat. Add onion and sauté until translucent, about 5 minutes. Add vinegar, sugar, and cloves; bring to boil, stirring constantly. Mix in cabbage. Reduce heat to low, cover, and cook until cabbage is very tender and almost all liquid evaporates, stirring occasionally, about 30 minutes. Season to taste with salt and pepper.

DO AHEAD *Can made 1 day ahead. Cover and chill. Rewarm over low heat.*

Celery root puree

6 SERVINGS *Despite its gnarled appearance, celery root is a delicately flavored vegetable. The potato gives the puree an extra-creamy texture.*

3 cups whole milk
3 cups water
1 tablespoon salt
2 large celery roots (celeriac; about 2½ pounds total), peeled, cut into 2-inch cubes
1 medium russet potato (about 10 ounces), peeled, cut into 2-inch cubes
1 small onion, peeled, quartered

5 tablespoons butter, cut into 5 pieces
Freshly ground white pepper

Chopped fresh chives

BRING milk, 3 cups water, and 1 tablespoon salt just to boil in heavy large saucepan over high heat. Add celery root cubes, potato, and onion; bring to boil. Reduce heat to medium and simmer until vegetables are tender, about 30 minutes. Drain, discarding cooking liquid.

COMBINE vegetables and butter in processor and puree until smooth. Season to taste with salt and white pepper.

DO AHEAD *Can be made 1 day ahead. Cover and chill. Rewarm in microwave before serving.*

TRANSFER celery root puree to bowl. Sprinkle with chopped chives.

Sautéed celery root with Swiss chard

4 SERVINGS *If you cut up the celery root ahead of time, be sure to place it in a bowl of cold water with a squeeze of lemon juice. This will prevent the celery root from browning. Drain and pat dry before using.*

- 3 tablespoons olive oil
- 1 medium onion, coarsely chopped
- 2 garlic cloves, finely chopped
- 12 ounces celery root (celeriac), peeled, cut into matchstick-size strips
- 1 pound Swiss chard, stems trimmed, leaves cut into ½-inch-wide strips
- 2 teaspoons fresh lemon juice

HEAT oil in heavy large pot over medium heat. Add onion and garlic; sauté 3 minutes. Add celery root and sauté until crisp-tender, about 8 minutes. Add chard; cover and cook until wilted and tender, about 5 minutes. Stir in lemon juice. Season to taste with salt and pepper.

Spiced winter squash with fennel

4 SERVINGS *Any winter squash, such as acorn or kabocha, would work well in this recipe. Serve this aromatic side dish with roasted chicken and cous-cous with pine nuts and currants.*

- 1 1½-pound butternut squash, peeled, halved lengthwise, seeded, halved crosswise, then cut lengthwise into ¾-inch-wide wedges
- 1 fennel bulb, trimmed, cut lengthwise into 1-inch-wide wedges
- 1 large onion, root end left intact, then cut lengthwise into ½-inch-wide wedges
- 3 tablespoons olive oil
- 1 teaspoon ground cumin
- 1 teaspoon ground cinnamon
- 1 teaspoon chili powder
- ½ teaspoon turmeric

POSITION rack in bottom third of oven and preheat to 450°F. Combine squash, fennel, and onion on heavy large rimmed baking sheet. Drizzle with oil and toss to coat. Mix all spices in small bowl to blend. Sprinkle spice mixture over vegetables and toss to coat. Sprinkle with salt and generous amount of pepper. Roast until vegetables are tender and browned, turning once, about 45 minutes. Transfer to shallow dish.

Baked squash with yogurt and mint

6 SERVINGS *If you can't find kabocha squash, acorn squash is a great substitute. You could also use delicata squash halved lengthwise and seeded; because it is a thinner-flesh squash, it will cook a little faster. Either whole-milk yogurt or nonfat yogurt works well in this recipe.*

  1   cup plain yogurt
  1   cup sour cream
  2   tablespoons minced fresh mint
  3   garlic cloves, minced

  2½   pounds kabocha squash or other orange-flesh winter squash, cut into 6 pieces total, seeded

COMBINE yogurt, sour cream, mint, and garlic in small bowl. Season yogurt sauce to taste with salt and pepper. Cover and refrigerate until well chilled, about 1 hour.

DO AHEAD *Can be made 1 day ahead. Keep chilled.*

PREHEAT oven to 350°F. Arrange squash, flesh side up, in baking dish. Sprinkle lightly with salt. Cover dish with foil and bake until squash is tender when pierced with knife, about 1 hour.

TRANSFER squash to platter. Spoon dollop of yogurt sauce into center of each squash piece. Serve, passing extra sauce separately.

KABOCHA SQUASH Kabocha squash has a dark-green rind with deep-orange flesh that is sweet and dense when cooked. Choose squash that are heavy for their size and have no blemishes or soft spots. Because kabocha is a very hard squash, the best way to cut it is to place it on a level surface, lift a large, sharp knife a few inches above the squash, and firmly cut into squash (be very careful and be sure to keep your other hand out of the way!). Once the knife has broken through the surface, place the hand that is not holding the knife atop the blade and rock back and forth to cut through the squash. Cut the squash in half first, scoop out the seeds, and then cut into slices or chunks.

Butternut squash with onions and pecans

8 SERVINGS *Many supermarkets sell packages of cut, peeled butternut squash—a great kitchen time-saver. Serve with cheese ravioli tossed in browned butter and an arugula salad.*

- 3 tablespoons butter
- 1 large onion, finely chopped
- 2¼ pounds butternut squash, peeled, seeded, cut into ½-inch cubes (about 6 cups)
- 1 cup coarsely chopped pecans (about 4 ounces), toasted, divided
- 3 tablespoons minced fresh parsley, divided

MELT butter in heavy large skillet over low heat. Add onion and sauté until very tender, about 15 minutes. Add squash and toss to coat. Cover and cook until squash is tender but still holds its shape, stirring frequently, about 15 minutes. Season to taste with salt and pepper.

DO AHEAD *Can be made 4 hours ahead. Let stand at room temperature. Rewarm over medium heat before continuing.*

STIR in half of pecans and half of parsley. Transfer to bowl. Sprinkle with remaining pecans and parsley.

Roasted radicchio with balsamic vinegar

4 SERVINGS *Cutting the radicchio through the core helps the wedges stay intact while being roasted. Serve with pork loin roast and herbed polenta.*

- 2 large heads of radicchio (about 1 pound total), halved through core end, each half cut into 3 wedges with some core still attached
- 3 tablespoons olive oil
- 1 tablespoon chopped fresh thyme

  Balsamic vinegar (for drizzling)

PREHEAT oven to 450°F. Rinse radicchio wedges in cold water; gently shake off excess water (do not dry completely). Place radicchio in large bowl. Drizzle with olive oil and sprinkle with thyme, salt, and pepper; toss to coat.

ARRANGE radicchio wedges, 1 cut side up, on rimmed baking sheet. Roast until wilted, about 12 minutes. Turn and roast until tender, about 8 minutes longer.

ARRANGE radicchio on platter and drizzle with balsamic vinegar.

YEAR-ROUND

Broccoli and rapini with lemon and shallots

6 SERVINGS *Rapini, often called broccoli rabe, is a slightly bitter leafy green Italian vegetable with scattered clusters of tiny, broccoli-like florets. It is available at some supermarkets and at specialty foods stores.*

- ¼ cup (½ stick) butter
- ½ cup chopped shallots
- 1½ teaspoons finely grated lemon peel
- ¾ pound broccoli crowns, cut into florets
- 2 tablespoons water
- ¾ pound rapini (broccoli rabe), cut into ½-inch pieces

MELT butter in heavy large skillet over medium-high heat. Add shallots and lemon peel; sauté 2 minutes. Mix in broccoli and 2 tablespoons water. Sprinkle with salt. Cover; cook until broccoli is almost crisp-tender, about 3 minutes. Add rapini. Sprinkle with salt, cover, and cook until rapini wilts, about 2 minutes. Uncover and sauté until tender and water evaporates, about 1 minute longer. Season to taste with salt and pepper.

Broccoli with garlic and Parmesan cheese

4 SERVINGS *Serve this cheesy broccoli dish with roast chicken and soft polenta.*

- 2 tablespoons olive oil
- 6 garlic cloves, chopped
- 2 teaspoons finely grated lemon peel
- 2 pounds broccoli, crowns cut into florets (stems reserved for another use)
- ½ cup water
- ½ cup grated Parmesan cheese (about 1½ ounces)

HEAT oil in large skillet over high heat. Add garlic and lemon peel and stir 30 seconds. Add broccoli and toss to coat. Add ½ cup water. Cover skillet and cook until broccoli is crisp-tender and water evaporates, about 5 minutes. Add cheese and toss to coat. Season to taste with salt and pepper.

Broccoli in brown butter

6 SERVINGS *Brown butter is made by gently simmering butter until the milk solids turn a deep golden brown color. It imparts a lovely nutty flavor to the broccoli.*

- 2 pounds broccoli

- ⅓ cup butter
- 3 garlic cloves, halved
- 1 tablespoon fresh lemon juice

CUT broccoli floret clusters from stems. Separate florets. Peel stems, then cut into ½-inch-thick slices. Steam florets and stem slices until crisp-tender, about 4 minutes.

COOK butter with garlic in heavy large skillet over medium-low heat until foam subsides and butter is deep amber color, stirring occasionally, about 5 minutes. Immediately remove from heat. Discard garlic. Stir in lemon juice. Add broccoli and toss to coat. Season to taste with salt and pepper.

Cauliflower with mustard-lemon butter

6 SERVINGS *Using whole grain mustard adds not only great flavor but also a lovely texture to the sauce. Serve with broiled smoked ham steaks.*

- 1 small head of cauliflower (about 1¾ pounds)
- 1 teaspoon coarse kosher salt

- 6 tablespoons (¾ stick) butter
- 2 tablespoons whole grain Dijon mustard
- 2 tablespoons fresh lemon juice
- 1½ teaspoons finely grated lemon peel

- 1 tablespoon chopped fresh parsley

PREHEAT oven to 400°F. Butter rimmed baking sheet. Cut cauliflower in half, then cut crosswise into ¼-inch-thick slices. Arrange slices in single layer on prepared baking sheet; sprinkle with coarse salt. Roast until cauliflower is slightly softened, about 15 minutes.

MEANWHILE, melt butter in small saucepan over medium heat. Whisk in mustard, lemon juice, and lemon peel.

SPOON mustard-lemon butter evenly over cauliflower and roast until crisp-tender, about 10 minutes longer.

DO AHEAD *Can be made 2 hours ahead. Let stand at room temperature. If desired, rewarm in 350°F oven until heated through, about 10 minutes.*

TRANSFER cauliflower to platter. Sprinkle with parsley and serve warm or at room temperature.

Roasted cauliflower with onions and fennel

6 SERVINGS *Roasting cauliflower completely transforms it, giving it a rich, nutty flavor. For a colorful presentation, try using one (or more) of the many colorful varieties of cauliflower, such as green, purple, or orange, which are available at select supermarkets and many farmers' markets.*

 1 medium head of cauliflower (about
   1¼ pounds), cored, cut into 1-inch florets
 6 tablespoons olive oil, divided

 2 medium onions (about 1 pound total),
   halved lengthwise, cut into ¾-inch-wide
   wedges with some core still attached
 2 fennel bulbs (about 1 pound total), halved
   lengthwise, cut lengthwise into ½-inch-
   wide wedges with some core still attached
 8 unpeeled garlic cloves
15 fresh marjoram sprigs

POSITION rack in center of oven; preheat to 425°F. Toss cauliflower with 2 tablespoons oil in large bowl. Heat heavy large skillet over medium-high heat. Add cauliflower and sauté until beginning to brown, about 5 minutes. Transfer cauliflower to rimmed baking sheet.

ADD 2 tablespoons oil to same skillet. Add onion wedges. Cook until browned on 1 side, about 3 minutes. Using spatula, carefully transfer onions to baking sheet with cauliflower, arranging wedges browned side up. Add remaining 2 tablespoons oil to same skillet. Add fennel; sauté until fennel softens slightly and starts to brown, about 5 minutes. Transfer to same baking sheet. Scatter garlic and marjoram over vegetables. Sprinkle with salt and pepper. Roast until vegetables are caramelized, about 25 minutes. Discard marjoram sprigs. Serve hot or at room temperature.

Thyme-roasted carrots

Roasting concentrates the sugars in carrots, deepening the flavors. Serve with broiled halibut and mashed potatoes.

6 SERVINGS

 2 pounds medium carrots, peeled, cut on
   deep diagonal into ½-inch-thick slices
1½ tablespoons olive oil
1½ teaspoons fresh thyme leaves
1½ tablespoons butter

PREHEAT oven to 400°F. Toss carrots, oil, and thyme in large bowl. Sprinkle generously with salt and pepper. Spread carrots in single layer on large rimmed baking sheet; dot with butter. Roast until carrots are tender and brown, turning occasionally, about 40 minutes.

Sweet maple carrots

6 SERVINGS *This recipe couldn't be easier—just cook all of the ingredients in a skillet until the carrots are tender and a sweet syrupy glaze forms. Use Grade B maple syrup, which is dark with deep flavor.*

1½ pounds carrots, peeled, cut
   into ½-inch-thick rounds
 ⅓ cup water
 3 tablespoons butter
 2 tablespoons pure maple syrup
 1 tablespoon (packed) dark brown sugar

BRING all ingredients to boil in heavy large skillet. Reduce heat to medium, cover, and simmer until carrots are crisp-tender, about 8 minutes. Uncover; cook until juices are reduced to glaze, about 5 minutes. Season to taste with salt and pepper.

Glazed carrots with molasses and marjoram

12 SERVINGS *Try this with different colors of carrots, such as the pale yellow and red varieties available at some supermarkets and at farmers' markets. (Leave the red ones unpeeled to preserve their color.)*

3	large fresh marjoram sprigs
2	tablespoons (¼ stick) butter
2	tablespoons extra-virgin olive oil
3	pounds medium carrots, peeled, halved lengthwise, cut crosswise into 1½-inch lengths
½	cup fresh orange juice
½	cup water
¼	cup mild-flavored (light) molasses
2	tablespoons chopped fresh Italian parsley

REMOVE leaves from marjoram sprigs. Chop enough leaves to measure 2 teaspoons; reserve stems. Melt butter with oil in large skillet over medium-high heat. Add carrots; season with salt and pepper. Toss with tongs until evenly coated and sizzling, about 4 minutes. Add orange juice, ½ cup water, molasses, and marjoram stems. Reduce heat to medium-low, cover, and simmer until carrots are almost tender, about 12 minutes. Uncover; increase heat to high and boil until juices are reduced to syrup and carrots are tender, about 5 minutes. Discard marjoram stems. Add parsley and chopped marjoram; toss to coat. Season to taste with salt and pepper.

THE WHOLE HERB The stems of herbs impart wonderful flavor to simmering sauces, then are removed before serving. It's a great way to use the whole herb—the stem to flavor the sauce, the chopped leaves to add flavor, aroma, and color to the finished dish.

Spiced butter-glazed carrots

6 SERVINGS *These carrots are seasoned with a little white pepper at the end. It is the kinder, gentler pepper—often used when you want the spice to be subtly noted and not seen. To smash the cardamom pods, place them in a resealable plastic bag and crush them with the flat side of a meat tenderizer or mallet.*

2	tablespoons (¼ stick) butter
¾	cup finely chopped onion
1	½-inch piece peeled fresh ginger, thinly sliced crosswise, then lengthwise into strips
4	whole green cardamom pods, smashed
1	garlic clove, thinly sliced
1½	pounds medium carrots (about 14), peeled, cut on deep diagonal into ⅓-inch-thick ovals
1	cup (or more) low-salt chicken broth
	Ground white pepper

MELT butter in medium skillet over medium heat. Add onion, ginger, cardamom pods with seeds, and garlic; sprinkle with salt and pepper. Cook until onion is soft, stirring frequently, about 4 minutes. Add carrots; stir to coat. Add 1 cup chicken broth; bring to boil. Reduce heat to medium-low, cover, and simmer until just tender, about 8 minutes. Uncover, increase heat to high, and boil until sauce glazes carrots, tossing occasionally, about 5 minutes. Season to taste with salt and white pepper.

DO AHEAD *Can be made 2 hours ahead. Rewarm over medium heat, adding more broth by tablespoonfuls as needed to thin glaze.*

FADE TO WHITE When the outer coating of whole peppercorns is removed, white peppercorns are revealed.

breakfast
andbrunch

FRENCH TOAST, PANCAKES, AND WAFFLES

Cinnamon French Toast

Croissant French Toast

Cardamom and Orange Panettone Toast

Oatmeal-Buttermilk Pancakes

Spiced Pumpkin Pancakes

Banana Pancakes with Caramel-Banana Syrup

Bread Pudding Pancakes

Puffed Apple Pancake

Easy Crepes

Waffles with Frizzled Ham and Maple-Mustard Cream

Crispy Cornmeal-Bacon Waffles

OMELETS, FRITTATAS, AND SCRAMBLES

Chard and Cheddar Omelet

Giant Southwestern Omelet

Mediterranean Supper Omelet with Fennel, Olives, and Dill

Four-Herb Omelet

Smoked Salmon Omelet with Herbs

Herbed Gruyère Omelet

Potato and Green Onion Frittata with Sour Cream and Caviar

Shiitake, Fontina, and Prosciutto Frittata

Frittata with Bacon, Fresh Ricotta, and Greens

Spaghetti Frittata

Baby Eggplant, Olive, and Herb-Cheese Frittata

Herbed Cheese Scrambled Eggs on Asparagus

Scrambled Eggs with Poblano Chiles and Cheese

Smoked Salmon and Leek Scramble with Meyer Lemon Crème Fraîche

Creamy Scrambled Eggs with Smoked Trout and Green Onions

Chorizo and Scrambled Egg Breakfast Tacos

BRUNCH DISHES

Apricot-Buttermilk Noodle Pudding

Canadian Bacon, Asparagus, and Egg Gratin with Fontina Cheese

Cheddar Cheese and Red Bell Pepper Strata

Arizona Cheese Strata

Sausage and Potato Breakfast Casserole

Smoked Sausage and Red Pepper Quesadillas

Breakfast Polenta with Chorizo and Queso Fresco

Fried Eggs on Toast with Pepper Jack and Avocado

Ham and Sweet Potato Hash with Fried Eggs

Poached Eggs in Pipérade

Scottish Farmhouse Eggs

Asparagus and Swiss Cheese Soufflés

Cabbage-Caraway Quiche

Bacon and Green Chile Quiche

Toasted Mini Bagels with Smoked Salmon and Caviar

Fried Corn Cakes with Green Onions

ON THE SIDE

Spicy Bacon, Onion, and Cheese Potatoes

Pork and Bacon Sausage

Rosemary and Mustard Breakfast Sausages

Cranberry-Almond Granola

Mixed Grain and Wild Rice Cereal

Cantaloupe Salad with Lime, Mint, and Ginger

Spiced Dried-Fruit Compote

Spiced Fig Preserves

Warm Berry Preserves

Cranberry-Orange Preserves

tool kit Contrary to popular belief, "fast and easy breakfast" is not synonymous with "cold cereal." It is possible to make a fresh, delicious breakfast quickly—and the recipes in this chapter are here to prove it. Meanwhile, a few tricks will come in handy on any weekday morning.

EGGS FOR EVERY OCCASION

Different egg dishes are best suited to certain situations. When serving just one or two, whip up an omelet. For a hungry family, pull out a larger skillet for a quick one-pan scramble or frittata. When entertaining, make a quiche, strata, or casserole the day before, so all you'll need to do before guests arrive is to bake it or rewarm it in the oven. Once you've selected the perfect egg dish, use pan-ready ingredients from the fridge, freezer, and pantry to pull it together quickly.

FROM THE FRIDGE

— Use cheeses that don't require any prep time, such as pre-shredded mozzarella, cheddar, or Monterey Jack, or soft cream cheese, ricotta, feta, or goat cheese.
— Select already cooked meats like smoked sausage, ham, cooked bacon strips, smoked salmon, cooked peeled shrimp, crabmeat, or vegetarian breakfast links.
— Jazz up the eggs with fresh herbs like parsley, chives, thyme, and dill.

FROM THE FREEZER

— Peas and corn kernels defrost right in a hot pan and add a splash of color; using frozen spinach eliminates the need to wash and cook fresh spinach leaves.
— For a quick quiche, add the egg mixture to a ready-made pie crust.

FROM THE PANTRY

— Add the robust flavors of roasted bell peppers, diced green chiles, capers, olives, salsas, sun-dried tomatoes, and canned beans. ➔

SHORTCUTS FOR EASY A.M. ENTERTAINING

PANCAKES AND WAFFLES

— Mix the dry and wet ingredients separately the night before; all you'll need to do in the morning is stir them together.

— Set up your griddle or waffle iron ahead of time, and line the counter with paper towels to catch any drips.

— Use a tortilla warmer to keep your pancakes hot as they come off the griddle.

BACON

— Save stovetop space by cooking bacon in the oven. Lay bacon strips in a single layer on rimmed baking sheets the night before, then cover and chill. In the morning, pop them into a 400°F oven for about 12 minutes, turning the baking sheets halfway through.

FRITTATAS AND SCRAMBLES

— Have all your mix-ins at the ready—cheese shredded, vegetables diced, and ham or bacon chopped.

POTATOES

— Doctor up a package of shredded or diced potatoes with freshly chopped onions, bell peppers, smoked fish, or ham for an easy hash.

TOPPINGS

— Create new syrup flavors by adding citrus zests and juice, pureed berries, spices, brown butter, or a touch of brandy, Grand Marnier, or amaretto to maple syrup.

— Or dilute jams and preserves with a little water or orange juice, then warm them up in the microwave for a quick accompaniment to pancakes, waffles, and French toast.

FRENCH TOAST, PANCAKES, AND WAFFLES

Cinnamon French toast

2 TO 4 SERVINGS *This can be assembled a day ahead and then cooked in the morning. Serve two slices to those with big appetites; one slice each is good for a lighter breakfast or if French toast is part of a bigger spread. Just about any of the "baking" spices would work with the cinnamon: Try a dash of nutmeg, ginger, cloves, or allspice. This would also be delicious with the Warm Berry Preserves on page 527.*

- 3 **large eggs**
- 6 **tablespoons half and half**
- 1 **tablespoon sugar**
- 3 **teaspoons ground cinnamon, divided**
- ¼ **teaspoon vanilla extract**
- 4 **¾-inch-thick slices soft-crusted French bread or egg bread**

- 2 **tablespoons (¼ stick) butter**
- ¼ **cup powdered sugar**
  Warm pure maple syrup (optional)

WHISK eggs, half and half, sugar, 2 teaspoons cinnamon, and vanilla in 13×9×2-inch glass baking dish to blend. Add bread and turn to coat. Cover and chill until bread absorbs egg mixture, at least 30 minutes and up to 1 day.

MELT butter in heavy large skillet over medium heat. Add bread and cook until golden and cooked through, about 3 minutes per side. Transfer to plates. Combine powdered sugar with remaining 1 teaspoon cinnamon and sift over toast. Serve with maple syrup, if desired.

MAPLE SYRUP REPORT CARD Maple syrup is the reduced sap of maple trees (most often from Quebec and New England) and is classified by grades A (Light, Medium, and Dark Amber) and B, categorizing their color and flavor. The BON APPÉTIT Test Kitchen actually prefers the lower-grade syrups (B's) for their deeper maple flavor and more intense color. They're great to cook with or to simply drizzle on pancakes or French toast (plus we like the fact that grade B's are less expensive).

493

Croissant French toast

4 SERVINGS *Replacing bread with croissants is especially delicious in this luscious take on French toast. Be sure to use day-old croissants as their texture will hold up better than fresh ones.*

- ⅔ **cup half and half or whole milk**
- 3 **large eggs**
- ⅓ **cup orange juice**
- 1 **teaspoon sugar**
- 2 **teaspoons vanilla extract**
- 1 **teaspoon finely grated orange peel**
- ½ **teaspoon ground cinnamon**
- ⅛ **teaspoon ground nutmeg**
- ⅛ **teaspoon salt**
- 4 **day-old croissants, halved horizontally**

- 4 **tablespoons (½ stick) unsalted butter, divided**
  Powdered sugar
  Pure maple syrup

WHISK first 9 ingredients in 15×10×2-inch glass baking dish. Add croissants to egg batter and turn until thoroughly coated.

MELT 2 tablespoons butter in each of two large nonstick skillets over medium heat. Add 4 croissant halves to each skillet and cook until deep golden brown, about 3 minutes per side. Transfer to plates. Sift powdered sugar over croissants. Serve with maple syrup.

> **ORANGE APPEAL** Orange peel and juice add a lovely aroma and flavor to the French toast. Intensify the flavor by simmering the maple syrup with some grated orange peel before drizzling.

Cardamom and orange panettone toast

6 SERVINGS *Thick slices of panettone—a tall, dried-fruit-studded Italian egg bread—are slathered in orange-scented butter, then topped with cardamom-spiced sugar and caramelized in the oven. This would be a great addition to a brunch buffet, and surprisingly, it only takes about 15 minutes to put together. Panettone is traditionally eaten at Christmas. It can be found in season at some supermarkets and specialty foods stores, and sometimes throughout the year at Italian markets.*

- ½ **cup (1 stick) unsalted butter, room temperature**
- 2 **teaspoons finely grated orange peel**
- 5 **tablespoons sugar**
- 1 **teaspoon ground cardamom**

- 8 **½-inch-thick slices small panettone or four ½-inch-thick slices large panettone, cut crosswise in half**

PREHEAT oven to 400°F. Blend butter and orange peel with fork in small bowl. Mix sugar and cardamom on small plate.

PLACE panettone on rimmed baking sheet. Toast in oven until light golden brown, turning once, about 10 minutes. Remove panettone from oven, spread 1 side of each slice with butter mixture, then press into sugar mixture. Return slices to baking sheet and bake until topping bubbles, about 4 minutes. Divide toasts among plates.

Oatmeal-buttermilk pancakes

MAKES ABOUT 16 *These incredibly light pancakes have a Swedish accent thanks to the use of buttermilk in the batter and the nicely tart lingonberry preserves served as an accompaniment. In the summer, serve the pancakes with fresh blueberries and whipped cream for an extra festive touch.*

2	cups old-fashioned oats or quick-cooking oats
½	cup all purpose flour
3	tablespoons sugar
1	teaspoon baking soda
1	teaspoon baking powder
½	teaspoon salt
2½	cups buttermilk
2	large eggs
¼	cup (½ stick) unsalted butter, melted, plus additional melted butter for brushing skillet
1	teaspoon vanilla extract
	Lingonberry preserves

COMBINE first 6 ingredients in large bowl. Whisk buttermilk, eggs, ¼ cup melted butter, and vanilla in medium bowl. Add to dry ingredients; whisk until blended but some small lumps still remain. Let batter stand to thicken, about 2 hours.

DO AHEAD *Can be made 1 day ahead. Cover and chill.*

PREHEAT oven to 250°F. Heat heavy large skillet over medium heat. Brush skillet with melted butter. Working in batches, ladle batter by ¼ cupfuls into skillet. Cook pancakes until bottoms are golden brown and bubbles form on top, about 2 minutes per side. Transfer to baking sheet. Keep warm in oven. Repeat with remaining batter, brushing skillet with more butter as necessary. Serve with lingonberry preserves.

GRIDDLE ME THIS A griddle, which is flat with no sides, makes for wide-open spatula access and easy pancake flipping. If you don't have a griddle, use the largest skillet you have so there will be plenty of room to maneuver around the sides and get under the pancakes.

Spiced pumpkin pancakes

MAKES ABOUT 12 *Perfect for Thanksgiving or Halloween morning. Pumpkin pie spice is a mix of cinnamon, ginger, allspice, and nutmeg. You can make your own mixture, keeping in mind that some of the spices, like nutmeg and allspice, are stronger than others; adjust the ratio to your taste.*

1¼   cups unbleached all purpose flour
3   tablespoons sugar
2   teaspoons baking powder
1¼   teaspoons pumpkin pie spice
¾   teaspoon salt
1⅓   cups whole milk
¾   cup canned pure pumpkin
4   large eggs, separated
¼   cup (½ stick) unsalted butter, melted
1   teaspoon vanilla extract

    Vegetable oil (for brushing skillet)
    Pure maple syrup

WHISK first 5 ingredients in large bowl to blend. Whisk milk, pumpkin, egg yolks, melted butter, and vanilla in medium bowl to blend well. Add pumpkin mixture to dry ingredients; whisk just until smooth (batter will be thick). Using electric mixer, beat egg whites in another medium bowl until stiff but not dry. Fold whites into batter in 2 additions.

BRUSH large nonstick skillet with oil; heat over medium heat. Working in batches, pour batter by ⅓ cupfuls into skillet. Cook until bubbles form on surface of pancakes and bottoms are brown, about 1½ minutes per side. Repeat with remaining batter, brushing skillet with oil between batches. Serve with maple syrup.

PANCAKES WITH STYLE In keeping with the holiday feel of these pumpkin-spiced pancakes, go all out with pumpkin- or turkey-shaped pancake molds, available from specialty cookware shops. They look like cookie cutters, but they have a little tab that sticks up so you can lift them off the griddle without burning your fingers. Just pour the batter into the mold, and when the first side is cooked (bubbles will surface on the top side), remove the mold and flip the pancake to brown the other side.

Banana pancakes with caramel-banana syrup

4 SERVINGS *These pancakes have bananas mashed into the batter and sliced into the syrup. Self-rising flour contains salt and baking powder, so there's no need for those ingredients in this recipe.*

- 3 large bananas, peeled, divided
- ½ cup (1 stick) butter, melted, divided, plus additional melted butter for brushing skillet
- ¾ cup (packed) golden brown sugar, divided
- ¼ cup water
- 1 teaspoon vanilla extract

- 2 cups self-rising flour
- 2 cups buttermilk
- 2 large eggs

CUT 2 bananas into ¼-inch-thick rounds. Combine ¼ cup melted butter, ½ cup brown sugar, and ¼ cup water in heavy large skillet. Boil over medium-high heat until mixture thickens slightly, about 2 minutes. Stir in vanilla and sliced bananas. Remove syrup from heat.

WHISK flour and remaining ¼ cup brown sugar in large bowl. Mash remaining banana in medium bowl, then whisk in buttermilk and eggs. Stir banana mixture into dry ingredients (some lumps will remain). Mix in ¼ cup melted butter.

HEAT griddle or heavy large skillet over medium heat; brush with additional melted butter. Working in batches, pour batter by ⅓ cupfuls onto griddle or into skillet. Cook pancakes until bubbles form on surface and bottoms are golden brown, about 2 minutes per side. Serve pancakes with caramel-banana syrup.

Let them eat pancakes A few tips on creating top-notch flapjacks:

- Use a nonstick or seasoned cast-iron skillet or other heavy skillet.
- Mix the dry ingredients into the wet ingredients just until blended (don't overwork the batter; some small lumps are okay).
- Make sure the skillet is nice and hot; add butter or oil.
- Drop the batter into the skillet in one single pour from a ladle so that it forms neat circles.
- Flip when you see bubbles rise to the surface and edges are dry and golden underneath.
- The second side will cook more quickly, so check for golden edges sooner than you think.
- The first batch never browns the best because the first pancakes help to season the pan for later batches. (But there's no reason why the cook can't eat the first batch while tending to the rest.)

Bread pudding pancakes

MAKES ABOUT 14 *Dessert for breakfast: The springy, custardy texture of these pancakes comes from pieces of white sandwich bread incorporated into the batter. A handful of chocolate chips or a sprinkle of cinnamon never hurt any pancake, and they'd be especially appropriate in this bread pudding variety.*

- ¾ cup all purpose flour
- 2 tablespoons sugar
- 1 tablespoon baking powder
- ½ teaspoon salt
- 7 ounces (about 7 slices) firm white sandwich bread, crusts trimmed, cut into ½-inch pieces
- 2 cups whole milk
- 2 large eggs, beaten to blend
- 5 tablespoons (or more) butter, melted, divided

   Pure maple syrup or fruit syrup

WHISK flour, sugar, baking powder, and salt in small bowl to blend. Place bread in large bowl; pour milk over. Let stand until bread is very soft and beginning to fall apart, stirring occasionally, about 15 minutes. Add flour mixture to bread mixture and stir to blend. Mix in eggs and 3 tablespoons melted butter. Let batter stand 15 minutes.

PREHEAT oven to 250°F. Heat 2 tablespoons melted butter in heavy large skillet over medium heat. Drop batter by ¼ cupfuls into skillet. Cook pancakes until bubbles form on surface and bottoms are golden brown, about 2 minutes per side. Transfer to baking sheet. Keep warm in oven. Repeat with remaining batter, adding more butter to skillet as needed. Serve pancakes with syrup.

Puffed apple pancake

4 SERVINGS *Here's a big pancake for everyone to share. It will rise in the oven like a Yorkshire pudding or a savory soufflé, then fall when cut, so be sure to present it to guests before slicing into it. Serve it with jam, apple sauce, maple syrup, or simply a dusting of powdered sugar.*

- 1 cup whole milk
- 4 large eggs
- 3 tablespoons sugar
- 1 teaspoon vanilla extract
- ½ teaspoon salt
- ¼ teaspoon ground cinnamon
- ⅔ cup all purpose flour
- ¼ cup (½ stick) unsalted butter
- 2 6-ounce Golden Delicious apples, peeled, cored, thinly sliced
- 3 tablespoons (packed) golden brown sugar

PREHEAT oven to 425°F. Whisk first 6 ingredients in large bowl until well blended. Add flour and whisk until batter is smooth. Place butter in 13×9×2-inch glass baking dish. Place dish in oven until butter melts, about 5 minutes. Remove dish from oven. Place apple slices in overlapping rows atop melted butter in baking dish. Return to oven and bake until apples begin to soften slightly and butter is bubbling and beginning to brown around edges of dish, about 10 minutes.

POUR batter over apples in dish and sprinkle with brown sugar. Bake pancake until puffed and brown, about 20 minutes. Serve warm.

IT'S DUTCH, BABY This recipe is based on the classic Dutch pancake (or Dutch baby, as it's sometimes called). Traditionally, the large, oven-baked pancake is cooked in a cast-iron skillet, then doused with lemon juice and powdered sugar before being devoured.

Easy crepes

MAKES ABOUT 20 CREPES *The thin French pancakes known as crepes are easier to make than they seem: Just swirl the batter in the pan to coat it evenly, let it cook for just a minute, slide a spatula around the edges to ease the crepe away from the pan (use your fingers if you need to, being careful not to burn yourself), then flip and cook about 30 seconds. And they work beautifully with both sweet and savory fillings.*

1⅓   cups whole milk, room temperature
1   cup all purpose flour
3   large eggs
3   tablespoons unsalted butter, melted
1   tablespoon sugar
¼   teaspoon salt

    Nonstick vegetable oil spray

MIX first 6 ingredients in blender just until smooth. Cover batter and chill at least 15 minutes and up to 1 day.

SPRAY 7-inch-diameter nonstick skillet with nonstick spray and heat over medium heat. Pour 2 tablespoons batter into pan and swirl to coat bottom. Cook until edge of crepe is light brown, about 1 minute. Loosen edges gently with spatula. Carefully turn crepe over. Cook until bottom begins to brown in spots, about 30 seconds. Transfer to plate. Cover with paper towel. Repeat with remaining batter, spraying pan with nonstick spray as needed and covering each crepe with paper towel.

DO AHEAD *Can be made 1 day ahead. Cover and refrigerate. Rewarm crepes in stacks wrapped in paper towels in microwave in 20-second intervals just until heated through.*

Waffles with frizzled ham and maple-mustard cream

4 SERVINGS *The ham gets "frizzled" by sautéing it until the edges crisp and curl up. This savory waffle is a great candidate when you're in the mood for breakfast at dinnertime. Just add an herby green salad and a nice glass of Alsatian Riesling.*

2   tablespoons (¼ stick) unsalted butter
12   ounces sliced Black Forest ham, cut into 2-inch-long, ¼-inch-wide strips
1   cup heavy whipping cream
¼   cup pure maple syrup
3   tablespoons coarse-grained Dijon mustard
½   cup thinly sliced green onions, divided

8   frozen Belgian toaster waffles, toasted; or 4 whole English muffins, split, toasted

MELT butter in large nonstick skillet over medium-high heat. Add ham and sauté until ham is heated through and ends are curled, about 5 minutes. Stir in cream, maple syrup, and mustard. Simmer until sauce is slightly thickened and coats ham, about 3 minutes. Stir in ⅓ cup green onions.

TOP toasted waffles with ham mixture. Sprinkle with remaining green onions.

Crispy cornmeal-bacon waffles

6 SERVINGS *The two best things about breakfast—bacon and waffles—come together in one recipe. After you've cooked the bacon, save the drippings in the skillet and fry or scramble eggs in them to go with the waffles.*

8	bacon slices
1¼	cups all purpose flour
¾	cup yellow cornmeal
2¼	teaspoons baking powder
½	teaspoon baking soda
2	cups buttermilk
2	large eggs
3	tablespoons pure maple syrup plus additional for serving
¼	cup (½ stick) unsalted butter, melted, cooled
	Additional melted butter or nonstick vegetable oil spray

COOK bacon in large skillet over medium heat until crisp, about 6 minutes. Transfer to paper towels. Crumble bacon.

WHISK flour and next 3 ingredients in large bowl to blend. Whisk buttermilk, eggs, and 3 tablespoons maple syrup in medium bowl to blend. Add buttermilk mixture to dry ingredients; stir just until blended. Fold in ¼ cup melted butter and crumbled bacon.

PREHEAT waffle iron (medium heat). Lightly brush waffle iron with melted butter or spray with nonstick spray. Working in batches, spoon batter onto hot waffle iron, spreading evenly over grid. Close waffle iron and cook until waffle is brown, crisp, and set, about 6 minutes, depending on type of waffle iron. Transfer waffles to plates. Serve with maple syrup.

Waffle do's and don'ts

DO preheat the waffle iron—a properly heated cooking surface is key to a properly cooked waffle (or anything, for that matter).

DON'T overwork the batter—mix the dry ingredients into the wet ingredients just until they are combined. When it comes to waffle chemistry, a little lumpy is better than smooth.

DON'T mix the batter ahead—the baking soda will lose its zing and the waffles won't puff to their potential.

DO serve waffles fresh and hot—ideally, straight off the waffle iron. But if you're serving a group, you can keep waffles warm on a baking sheet in a 300°F oven (for only as long as it takes to make the remaining waffles).

DON'T try to make waffles ahead of time and reheat—they'll just get soggy.

OMELETS, FRITTATAS, AND SCRAMBLES

Chard and cheddar omelet

2 SERVINGS; CAN BE DOUBLED *Serve corn muffins or grits and andouille sausage with this hearty omelet. The slight bitterness of the chard is the perfect complement to the richness of the cheddar cheese.*

- 2 tablespoons (¼ stick) butter, divided
- 2 garlic cloves, minced
- 4 ounces red Swiss chard, stemmed, chopped (about 3 cups packed)
- ¾ teaspoon hot pepper sauce

- 5 large eggs
- ¾ cup grated sharp cheddar cheese (about 3 ounces), divided
- ¼ teaspoon salt
- ¼ teaspoon ground black pepper

MELT 1 tablespoon butter in 8-inch-diameter non-stick skillet over medium-low heat. Add garlic; sauté until soft, about 2 minutes. Stir in chard; cover and cook until tender, about 4 minutes. Stir in hot sauce. Season to taste with salt and pepper. Transfer to small bowl. Wipe skillet clean.

WHISK eggs, ¼ cup cheese, salt, and pepper in medium bowl to blend. Melt ½ tablespoon butter in same skillet over medium-high heat. Add half of egg mixture and cook until eggs are just set in center, tilting pan and lifting edge of omelet with spatula to let uncooked portion flow underneath, about 2 minutes. Scatter half of chard mixture over half of omelet. Sprinkle ¼ cup cheese over chard.

Fold omelet over cheese; slide out onto plate. Repeat with remaining butter, egg mixture, chard mixture, and cheese.

CHARD CHOICES You may have a few varieties to choose from, especially at farmers' markets. Swiss chard has dark green leaves and white stalks; rhubarb chard has green leaves and red stalks; and ruby chard has red leaves and red stalks. A mix would make a very pretty omelet. Or try a multicolored bunch of rainbow or Bright Lights Swiss chard to get the whole spectrum at once.

Giant southwestern omelet

2 SERVINGS *Serve this with salsa, guacamole, sour cream, and warm tortillas.*

- 1 15- to 15.5-ounce can black beans, rinsed, drained
- ¾ cup purchased tomatillo salsa

- 4 large eggs
- 2 green onions, chopped
- ¼ teaspoon salt
- ¼ teaspoon freshly ground black pepper
- 3 tablespoons butter, divided
- ½ red bell pepper, cut into strips
- 2 cups sliced mushrooms (about 5 ounces)

- 1 cup (packed) coarsely grated Monterey Jack cheese (about 4 ounces)
- 3 tablespoons chopped fresh cilantro, divided

STIR beans and salsa in heavy medium saucepan over medium heat until heated through. Remove bean and salsa mixture from heat. Cover and keep warm while preparing omelet.

WHISK eggs, green onions, salt, and pepper in medium bowl to blend. Melt 2 tablespoons butter in medium nonstick skillet over medium heat. Add bell pepper and mushrooms to skillet; sauté until mushrooms are brown, about 8 minutes. Transfer vegetables to bowl.

MELT remaining 1 tablespoon butter in same skillet over medium heat. Add egg mixture. Cook without stirring until beginning to set, about 4 minutes. Sprinkle with vegetables, cheese, and 1 tablespoon cilantro. Cover skillet and cook until cheese melts and eggs are set, about 2 minutes. Slide large spatula around edges and under omelet to loosen. Fold omelet in half; slide out onto platter. Top omelet with bean and salsa mixture. Sprinkle with remaining 2 tablespoons cilantro.

Mediterranean supper omelet with fennel, olives, and dill

2 SERVINGS *A nice, big omelet for two (breakfast—or supper—in bed, perhaps?). Fresh fennel is a two-for-one treat: The white bulb end adds a crisp, onion-like texture and anise flavor; the chopped green tops (fronds) make a nice garnish for the omelet with an extra herbal hit of anise. You can also add prosciutto or Serrano ham to the omelet.*

- 2 tablespoons olive oil, divided
- 2 cups thinly sliced fresh fennel bulb, fronds chopped and reserved
- 8 cherry tomatoes
- ¼ cup chopped pitted brine-cured green olives

- 5 large eggs, beaten to blend with ¼ teaspoon salt and ¼ teaspoon ground black pepper
- ½ 4-ounce package crumbled goat cheese Provençal (with thyme, basil, and sweet red pepper) or any herbed or peppered goat cheese
- 1½ tablespoons chopped fresh dill

HEAT 1 tablespoon oil in 10-inch-diameter nonstick skillet over medium-high heat. Add fennel bulb; sauté until beginning to brown, about 5 minutes. Cover and cook until soft, stirring occasionally, about 4 minutes. Add tomatoes and mash with fork; mix in olives. Transfer to medium bowl.

ADD remaining 1 tablespoon oil to same skillet; heat over medium-high heat. Add beaten eggs; cook until eggs are set in center, tilting skillet and lifting edges of omelet with spatula to let uncooked portion flow underneath, about 3 minutes. Sprinkle half of cheese over half of omelet; top with fennel mixture. Sprinkle dill over, then remaining cheese. Using spatula, fold uncovered half of omelet over cheese; slide onto platter. Garnish with chopped fennel fronds.

Four-herb omelet

2 SERVINGS *This classic is delicious for breakfast, lunch, or dinner. Try any mix of subtle, sweet herbs, such as basil, mint, or chervil. A soft goat cheese or some grated Gruyère would also be a delicious addition. Mixed greens with a mustardy vinaigrette and a glass of Sauvignon Blanc turn this omelet into a light, French-style supper.*

- **6 large eggs**
- **4 teaspoons water**
- **2 teaspoons chopped fresh parsley**
- **2 teaspoons chopped fresh chives plus whole fresh chives for garnish**
- **2 teaspoons chopped fresh tarragon or ½ teaspoon dried**
- **2 teaspoons chopped fresh thyme or ½ teaspoon dried**
- **4 teaspoons butter, divided**

WHISK eggs and 4 teaspoons water in medium bowl to blend. Sprinkle with salt and pepper. Mix in parsley, chopped chives, tarragon, and thyme. Melt 2 teaspoons butter in 8-inch-diameter omelet pan or small nonstick skillet over high heat. Add half of eggs to pan and stir briefly. Let eggs begin to set around edges. Using spatula, lift edges of omelet and tilt pan, allowing uncooked portion to flow underneath. Cook until eggs are almost set but still slightly moist, about 30 seconds. Using spatula as aid, roll ⅓ of omelet to center. Tilt pan; slide omelet onto plate while folding over second ⅓. Make second omelet with remaining 2 teaspoons butter and eggs. Garnish with whole chives.

Good eggs The egg case at the supermarket just keeps growing, with new variations cropping up all the time. Here are some of the choices you'll be presented with:

FREE-RANGE: Eggs laid by hens that have regular access to outdoor space.

ORGANIC: Eggs produced by hens that have been given only organic feed, thereby reducing the hens' (and eggs') exposure to pesticides and other harmful chemicals.

NUTRIENT-ENHANCED: Eggs that are higher in omega-3 fatty acids and sometimes other vitamins and minerals as a result of feeding hens nutrient-rich diets. The flavor and cooking properties are theoretically the same, but you might want to make a trial run with that favorite cake before serving it to guests.

VEGETARIAN: Eggs produced by hens that have been fed no meat or meat by-products.

BROWN VS. WHITE: Simply a reflection of the breed of chicken that laid the egg (there's no difference in culinary performance or nutritional value).

Smoked salmon omelet with herbs

2 SERVINGS; CAN BE DOUBLED *Dill would be a natural substitute for the tarragon, if necessary. If you're feeling decadent, stir some caviar into the sour cream. Toasted bagels or croissants would be delicious partners with this omelet.*

    3 tablespoons reduced-fat sour cream
    1 tablespoon coarse-grained Dijon mustard
    4 large eggs
    2 tablespoons water
    2 tablespoons finely chopped fresh
       chives or green onion tops
 1½ tablespoons minced fresh
       tarragon or 1 teaspoon dried
    2 teaspoons butter, divided
    2 ounces thinly sliced smoked salmon,
       cut into strips, divided

WHISK sour cream and mustard in small bowl to blend. Whisk eggs, 2 tablespoons water, chives, and tarragon in medium bowl to blend. Sprinkle egg mixture with salt and pepper.

MELT 1 teaspoon butter in small nonstick skillet over medium-high heat. Add half of egg mixture and stir briefly. Let eggs begin to set at edges. Using spatula, lift edges of omelet and tilt pan, allowing uncooked portion to flow underneath. Cook until eggs are set but still moist, about 1 minute. Spread half of sour cream mixture and half of salmon over half of omelet. Using spatula, fold unfilled portion over filling. Slide omelet out onto plate. Repeat with remaining butter, egg mixture, and fillings to make second omelet.

10 steps to amazing omelets

1. Use a nonstick skillet or a well-seasoned cast-iron skillet (preferably with rounded or slanted sides) and heat it to medium.
2. Add butter or oil (or a combination) to the pan to help with the non-stickiness.
3. Add beaten eggs and cook until bottom is just set.
4. Using spatula, lift edges of cooked egg and let uncooked egg run underneath and cook, repeating until all of egg is set.
5. Add fillings late enough that most of egg is set, but early enough that flavors can blend and cheese can melt.
6. When eggs are cooked (but not too dry), jiggle the pan to loosen the omelet (using spatula to free it up if necessary).
7. Move the omelet to the left side of the pan, making the left edge of the omelet flush with the left edge of the pan.
8. Fold the right third of the omelet over center of omelet and fillings.
9. Tilt the pan to the left and rest the left side of the pan on the plate.
10. Slide the unfolded portion of the omelet onto the plate, then turn the pan over and flip the omelet completely onto itself. Voila!

Even easier: Skip steps 8 through 10. Fold the omelet in half in the skillet, then slide out onto the plate.

Herbed Gruyère omelet

2 SERVINGS *An excellent addition to the breakfast repertoire for sure: Delicious as is, it's also perfectly suited to experimentation with different herbs and cheeses—the potential combinations are infinite.*

- 6 **large eggs, divided**
- 2 **teaspoons chopped fresh chives, divided**
- 2 **teaspoons chopped fresh tarragon, divided**
- 2 **teaspoons chopped fresh parsley, divided**

- 2 **teaspoons butter, divided**
- 1 **cup (packed) grated Gruyère cheese (about 4 ounces), divided**

WHISK 3 eggs, 1 teaspoon chives, 1 teaspoon tarragon, and 1 teaspoon parsley in bowl. Sprinkle with salt and pepper.

PREHEAT broiler. Melt 1 teaspoon butter in 8- to 9-inch-diameter nonstick skillet over medium heat. Pour egg mixture into skillet. Stir until eggs begin to set, lifting edge of omelet with spatula and tilting skillet to allow uncooked portion to flow underneath. Cook until omelet is softly set, about 2 minutes. Sprinkle ⅓ cup cheese down center of omelet. Roll up omelet; place in broilerproof baking dish large enough to hold 2 omelets. Repeat with remaining eggs, herbs, butter, and ⅓ cup cheese to form second omelet. Sprinkle remaining ⅓ cup cheese over omelets.

BROIL omelets until cheese is bubbling and slightly brown, about 2 minutes.

Potato and green onion frittata with sour cream and caviar

2 SERVINGS; CAN BE DOUBLED *A frittata is an Italian open-face style of omelet. This one is like a steakhouse baked potato in the form of a frittata: Paired with a juicy rib eye, it would be the ultimate version of steak and eggs.*

- 3 **tablespoons butter, divided**
- 2 **medium unpeeled red-skinned potatoes (about 10 ounces), quartered lengthwise, thinly sliced crosswise**
- 4 **green onions, sliced, plus minced green onion tops for garnish**

- 6 **large eggs**
  Sour cream
  Caviar

MELT 1 tablespoon butter in broilerproof 9-inch-diameter skillet (if doubling recipe, use 12-inch skillet) over medium-high heat. Add potatoes; sprinkle generously with freshly ground black pepper and sauté until potatoes are crusty and tender, stirring frequently and reducing heat if browning too quickly, about 8 minutes. Add sliced green onions and stir 2 minutes. Cool potatoes slightly.

WHISK eggs in medium bowl to blend. Stir in potatoes. Sprinkle with salt. Wipe out same skillet. Add remaining 2 tablespoons butter to skillet and melt over medium heat. Add egg mixture and cook without stirring, lifting up edges with spatula and tilting skillet to allow uncooked portion to flow underneath until sides and bottom are set, about 1 minute. Reduce heat to low. Cover skillet and cook until eggs are almost set, about 5 minutes.

MEANWHILE, preheat broiler. Uncover skillet and broil frittata until eggs are set, about 2 minutes. Garnish with sour cream, minced green onion tops, and caviar.

Shiitake, Fontina, and prosciutto frittata

8 SERVINGS *In a frittata, meats, veggies, and cheese are incorporated into the egg mixture, which is poured into a skillet and cooked until the bottom and sides are set; it is then baked and/or broiled in the oven until the top is set. The frittata is sliced into wedges like a tart (rather than being folded over like a French omelet). Frittatas can be made ahead and served at room temperature, making them one of the best candidates for a brunch menu. Be sure to cut the stems off the shiitakes before cooking; they're woody and tough.*

 4 tablespoons (½ stick) butter, divided

 1 cup thinly sliced shallots (about 4 large)

 1 3-ounce package thinly sliced prosciutto, slivered (about ¾ cup)

 8 ounces shiitake mushrooms, stemmed, caps thinly sliced

12 large eggs

 2 cups (packed) coarsely grated Fontina cheese (about 8 ounces), divided

¼ cup chopped fresh Italian parsley

½ teaspoon salt

¼ teaspoon freshly ground black pepper

PREHEAT oven to 350°F. Melt 3 tablespoons butter in 12-inch nonstick ovenproof skillet over medium heat. Add shallots; sauté 2 minutes. Add prosciutto; sauté until almost crisp, about 3 minutes. Add mushrooms; sauté until brown and tender, about 6 minutes. Cool mushroom mixture in skillet 10 minutes.

WHISK eggs, 1 cup cheese, parsley, salt, and pepper in large bowl. Stir in mushroom mixture. Melt remaining 1 tablespoon butter in same skillet over medium heat. Pour egg mixture into skillet. Cook without stirring until bottom and sides are set (top will be undercooked), about 10 minutes.

BAKE frittata in skillet until top is set, about 20 minutes.

PREHEAT broiler. Sprinkle frittata with remaining 1 cup cheese. Broil until cheese melts, about 2 minutes. Using heatproof spatula, loosen frittata on all sides. Slide out onto platter.

DO AHEAD *Can be made 2 hours ahead. Let stand at room temperature.*

Frittata with bacon, fresh ricotta, and greens

6 SERVINGS *Here's a brilliant way to get those good-for-you greens: Encase them in eggs with bacon and cheese. Use whatever greens look freshest at the market. Most are available year-round, which makes this recipe perfect for any season.*

12 ounces applewood-smoked bacon, cut into ½- to ¾-inch pieces
1 cup sliced shallots
12 cups (packed) assorted coarsely chopped greens, such as kale, chard, and mustard greens (about 12 ounces)

12 large eggs
½ teaspoon coarse kosher salt
1 cup freshly grated Parmesan cheese, divided
12 ounces fresh whole-milk ricotta cheese (about 1¾ cups)

PREHEAT oven to 350°F. Cook bacon in 12-inch-diameter ovenproof nonstick skillet over medium-high heat until crisp. Using slotted spoon, transfer bacon to paper towels to drain. Pour bacon drippings into bowl; reserve. Return 2 tablespoons drippings to skillet. Add shallots and sauté over medium heat until golden, about 4 minutes. Add half of greens and toss until beginning to wilt, about 1 minute. Add remaining greens and sauté until wilted, tender, and dry, about 10 to 15 minutes, depending on greens used. Transfer greens to plate; cool.

RINSE and dry skillet. Whisk eggs and coarse kosher salt to blend in large bowl. Whisk in ¾ cup Parmesan, then greens and half of bacon. Stir in ricotta, leaving some clumps. Heat 1 tablespoon reserved drippings in skillet over medium heat. Pour in egg mixture; spread greens evenly. Sprinkle remaining bacon and ¼ cup Parmesan over eggs. Cook over medium heat until frittata is just set at edges, about 10 minutes. Transfer to oven and bake until just set, about 20 minutes. Cut around frittata to loosen; slide out onto platter. Let cool 30 minutes. Slice into wedges.

Spaghetti frittata

4 SERVINGS *This recipe comes from Armandino Batali (Mario's dad and the owner of Salumi Artisan Cured Meats shop in Seattle). If anyone knows how to use leftover pasta and tomato sauce the next morning, it's the Batali family.*

8 ounces spaghetti, cooked, rinsed, cooled
2 cups tomato-based pasta sauce, divided
5 large eggs
½ cup chopped fresh Italian parsley, divided
½ teaspoon salt
½ teaspoon ground black pepper
⅛ teaspoon cayenne pepper

5 tablespoons olive oil
1 cup grated Parmesan cheese

PREHEAT broiler. Toss pasta and 1 cup pasta sauce in medium bowl to blend. Combine eggs, ¼ cup parsley, salt, black pepper, and cayenne in small bowl; whisk to blend.

HEAT oil in large broilerproof nonstick skillet over medium-high heat. Add pasta and toss until warmed through, about 4 minutes. Pour egg mixture over; do not stir. Reduce heat to medium-low. Cook until eggs start to firm and bottom begins to brown, lifting sides occasionally to let uncooked egg portion flow underneath, about 8 minutes. Remove skillet from heat. Sprinkle frittata with cheese. Broil until cheese melts, about 3 minutes.

MEANWHILE, heat remaining 1 cup pasta sauce in saucepan over low heat.

USING flexible spatula, loosen edges and bottom of frittata. Slide out onto plate. Sprinkle with remaining ¼ cup parsley. Cut frittata into wedges. Serve, passing warm sauce separately.

507

Baby eggplant, olive, and herb-cheese frittata

2 SERVINGS *If you can't find Boursin, a French herbed spreadable cheese, soft fresh goat cheese will do. Just throw in some extra herbs (like oregano or marjoram) and sauté a minced clove of garlic in the skillet and add it to the goat cheese before cooking the eggplant.*

2 tablespoons olive oil
5 baby (plum-size) purple eggplants, stemmed, split lengthwise

4 large eggs
3 tablespoons coarsely chopped pitted brine-cured green olives
2 tablespoons chopped fresh basil
¼ teaspoon salt
1 5.2-ounce package Boursin cheese with herbs and garlic, divided

HEAT oil in 10-inch-diameter nonstick skillet over medium heat. Add eggplant halves, cut side down, spacing evenly. Cover and cook until tender, about 10 minutes.

WHISK eggs, olives, basil, and salt in medium bowl. Sprinkle with pepper. Coarsely crumble half of cheese into eggs; stir to blend. Pour over eggplants, rearranging evenly in pan. Cook uncovered over medium heat until sides are set and bottom begins to brown, loosening sides occasionally with spatula, about 5 minutes. Sprinkle with remaining cheese. Cover and cook until set, about 7 minutes.

EGGPLANT SHOPPING Look for small baby eggplants (purple or white) at supermarkets, specialty foods stores, and farmers' markets, and even at Indian and Asian markets. They're available year-round, and they're worth seeking out for their softer, more delicate skin.

Herbed cheese scrambled eggs on asparagus

4 SERVINGS *With such a pretty breakfast, you'll want to invite friends over to share it. A mix of white and green asparagus would make this truly elegant.*

1 pound slender asparagus spears, trimmed
½ cup creamy garlic and herb cheese (such as Boursin)
1 tablespoon minced fresh basil
10 large eggs
2½ tablespoons butter, divided

COOK asparagus in medium skillet of boiling water until just tender, about 3 minutes. Drain; return asparagus to skillet. Mix cheese and basil in small bowl. Whisk eggs in large bowl to blend. Melt 1½ tablespoons butter in heavy large skillet over medium heat. Add eggs; stir until eggs are almost set, about 1 minute. Add cheese mixture and stir until cheese melts and eggs are softly set, about 2 minutes.

MEANWHILE, add remaining 1 tablespoon butter to asparagus in skillet and stir over medium heat until asparagus is heated through. Divide asparagus among 4 plates; spoon eggs over and serve.

Scrambled eggs with poblano chiles and cheese

4 SERVINGS *Create a Southwest theme with hot buttered tortillas, rice and beans, salsa, and guacamole. Poblano chiles (sometimes called pasilla chiles) are large fresh green chiles with subtle heat and deep flavor. You'll find them and* queso fresco *at supermarkets or Latin markets.*

6	tablespoons (¾ stick) butter, divided
1	cup chopped onion
2	garlic cloves, chopped
½	teaspoon dried oregano
1	14.5-ounce can petite diced tomatoes in juice
¼	teaspoon chili powder
2	large fresh poblano chiles, seeded, diced
½	cup chopped green onions
½	cup chopped fresh cilantro, divided
8	large eggs, beaten to blend
1	cup crumbled queso fresco or feta cheese (about 4 ounces)

MELT 2 tablespoons butter in large saucepan over medium heat. Add onion, garlic, and oregano; sauté until onion is soft, about 3 minutes. Add tomatoes with juice and chili powder. Cover and simmer 5 minutes to blend flavors. Transfer sauce to blender and puree until smooth. Season to taste with salt and pepper. Return sauce to pan and keep warm.

MELT remaining 4 tablespoons butter in large skillet over medium heat. Add poblano chiles; sauté until tender, about 6 minutes. Add green onions and ¼ cup cilantro. Add eggs and cheese. Cook until eggs are softly set, stirring occasionally, about 4 minutes. Divide eggs among 4 plates. Spoon sauce over; sprinkle with remaining ¼ cup cilantro.

Scrambled eggs, unscrambled If you're a fan of softly scrambled eggs, try this ultra-indulgent method:

1. Use about a half tablespoon of butter in the skillet (nonstick or seasoned cast-iron) per egg.

2. Melt the butter and heat the pan over medium-low heat.

3. Whisk the eggs in a bowl and season as you like.

4. Pour the eggs into the pan, and give them a minute or two to start cooking.

5. Using a heatproof rubber or silicone spatula, gently pull the spatula along the bottom surface of the pan, scraping up the cooked egg in strips.

6. Continue over medium-low heat, constantly running the spatula over the bottom of the pan, until eggs have set but are still moist and fluffy.

7. Take the eggs off the heat and plate them a second or two before you think you should; they'll keep cooking (and drying out) even after being removed from the heat.

Smoked salmon and leek scramble with Meyer lemon crème fraîche

6 SERVINGS *This recipe showcases subtle flavors: leeks rather than harsher onions, sweet Meyer lemons rather than more tart and acidic regular lemons, and crème fraîche rather than the less refined sour cream. Leeks look like overgrown green onions, but they have an earthy-sweet, very mild onion flavor. Wash them thoroughly, and use the white and pale green parts of the leek only (the bottom third or half)—the darker green tops can be used for some dishes, but are a bit tough and take a little longer to cook.*

 1 cup crème fraîche or sour cream
 2 teaspoons finely grated Meyer lemon
    peel or regular lemon peel
1½ teaspoons salt, divided

 12 large eggs
 ¾ cup heavy whipping cream
 3 tablespoons olive oil, divided
2¼ cups thinly sliced leeks (white
    and pale green parts only)

 12 slices smoked salmon (about 8 ounces)
 1 tablespoon chopped fresh chives

MIX crème fraîche, lemon peel, and ½ teaspoon salt in small bowl.

DO AHEAD *Can be made 4 days ahead. Cover and chill.*

WHISK eggs, cream, and remaining 1 teaspoon salt in large bowl to blend. Heat 2 tablespoons oil in large nonstick skillet over medium heat. Add leeks, cover, and cook until leeks are soft, stirring occasionally, about 10 minutes. Add remaining 1 tablespoon oil to same skillet with leeks; increase heat to medium-high. Pour egg mixture into skillet and stir with heat-proof rubber spatula until light, fluffy, and softly set, about 8 minutes.

SPOON eggs onto serving platter. Top with some of Meyer lemon crème fraîche mixture, smoked salmon slices, and chives. Serve, passing remaining Meyer lemon crème fraîche mixture separately.

ON RAMPS If you're making this dish in early spring and you're lucky enough to find ramps—wild leeks in season for only a few weeks of the year—grab a bunch. Their subtle flavor and tender texture would be outstanding in this dish. Look for them at farmers' markets: They look like short green onions and have a very soft, delicate texture. Ramps can be pricey, but they're worth it for a special occasion or just to take advantage of a truly fleeting seasonal ingredient.

Creamy scrambled eggs with smoked trout and green onions

4 SERVINGS *Cream cheese puts the "creamy" in these scrambled eggs. Toast bagels to serve alongside. Smoked trout is available at some supermarkets and at specialty foods stores and delicatessens.*

- 8 **large eggs**
- 1 **4.5-ounce package smoked trout fillets, broken into ½-inch pieces**
- 4 **ounces cream cheese, cut into ½-inch pieces, room temperature**
- ½ **cup chopped green onions**
- 1½ **tablespoons chopped fresh dill plus sprigs for garnish**
- 2½ **tablespoons butter**

WHISK eggs in large bowl to blend. Add trout, cream cheese, green onions, and chopped dill. Season lightly with salt and generously with pepper; stir to mix.

MELT butter in large nonstick skillet over medium heat. Add egg mixture and stir slowly until eggs just hold together and are cooked through but still moist, about 4 minutes. Divide egg mixture among 4 plates. Garnish with dill sprigs and serve.

GONE FISHING If you'd like to cast your net wider, try smoked salmon, smoked mackerel, or smoked whitefish in place of the trout. Green onions and dill will complement all of these very well.

Chorizo and scrambled egg breakfast tacos

2 SERVINGS *Fresh (not fully cooked or smoked) Mexican or Spanish chorizo can be used in this recipe. You can even use soy chorizo if you're in the mood for meatless. Serving these for dinner? Margaritas or Mexican beers with lime would be the perfect drinks.*

- **Olive oil or vegetable oil**
- 4 **5- to 6-inch corn tortillas**
- 1 **cup grated extra-sharp white cheddar cheese (about 4 ounces)**
- 4 **large eggs**
- 4 **tablespoons chopped fresh cilantro, divided**
- 7 **ounces fresh chorizo sausages, casings removed if necessary**
- 4 **green onions, sliced**

  Sour cream (optional)
  Hot sauce or salsa (optional)

BRUSH large nonstick skillet with oil. Char tortillas over gas flame or directly on electric burner until blackened in spots, turning with tongs. Arrange tortillas in single layer in skillet. Sprinkle each tortilla with ¼ cup cheese and set aside.

WHISK eggs and 2 tablespoons cilantro in medium bowl. Season with salt and pepper. Sauté chorizo sausages in medium nonstick skillet over medium-high heat until cooked through, breaking up with back of spoon, about 5 minutes. Add green onions and sauté 2 minutes. Add egg mixture and stir until very softly set, about 1 minute. Remove egg mixture from heat.

COOK tortillas in skillet over high heat until beginning to crisp on bottom, but still soft and pliable, about 1 minute. Divide egg mixture among tortillas and sprinkle with remaining 2 tablespoons cilantro. Fold each tortilla in half. Transfer to plates. Serve with sour cream and hot sauce, if desired.

BRUNCH DISHES

Apricot-buttermilk noodle pudding

12 SERVINGS *This is a sweet riff on kugel, the traditional Jewish pudding made with noodles or potatoes. Savory versions usually include meat and vegetables; this brunch variety leans to the sweet side with dried apricots, raisins, and green apple. The pudding needs to chill at least 2 hours, so begin making this ahead. To crush the cornflakes, use a processor or enclose them in a resealable plastic bag and crush with a mallet. Serve the pudding with sour cream.*

    1 pound wide egg noodles
    ½ cup (1 stick) butter, room temperature
    5 large eggs
    ½ cup sugar
    1 large tart green apple, peeled, cored, chopped
    ¾ cup (packed) quartered dried apricots
       (about 5 ounces)
    2 tablespoons golden raisins
    4 cups buttermilk

    1 cup cornflake crumbs (about 4 cups
       whole cornflakes)
    ¾ cup (lightly packed) golden brown sugar
    5 tablespoons butter, melted

BUTTER 13×9×2-inch glass baking dish. Cook noodles in large pot of boiling salted water until almost tender. Drain noodles; return to same pot. Add ½ cup butter and toss until butter melts. Whisk eggs and sugar in medium bowl to blend; mix into noodles. Mix in apple, apricots, and raisins. Transfer noodle mixture to prepared baking dish. Pour buttermilk evenly over. Cover and chill at least 2 hours or overnight.

PREHEAT oven to 350°F. Uncover pudding and bake 45 minutes.

MIX cornflake crumbs, brown sugar, and 5 tablespoons melted butter in medium bowl. Remove pudding from oven. Spoon cornflake topping evenly over pudding. Return pudding to oven and bake until topping is golden brown and crisp, about 30 minutes longer. Let stand 10 minutes. Cut pudding into squares and serve.

Canadian bacon, asparagus, and egg gratin with Fontina cheese

2 SERVINGS; CAN BE DOUBLED OR TRIPLED *A gratin is a yummy, creamy dish that's baked and browned. In this case, onion, asparagus, and Canadian bacon make a delicious bed for eggs that are cracked into the mixture and then set when baked. Fontina, a nutty ewe's milk Italian cheese, is grated and sprinkled over the top, then gratinéed under the broiler just before serving.*

1 tablespoon butter

1 onion, chopped

8 ounces asparagus spears, trimmed, cut on diagonal into 1-inch pieces

6 ounces unsliced Canadian bacon, cut into ½-inch cubes

⅓ cup plus 4 teaspoons heavy whipping cream
Cayenne pepper

1 tablespoon Dijon mustard

4 large eggs

1 cup (packed) grated Fontina cheese (about 4 ounces)

PREHEAT oven to 375°F. Butter 9½-inch oval gratin pan. Melt butter in heavy medium skillet over medium heat. Add onion and sauté until beginning to soften, about 5 minutes. Add asparagus; sprinkle with salt and pepper. Cook until asparagus begins to soften, about 4 minutes. Add bacon and stir 1 minute. Add ⅓ cup cream and pinch of cayenne. Stir until heated through, 1 minute. Mix in mustard. Transfer to prepared pan.

MAKE 4 nests in mixture, spacing evenly. Break 1 egg into each nest. Drizzle 1 teaspoon cream over each egg. Sprinkle with salt, pepper, and cayenne. Bake until whites are beginning to set but are still runny, about 12 minutes.

PREHEAT broiler. Sprinkle cheese over dish. Immediately broil until melted and beginning to brown, about 30 seconds. Serve immediately.

O, CANADIAN BACON Canadian bacon is a lean, ham-like cut of smoked pork loin. It's a salty, smoky addition to this gratin. You'll find it by the regular bacon and breakfast meats in the refrigerator case at the supermarket, or in the deli section.

Cheddar cheese and red bell pepper strata

4 TO 6 SERVINGS *Stratas get their name from the Italian word for "layers," and they're made up of vegetables, cheese, herbs, and sometimes meats layered with bread, then drowned in an eggy batter and baked, resulting in a sort of savory bread pudding. This one features bell peppers and cheddar cheese, but stratas are so versatile that you could use almost any veggies and cheese you've got on hand.*

- 3 tablespoons butter, room temperature, divided
- 1 medium-size red bell pepper, thinly sliced
- 1 cup chopped green onions

- 5 slices white sandwich bread, divided
- 1½ cups grated sharp cheddar cheese (about 6 ounces), divided
- 2 cups whole milk
- 3 large eggs
- 1 tablespoon Dijon mustard
- ½ teaspoon dry mustard
- ½ teaspoon salt
- ¼ teaspoon pepper

PREHEAT oven to 350°F. Melt 1½ tablespoons butter in heavy large skillet over medium-high heat. Add bell pepper to skillet and sauté until just tender, about 4 minutes. Mix in green onions; sauté 1 minute longer. Remove from heat.

SPREAD remaining 1½ tablespoons butter thinly on bread. Cut bread into ½-inch pieces. Layer half of bread in 8×8×2-inch glass baking dish. Cover with half of cheese, then half of bell pepper mixture. Repeat layering with bread, cheese, and bell pepper mixture. Whisk milk, eggs, Dijon mustard, dry mustard, salt, and pepper in medium bowl to blend. Pour over strata.

BAKE strata until lightly browned on top and set in center (knife inserted into center comes out clean), about 45 minutes. Let stand 10 minutes.

GET AHEAD To make this the night before the big brunch, use a heartier bread, like sourdough. Assemble the strata and refrigerate it for up to 12 hours. Then all that's left to do is pop it in the oven.

Arizona cheese strata

2 SERVINGS; CAN BE DOUBLED *Go Tex-Mex all the way with this one: Serve it with an avocado and orange salad on the side, and lime sorbet to finish. Also, feel free to experiment with salsas—offer guests mild and spicy varieties, plus a green tomatillo version. If you're serving this strata for brunch or supper, Bloody Marys would also be delicious.*

1	cup whole milk
2	large eggs
½	teaspoon salt
½	teaspoon pepper
1	cup (packed) grated Monterey Jack cheese (about 4 ounces)
3	tablespoons sliced green onion
2	teaspoons minced jalapeño chile
2	cups cubed white sandwich bread (about 3 slices)
½	cup purchased chunky salsa
2	tablespoons chopped fresh cilantro

PREHEAT oven to 400°F. Lightly butter 9-inch-diameter glass pie dish. Whisk first 4 ingredients in medium bowl to blend. Mix in cheese, green onion, and chile. Add bread; stir until moistened. Transfer mixture to prepared pie dish. Let stand until bread absorbs most of custard, pressing several times to submerge cubes, about 5 minutes.

BAKE strata uncovered until light brown around edges, top is crusty, and knife inserted into center comes out clean, about 20 minutes.

COMBINE salsa and cilantro in small bowl. Cut strata into wedges. Serve with salsa.

Sausage and potato breakfast casserole

6 SERVINGS *Ground sausage, frozen hash browns, chopped green onions, and cheese combine in a super easy a.m. casserole. While it's in the oven, cook eggs to order and serve them alongside.*

1	pound bulk breakfast sausage
2	tablespoons all purpose flour
1½	cups whole milk
1	1-pound package frozen shredded hash brown potatoes
4	green onions, finely chopped, divided
1¼	cups grated sharp cheddar cheese (about 5 ounces), divided

PREHEAT oven to 350°F. Butter 8×8×2-inch glass baking dish. Cook sausage in heavy large skillet over medium-high heat until brown, breaking into small pieces with back of fork, about 5 minutes. Mix in flour, then milk. Cook until mixture boils and thickens, stirring occasionally, about 5 minutes.

ARRANGE potatoes in prepared baking dish. Top with ⅓ of green onions, 1 cup cheese, ⅓ of green onions, sausage mixture, and remaining ¼ cup cheese.

BAKE casserole until potatoes are tender, about 45 minutes. Sprinkle with remaining green onions.

Smoked sausage and red pepper quesadillas

MAKES 6 *The great thing about this recipe is that you can slice the quesadillas into thin wedges for appetizers or a snack, or into larger wedges for a substantial breakfast or supper. The quesadillas are topped with a tangy, spicy mixture of salsa verde, chopped avocados, and cilantro that would be wonderful on any quesadilla or taco, or just with tortilla chips.*

Olive oil

1 cup purchased salsa verde

2 ripe avocados, halved, pitted, peeled, chopped

½ cup chopped fresh cilantro, divided

8 ounces spicy smoked sausages (such as hot links or andouille), thinly sliced

12 5- to 6-inch corn tortillas, divided

2 cups (packed) grated Monterey Jack cheese (about 8 ounces), divided

½ cup crumbled feta cheese (about 2 ounces)

1 7-ounce jar roasted red peppers, drained, thinly sliced

PREHEAT oven to 350°F. Brush baking sheet with oil. Gently mix salsa, avocado, and ¼ cup cilantro in medium bowl.

SAUTÉ sausage slices in heavy large skillet over medium-high heat until just brown, about 2 minutes. Set aside. Cook tortillas, 1 at a time, directly over gas flame until beginning to brown in spots, about 20 seconds per side. Arrange 6 tortillas on prepared sheet. Layer tortillas on sheet with 1 cup Monterey Jack cheese, feta cheese, sausage slices, red peppers, remaining ¼ cup cilantro, then remaining 1 cup Monterey Jack cheese, dividing equally. Press each remaining tortilla atop filling and brush with oil.

BAKE quesadillas until golden and cheeses melt, about 15 minutes. Cut into wedges; serve with salsa mixture.

Toasty tortillas When you want to serve nice warm tortillas alongside a Mexican or Tex-Mex dish, here are three ways to heat 'em up:

— Drape one tortilla at a time over a gas burner on medium-high heat, turning frequently with tongs as it toasts.

— Put a stack of tortillas in the microwave on a plate (no water, no covering, no paper towels in between); heat on high at 10-second intervals until warm.

— Wrap a stack of tortillas in aluminum foil and warm them in a 350°F oven for about 10 minutes.

Breakfast polenta with chorizo and queso fresco

4 SERVINGS *Warm and comforting, this would be great for breakfast on its own, or with fried eggs and chips and salsa alongside. Make sure to buy uncooked chorizo (the spicy ground-pork sausage) in links, so that when you remove the casings, the raw sausage breaks apart easily; fully cooked chorizo will be too firm. Queso fresco, a salty, crumbly Mexican cheese, can be found either in the cheese section of the market or near the refrigerated salsas and guacamoles. Feta is the perfect substitute.*

1⅓ cups crumbled queso fresco or
     feta cheese (about 6 ounces)
 ½ cup chopped fresh cilantro
3¼ cups water
 1 cup polenta (coarse cornmeal)
     or regular cornmeal
 1 1-pound bag frozen yellow corn
     kernels, thawed
 1 pound fresh link chorizo
     sausage, casings removed
 1 pound cherry tomatoes

PREHEAT oven to 425°F. Toss cheese and cilantro in small bowl. Mix 3¼ cups water, polenta, and corn kernels in 13×9×2-inch glass baking dish. Sprinkle generously with salt and pepper; stir to blend well. Bake until water is absorbed and polenta is tender, stirring once, about 25 minutes.

MEANWHILE, sauté chorizo in heavy large skillet over medium-high heat until browned, breaking into small pieces with side of wooden spoon, about 6 minutes. Add cherry tomatoes to skillet. Cover, reduce heat to medium, and simmer until tomatoes soften, about 6 minutes. Uncover; crush some tomatoes with fork. Simmer until tomatoes release juices and sauce thickens slightly, about 10 minutes.

SPOON polenta onto plates. Top with chorizo mixture, then cheese mixture.

Fried eggs on toast with pepper Jack and avocado

4 SERVINGS *Here's the perfect breakfast to follow some California dreaming: Monterey Jack cheese (spiked with hot peppers) and avocados (preferably the Golden State's own Hass variety) top fried eggs on toast. Make sure the avocado gives slightly when squeezed; hard, underripe avocados will taste grassy.*

3 tablespoons butter, room temperature, divided
4 large eggs
4 slices hot pepper Monterey Jack cheese
4 ½-inch-thick slices country bread, toasted
1 ripe avocado, peeled, pitted, sliced
  Chopped fresh cilantro

PREHEAT broiler. Melt 1 tablespoon butter in heavy large broilerproof skillet over medium heat. Crack eggs into skillet; sprinkle with salt and pepper. Cook until egg whites are just set on bottom, about 2 minutes. Remove skillet from heat; top each egg with 1 cheese slice. Broil until cheese just melts, about 1 minute.

SPREAD remaining 2 tablespoons butter on toast; top with fried eggs, then avocado slices. Sprinkle with cilantro.

Ham and sweet potato hash with fried eggs

4 SERVINGS *This one has "Thanksgiving leftovers" written all over it.*

- 4 tablespoons olive oil, divided
- 2½ cups ⅓-inch cubes peeled red-skinned sweet potato (yam)
- 2 cups ½-inch cubes ham
- 1 large white onion, chopped
- ¼ cup Dijon mustard with horseradish
- 2 cups coarsely chopped watercress tops plus 4 sprigs for garnish

- 4 large eggs

HEAT 3 tablespoons oil in large nonstick skillet over medium-high heat. Add yam cubes; cover and cook 5 minutes. Mix in ham, onion, and mustard. Cover and cook until yam is tender and bottom of hash begins to brown, about 8 minutes. Sprinkle with pepper. Using spatula, turn hash over in portions and press to compact. Cook uncovered until golden, turning and pressing occasionally, about 10 minutes longer. Add chopped watercress and stir until wilted, about 1 minute.

MEANWHILE, heat remaining 1 tablespoon oil in another large nonstick skillet over medium-high heat. Crack eggs into skillet and fry as desired.

DIVIDE hash among 4 plates. Top with eggs. Garnish with watercress sprigs.

Poached eggs in pipérade

2 SERVINGS *Eggs are "poached" in* pipérade, *a Basque mixture of bell peppers and tomatoes. Crusty bread would soak up all the juices nicely.*

- 2 tablespoons olive oil
- 1 small onion, coarsely chopped (about 1¼ cups)
- 1 cup coarsely chopped bell peppers (preferably a mix of red, yellow, and green)
- 3 garlic cloves, finely chopped
- 2 large plum tomatoes, seeded, coarsely chopped
- 4 large eggs

- ¼ cup crumbled feta cheese

HEAT oil in heavy 10-inch-diameter skillet over medium heat. Add onion, bell peppers, and garlic; sauté until vegetables begin to soften, about 5 minutes. Add tomatoes and sauté until soft, about 3 minutes. Season to taste with salt and pepper. Spread mixture evenly in skillet. Carefully break eggs over vegetable mixture, spacing evenly. Sprinkle eggs with salt and pepper; cover skillet and reduce heat to low. Cook eggs until whites are set but yolks are still soft, about 5 minutes.

USING wide spatula, transfer 2 eggs with vegetable mixture underneath to each plate. Spoon remaining vegetables around eggs. Sprinkle pipérade with feta cheese and serve.

Scottish farmhouse eggs

4 SERVINGS *This creamy baked-egg dish is a typical treat on the Scottish breakfast table. Hearty and versatile, it also makes a good supper dish. Pair it with smoked fish and some bread or English muffins to soak up the eggs. Dunlop is a Scottish cheese that's similar in taste and texture to cheddar. If you can't find Dunlop at the cheese shop, a good cheddar would be the best (and most geographically appropriate) substitute.*

1½ cups fresh white breadcrumbs, divided

3 tablespoons chopped fresh chives or green onions, divided, plus fresh chive pieces for garnish

3 ounces Dunlop, sharp cheddar, or Cheshire cheese, grated (about ⅞ cup), divided

4 large eggs
   Cayenne pepper

1 cup half and half

PREHEAT oven to 350°F. Butter 10-inch-diameter glass pie dish. Sprinkle half of breadcrumbs over bottom of prepared pie dish. Sprinkle with half of chopped chives and half of cheese. Carefully break eggs into pie dish, spacing evenly. Top with remaining half of breadcrumbs, chopped chives, and cheese. Sprinkle with cayenne and salt. Pour half and half over. Bake until eggs are softly set, about 20 minutes. Garnish eggs with fresh chive pieces and serve immediately.

Asparagus and Swiss cheese soufflés

2 SERVINGS; CAN BE DOUBLED *Welcome spring with these beautiful breakfast soufflés. Sliced ham or morel mushrooms would be delicious seasonal add-ins.*

10 thin asparagus spears, trimmed, cut into 1-inch pieces

2½ tablespoons butter, divided

⅔ cup whole milk

2 large eggs, separated

2 tablespoons all purpose flour

1 teaspoon dry mustard

⅔ cup (packed) grated Swiss cheese (about 3 ounces)

¼ teaspoon salt

¼ teaspoon freshly ground black pepper

PREHEAT oven to 450°F. Generously butter two 1¼-cup soufflé dishes or custard cups. Divide asparagus pieces between prepared dishes. Melt butter in heavy medium saucepan. Drizzle ¾ teaspoon butter over asparagus in each dish. Reserve remaining butter in pan. Bake asparagus until just tender and beginning to brown, about 6 minutes. Maintain oven temperature.

MEANWHILE, whisk milk and yolks to blend in small bowl. Add flour and mustard to remaining butter in saucepan and whisk until smooth paste forms. Set over medium heat and whisk 1 minute. Whisk milk mixture into flour mixture. Cook until sauce thickens, whisking constantly, about 2 minutes. Remove pan from heat. Add cheese, salt, and pepper; stir until cheese melts.

BEAT egg whites in medium bowl until stiff but not dry. Fold whites into warm cheese mixture in pan. Spoon soufflé batter over asparagus in dishes.

BAKE soufflés until puffed and golden, about 14 minutes. Serve immediately.

Cabbage-caraway quiche

4 SERVINGS *Quiche—a savory egg-based tart—has its roots in the Alsace and Lorraine regions of France. The classic, of course, is quiche Lorraine, which is made with bacon and Gruyère (a nutty Swiss cheese also produced in France). This version has the flavors of Eastern Europe and Scandinavia, thanks to the cabbage and caraway. If serving this for lunch or dinner, borscht (cold beet soup) or a beet salad would be a colorful, delicious accompaniment.*

4	bacon slices, chopped
½	large onion, chopped
3½	cups chopped cabbage
3	large eggs
1	cup half and half
1	cup grated Gruyère cheese (about 4 ounces)
1	teaspoon salt
¾	teaspoon caraway seeds
1	9-inch frozen deep-dish pie crust, baked according to package directions

PREHEAT oven to 375°F. Cook bacon in heavy large skillet over medium heat 5 minutes. Add onion and sauté until tender, about 5 minutes. Add cabbage and cook until all liquid evaporates and cabbage is golden brown, stirring frequently, about 16 minutes.

WHISK eggs, half and half, cheese, salt, and caraway seeds in medium bowl; sprinkle generously with pepper. Stir in cabbage mixture. Pour into crust. Bake until filling puffs and starts to brown and knife inserted into center comes out clean, about 40 minutes. Serve warm or at room temperature.

Bacon and green chile quiche

6 SERVINGS *A refrigerated pie crust makes this quiche a snap to assemble. Most of the ingredients are kitchen staples, so you could whip this together at a moment's notice.*

1	refrigerated pie crust (half of 15-ounce package), room temperature
8	bacon slices
1	4-ounce can diced green chiles, drained
4	green onions, chopped
1	cup grated Monterey Jack cheese (about 4 ounces)
1	cup grated sharp cheddar cheese (about 4 ounces)
4	large eggs
1¼	cups half and half
½	teaspoon salt

PREHEAT oven to 425°F. Unfold crust. Using fingertips, press together any tears. Press crust into 9-inch-diameter deep-dish glass pie dish. Press foil onto crust to hold shape. Bake 5 minutes. Remove from oven; remove foil. Reduce oven temperature to 400°F.

COOK bacon in heavy large skillet over medium-high heat until brown and crisp. Transfer to paper towels to drain. Crumble bacon. Sprinkle bacon, then chiles and green onions over crust. Mix Monterey Jack cheese and cheddar cheese and sprinkle over. Whisk eggs, half and half, and salt in medium bowl to blend; pour mixture into crust.

BAKE quiche until knife inserted into center comes out clean, about 45 minutes. Let quiche stand 5 minutes. Cut quiche into wedges.

Toasted mini bagels with smoked salmon and caviar

8 TO 10 SERVINGS *Cuter than regular bagels, these dressed-up minis are great for a brunch or even a cocktail party. Mix up the recipe with as many different bagel varieties as you can find (sesame, poppy seed, onion) and with different colors of caviar (orange, black, golden). And keep the Champagne close by no matter what time of day it is. Look for mini bagels at supermarkets, delis, and bagel shops. If you can't find them, there's nothing wrong with supersizing these.*

12   plain mini bagels, cut in half horizontally
¼   cup (½ stick) unsalted butter, melted

    Fresh spinach leaves
    Sour cream
4   ounces thinly sliced smoked salmon
    Caviar

PREHEAT oven to 300°F. Arrange bagel halves, cut side up, on large baking sheet. Brush bagels generously with melted butter. Bake until light golden brown, about 8 minutes. Cool slightly.

ARRANGE spinach decoratively on large platter. Spread each bagel half with sour cream. Cover with salmon. Top with small dollop of sour cream and some caviar. Sprinkle with freshly ground black pepper. Place bagels atop spinach-lined platter.

Fried corn cakes with green onions

MAKES ABOUT 10 *Serve these savory corn cakes with andouille sausages and fried eggs for breakfast—or with a nice, juicy porterhouse steak for dinner.*

1   cup all purpose flour
1   tablespoon sugar
1½   teaspoons baking powder
½   teaspoon salt
⅛   teaspoon cayenne pepper
⅔   cup whole milk
1   large egg
½   teaspoon white distilled vinegar
2   cups frozen corn kernels, thawed
½   cup chopped green onions

2   tablespoons (or more) vegetable oil

PREHEAT oven to 300°F. Blend first 5 ingredients in large bowl. Add milk, egg, and vinegar to bowl and whisk to blend. Mix in corn and green onions.

HEAT 2 tablespoons oil in heavy large skillet over medium heat. Drop batter by scant ¼ cupfuls into skillet. Cook cakes until brown and cooked through, about 3 minutes per side. Transfer to baking sheet. Place in oven to keep warm. Repeat with remaining batter, adding more oil to skillet as needed. Serve cakes hot.

ONTHESIDE

Spicy bacon, onion, and cheese potatoes

8 SERVINGS *Breakfast potatoes get serious. These are so good you could also serve them for dinner with a juicy grilled steak or pan-fried pork chops.*

- 8 bacon slices, coarsely chopped
- 2 pounds russet potatoes, peeled, cut into ½-inch pieces
- 1 large onion, chopped
- 1 cup (packed) grated hot pepper Monterey Jack cheese (about 4 ounces)
- 2 tablespoons (¼ stick) butter, cut into ½-inch cubes

PREHEAT oven to 350°F. Butter 13×9×2-inch glass baking dish. Cook bacon in heavy large skillet over medium heat until brown and crisp. Using slotted spoon, transfer bacon to paper towels to drain. Combine bacon, potatoes, and onion in prepared baking dish. Sprinkle with salt and pepper. Sprinkle cheese over and dot with butter. Cover dish tightly with foil. Bake until potatoes and onions are very tender, about 1 hour.

PREHEAT broiler. Uncover baking dish and broil until top of potato mixture is brown and crisp, about 2 minutes.

Pork and bacon sausage

2 SERVINGS; CAN BE DOUBLED OR TRIPLED *Chopped bacon adds oomph to these sausage patties. Serve them with eggs and breakfast potatoes, or make them part of an elegant sausage-and-egg sandwich: Butter toasted English muffins and top each with a sausage patty, a poached egg, and some shaved Pecorino Romano or Parmesan cheese (a few arugula leaves would be a nice touch, too).*

- 3 bacon slices, cut into 1-inch pieces
- ½ pound ground pork
- ½ teaspoon dried thyme
- ½ teaspoon finely grated orange peel
- ½ teaspoon freshly ground black pepper
- ¼ teaspoon salt
- ⅛ to ¼ teaspoon ground mace

- 1 tablespoon butter

FINELY chop bacon in processor. Add remaining ingredients except butter; process using on/off turns until sausage mixture is blended.

DIVIDE sausage mixture into 4 pieces. Flatten each to ⅓-inch-thick round. Melt butter in heavy small skillet over medium-high heat. Add sausage and fry until cooked through and just firm to touch, 2½ to 3 minutes per side. Transfer to plates.

Rosemary and mustard breakfast sausages

MAKES 12 *Fresh rosemary and whole grain mustard elevate these sausage patties. They can be assembled the night before, which makes them perfect for a brunch or holiday breakfast. And they're baked rather than sautéed, leaving plenty of room on the stove to make the scrambled eggs and hash browns you'll surely want alongside. Garnish with fresh rosemary sprigs, if desired.*

 1 tablespoon olive oil
 1 medium onion, finely chopped
 1 teaspoon chopped fresh rosemary
14 ounces bulk breakfast sausage
 2 teaspoons whole grain mustard

HEAT oil in small skillet over medium-high heat. Add onion and rosemary; sauté until onion is golden, about 10 minutes. Transfer to medium bowl. Add sausage and mustard; sprinkle with generous amount of freshly ground black pepper. Mix gently. Form into twelve 2-inch-diameter patties. Arrange sausages on large rimmed baking sheet.

DO AHEAD *Can be made 1 day ahead. Cover and chill.*

SET rack at lowest position in oven and preheat to 500°F. Bake sausages until just cooked through, about 6 minutes. (If sausages have not browned, broil 2 minutes.) Transfer sausages to paper towels to drain. Arrange on platter.

Cranberry-almond granola

MAKES ABOUT 4 CUPS *Feeling creative? This recipe is the perfect vehicle for experimentation. Try different dried fruits (currants, dried cherries, chopped dried apricots) or seeds (pumpkin or sunflower), or add a touch of honey or maple syrup to give the sweetness a little more depth.*

    Nonstick vegetable oil spray
 2 cups old-fashioned oats
⅓ cup slivered almonds
⅓ cup sweetened flaked coconut
⅓ cup pecan halves
⅓ cup frozen concentrated
    cranberry juice cocktail, thawed
⅓ cup (packed) golden brown sugar
 2 tablespoons vegetable oil
 1 teaspoon ground cinnamon
½ teaspoon ground allspice
 1 cup dried sweetened cranberries

PREHEAT oven to 325°F. Spray heavy large rimmed baking sheet with nonstick spray. Combine oats, almonds, coconut, and pecans in large bowl. Combine cranberry juice concentrate, brown sugar, oil, cinnamon, and allspice in medium saucepan. Bring to boil, whisking until sugar dissolves. Pour hot syrup over oat mixture; stir to coat evenly. Spread mixture out on prepared sheet. Bake until golden brown at edges, about 20 minutes. Add dried cranberries; using metal spatula, stir to blend. Bake until granola is golden and beginning to dry, stirring occasionally, about 12 minutes longer. Cool completely on baking sheet.

DO AHEAD *Can be made 1 week ahead. Store airtight at room temperature.*

Mixed grain and wild rice cereal

8 SERVINGS *This is a hot, oatmeal-like cereal with a hearty mix of grains and dried fruit. Make a batch of it and store it in the fridge for a week's worth of fortifying breakfasts (just reheat in the microwave as needed). Serve it as is or with some milk and a little extra brown sugar, honey, or maple syrup added.*

8 cups water, divided
½ cup wild rice
½ cup pearl barley
½ cup steel-cut oats (Irish oatmeal)
½ cup bulgur
½ cup raisins
½ cup chopped pitted dates
6 tablespoons (packed) dark brown sugar
3 tablespoons unsalted butter
¾ teaspoon salt
½ teaspoon ground cinnamon

PREHEAT oven to 375°F. Butter 2½-quart baking dish. Simmer 2 cups water and wild rice in small saucepan 20 minutes. Drain. Transfer rice to prepared baking dish; mix in remaining 6 cups water and all remaining ingredients. Cover loosely with foil and bake until grains are tender, water is absorbed, and cereal is creamy, stirring occasionally, about 1½ hours. Serve hot.

GRAINS OF STEEL Steel-cut oats are literally whole oats that have been sliced into two or three pieces with a steel blade. Often called Irish or Scottish oats, they require longer cooking time than the more thinly sliced rolled oats or quick-cooking oats.

Cantaloupe salad with lime, mint, and ginger

4 TO 6 SERVINGS *An inspired way to dress up cantaloupe, this can be served on its own, as a salad on a big brunch spread, or with a scoop of lime sorbet for dessert. Use half cantaloupe and half honeydew for a little variety.*

1 cantaloupe, halved, seeded, peeled
3 tablespoons fresh lime juice
3 tablespoons chopped fresh mint
2 teaspoons finely grated lime peel
2 tablespoons sugar
2½ teaspoons grated peeled fresh ginger
2 teaspoons honey

CUT cantaloupe into ¾- to 1-inch cubes (about 5 cups) and place in large bowl. Add lime juice, mint, and lime peel; toss to blend. Mix in sugar, ginger, and honey. Refrigerate salad until ready to serve, stirring occasionally, up to 3 hours.

Spiced dried-fruit compote

12 SERVINGS *An all-purpose compote for pancakes, waffles, crepes, or even as a topping for granola or oatmeal. With so many options for the dried fruits, you could make endless combinations. When it comes to the sweet white wine, this isn't the place to break the bank. A mid-range Johannisberg Riesling or Muscat will do (pour a nicer dessert wine if serving the compote over crepes for dessert).*

- 3 **cups water**
- 1 **cup sugar**
- 1 **pound mixed dried fruits (such as pitted prunes, pears, apricots, peaches, apples, and figs), cut into ½-inch pieces**
- 1 **cup sweet white wine (such as Johannisberg Riesling or Muscat)**
- 1 **orange, unpeeled, thinly sliced**
- 1 **lemon, unpeeled, thinly sliced**
- ½ **cup raisins**
- ½ **cup dried cherries, cranberries, or currants**
- 8 **whole cloves**
- 4 **cinnamon sticks**
- 1 **cup seedless grapes**

COMBINE 3 cups water and sugar in heavy large saucepan. Stir over medium heat until sugar dissolves. Add mixed dried fruits, white wine, orange, lemon, raisins, dried cherries, cloves, and cinnamon sticks. Simmer compote until fruits are tender and liquid is reduced to syrup, stirring occasionally, about 20 minutes. Mix in grapes. Cool compote to room temperature. Discard whole cloves and cinnamon sticks. Cover tightly and chill.

DO AHEAD *Can be made 3 days ahead. Keep chilled.*

SPOON compote into stemmed goblets and serve.

Spiced fig preserves

MAKES ABOUT 3⅓ CUPS *If you have a fig tree, this is a great way to use up a summer bumper crop. The spices and lemon make this delicious on everything from toast to crepes to pancakes; you could even try it like a chutney with roast duck or pork. Make a full batch and give a jar or two as gifts, or halve the recipe for a two-week supply.*

½ lemon (unpeeled), thickly sliced, seeded
1½ pounds fresh ripe figs, halved (about 4 cups)
2¼ cups sugar
1 cinnamon stick
2¼ teaspoons minced peeled fresh ginger
⅛ teaspoon ground cloves

FINELY chop lemon in processor. Add figs. Using on/off turns, process until figs are coarsely pureed. Transfer mixture to heavy large saucepan. Add sugar, cinnamon stick, ginger, and cloves. Simmer until mixture thickens to jam consistency, stirring often, about 20 minutes. Discard cinnamon stick.

TRANSFER mixture to clean jars. Cover tightly and chill until cold.

DO AHEAD *Can be made 2 weeks ahead. Keep chilled.*

GET FIGGY WITH IT Fresh figs are available in markets (and backyards everywhere) throughout the summer months and into early fall. Ripe figs will be plump, sometimes with split skins. Whether you grow your own or shop for them, you'll likely be working with one of three types: Calimyrna, a green-skinned variety with white flesh; the deep purple Mission fig; or the green-skinned, raspberry-fleshed Kadota. Any of them would be lovely in this recipe, but the purple Mission figs will produce the "figgiest"-looking preserves.

Warm berry preserves

MAKES ABOUT 3½ CUPS *This recipe couldn't be easier. It requires a little lead time (start it a couple of hours ahead), but the active time is only about 10 minutes. Keep frozen berries in your freezer and this can be made on a whim at any time of year. It's delicious warm on toast or crepes, but it can also be chilled and served cold.*

  1 **1-pound bag frozen unsweetened strawberries**
  1 **1-pound bag frozen unsweetened mixed berries**
 ⅔ **cup red currant jelly**
 ⅓ **cup sugar**

MIX all ingredients in large nonstick skillet. Let stand until berries thaw and mixture is juicy, stirring occasionally and breaking strawberries into smaller pieces with spoon, about 2 hours.

BOIL until mixture thickens but is still chunky, stirring frequently, about 7 minutes.

DO AHEAD *Can be made 3 days ahead. Cover and chill. Rewarm over medium heat, stirring frequently.*

Cranberry-orange preserves

MAKES 3 CUPS *Try this tart jam on pumpkin bread, pancakes, or even on a turkey or ham sandwich. Fresh cranberries are available in the produce section around Thanksgiving. To guarantee that you can make this all year long, buy a few bags of fresh cranberries in the fall and keep them in the freezer until you need them.*

 ¾ **cup orange juice**
 ½ **cup sugar**
  2 **cups fresh or frozen cranberries**
  2 **cups orange marmalade**
 ¾ **cup dried cranberries**
  1 **tablespoon finely grated orange peel**
  1 **teaspoon finely grated lemon peel**
 ¼ **teaspoon ground cloves**

STIR juice and sugar in medium saucepan over medium-high heat until sugar dissolves. Add all remaining ingredients and bring to boil. Reduce heat to medium; simmer until mixture is reduced to 3 cups, stirring occasionally, about 15 minutes. Cool.

DO AHEAD *Can be made 1 week ahead. Cover and chill.*

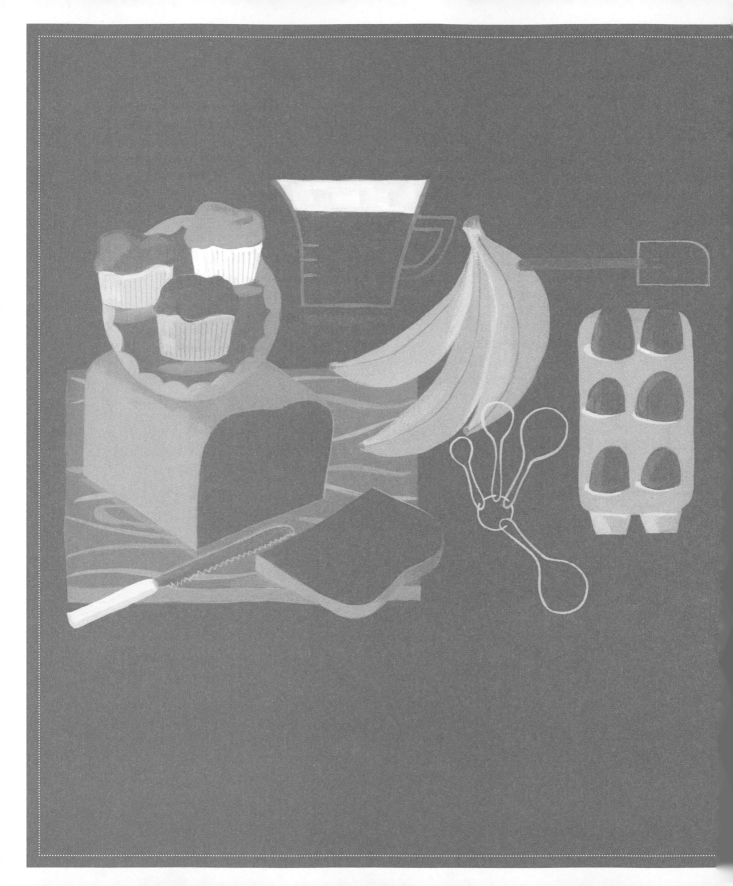

quickbreads

SCONES AND MUFFINS

Meyer Lemon and Dried
Blueberry Scones

Lemon-Scented Thumbprint
Scones with Berry Jam Filling

Chocolate Chip and Ginger
Heart-Shaped Scones

Maple Tea Scones

Walnut, Golden Raisin, and
Fennel Seed Scones

Banana-Macadamia Nut Muffins

Giant Pumpkin Muffins with
Molasses-Ginger Glaze

Old-Fashioned Blueberry Muffins

Honey Bran Muffins with Figs

Poppy Seed-Almond Muffins

Mocha Muffins with Chocolate
Chips and Pecans

Popovers with Gruyère

LOAF BREADS AND CORNBREAD

Best Ever Banana Bread

Spiced Pumpkin Bread

Glazed Lemon Bread

Cinnamon Swirl Coffee Cake

Mini Walnut Soda Breads

White Soda Bread

Buttery Cornbread

Buttermilk Cornbread with
Monterey Jack Cheese

Chipotle Cornbread

Blue Cheese Cornbread

Double-Corn and Cheese Muffins

Virginia Spoon Bread

ROLLS, BUNS, AND BISCUITS

Petits Pains Au Chocolat

Quick Sticky Buns

Prosciutto Crescent Rolls

Sweet-Cream Biscuits

Three-Cheese Drop Biscuits

Green-Onion Biscuits

Buttermilk Biscuits

Sage and Pancetta Biscuits
with Fontina Cheese

SAVORY BREADS

Parsley-Pepper Skillet Bread

Three-Cheese Garlic Bread

Zucchini, Red Onion, and
Two-Cheese Flatbread

Pesto and Cheese French Bread

Fig Focaccia with
Gorgonzola Cheese

Onion and Poppy Seed Focaccia

Curry Naan

Herbed Peasant Bread

Shallot Bruschetta

Grilled Bread with Olive Oil

Grilled Olive Bread with
Garlic-Fennel Butter

tool kit Quick breads are a great way to have delicious homemade breads in a hurry—they take minutes to put together, unlike yeast breads, which can take hours just to rise. A few essential bakers' tips will ensure that these quick breads will be rich in flavor and light in texture.

Preheat the oven and prepare the pans before you begin to measure and mix ingredients. Because the baking powder in quick breads will begin leavening the batter as soon as the wet ingredients are added, the breads should be baked as soon as the batter is mixed. Measure the ingredients carefully: In baking, accurate measurements are crucial in order to get the best results. For dry ingredients, use the "scoop and level" technique: Dip your measuring cup or spoon into the sack, box, or jar; scoop out a rounded cupful or spoonful; and use a straight edge to level it off. For wet ingredients, place the liquid measuring cup on a flat surface, let the liquid settle, and then read the measurement at eye level.

Make sure you have fresh (unexpired) baking soda and baking powder on hand—these are the key elements that leaven quick breads.

Use all purpose flour for tender, moist, light breads. Bread flour has more gluten-forming protein, and when gluten is developed it will give these cake-like breads a tough, heavy texture.

Whisk or sift all the dry ingredients together so that they are evenly distributed and less mixing of the dough will be necessary.

Do not overmix the batter or overknead the dough—the less the flour is handled, the more delicate the breads will be.

JUST FOR MUFFINS

Use room-temperature or melted butter (or vegetable oil) to mix with the other ingredients; this will result in moist, light muffins.

Bake the batter immediately to avoid loss of volume.

Use an ice cream scoop to spoon batter into muffin cups evenly and easily.

Test for doneness by inserting a skewer into the center of the muffins. The skewer should come out clean or with just a few flecks of crumbs attached.

Once the muffins finish baking, let them cool in their pans for about 10 minutes so that they firm up a bit and can be removed without breaking. Finish cooling them on a rack to avoid steaming in the pans and becoming soggy.

Turn zucchini bread, banana bread, cornbread, and gingerbread into muffins—they make great single-serving treats and the cooking time is shorter.

JUST FOR SCONES AND BISCUITS

Use chilled butter to cut or rub into the flour; this results in tender, flaky biscuits and scones.

Steam helps these breads rise, so make sure the dough is moist. Use floured hands and cutters to prevent the dough from sticking.

When done, biscuits and scones should be puffed and golden brown on the top and bottom.

531

SCONESANDMUFFINS

Meyer lemon and dried blueberry scones

MAKES 12 *Meyer lemons are sweeter than regular lemons, making them great for baking. They have a smooth peel that ranges in color from deep yellow to orange-yellow, and are available at some supermarkets and at specialty foods stores from November through May. Look for dried wild blueberries or regular dried blueberries at some supermarkets, specialty foods stores, and Trader Joe's markets. Dried currants make a good substitute.*

    3 cups self-rising flour
    ½ cup plus 1½ tablespoons sugar
    ¾ cup (1½ sticks) chilled unsalted
       butter, cut into small cubes
   1½ cups dried wild blueberries (about 10 ounces)
    1 cup plus 1 tablespoon buttermilk
   1½ tablespoons finely grated Meyer lemon
       peel or regular lemon peel

POSITION rack in top third of oven and preheat to 425°F. Line large baking sheet with parchment paper. Whisk flour and ½ cup sugar in large bowl. Using fingertips, rub in butter until pieces are size of small peas. Add dried blueberries and toss to coat. Mix 1 cup buttermilk and lemon peel in glass measuring cup. Pour buttermilk mixture into dry ingredients and stir until dough begins to form (some of flour will not be incorporated). Transfer dough to lightly floured work surface and gather together.

Knead dough briefly, about 5 turns. Divide dough in half. Form each dough half into ball and flatten into 1-inch-thick disk. Cut each disk into 6 wedges.

TRANSFER scones to prepared baking sheet, spacing 1 inch apart. Brush tops with remaining 1 tablespoon buttermilk and sprinkle with remaining 1½ tablespoons sugar. Bake until scones are golden brown on top and toothpick inserted into center comes out clean, about 25 minutes. Cool slightly. Serve warm or at room temperature.

MORE TO TRY This is a versatile recipe: Pretty much any citrus peel and dried fruit can be used—try orange peel with dried tart cherries or lime peel with dried cranberries.

Lemon-scented thumbprint scones with berry jam filling

MAKES ABOUT 12 *These pretty lemon-flavored scones are filled with bright berry jam and drizzled with a lemon glaze. Use a few different preserves to create a colorful mix of scones. Orange marmalade also makes a great thumbprint filling.*

- 2 lemons
- ½ cup sugar
- 2 cups unbleached all purpose flour
- 2 teaspoons baking powder
- ¾ teaspoon salt
- ½ teaspoon baking soda
- ½ cup (1 stick) chilled unsalted butter, cut into small cubes
- ¼ cup chilled buttermilk

- 12 teaspoons assorted berry preserves (such as raspberry, blackberry, and blueberry)

- ¾ cup powdered sugar

PREHEAT oven to 400°F. Line heavy large baking sheet with parchment paper or silicone baking mat. Using sharp vegetable peeler, remove peel (yellow part only) from lemons. Squeeze enough juice from lemons to measure 3 tablespoons and set juice aside. Blend ½ cup sugar and lemon peel in processor until peel is very finely chopped. Add flour, baking powder, salt, and baking soda; pulse to blend, scraping down sugar from sides of processor bowl. Add butter. Using on/off turns, pulse until mixture resembles coarse meal. Stir buttermilk and 2 tablespoons of reserved lemon juice in small bowl; pour over flour mixture and pulse just until dough forms.

TRANSFER dough to lightly floured work surface and knead just until dough comes together. Pat out to ¾-inch-thick round. Using 2-inch-diameter biscuit or cookie cutter, cut out scones. Gather dough scraps; press out to ¾-inch-thick round and cut out additional scones, forming about 12 scones total. Transfer scones to prepared baking sheet, spacing evenly apart.

PRESS back of teaspoon into center of each scone, creating indentation. Spoon 1 teaspoon preserves into each indentation. Bake scones until golden, about 20 minutes. Transfer scones to rack and cool slightly.

MEANWHILE, stir powdered sugar and remaining 1 tablespoon reserved lemon juice in small bowl to blend. Drizzle lemon icing around preserves on scones and cool.

Chocolate chip and ginger heart-shaped scones

MAKES ABOUT 15 *The perfect Valentine's Day break-fast, these scones are delicious warm or at room tem-perature. Diced crystallized ginger adds a bit of spice; you'll find it in the spice aisle and sometimes in the Asian foods section of the supermarket. Raw sugar, also called turbinado or demerara sugar, is avail-able in the baking aisle of most supermarkets and at natural foods stores.*

- 2 cups all purpose flour
- ⅓ cup sugar
- 1 tablespoon baking powder
- ¼ teaspoon salt
- 6 tablespoons (¾ stick) chilled unsalted butter, cut into small cubes
- 1 cup semisweet chocolate chips
- ½ cup diced crystallized ginger
- 1 cup plus 2 tablespoons chilled heavy whipping cream
- 2 tablespoons raw sugar

POSITION rack in center of oven and preheat to 400°F. Line heavy large baking sheet with parch-ment paper or silicone baking mat. Whisk first 4 ingredients in large bowl to blend. Add butter and rub in with fingertips until coarse meal forms. Stir in chocolate chips and ginger. Drizzle 1 cup cream over and toss to form soft dough. Gather dough together and transfer to lightly floured work surface. Press out dough to ½-inch thickness.

USING floured 3-inch heart-shaped cookie cutter, cut out scones. Gather scraps, press out dough to ½-inch thickness, and cut out additional scones. Transfer to prepared baking sheet, spacing evenly apart. Brush tops of scones lightly with remaining 2 tablespoons cream and sprinkle with raw sugar. Bake until scones are golden brown, about 18 minutes. Transfer to rack and cool slightly. Serve warm or at room temperature.

Maple tea scones

MAKES 8 *For the best maple flavor, use Grade B maple syrup. It's darker and more flavorful than Grade A.*

- 3 cups all purpose flour
- 4 tablespoons (packed) dark brown sugar, divided
- 1½ teaspoons baking powder
- ½ teaspoon baking soda
- ½ teaspoon salt
- ¾ cup (1½ sticks) chilled unsalted butter, cut into small cubes
- ½ cup (or more) plus 6 tablespoons heavy whipping cream
- ½ cup plus 2 tablespoons pure maple syrup
- ⅔ cup (about) powdered sugar

PREHEAT oven to 375°F. Whisk flour, 2 tablespoons brown sugar, baking powder, baking soda, and salt in large bowl to blend. Add butter and rub in with fingertips until mixture resembles coarse meal. Stir ½ cup whipping cream and ½ cup maple syrup in small bowl to blend. Gradually add cream mixture to flour mixture, stirring just until dough comes together and adding more cream by tablespoonfuls if dough is dry. Turn dough out onto lightly floured work surface. Knead dough gently just until smooth, about 5 turns. Using floured hands, pat out dough to 8-inch round; cut dough into 8 wedges. Transfer wedges to baking sheet, spacing 2 inches apart.

BAKE scones until golden and tester inserted into center comes out clean, about 20 minutes. Transfer to rack.

MEANWHILE, whisk remaining 2 tablespoons brown sugar, 6 tablespoons whipping cream, and 2 tablespoons maple syrup in medium bowl to blend. Gradually whisk in enough powdered sugar to form thick glaze.

DRIZZLE or spread glaze over warm scones. Let stand until glaze sets.

Walnut, golden raisin, and fennel seed scones

MAKES 12 *Fennel seeds give these simple scones a sophisticated flavor. The dough is just shaped into disks and cut into wedges, so the scones can be ready in less than half an hour.*

- 2　cups all purpose flour
- ⅓　cup sugar
- 2　teaspoons baking powder
- ½　teaspoon salt
- 6　tablespoons (¾ stick) chilled unsalted butter, cut into small cubes
- 2　large egg yolks
- ½　cup chilled buttermilk
- ½　cup golden raisins
- ⅓　cup chopped toasted walnuts
- 1　tablespoon fennel seeds
- 1　large egg, beaten to blend with 1 tablespoon water (for glaze)

PREHEAT oven to 400°F. Butter large baking sheet. Whisk flour, sugar, baking powder, and salt in large bowl to blend. Add butter and rub in with fingertips until mixture resembles coarse meal. Whisk egg yolks and buttermilk in small bowl to blend. Stir egg mixture into flour mixture, then stir in raisins, walnuts, and fennel seeds. Turn dough out onto lightly floured work surface and knead gently just until smooth, about 4 turns. Divide dough in half; pat each half into 6-inch round. Cut each round into 6 wedges. Transfer scones to prepared baking sheet, spacing evenly apart. Brush scones with egg glaze. Bake until scones are light brown, about 17 minutes. Serve warm or at room temperature.

Banana-macadamia nut muffins

MAKES 12 *Macadamia nuts give these moist and flavorful muffins a tropical twist—and a crunchy topping. Store macadamia nuts in the freezer so they'll keep longer.*

- 1½　cups unbleached all purpose flour
- 1½　teaspoons baking soda
- ¼　teaspoon salt
- ⅛　teaspoon ground nutmeg
- 1¼　cups mashed ripe bananas (about 3 large)
- ½　cup sugar
- ¼　cup (packed) dark brown sugar
- ½　cup (1 stick) unsalted butter, melted
- ¼　cup whole milk
- 1　large egg
- 1　cup unsalted macadamia nuts, toasted, chopped, divided

PREHEAT oven to 350°F. Butter 12 muffin cups or line with paper liners. Sift first 4 ingredients into large bowl. Stir bananas, both sugars, melted butter, milk, and egg in medium bowl to blend. Mix into dry ingredients. Fold in ½ cup macadamia nuts. Divide batter among prepared muffin cups. Sprinkle tops of muffins with remaining ½ cup macadamia nuts. Bake until muffins are golden brown and tester inserted into center comes out clean, about 25 minutes. Transfer muffins to rack and cool.

Giant pumpkin muffins with molasses-ginger glaze

MAKES 6 GIANT MUFFINS OR 18 STANDARD MUFFINS

These are the perfect fall muffins—like pumpkin pie in muffin form, with a delicious molasses glaze and a sprinkling of chopped crystallized ginger on top.

	Nonstick vegetable oil spray
2¾	cups all purpose flour
2	teaspoons ground ginger
1½	teaspoons baking soda
1	teaspoon salt
1	cup sugar
½	cup canola oil
3	large eggs
1	15-ounce can pure pumpkin
½	cup plus 1 tablespoon mild-flavored (light) molasses
½	cup buttermilk
½	cup chopped crystallized ginger, divided
1½	cups powdered sugar
1½	tablespoons (or more) water

PREHEAT oven to 350°F. Spray 6 giant (1¼-cup) muffin cups or 18 standard (⅓-cup) muffin cups with nonstick spray. Sift flour, ginger, baking soda, and salt into medium bowl. Using electric mixer, beat 1 cup sugar and oil in large bowl to blend. Beat in eggs 1 at a time, blending well after each addition. Beat in pumpkin, ½ cup molasses, buttermilk, and ¼ cup crystallized ginger. Stir in flour mixture until just blended.

DIVIDE batter among prepared muffin cups. Bake muffins until tester inserted into center comes out clean, about 40 minutes for giant muffins and 30 minutes for standard muffins. Transfer muffins to rack; cool completely.

WHISK powdered sugar, 1½ tablespoons water, and remaining 1 tablespoon molasses in medium bowl, adding more water as needed to form thick glaze. Dip muffin tops in glaze; transfer to rack, allowing glaze to drip down sides. Sprinkle with remaining ¼ cup crystallized ginger. Let stand until glaze is set, about 1 hour.

Old-fashioned blueberry muffins

MAKES 12 *Grated orange peel gives fresh flavor to these classic breakfast treats, which would also be delicious made with fresh or frozen raspberries.*

- 1 **cup whole milk**
- ½ **cup (1 stick) unsalted butter**
- 1½ **teaspoons finely grated orange peel**
- 1 **teaspoon vanilla extract**
- 2 **large eggs**

- 2 **cups unbleached all purpose flour**
- ¾ **cup sugar**
- 2½ **teaspoons baking powder**
- ¾ **teaspoon salt**
- 1⅓ **cups fresh blueberries or unthawed frozen blueberries**

PREHEAT oven to 400°F. Line 12 muffin cups with paper liners. Combine first 4 ingredients in heavy small saucepan. Stir over medium heat until butter melts. Cool until mixture is just slightly warm to touch. Whisk in eggs.

SIFT flour, sugar, baking powder, and salt into large bowl. Add milk mixture and stir just until blended. Fold in blueberries. Divide batter among prepared muffin cups. Bake until golden and tester inserted into center of muffins comes out clean, about 20 minutes. Transfer to racks and cool.

Honey bran muffins with figs

MAKES 24 *A light texture and honey-sweet flavor make these fiber-rich muffins taste like something much more sinful.*

- 2½ **cups all purpose flour**
- 2 **teaspoons baking soda**
- 1½ **teaspoons salt**
- 2 **cups toasted wheat bran (about 4 ounces)**
- ¾ **cup chopped dried figs**
- 1 **cup boiling water**

- ½ **cup (1 stick) unsalted butter, room temperature**
- 1 **cup sugar**
- ½ **cup honey**
- 2 **large eggs**
- 2 **cups buttermilk**

PREHEAT oven to 400°F. Line 24 muffin cups with paper liners. Whisk flour, baking soda, and salt in small bowl to blend. Combine bran and figs in another small bowl; mix in 1 cup boiling water.

BEAT butter in large bowl until smooth. Gradually beat in sugar, then honey. Beat in eggs 1 at a time. Beat in buttermilk alternately with flour mixture in 3 additions each. Mix in bran mixture. Divide batter among prepared muffin cups.

BAKE muffins until tester inserted into center comes out clean, about 20 minutes. Turn muffins out onto racks and cool completely.

Poppy seed-almond muffins

MAKES 12 *To turn these into lemon–poppy seed muffins, replace the almonds and almond extract with 2 teaspoons or more finely grated lemon peel.*

1¾ cups all purpose flour
¼ cup poppy seeds
½ teaspoon salt
¼ teaspoon baking soda
½ cup (1 stick) unsalted butter, room temperature
1 cup sugar
2 large eggs
¾ cup buttermilk
1 teaspoon almond extract
1 cup sliced almonds, divided

PREHEAT oven to 375°F. Butter 12 muffin cups or line with paper liners. Whisk flour, poppy seeds, salt, and baking soda in small bowl to blend. Using electric mixer, beat butter and sugar in medium bowl until thick and light. Beat in eggs 1 at a time. Mix in buttermilk and almond extract. Gradually beat in dry ingredients. Stir in ½ cup almonds.

SPOON batter into prepared muffin cups. Sprinkle remaining ½ cup almonds over muffins. Bake muffins until tester inserted in center comes out clean, about 20 minutes. Cool 5 minutes in muffin cups. Transfer muffins to rack and cool completely.

Mocha muffins with chocolate chips and pecans

MAKES 12 *These double-chocolate, pecan, and coffee muffins are a decadent start to the day—not that there's anything wrong with that. They're the perfect accompaniment to your morning cup of joe.*

¾ cup buttermilk
1 tablespoon instant espresso powder
½ cup vegetable oil
2 large eggs
1 teaspoon vanilla extract
1¾ cups all purpose flour
1 cup (packed) golden brown sugar
3 tablespoons unsweetened cocoa powder
1 teaspoon baking powder
1 teaspoon baking soda
1 teaspoon salt
1½ cups milk chocolate chips
1 cup coarsely chopped toasted pecans (about 4 ounces)

PREHEAT oven to 375°F. Line 12 muffin cups with paper liners. Stir buttermilk and espresso powder in medium bowl until espresso powder dissolves. Whisk in oil, eggs, and vanilla. Whisk flour, brown sugar, cocoa, baking powder, baking soda, and salt in large bowl to blend. Add buttermilk mixture and stir just until combined. Stir in chocolate chips and chopped pecans.

DIVIDE batter among prepared muffin cups. Bake until tester inserted into center of muffins comes out clean, about 25 minutes. Transfer muffins to rack and cool.

Popovers with Gruyère

MAKES 16 *A popover is a light, muffin-shaped bread that gets nicely crisp and browned on the outside, and remains moist and airy on the inside. Preheating the muffin tins in the oven ensures that the popovers are extra crispy.*

    2 cups all purpose flour
 1¼ teaspoons salt
    2 cups whole milk
    4 large eggs

        Nonstick vegetable oil spray
 1½ cups grated Gruyère cheese (about 6 ounces)

PLACE one 12-cup muffin pan and one 6-cup muffin pan in oven. Preheat oven to 350°F. Whisk flour and salt in medium bowl to blend. Heat milk in heavy small saucepan over medium heat until very warm, about 125°F. Whisk eggs in large bowl to blend. Gradually whisk warm milk into eggs. Gradually stir flour mixture into milk mixture just to blend (batter may still be slightly lumpy).

REMOVE hot muffin pans from oven. Spray pans with nonstick spray. Spoon ¼ cup batter into each of 16 muffin cups. Top each with 1½ tablespoons cheese. Bake until puffed and deep brown, about 40 minutes. Remove popovers from pan and serve immediately.

SWISS CHEESE Gruyère is a wonderfully rich and nutty cow's-milk cheese from Switzerland. It's available at most supermarkets and at specialty foods stores and cheese shops.

LOAFBREADSAND CORNBREAD

Best ever banana bread

MAKES 1 LOAF *Here's a great use for very ripe bananas. The walnuts can be omitted—or replaced with pecans—if you prefer. Try a warm slice with orange-zest cream cheese on top.*

    2 ripe medium bananas, mashed
    2 large eggs
 1¾ cups all purpose flour
 1½ cups sugar
    1 cup chopped walnuts
  ½ cup vegetable oil
  ¼ cup plus 1 tablespoon buttermilk
    1 teaspoon baking soda
    1 teaspoon vanilla extract
  ½ teaspoon salt

PREHEAT oven to 325°F. Butter and flour 9×5×3-inch metal loaf pan. Whisk bananas and eggs in large bowl to blend. Add all remaining ingredients and stir to blend well. Transfer batter to prepared pan. Bake bread until top is golden brown and splits slightly and tester inserted into center comes out clean, about 1 hour 20 minutes. Cool in pan on rack 20 minutes. Turn bread out onto rack and cool slightly. Serve warm or at room temperature.

ONE AT A TIME This recipe doesn't double well. To make two loaves, you'll need to make two separate batches of batter.

Spiced pumpkin bread

MAKES 2 LOAVES *Because this recipe makes two loaves, you can keep one loaf and give the other to a friend. Or wrap one in foil, then enclose in a resealable plastic bag and freeze it for up to a month. If desired, the ground cloves, cinnamon, and nutmeg can be replaced with 1 tablespoon of pumpkin pie spice, which contains cinnamon, nutmeg, ginger, and allspice.*

    3 cups all purpose flour
    1 teaspoon ground cloves
    1 teaspoon ground cinnamon
    1 teaspoon ground nutmeg
    1 teaspoon baking soda
  ½ teaspoon salt
  ½ teaspoon baking powder
    3 cups sugar
    1 cup vegetable oil
    3 large eggs
    1 15-ounce can pure pumpkin
    1 cup coarsely chopped walnuts (optional)

PREHEAT oven to 350°F. Butter and flour two 9×5×3-inch metal loaf pans. Sift first 7 ingredients into large bowl. Beat sugar and oil in another large bowl to blend. Mix in eggs and pumpkin. Stir dry ingredients into pumpkin mixture in 2 additions just until blended. Mix in walnuts, if desired.

DIVIDE batter between prepared pans. Bake breads until tester inserted into center comes out clean, about 1 hour 10 minutes. Transfer to racks and cool in pans 10 minutes. Using knife, cut around sides of loaves to loosen. Turn loaves out onto rack and cool completely.

Glazed lemon bread

MAKES 1 LOAF *This is a great breakfast or afternoon treat—and would make a nice hostess gift, too. The lemon glaze soaks into the bread, which becomes very moist. If you want more tartness in the bread, add a little lemon juice (about 2 tablespoons) to the batter and increase the lemon peel to 1 tablespoon.*

1⅔ cups all purpose flour
1 teaspoon baking powder
½ teaspoon salt
1½ cups sugar, divided
½ cup (1 stick) unsalted butter, room temperature
2 large eggs
2 teaspoons finely grated lemon peel
½ cup whole milk

¼ cup fresh lemon juice

PREHEAT oven to 350°F. Lightly butter 8½×4½×2½-inch metal loaf pan. Whisk flour, baking powder, and salt in medium bowl to blend. Using electric mixer, beat 1 cup sugar and butter in large bowl until light and fluffy. Beat in eggs 1 at a time. Mix in lemon peel. Beat in dry ingredients alternately with milk in 3 additions each. Transfer batter to prepared pan. Bake until tester inserted into center of bread comes out clean, about 1 hour.

MEANWHILE, combine remaining ½ cup sugar and lemon juice in heavy small saucepan and stir over low heat until sugar dissolves.

TRANSFER bread in pan to rack. Pierce top of bread all over with wooden skewer. Gradually spoon lemon glaze over hot bread, adding more as glaze is absorbed. Cool lemon bread completely in pan on rack.

DO AHEAD *Can be made 1 day ahead. Turn bread out onto rack. Wrap loosely in foil and store at room temperature.*

Cinnamon swirl coffee cake

12 SERVINGS *Here's the ultimate coffee cake, perfect for breakfast, afternoon tea, or a casual dessert. The cinnamon-sugar swirl has some cocoa powder for added flavor and chopped walnuts for a bit of crunch.*

1¾ cups sugar, divided
½ cup chopped toasted walnuts
1 tablespoon ground cinnamon
1 tablespoon unsweetened cocoa powder
3 cups all purpose flour
1 tablespoon baking powder
¾ teaspoon salt

¾ cup (1½ sticks) unsalted butter, room temperature
4 large eggs
1 tablespoon vanilla extract
1 cup whole milk

PREHEAT oven to 350°F. Butter 10-inch-diameter angel food cake pan with 4-inch-high sides; dust with flour. Mix ½ cup sugar, walnuts, cinnamon, and cocoa powder in small bowl. Sift flour, baking powder, and salt into medium bowl.

USING electric mixer, beat butter in large bowl until smooth. Gradually beat in remaining 1¼ cups sugar. Beat in eggs 1 at a time, then vanilla. Mix in dry ingredients in 3 additions alternately with milk in 2 additions. Spoon ⅓ of batter into prepared pan. Sprinkle with half of walnut mixture. Top with half of remaining batter, then remaining walnut mixture and remaining batter. Using knife, cut through batter to swirl walnut mixture.

BAKE cake until tester inserted near center comes out clean, about 55 minutes. Cool cake in pan on rack.

DO AHEAD *Can be made 1 day ahead. Cover pan with foil and store at room temperature.*

CUT around pan sides and center tube to loosen cake. Turn cake out; transfer cake, round side up, to plate.

Mini walnut soda breads

MAKES 6 *Spread with butter and jam, these make a great teatime treat. They can also be served with slices of aged white cheddar or paired with a main-course salad.*

- 2 **cups whole wheat flour**
- 1 **cup unbleached all purpose flour**
- ¼ **cup (packed) dark brown sugar**
- 1 **teaspoon baking soda**
- 1 **teaspoon salt**
- ¼ **cup (½ stick) chilled unsalted butter, cut into small cubes**
- 1 **cup walnuts, toasted, chopped**
- 1 **cup chilled buttermilk**
- 1 **large egg**
- 2 **tablespoons mild-flavored (light) molasses**

PREHEAT oven to 375°F. Lightly flour large baking sheet. Whisk first 5 ingredients in large bowl to blend well. Add butter and rub in with fingertips until mixture resembles coarse meal. Mix in walnuts. Whisk buttermilk, egg, and molasses in small bowl to blend. Gradually add buttermilk mixture to flour mixture, stirring until medium-firm dough forms. Turn dough out onto lightly floured work surface. Knead just until dough comes together, about 6 turns. Flatten dough into disk. Cut into 6 wedges. Shape each wedge into ball. Place on prepared sheet, spacing evenly apart. Flatten each to 3-inch round. Using sharp knife, cut shallow X in top of each round.

BAKE soda breads until golden brown and tester inserted into center comes out clean, about 30 minutes. Transfer to rack. Serve warm or at room temperature.

FLOUR POWER Whole wheat flour is higher in fiber and nutrients than all purpose flour. It also has more fat, so it should be stored in the refrigerator or freezer to avoid spoiling.

White soda bread

MAKES 1 LOAF *This traditional Irish bread gets its name from the baking soda that makes it rise. Caraway seeds give the bread a light anise flavor. Dried currants can also be mixed into the dough.*

- 3½ **cups all purpose flour**
- 2 **tablespoons caraway seeds (optional)**
- 1 **teaspoon baking soda**
- ¾ **teaspoon salt**
- 1½ **cups (about) buttermilk**

PREHEAT oven to 425°F. Lightly flour baking sheet. Mix flour, caraway seeds, if desired, baking soda, and salt in large bowl. Mix in enough buttermilk to form moist clumps. Gather dough into ball. Turn out onto lightly floured work surface and knead just until dough holds together, about 1 minute. Shape dough into 6-inch-diameter round, about 2 inches high. Place on prepared baking sheet. Cut 1-inch-deep X in top of dough round, extending almost to edges. Bake bread until golden brown, loaf sounds hollow when tapped on bottom, and tester inserted into center comes out clean, about 35 minutes. Transfer bread to rack and cool completely.

Buttery cornbread

MAKES 1 LOAF *This would be delicious served with honey butter or used for Thanksgiving stuffing.*

1⅓ cups coarse stone-ground yellow cornmeal
1 cup unbleached all purpose flour
¼ cup sugar
2 teaspoons baking powder
¾ teaspoon coarse kosher salt
1 cup plus 2 tablespoons buttermilk
9 tablespoons (1 stick plus 1 tablespoon) unsalted butter, melted
1 large egg plus 1 large egg yolk, beaten to blend

BUTTER 9×5×3-inch metal loaf pan. Mix cornmeal, flour, sugar, baking powder, and coarse salt in large bowl. Add buttermilk, melted butter, and beaten eggs. Stir with wooden spoon until well blended. Let mixture stand 30 minutes to absorb liquid. Meanwhile, preheat oven to 375°F.

TRANSFER batter to prepared pan. Bake bread until browned around edges and tester inserted into center comes out clean, about 40 minutes. Cool bread in pan 5 minutes. Turn bread out onto rack and cool completely.

DO AHEAD *Can be made 2 days ahead. Wrap in foil and store at room temperature.*

Buttermilk cornbread with Monterey Jack cheese

MAKES ONE 8-INCH SQUARE CORNBREAD *A little firmer and denser than regular cornbread, this one is perfect for toasting. Or cut thick slices, brush them with oil, and put them on the grill for one minute per side.*

1 cup all purpose flour
1 cup yellow cornmeal
2 teaspoons baking soda
1 teaspoon baking powder
1 teaspoon salt
½ cup (packed) coarsely grated Monterey Jack cheese (about 2 ounces)
¾ cup buttermilk
2 large eggs
3 tablespoons honey
¼ cup (½ stick) unsalted butter, melted

PREHEAT oven to 425°F. Butter 8×8×2-inch metal baking pan. Whisk first 5 ingredients in medium bowl to blend. Stir in cheese. Whisk buttermilk, eggs, and honey in another medium bowl to blend. Add melted butter; whisk until blended. Add buttermilk mixture to dry ingredients; stir just until combined (do not overmix).

TRANSFER batter to prepared pan. Bake until tester inserted into center of bread comes out clean, about 15 minutes. Cool completely in pan on rack.

DO AHEAD *Can be made 1 day ahead. Cover and store at room temperature.*

Chipotle cornbread

MAKES 1 LOAF *This recipe gets subtle heat from chipotle chiles—dried smoked jalapeños canned in a spicy tomato sauce called adobo. Canned chipotles can be found at some supermarkets and at specialty foods stores and Latin markets.*

- 1 cup yellow cornmeal
- 1 cup all purpose flour
- ¼ cup sugar
- 2 teaspoons baking powder
- 1 teaspoon baking soda
- 1 teaspoon salt
- 1 cup grated Monterey Jack cheese (about 4 ounces)
- 1 cup buttermilk
- 3 large eggs
- 6 tablespoons (¾ stick) unsalted butter, melted, cooled
- 2 tablespoons minced canned chipotle chiles

PREHEAT oven to 375°F. Butter 9×5×2½-inch metal loaf pan. Mix first 6 ingredients in large bowl. Stir in cheese. Whisk buttermilk, eggs, melted butter, and chipotles in medium bowl. Add buttermilk mixture to dry ingredients; stir until blended. Spoon batter into prepared pan. Bake bread until tester inserted into center comes out clean, about 35 minutes. Cool in pan on rack 15 minutes. Turn bread out onto rack and cool completely.

Blue cheese cornbread

6 SERVINGS *Cornbread mix gets a kick from crumbled blue cheese. To make this recipe even easier, look for already-crumbled blue cheese, available at most supermarkets.*

- ⅓ cup whole milk
- 1 large egg
- 1 8.5-ounce box corn muffin mix
- ½ cup crumbled blue cheese (about 2 ounces)
- 2 green onions, chopped
- 1 teaspoon freshly ground black pepper

PREHEAT oven to 350°F. Butter 8×8×2-inch metal baking pan. Whisk milk and egg in medium bowl to blend. Add all remaining ingredients and stir until blended. Spread batter in prepared pan. Bake until firm to touch and golden brown and tester inserted into center comes out clean, about 30 minutes. Cool slightly. Cut into squares and serve warm.

Double-corn and cheese muffins

MAKES 8 *Frozen corn kernels, shredded cheese, and fresh basil transform a simple boxed corn muffin mix. Bags of already-grated mixed Italian cheeses are available at most supermarkets, in the deli case where other cheeses are sold. They sometimes contain a mixture of mozzarella, Parmesan, Romano, and Asiago cheeses.*

⅓ **cup whole milk**

1 **large egg**

1 **8.5-ounce box corn muffin mix**

⅓ **cup (packed) grated Italian cheese mix or mozzarella cheese**

⅓ **cup frozen corn kernels, thawed**

3 **tablespoons chopped fresh basil**

PREHEAT oven to 400°F. Line 8 muffin cups with paper liners. Whisk milk and egg in large bowl. Add remaining ingredients and stir until just moistened (do not overmix). Divide batter among prepared muffin cups.

BAKE muffins until golden and tester inserted into center comes out clean, about 20 minutes. Serve muffins warm.

Virginia spoon bread

4 SERVINGS *Spoon bread is a southern specialty—a cornmeal-based side dish that's so soft and creamy it's more like a soufflé than a bread. It would be delicious served with ham.*

2 **cups water**

1 **cup yellow cornmeal**

¼ **cup (½ stick) unsalted butter, room temperature**

¾ **cup whole milk**

1 **teaspoon salt**

¼ **teaspoon freshly ground black pepper**

3 **large eggs, separated**

PREHEAT oven to 400°F. Butter 6-cup soufflé dish. Bring water to boil in heavy medium saucepan. Gradually add cornmeal and whisk over medium heat until mixture is very thick, about 1 minute. Remove from heat. Mix in butter, then milk, salt, and pepper. Cool 10 minutes. Mix in egg yolks. Using electric mixer, beat egg whites in medium bowl until stiff but not dry. Fold whites into lukewarm cornmeal mixture in 2 additions.

TRANSFER batter to prepared dish. Bake until puffed, golden on top, and set in center, about 45 minutes. Serve hot.

ROLLS, BUNS, AND BISCUITS

Petits pains au chocolat

MAKES 24 *Here's a quick version of the French choco-late-filled pastry; this one is made with frozen puff pastry instead of homemade dough. Use a high-quality chocolate, such as Lindt or Perugina, for the best flavor. These make an indulgent brunch or after-school treat.*

 1 17.3-ounce package frozen puff pastry
    (2 sheets), thawed, each sheet cut into
    12 squares
 1 large egg, beaten to blend with
    1 tablespoon water (for glaze)
 4 3.5-ounce bars imported bittersweet or
    milk chocolate, each cut into six
    2×¾-inch pieces

    Sugar (for sprinkling)

LINE baking sheet with parchment paper. Brush top of each puff pastry square with egg glaze. Place 1 chocolate piece on edge of 1 pastry square. Roll up dough tightly, enclosing chocolate. Repeat with remaining pastry and chocolate. Place pastry rolls, seam side down, on prepared baking sheet.

DO AHEAD *Can be made 1 day ahead. Cover pastry rolls with plastic wrap and chill. Cover and chill remaining egg glaze.*

PREHEAT oven to 400°F. Brush tops of pastry rolls with remaining egg glaze. Sprinkle lightly with sugar. Bake until pastries are golden brown, about 15 minutes. Serve warm or at room temperature.

Quick sticky buns

MAKES 8 *Refrigerated crescent roll dough takes much of the work out of this recipe. Serve the buns for breakfast or dessert, or as a side dish on Thanksgiving.*

 2½ tablespoons unsalted butter
 ½   cup (packed) golden brown sugar, divided
 2   tablespoons light corn syrup
 2   teaspoons fresh lemon juice
 ⅓   cup coarsely chopped walnuts
 1   8-ounce tube refrigerated crescent roll dough
 ¾   teaspoon ground cinnamon

PREHEAT oven to 375°F. Butter 9-inch-diameter cake pan. Melt 2½ tablespoons butter in small saucepan over low heat. Whisk in ¼ cup brown sugar, corn syrup, and lemon juice. Increase heat to medium and whisk until sugar melts and syrup boils. Pour syrup evenly over bottom of prepared pan. Sprinkle with walnuts.

UNROLL dough onto floured work surface; press perforations together. Roll out dough to 8×12-inch rectangle. Sprinkle with remaining ¼ cup brown sugar and cinnamon. Starting at 1 short side, roll up dough jelly-roll style. Cut crosswise into eight 1-inch-thick rounds. Arrange rounds, cut side down, in syrup in pan.

BAKE buns until golden brown, about 20 minutes. Cool in pan 1 minute. Place plate over pan. Invert buns onto plate. Remove pan. Spoon any syrup in pan over buns and serve.

Prosciutto crescent rolls

MAKES 16 *Here's a grown-up version of pigs in a blanket. Salty, thin slices of prosciutto are rolled up in refrigerated crescent-roll dough and brushed with a honey-mustard glaze. Serve them on their own for breakfast, with a salad for lunch, or as an appetizer before dinner.*

　　Nonstick vegetable oil spray
2　8-ounce tubes refrigerated crescent roll dough
8　thin slices prosciutto

2　tablespoons honey
2　tablespoons country-style Dijon mustard

PREHEAT oven to 375°F. Spray heavy large baking sheet with nonstick spray. Open 1 tube of dough. Unroll dough onto floured work surface and separate into 4 rectangles (do not separate dough into triangles); press perforations together. Top each dough rectangle with 1 slice prosciutto. Starting at 1 long side, roll up dough rectangles jelly-roll style. Cut each crosswise in half. Transfer rolls, seam side down, to prepared baking sheet. Repeat with second tube of dough.

DO AHEAD *Can be made 1 day ahead. Cover and chill.*

WHISK honey and mustard in small bowl to blend. Brush rolls with honey mixture. Bake until golden brown, about 12 minutes. Cool slightly.

Sweet-cream biscuits

MAKES ABOUT 6 DOZEN *These cute biscuits have a nice rich flavor, thanks to the butter and whipping cream. In the unlikely event you have any left over, they will freeze well, too. The flour is sifted twice: first before it's measured, then again with the sugar, baking powder, and salt to ensure very light, tender biscuits.*

1¾　cups sifted all purpose flour
　　(sifted, then measured)
1　tablespoon sugar
1　tablespoon baking powder
½　teaspoon salt
6　tablespoons (¾ stick) chilled unsalted butter, cut into small cubes
¾　cup chilled heavy whipping cream

PREHEAT oven to 450°F. Sift flour, sugar, baking powder, and salt into large bowl. Rub in butter with fingertips until mixture resembles coarse meal. Add whipping cream and stir until just combined (do not overmix). Turn dough out onto lightly floured work surface and knead just until dough holds together, about 5 turns. Pat out dough to ¼-inch thickness. Using floured ¾- to 1-inch-diameter cutter, cut out biscuits. Gather dough scraps and pat out to ¼-inch thickness. Cut out additional biscuits. Repeat gathering, patting out, and cutting out biscuits until all dough is used. Transfer biscuits to ungreased baking sheets. Bake until golden brown, about 10 minutes. Serve warm or at room temperature.

Three-cheese drop biscuits

MAKES ABOUT 10 *Serve these easy-to-make drop biscuits straight out of the oven with a bowl of soup or a main-course salad.*

1¼ cups all purpose flour

1½ tablespoons sugar

  1 teaspoon baking powder

¼ teaspoon baking soda

¼ teaspoon salt

  3 tablespoons chilled unsalted butter, cut into small cubes

½ cup (packed) grated sharp cheddar cheese (about 2 ounces)

½ cup (packed) grated Monterey Jack cheese (about 2 ounces)

½ cup grated Parmesan cheese (about 1½ ounces)

⅔ cup chilled buttermilk

PREHEAT oven to 400°F. Lightly butter baking sheet. Whisk first 5 ingredients in medium bowl to blend. Add butter and rub in with fingertips until mixture resembles coarse meal. Add all cheeses and toss to coat well. Gradually mix in buttermilk. Drop dough by ¼ cupfuls onto prepared sheet, spacing 2 inches apart.

BAKE biscuits until golden brown on top, about 16 minutes. Transfer to platter. Serve warm or at room temperature.

Green-onion biscuits

MAKES 16 *Ground black pepper and sliced green onions make these biscuits savory. They're the perfect bread for mini ham sandwiches.*

  3 cups all purpose flour

1½ tablespoons baking powder

1½ teaspoons salt

  1 teaspoon freshly ground black pepper

2⅓ cups chilled heavy whipping cream

1½ cups thinly sliced green onions

  2 tablespoons (¼ stick) unsalted butter, melted

PREHEAT oven to 425°F. Mix flour, baking powder, salt, and pepper in large bowl. Mix cream and green onions in medium bowl. Add cream mixture to dry ingredients. Stir until moist clumps form.

TRANSFER dough to floured work surface. Knead just until dough holds together, about 8 turns. Shape into 8-inch square. Cut out sixteen 2-inch square biscuits. Transfer biscuits to large ungreased baking sheet, spacing 1½ inches apart. Brush top of biscuits with melted butter.

BAKE biscuits until golden brown on top, about 18 minutes. Serve warm or at room temperature.

Buttermilk biscuits

MAKES ABOUT 24 *Here's a great basic biscuit recipe. Serve the biscuits with fried chicken or on their own with butter and honey. Chopped fresh herbs, such as thyme, sage, or dill, would also be a nice addition. Or, if you prefer biscuits with a little sweetness, add 2 to 4 tablespoons sugar to the flour mixture before adding the butter.*

- 4 cups all purpose flour
- 2 tablespoons baking powder
- 1½ teaspoons salt
- ½ teaspoon baking soda
- ½ cup (1 stick) chilled unsalted butter, cut into small cubes
- 2 cups chilled buttermilk plus additional for brushing

PREHEAT oven to 400°F. Whisk first 4 ingredients in large bowl to blend. Add butter and rub in with fingertips until mixture resembles coarse meal. Gradually mix in 2 cups buttermilk; toss until dough comes together in large clumps. Gather dough into ball. Pat out on floured work surface to ½-inch thickness. Using floured 2½-inch-diameter cutter, cut out biscuits. Gather dough scraps; press out to ½-inch thickness and cut out more biscuits. Repeat until all dough is used.

TRANSFER biscuits to 2 large ungreased baking sheets. Brush tops of biscuits with additional buttermilk. Bake until tester inserted into center comes out clean, about 18 minutes. Cool biscuits 10 minutes. Serve warm or at room temperature.

Sage and pancetta biscuits with Fontina cheese

MAKES ABOUT 12 *Pancetta is unsmoked cured Italian bacon. It's available in the deli case of many supermarkets and at Italian markets. Here, it's crisped in a skillet and then added to the sage-flavored biscuit batter. Serve the biscuits with eggs for a great, filling breakfast—or with your turkey on Thanksgiving.*

- 1 3-ounce package thinly sliced pancetta (Italian bacon), chopped
- 2 cups all purpose flour
- 2 tablespoons sugar
- 3½ teaspoons baking powder
- ½ teaspoon salt
- 6 tablespoons (¾ stick) chilled unsalted butter, cut into small cubes
- 1 cup coarsely grated Fontina cheese
- 1 tablespoon chopped fresh sage
- ¾ cup plus 2 tablespoons chilled buttermilk

PREHEAT oven to 450°F. Sauté pancetta in medium nonstick skillet over medium heat until crisp, about 8 minutes. Remove skillet from heat and cool.

WHISK flour, sugar, baking powder, and salt in large bowl to blend. Rub in butter with fingertips until mixture resembles coarse meal. Stir in Fontina and sage, separating strands of cheese. Add ¾ cup buttermilk and pancetta with any pan drippings and stir until moist clumps form. Turn dough out onto floured work surface and knead just until dough holds together, about 4 to 6 turns. Flatten dough to ¾-inch thickness. Using floured 2¼-inch-diameter biscuit or cookie cutter, cut out rounds. Flatten dough to ¾-inch thickness and cut out more rounds until all dough is used.

TRANSFER biscuits to large ungreased baking sheet, spacing apart. Brush biscuit tops with remaining 2 tablespoons buttermilk. Bake until biscuits are puffed and golden, about 14 minutes. Serve warm or at room temperature.

SAVORYBREADS

Parsley-pepper skillet bread

8 SERVINGS *In pioneer days, this type of bread would have been cooked in a skillet over an open fire. Fortunately, it can also be made with less hassle in the oven, as in this recipe. This bread—really more like a giant biscuit with a nice peppery kick—turns bright green from the parsley, making it perfect for St. Patrick's Day.*

   4 cups unbleached all purpose flour
   1 cup chopped fresh Italian parsley
   2 tablespoons baking powder
   1 tablespoon freshly ground black pepper
   1 teaspoon salt
   ½ cup (1 stick) chilled unsalted butter,
       cut into small cubes
   1½ cups chilled heavy whipping cream
   1 tablespoon olive oil

POSITION rack in center of oven and preheat to 425°F. Generously butter 10-inch-diameter cast-iron skillet or other heavy ovenproof skillet. Blend flour, parsley, baking powder, 1 tablespoon pepper, and 1 teaspoon salt in processor. Add butter and process until mixture resembles coarse meal. With machine running, blend in cream through feed tube (do not overmix). Turn dough out onto lightly floured work surface. Pat into 10-inch disk. Transfer dough to prepared skillet. Brush top with oil; sprinkle lightly with pepper. Bake until puffed, golden brown, and crisp around edges, about 35 minutes. Turn bread out onto rack and cool until lukewarm, about 1 hour.

Three-cheese garlic bread

MAKES 12 SLICES *These delicious, gooey toasts will disappear quickly, so you might want to double the recipe.*

   2 tablespoons mayonnaise
   2 tablespoons (¼ stick) butter, room temperature
   1 garlic clove, pressed
   1⅓ cups crumbled feta cheese (about 5½ ounces)
   1¼ cups (about) grated Parmesan cheese
       (about 4 ounces), divided
   ½ cup (packed) grated Monterey Jack
       cheese (about 2 ounces)
   ½ cup finely chopped green onions
   12 ¾-inch-thick slices pain rustique
       or ciabatta bread

POSITION rack in center of oven and preheat to 475°F. Mix first 3 ingredients in medium bowl. Mix in feta, ½ cup Parmesan, Jack cheese, and green onions. Spread 2 tablespoons cheese mixture over each bread slice. Top each with 1 tablespoon Parmesan; press to adhere. Place on baking sheet. Sprinkle lightly with salt and pepper. Bake until cheese is golden and bubbly, about 12 minutes.

SAY CHEESE The cheese mixture also makes a great spread for bread and crackers, or it can be used as a dip for veggies. It can be frozen for up to one month (thaw it before using).

Zucchini, red onion, and two-cheese flatbread

4 TO 6 SERVINGS *With refrigerated pizza dough and flavorful purchased cheese spread, this bread is simple to make. Use both green and yellow zucchini for an extra splash of color.*

> Nonstick vegetable oil spray
> 1 13.8-ounce tube refrigerated pizza dough
> ¾ cup garlic-and-herb cheese spread (such as Alouette), divided
> ¾ cup finely grated Parmesan cheese, divided
> 3 tablespoons chopped fresh Italian parsley, divided
> 1 small red onion
> 1 7- to 8-inch-long zucchini (yellow or green), cut crosswise into ⅛-inch thick rounds, divided
> Olive oil

PREHEAT oven to 400°F. Line baking sheet with parchment paper; spray with nonstick spray. Unroll dough onto parchment. Spread half of herb cheese over 1 long half of dough, leaving ½-inch plain border. Sprinkle with half of Parmesan and 2 tablespoons parsley. Using parchment as aid, fold plain half of dough over filled half (do not seal edges). Spread remaining herb cheese over top; sprinkle with remaining Parmesan. Remove enough outer layers of onion to yield 2-inch diameter core; cut into ⅛-inch-thick rounds. Arrange 1 row of zucchini down 1 long side of dough. Arrange onion rounds in row alongside zucchini. Arrange 1 more row of zucchini alongside onion. Brush vegetables with oil; sprinkle with salt and pepper. Bake bread until puffed and deep brown at edges, about 24 minutes. Sprinkle with remaining 1 tablespoon parsley.

Pesto and cheese French bread

2 SERVINGS; CAN BE DOUBLED OR TRIPLED *This rich and delicious bread is great for a dinner party; just double or triple the recipe. Look for pesto near the refrigerated pasta sauces in the supermarket—or make your own, with the recipe on page 320.*

> ½ cup mayonnaise
> ½ cup freshly grated Romano or Parmesan cheese (about 2 ounces)
> 1 tablespoon (or more) purchased pesto
> ½ 1-pound loaf French bread, cut horizontally

MIX first 3 ingredients in small bowl. Add more pesto to taste, if desired. Preheat broiler. Broil bread, cut side up, until beginning to brown. Spread each bread half generously with mayonnaise mixture. Broil until bubbling and beginning to brown, watching closely to prevent burning. Cut bread crosswise into 1½-inch pieces and serve.

Fig focaccia with Gorgonzola cheese

4 TO 6 SERVINGS *This sweet and peppery bread can be cut into squares and served as an appetizer or cut into wedges and served with a radicchio and arugula salad.*

1   **13.8-ounce tube refrigerated pizza dough**

½   **cup finely chopped stemmed dried Calimyrna figs (about 5), divided**

4   **canned figs, drained, patted dry, sliced**

¾   **cup crumbled Gorgonzola cheese (about 3 ounces)**

1   **tablespoon (packed) dark brown sugar**

1   **teaspoon freshly ground black pepper**

PREHEAT oven to 425°F. Roll out dough on work surface to 12×9-inch rectangle. Sprinkle ¼ cup dried figs down center third of dough. Fold left side of dough over figs. Sprinkle with remaining ¼ cup dried figs. Fold right side of dough over second layer of figs to cover. Using rolling pin, gently flatten dough to 12×7-inch rectangle; place on baking sheet. Arrange fig slices atop dough. Sprinkle with cheese, then brown sugar and pepper. Bake bread until golden brown and cheese melts, about 25 minutes. Serve warm.

Onion and poppy seed focaccia

6 SERVINGS *Purchased bread dough makes this focaccia incredibly easy to prepare. It's delicious on its own, or served with warm marinara dipping sauce.*

2   **tablespoons olive oil, divided**

1   **cup finely chopped onion**

1   **11-ounce package refrigerated French bread dough**

¼   **cup freshly grated Parmesan cheese**

2   **teaspoons poppy seeds**

PREHEAT oven to 400°F. Oil baking sheet. Heat 1 tablespoon oil in medium skillet over medium heat. Add onion and sauté until golden, about 7 minutes. Cool.

PLACE dough on floured work surface. Fold dough in half. Using rolling pin, roll out dough to 10×8-inch rectangle. Transfer to prepared baking sheet. Drizzle remaining 1 tablespoon oil over dough. Spread onion atop dough. Sprinkle with Parmesan and poppy seeds; sprinkle lightly with salt. Bake until bread is golden brown, about 18 minutes. Serve warm or at room temperature.

Curry naan

MAKES 8 *Traditional Indian flatbread is baked in a tandoor (clay) oven. Here, the bread gets its browned exterior on an oiled griddle. A large griddle, which is flat with no sides and often made of cast iron, works great here and is a timesaver, because the bread can be made in two batches instead of cooking one bread round at a time in a skillet. Naan is great with any Indian meal or as a snack, dipped in sweet mango chutney. There are plenty of variations to try: For a plain naan, omit the curry powder—or replace it with cumin. Add chopped herbs (such as cilantro, mint, or parsley) or chopped green onions to the dough. You can also brush the naan with garlic oil or garlic butter and sprinkle with cilantro after cooking.*

3	cups sifted all purpose flour (sifted, then measured)
2	teaspoons curry powder
1½	teaspoons salt
¾	teaspoon baking soda
½	teaspoon baking powder
1½	cups (about) plain whole-milk yogurt
	Vegetable oil

SIFT flour, curry powder, salt, baking soda, and baking powder into large bowl. Stir in enough yogurt to make dough soft but not too sticky. Turn dough out onto lightly floured work surface and divide into 8 pieces. Form each piece into ball and roll out to 6- to 7-inch round about ⅛ inch thick.

OIL heavy large griddle and place over 2 burners set at medium heat. Add dough rounds in batches and cook until lightly browned on both sides, turning frequently and adjusting heat to prevent burning, about 8 minutes. Serve immediately or cool completely; wrap in foil and freeze up to 2 weeks, then rewarm in oven wrapped in foil.

Herbed peasant bread

2 SERVINGS; CAN BE DOUBLED *These flavorful toasts are perfect with so many main courses—from Greek-style lamb to spaghetti with meatballs or fried chicken. Use any herbs you have on hand.*

3	tablespoons minced assorted fresh herbs (such as chives, parsley, basil, marjoram, and sage)
3	tablespoons olive oil
4	large slices crusty country-style bread (about ½ to ¾ inch thick)
2	tablespoons freshly grated Parmesan cheese

COMBINE herbs and oil in small bowl. Let stand 15 minutes.

PREHEAT broiler. Place bread on baking sheet. Brush bread lightly with half of herb oil. Broil until bread is just beginning to color, watching closely to prevent burning, about 3 minutes. Turn bread over and brush with remaining herb oil. Sprinkle with grated Parmesan cheese. Broil until cheese topping is golden brown, watching closely to prevent burning, about 3 minutes. Serve bread warm.

TAKE IT OUTDOORS You can also toast the bread on the grill. Just grill the bread plain, then brush it with herb oil and sprinkle with Parmesan cheese before serving.

Shallot bruschetta

2 SERVINGS; CAN BE DOUBLED OR TRIPLED *Here's a simple Italian appetizer or a great side for pasta. The recipe can easily be doubled or tripled.*

- 3   tablespoons olive oil
- 5   large shallots or green onions, thinly sliced
- 4   3×5-inch slices French bread
     Freshly grated Pecorino Romano cheese

PREHEAT broiler. Heat oil in heavy small skillet over medium heat. Add shallots and sauté until tender, stirring frequently, about 5 minutes.

BROIL 1 side of bread until toasted. Spread shallot mixture on second side of bread. Sprinkle generously with freshly ground black pepper and cheese. Broil until beginning to brown. Serve immediately.

Grilled bread with olive oil

6 SERVINGS *Next time you fire up the barbecue, throw some bread on the grill. The baguette will take on a nice smoky flavor as it crisps. Instead of plain olive oil, you can use any flavored oil. Supermarkets, specialty foods stores, and cookware shops often carry great garlic, basil, and rosemary oils. Or, for quick garlic bread, simply rub half a clove of garlic over the bread after you take it off the grill.*

- 1   baguette, cut into 1-inch diagonal slices
- ¼   cup extra-virgin olive oil

PREPARE barbecue (medium-high heat). Brush both sides of bread generously with oil; sprinkle with salt and pepper. Grill until golden, about 1 minute per side.

Grilled olive bread with garlic-fennel butter

10 SERVINGS *Here's a great modern take on classic garlic bread. If it's not grilling weather, broil the bread on one side until it's crisp. Turn it over, spread it with the seasoned butter, and broil it until the topping is bubbling. Use a mortar with pestle to crush the fennel seeds or enclose them in a resealable plastic bag and crush with a meat mallet.*

½ **cup (1 stick) butter, room temperature**

3 **garlic cloves, peeled, mashed**

1 **tablespoon fennel seeds, crushed**

½ **cup mayonnaise**

20 **½-inch-thick slices olive bread**

COMBINE butter, garlic, and fennel seeds in medium bowl. Beat until mixture is blended and fluffy. Beat in mayonnaise. Season to taste with salt and pepper.

DO AHEAD *Can be made 1 day ahead. Cover and chill. Bring to room temperature before using.*

PREPARE barbecue (medium-high heat). Coat 1 side of bread with garlic-fennel butter. Grill uncoated side until crisp, then turn and grill until buttered side is beginning to brown, about 2 minutes. Transfer grilled bread to platter and serve.

frozendesserts

GRANITAS

Tangerine Granita with
Vanilla Bean Cream

Summer Melon with
Basil-Mint Granita

Cranberry Granita

Root Beer Granita Float

Watermelon Granita
with Campari

Icy Lemon-Mint Parfaits

Peach and Prosecco Ice

Mango Ice with Tequila and Lime

Lemon-Buttermilk Ice Pops

SORBETS

Ginger-Pear Sorbet

Kiwi-Lime Sorbet

Raspberry-Plum Sorbet

Chocolate-Orange Sorbet

Burgundy Cinnamon Sorbet

Fresh Strawberry Sorbet

Blackberry Sorbet

Key Lime Pie Sorbet

Sorbet and Ice Cream Terrine
with Blackberry Compote

GELATO AND ICE CREAM

Pistachio Gelato

Chocolate-Cinnamon
Gelato with Toffee Bits

Zabaglione Gelato

Banana Ice Cream

Frozen Meyer Lemon Cream
with Blackberry Sauce

Grapefruit-Ginger Sherbet

Rum-Raisin Ice Cream

Cadbury Crunch Ice Cream

Amaretto Amaretti
Crunch Ice Cream

Spiced Peach Sundaes

Red, White, and Blueberry
Ice Cream Sundaes

Tropical Fruit Sundaes with
Pineapple-Rum Sauce

Sesame Seed–Peanut
Brittle Coupes

Coffee, Chocolate, and
Marshmallow Sundaes

Chocolate-Orange Ice
Cream Sundaes

FROZEN DESSERTS

Chestnut and Kahlúa Ice
Cream with Kahlúa Sauce

Dulce de Leche Ice Cream
with Fresh Strawberries and
Mexican Chocolate Sauce

Brown Sugar-Bourbon Peaches
with Vanilla Ice Cream

Prune and Armagnac
Compote with Ice Cream

Ice Cream with Sautéed
Pineapple and Bourbon

Brandy-Glazed Apples
with Vanilla Ice Cream

Vanilla Ice Cream with Lychees
and Crystallized Ginger

Balsamic Berries over
Vanilla Ice Cream

Ice Cream with Marsala
and Currants

Strawberry and Macaroon Parfaits

Biscotti Parfaits

Warm Doughnuts à la
Mode with Bananas and
Spiced Caramel Sauce

Butter Pecan Ice Cream Pie
with Caramel Topping

Chocolate Cookie and
Coffee Ice Cream Pie

Frozen Peanut Butter Pie

Macadamia Ice Cream and
Mango Sorbet Swirl Pie

Goober Ice Cream Sandwiches

Chocolate Chip Cookie and
Mint Ice Cream Sandwiches

Valentine Chocolate-Cherry
Ice Cream Bombe

Frozen Lemon-Ginger Yogurt

White Peach, Cassis, and
Champagne Floats

Affogato Mocha

tool kit Is there any dessert that is faster or easier to pull off than purchased ice cream? All you have to do is take the top off the carton and start scooping. But sometimes you want something a little more creative. Here are six ways to turn a pint of ice cream into a truly inventive dessert:

ICE CREAM BONBONS

Freeze small balls of your favorite ice cream. Melt 8 ounces of chocolate with 4 teaspoons of nonhydrogenated vegetable shortening in a small bowl in the microwave and cool until just barely lukewarm. Pierce the ice cream balls with a toothpick and dip them into the melted chocolate to coat, then coat them in finely chopped almonds. Place them on a baking sheet lined with waxed paper, remove the toothpicks, and freeze until firm.

PARTY BOWL

Here's a take on an ice cream parlor extravaganza that's great for kids. Pile a large serving bowl with scoops of assorted ice creams, such as chocolate, vanilla, and strawberry. (See page 576 for tips on scooping ice cream ahead of time.) Cover the bowl of ice cream and freeze. When you're ready to serve, drizzle the scoops of ice cream with chocolate sauce, then top it all with whipped cream and multicolored sprinkles.

BREAKFAST FOR DESSERT

Some breakfast favorites make natural desserts: French toast made with brioche bread, Belgian waffles, crepes. Just top them with ice cream, then roasted or sautéed peaches, bananas, or apples, and a drizzle of warm maple syrup or caramel sauce. →

SHORTCUT *SEMIFREDDO*

Semifreddo, meaning "half cold" in Italian, is a half-frozen dessert of ice cream, custard, or whipped cream that often includes fruit and cake. For a shortcut version, mix slightly softened purchased vanilla ice cream with finely grated orange peel, chopped toasted hazelnuts, and a splash of Frangelico (hazelnut liqueur) if you like. Line a small loaf pan with plastic wrap, allowing some to extend beyond the edge of the pan; pack the flavored ice cream into the pan. Fold the excess plastic wrap over to cover and freeze. When ready to serve, unmold the *semifreddo,* cut it into slices, and serve with chocolate sauce, if desired.

ICE CREAM INSTEAD OF WHIPPED CREAM

Use ice cream in desserts where whipped cream is usually the star, like strawberry shortcakes, cream puffs, or *clafouti.*

LIMONCELLO PARFAITS

Scoop vanilla ice cream into a parfait glass, followed by a scoop of lemon sorbet and a second scoop of vanilla ice cream. Sprinkle raspberries into the glass. Drizzle with limoncello (a lemon liqueur) and serve.

GRANITAS

Tangerine granita with vanilla bean cream

6 SERVINGS *With sweetened vanilla cream adding luscious contrast to the icy tangerine crystals, this super-easy dessert is like a sophisticated Creamsicle. The tangerine juice can be replaced with other sweet fruit juice such as orange, mango, or peach juice.*

 3 **cups fresh tangerine juice**
 ⅔ **cup plus 2 tablespoons sugar**

 ¾ **cup heavy whipping cream**
 1 **vanilla bean, split lengthwise**

COMBINE tangerine juice and ⅔ cup sugar in 8-inch square metal baking pan and whisk until sugar dissolves. Freeze tangerine mixture 2 hours, then stir well. Cover and freeze until solid, at least 3 hours or overnight.

PLACE cream in small bowl. Scrape in seeds from vanilla bean; add bean. Mix in remaining 2 tablespoons sugar. Cover bowl and refrigerate vanilla cream for at least 2 hours or overnight.

SPOON 2 tablespoons vanilla cream into each of 6 glasses. Using fork, scrape granita into flakes. Mound granita into glasses and serve.

WHIP IT UP If desired, the chilled vanilla cream can be beaten until soft peaks form before serving.

Sweet, icy, easy Ice, *granité*, and granita all refer to the same thing in different languages: a dessert in which a sweetened liquid is placed in a shallow pan and stored in the freezer until it becomes semi-firm. When it freezes, it is scraped with a fork to form the icy crystals. These are among the easiest frozen desserts to make—and best of all, they don't require any special equipment. Sorbets may contain similar ingredients but have smoother textures because they're usually churned in an ice cream maker. If you see a sorbet recipe you like but don't have an ice cream maker, turn it into a granita instead. If a certain granita sounds good but you prefer the smoother texture of ice cream, it can easily become a sorbet by churning it in an ice cream maker.

Summer melon with basil-mint granita

8 SERVINGS *Mashing (or "muddling") the mint and basil with sugar helps release their essential oils and flavors. Any combination of melons will work well with this granita. Look for Charentais (or Cavaillon), delicious French melons with orange flesh, at farmers' markets during the summer.*

- ¾ **cup plus 2 tablespoons sugar**
- ¾ **cup chopped fresh mint leaves**
- ¾ **cup chopped fresh basil leaves**
- 2 **tablespoons finely grated lime peel**
- 1½ **cups fresh lime juice**
- 1¼ **cups water**

- 3 **small melons, halved lengthwise, seeded, each half cut into 8 wedges (about ¾ inch wide), peeled**
- 2 **tablespoons thinly sliced fresh mint leaves plus 8 fresh sprigs for garnish**

MIX first 4 ingredients in medium bowl. Mash with wooden spoon until herbs turn dark green, about 3 minutes. Stir in lime juice and 1¼ cups water. Let stand 1 hour. Strain into large bowl, pressing on solids. Transfer ½ cup lime syrup to small pitcher; cover and refrigerate. Pour remaining lime syrup into 13×9×2-inch metal baking dish. Place dish in freezer. Stir syrup with fork after 2 hours. Freeze until frozen, about 4 hours.

DO AHEAD *Can be prepared 1 day ahead. Cover and keep frozen.*

DIVIDE melon wedges among 8 shallow soup bowls. Drizzle melon with reserved lime syrup. Scrape granita into flakes with fork. Spoon generous ½ cup granita atop melon in each bowl. Sprinkle with sliced mint leaves and garnish with mint sprigs.

DRINK IT UP If you like the flavor of this granita, try mixing the lime syrup with a little clear rum or silver tequila and a splash of club soda for a refreshing summertime cocktail.

Cranberry granita

10 SERVINGS *Sugar sweetens up the tart cranberry juice, and corn syrup helps soften the granita to make it a little slushy. Either fresh-squeezed or prepared orange juice is fine in this recipe.*

- 4 **cups cranberries (about 1 pound)**
- 4 **cups cold water**
- 2 **cups sugar**
- 1 **cup light corn syrup**
- ½ **cup orange juice**

COMBINE all ingredients in heavy large saucepan. Bring to boil, stirring until sugar dissolves. Remove from heat, cover, and let steep 30 minutes. Working in batches, puree mixture in processor. Strain puree into large bowl, pressing on solids to extract as much liquid as possible.

POUR strained puree into 15×10×2-inch dish. Freeze 2 hours. Using fork, stir to blend in any frozen portions. Freeze until granita has uniformly slushy consistency, about 5 hours. Cover and keep frozen up to 1 day.

USING fork, scrape granita to form icy flakes. Spoon into goblets.

Root beer granita float

6 SERVINGS *Everyone's childhood favorite grows up. Root beer is frozen to make the granita and boiled to make the syrup that's drizzled over vanilla ice cream.*

- 8 **cups root beer, divided**
- 1 **pint vanilla ice cream**

POUR 4 cups root beer into 13×9×2-inch baking pan; freeze until set, about 4 hours or overnight.

MEANWHILE, boil remaining 4 cups root beer in large saucepan until reduced to ½ cup, about 30 minutes. Cool root beer syrup.

USING fork, scrape frozen root beer into icy flakes, then mix gently in pan to blend. Spoon root beer granita into each of 6 clear glasses or dessert cups. Top granita with scoop of ice cream. Drizzle each with 4 teaspoons root beer syrup and serve.

Watermelon granita with Campari

4 SERVINGS *A little Campari lends color and a bitter-sweet flavor that contrasts with the summery sweetness of watermelon.*

- ¼ **cup sugar**
- ¼ **cup water**

- 3½ **cups 1-inch cubes watermelon**
- 2 **teaspoons fresh lime juice**
- 1 **to 2 teaspoons Campari**

COOK sugar and ¼ cup water in heavy small saucepan over low heat, stirring until sugar dissolves. Increase heat and bring to boil. Cool.

PUREE melon in processor in batches using on/off turns. Measure 2 cups pulp. Stir in sugar syrup and lime juice. Pour into 8×8×2-inch metal baking pan. Freeze 2 hours. Stir with fork, then freeze until solid, about 3 hours. Using fork, scrape granita to form crystals. Spoon into bowls. Drizzle ¼ to ½ teaspoon Campari over each.

Icy lemon-mint parfaits

6 SERVINGS Parfait, *meaning "perfect" in French, is what you'll think when tasting the refreshing combination of lemon and mint flavors in this dessert. Use clear glasses to show off the parfait's layers of sliced strawberries, whipped cream, and slushy* granité *(French for "ice").*

Lemon-Mint Granité

- **2 cups (loosely packed) fresh mint leaves plus 6 leaves for garnish**
- **1¼ cups water**
- **1 cup sugar**
- **¾ cup fresh lemon juice**

Minted Whipped Cream

- **¾ cup chilled heavy whipping cream**
- **1½ tablespoons sugar**
- **1½ tablespoons finely chopped fresh mint leaves**

- **1 1-pint container fresh strawberries, hulled, thinly sliced**

FOR GRANITÉ: Combine 2 cups mint leaves, 1¼ cups water, and sugar in medium saucepan. Stir over medium heat until sugar dissolves. Reduce heat to very low; cook 5 minutes without simmering. Pour syrup through fine strainer into 8×8×2-inch glass baking dish. Cool to room temperature; mix in lemon juice. Cover and freeze until firm, stirring occasionally, at least 6 hours or overnight.

FOR WHIPPED CREAM: Using electric mixer, beat cream, sugar, and chopped mint in medium bowl until peaks form.

DO AHEAD *Can be made 4 hours ahead. Cover and chill. Rewhisk to thicken before using.*

USING fork, scrape granité to form crystals. Place 4 berry slices in each of 6 glasses. Top with 1 generous tablespoon minted cream, then 4 berry slices. Spoon ¼ cup granité over. Repeat layering with berry slices, minted cream, and granité. Garnish each parfait with berry slice and mint leaf.

Peach and Prosecco ice

MAKES ABOUT 4 CUPS *This elegant treat is inspired by the Bellini, a mix of peach nectar and Prosecco (sparkling white wine) made famous at Harry's Bar in Venice. Scoop it into flutes and top with Prosecco for a lovely aperitif. As an alternative to the peaches, try it with frozen mangoes.*

- **¾ cup sugar**
- **½ cup hot water**
- **¼ cup fresh orange juice**
- **1 16-ounce bag frozen sliced peaches, thawed, juices reserved**
- **1 cup chilled Prosecco or other sparkling white wine**

STIR first 3 ingredients in medium bowl until sugar dissolves. Blend peaches and reserved peach juices in processor until peaches are finely chopped. With machine running, gradually pour in orange sugar syrup; process until smooth. Add Prosecco and blend well. Transfer mixture to container. Cover and freeze until firm, at least 3 hours.

DO AHEAD *Can be prepared 2 days ahead. Keep frozen. If necessary, let soften slightly at room temperature before serving.*

Mango ice with tequila and lime

4 SERVINGS *For a nonalcoholic version, replace the tequila with the same amount of orange juice; you can also use lemon juice in place of the lime juice.*

¼ **cup water**
3 **tablespoons tequila**
2 **tablespoons sugar**

2 **large ripe mangoes, peeled, pitted**
2 **tablespoons fresh lime juice**

COMBINE first 3 ingredients in heavy small saucepan. Stir over medium heat until sugar dissolves and mixture boils. Cool syrup slightly.

PUREE mangoes, lime juice, and sugar syrup in processor until smooth. Transfer mixture to pie plate. Freeze 2 hours; stir. Continue freezing until firm. Let stand 10 minutes at room temperature. Break up into chunks. Return to processor and process until smooth.

Lemon-buttermilk ice pops

MAKES 8 *You can find ice pop molds in fun shapes at specialty cookware stores and some supermarkets. To unmold the ice pops easily, dip the molds in hot water for a few seconds, then remove the pops. You can also simply freeze fruit juice in the molds to make healthful treats for kids.*

¾ **cup sugar**
5 **tablespoons fresh lemon juice**
2 **tablespoons finely grated lemon peel**
    Pinch of salt
1⅔ **cups buttermilk**

WHISK first 4 ingredients in 4-cup measuring cup until sugar dissolves. Whisk in buttermilk. Divide mixture among 8 ice pop molds (each about ¼ to ⅓ cup capacity). Cover and freeze until firm, at least 4 hours and up to 5 days.

IN A PAPER CUP If the molds are not available, divide the buttermilk mixture among paper cups, such as Dixie cups, then cover the cups with foil and insert wooden sticks into the center of the cups (the foil will help keep the sticks in place). Once the ice pops are frozen, just remove the foil and peel off the paper cups.

SORBETS

Ginger-pear sorbet

4 SERVINGS *The pear and ginger combination makes this sorbet a light and refreshing ending to any meal. Canned pears taste great and eliminate the extra steps of peeling, coring, and cooking the pears. Look for crystallized ginger in the spice section or Asian foods section of the supermarket. Use a large sharp knife to cut the frozen pear mixture into large chunks to help blend it more easily in the food processor.*

1   **15- to 16-ounce can pear halves in heavy syrup**
¼   **cup sugar**
1   **tablespoon (packed) finely chopped crystallized ginger**
1   **teaspoon finely grated lemon peel**

LINE 9-inch glass pie dish with plastic wrap. Drain syrup from pears into small bowl; transfer pears to prepared dish. Add sugar, ginger, and lemon peel to syrup and stir until sugar dissolves. Pour syrup mixture over pears. Cover and freeze until solid, at least 6 hours.

TURN pear mixture out onto work surface; peel off plastic wrap. Cut into 1-inch pieces. Place in processor; blend until smooth. Freeze in covered container 1 hour.

DO AHEAD *Sorbet can be made 2 days ahead. Keep frozen. If necessary, let soften slightly at room temperature before serving.*

Kiwi-lime sorbet

MAKES ABOUT 3½ CUPS *Using frozen limeade concentrate makes this a very simple dessert; you can find it in the frozen foods section next to the frozen lemonade and orange juice concentrates.*

1¾   **pounds kiwis (about 8), peeled**
¾   **cup sugar**
½   **cup frozen limeade concentrate**

PUREE all ingredients in processor. Process in ice cream maker according to manufacturer's instructions. Transfer to container, cover, and freeze until solid, at least 3 hours.

DO AHEAD *Sorbet can be made 2 days ahead. Keep frozen. Let stand at room temperature 30 minutes before serving to soften.*

NO ICE CREAM MAKER? If you don't have an ice cream maker, freeze the puree in a shallow metal baking pan until almost set, about 2 hours. Break it into pieces, then blend in processor until smooth. Cover and freeze. Let soften slightly at room temperature before serving.

Raspberry-plum sorbet

6 SERVINGS *This is a great summertime sorbet, when plums and raspberries are fresh and juicy. If you don't have an ice cream maker, freeze the fruit mixture, then break it into large chunks and blend it in a food processor until it is smooth and icy like a sorbet.*

1⅓ cups sugar
1⅓ cups water

2 pounds plums, pitted, cut into large chunks
3½ cups fresh raspberries or frozen
    unsweetened raspberries, thawed

COMBINE sugar and 1⅓ cups water in medium saucepan. Bring to boil, stirring to dissolve sugar. Remove from heat. Cool sugar syrup completely.

BLEND plums and raspberries in processor until smooth. Strain through coarse sieve into large bowl, pressing on solids to extract as much liquid as possible. Stir in cooled sugar syrup. Refrigerate until chilled, about 2 hours.

PROCESS sorbet in ice cream maker according to manufacturer's instructions. Transfer sorbet to container. Cover and freeze.

DO AHEAD *Sorbet can be made 1 week ahead. Keep frozen. If necessary, let soften slightly at room temperature before serving.*

Chocolate-orange sorbet

MAKES ABOUT 7 CUPS *Get your chocolate fix without the guilt with this low-fat sorbet. Use good-quality chocolate in order to get a sorbet with a silky-smooth texture. To cool the chocolate mixture in a matter of minutes rather than hours, transfer it to a wide metal bowl and set the bowl over another large bowl of ice water so that the base of the bowl of chocolate rests in the ice water. Stirring the chocolate mixture will also help dissipate the heat even more quickly.*

4 cups water
⅔ cup sugar
1 tablespoon instant coffee crystals
½ cup frozen orange juice concentrate, thawed
1 pound bittersweet or
   semisweet chocolate, chopped

BRING first 3 ingredients to boil in large saucepan over medium-high heat, stirring until sugar dissolves. Mix in orange juice concentrate. Reduce heat to low. Add chocolate and whisk until smooth. Chill uncovered until cold, stirring occasionally, about 3 hours.

PROCESS sorbet mixture in ice cream maker according to manufacturer's instructions. Transfer to container. Cover; freeze at least 6 hours and up to 3 days.

Burgundy cinnamon sorbet

MAKES ABOUT 3 CUPS *Bringing the wine mixture to a boil cooks off most of the alcohol, dissolves the sugar, and helps extract more flavor from the cinnamon sticks. You can chill the mixture faster by placing it in the freezer rather than the refrigerator; stir it occasionally so that it cools evenly and doesn't freeze.*

2¼ cups red Burgundy wine (from one 750-ml bottle)
1¼ cups water
⅔ cup sugar
4 3-inch-long cinnamon sticks

COMBINE all ingredients in heavy medium saucepan. Stir over medium heat until sugar dissolves. Increase heat and bring to boil. Remove from heat. Cover and let steep 45 minutes. Discard cinnamon sticks. Cover and refrigerate until cold.

TRANSFER sorbet mixture to ice cream maker and process according to manufacturer's instructions. Freeze sorbet in covered container until firm, about 30 minutes.

DO AHEAD *Can be made 1 day ahead. Keep frozen.*

Fresh strawberry sorbet

6 SERVINGS *This sorbet can easily become a granita. After blending the strawberry mixture with the sugar syrup, place it in a 13×9×2-inch metal or glass baking dish and freeze it until it becomes semi-firm, stirring occasionally. As the mixture hardens, scrape the surface to form the icy crystals.*

2 cups water
1 cup sugar

1 quart fresh strawberries, hulled
⅓ cup fresh orange juice
⅓ cup fresh lemon juice

STIR 2 cups water and sugar in heavy medium saucepan over high heat until sugar dissolves. Boil 5 minutes.

WORKING in batches, puree strawberries in processor until smooth. Add strawberry puree and orange and lemon juices to sugar syrup; stir to blend. Cover and refrigerate until cold, about 2 hours.

PROCESS strawberry mixture in ice cream maker according to manufacturer's instructions.

DO AHEAD *Can be made 3 days ahead. Cover and freeze in airtight container. If sorbet is frozen solid, place in refrigerator for 15 minutes to soften before serving.*

Blackberry sorbet

8 SERVINGS *This would also be delicious with frozen raspberries instead of the blackberries.*

1¼   cups sugar

1   cup water

1½   pounds frozen unsweetened blackberries, thawed, juices reserved

2   tablespoons fresh lemon juice

½   small watermelon

16   fresh blackberries

STIR sugar and 1 cup water in small saucepan. Bring to boil over high heat, stirring until sugar dissolves. Boil 1 minute. Transfer syrup to large bowl. Chill until syrup is cold, about 3 hours.

WORKING in batches, puree blackberries with juices and cold syrup in blender until smooth. Strain into another large bowl; discard seeds. Stir in lemon juice.

PROCESS blackberry mixture in ice cream maker according to manufacturer's instructions. Transfer sorbet to container; cover and freeze until firm, about 3 hours.

DO AHEAD *Can be made 1 week ahead. Keep frozen.*

USING large spoon, scoop out flesh from watermelon, leaving rind intact and forming bowl (reserve melon for another use or serve alongside sorbet, if desired). Drain excess juice from watermelon bowl. Cover and chill watermelon bowl until cold.

SCOOP sorbet into watermelon bowl. Garnish with fresh blackberries.

Key lime pie sorbet

MAKES ABOUT 3 CUPS *Sweetened condensed milk is a vital ingredient in Key lime pie. When mixed with the lime juice it becomes thicker, and in this sorbet it lends a rich and luxurious texture. If you can't find Key limes (which look like mini limes) or bottled Key lime juice at the supermarket or Latin market, use regular limes instead.*

¾   cup water

½   cup sugar

1   14-ounce can sweetened condensed milk

1   cup fresh or bottled Key lime juice

BRING ¾ cup water and sugar to boil in heavy medium saucepan, stirring until sugar dissolves. Mix in condensed milk, then Key lime juice. Transfer mixture to medium bowl; place over large bowl filled with ice and water and cool, stirring often, about 30 minutes.

PROCESS lime mixture in ice cream maker according to manufacturer's instructions. Transfer sorbet to medium container, cover, and freeze until firm, at least 4 hours and up to 2 days.

PIE IN A GLASS Spoon the sorbet into dessert glasses, sprinkle with coarsely crushed graham crackers, and top with a spoonful of whipped cream.

Sorbet and ice cream terrine with blackberry compote

10 SERVINGS *A rainbow of four purchased sorbets plus vanilla ice cream makes this beauty one of the easiest and most versatile desserts ever. Try chocolate ice cream instead of boysenberry sorbet and orange sorbet instead of mango. Freeze each layer of sorbet before adding the next to create clearly defined layers. To soften the sorbets and ice cream quickly, microwave each container at five-second intervals just before using.*

Terrine

1 **pint raspberry sorbet, slightly softened**
1 **pint lemon sorbet, slightly softened**
1 **pint vanilla ice cream, slightly softened**
1 **pint mango sorbet, slightly softened**
1 **pint boysenberry sorbet, slightly softened**

Compote

½ **cup seedless blackberry jam**
2 **teaspoons finely grated lemon peel**
1 **teaspoon fresh lemon juice**
2 **½-pint containers fresh blackberries**

1 **tablespoon thinly sliced fresh mint leaves**

FOR TERRINE: Line 9×5×2¾-inch metal loaf pan with 2 layers of plastic wrap, extending 3 inches over sides. Spread raspberry sorbet evenly in bottom of prepared loaf pan. Freeze until firm, about 20 minutes. Spoon lemon sorbet in large dollops atop raspberry sorbet, then spread in even layer. Freeze until firm, about 20 minutes. Repeat procedure with vanilla ice cream, then mango sorbet, and finally boysenberry sorbet. Fold plastic wrap overhang over terrine; cover with aluminum foil. Freeze terrine overnight.

DO AHEAD *Can be made 4 days ahead. Keep frozen.*

FOR COMPOTE: Stir blackberry jam in heavy medium saucepan over medium-low heat until melted. Stir in lemon peel and lemon juice. Cool to room temperature. Stir in fresh blackberries, crushing some with fork to release juices. Refrigerate compote until cold, at least 2 hours and up to 1 day.

STIR mint into blackberry compote. Invert terrine onto platter; peel off plastic wrap. Cut terrine into slices. Serve with blackberry compote.

Pistachio gelato

6 SERVINGS *Most pistachio ice creams are green due to the addition of green food coloring, as in this recipe. You can leave it out if you'd like a more natural-colored gelato.*

¾   **cup unsalted shelled pistachios (about 3¾ ounces)**

¾   **cup sugar, divided**

2   **cups whole milk**

1   **teaspoon almond extract**

5   **large egg yolks**

2   **drops green food coloring (optional)**

   Chopped unsalted pistachios

FINELY grind ¾ cup pistachios and ¼ cup sugar in processor. Combine pistachio mixture, milk, and almond extract in heavy medium saucepan. Bring to boil. Whisk yolks and remaining ½ cup sugar in large bowl to blend. Gradually whisk milk mixture into yolk mixture. Return mixture to saucepan. Stir over medium-low heat until custard thickens slightly and leaves path on back of spoon when finger is drawn across, about 8 minutes (do not boil). Remove from heat. Whisk in food coloring, if desired. Refrigerate custard until cold, about 3 hours.

PROCESS custard in ice cream maker according to manufacturer's instructions. Transfer to covered container and freeze.

DO AHEAD *Can be made 1 week ahead. Keep frozen.*

SCOOP into glasses or bowls. Garnish with chopped pistachios.

Gelato vs. ice cream What's the difference? Even though gelato may seem richer, the opposite is true: Gelato is traditionally made with whole milk and a minimal amount of cream, whereas ice cream is made with much more cream. But the biggest difference is actually in the amount of *air*; the typical ice cream processing method mixes in a lot of air while it's churning. Softer in texture and more intense in taste and color than most ice cream, gelato is one of Italy's greatest culinary creations.

Chocolate-cinnamon gelato with toffee bits

MAKES ABOUT 3 CUPS *Cornstarch, not eggs, makes this gelato thick and creamy. If you're really rushed, stir a little ground cinnamon and toffee bits into purchased chocolate gelato or ice cream.*

½	**cup sugar**
2	**tablespoons cornstarch**
1¼	**teaspoons ground cinnamon**
	Pinch of salt
2	**cups whole milk, divided**
5	**ounces bittersweet or semisweet chocolate, finely chopped**
½	**cup chilled heavy whipping cream**
⅓	**cup coarsely crushed toffee candy (such as Skor, Heath, or Almond Roca)**

WHISK first 4 ingredients in heavy medium saucepan until blended. Gradually add ¼ cup milk, whisking until cornstarch is dissolved. Whisk in remaining 1¾ cups milk. Whisk over medium-high heat until mixture thickens and comes to boil, about 6 minutes. Reduce heat to medium and cook 1 minute longer, whisking occasionally. Remove from heat; add chocolate. Let stand 1 minute, then whisk until melted and smooth.

TRANSFER gelato base to medium bowl. Mix in cream. Place bowl over large bowl filled with ice and water and cool, stirring often, about 30 minutes.

PROCESS gelato base in ice cream maker according to manufacturer's instructions, adding toffee during last minute of churning. Transfer to container; cover. Freeze at least 3 hours and up to 2 days.

Ice cream basics Custard—the egg and milk (and/or cream) mixture that serves as the base of most ice creams and gelatos—must be stirred constantly as it cooks over low heat to prevent the egg yolks from curdling into scrambled eggs. Use a heat-resistant silicone spatula or wooden spoon to scrape the bottom and sides of the saucepan as the custard cooks. In order to get a smooth and creamy texture, be sure to cook the custard until it thickens to the consistency of heavy whipping cream or a thin gravy.

Zabaglione gelato

MAKES ABOUT 3½ CUPS *Zabaglione, a light Italian dessert custard (called* sabayon *in France), is traditionally flavored with Marsala, a Sicilian fortified wine. Because the zabaglione will curdle if it gets too hot, it's important to know when it's reached the right temperature—use an instant-read thermometer to eliminate the guesswork. The zabaglione is frozen in this recipe, but you can also serve it warm or chilled over fresh berries.*

- 4 **large egg yolks**
- ½ **cup sugar**
- 1 **cup whole milk**
- 1 **cup heavy whipping cream**
- 6 **tablespoons imported dry Marsala**
- 2 **tablespoons dark rum**
- 1 **teaspoon vanilla extract**

WHISK yolks and sugar in medium bowl until thick, about 2 minutes. Heat milk and cream in medium saucepan over medium heat until mixture bubbles at edges. Gradually whisk hot milk mixture into yolk mixture; return to saucepan. Stir over medium heat until custard leaves path on back of spoon when finger is drawn across and temperature registers 170°F, about 6 minutes. Immediately pour custard through sieve set over another medium bowl. Stir Marsala, rum, and vanilla into custard. Cover and chill at least 3 hours.

PROCESS custard in ice cream maker according to manufacturer's instructions. Transfer gelato to container. Cover and freeze until firm, at least 6 hours.

DO AHEAD *Can be made 2 days ahead. Keep frozen.*

WINE NOT? In this recipe, rum is added to the Marsala for a more intense flavor, but it can be replaced with more Marsala, if desired. In fact, both the Marsala and rum can be replaced with other wines, including Essensia, Moscato, Vin Santo, or Madeira.

Banana ice cream

6 SERVINGS *This is an excellent use for bananas that are just a little past their prime. It's a remarkably easy dessert to make and doesn't even require an ice cream maker.*

- 4 **ripe bananas, peeled, mashed**
- 1 **14-ounce can sweetened condensed milk**
- ¾ **cup heavy whipping cream**

COMBINE bananas and condensed milk in large bowl. Whisk in cream. Pour banana mixture into 8×8×2-inch glass baking dish. Cover and freeze until softly set, about 2 hours. Transfer to large bowl. Using electric mixer, beat ice cream just until fluffy. Return to same glass baking dish. Cover and freeze until firm, about 6 hours.

DO AHEAD *Can be made 3 days ahead. Keep frozen.*

Frozen Meyer lemon cream with blackberry sauce

6 SERVINGS *This lemon cream has a heavenly mousse-like texture due to the whipped cream that is folded into the lemon curd. Meyer lemons are not quite as tart as regular lemons and lend a little more fragrance to this cream, which needs to freeze for about four hours.*

½   cup plus 2 tablespoons sugar

5   tablespoons plus 1½ teaspoons
strained fresh Meyer lemon juice

3   large egg yolks

1   tablespoon light corn syrup

1   cup chilled heavy whipping cream

1¾ teaspoons finely grated
Meyer lemon peel, divided

1   cup frozen unsweetened blackberries, thawed

WHISK ½ cup sugar, 5 tablespoons lemon juice, yolks, and corn syrup in small metal bowl to blend. Set bowl over saucepan of boiling water; whisk until mixture is thick and fluffy and thermometer inserted into mixture registers 180°F, about 3 minutes. Place bowl with yolk mixture over larger bowl filled with ice and water until mixture is cool, stirring occasionally, about 8 minutes.

MEANWHILE, using electric mixer, beat cream, 1½ teaspoons lemon peel, and 1 tablespoon sugar in medium bowl until stiff peaks form. Fold cooled yolk mixture into cream in 3 additions. Cover and freeze until firm, about 4 hours.

MIX berries and any accumulated juices, remaining 1 tablespoon sugar, 1½ teaspoons lemon juice, and ¼ teaspoon lemon peel in small bowl; let stand 10 minutes. Coarsely mash half of berries in bowl to thicken juices. Scoop lemon cream into small bowls. Top each with 1 rounded tablespoon berry sauce.

FOLD IT When folding, the goal is to blend two parts together—in this case, the curd and whipped cream—while maintaining the mixture's delicate airy texture. Use the side edge of a large flat rubber spatula to guide the curd down through the whipped cream and the flat part of the spatula to lift it up and over the whipped cream, repeating this motion until the mixtures are just blended.

Grapefruit-ginger sherbet

MAKES ABOUT 4¼ CUPS *Sherbet sounds like an old-fashioned frozen dessert, but it's actually perfect for our contemporary tastes; it's lighter than ice cream but richer than sorbet. Buttermilk and lots of fresh grapefruit juice help keep it light, ginger gives it a nice zing, and a touch of cream lends just the right richness. Add the cream to the sherbet when it's almost finished churning so it will stay creamy—overmixing the cream will make it curdle.*

3	cups strained fresh Ruby Red grapefruit juice, divided
¾	cup sugar
¼	cup grated peeled fresh ginger with juices
1	tablespoon finely grated grapefruit peel
¼	cup light corn syrup
1	cup buttermilk
½	cup whipping cream

STIR 1 cup grapefruit juice, sugar, ginger with juices, and grapefruit peel in heavy medium saucepan over medium-high heat until sugar dissolves. Bring to boil; remove from heat. Cool 30 minutes.

WHISK corn syrup, then buttermilk into ginger mixture. Stir in remaining 2 cups grapefruit juice. Strain mixture into large bowl, pressing on solids to extract juices. Process in ice cream maker according to manufacturer's instructions. When sherbet is softly set, gradually pour in cream. Process 5 minutes longer to blend well. Transfer sherbet to container; cover and freeze.

Rum-raisin ice cream

10 SERVINGS *Marinating (or macerating) the raisins in rum makes them plump and full of flavor. Since dark rums have a richer, sweeter flavor and more body than light or clear rums, they work best here.*

1	cup (packed) raisins
⅔	cup dark rum
8	large egg yolks
1	cup sugar
3	cups whole milk
1½	cups heavy whipping cream

COMBINE raisins and rum in small bowl. Cover; let stand at room temperature 2 hours. Drain all but 6 tablespoons rum from raisins.

WHISK yolks and sugar in large bowl until blended. Bring milk and cream to boil in heavy large saucepan over medium heat. Gradually whisk into yolk mixture. Return mixture to saucepan; stir over medium-low heat until custard thickens and finger leaves path when drawn across back of spoon, about 15 minutes (do not boil). Strain custard into bowl. Cool. Add raisin mixture to custard. Refrigerate until cold.

TRANSFER custard to ice cream maker and process according to manufacturer's instructions. Freeze ice cream in covered container until firm, about 4 hours.

DO AHEAD *Can be made 3 days ahead. Keep frozen.*

Cadbury crunch ice cream

2 TO 4 SERVINGS *Once the ice cream is blended, refreeze it until firm so it will be easy to scoop.*

1	**pint coffee ice cream, slightly softened**
2½	**ounces Cadbury Fruit & Nut bar, coarsely chopped**
2	**tablespoons dark rum**
2	**teaspoons instant espresso powder**

MIX all ingredients in large bowl. Cover and freeze until firm, about 1 hour.

DO AHEAD *Can be made 1 day ahead. Keep frozen.*

SCOOP into bowls and serve.

Amaretto amaretti crunch ice cream

2 TO 4 SERVINGS *Amaretti are delicious little Italian macaroons available at Italian markets and at many supermarkets. They have a sweet almond flavor that adds a lot of personality to vanilla ice cream, and the splash of amaretto liqueur adds more almond flavor with a kick.*

1	**pint vanilla ice cream, slightly softened**
½	**cup chopped amaretti cookies or other almond macaroons**
¼	**cup amaretto**

MIX all ingredients in medium bowl. Transfer to container and freeze until firm, about 1 hour. Scoop ice cream into bowls.

Easy scoops

— Dip ice cream scoop into lukewarm water before scooping.

— When entertaining a crowd, scoop ice cream ahead of time. Line a small baking sheet or muffin pan with plastic wrap, then scoop the ice cream onto the pan or into the cups. Cover with plastic wrap and keep frozen.

— Let ice cream soften slightly for 30 minutes in fridge before scooping, or microwave in 5-second intervals to soften.

Spiced peach sundaes

8 SERVINGS *Cardamom and nutmeg are lovely notes of spice in these super sundaes. Grating fresh nutmeg is easy to do with a Microplane grater and would add a lively flavor to the peach mixture. Vanilla ice cream is excellent with the peaches, but dulce de leche or butter pecan would be good here, too.*

¼ cup (½ stick) unsalted butter
6 tablespoons (packed) dark brown sugar
1 teaspoon vanilla extract
½ teaspoon ground cardamom
⅛ teaspoon ground nutmeg
2½ pounds ripe peaches, pitted, cut into ¼-inch-thick slices

½ gallon vanilla ice cream
Whole pecans, toasted
Sweetened whipped cream

MELT butter in heavy large skillet over medium heat. Add brown sugar; stir to blend. Add vanilla, cardamom, and nutmeg. Stir 1 minute. Add peaches; toss gently to coat. Cook until sugar mixture melts and peaches are tender but do not fall apart, tossing occasionally, about 5 minutes.

DO AHEAD *Can be made 8 hours ahead. Cover and chill. Rewarm over low heat before using.*

PLACE 2 scoops ice cream in each of 8 bowls. Spoon peach mixture over ice cream, dividing equally. Garnish with pecans and whipped cream.

Red, white, and blueberry ice cream sundaes

6 SERVINGS *These "patriotic" sundaes with their terrific blueberry-caramel sauce, vanilla and strawberry ice creams, and raspberry sorbet would be the perfect dessert for a Fourth of July party.*

1 cup plus two ½-pint baskets blueberries
2 teaspoons fresh lemon juice
2 cups powdered sugar
1¾ cups chilled heavy whipping cream, divided
¼ cup water

1 pint vanilla ice cream
1 pint raspberry sorbet
1 pint strawberry ice cream

COMBINE 1 cup blueberries and lemon juice in medium bowl; mash well. Sift powdered sugar into heavy medium nonstick skillet. Cook over medium heat until sugar begins to dissolve, stirring occasionally, about 5 minutes. Continue to cook until syrup turns deep golden brown, stirring often, about 5 minutes longer. Whisk in 1 cup cream and ¼ cup water (mixture will bubble). Reduce heat to medium-low, cover, and cook until most hard caramel bits dissolve, stirring occasionally, about 20 minutes. Remove from heat. Stir in mashed blueberries; strain into medium saucepan, pressing on solids in strainer.

DO AHEAD *Can be made 3 days ahead. Cover and chill.*

REWARM sauce over low heat. Beat remaining ¾ cup cream in medium bowl to soft peaks. Place 1 scoop each of vanilla ice cream, raspberry sorbet, and strawberry ice cream in each of 6 sundae dishes. Spoon warm sauce over. Top with remaining blueberries and whipped cream.

Tropical fruit sundaes with pineapple-rum sauce

4 SERVINGS *Meet the new sundae: A rich caramel sauce replaces traditional chocolate fudge sauce and diced fresh tropical fruits replace the lonesome maraschino cherry. A banana-strawberry frozen yogurt keeps things light, but try a macadamia nut ice cream or a coconut sorbet to keep it tropical.*

- ½ cup sugar
- ½ cup (packed) dark brown sugar
- ⅓ cup water
- ¼ cup frozen pineapple juice concentrate, thawed
- 3 tablespoons unsalted butter
- 2 tablespoons dark rum

   Banana-strawberry frozen yogurt or vanilla ice cream

   Mixed tropical fruits (such as mango, papaya, banana, and pineapple), cut into ½-inch pieces

COMBINE first 5 ingredients in heavy medium saucepan. Stir over medium heat until sugars dissolve. Boil gently until reduced to 1 cup, about 10 minutes. Cool to lukewarm. Mix in rum.

DO AHEAD *Can be made 2 days ahead. Cover and chill. Reheat to lukewarm and whisk to blend before serving.*

SCOOP frozen yogurt into balloon-shaped glasses or sundae dishes. Spoon lukewarm sauce over. Top with fruit and serve immediately.

Sesame seed–peanut brittle coupes

8 SERVINGS *When making the caramel (the sugar-water combination), keep the sides of the saucepan free of any clinging sugar granules by brushing down the sides of the pan with a wet pastry brush. A few granules can cause a chain reaction of crystallization, which makes the caramel syrup grainy. Once you've mixed in the peanuts, butter, and sesame seeds, quickly pour the caramel onto a buttered baking sheet so that it spreads into a thin layer, which will make a more delicate brittle.*

- 1 cup sugar
- ⅓ cup water
- ¾ cup lightly salted husked cocktail peanuts (about 4 ounces)
- 1½ teaspoons butter
- ¼ cup sesame seeds, toasted

   Vanilla ice cream or frozen yogurt
   Rum

BUTTER baking sheet. Cook sugar and ⅓ cup water in heavy medium saucepan over low heat, stirring until sugar dissolves. Increase heat and boil without stirring until syrup turns dark amber color, swirling pan occasionally and brushing down sides of pan with wet pastry brush, about 13 minutes. Mix in peanuts and butter, then sesame seeds. Immediately pour mixture onto prepared sheet. Cool completely. Break into pieces. Using on/off turns, coarsely grind brittle in processor.

DO AHEAD *Can be made 2 weeks ahead. Chill in airtight container.*

SCOOP ice cream into dishes. Top with brittle and drizzle with rum.

Cinnamon French Toast
Warm Berry Preserves

Giant Pumpkin Muffins with Molasses-Ginger Glaze

Chocolate Chip Cookie and Mint Ice Cream Sandwich

CLOCKWISE FROM TOP LEFT: Dark Chocolate Fondue;
Dark Chocolate Brownies with White Chocolate Chunks;
Red Velvet Cupcakes with Coconut and Cream Cheese
Frosting; Fudgy Chocolate Mint Cupcakes

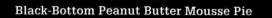
Black-Bottom Peanut Butter Mousse Pie

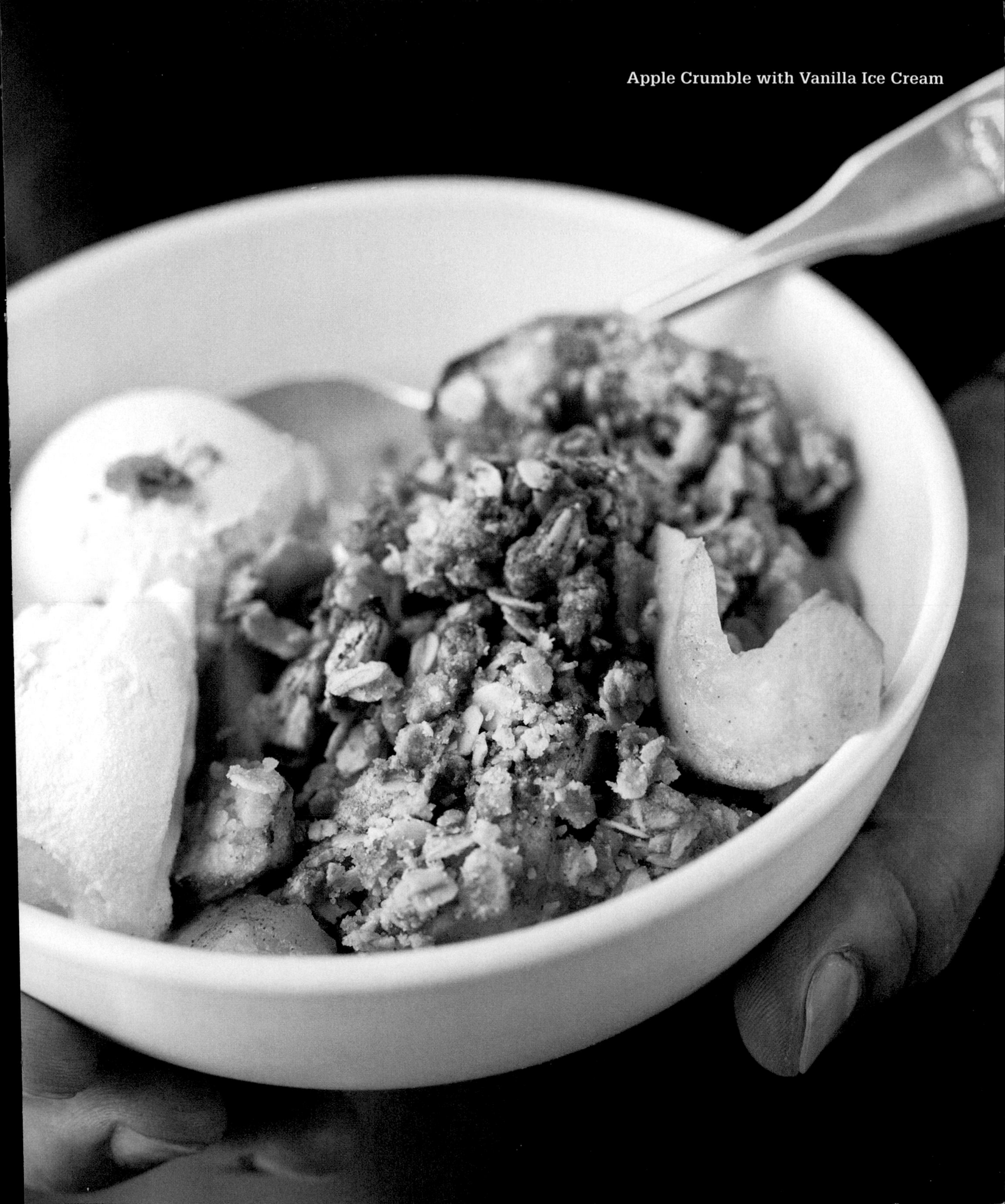

Apple Crumble with Vanilla Ice Cream

Strawberry Shortcakes with
Mint and Whipped Cream

Coffee, chocolate, and marshmallow sundaes

6 SERVINGS *If you can't find a good-quality coffee ice cream with almonds and chocolate (sometimes la-beled coffee almond fudge), mix a few more almonds into another high-quality coffee ice cream.*

- ½ **cup heavy whipping cream**
- ½ **cup marshmallow creme, plus more for topping**
- 6 **ounces bittersweet or semisweet chocolate, chopped**

- 1½ **pints (about) coffee ice cream with almonds and chocolate**
- ⅔ **cup sliced almonds, toasted**

BRING cream and ½ cup marshmallow creme to simmer in small saucepan. Remove from heat. Add chocolate and whisk until melted and smooth. Cool marshmallow sauce at least 10 minutes and up to 1 hour.

PLACE 1 scoop of ice cream in each bowl. Pour marshmallow sauce over. Sprinkle sundaes with almonds and top with dollop of marshmallow creme.

DON'T STICK To keep marshmallow creme from sticking to your measuring cup, spray the cup with nonstick cooking spray first, or spray a trigger ice cream scoop and use it to scoop out the marshmallow creme from its container.

Chocolate-orange ice cream sundaes

4 SERVINGS *Corn syrup is the secret ingredient that gives chocolate fudge sauce its wonderfully gooey texture, making it different than a syrupy chocolate sauce. The orange peel gives this sauce a citrus twist that pairs nicely with a Creamsicle-flavored sorbet, but it can be omitted to make a multipurpose choco-late fudge sauce that pairs well with any ice cream.*

- ¾ **cup heavy whipping cream**
- ¼ **cup light corn syrup**
- 2 **teaspoons finely grated orange peel**
- 8 **ounces bittersweet or semisweet chocolate, chopped**

- 1 **pint orange sorbet and vanilla ice cream swirl, or 1 cup orange sherbet and 1 cup vanilla ice cream**

BRING cream, corn syrup, and orange peel to simmer in heavy medium saucepan. Reduce heat to low. Add chocolate and whisk until melted and smooth. Cool mixture to lukewarm.

DO AHEAD *Sauce can be made 2 weeks ahead. Cover and chill. Rewarm over low heat before continuing.*

SCOOP ice cream into dishes. Spoon sauce over ice cream.

FROZENDESSERTS

Chestnut and Kahlúa ice cream with Kahlúa sauce

2 TO 4 SERVINGS; CAN BE DOUBLED Marrons glacés is French for "chestnuts in syrup." You'll find them in jars and cans at specialty markets and some supermarkets during the holidays. Be sure to save some of the syrup, since it doubles as a sauce for this very elegant sundae. If you don't have Kahlúa, you can use another coffee-flavored liqueur.

- 1 pint rich vanilla ice cream, slightly softened
- 8 chestnuts in vanilla syrup, drained (syrup reserved) and chopped
- 2½ tablespoons Kahlúa, divided
- 2 tablespoons coarsely grated bittersweet or semisweet chocolate
- ¼ teaspoon instant espresso powder

STIR ice cream, chestnuts, and 2 tablespoons Kahlúa in medium bowl. Freeze until firm, about 1 hour.

COMBINE 1 tablespoon chestnut syrup and remaining ½ tablespoon Kahlúa in small bowl. Combine chocolate and espresso powder in small bowl. Scoop ice cream into glass goblets. Spoon syrup over. Sprinkle with chocolate mixture.

Dulce de leche ice cream with fresh strawberries and Mexican chocolate sauce

6 SERVINGS Ten years ago most Americans couldn't pronounce dulce de leche (DOOL-say de LE-chay)—now we can't get enough of it. This "sweetened milk," used as sauce and candy in many Latin countries, as well as in Spain and Portugal, has an irresistible caramel-like appeal. This flavor pairs well with the chocolate sauce, which has its own Latin vibe with cinnamon and a dash of cayenne.

- 6 ounces bittersweet or semisweet chocolate, chopped
- ⅔ cup heavy whipping cream
- 1 teaspoon ground cinnamon
- ⅛ teaspoon cayenne pepper

- 2 pints dulce de leche ice cream
- 4 cups fresh strawberries (about 1 pound), hulled, quartered

PLACE first 4 ingredients in medium metal bowl. Set bowl over saucepan of simmering water; stir until smooth.

DIVIDE ice cream among 6 bowls. Sprinkle berries over. Spoon warm or room-temperature sauce over.

Brown sugar–bourbon peaches with vanilla ice cream

2 SERVINGS; CAN BE DOUBLED OR TRIPLED *To peel peaches, place them in boiling water for 30 seconds to one minute (this is called "blanching"), then rinse them under cold water to stop them from cooking. The skins will slip right off. Use freestone peaches rather than the clingstone variety, and the pits will come out easily. If using very ripe peaches, the skins can be peeled off easily (no need to blanch first).*

- 6 tablespoons bourbon
- ¼ cup (packed) dark brown sugar
- 2 tablespoons (¼ stick) butter
- 1 tablespoon fresh lemon juice
- 1 teaspoon vanilla extract
- 2 peaches, peeled, pitted, sliced

  Vanilla ice cream

COMBINE first 5 ingredients in heavy medium skillet over medium-low heat. Stir until brown sugar dissolves. Add peaches and stir until heated through.

SCOOP ice cream into bowls. Spoon peaches and sauce over.

Prune and Armagnac compote with ice cream

4 SERVINGS *Armagnac is a truly luxurious French brandy with a rich, full-bodied flavor and smooth finish. As it simmers with the prunes it becomes infused with cinnamon and orange notes and creates a compote that is delicious on its own, and even better over ice cream. If you have any leftover compote, serve it with French toast for a special brunch.*

- 1½ cups water
- ¾ cup sugar
- 3 orange slices
- 1 cinnamon stick
- 1 12-ounce bag pitted prunes
- 3 tablespoons Armagnac, Cognac, or brandy (optional)

  Chocolate or vanilla ice cream
  Sliced toasted almonds

SIMMER first 4 ingredients in heavy medium saucepan over medium heat for flavors to blend, stirring until sugar dissolves, about 15 minutes. Add prunes and simmer until tender, about 20 minutes. Remove from heat and mix in Armagnac.

DO AHEAD *Can be made 3 days ahead. Cover and chill.*

DISCARD orange slices and cinnamon stick. Serve compote warm or at room temperature over ice cream. Top with almonds.

Ice cream with sautéed pineapple and bourbon

2 SERVINGS; CAN BE DOUBLED OR TRIPLED *Use a sharp chef's knife or serrated knife to cut through the rough pineapple peel—or skip the peeling altogether and look for peeled, cored fresh pineapple in rings or cubes in the refrigerated produce section of the supermarket. As the pineapple chunks cook in the sugar mixture they exude their juices to create a delicious syrupy caramel sauce for the ice cream.*

- 2 tablespoons (¼ stick) butter
- 3 tablespoons (packed) dark brown sugar
- ⅛ teaspoon ground cloves
- 1½ cups ½-inch cubes peeled fresh pineapple
- ¼ cup bourbon
  Vanilla ice cream

MELT butter in heavy medium saucepan over medium heat. Add brown sugar and cloves; bring to boil, stirring until sugar dissolves. Add pineapple and cook until heated through and liquid is syrupy, stirring constantly, about 2 minutes. Remove from heat. Stir in bourbon. Cook over medium heat until syrupy, about 2 minutes. Scoop ice cream into bowls. Spoon pineapple and syrup over.

Brandy-glazed apples with vanilla ice cream

2 SERVINGS; CAN BE DOUBLED OR TRIPLED *Granny Smith or Pippin apples provide a tart backdrop to the sweet ice cream in this dessert.*

- 2 small tart green apples (such as Granny Smith or Pippin), peeled, cored, cut into ¼-inch-thick rings
- 1½ tablespoons butter, melted
- ¼ cup (packed) brown sugar
- 1½ tablespoons applejack or other brandy
  Vanilla ice cream

PREHEAT oven to 350°F. Lightly butter 9-inch square baking pan. Arrange apple rings in pan, overlapping slightly. Brush with butter. Bake until just tender, about 40 minutes.

PREHEAT broiler. Sprinkle apples with brown sugar. Broil until sugar melts and begins to caramelize, watching carefully. Sprinkle with applejack. Arrange apples in ring on each of 2 plates. Place scoop of ice cream in center of each. Drizzle juices from bottom of pan over ice cream.

KITCHEN TOYS Use an apple corer to remove the core and keep the apple intact so you can cut the apple into rings. To really impress your dinner guests, caramelize the brown sugar topping with a small culinary torch.

Vanilla ice cream with lychees and crystallized ginger

2 SERVINGS; CAN BE DOUBLED *Canned lychees are available in the Asian foods section of most supermarkets; they're packed in a syrup that also doubles as a sauce. For a fragrant floral addition, steep a couple of jasmine tea bags in the syrup as it simmers; after a few minutes, remove the tea bags and continue simmering the syrup until it thickens.*

1   15-ounce can lychees in syrup
2   orange slices
2   tablespoons Cointreau or other orange liqueur
1   tablespoon (generous) minced crystallized ginger

    Vanilla ice cream

DRAIN syrup from lychees into heavy small saucepan. Place lychees in medium bowl. Add orange slices to syrup and boil until syrup thickens, about 10 minutes. Discard orange slices. Pour syrup over lychees. Mix in Cointreau and ginger.

DO AHEAD *Can be made 2 days ahead. Cover and chill.*

SCOOP ice cream into bowls. Spoon lychees and syrup over.

Balsamic berries over vanilla ice cream

2 SERVINGS; CAN BE DOUBLED OR TRIPLED *In a simple recipe like this, it's important to use the best quality ingredients you can get your hands on. Use fresh seasonal strawberries (try the wild ones that you can find at your farmers' market during spring and summer) and aged balsamic vinegar. The clove-scented pine nuts add a surprising final touch.*

1   ½-pint basket fresh strawberries, hulled, sliced
1   tablespoon balsamic vinegar
2   tablespoons sugar, divided

2   tablespoons pine nuts
    Pinch of ground cloves

    Vanilla ice cream

PLACE berries, vinegar, and 1 tablespoon sugar in small bowl; toss to coat.

COMBINE remaining 1 tablespoon sugar, pine nuts, and cloves in heavy small skillet. Stir over medium-low heat until sugar melts and pine nuts are golden brown, about 4 minutes. Transfer to sheet of foil and cool.

SCOOP ice cream into bowls. Top with berries, then with pine nuts.

Ice cream with Marsala and currants

2 SERVINGS; CAN BE DOUBLED OR TRIPLED *You may be tempted to substitute raisins for the dried currants, but you'll miss the delicate speckling and intense flavor that currants (tiny dried Zante grapes) contribute. Look for currants at the supermarket—they are sold right alongside the raisins.*

- ¼ cup dried currants
- ¼ cup fresh orange juice
- ¼ cup sweet Marsala
- 2 tablespoons sugar
- ½ cinnamon stick (about 2 inches)
- ½ teaspoon finely grated orange peel

   Vanilla ice cream
   Amaretti or other cookies, crumbled

COMBINE first 6 ingredients in heavy small saucepan. Boil until syrupy, stirring frequently, about 10 minutes. Cool slightly. Discard cinnamon stick.

SCOOP ice cream into bowls. Spoon warm currant mixture over ice cream. Sprinkle with cookies.

Strawberry and macaroon parfaits

6 SERVINGS *There are two distinctly different types of macaroons: soft coconut macaroons, and dry, airy, crisp macaroons made with almonds, sugar, and egg whites and sometimes called amaretti. This recipe calls for the latter (they're available at some supermarkets and at Italian markets); their texture contrasts nicely with the fresh fruit and frozen yogurt in this parfait. As an alternative to the frozen yogurt, use vanilla ice cream or sweetened crème fraîche or whipped cream.*

- 3 cups sliced hulled fresh strawberries (about 18 ounces), plus 6 whole strawberries for garnish
- 1 16-ounce package frozen strawberries in sugar, thawed
- 2 cups coarsely crushed Italian-style almond macaroons or crushed almond biscotti
- 1½ pints vanilla frozen yogurt

MIX sliced strawberries and frozen strawberries in sugar in medium bowl. Divide half of strawberry mixture among six 10- to 12-ounce goblets or wineglasses. Top with half of macaroons and small scoops of frozen yogurt. Repeat layering. Garnish each with 1 fresh strawberry.

Biscotti parfaits

2 SERVINGS; CAN BE DOUBLED *This combination of flavors and textures, not to mention the elegant presentation in wineglasses or brandy snifters, makes it a special dessert for two or four. Try different flavors—chocolate or coffee ice cream, for example, and dried cherries, figs, and currants. For more liqueur flavor, soak the fruit in the sambuca for an hour before assembling the dessert.*

4 purchased almond biscotti
12 teaspoons sambuca or other anise liqueur
1 cup (½ pint) vanilla ice cream or frozen yogurt
4 tablespoons diced mixed dried fruit

PLACE biscotti in heavy sealable plastic bag. Crush biscotti coarsely with rolling pin. Divide half of crumbs between 2 brandy snifters or tall wine goblets. Drizzle each with 2 teaspoons liqueur. Divide half of ice cream and half of diced fruit between glasses. Drizzle each with 2 teaspoons liqueur. Divide remaining ice cream and remaining crumbs between glasses. Drizzle each with 2 teaspoons liqueur. Serve immediately or cover and freeze up to 1 hour.

Warm doughnuts à la mode with bananas and spiced caramel sauce

2 SERVINGS *Doughnuts meet bananas Foster in this playful treat. Use supermarket doughnuts or freshly baked ones from the doughnut shop.*

2 cinnamon crumb or glazed doughnuts
3 tablespoons butter
3 tablespoons (packed) golden brown sugar
2 teaspoons fresh lemon juice
¾ teaspoon ground cinnamon
⅛ teaspoon ground nutmeg
1 tablespoon dark rum

2 small ripe bananas, peeled, cut on diagonal into ½-inch-thick slices
Vanilla ice cream
Toasted pecans

PREHEAT broiler. Place doughnuts on small baking sheet; set aside. Stir butter and brown sugar in heavy medium skillet over medium heat until butter is melted. Boil 1 minute, stirring occasionally. Remove from heat. Mix in lemon juice and spices, then rum; stir to blend. Cool caramel sauce 3 minutes.

MEANWHILE, broil doughnuts just until hot and bubbly, watching closely to avoid burning, 1 to 2 minutes per side. Transfer doughnuts to 2 plates. Toss bananas with caramel sauce in skillet. Top each doughnut with scoop of ice cream, flattening slightly in center. Spoon bananas and caramel sauce over. Sprinkle with pecans.

Butter pecan ice cream pie with caramel topping

8 SERVINGS *This variation of the American mud pie is made with butter pecan ice cream and purchased caramel topping.*

¾ cup pecans, toasted
1½ cups graham cracker crumbs
2 tablespoons (packed) golden brown sugar
6 tablespoons (¾ stick) unsalted butter, melted

2 quarts butter pecan ice cream, slightly softened

   Purchased caramel ice cream topping

COARSELY chop pecans in processor. Set aside ¼ cup pecans for garnish. Add graham cracker crumbs and brown sugar to remaining pecans in processor and blend until nuts are finely ground. Add melted butter and process until moist clumps form. Press pecan mixture onto bottom and up sides of 9-inch pie dish. Freeze crust until firm, about 15 minutes.

SPOON ice cream into crust, packing firmly and mounding slightly in center. Freeze pie until ice cream is firm, about 1 hour.

DRIZZLE some caramel topping over pie. Sprinkle with reserved chopped pecans. Serve pie immediately or cover and freeze up to 2 days.

Chocolate cookie and coffee ice cream pie

8 TO 10 SERVINGS *Look for the ready-made chocolate cookie pie crust alongside the canned fruits and pie fillings at the supermarket.*

1 cup heavy whipping cream
8 ounces semisweet chocolate chips
1 teaspoon instant coffee crystals
½ teaspoon vanilla extract

1 pint coffee ice cream, slightly softened
1 9-inch-diameter purchased chocolate cookie crumb crust
10 chocolate sandwich cookies, coarsely crushed (about 1 cup), plus additional whole sandwich cookies
1 pint chocolate ice cream

BRING cream to simmer in small saucepan over medium heat. Remove from heat. Add chocolate chips; whisk until chocolate is melted. Whisk in coffee and vanilla. Let sauce cool.

SPREAD coffee ice cream evenly in cookie crumb crust. Pour ¾ cup chocolate sauce over; sprinkle with crushed cookies. Freeze until ice cream is firm, about 20 minutes. Drizzle ⅓ cup sauce over pie. Arrange chocolate ice cream in side-by-side scoops around edge of pie. Wedge 1 whole cookie between each scoop. Freeze pie until firm, at least 2 hours and up to 1 day. Cover and chill remaining sauce.

REWARM sauce. Cut pie into wedges. Serve, passing sauce separately.

Frozen peanut butter pie

8 SERVINGS *This larger-than-life peanut butter cup blends cream cheese, peanut butter, sugar, and whipped cream for a rich and decadent filling. Old-fashioned-style peanut butter and freshly ground peanut butter, while delicious, don't have the right consistency for this pie filling, so be sure to use a creamy peanut butter. As with most frozen pies, you can make this dessert a day ahead and keep it in the freezer, covered.*

¾ **cup graham cracker crumbs**
1 **cup sugar, divided**
2 **tablespoons (packed) golden brown sugar**
¼ **cup (½ stick) unsalted butter, melted**

1 **8-ounce package cream cheese, room temperature**
1 **cup creamy peanut butter**
1 **tablespoon vanilla extract**
1½ **cups chilled heavy whipping cream**

Purchased hot fudge sauce

MIX graham cracker crumbs, ¼ cup sugar, and brown sugar in medium bowl. Add butter and stir until blended. Press mixture onto bottom and up sides of 9-inch-diameter glass pie dish. Refrigerate while preparing filling.

USING electric mixer, beat cream cheese, peanut butter, vanilla, and remaining ¾ cup sugar in large bowl until smooth. Using electric mixer with clean dry beaters, beat cream in another large bowl until peaks form. Gently fold whipped cream into peanut butter mixture in 4 additions. Spoon filling into prepared crust, mounding slightly in center. Freeze until firm, about 2 hours.

DO AHEAD *Can be prepared 1 day ahead. Cover and keep frozen.*

WARM hot fudge according to package directions, if desired. Cut pie into wedges; serve with hot fudge sauce.

Crowning touch Piping rosettes of whipped cream around the edge of a pie just before serving is a smart way to give any pie (even a purchased one) a professional look. Plus, it's easy. Using an electric mixer, beat heavy whipping cream in a large bowl with just a touch of sugar, brown sugar, maple syrup, or honey until the cream is soft and fluffy. Spoon the whipped cream into a resealable plastic bag, cut off one corner, grasp the bag firmly to push the whipped cream down toward the corner, and pipe away.

Macadamia ice cream and mango sorbet swirl pie

8 SERVINGS *Grinding purchased ice cream sugar cones in a food processor with sugar and butter is a clever way of making the delicious crust for this pie. Feel free to create your own ice cream filling combination—supermarket freezers are full of new ice cream flavors.*

Nonstick vegetable oil spray
12 purchased ice cream sugar cones (about 5 to 6 ounces), coarsely broken
4 tablespoons sugar, divided
6 tablespoons (¾ stick) unsalted butter, melted

1 pint macadamia brittle ice cream, slightly softened
1 pint mango sorbet, slightly softened

1 cup chilled heavy whipping cream
½ teaspoon vanilla extract
Toasted shredded coconut

SPRAY 9-inch-diameter glass pie dish with nonstick spray. Using on/off turns, grind cones with 3 tablespoons sugar in processor until fine crumbs form. Add butter and blend until crumbs stick together. Press crumb mixture onto bottom and up sides of prepared dish. Freeze until firm, at least 30 minutes.

SCOOP ice cream into large bowl. Scoop sorbet atop ice cream. Using spatula, fold and stir ice cream and sorbet briefly to swirl (do not overmix). Transfer mixture to prepared pie crust. Freeze pie until filling is hard, at least 2 hours.

DO AHEAD *Can be prepared 1 day ahead. Cover and keep frozen.*

USING electric mixer, beat cream, vanilla, and remaining 1 tablespoon sugar in medium bowl until peaks form. Spread over ice cream pie. Sprinkle with coconut. Cut pie into wedges.

Goober ice cream sandwiches

2 SERVINGS; CAN BE DOUBLED *"Goober" is a southern colloquialism for the peanut. Be sure to put these together before dinner so that they'll be frozen and ready for dessert. Or make them up to two days ahead and wrap them tightly in plastic wrap before freezing. The chocolate wafer cookies called for here are very thin and flat.*

⅓ cup chopped roasted salted cocktail peanuts
1 cup vanilla ice cream, slightly softened
12 chocolate wafer cookies (from 9-ounce package)

PLACE peanuts in shallow bowl. Spoon 1 heaping tablespoon ice cream onto flat side of 1 cookie. Place flat side of another cookie onto ice cream and press until ice cream spreads to edge of sandwich. Smooth ice cream. Roll edge of sandwich in peanuts to coat ice cream filling. Place sandwich on plate and put in freezer. Repeat with remaining cookies, ice cream, and peanuts, forming 6 sandwiches total. Freeze sandwiches until ice cream firms, at least 15 minutes.

DO AHEAD *Can be made 2 days ahead. Wrap tightly and keep frozen.*

Chocolate chip cookie and mint ice cream sandwiches

MAKES 8 *Dipping the sandwiches in melted chocolate is decadent and fun; melting the chocolate in a small bowl creates a deeper pool of chocolate, which makes dipping easy. As you melt the chocolate in the microwave, stir it every 15 seconds so that it melts evenly, even if it doesn't look melted after the first 15 to 30 seconds. You can use purchased chocolate chip cookies to make these even more quickly.*

16   **ready-to-bake chocolate chip cookie dough pieces**

¾   **cup chopped toasted hazelnuts**

1   **pint vanilla ice cream, slightly softened**

2   **tablespoons chopped fresh mint**

¼   **teaspoon peppermint extract**

6   **ounces (1 cup) semisweet or bittersweet chocolate chips**

PREHEAT oven to 350°F. Shape dough pieces into balls. Arrange on baking sheet and flatten to ½-inch thickness; press nuts onto each. Bake until golden, 12 to 18 minutes, depending on brand of cookie. Cool completely on sheet.

MEANWHILE, mix ice cream, fresh mint, and extract in small bowl; place in freezer until ready to use.

LINE baking sheet with foil. Place ¼ cup ice cream on flat side of 1 cookie. Top with flat side of second cookie. Place on prepared sheet and freeze. Repeat to form 7 more sandwiches. Freeze until ice cream begins to firm, about 10 minutes.

MELT chocolate chips in small microwave-safe bowl on low setting in 15-second intervals, stirring often. Dip sandwiches halfway into chocolate. Return to sheet. Freeze at least 30 minutes and up to 1 day.

Simple sandwiches Ice cream sandwiches are quick, easy, and fun desserts. Here's another to try: Spread softened chocolate or vanilla ice cream over the flat side of one peanut butter cookie. Add thin slices of banana and a little peanut butter. Top with another cookie, flat side down, and press gently to adhere. Freeze the sandwiches until they're firm. If you like, you can then dip them in melted chocolate.

589

Valentine chocolate-cherry ice cream bombe

12 TO 16 SERVINGS *A bombe sounds and looks fancy, but it's really just frozen layers of ice cream made in a rounded mold. Here, the ice cream and sorbet are purchased, topped with cookies (which form a bottom crust once the bombe is unmolded), and finished with a store-bought fudge sauce spruced up with chocolate chips and brandy. Begin preparing this a day ahead.*

- 1 16-ounce jar purchased hot fudge sauce
- 1 12-ounce package semisweet chocolate chips
- 3 tablespoons water
- ¼ cup brandy

- 3 pints cherry-vanilla ice cream with chocolate chunks or fudge flakes, slightly softened
- 1½ pints chocolate sorbet or chocolate-cherry sorbet, slightly softened
- 1 9-ounce package chocolate wafer cookies

STIR first 3 ingredients in heavy medium saucepan over medium-low heat until melted and smooth. Remove from heat. Whisk in brandy. Cool.

LINE 10-inch-diameter, 10-cup metal bowl with plastic wrap, extending over sides. Spread cherry-vanilla ice cream over inside of bowl to within ¾ inch of top edge, leaving center 6-inch-diameter hollow. Freeze 30 minutes. Fill hollow completely with sorbet; smooth top. Overlap half of cookies (about 22) atop ice cream and sorbet, covering completely and pressing gently. Spread 1⅓ cups fudge-brandy sauce over cookies. Overlap remaining cookies atop sauce. Cover; freeze bombe overnight. Cover and chill remaining sauce.

DO AHEAD *Can be made 3 days ahead. Keep bombe frozen. Keep sauce chilled.*

REWARM remaining sauce over low heat, stirring often. Turn bombe out onto platter. Peel off plastic. Cut bombe into wedges. Serve with remaining sauce.

Frozen lemon-ginger yogurt

MAKES ABOUT 6 CUPS *Light, refreshing, and tangy-sweet yogurt is easy to make—just stir all the ingredients together and process in an ice cream machine until frosty and creamy. Scoop it into bowls and top it with cubes of fresh mango, strawberry slices, and blackberries.*

- 1 16-ounce container plain low-fat yogurt
- 2 cups heavy whipping cream
- ½ cup sugar
- ¼ cup honey
- 3 tablespoons fresh lemon juice
- 1 tablespoon minced peeled fresh ginger
- 2 teaspoons finely grated lemon peel
- ½ teaspoon vanilla extract
- ¼ teaspoon ground ginger

COMBINE all ingredients in large bowl and stir to blend. Transfer yogurt mixture to ice cream maker. Process according to manufacturer's instructions. Spoon into large covered container and freeze.

DO AHEAD *Can be made 2 days ahead. Keep frozen.*

White peach, cassis, and Champagne floats

MAKES 6 *This super-easy and refreshing dessert is like a peach parfait cocktail. For a very cool treat, layer the fruit and ice cream in frosty Collins or pilsner glasses straight from the freezer. Serve with iced-tea spoons.*

- 6 medium white peaches, halved, pitted, each half cut into 4 wedges
- 2 pints peach ice cream
- ¾ cup crème de cassis (black-currant liqueur) plus additional for drizzling
- 2 cups chilled brut Champagne or sparkling wine

PLACE 3 peach wedges in bottom of each of 6 tall glasses. Top with 1 scoop ice cream, then another 3 peach wedges. Add second scoop ice cream and top with 2 more peach wedges. Drizzle each with 2 tablespoons crème de cassis. Pour ⅓ cup Champagne into each glass. Top with 1 scoop ice cream and drizzle with additional crème de cassis.

Affogato mocha

4 SERVINGS *Affogato is a typically Italian way to enjoy ice cream—it's "drowned" in espresso or another liquid topping. This recipe uses chocolate ice cream and rum, but vanilla ice cream and Kahlúa work well, too. Be sure to chop the chocolate very finely so that it melts from the heat of the espresso.*

- 1 pint chocolate ice cream
- 8 tablespoons finely chopped bittersweet or semisweet chocolate
- 8 tablespoons hot freshly brewed espresso coffee
- 8 tablespoons dark rum

DIVIDE ice cream among 4 dessert bowls or coffee cups. Spoon 2 tablespoons each of chopped chocolate, hot espresso, and rum over ice cream and serve immediately.

HOT CHOCOLATE, *AFFOGATO* STYLE An *affogato* is traditionally made by drowning a scoop of vanilla ice cream in a shot of hot espresso. Why not reverse it: Drown a scoop of coffee ice cream in hot white chocolate. You can even add a splash of your favorite liqueur.

cookiesand
brownies,
piesandtarts, andeasycakes

COOKIES AND BROWNIES

No-Fail Chocolate Chippers

Giant Chocolate Chip Cookies

Sugar Cookies

Chai-Spiced Almond Cookies

Chocolate Macaroons

Currant and Spice
Oatmeal Cookies

Soft Ginger Cookies

Peppermint Crunch
Chocolate Chip Meringues

Chewy Pine Nut Cookies

Double Chocolate Mint Cookies

Outrageous Peanut
Butter Cookies

Lemon and Anise Sugar Twists

Lemon Thumbprint Cookies

Lemon Shortbread

Ginger Almond Wafers

Brown Sugar and Nutmeg Snaps

S'mores with a Twist

Dark Chocolate Brownies with
White Chocolate Chunks

Brownies with Chocolate-
Covered Raisins

Mocha Brownies

Fudgy Peanut Brownies

Heath Bar Brownies

Raspberry-Pecan Blondies

Double-Lemon Bars

Berry-Berry Streusel Bars

Raisin and Cardamom
Granola Bars

Pumpkin-Raisin Bars

PIES AND TARTS

Citrus Galette

Raspberry Sour Cream Tart

Chocolate-Hazelnut Ganache Tart

No-Bake Lemon Cream Tart

Mascarpone Tart with Honey,
Oranges, and Pistachios

Pear and Frangipane Crostata
with Raspberry Vinegar Glaze

Caramelized Walnut Tart

Almond, Apricot, and
Cream Cheese Crostata

Fruit and Cookie-Crust Pizza

Scottish Apple Pie

Old-Fashioned Lime Pie

Peach Pie with Berry Jam

Chocolate-Pecan Chess Pie

Black-Bottom Peanut
Butter Mousse Pie

Chocolate Mousse Pie

Pineapple-Coconut Pie

Sweet Potato–Pecan Pie

Fresh Blackberry Napoleons
with Cream Cheese Mousse

Chocolate-Orange Cookie Stacks

EASY CAKES

Red Velvet Cupcakes
with Coconut and Cream
Cheese Frosting

Fudgy Chocolate Mint Cupcakes

Pear-Gingerbread
Upside-Down Cake

Old-Fashioned Gingerbread
with Molasses Whipped Cream

Mississippi Mud Cake

Chocolate-Raspberry Cakes

Bittersweet Molten Chocolate
Cakes with Coffee Ice Cream

Chocolate Terrine with
Cookies and Dried Cherries

Almond Cake with Kirsch

Orange-Pineapple Carrot Cake

Banana Cake with Sour
Cream Frosting

Apple and Walnut Sheet
Cake with Caramel Sauce

Spiced Nectarine Cake

Lemon-Lime Pound Cake

tool kit The delicious baked desserts in this chapter come in all shapes, sizes, categories, and flavor combinations, from the simple chocolate chip cookie to elegant napoleons. One easy way to put a finishing touch on any of them—or to dress up purchased baked goods so that they'll look and taste homemade—is with luxurious dessert sauces. And since batches of brownies or whole cakes will likely last a day or two, these sauces offer ways to make leftovers look like brand-new desserts.

BERRY SAUCE

HOW TO MAKE IT: Blend thawed frozen berries (raspberries, blackberries, blueberries, stemmed strawberries) in a food processor or blender just until the fruit is pureed. Strain to remove the seeds. Sweeten to taste with sugar, honey, or maple syrup.

WAYS TO USE IT: Spoon over brownies or pound cake; drizzle between layers of cubed angel food cake and sweetened crème fraîche in clear glasses for pretty parfaits.

CARAMEL SAUCE

HOW TO MAKE IT: Combine 1 cup firmly packed light or dark brown sugar with ⅔ cup heavy whipping cream, ¼ cup butter, 2 tablespoons dark corn syrup, and a generous pinch of salt in a heavy medium saucepan. Stir over medium heat until sugar dissolves. Increase heat to high and boil until slightly thickened, stirring occasionally, about 4 minutes. Cool at least 10 minutes before using.

WAYS TO USE IT: While it's still warm, drizzle the sauce over warm purchased gingerbread so that it soaks through. Spoon it over apple pie. Or chill it and spread it between butter cookies.

CHOCOLATE SAUCE

HOW TO MAKE IT: Bring ½ cup water to a simmer in a heavy small saucepan over high heat. Remove from heat and add 8 ounces of bittersweet or semisweet chocolate chips. Whisk until melted and smooth.

WAYS TO USE IT: Pour it over brownies and chill until the sauce hardens before cutting. Spoon it into purchased pastry shells and chill until cold, then dollop with whipped cream. →

SWEETENED CREAM

HOW TO MAKE IT: Sweeten chilled heavy whipping cream with sugar to taste and stir until the sugar dissolves. This sweet cream is delicious as is, but can be flavored with finely grated orange peel, a drop or two of almond extract, ground cinnamon, grated nutmeg, liqueur, or small pieces of vanilla bean.

WAYS TO USE IT: Drizzle it around plated brownies, or over slices of virtually any cake, tart, or pie.

JAM SAUCE

HOW TO MAKE IT: Combine ½ cup of your favorite preserves or jam with 2 to 3 tablespoons water in a small saucepan over low heat until it is warm and saucy. Strain the sauce, if desired, to remove any fruit pieces. Stir in your favorite liqueur, if desired.

WAYS TO USE IT: Spoon it over pound cake and top with fresh fruit, or brush it over a fruit tart for a pretty glaze.

Cookies 101 How to bake great cookies, batch after batch:

— To make sure that the temperature inside the oven is the same as the number you selected on the dial, invest in an oven thermometer. Most home ovens are off by between 25 and 50 degrees, which can greatly affect baking times.

— After years of baking cookies for the magazine, the BON APPÉTIT Test Kitchen has found that light-colored, non-insulated, metal cookie sheets work best—particularly "half-sheets," which are 17×12-inch aluminum pans with 1-inch-high sides. These are very sturdy and can accommodate about a dozen 2-inch cookies. Look for baker's half-sheets at well-stocked supermarkets, cookware stores, and restaurant supply stores.

— To prevent cookies from sticking (and to make cleanup a breeze), line the baking sheets with parchment paper or a silicone baking mat.

— If you are baking two sheets of cookies at a time, switch them from the top rack to the bottom rack and turn them from front to back halfway through baking. This will ensure that the cookies are evenly browned.

— Don't place cookie dough on a warm cookie sheet—the dough will melt and spread too quickly. To cool baking sheets in a hurry, wipe them with a cold, wet sponge or rinse them under cold running water.

— Cool cookies completely before storing them in airtight containers. If they are still warm, the trapped steam will make them soggy.

COOKIESANDBROWNIES

No-fail chocolate chippers

MAKES ABOUT 2 DOZEN *Almost any combination of nuts and chocolate chips would be good in this simple recipe. Two to try: pecans and semisweet chips, or macadamia nuts and white chocolate chips.*

- 2 **cups old-fashioned oats**
- 1¾ **cups all purpose flour**
- 1 **teaspoon baking soda**
- ½ **teaspoon salt**

- ½ **cup (1 stick) unsalted butter, room temperature**
- 1 **cup (packed) golden brown sugar**
- ½ **cup sugar**
- 2 **large eggs**
- 1 **teaspoon vanilla extract**
- 1 **cup chopped walnuts**
- 1 **11.5-ounce package (about 2 cups) milk chocolate chips**

PREHEAT oven to 375°F. Finely grind oats in processor. Add flour, baking soda, and salt; blend 5 seconds.

BEAT butter and both sugars in large bowl until well blended. Beat in eggs and vanilla. Mix in dry ingredients. Mix in walnuts and chocolate chips.

FOR each cookie, form 2 rounded tablespoons dough into ball and place on ungreased baking sheet; flatten slightly. Bake until cookies are golden brown, about 12 minutes. Cool on sheets 5 minutes. Transfer to racks; cool completely.

Giant chocolate chip cookies

MAKES ABOUT 20 *This recipe calls for both shortening and butter. The shortening gives the oversize cookies a chewy texture; butter adds a rich flavor.*

- 2¼ **cups all purpose flour**
- 1 **teaspoon baking soda**
- 1 **teaspoon salt**
- ½ **cup (1 stick) unsalted butter, room temperature**
- ½ **cup nonhydrogenated solid vegetable shortening**
- ¾ **cup sugar**
- ¾ **cup (packed) golden brown sugar**
- 1 **tablespoon sour cream**
- 1½ **teaspoons vanilla extract**
- 2 **large eggs**
- 2⅔ **cups semisweet chocolate chips**

PREHEAT oven to 350°F. Sift flour, baking soda, and salt into medium bowl. Using electric mixer, beat butter and shortening in large bowl until fluffy. Add sugar, brown sugar, sour cream, and vanilla; beat to blend well. Beat in eggs 1 at a time, then flour mixture. Stir in chocolate chips. Drop half of batter by generous ¼ cupfuls onto 2 large ungreased baking sheets (5 mounds per sheet, spaced 3 inches apart). Using moistened fingertips, flatten each mound to 2½-inch round.

BAKE cookies until golden brown, about 14 minutes. Cool on sheets 5 minutes. Transfer cookies to racks and cool completely. Repeat with remaining batter using cooled baking sheets.

Sugar cookies

MAKES ABOUT 36 *Using vegetable oil instead of butter or shortening makes these cookies especially tender. For best results, use a mild-tasting oil, such as canola, sunflower, or corn oil. Since the dough for this cookie is very soft, it's necessary to chill the dough. After a little while in the refrigerator (at least 30 minutes and up to 1 day), the dough will be easier to work with.*

- ½ **cup (1 stick) unsalted butter, room temperature**
- ½ **cup vegetable oil**
- ½ **cup sugar plus additional for dipping**
- ½ **cup powdered sugar**
- 1 **egg**
- 1 **teaspoon vanilla extract**
- 2¼ **cups all purpose flour**
- ½ **teaspoon baking soda**
- ½ **teaspoon cream of tartar**
- ½ **teaspoon salt**

USING electric mixer, beat first 4 ingredients in large bowl until well blended. Mix in egg and vanilla. Sift flour, baking soda, cream of tartar, and salt over and mix in. Cover mixture and chill until firm, about 30 minutes or up to 1 day.

PREHEAT oven to 350°F. Butter 2 heavy large baking sheets. Roll 1 tablespoon dough into ball. Place on prepared sheet. Repeat with remaining dough, spacing balls evenly on sheets. Dip flat-bottomed glass into water to moisten, then dip into sugar and press dough to ¼-inch-thick round. Repeat with remaining dough balls, dipping bottom of glass into sugar before pressing each.

BAKE cookies until light brown, about 15 minutes. Transfer cookies to racks and cool completely.

PICTURE-PERFECT Flattening the cookies with the bottom of a glass causes the dough to crack slightly, forming a pretty scalloped edge.

Butter for baking Using unsalted butter allows the cook to adjust the level of salt in the recipe more precisely. Keep in mind that unsalted butter is more perishable than salted butter (salt acts as a preservative), so watch the expiration date.

Chai-spiced almond cookies

MAKES ABOUT 22 *Chai, the spiced Indian tea brewed in milk that's a coffeehouse favorite, was the inspiration for the flavors in this cookie.*

½ **cup (1 stick) unsalted butter, room temperature**

1⅓ **cups powdered sugar, divided**

2 **teaspoons vanilla extract**

1 **teaspoon almond extract**

¾ **teaspoon ground allspice**

¾ **teaspoon ground cardamom**

½ **teaspoon ground cinnamon**

¼ **teaspoon salt**

1 **cup all purpose flour**

¾ **cup finely chopped toasted almonds**

PREHEAT oven to 350°F. Using electric mixer, beat butter, ⅓ cup powdered sugar, both extracts, spices, and salt in medium bowl. Beat in flour, then stir in almonds.

USING hands, roll dough into tablespoon-size balls. Place on large baking sheet, spacing apart. Bake until pale golden, about 25 minutes. Cool on sheet 5 minutes. Place remaining 1 cup powdered sugar in large bowl. Working in batches, gently coat hot cookies in sugar. Cool cookies on rack. Roll again in sugar.

Measure for measure Baking is a science, so it's important to measure all of the ingredients carefully if you want the recipe to turn out well:

— Use the proper tools to measure dry and wet ingredients. Dry ingredients are measured in measuring cups or spoons in which the ingredient can come all the way up to the top. Wet ingredients should be measured in liquid measuring cups, which are usually clear with a handle and spout for pouring and have measures marked on the side of the container.

— When measuring dry ingredients (such as flour and sugar), dip the measuring cup or spoon into the container, filling above the rim. Gently sweep off the excess with the flat side of a knife, making the ingredient level with the top of the cup or spoon.

— When measuring liquid ingredients, place the measuring cup on a flat surface. Pour the ingredient in until it reaches the desired mark; view the measuring cup from the side to make sure the ingredient aligns with the correct measurement.

Chocolate macaroons

MAKES ABOUT 30 *There are two styles of macaroons: the crisp cookie that is a close relative of the meringue (sometimes called amaretti) and the chewy coconut-based macaroon, as in this recipe. This version is packed with chocolate flavor.*

1⅓ **cups mini semisweet chocolate chips (about 8 ounces), divided**

2 **large egg whites**
¼ **teaspoon salt**
½ **cup sugar**
½ **teaspoon vanilla extract**
1½ **cups sweetened flaked coconut**

PREHEAT oven to 325°F. Line 2 large rimmed baking sheets with parchment paper. Place 1 cup chocolate chips in microwave-safe bowl; microwave on low setting at 10-second intervals until chocolate is melted, stirring occasionally. Cool just to room temperature.

USING electric mixer, beat egg whites and salt in medium bowl until soft peaks form. Gradually add sugar, then vanilla, beating until whites are thick and glossy. Fold in melted chocolate and coconut, then remaining ⅓ cup chocolate chips.

DROP batter by heaping teaspoonfuls onto prepared sheets, spacing 1½ inches apart. Bake cookies 10 minutes. Reverse sheets. Bake until tops are dry and cracked and tester inserted into centers comes out with moist crumbs attached, about 10 minutes longer. Cool cookies on sheets on racks.

DO AHEAD *Can be made 2 days ahead. Store in airtight container at room temperature.*

BEAT IT To get the most loft from beaten egg whites, make sure the bowl and beaters are free of grease (fat of any kind will prevent whites from reaching their maximum volume). Use a metal, ceramic, or glass bowl (plastic bowls are porous and may hold on to oils). And make sure the whites are at room temperature. They will whip up more easily, and higher, than chilled whites.

Currant and spice oatmeal cookies

MAKES ABOUT 45 *We call for old-fashioned oats—oat berries that have been steamed and then rolled flat. These oats are sometimes labeled "rolled oats" at the supermarket. They produce oatmeal cookies with the familiar craggy texture and hearty flavor. Don't substitute instant oatmeal or steel-cut oats, which will affect the cookies' texture.*

2	large eggs
1½	teaspoons vanilla extract
⅔	cup dried currants
1⅔	cups all purpose flour
1	teaspoon baking soda
¾	teaspoon salt
¾	teaspoon ground cardamom
½	teaspoon ground cinnamon
¼	teaspoon ground allspice
1	cup (2 sticks) unsalted butter, room temperature
1½	cups (packed) dark brown sugar
2	cups old-fashioned oats

PREHEAT oven to 350°F. Butter and flour 3 large baking sheets. Whisk eggs and vanilla in small bowl to blend. Mix in currants; let mixture stand 15 minutes.

SIFT flour, baking soda, salt, and spices into medium bowl. Using electric mixer, beat butter in large bowl until fluffy. Add brown sugar and beat until smooth. Add currant mixture and beat to blend. Stir in flour mixture. Mix in oats. Drop batter by level tablespoonfuls onto prepared sheets, spacing 1½ inches apart. Using moistened fingertips, flatten cookies slightly. Bake 1 sheet at a time until cookies are golden brown, about 12 minutes. Cool cookies on sheets.

DO AHEAD *Can be made 1 day ahead. Store in airtight container at room temperature.*

MORE TO TRY Currants are great in this recipe, but feel free to use other dried fruits: Raisins, dried cherries, or chopped dried apricots would also be delicious.

Soft ginger cookies

MAKES ABOUT 40 *This old-fashioned cookie is deep and dark, with intense spice flavors. Rolling the cookies in sugar before baking gives them a sparkly, crispy exterior. The dough is very sticky, so be sure to chill it thoroughly before forming the cookies.*

4	cups all purpose flour
1	cup sugar plus additional for rolling
2	teaspoons baking soda
2	teaspoons ground ginger
1	teaspoon ground nutmeg
1	teaspoon ground cinnamon
1	teaspoon ground cloves
½	teaspoon salt
1	cup robust-flavored (dark) molasses
½	cup nonhydrogenated solid vegetable shortening
1	large egg, beaten to blend
½	cup boiling water

COMBINE first 8 ingredients in large bowl. Add molasses, shortening, and egg; beat to blend. Beat in ½ cup boiling water. Chill 3 hours.

PREHEAT oven to 400°F. Roll chilled dough by tablespoonfuls into balls. Roll in additional sugar. Space balls 2 inches apart on ungreased baking sheets. Bake until cookies are puffed and cracked on top and centers still feel soft, about 12 minutes. Transfer to racks and cool.

DO AHEAD *Can be made 2 days ahead. Store in airtight container at room temperature.*

Peppermint crunch chocolate chip meringues

MAKES ABOUT 21 *For a pretty pink color, mix a drop or two of red food coloring into the meringue batter. These cookies will be crisp outside and soft inside.*

    3 large egg whites, room temperature
    1 cup sugar
    ¼ teaspoon peppermint extract
    ¾ cup bittersweet or semisweet chocolate chips
    8 red-and-white-striped hard
       peppermint candies, crushed

PREHEAT oven to 275°F. Line 2 large baking sheets with parchment paper. Using electric mixer, beat egg whites in large bowl to soft peaks. Gradually add sugar, beating until thick and fluffy. Fold in extract, then chocolate chips. Drop meringue by slightly mounded tablespoonfuls onto prepared sheets, spacing 2 inches apart. Sprinkle with candy. Bake 1 hour. Transfer sheets to racks and cool.

DO AHEAD *Can be made 2 days ahead. Store in airtight container at room temperature.*

CANDY BASH Using a rolling pin, firmly break the candies into pieces while still in their wrappers. Twist the ends open, then sprinkle the candy over the meringues.

Chewy pine nut cookies

MAKES ABOUT 28 *The pine nut flavor permeates these cookies—half of the nuts are ground into the dough, while the rest are kept whole for coating the cookies. And that other nutty flavor? That's from the almond paste, an ingredient available at specialty foods stores and in the baking section of most supermarkets.*

    1½ cups pine nuts (about 7 ounces), divided
     1 cup sugar
     ¼ cup (packed) almond paste, crumbled
    1½ teaspoons finely grated lemon peel
     ¾ teaspoon vanilla extract
     3 large egg whites
    1⅓ cups all purpose flour
     ½ teaspoon baking powder
     ¼ teaspoon salt

     ½ cup powdered sugar (for dusting)

PREHEAT oven to 350°F. Butter 2 large baking sheets. Using on/off turns, blend ¾ cup pine nuts and next 4 ingredients in processor until crumbly mixture forms. Transfer mixture to large bowl; add egg whites. Using electric mixer, beat until mixture is smooth. Whisk flour, baking powder, and salt in small bowl to blend. Add to pine nut mixture; beat until smooth (dough will be soft and sticky).

PLACE remaining ¾ cup pine nuts in shallow bowl. Spoon generous tablespoonful dough into pine nuts in shallow bowl, coating 1 side of dough with pine nuts. Using floured fingertips, transfer dough to prepared baking sheet, pine nut side up. Smooth edges of dough to form even round. Repeat with remaining dough, flouring fingertips as needed to prevent sticking and spacing cookies 2 inches apart on prepared baking sheets.

BAKE cookies 1 baking sheet at a time until golden, about 20 minutes. Cool completely. Dust with powdered sugar and transfer to plate.

DO AHEAD *Can be made 1 day ahead. Store in airtight container at room temperature.*

Double chocolate mint cookies

MAKES 21 *Made with a lot of chocolate and just a little bit of flour, these cookies are a chocolate lover's dream. Freezing the dough for 10 minutes will make it firm enough to scoop onto the baking sheet.*

2½   **cups bittersweet or semisweet chocolate chips, divided**

6   **tablespoons all purpose flour**
½   **teaspoon baking powder**
¾   **cup sugar**
2   **large eggs**
2   **tablespoons dark corn syrup**
½   **teaspoon peppermint extract**

PREHEAT oven to 350°F. Line 3 large baking sheets with foil; butter foil. Place 1¼ cups chocolate chips in medium glass bowl. Microwave on medium-high until melted, stirring every 30 seconds, about 2 minutes. Cool 15 minutes.

MIX flour and baking powder in small bowl. Using electric mixer, beat sugar, eggs, corn syrup, and peppermint extract in medium bowl until thick, about 3 minutes. Gradually beat in melted chocolate, then dry ingredients. Mix in remaining 1¼ cups chocolate chips; freeze 10 minutes.

DROP 7 heaping tablespoons batter on each prepared baking sheet, spacing 3 inches apart (cookies will spread). Bake until cookies are cracked on top and softly set, about 15 minutes. Cool cookies on baking sheets 5 minutes. Using metal spatula, transfer cookies to racks and cool completely.

DO AHEAD *Can be made 1 day ahead. Store in airtight container at room temperature.*

HOW TO MELT The easiest way to melt chocolate is in the microwave, but keep a close eye on it—chocolate burns easily. Heat the chocolate on medium-high heat in 30-second intervals, and take it out of the microwave once the chocolate is melted about three-quarters of the way; the residual heat will melt the rest. Stir the chocolate several times as it melts and be sure that there is no water on the spoon you're using. Chocolate will seize (become thick and lumpy) if it comes into contact with liquid. No microwave? You can also place chopped chocolate (or chocolate chips) in a heat-proof bowl set over a saucepan of simmering water. Stir the chocolate until it's melted and smooth.

Outrageous peanut butter cookies

MAKES 30 *The cookie jar meets the candy jar in this decadent treat. Lining the baking sheets with foil prevents the cookies from sticking. Silicone baking mats or parchment paper would work well, too.*

 1 **cup super chunky peanut butter**
 1 **cup (packed) dark brown sugar**
 6 **tablespoons (¾ stick) unsalted butter, room temperature**
 1 **large egg**
 2 **tablespoons dark corn syrup**
 2 **teaspoons vanilla extract**
 1 **cup all purpose flour**
 ⅓ **cup old-fashioned oats**
 1 **teaspoon baking soda**
 3 **1.8- to 2-ounce candy bars with peanuts, peanut butter, chocolate, and caramel (such as NutRageous), cut into ½-inch cubes**

PREHEAT oven to 325°F. Line 2 large baking sheets with foil. Using electric mixer, beat first 6 ingredients in large bowl until well blended. Stir flour, oats, and baking soda in small bowl to blend; mix into peanut butter mixture. Gently mix in candy bar cubes.

DROP dough by heaping tablespoonfuls onto prepared sheets (15 per sheet), spacing 1½ inches apart. Flatten cookies slightly with moistened fingertips. Freeze cookies on sheets 15 minutes.

BAKE cookies 10 minutes. Reverse sheets and bake until golden, about 10 minutes longer. Let cookies cool on sheets until beginning to firm, about 5 minutes. Using metal spatula, transfer cookies to racks and cool completely.

WHY CORN SYRUP? This recipe calls for a few tablespoons of corn syrup—a thick, sweet syrup made from cornstarch. Because corn syrup inhibits crystallization of the sugar, it makes the cookies soft, moist, and chewy. Corn syrup comes in two varieties: light and dark (light corn syrup with a little molasses or caramel color mixed in).

Lemon and anise sugar twists

MAKES 12 *Purchased puff pastry, which is available in the frozen foods section of the supermarket, is the base for these elegant sweets. Serve the twists on their own or with a cup of hot cocoa.*

    Sugar
 1 **sheet frozen puff pastry (half of 17.3-ounce package), thawed**
 1 **egg beaten with 1 teaspoon milk (glaze)**
 3 **tablespoons sugar**
 1 **teaspoon finely grated lemon peel**
 2 **teaspoons aniseed**

PREHEAT oven to 350°F. Sprinkle work surface with sugar. Set pastry atop sugar and roll out to thickness of ⅛ inch. Brush with egg glaze. Combine 3 tablespoons sugar and lemon peel in small bowl. Sprinkle over pastry. Sprinkle with aniseed. Cut pastry crosswise into 1-inch-wide strips. Pick up each pastry strip, twist several times, and place on ungreased cookie sheet, pressing ends onto sheet. Bake until golden brown and crisp, about 20 minutes. Cool pastries on rack.

Lemon thumbprint cookies

MAKES ABOUT 36 *Lemon peel and lemon juice give these cookies their citrusy zing. Fill with your favorite jam—apricot and raspberry work well.*

- 1 **cup (2 sticks) unsalted butter, room temperature**
- ½ **cup sugar**
- 2 **large egg yolks**
- 3 **tablespoons finely grated lemon peel**
- 1 **tablespoon fresh lemon juice**
- ¼ **teaspoon salt**
- 2½ **cups all purpose flour**

- 6 **tablespoons (about) jam**

PREHEAT oven to 350°F. Lightly butter 2 baking sheets. Using electric mixer, beat butter and sugar in large bowl until well blended. Beat in yolks, lemon peel, lemon juice, and salt. Add flour in 2 additions and beat just until moist clumps form. Gather dough together in bowl to bind dough. Form dough into 1-inch balls. Place balls on prepared baking sheets, spacing 1 inch apart. Using finger, make deep indentation in center of each ball.

BAKE cookies until firm to touch and golden on bottom, about 22 minutes. Remove from oven. Immediately fill indentation in each cookie with scant ½ teaspoon jam. Transfer cookies to racks and cool completely.

DO AHEAD *Can be made 2 days ahead. Store between sheets of waxed paper in airtight container at room temperature. Cookies will soften slightly.*

Lemon shortbread

MAKES 24 WEDGES *Shortbread is a traditional Scottish treat that has become popular the world over. The secret to tender shortbread is to avoid overworking the dough. Substitute orange or lime peel for the lemon, if desired.*

- 1½ **cups all purpose flour**
- ⅔ **cup sugar**
- ¼ **cup cornstarch**
- 2½ **teaspoons finely grated lemon peel**
- ½ **teaspoon salt**
- ¾ **cup (1½ sticks) chilled unsalted butter, cut into ½-inch cubes**

PREHEAT oven to 300°F. Blend first 5 ingredients in processor. Add butter; cut in using on/off turns until moist clumps form. Gather dough into ball; divide in half. Press 1 dough half onto bottom of each of two 8-inch-diameter cake pans. Pierce dough all over with fork.

BAKE until cooked through and pale golden, about 40 minutes. Cool shortbread in pans on racks 5 minutes. Cut each warm shortbread in pan into 12 wedges. Cool completely. Using spatula, carefully transfer to platter.

DO AHEAD *Can be made up to 4 days ahead. Store in airtight container at room temperature.*

THE HOLE STORY Be sure to pierce the dough with a fork before baking. The holes will prevent the shortbread from puffing up and will help it bake evenly.

Ginger almond wafers

MAKES ABOUT 26 *These spicy-nutty cookies would be great with tea or served with mango sorbet.*

1½   cups powdered sugar plus additional for dipping

1¼   cups all purpose flour

½   cup (1 stick) chilled unsalted butter, diced

1   tablespoon minced peeled fresh ginger

1   tablespoon ground ginger

½   teaspoon ground cinnamon

½   teaspoon salt

¾   cup whole almonds, toasted

3   tablespoons heavy whipping cream

3   tablespoons chopped crystallized ginger

PREHEAT oven to 325°F. Line 2 heavy large baking sheets with parchment paper. Combine first 7 ingredients in processor and blend using on/off turns until mixture resembles coarse meal. Add almonds, cream, and crystallized ginger; process just until moist clumps form. Shape dough into 1¼-inch-diameter balls. Place on prepared sheets. Moisten bottom of glass; dip into powdered sugar and press each dough ball to ¼-inch thickness, dipping in powdered sugar before each pressing.

BAKE cookies until brown on bottom and at edges, about 28 minutes. Transfer cookies to rack; cool.

DO AHEAD *Can be made 4 days ahead. Store in airtight container at room temperature.*

Brown sugar and nutmeg snaps

MAKES ABOUT 3 DOZEN *Intensify the flavor by using freshly ground nutmeg. Look for whole nutmeg in the spice aisle, and for nutmeg graters and grinders at kitchenwares stores; or use a Microplane grater.*

1¼   cups (packed) golden brown sugar

½   cup (1 stick) unsalted butter, room temperature

1   large egg

1¾   cups all purpose flour

1   teaspoon ground nutmeg

1   teaspoon baking soda

½   teaspoon salt

    Sugar

USING electric mixer, beat brown sugar and butter in bowl until fluffy. Mix in egg. Add flour, nutmeg, baking soda, and salt; beat until well blended. Chill 1 hour.

PREHEAT oven to 350°F. Butter 3 heavy large baking sheets. Roll dough into 1-inch balls. Roll balls in sugar, coating completely. Arrange on prepared baking sheets, spacing balls 2 inches apart. Using bottom of glass, flatten cookies to 1¾-inch rounds. Bake until cookies are golden, about 13 minutes. Cool on baking sheets.

DO AHEAD *Can be made 1 week ahead. Store in airtight container at room temperature.*

PACK IT IN It's important to firmly pack brown sugar in a measuring cup to get the correct amount.

S'mores with a twist

12 SERVINGS *The name of this Girl Scout campfire favorite comes from "some more," as in "These treats are so good you'll want some more." If you don't have a campfire or fireplace handy, toast the marshmallows over a gas flame. The "twist" comes from the filled chocolate bars—try those with orange, pistachio, or caramel filling. You'll find them in most supermarkets.*

12 whole regular or cinnamon-coated graham crackers, broken in half, or 24 chocolate wafer cookies

6 3.5-ounce imported filled chocolate bars, broken into pieces

12 large marshmallows

PLACE 2 cracker halves or 2 cookies on each of 12 plates. Top 1 on each plate with chocolate pieces in single layer. Skewer 1 marshmallow onto each of 12 skewers. Cook marshmallows directly over fire or gas flame until toasted to desired doneness. Using fork, push 1 marshmallow onto each chocolate layer. Press second cracker half or cookie onto each hot marshmallow to form sandwich.

Dark chocolate brownies with white chocolate chunks

MAKES 16 *To make sure that the brownies are moist, bake them only until a tester comes out with moist crumbs attached. Overbaking will result in dry, crumbly brownies.*

4 ounces unsweetened chocolate, coarsely chopped

6 tablespoons (¾ stick) unsalted butter

⅔ cup all purpose flour

½ teaspoon baking powder

¼ teaspoon salt

1 cup sugar

2 large eggs

1 teaspoon vanilla extract

5 ounces high-quality white chocolate (such as Lindt or Perugina), cut into ½-inch pieces

Fresh large strawberries

PREHEAT oven to 325°F. Butter 8-inch square baking pan. Stir chocolate and butter in heavy medium saucepan over low heat until melted and smooth. Cool to room temperature.

COMBINE flour, baking powder, and salt in small bowl. Whisk sugar, eggs, and vanilla in medium bowl until mixture is very thick, about 3 minutes. Whisk in melted chocolate mixture, then flour mixture. Stir in white chocolate. Transfer to prepared baking pan.

BAKE brownies until tester inserted into center comes out with moist crumbs attached, about 28 minutes. Transfer brownies in pan to rack; cool completely.

DO AHEAD *Can be prepared 1 day ahead. Store in airtight container at room temperature.*

CUT brownies into 16 squares. Serve brownies with strawberries.

Brownies with chocolate-covered raisins

MAKES ABOUT 12 *As the brownies bake, the chocolate-covered raisins turn into fudgy pockets of chocolate with plump raisins in the center.*

¾ cup (1½ sticks) unsalted butter, cut into pieces
6 ounces semisweet chocolate, chopped
1 ounce unsweetened chocolate, chopped

¾ cup sugar
2 large eggs
1 teaspoon vanilla extract
⅔ cup all purpose flour
¾ teaspoon baking powder
¼ teaspoon salt
1 cup chocolate-covered raisins

PREHEAT oven to 350°F. Butter 8-inch square pan with 2-inch-high sides. Stir butter and both chocolates in medium saucepan over low heat until melted. Remove from heat; cool to lukewarm.

USING electric mixer, beat sugar and eggs in medium bowl until very thick and pale, about 3 minutes. Stir in melted chocolate mixture and vanilla. Mix flour, baking powder, and salt in another medium bowl. Stir into chocolate mixture. Mix in chocolate-covered raisins.

POUR batter into prepared pan. Bake until tester inserted into center comes out with moist crumbs attached and top cracks in places, about 30 minutes. Transfer to rack and cool in pan.

DO AHEAD *Can be made 1 day ahead. Cover with foil and let stand at room temperature.*

CUT brownies into squares.

Mocha brownies

MAKES ABOUT 24 *Coffee and chocolate are a winning combination and create a sophisticated version of our favorite dessert. Lining the pan with waxed paper or parchment paper makes it super-easy to remove the brownies from the pan.*

Nonstick vegetable oil spray
8 ounces bittersweet or semisweet chocolate, chopped
¾ cup (1½ sticks) unsalted butter

2 cups sugar
6 large eggs
2 teaspoons vanilla extract
½ cup all purpose flour
⅓ cup unsweetened cocoa powder
1 teaspoon instant espresso powder or instant coffee granules
½ teaspoon salt
¼ cup sour cream
¾ cup chopped walnuts

Powdered sugar

PREHEAT oven to 375°F. Spray 13×9×2-inch metal baking pan with nonstick spray. Line with waxed paper, extending over 2 long sides of pan. Spray paper. Stir chocolate and butter in heavy small saucepan over low heat until melted. Cool to lukewarm.

USING electric mixer, beat sugar, eggs, and vanilla in medium bowl until fluffy, about 5 minutes. Add chocolate mixture; beat just until blended. Add flour, cocoa powder, espresso powder, and salt; beat just until blended. Stir in sour cream and walnuts.

TRANSFER batter to pan. Bake until tester inserted into center comes out with moist crumbs attached, about 35 minutes. Transfer pan to rack; cool completely. Fold down waxed paper. Cut brownies into squares. Sprinkle with powdered sugar.

DO AHEAD *Can be made 1 day ahead. Store in single layer in airtight container at room temperature.*

Fudgy peanut brownies

MAKES 9 *The chocolate in these brownies is balanced by peanut butter chips and salted peanuts.*

    1 cup (2 sticks) unsalted butter
 1¼ cups semisweet chocolate chips
    3 ounces unsweetened chocolate, chopped
    1 cup plus 2 tablespoons sugar
    3 large eggs
 1½ tablespoons instant coffee granules
    1 tablespoon vanilla extract

 ⅔ cup all purpose flour
 1½ teaspoons baking powder
 ½ teaspoon salt
    1 10-ounce package peanut butter chips
 ½ cup chopped salted peanuts

PREHEAT oven to 350°F. Butter and flour 9-inch square metal baking pan. Combine butter, chocolate chips, and unsweetened chocolate in heavy medium saucepan. Stir over low heat until chocolate mixture is melted and smooth. Remove from heat. Whisk sugar, eggs, instant coffee, and vanilla in large bowl just until combined. Add warm chocolate mixture; whisk to combine. Cool just to room temperature.

WHISK flour, baking powder, and salt in medium bowl. Whisk into chocolate mixture. Mix in peanut butter chips and peanuts. Pour batter into prepared pan. Bake until tester inserted into center comes out with moist crumbs still attached, about 35 minutes (do not overbake). Cool completely. Cut into 9 squares.

DO AHEAD *Can be made 1 day ahead. Store in airtight container at room temperature.*

Brownies, deluxe For an even more decadent dessert, add a scoop of ice cream and a drizzle of hot fudge or fruit sauce to any of the brownies here to make it a brownie sundae.

Heath bar brownies

MAKES ABOUT 18 *Toasted walnuts and chopped toffee bars add a satisfying crunch.*

¾ cup (1½ sticks) unsalted butter,
   cut into ½-inch cubes
3½ ounces unsweetened chocolate, chopped

¾ cup all purpose flour
½ teaspoon salt
¼ teaspoon baking soda
1⅔ cups sugar
3 large eggs
1 teaspoon vanilla extract
1 cup walnut pieces (about 4 ounces), toasted

5 1.4-ounce Heath English toffee
   candy bars, chopped

PREHEAT oven to 350°F. Butter and flour 13×9×2-inch metal baking pan. Stir butter and chocolate in heavy small saucepan over low heat until melted and smooth. Cool to lukewarm.

WHISK flour, salt, and baking soda in small bowl to blend. Using electric mixer, beat sugar, eggs, and vanilla in large bowl until thick and billowy, about 3 minutes. Beat in chocolate mixture, then flour mixture. Fold in walnuts. Transfer to pan.

BAKE brownies until puffed and tester inserted into center comes out with moist crumbs attached, about 28 minutes. Sprinkle brownies evenly with chopped toffee bars. Cool in pan on rack.

DO AHEAD *Can be made 1 day ahead. Cover and store at room temperature.*

CUT into squares.

Raspberry-pecan blondies

MAKES 16 *A blondie is a brownie minus the chocolate. In this version, fresh raspberries are sprinkled on top of the batter before the blondies go into the oven.*

2 cups all purpose flour
1 teaspoon baking powder
½ teaspoon salt
¼ teaspoon baking soda
2 cups (packed) golden brown sugar
¾ cup (1½ sticks) unsalted butter,
   room temperature
2 large eggs
2 teaspoons vanilla extract
1 cup coarsely chopped pecans (about 3 ounces)
1 ½-pint basket fresh raspberries

PREHEAT oven to 350°F. Line 9×9×2-inch metal baking pan with foil, extending foil over sides by 2 inches. Butter and flour foil. Whisk first 4 ingredients in medium bowl to blend. Using electric mixer, beat brown sugar and butter in large bowl until light and fluffy. Beat in eggs 1 at a time, then vanilla. Add flour mixture and beat just until blended. Stir in pecans. Spread batter evenly in prepared pan. Sprinkle raspberries over top.

BAKE dessert until top is golden and tester inserted into center comes out clean, about 50 minutes. Cool completely in pan on rack.

DO AHEAD *Can be made 1 day ahead. Cover and refrigerate. Bring to room temperature before serving.*

CUT into 16 squares.

Double-lemon bars

MAKES 24 *This take on the classic dessert offers twice the lemon flavor by using both lemon peel and lemon juice with the pulp. To make the bars easy to cut, chill them for a few minutes.*

- 1 cup (2 sticks) unsalted butter, room temperature
- ⅔ cup powdered sugar plus additional for dusting
- 2¼ cups all purpose flour, divided

- 2 cups sugar
- 4 large eggs
- 3 large lemons, halved
- ¼ cup finely grated lemon peel (from about 6 large lemons)
- 1 teaspoon baking powder

PREHEAT oven to 350°F. Using electric mixer, beat butter in large bowl until fluffy. Beat in powdered sugar. Add 2 cups flour, 1 cup at a time, beating until moist clumps form. Using back of fork, press dough over bottom of nonstick 13×9×2-inch metal baking pan. Bake crust until light golden, about 20 minutes.

MEANWHILE, beat sugar and eggs in medium bowl until blended. Scrape enough pulp and juice from lemon halves to measure 7 tablespoons; add to egg mixture. Beat in lemon peel and baking powder, then remaining ¼ cup flour.

POUR lemon filling over hot crust. Bake until filling is set in center and begins to brown on top, about 20 minutes. Transfer pan to rack; cool completely.

DO AHEAD *Can be made 1 day ahead. Cover and chill.*

CUT pastry into 24 bars. Transfer bars to serving platter and dust with additional powdered sugar.

Berry-berry streusel bars

MAKES ABOUT 24 *Half of the crust mixture is pressed into the bottom of the pan; the other half is sprinkled over the top of the bars to make a streusel. Any leftover bars would be great for breakfast.*

Crust
- 1½ cups old-fashioned oats
- 1½ cups all purpose flour
- 1 cup (packed) brown sugar
- ½ teaspoon baking soda
- 1 cup (2 sticks) chilled unsalted butter, cut into small pieces

Filling
- 1 12-ounce package frozen blueberries, thawed
- ⅔ cup raspberry jam
- 5 teaspoons all purpose flour
- 1½ teaspoons minced lemon peel

FOR CRUST: Preheat oven to 375°F. Butter 13×9×2-inch glass baking dish. Combine first 4 ingredients in medium bowl. Add butter; rub with fingertips until mixture resembles coarse meal. Press half of crumb mixture onto bottom of prepared pan (reserve remaining mixture for streusel). Bake crust until light brown, about 15 minutes. Cool slightly.

FOR FILLING: Mix all ingredients in bowl.

SPREAD filling over crust. Sprinkle remaining crumb mixture over. Bake until topping is golden, about 35 minutes. Cool in pan. Cut into squares.

Raisin and cardamom granola bars

MAKES 18 *You could buy granola bars at the store but when they are this easy to put together, why not make your own? Feel free to customize: Try dried cranberries with chopped almonds and cinnamon, or for a sweeter treat, sprinkle some chocolate chips over the bars when they come out of the oven.*

  2 **cups old-fashioned oats**
  ½ **cup raisins**
  ½ **cup chopped pecans, toasted**
1¼ **teaspoons ground cardamom**
  6 **tablespoons (¾ stick) unsalted butter**
  ⅓ **cup (packed) dark brown sugar**
  3 **tablespoons honey**

PREHEAT oven to 350°F. Line 9-inch square baking pan with foil, allowing foil to extend over sides. Butter foil. Mix first 4 ingredients in bowl. Combine butter, brown sugar, and honey in medium saucepan. Stir over medium heat until butter melts and mixture is smooth and begins to boil. Pour butter mixture over oat mixture and stir until well coated. Transfer to prepared pan. Using spatula, press mixture evenly into pan.

BAKE oat mixture until top is golden brown, about 30 minutes. Transfer to rack and cool. Using foil as aid, lift out of pan; place on work surface. Using large sharp knife, cut into 18 bars.

DO AHEAD *Can be made 2 days ahead. Store in airtight container at room temperature.*

Pumpkin-raisin bars

MAKES 24 *These bars are more like a moist pumpkin cake topped with a rich cream cheese frosting. To add a little crunch, sprinkle the frosting with chopped toasted pecans or walnuts.*

2 **cups all purpose flour**
2 **cups sugar**
1 **tablespoon ground cinnamon**
2 **teaspoons baking powder**
1 **teaspoon baking soda**
1 **teaspoon salt**
½ **teaspoon ground nutmeg**
½ **teaspoon ground cloves**
1 **15-ounce can pure pumpkin**
4 **large eggs**
¾ **cup vegetable oil**
1 **cup raisins**

6 **ounces cream cheese, room temperature**
1 **cup powdered sugar**
⅓ **cup butter, room temperature**

PREHEAT oven to 350°F. Grease 15½x10½x1-inch baking sheet. Stir first 8 ingredients in large bowl to blend. Add pumpkin, eggs, and oil; beat until blended. Mix in raisins. Spread batter in prepared pan. Bake until tester inserted into center comes out clean, about 25 minutes. Cool in pan on rack.

BEAT cream cheese, powdered sugar, and butter in medium bowl to blend. Spread frosting over cake in thin layer.

DO AHEAD *Can be prepared 1 day ahead. Refrigerate until cold, then cover and keep refrigerated.*

CUT cake into bars.

PIESANDTARTS

Citrus galette

4 SERVINGS *Thawed frozen bread dough from the supermarket serves as a crust in this rustic dessert.*

- 1 **1-pound loaf frozen white bread dough, thawed**
- ¼ **cup sugar**
- 3 **tablespoons all purpose flour**
- 2 **teaspoons finely grated lemon peel**
- ½ **teaspoon freshly grated nutmeg**
- 3 **tablespoons chilled butter, cut into ½-inch pieces**

GREASE baking sheet or 12-inch pizza pan. Knead dough on lightly floured surface 3 minutes to warm slightly. Let rest 10 minutes. Roll out on lightly floured surface to 12-inch round. Transfer to prepared pan. Combine sugar, flour, lemon peel, and nutmeg in processor. Using on/off turns, cut in butter until mixture resembles fine meal. Sprinkle over dough. Let dough rise in warm draft-free area until doubled in volume, about 30 minutes.

PREHEAT oven to 375°F. Bake galette until edges are golden brown, about 25 minutes. Cool slightly on rack.

GIVE IT A REST If the dough resists when you're trying to roll it out, let it rest for a few minutes. When you return, the dough should have relaxed enough for you to roll it to the right size. If the rolling pin isn't working, use your hands to gently pull and stretch the dough.

Raspberry sour cream tart

8 SERVINGS *Get creative with the topping by using whatever berries look best at the market. Try blueberries, blackberries, whole or sliced strawberries—or a combination of several different berries.*

Crust
- 8 **whole graham crackers, coarsely broken**
- ¼ **cup (packed) golden brown sugar**
- ¼ **cup (½ stick) unsalted butter, melted**

Filling and Topping
- 6 **ounces cream cheese, room temperature**
- ⅓ **cup sugar**
- ½ **cup sour cream**
- 2 **teaspoons fresh lemon juice**
- ½ **teaspoon vanilla extract**

- 2 **½-pint baskets raspberries**
- ¼ **cup seedless raspberry jam**

FOR CRUST: Preheat oven to 375°F. Grind crackers and brown sugar in processor until coarse crumbs form. Add butter and process until crumbs are evenly moistened. Press crumb mixture firmly onto bottom and up sides of 9-inch-diameter tart pan with removable bottom. Bake until crust is firm to touch, about 8 minutes. Cool crust on rack.

FOR FILLING AND TOPPING: Using electric mixer, beat cream cheese and sugar in medium bowl until smooth. Beat in sour cream, lemon juice, and vanilla. Spread filling in cooled crust. Chill until firm, at least 4 hours.

DO AHEAD *Can be prepared 1 day ahead. Cover and keep chilled.*

ARRANGE berries over filling. Whisk jam in small bowl to loose consistency. Drizzle over berries. Serve immediately or chill up to 3 hours.

613

Chocolate-hazelnut ganache tart

8 TO 12 SERVINGS *Ganache is a rich mixture of choco-*
late and whipping cream. Here, it is flavored with
hazelnut liqueur and poured into a hazelnut-
graham cracker crust. The ganache can also be
spread between cake layers. Just chill until firm,
then stir until spreadable.

	Nonstick vegetable oil spray
1¼	cups hazelnuts, toasted, divided
9	whole graham crackers, broken in half to form 18 squares
3	tablespoons sugar
¼	teaspoon salt
7	tablespoons unsalted butter, melted
1	cup heavy whipping cream
6	ounces bittersweet or semisweet chocolate, chopped
3	tablespoons Frangelico (hazelnut liqueur)

PREHEAT oven to 350°F. Spray 9-inch-diameter tart
pan with removable bottom with nonstick spray.
Combine ¾ cup hazelnuts, graham crackers, sugar,
and salt in food processor and blend using on/off
turns just until nuts and crackers are finely ground.
Drizzle melted butter over and blend using on/off
turns just until moistened. Press crumbs evenly
onto bottom and up sides of prepared pan (crust
will be thick). Bake until set and just beginning to
turn golden brown, about 10 minutes. Cool completely on rack.

COARSELY chop remaining ½ cup hazelnuts.
Sprinkle evenly over bottom of crust. Bring cream
to simmer in heavy small saucepan over medium
heat. Remove from heat. Add chocolate and whisk
until melted and smooth. Whisk in Frangelico.
Carefully pour chocolate mixture evenly over hazelnuts in crust. Refrigerate until chocolate mixture is
set, at least 3 hours.

DO AHEAD *Can be prepared 2 days ahead. Cover and*
keep refrigerated.

No-bake lemon cream tart

6 TO 8 SERVINGS *For a chocolate version, brush melted*
bittersweet chocolate over the crust before filling.

10	tablespoons (1¼ sticks) unsalted butter, divided
¼	cup (packed) golden brown sugar
7	whole graham crackers, finely crushed
½	cup whole milk
1	teaspoon unflavored gelatin
1	cup plus 1 tablespoon sugar
½	cup fresh lemon juice
2	teaspoons finely grated lemon peel
2	large eggs
1¼	cups chilled heavy whipping cream

MELT 6 tablespoons butter in medium skillet over
medium-high heat. Whisk in brown sugar. Whisk
until mixture bubbles thickly, about 2 minutes. Mix
in cracker crumbs; stir 1 minute. Using back of fork,
press warm crumb mixture over bottom and up
sides of 9-inch-diameter tart pan with removable
bottom. Cool crust completely.

POUR milk into small custard cup. Sprinkle gelatin
over. Let stand until gelatin softens, about 15 minutes. Whisk 1 cup sugar, lemon juice, and lemon
peel in heavy medium saucepan to blend well.
Whisk in eggs, then remaining 4 tablespoons butter. Whisk over medium heat until custard thickens
and just begins to boil, about 5 minutes; remove
from heat. Add gelatin mixture; whisk until gelatin
dissolves. Let stand until beginning to set, about
10 minutes. Pour warm filling into crust. Chill until
filling is firm, at least 3 hours and up to 1 day.

BEAT cream and remaining 1 tablespoon sugar
in medium bowl until peaks form. Pipe or spoon
whipped cream over tart. Serve immediately or
chill up to 4 hours.

Mascarpone tart with honey, oranges, and pistachios

8 SERVINGS *If you don't have a tart pan, a nine-inch pie dish makes a good substitute. Keep in mind that the tart will have a slightly different look. Mascarpone cheese (Italian cream cheese) is available at many supermarkets and Italian markets.*

1 refrigerated pie crust (half of 15-ounce package)

2 large navel oranges

1 8- to 8.8-ounce container chilled mascarpone cheese

½ cup chilled heavy whipping cream

¼ cup sugar

2 tablespoons honey, divided

¼ teaspoon (generous) ground cardamom

2 tablespoons chopped pistachios

PREHEAT oven to 400°F. Press pie crust onto bottom and up sides of 9-inch-diameter tart pan with removable bottom; fold sides in and press to extend sides ¼ inch above rim of pan. Pierce crust all over with fork. Bake until golden brown, about 24 minutes. Cool completely on rack.

MEANWHILE, grate enough orange peel to measure 1¼ teaspoons. Cut off remaining peel and pith from oranges. Slice oranges into thin rounds, then cut rounds crosswise in half. Place orange slices on paper towels to drain slightly.

COMBINE mascarpone, cream, sugar, 1 tablespoon honey, cardamom, and orange peel in medium bowl. Using electric mixer, beat just until blended and peaks form (do not overbeat or mixture will curdle). Spread filling evenly in cooled crust. Arrange orange slices atop tart in concentric circles; sprinkle with pistachios. Drizzle with remaining 1 tablespoon honey.

D.I.Y. MASCARPONE If you can't find mascarpone cheese, you can make a quick and delicious substitute from ingredients that are easily found at the supermarket. Mix 8 ounces cream cheese with ¼ cup heavy whipping cream and 2½ tablespoons sour cream.

Pie crust perfection Many of the pies and tarts in this chapter call for premade pie crusts from the supermarket. These tips will make working with the dough even easier.

— Remove the dough from the fridge about 15 minutes before you line your pan. The crust will be easier to handle when it has warmed up slightly.

— If the crust cracks when you unfold it or while you're putting it in the pan, wet your fingers with cold water and pinch the cracks together.

— Some cooks find that purchased pie crust browns more quickly than homemade crust. If the edges of the crust are getting too brown, cover the edges with foil. To make a foil ring to cover a 9-inch pie crust, cut a 7-inch circle from the center of a 12-inch square piece of foil. Carefully fold the ring around the edges of the crust.

Pear and frangipane crostata with raspberry vinegar glaze

6 TO 8 SERVINGS *Frangipane is a pastry cream flavored with almonds. Raspberry vinegar is available at some supermarkets and specialty foods stores, and almond paste at specialty foods stores and in the baking section of most supermarkets.*

5   ounces almond paste, crumbled
    (about 3¾ inches of a 5½-inch log)

3   tablespoons butter, room temperature

2   tablespoons all purpose flour

1   large egg

1   sheet frozen puff pastry (half of
    17.3-ounce package), thawed

3   large firm but ripe Bosc pears, peeled,
    halved, cored, cut into ⅓-inch slices

5   tablespoons sugar, divided

½   cup raspberry vinegar

    Crushed pink peppercorns (optional)

FINELY grind almond paste in processor. Add butter, flour, and egg; blend until smooth.

PREHEAT oven to 400°F. Roll out puff pastry on floured surface to 13×11-inch rectangle. Fold ¾ inch of edges over; press to adhere to make 11½×9½-inch rectangle. Transfer to rimmed baking sheet. Pierce surface evenly with fork, avoiding folded edges. Spread almond paste mixture evenly over crust within folded edges. Arrange pear slices atop filling, overlapping slightly. Sprinkle with 1 tablespoon sugar. Bake until crust is deep golden and pears are tender, about 38 minutes. Cool slightly.

MEANWHILE, stir vinegar and remaining 4 tablespoons sugar in heavy small saucepan over medium heat until sugar dissolves. Increase heat; boil until syrup is reduced to ¼ cup, about 6 minutes.

PLACE tart on platter. Drizzle syrup over. Sprinkle lightly with peppercorns, if using. Serve warm.

Caramelized walnut tart

6 SERVINGS *Freezing the crust for a few minutes prevents it from shrinking as it bakes.*

1   refrigerated pie crust (half of
    15-ounce package)

½   cup heavy whipping cream

½   cup (packed) golden brown sugar

¼   cup dark corn syrup

1   teaspoon vanilla extract

½   teaspoon ground cinnamon

1¼ cups coarsely chopped toasted
    walnuts (about 5 ounces)

PREHEAT oven to 400°F. Transfer crust to 9-inch tart pan with removable bottom, folding in overhang to form double-thick sides. Freeze crust while preparing filling.

WHISK cream, sugar, corn syrup, vanilla, and cinnamon in heavy large saucepan. Stir in walnuts. Simmer over medium heat until mixture is bubbling and darkens slightly, stirring until sugar dissolves, about 3 minutes. Spread filling evenly in crust. Bake tart until filling is deep golden brown and crust is golden, about 25 minutes. Cool completely in pan on rack.

DO AHEAD *Can be made 1 day ahead. Cover and store at room temperature.*

REMOVE tart from pan.

Almond, apricot, and cream cheese crostata

8 SERVINGS *A little melted apricot jam makes an instant glaze for this dessert. You'll find almond paste at most supermarkets (look in the baking aisle) and at specialty foods stores. Light, airy amaretti cookies are available at some supermarkets and at Italian markets.*

- ½ 7-ounce log almond paste
- 3½ tablespoons sugar, divided
- 3 ounces cream cheese, cut into ½-inch cubes
- 1 large egg yolk
- 1 teaspoon vanilla extract
- 1 refrigerated pie crust (half of 15-ounce package), room temperature
- 5 to 6 large apricots, quartered, pitted
- ¼ cup apricot jam, heated
- 3 crushed amaretti cookies (Italian macaroons)

PREHEAT oven to 400°F. Blend almond paste and 3 tablespoons sugar in processor until finely chopped. Add cream cheese, yolk, and vanilla; blend until filling is smooth. Unroll crust on heavy rimmed baking sheet. Spread filling over crust, leaving 1½-inch plain border. Arrange apricot quarters, rounded side down, in spoke pattern in 2 concentric circles atop filling. Fold dough border up over edge of filling. Brush exposed apricots with warm jam. Sprinkle apricots with remaining ½ tablespoon sugar.

BAKE crostata until crust is golden brown and apricots are tender and slightly browned, about 43 minutes. Sprinkle with crushed amaretti. Cool 30 minutes. Serve warm or at room temperature.

Fruit and cookie-crust pizza

8 SERVINGS *A giant sugar cookie is the "dough" for this dessert pizza and sliced fruits are the toppings. This is a fun recipe to involve the kids in. They can help press the dough into the pan and get creative with the decorating.*

- 1 16.5-ounce roll refrigerated sugar-cookie dough
- 1 8-ounce package cream cheese, room temperature
- 1 7-ounce jar marshmallow creme

  Sliced fruits (such as hulled strawberries, peeled kiwis, peeled bananas, peeled cored pineapple), plus whole raspberries
  Purchased caramel sauce, warmed

PREHEAT oven to 350°F. Butter and flour 12-inch-diameter pizza pan. Cut cookie dough roll crosswise into ⅓-inch-thick slices; arrange on prepared pan. Using wet fingertips, press dough evenly into pan to form pizza crust.

BAKE crust until deep golden brown, about 15 minutes. Transfer to rack. Using edge of metal spatula, press in crust edges to form even round. Cool completely.

BEAT cream cheese in medium bowl until smooth. Beat in marshmallow creme. Spread filling evenly over crust, leaving ½-inch plain border.

DO AHEAD *Can be made 45 minutes ahead. Let stand at room temperature.*

TOP with fruits as desired; drizzle with warm caramel sauce.

Scottish apple pie

8 SERVINGS *The all-American dessert gets a Scottish flavor from crushed gingersnaps, orange marmalade, orange peel, and raisins. Serve with vanilla ice cream—or sweetened whipped cream spiked with a touch of whiskey.*

1	15-ounce package refrigerated pie crusts (2 crusts), room temperature
1½	pounds Granny Smith apples, peeled, cored, cut into ⅓-inch cubes
9	tablespoons sugar, divided
½	cup gingersnap cookie crumbs
⅓	cup orange marmalade
⅓	cup golden raisins
1	teaspoon finely grated orange peel
1	tablespoon heavy whipping cream

PREHEAT oven to 375°F. Line 9-inch-diameter glass pie dish with 1 pie crust. Mix apples, 8 tablespoons sugar, cookie crumbs, marmalade, raisins, and orange peel in large bowl. Spoon filling into crust-lined dish. Top with remaining crust. Press crust edges together to seal; crimp edge decoratively. Cut 1-inch hole in center.

BLEND cream and remaining 1 tablespoon sugar in small bowl; brush over crust. Bake pie until crust is golden and filling bubbles thickly, about 45 minutes. Serve warm.

HOW THE COOKIE CRUMBLES The easiest way to make cookie crumbs is by finely grinding broken cookies in a food processor.

Old-fashioned lime pie

8 SERVINGS *To make sure the filling is firm, the pie needs to chill for a few hours before serving.*

36	vanilla wafer cookies (about 4¾ ounces)
¼	cup (½ stick) unsalted butter, melted
½	teaspoon plus 1 tablespoon finely grated lime peel
1	14-ounce can sweetened condensed milk
¾	cup fresh lime juice
2	large eggs
	Lime slices

PREHEAT oven to 350°F. Finely grind vanilla wafers in processor. Add butter and ½ teaspoon lime peel; process until moist crumbs form. Transfer to 9-inch-diameter glass pie dish. Using plastic wrap as aid, press crumbs onto bottom and up sides of dish (crust will be thin). Bake just until crust begins to turn golden on edges, about 10 minutes. Remove from oven. Maintain oven temperature.

MEANWHILE, whisk condensed milk, lime juice, and remaining 1 tablespoon lime peel in medium bowl to blend. Whisk in eggs.

POUR filling into warm crust. Bake until filling is set, about 20 minutes. Cool. Refrigerate until chilled, about 3 hours.

DO AHEAD *Can be prepared 1 day ahead. Cover and keep refrigerated.*

GARNISH with lime slices. Cut into wedges.

Peach pie with berry jam

8 SERVINGS *Granola soaks up some of the peach juices and creates an instant streusel topping on this pie. To peel peaches, place them in boiling water for 30 seconds to one minute, then rinse them under cold water to stop them from cooking. The skins will slip right off.*

　5　**cups thickly sliced peeled and pitted peaches (about 2 pounds)**
　⅓　**cup boysenberry or raspberry jam**
　2　**tablespoons sugar**
　1　**tablespoon cornstarch**
　¼　**teaspoon ground cinnamon**
　1　**9-inch frozen deep-dish pie crust, thawed**
　1　**tablespoon butter**
　½　**cup granola**

POSITION rack in lower third of oven and preheat to 425°F. Combine first 5 ingredients in medium bowl and mix to blend. Transfer to crust. Cut butter into small pieces and dot over surface of pie. Place pie on rimmed baking sheet. Bake until filling bubbles, about 35 minutes. Sprinkle granola over pie. Continue baking until granola is brown, about 8 minutes. Cool on rack. Serve slightly warm.

Chocolate-pecan chess pie

8 SERVINGS *There are myriad legends about the origins of the name chess pie ("chess" could have evolved from "cheese" due to the texture of the filling, or from "chest" because it kept well in a pie chest, or from a modest southern cook insisting it's "jes' pie"), but no one argues the merits of this luscious specialty. The original starts with a simple eggs, butter, and sugar mixture; here, it gets a chocolate-pecan twist. The baking sheet under the pie will catch any filling that bubbles over the edge of the crust.*

　½　**cup (1 stick) unsalted butter**
　2　**ounces unsweetened chocolate, chopped**

　1　**cup sugar**
　2　**large eggs**
　1　**tablespoon bourbon**
　1　**teaspoon vanilla extract**
　¼　**teaspoon salt**
　1　**cup chopped pecans**
　1　**9-inch frozen deep-dish pie crust, thawed**

　　Whipped cream

POSITION rack in lower third of oven and preheat to 325°F. Place baking sheet in oven. Stir butter and chocolate in heavy small saucepan over low heat until melted and smooth. Remove from heat; cool 10 minutes.

WHISK sugar and eggs in medium bowl to blend. Whisk in chocolate mixture, then bourbon, vanilla, and salt. Stir in pecans (filling will be thick). Spoon filling into crust.

PLACE pie on baking sheet in oven. Bake until edges of filling puff and begin to crack and center is just set, about 30 minutes. Transfer pie to rack and cool completely. Serve with whipped cream.

619

Black-bottom peanut butter mousse pie

8 TO 10 SERVINGS *Be careful not to overbeat the whipped cream or it won't fold smoothly into the peanut butter mousse base. The pie needs to chill at least an hour and up to a day, so plan accordingly.*

       Nonstick vegetable oil spray
   7   whole graham crackers, coarsely broken
   ¼   cup (½ stick) unsalted butter, melted
   4   tablespoons sugar, divided

   1⅓ cups bittersweet or semisweet chocolate chips (about 8 ounces)
   ⅔   cup plus 1¾ cups chilled heavy whipping cream
   2   tablespoons light corn syrup
   2   teaspoons vanilla extract, divided

   6   ounces peanut butter chips (1 cup)
   2   tablespoons creamy peanut butter (do not use old-fashioned style or freshly ground)

PREHEAT oven to 350°F. Spray 9-inch-diameter glass pie dish with nonstick spray. Blend graham crackers, butter, and 2 tablespoons sugar in processor until moist clumps form. Press crumb mixture over bottom and up sides of prepared pie dish. Bake crust until lightly browned, about 15 minutes.

MEANWHILE, combine chocolate chips, ⅔ cup cream, corn syrup, and 1 teaspoon vanilla in microwave-safe bowl. Microwave on medium heat until chocolate softens, about 3 minutes. Whisk until melted and smooth. Spread chocolate mixture over bottom of crust. Freeze 10 minutes.

MICROWAVE peanut butter chips and ¾ cup cream in large microwave-safe bowl on medium heat at 15-second intervals just until chips soften, stirring often. Whisk in peanut butter and remaining 1 teaspoon vanilla. Cool to barely lukewarm. Beat remaining 1 cup cream and 2 tablespoons sugar in medium bowl until very thick but not yet holding peaks; fold into peanut butter mixture in 3 additions. Spoon mousse over chocolate layer. Chill at least 1 hour and up to 1 day.

Chocolate mousse pie

8 SERVINGS *For a different version of this dessert, use peanut butter sandwich cookies to make the crust and sprinkle the finished pie with salted peanuts.*

Crust
   21 chocolate sandwich cookies (such as Oreos)
   ¼   cup (½ stick) unsalted butter, room temperature, cut into pieces

Mousse
   12 ounces semisweet chocolate, finely chopped
   1   teaspoon vanilla extract
       Pinch of salt
   3¾ cups chilled heavy whipping cream, divided
   ¼   cup sugar

FOR CRUST: Preheat oven to 350°F. Butter 9-inch-diameter springform pan with 2¾-inch-high sides. Finely grind cookies in processor. Add butter and process until mixture is evenly moistened. Press crumb mixture onto bottom and up sides of prepared pan to form thin crust. Bake crust 5 minutes. Transfer crust to rack and cool completely.

FOR MOUSSE: Combine chocolate, vanilla, and salt in processor. Bring 1 cup cream to boil in heavy small saucepan. With processor running, gradually pour hot cream through feed tube and process until chocolate is melted and smooth. Transfer mixture to large bowl. Cool to room temperature, stirring occasionally.

BEAT 2 cups cream and sugar in large bowl to stiff peaks. Fold into chocolate mixture. Pour mousse into prepared crust. Chill until set, about 6 hours.

DO AHEAD *Can be prepared 1 day ahead. Keep chilled.*

BEAT remaining ¾ cup cream in medium bowl to firm peaks. Transfer to pastry bag fitted with medium star tip. Pipe rosettes of whipped cream around edge of pie.

THE LOOK FOR LESS If you don't have a pastry bag to pipe cream around the edge of a pie, use a resealable plastic bag instead. Spoon the whipped cream into one bottom corner of the bag, then twist at the top, grasping top firmly. Using scissors, cut ¾ inch off the filled corner to form opening; turn bag so that one seam faces up (the seam will leave a decorative line in the piped cream). Pipe ovals along edge of tart and serve.

Pineapple-coconut pie

8 SERVINGS *Look for precut fresh pineapple in the produce section of the grocery store. Be sure to drain the pineapple before placing it in the crust. Excess pineapple juice could cause the crust to be soggy.*

- 1 refrigerated pie crust (half of 15-ounce package), room temperature
- 3 cups ½-inch pieces fresh pineapple, well drained
- ⅔ cup sugar
- ¼ cup all purpose flour
- ⅛ teaspoon salt
- 3 eggs, beaten to blend
- ¼ cup (½ stick) unsalted butter, melted
- ½ cup sweetened flaked coconut
- ⅓ cup chopped macadamia nuts

PREHEAT oven to 325°F. Flatten crust on lightly floured surface; press seams together if necessary. Fit into 9-inch-diameter glass pie dish; crimp edges.

ARRANGE pineapple in crust. Combine sugar, flour, and salt in medium bowl. Add eggs and butter and blend well. Pour batter evenly over pineapple. Sprinkle coconut and macadamia nuts over and press lightly into batter. Bake until light brown and center is firm to touch, about 1 hour 15 minutes. Transfer to rack and cool completely.

Sweet potato–pecan pie

8 SERVINGS *Two favorites in one deep dish—sweet potato on the bottom and pecan on the top.*

- 1 9-inch frozen deep-dish pie crust, thawed, pierced all over with fork
- 1 1-pound red-skinned sweet potato (yam), pierced with fork
- ½ cup (packed) golden brown sugar
- 2 tablespoons (¼ stick) unsalted butter, melted
- 1 tablespoon vanilla extract
- ½ teaspoon ground cinnamon
- ¼ teaspoon ground allspice
- ¼ teaspoon salt
- ¾ cup light corn syrup
- 2 large eggs
- 1 cup pecan halves (about 4 ounces)

PREHEAT oven to 400°F. Bake crust until pale golden, about 8 minutes; set aside. Reduce oven temperature to 350°F.

COOK yam in microwave on high until tender, about 6 minutes per side. Cut yam in half; scoop flesh into medium bowl and mash. Measure 1 cup mashed yam; place in large bowl. Whisk brown sugar and next 5 ingredients into mashed yam; spread mixture in prepared crust. Whisk corn syrup and eggs in bowl to blend. Stir in pecans. Pour syrup mixture over potato mixture.

BAKE pie until filling is set, puffed, and brown, about 45 minutes. Cool pie completely. Serve at room temperature or refrigerate up to 1 day and serve cold.

621

Fresh blackberry napoleons with cream cheese mousse

6 SERVINGS *A napoleon is a classic French dessert (although it goes by the name* mille-feuille *in France) made by layering puff pastry with pastry cream. Blackberries glazed with blackberry preserves add a freshness to this version.*

- 6 ounces cream cheese, room temperature
- ¾ cup powdered sugar, divided
- 1 teaspoon vanilla extract
- ⅔ cup chilled heavy whipping cream

- 1 sheet frozen puff pastry (half of 17.3-ounce package), thawed

- ½ cup blackberry preserves
- 3 ½-pint containers fresh blackberries

  Fresh mint sprigs

PREHEAT oven to 375°F. Using electric mixer, beat cream cheese, ¼ cup powdered sugar, and vanilla in medium bowl until fluffy. Using same beaters, beat whipping cream in another medium bowl until peaks form. Fold whipped cream into cream cheese mixture in 3 additions. Cover mousse and refrigerate.

ROLL out pastry sheet on lightly floured surface to 14×10½-inch rectangle. Cut sheet into twelve 3½-inch squares. Pierce squares all over with fork. Sift ¼ cup powdered sugar over squares. Place squares on ungreased baking sheet. Bake 12 minutes. Using metal spatula, flatten squares and continue baking until crisp and brown, about 5 minutes longer. Cool pastry squares on sheet.

HEAT preserves in small saucepan until just melted. Transfer to medium bowl. Add berries and toss to coat.

PLACE 6 pastry squares on work surface. Spread each with ¼ cup mousse. Top with 6 to 8 coated berries. Cover with remaining pastry squares. Dust napoleons with remaining ¼ cup powdered sugar. Top each with berry and mint sprig. Place napoleons on plates. Serve, passing remaining berries.

Chocolate-orange cookie stacks

8 SERVINGS *Four simple ingredients never looked so impressive. Because the cookie stacks need to chill for at least six hours, you'll need to start this recipe early in the day (or the night before).*

- 1 cup chilled heavy whipping cream
- ⅔ cup frozen orange juice concentrate, partially thawed

- 40 chocolate wafer cookies (about one 9-ounce package)

  Finely grated orange peel

USING electric mixer, beat cream and orange juice concentrate in medium bowl until stiff peaks form.

PLACE 8 cookies on rimmed baking sheet, spacing apart. Spoon about 1 level tablespoon whipped orange cream atop each cookie, then top each with second cookie and another tablespoon cream. Repeat 2 more times with cookies and cream, creating 8 stacks of 4 cookies with 4 layers of orange cream. Top each stack with fifth cookie. Transfer remaining orange cream to small bowl; cover and chill. Cover and chill stacks at least 6 hours or overnight (cookies will soften).

CAREFULLY transfer 1 stack to each of 8 plates. Rewhisk reserved orange cream, if necessary, until stiff peaks form. Spoon dollop of orange cream atop each stack and sprinkle with orange peel.

EASYCAKES

Red velvet cupcakes with coconut and cream cheese frosting

MAKES 18 *Here's a miniature version of the popular southern dessert.*

1¾ **cups self-rising flour**

¼ **cup unsweetened cocoa powder**

1½ **cups sugar**

1 **cup (2 sticks) unsalted butter, room temperature, divided**

2 **large eggs**

1 **tablespoon red food coloring**

2 **teaspoons vanilla extract, divided**

1 **cup buttermilk, divided**

1 **teaspoon distilled white vinegar**

¼ **teaspoon baking soda**

2 **8-ounce packages cream cheese, room temperature**

1½ **cups powdered sugar**

2 **cups sweetened flaked coconut (about 6 ounces), divided**

PREHEAT oven to 350°F. Line 18 muffin cups with paper liners. Sift flour and cocoa into small bowl. Using electric mixer, beat 1½ cups sugar and ¾ cup butter in large bowl until smooth. Beat in eggs 1 at a time, then red food coloring and 1 teaspoon vanilla. Mix in dry ingredients in 3 additions alternately with ⅔ cup buttermilk in 2 additions. Make well in center; pour in remaining ⅓ cup buttermilk, vinegar, and baking soda. When bubbles form, stir into batter.

DIVIDE batter equally among paper liners. Bake cupcakes until tester inserted into center comes out clean, about 20 minutes. Cool 10 minutes; transfer to rack and cool completely.

BEAT cream cheese, remaining ¼ cup butter, and remaining 1 teaspoon vanilla in medium bowl until smooth. Beat in powdered sugar; fold in 1 cup coconut. Spread frosting on cupcakes, leaving ½-inch plain border; sprinkle with remaining 1 cup coconut.

Fudgy chocolate mint cupcakes

MAKES 18 *The boxed cake mix never had it so good. Tint the frosting any color you like—or leave it white and top with chocolate shavings.*

Cupcakes

- 1 box devil's food cake mix (1 pound 2.25 ounces)
- 1⅓ cups water
- ½ cup vegetable oil
- 3 large eggs
- 1 tablespoon vanilla extract
- 1½ cups semisweet chocolate chips

Frosting

- 12 ounces cream cheese, room temperature
- ¼ cup (½ stick) unsalted butter, room temperature
- 1¾ cups powdered sugar
- ½ teaspoon peppermint extract
- 2 drops green food coloring

FOR CUPCAKES: Preheat oven to 350°F. Line eighteen ⅓-cup muffin cups with paper liners. Combine first 5 ingredients in large bowl. Using electric mixer, beat 2 minutes. Mix in chocolate chips. Pour batter into cups. Bake until tester inserted into center comes out with crumbs attached, about 25 minutes. Cool on racks.

FOR FROSTING: Using electric mixer, beat all ingredients in medium bowl until light and fluffy.

SPREAD frosting over cupcakes.

DO AHEAD *Can be made 1 day ahead. Cover and chill.*

Pear-gingerbread upside-down cake

8 TO 10 SERVINGS *Ginger preserves (like orange marmalade, but made with ginger) add a sweet-spicy note to this cake. Any leftover preserves would be great on toast, English muffins, or waffles.*

- ¾ cup (1½ sticks) unsalted butter
- 1 cup (packed) golden brown sugar, divided
- 3 Anjou pears, peeled, halved, cored, cut crosswise into ⅓-inch-thick slices
- ⅔ cup mild-flavored (light) molasses
- 2 large eggs
- ¾ cup ginger preserves (such as Robertson's)
- 1½ cups self-rising flour
- 1 tablespoon pumpkin pie spice

PREHEAT oven to 325°F. Butter 9×9×2-inch non-stick baking pan. Melt butter in medium saucepan over medium heat. Transfer ⅓ cup melted butter to small bowl. Whisk ½ cup brown sugar into remaining butter in saucepan until blended (mixture may be grainy). Spread butter-sugar mixture in prepared pan; slightly overlap enough pear slices to cover mixture. Dice enough remaining pear to yield 1 cup.

USING electric mixer, beat molasses, reserved ⅓ cup butter, and remaining ½ cup brown sugar in large bowl to blend. Beat in eggs, then preserves. Beat in flour and pumpkin pie spice; stir in diced pears. Spread batter over pears in pan. Bake until tester inserted into center comes out clean, about 1 hour 15 minutes. Cool 5 minutes. Invert cake onto platter; cool slightly. Serve warm or at room temperature.

Old-fashioned gingerbread with molasses whipped cream

8 TO 10 SERVINGS *A slice of this cake is the perfect accompaniment to a cup of tea. For more ginger flavor, mix some chopped crystallized ginger into the batter.*

- 1 cup plus 1 tablespoon sugar
- ½ cup (1 stick) unsalted butter, room temperature
- ¾ cup plus 2 tablespoons mild-flavored (light) molasses
- 2 large eggs
- 2 cups all purpose flour
- 2 teaspoons baking soda
- 1¼ teaspoons ground cinnamon
- ¾ teaspoon ground ginger
- ½ teaspoon salt
- 1½ cups chilled heavy whipping cream, divided
- ¾ cup boiling water

PREHEAT oven to 350°F. Butter and flour 9×9×2-inch metal baking pan. Using electric mixer, beat 1 cup sugar and butter in large bowl until blended. Beat in ¾ cup molasses, then eggs 1 at a time. Sift in flour, baking soda, cinnamon, ginger, and salt; beat until blended. Beat in ¼ cup cream, then ¾ cup boiling water. Transfer batter to prepared pan.

BAKE cake until tester inserted into center comes out clean, about 45 minutes. Cool in pan on rack.

BEAT remaining 1¼ cups cream and 1 tablespoon sugar in medium bowl until peaks form. Fold in remaining 2 tablespoons molasses just until streaks appear (do not overmix). Cut cake into slices; transfer to plates. Serve with molasses whipped cream.

Mississippi mud cake

24 SERVINGS *This dark, rich chocolate cake gets its name from the muddy Mississippi River. For a more casual look, sprinkle chopped toasted pecans over the top of the cake.*

- 2¼ cups sugar
- 2 cups unbleached all purpose flour
- 1 teaspoon baking soda
- ½ teaspoon salt
- 1½ cups whole milk
- 1 cup (2 sticks) unsalted butter, cut into pieces
- ¾ cup unsweetened cocoa powder
- 2 large eggs
- 2 teaspoons vanilla extract
- 2⅓ cups semisweet chocolate chips (about 14 ounces), divided
- 1½ cups pecan halves (about 7 ounces), toasted

- 6 tablespoons heavy whipping cream
- 6 tablespoons dark corn syrup

PREHEAT oven to 350°F. Butter and flour 15½x10½x1-inch baking sheet. Whisk first 4 ingredients in large bowl to blend. Whisk milk, butter, and cocoa powder in heavy medium saucepan over medium heat just until butter melts and mixture is smooth. Remove saucepan from heat. Whisk cocoa mixture, then eggs and vanilla into dry ingredients. Spread batter in prepared pan and sprinkle with 1 cup chocolate chips. Bake cake until tester inserted into center comes out clean, about 25 minutes. Arrange toasted pecans atop cake. Cool cake in pan.

MEANWHILE, bring cream and corn syrup to simmer in heavy medium saucepan. Add remaining 1⅓ cups chocolate chips. Whisk until chocolate chips have melted and glaze is smooth. Cool glaze 15 minutes.

POUR glaze evenly over cake. Chill at least 1 hour and up to 2 days.

Chocolate-raspberry cakes

MAKES 6 *Top these individual molten chocolate cakes with whipped cream and fresh raspberries. Using seedless preserves makes the cake centers smooth.*

8	ounces bittersweet or semisweet chocolate, coarsely chopped
14	tablespoons (1¾ sticks) unsalted butter, diced
2	tablespoons seedless raspberry preserves
4	large eggs
¼	cup sugar
1	tablespoon vanilla extract

PREHEAT oven to 325°F. Butter six ¾-cup soufflé dishes or custard cups. Arrange dishes on baking sheet. Mix chocolate, butter, and preserves in saucepan. Stir over low heat until chocolate melts. Remove from heat; cool to lukewarm, stirring often, about 10 minutes.

WHISK eggs, sugar, and vanilla in large bowl to blend well, about 1 minute. Gradually whisk in chocolate mixture. Divide batter among prepared dishes.

BAKE cakes until tester inserted into center comes out with some moist batter still attached, about 20 minutes. Let cool 30 minutes (centers may fall). Serve cakes warm or at room temperature.

Bittersweet molten chocolate cakes with coffee ice cream

MAKES 8 *For the most delicious results, use the best quality chocolate you can afford. Try Scharffen Berger, Lindt, Callebaut, or Valrhona. Make sure the chocolate has a cacao content between 60 and 70 percent (this number will be marked on the package).*

12	teaspoons plus 5 tablespoons sugar
8	ounces bittersweet or semisweet chocolate, chopped
¾	cup (1½ sticks) unsalted butter
3	large eggs
3	large egg yolks
1	tablespoon all purpose flour
1	quart coffee ice cream

GENEROUSLY butter eight ¾-cup soufflé dishes or custard cups. Sprinkle inside of each dish with 1½ teaspoons sugar.

STIR chocolate and butter in heavy medium saucepan over low heat until smooth. Remove from heat. Using electric mixer, beat eggs, yolks, and remaining 5 tablespoons sugar in large bowl until thick and pale yellow, about 8 minutes. Fold ⅓ of warm chocolate mixture into egg mixture, then fold in remaining chocolate. Fold in flour. Divide batter among prepared dishes.

DO AHEAD *Can be made 1 day ahead. Cover and refrigerate. Bring to room temperature before continuing.*

PREHEAT oven to 425°F. Place soufflé dishes on baking sheet. Bake cakes uncovered until edges are puffed and slightly cracked but center 1 inch of each moves slightly when dishes are shaken gently, about 13 minutes.

TOP each cake with scoop of coffee ice cream and serve immediately.

Chocolate terrine with cookies and dried cherries

12 SERVINGS *Coarsely chopped cookies add crunch to this incredibly rich and easy dessert. How easy is it? Everything is mixed together in a saucepan, poured into a loaf pan, then chilled for a few hours.*

- 10 **ounces bittersweet or semisweet chocolate, chopped**
- 10 **tablespoons (1¼ sticks) unsalted butter**
- ¼ **cup heavy whipping cream**
- 2 **tablespoons Lyle's Golden Syrup or light corn syrup**
- 1 **7.5-ounce package Le Petit Beurre lightly toasted butter biscuits, coarsely chopped**
- 1 **cup chopped walnuts**
- ⅔ **cup dried tart cherries**

LINE 9×5×2-inch metal loaf pan with plastic wrap, extending over sides. Stir chocolate and butter in heavy large saucepan over low heat until melted and smooth. Mix in cream and golden syrup. Remove from heat. Stir in remaining ingredients. Pour chocolate mixture into prepared pan. Smooth top. Cover and refrigerate until set, at least 4 hours or overnight.

DO AHEAD *Can be prepared up to 3 days ahead. Keep refrigerated.*

UNCOVER pan. Place platter upside-down over pan. Invert terrine onto platter. Peel off plastic wrap. Using large knife dipped in hot water and wiped dry, cut terrine into slices.

Delicious imports This recipe has an international flair, thanks to a couple of imported ingredients:

— Lyle's Golden Syrup, a popular British sweetener with a mild butterscotch flavor, is available in many supermarkets near the syrups.

— Le Petit Beurre ("little butter" in French) are crispy, buttery, not-too-sweet cookies from France. Look for them in the cookie aisle.

Almond cake with kirsch

8 SERVINGS *The intense flavor in this nearly flourless cake comes from cherry brandy, almond extract, and almond paste; almond paste is available in the baking-products section of most supermarkets and at specialty foods stores.*

¾ **cup sugar**

½ **cup (1 stick) unsalted butter, room temperature**

1 **7-ounce package almond paste, broken into pieces**

3 **large eggs**

1 **tablespoon kirsch (clear cherry brandy)**

½ **teaspoon almond extract**

¼ **teaspoon salt**

⅓ **cup cake flour**

½ **teaspoon baking powder**

Powdered sugar

PREHEAT oven to 350°F. Butter 8-inch-diameter cake pan with 2-inch-high sides. Dust pan with flour; tap out excess. Using electric mixer, beat ¾ cup sugar and butter in large bowl until light and creamy. Add almond paste, 1 piece at a time, beating until well blended after each addition. Beat in eggs 1 at a time. Mix in kirsch, almond extract, and salt. Mix flour and baking powder in small bowl; add to batter. Beat just until blended. Spoon batter into prepared pan; smooth top.

BAKE cake until top is golden brown and tester inserted into center comes out clean, about 35 minutes. Cool in pan on rack.

TRANSFER cake to platter.

DO AHEAD *Can be made 1 day ahead. Store in airtight container at room temperature.*

DUST with powdered sugar.

Thinking outside the pan For most bakers, the most stressful part of baking a cake is inverting it. These tips should help calm your nerves.

— Be careful to cover every nook and cranny of the pan with butter and flour. This coating should keep the cake from sticking.

— To be extra sure that your cake will emerge from the pan in one piece, line the bottom of the pan with parchment paper. You can either cut the parchment to fit into the pan or buy precut parchment paper rounds. Look for them at cookware stores. Be sure to butter the parchment before pouring in the batter.

— Look for flexible silicone baking pans at cookware stores or in the cookware section of some supermarkets. They are available in a variety of styles, including loaf and Bundt, and require no greasing or flouring (muffin and loaf pans may benefit from a light coating of nonstick spray). Because they're so flexible, you'll want to use a cookie sheet underneath.

— After you place the cake on the cooling rack, start the timer. For best results, turn the cake out after it has cooled for 10 to 15 minutes. If the cake is removed when it is too hot, it will break apart because it is so soft and tender. If you allow the cake to cool completely in the pan, the butter will firm up and adhere the cake to the bottom of the pan. If this happens, hold the pan over one of the burners on your stove for several seconds. Heating the pan should help the cake release.

Orange-pineapple carrot cake

12 SERVINGS *For a moist, sweet cake, use organic carrots or sweet Nantes carrots, if available.*

- 2 cups all purpose flour
- 2 teaspoons baking powder
- 2 teaspoons ground cinnamon
- 1½ teaspoons baking soda
- 1 teaspoon salt
- 2 cups sugar
- 4 large eggs
- ¾ cup frozen pineapple-orange juice concentrate, thawed, divided
- ½ cup sour cream
- ½ cup vegetable oil
- 2 cups grated carrots
- 1 8-ounce can crushed pineapple in juice, well drained

- 1½ 8-ounce packages cream cheese, room temperature
- ½ cup (1 stick) unsalted butter, room temperature
- 2 cups powdered sugar

PREHEAT oven to 350°F. Butter and flour 13×9×2-inch metal baking pan. Combine first 5 ingredients in medium bowl; whisk to blend. Using an electric mixer, beat 2 cups sugar, eggs, ½ cup juice concentrate, sour cream, and oil in large bowl until smooth. Beat in dry ingredients; stir in carrots and pineapple. Pour batter into prepared pan. Bake cake until tester inserted into center comes out clean, about 50 minutes. Cool cake completely in pan on rack.

COMBINE cream cheese, butter, and remaining ¼ cup juice concentrate in medium bowl. Beat until blended. Add powdered sugar and beat until smooth. Spread frosting over cake.

DO AHEAD *Can be made 2 days ahead. Chill until frosting sets, then cover and keep chilled.*

Banana cake with sour cream frosting

10 TO 12 SERVINGS *Ripe bananas get a new life in this homey dessert.*

- 2 cups all purpose flour
- ¾ teaspoon baking soda
- ½ teaspoon baking powder
- ½ teaspoon salt
- ½ cup (1 stick) unsalted butter, room temperature
- 1½ cups sugar
- 2 large eggs
- 1¼ cups sour cream, divided
- 1⅓ cups mashed ripe bananas (about 3 large)
- 2 tablespoons fresh lemon juice

- 1 8-ounce package cream cheese, room temperature
- ⅔ cup powdered sugar

PREHEAT oven to 350°F. Lightly butter and flour 13×9×2-inch metal baking pan. Combine flour, baking soda, baking powder, and salt in medium bowl. Using electric mixer, beat butter and 1½ cups sugar in large bowl until blended. Add eggs and beat until fluffy. Mix in ¾ cup sour cream, bananas, and lemon juice. Add dry ingredients to banana mixture and beat until well blended. Transfer batter to prepared pan.

BAKE cake until top is golden and tester inserted into center comes out clean, about 30 minutes. Cool completely on rack.

BEAT cream cheese, powdered sugar, and remaining ½ cup sour cream in large bowl until well blended. Spread frosting over cooled cake.

Apple and walnut sheet cake with caramel sauce

12 SERVINGS *Any crisp, somewhat tart apples, such as Pippin, Jonagold, or Granny Smith, would work well in this recipe. To serve for breakfast or brunch, skip the caramel sauce and sprinkle the cake with powdered sugar.*

    2 cups sugar
    ½ cup plus 2 tablespoons (1¼ sticks)
       unsalted butter, room temperature
    2 large eggs
    2 teaspoons vanilla extract
    2 cups all purpose flour
    2 teaspoons ground cinnamon
    1 teaspoon baking soda
    1 teaspoon baking powder
    ½ teaspoon salt
    2 pounds Golden Delicious apples,
       peeled, cored, coarsely grated
    1 cup walnuts, toasted, chopped

       Purchased caramel sauce, heated

PREHEAT oven to 350°F. Butter and flour 13×9×2-inch metal baking pan. Using electric mixer, beat first 4 ingredients in large bowl until smooth. Add flour, cinnamon, baking soda, baking powder, and salt; beat just until blended. Stir in apples, then walnuts. Transfer batter to prepared pan.

BAKE cake until top browns and tester inserted into center comes out clean, about 55 minutes. Cool cake in pan.

CUT cake into squares and serve with warm caramel sauce.

Spiced nectarine cake

8 SERVINGS *This cake would also be delicious made with plums or pluots. The perfect finishing touch? A scoop of vanilla ice cream or a dollop of whipped cream.*

    ½ cup (1 stick) unsalted butter,
       room temperature
    ¾ cup plus 3 tablespoons sugar
    2 large eggs
    1 tablespoon fresh lemon juice
    1½ teaspoons finely grated lemon peel
    1¼ cups self-rising flour

    5 medium nectarines (about 1¾ pounds),
       halved, each half cut into 4 slices
    ¾ teaspoon ground cinnamon

PREHEAT oven to 350°F. Generously butter 9-inch-diameter springform pan. Using electric mixer, beat butter in large bowl until fluffy. Add ¾ cup sugar and beat until blended. Beat in eggs 1 at a time, then lemon juice and lemon peel. Beat in flour until smooth. Spread batter evenly in prepared pan.

ARRANGE enough nectarine slices atop batter in concentric circles to cover completely; press lightly to adhere. Mix cinnamon and remaining 3 tablespoons sugar in small bowl. Sprinkle over cake.

BAKE until cake is golden brown and tester inserted into center comes out clean, about 1 hour (50 minutes for plums or pluots). Cut around cake to loosen; remove pan sides. Serve cake slightly warm or at room temperature.

FORM AND FUNCTION This recipe calls for a springform pan, a round cake pan with sides that expand via a clamp or spring. After the cake is finished baking, you cut around the cake to loosen it, release the clamp, and remove the sides of the pan, leaving the bottom of the pan under the cake.

Lemon-lime pound cake

12 SERVINGS *Using soda in cakes is a southern tradition. In this recipe, the lemon-lime soda goes into the cake batter and is used to make the icing.*

    Nonstick vegetable oil spray
 3 cups all purpose flour
 ½ teaspoon salt
1½ cups (3 sticks) unsalted butter,
    room temperature
 3 cups sugar
 5 large eggs
1½ teaspoons finely grated lemon peel, divided
1½ teaspoons finely grated lime peel, divided
 ¾ cup plus 2 tablespoons (about)
    lemon-lime soda (such as 7UP)

1¼ cups powdered sugar

PREHEAT oven to 325°F. Spray 12-cup Bundt pan with nonstick spray. Whisk flour and salt in bowl to blend. Using electric mixer, beat butter in large bowl until fluffy. Gradually beat in 3 cups sugar. Beat in eggs, 1 at a time, then beat in 1 teaspoon each lemon peel and lime peel. Beat in flour mixture in 4 additions alternately with ¾ cup soda in 3 additions. Transfer batter to prepared pan.

BAKE cake until golden on top and tester inserted near center comes out clean, about 1 hour 15 minutes. Cool cake in pan 5 minutes. Turn cake out onto rack and cool completely.

COMBINE powdered sugar and remaining ½ teaspoon each lemon peel and lime peel in bowl. Whisk in enough of remaining 2 tablespoons soda to form thick, smooth icing. Drizzle icing over cake.

When bad things happen to good cakes Into each baker's life some crumbs must fall. After years of baking we've learned that, despite our best efforts, sometimes the edges of the cake will be burned—or it doesn't come out of the pan in one piece. Don't despair. We've got some quick fixes.

— **MAKE EXTRA FROSTING:** Whip up a batch of your favorite quick buttercream (a mixture of powdered sugar and butter) and use it to piece the cake back together.

— **TURN IT INTO A TRIFLE:** Cut the cake into cubes. Layer it with chocolate sauce or berry sauce, whipped cream, and berries.

— **SUNDAE TIME:** Cut the cake into squares. Serve with a scoop of ice cream, a drizzle of sauce, and some chopped nuts.

custards
puddings, and fruit desserts

CUSTARDS

Raspberry Custard

Low-Fat Vanilla Custard Sauce

Lime Mascarpone Panna
Cotta with Raspberries

Honey-Yogurt Panna Cotta with
Orange and Date Compote

Buttermilk Panna Cotta
with Tropical Fruit

Peach and Berry Trifle

Raspberry, White Chocolate,
and Almond Trifle

Tiramisù with Brandy Custard

Strawberry Tiramisù

Blackberries Brûlée with
Mascarpone Cream

Lemon Crème Brûlée
with Fresh Berries

Grand Marnier Crème Brûlée

Lime Fool with
Strawberries and Kiwis

Vanilla Pear Clafouti

Cherry-Almond Clafouti

Exotic Fruit with Ginger Sabayon

PUDDINGS

Sticky Toffee Pudding

Bread and Butter Pudding

Sugar-Crusted Chocolate Chip
and Cherry Bread Puddings

Banana Pudding

Amaretto Chocolate Pudding

Coconut Rice Pudding

Turkish Coffee Pudding

Strawberry, Mascarpone,
and Marsala Budini

Meyer Lemon Buttermilk Pudding
Cake with Fresh Berries

30-Minute Rice Pudding
with Dried Fruit

Dark Chocolate Mousse
with Sugared Kumquats

Mom's Blender Chocolate
Mousse with Lemon Cream

Simplest Chocolate
Honey Mousse

White Chocolate Mousse
with Dark Chocolate Sauce

FRUIT DESSERTS

Tropical Fruit Kebabs
with Lime Cream

Peaches In Spiced Red Wine

Sherry-Poached Pears with
Spanish Turrón Ice Cream

Blueberry Crisp with
Cinnamon-Streusel Topping

Almond-Peach Crisp

Mixed Berry Crisp

Double-Cherry Almond Crisp

Plum Crumble

Apple Crumble with
Vanilla Ice Cream

Nectarine Cobbler

Fresh Fruit with Mascarpone
and White Chocolate Dip

Dark Chocolate Fondue

Milk Chocolate Fondue
with Strawberries

Summer Fruit with
Praline Fondue

Berries In Sweet Fragolino
Wine with Biscotti

Mixed Berries with Mascarpone-
Limoncello Cream

Caramelized Chocolate, Banana,
and Marshmallow Sandwiches

Strawberries with Lemon
Sugar and Lavender Syrup

Grilled Cardamom-Glazed
Pineapple with Vanilla Ice Cream

Grilled Nectarines with
Honey-Balsamic Glaze

Grilled Brown-Sugar Peaches
with White Chocolate

Honey-Roasted Plums with
Thyme and Crème Fraîche

Apricot-Raspberry Pavlovas
with Sliced Almonds

Spiced Rhubarb and
Pear Compote

Caramel Oranges

Baked Apples with Mincemeat,
Cherries, and Walnuts

Ginger Baked Apples

Hazelnut-Stuffed Pears
with Maple Glaze

Fresh Pears with Port Zabaglione

Cinnamon Apple Ring Fritters

Dark Chocolate-Lime Soufflés

Vanilla-Infused Scharffen
Berger Bittersweet Soufflés

Strawberry Shortcakes with
Mint and Whipped Cream

Raspberry Salzburger Nockerl

tool kit Besides being delicious, the recipes in this chapter also provide the building blocks for an entire array of desserts. Just swap out a few ingredients, a couple of garnishes, and a topping or two, and you've created several new dishes. Consider these examples.

QUICK PARFAITS

The Italian *budini,* or pudding parfaits (page 650), feature layers of creamy mascarpone cheese, crunchy amaretti cookies, and fresh berries. Now mix them up.

CHANGE THE FLAVOR OF THE MASCARPONE CREAM:

— Replace the Marsala with different sweet liqueurs and wines, such as Chambord (black-raspberry liqueur), Frangelico (hazelnut liqueur), Grand Marnier (orange liqueur), crème de cassis (black-currant liqueur), sambuca (anise liqueur), Sherry, or Essencia (orange Muscat wine). Add the liqueur or wine to the mascarpone a little bit at a time (liqueurs are stronger and sweeter than wine, so you'll use less) and taste between additions to make sure it doesn't overwhelm the other flavors.

— Spice it up with freshly grated nutmeg, cinnamon, star anise, or cloves.

— Mix in finely grated citrus peel such as lemon, orange, or lime.

— Sweeten it with maple syrup or honey instead of sugar.

CHANGE THE TEXTURE:

— Use different types of purchased cookies or cake in place of the amaretti: Try biscotti, chocolate wafer cookies, chewy ginger cookies, soft sponge-cake ladyfingers, angel food cake, chocolate pound cake, or carrot cake.

— Sprinkle toasted coconut or chopped nuts on top just before serving.

CHANGE THE FRUIT WITH THE SEASONS:

— Try cooked rhubarb in the spring; cherries, mixed berries, nectarines, figs, or pineapple in the summer; sautéed apples or pears or a dried fruit compote in the fall; and banana slices or tangerine or orange segments in the winter. →

EASY CHOCOLATE PUDDING AND BEYOND

Semisweet chocolate chips and a splash of amaretto transform a chocolate pudding box mix into an elegant Amaretto Chocolate Pudding (page 648). Take it above and beyond the box with these easy changes.

— Replace the amaretto with raspberry liqueur, then layer the pudding in wineglasses with fresh raspberries and sweetened crème fraîche.

— Give it a mousse-like texture by folding in whipped cream.

— Make a double batch of pudding and layer it between cubes of toasted pound cake, spiced cranberry compote, or cherry jam and whipped cream for an impressive trifle.

— Replace the amaretto with two tablespoons of rum and spoon the pudding into Champagne coupes. Before serving, top it with whipped cream and raisins that have been soaked in rum.

— Spoon it into a chocolate-cookie pie crust and top it with whipped cream for a double-chocolate cream pie. Or replace the amaretto with peppermint schnapps and sprinkle the whipped cream with crushed peppermint candies to create a chocolate mint pie.

— Use Kahlúa and instant coffee instead of the chocolate chips and amaretto, to give the pudding a mocha flavor. Then chill it in demitasse cups and top with whipped cream.

— Prefer vanilla? Use vanilla pudding with white chocolate, a splash of Sherry, and finely grated orange peel.

COBBLER SWAP

A cobbler and a crisp start out the same: ripe fruit tossed with some sugar and a bit of flour, cornstarch, or tapioca to thicken the juices into a luxurious sauce when baked. When topped with sweet biscuits, it becomes a cobbler; when topped with sweet, streusel-like dough, it becomes a crisp or a crumble. Turn crisps and crumbles into cobblers by swapping the biscuit topping from the Nectarine Cobbler (page 658) with:

— The oaty streusel topping on the apple crumble (page 658)

— The cinnamon-streusel topping on the blueberry crisp (page 655)

— The almond topping on the cherry-almond crisp (page 657)

Or turn the Nectarine Cobbler into a crisp with any of the above toppings.

CUSTARDS

Raspberry custard

6 SERVINGS *This is a classic baked custard with a sweet raspberry surprise at the bottom. Have fun getting creative with this recipe: Try blueberry or blackberry preserves, for example, with 36 blueberries or blackberries in place of the raspberries.*

   6 tablespoons raspberry preserves
      or jam, divided
  36 fresh raspberries or frozen
      unsweetened, thawed
  ½ cup sugar
   2 large eggs
   2 large egg yolks
   2 teaspoons vanilla extract
      Pinch of salt
   2 cups half and half

PREHEAT oven to 350°F. Place 1 tablespoon preserves and 6 berries in each of six ¾-cup custard cups or ramekins. Whisk sugar, eggs, egg yolks, vanilla, and salt in medium bowl to blend. Heat half and half in small saucepan over medium heat until tiny bubbles form around edge of pan. Gradually whisk hot half and half into egg mixture. Divide custard mixture evenly among prepared cups. Set cups in 13×9×2-inch metal baking pan. Pour enough hot water into pan to reach halfway up sides of cups.

PLACE pan with custards in oven. Bake until custards are just set in center, about 35 minutes. Remove custards from water and cool 10 minutes. Chill uncovered until cold, at least 2 hours.

DO AHEAD *Can be made 1 day ahead. Cover and keep chilled.*

Low-fat vanilla custard sauce

MAKES ABOUT 2 CUPS *Use this versatile sauce on fruit, such as fresh berries, sliced peaches, or apricots, or with cakes, crisps, or cobblers. Vanilla bean—the aromatic pod from an orchid—imparts an intensely perfumed vanilla flavor to the sauce. If you prefer, you can substitute 1 teaspoon vanilla extract.*

   2 cups low-fat (1%) milk
   1 3-inch piece vanilla bean, split lengthwise
  ¼ cup sugar
   2 teaspoons cornstarch
   1 large egg

POUR milk into heavy medium saucepan. Scrape in seeds from vanilla bean; add bean. Bring to simmer. Whisk sugar and cornstarch in medium bowl until no lumps remain. Add egg; whisk until well blended. Gradually whisk hot milk mixture into egg mixture. Return to same saucepan; whisk over medium heat until sauce thickens and boils, about 5 minutes. Pour sauce into another medium bowl. Chill until cold, stirring occasionally, about 4 hours.

DO AHEAD *Can be made 2 days ahead. Cover and keep chilled. Discard vanilla bean and whisk sauce to loosen before serving.*

Lime mascarpone panna cotta with raspberries

6 SERVINGS Panna cotta *means "cooked cream" in Italian. In this version of the classic Italian custard, mascarpone (the Italian cream cheese sold at many supermarkets and Italian markets) adds incredible richness. The panna cotta can be made two days ahead of time.*

6	tablespoons fresh lime juice, divided
1½	teaspoons finely grated lime peel
1	teaspoon unflavored gelatin
1¼	cups heavy whipping cream, divided
½	cup mascarpone cheese or cream cheese
¾	cup sugar, divided
1	tablespoon butter
1½	½-pint containers raspberries (about 2 cups)
1	lime

COMBINE 4 tablespoons lime juice and lime peel in small saucepan; sprinkle gelatin over. Let stand until gelatin softens, about 10 minutes. Add ¼ cup cream to gelatin mixture; stir over low heat just until gelatin dissolves. Remove from heat.

WHISK mascarpone and ½ cup sugar in medium bowl just until blended; gradually whisk in remaining 1 cup cream, then gelatin mixture. Divide panna cotta among 6 Champagne coupes or small wineglasses. Chill until set, at least 4 hours or overnight.

STIR remaining 2 tablespoons lime juice, ¼ cup sugar, and butter in small skillet over medium-high heat until sugar dissolves, about 3 minutes. Cool 2 minutes. Fold berries into lime sauce and spoon over panna cotta. Grate peel from lime directly over panna cotta.

Custards 101

— Custards are made with eggs and milk or cream. Custards made with egg yolks are denser than those made with whole eggs. And custards made with cream are richer than those made with milk.

— They can be stirred on the stovetop or baked in the oven, often in a water bath (or bain-marie): The baking dish sits inside a larger pan and water is added to the pan until it comes halfway up the sides of the baking dish. The water insulates the custard while it's baking, so it cooks gently without curdling.

— When stirring, be careful not to boil custards that have no flour or cornstarch as thickeners, because eggs can curdle and create an unpleasant texture.

— When baking, unless the recipe instructs otherwise, be sure to remove the ramekin or dish from the water bath as soon as the custard is taken out of the oven, or the hot water will continue to bake the custard.

— To test for doneness, insert a small, sharp knife into the edge of the custard; if the knife comes out clean, remove the custard from the oven. Or slightly shake the pan to see whether the center of the custard is still very jiggly (not cooked enough). The custards will continue to set in the center as they cool.

— Store custards in the refrigerator. Once the custard has cooled, cover it so that the delicate dessert does not pick up flavors from the refrigerator.

Honey-yogurt panna cotta with orange and date compote

2 SERVINGS *Orange-flower water can be found in the liquor, Middle Eastern, or baking section of many supermarkets and at Middle Eastern markets.*

> Nonstick vegetable oil spray
> ¼ cup cold low-fat (1%) milk
> ½ teaspoon unflavored gelatin
>
> ½ cup heavy whipping cream, divided
> ¼ cup plain whole-milk yogurt
> 4 tablespoons honey, divided
>
> 1 orange, all peel and pith cut away
> ⅛ teaspoon orange-flower water or
>   1 teaspoon finely grated orange peel
> 4 pitted dates, thinly sliced into rounds

SPRAY two ½-cup ramekins with nonstick spray. Place milk in small bowl; sprinkle gelatin over. Let stand until gelatin softens, about 10 minutes.

MEANWHILE, stir ¼ cup cream and yogurt in medium bowl to blend. Bring remaining ¼ cup cream and 3 tablespoons honey to simmer in heavy small saucepan. Remove from heat; add gelatin mixture to hot cream mixture and stir until gelatin dissolves. Stir gelatin mixture into yogurt mixture. Divide between prepared ramekins. Chill panna cotta uncovered until set, at least 2 hours, then cover and chill up to 2 days.

WORKING over medium bowl, cut orange between membranes to release segments. Stir remaining 1 tablespoon honey and orange-flower water into orange segments. Carefully mix in dates.

DO AHEAD *Can be made 6 hours ahead. Cover; chill.*

CUT around each panna cotta to loosen. Invert each onto plate. Hold ramekin and plate together and shake gently, allowing panna cotta to settle onto plate. Spoon orange-date compote around panna cotta.

Buttermilk panna cotta with tropical fruit

6 SERVINGS *The tangy buttermilk flavor is a good foil for the sweet tropical fruit; sweetened, sliced strawberries would also be an excellent accompaniment.*

> 2 tablespoons water
> 2 teaspoons unflavored gelatin
>
> 1 cup heavy whipping cream
> 7 tablespoons sugar
>
> 2 cups reduced-fat (2%) buttermilk
> ¾ teaspoon vanilla extract
>
> 2 cups ½-inch cubes peeled assorted tropical fruits (such as mango, papaya, and kiwi)

POUR 2 tablespoons water into small custard cup; sprinkle gelatin over. Let stand until gelatin softens, about 10 minutes.

STIR cream and sugar in heavy medium saucepan over medium heat until sugar dissolves and mixture is hot but not yet boiling. Remove from heat; add gelatin mixture and stir until gelatin dissolves. Cool mixture to room temperature, about 45 minutes.

STIR buttermilk and vanilla extract into gelatin mixture. Strain buttermilk mixture through fine sieve into 4-cup measuring cup; divide among six ¾-cup custard cups or ramekins. Chill until panna cotta is set, at least 6 hours and up to 1 day.

CUT around each panna cotta to loosen. Working with 1 at a time, place bottom of cup in 1 inch of hot water for 30 to 45 seconds. Immediately invert cup onto plate. Hold cup and plate together and shake gently, allowing panna cotta to settle onto plate. Spoon fruit mixture around each panna cotta.

Peach and berry trifle

8 TO 10 SERVINGS *Trifle is an English dessert made with layers of fruit, sponge cake, and cream or custard. Trifle is traditionally a celebratory treat that's especially good with summer fruit, like the peaches and strawberries used in this easy version. Look for the soft ladyfingers at bakeries and in the bakery section of the supermarket. Wash and dry the peaches to remove the fuzz.*

- 4 peaches, halved, pitted, cut into ½-inch cubes or thinly sliced
- 2 1-pint containers strawberries, halved (or quartered if large)
- 2 ½-pint containers raspberries
- ¼ cup sugar
- 1 teaspoon vanilla extract
- 3 cups chilled heavy whipping cream
- 48 purchased sponge-cake-type ladyfingers (from two 3-ounce packages), divided
- 1 cup seedless raspberry jam, divided
  Additional whole strawberries for garnish (optional)

COMBINE first 5 ingredients in large bowl and toss to blend; let stand 10 minutes. Beat chilled cream in another large bowl until stiff peaks form.

ARRANGE 16 ladyfingers in 10- to 12-cup glass bowl or trifle dish to cover bottom. Spread with ⅓ cup raspberry jam. Top with 2 cups fruit mixture, then 2 cups whipped cream. Repeat layering 2 more times with ladyfingers, jam, fruit mixture, and cream. Garnish with whole strawberries, if desired. Refrigerate trifle at least 2 hours and up to 6 hours before serving.

Raspberry, white chocolate, and almond trifle

16 SERVINGS *The perfect holiday-party dessert—impressive, yet easy to assemble; you can even make it a day ahead. High-quality white chocolate contains cocoa butter, which is important for texture, proper melting, and flavor.*

- 3½ cups chilled heavy whipping cream, divided
- 12 ounces high-quality white chocolate (such as Lindt or Perugina), chopped
- 1¼ teaspoons almond extract, divided

- ½ cup sugar
- ½ cup water
- 7 ounces crisp ladyfingers (such as Boudoirs or Savoiardi), divided

- 1 cup raspberry jam, melted, divided
- 1½ 12-ounce packages frozen unsweetened raspberries, partially thawed, divided
- 2 ½-pint containers fresh raspberries
- ¾ cup sliced almonds, toasted

BRING 1 cup cream to simmer in medium saucepan. Remove from heat. Add white chocolate; whisk until smooth. Cool to barely lukewarm, about 10 minutes. Beat remaining 2½ cups cream and ½ teaspoon almond extract in large bowl until peaks form. Gradually fold in white chocolate mixture.

STIR sugar and ½ cup water in small saucepan over medium heat until sugar dissolves. Mix in remaining ¾ teaspoon almond extract; remove syrup from heat. Quickly submerge 1 ladyfinger in syrup; shake excess back into pan. Place dipped ladyfinger in 14-cup trifle dish. Repeat with enough ladyfingers to cover bottom of dish.

SPREAD ⅓ of melted jam over ladyfingers in dish. Top with ⅓ of partially thawed berries with juices, then ⅓ of whipped white chocolate cream. Repeat layering with ladyfingers, jam, berries, and white chocolate cream 2 more times. Mound fresh berries in center of trifle. Sprinkle almonds around edge. Cover and chill at least 5 hours and up to 24 hours.

Tiramisù with brandy custard

12 SERVINGS Tiramisù *means "pick-me-up" in Italian, and eating this light and creamy dessert is certain to lift your spirits. Mascarpone (Italian cream cheese, available at many supermarkets and Italian markets), ladyfingers, custard, coffee, and some liquor are the traditional components in the cocoa-dusted favorite. Here, brandy flavors the filling.*

 6 **large eggs**
1⅓ **cups sugar, divided**
 5 **tablespoons brandy**

1½ **pounds mascarpone cheese**
1½ **cups water**
 ½ **cup instant espresso powder**
 ¾ **cup heavy whipping cream**

14 **ounces (about) crisp ladyfingers (such as Boudoirs or Savoiardi), divided**
 ½ **cup unsweetened cocoa powder**
 ¼ **cup powdered sugar**

FILL large bowl with ice water. Whisk eggs and ⅓ cup sugar in medium metal bowl set over saucepan of simmering water until thermometer registers 160°F, about 10 minutes. Set custard over bowl of ice water and whisk until cool. Mix in brandy.

WHISK mascarpone in another large bowl just to loosen. Fold in custard. Bring 1½ cups water, remaining 1 cup sugar, and espresso powder to simmer in medium saucepan, whisking until sugar dissolves. Mix in cream. Refrigerate until cold.

SUBMERGE 3 ladyfingers in chilled espresso-cream mixture for 5 seconds. Place ladyfingers on bottom of 13×9×2-inch baking dish. Repeat with enough remaining ladyfingers to cover bottom of dish. Spread half of mascarpone mixture over ladyfingers. Repeat soaking process with remaining ladyfingers, placing them in single layer atop mascarpone mixture. Spread remaining mascarpone mixture over ladyfingers. Refrigerate tiramisù until set, about 2 hours.

WHISK cocoa and powdered sugar in small bowl to blend; sift over top of tiramisù. Cover and chill at least 2 hours.

DO AHEAD *Can be made 1 day ahead. Keep chilled.*

Strawberry tiramisù

8 SERVINGS *This fruit-filled version of the Italian classic is perfect for spring, with strawberries, orange liqueur, orange juice, and strawberry preserves taking the place of coffee and cocoa. Prepare this a day ahead so that all of the elements can meld and the ladyfingers get a chance to soften. Look for mascarpone (Italian cream cheese) at supermarkets or Italian markets.*

1¼ cups strawberry preserves
⅓ cup plus 4 tablespoons Cointreau or other orange liqueur, divided
⅓ cup orange juice
1 pound mascarpone cheese, room temperature
1⅓ cups chilled heavy whipping cream
⅓ cup sugar
1 teaspoon vanilla extract

1½ pounds fresh strawberries, divided
14 ounces (about) crisp ladyfingers (such as Boudoirs or Savoiardi), divided

WHISK preserves, ⅓ cup Cointreau, and orange juice in small bowl to blend. Place mascarpone and 2 tablespoons Cointreau in large bowl; stir just until blended. Using electric mixer, beat cream, sugar, vanilla, and remaining 2 tablespoons Cointreau in another large bowl until peaks form. Stir ¼ of whipped cream mixture into mascarpone mixture to lighten. Fold in remaining whipped cream mixture in 2 additions.

HULL and slice half of strawberries. Spread ½ cup preserves mixture over bottom of 3-quart oblong serving dish or 13×9×2-inch glass baking dish. Top with enough ladyfingers to cover. Spread with ¾ cup preserves mixture, then 2½ cups mascarpone mixture. Top with sliced strawberries. Repeat layering with remaining ladyfingers, preserves mixture, and mascarpone mixture. Cover dish with plastic and chill at least 8 hours or overnight.

HULL and slice remaining strawberries and arrange over tiramisù.

Blackberries brûlée with mascarpone cream

4 TO 6 SERVINGS *Summer's freshest berries are topped with sweetened mascarpone (Italian cream cheese), then browned in a hot oven. Another great way to enjoy this simple treat: Skip the vanilla bean and add ¼ teaspoon almond extract to the mascarpone cream. Use raspberries instead of blackberries, and sprinkle the cream with sliced almonds before baking. You'll find mascarpone in many supermarkets and at Italian markets.*

3 ½-pint containers blackberries (about 2 cups)
1 8- to 8½-ounce container mascarpone cheese
2 tablespoons powdered sugar
1 large egg yolk
1 vanilla bean, split lengthwise

PREHEAT oven to 450°F. Spread berries in single layer in 11×7×2-inch glass baking dish. Stir mascarpone in medium bowl to loosen. Mix in powdered sugar and egg yolk. Scrape in seeds from vanilla bean and blend gently.

SPOON mascarpone mixture over berries; spread slightly to even layer. Bake until mascarpone mixture is beginning to brown, about 10 minutes. Serve warm.

Lemon crème brûlée with fresh berries

8 SERVINGS *You can avoid turning on the broiler by using a small blowtorch, available at cookware stores for about $20 to $40 to caramelize the sugar.*

- 3 **cups heavy whipping cream**
- 5 **teaspoons finely grated lemon peel**
- ¾ **cup sugar**
- 6 **large egg yolks**
- 2 **teaspoons vanilla extract**
- ¼ **teaspoon salt**

- 8 **teaspoons (packed) golden brown sugar, divided**

- 2 **½-pint containers fresh raspberries**
- ¼ **cup black-raspberry liqueur (such as Chambord) or crème de cassis (black-currant liqueur)**

PREHEAT oven to 325°F. Arrange eight ¾-cup custard cups or ramekins in 13×9×2-inch metal baking pan. Combine cream and lemon peel in heavy small saucepan and bring to simmer. Whisk sugar and egg yolks in large bowl until thick, about 3 minutes. Gradually whisk in hot cream mixture, then vanilla and salt. Let stand 10 minutes. Strain custard, then divide among cups. Pour enough hot water into baking pan to come halfway up sides of cups.

BAKE custards until just set in center, about 55 minutes. Remove custards from water; chill uncovered until firm, at least 3 hours.

DO AHEAD *Can be made 1 day ahead. Cover; keep chilled.*

PREHEAT broiler. Place custard cups on baking sheet. Press 1 teaspoon brown sugar through small sieve onto each custard. Broil until sugar melts and browns, about 2 minutes. Chill until topping is hard and crisp, at least 1 hour and up to 2 hours.

COMBINE raspberries and liqueur in bowl. Let stand at room temperature at least 15 minutes and up to 1 hour. Spoon berry mixture atop custards.

Grand Marnier crème brûlée

6 SERVINGS *How can a dessert with a name that means "burnt cream" in French taste so good? Maybe because the rich, creamy custard is topped with a thin layer of caramelized (or "burnt") sugar. Be sure to chill the custard a second time, after broiling, so that the topping hardens to a brittle crust.*

- 6 **large egg yolks**
- 7 **tablespoons sugar**
- 2¼ **cups heavy whipping cream**
- 2 **tablespoons Grand Marnier or other orange liqueur**
- 2 **teaspoons vanilla extract**

- 3 **tablespoons (packed) golden brown sugar, divided**

PREHEAT oven to 325°F. Whisk egg yolks and sugar in medium bowl until thick and pale yellow, about 2 minutes. Bring cream to simmer in heavy small saucepan. Gradually whisk hot cream into yolk mixture. Whisk in Grand Marnier and vanilla; divide custard among six ¾-cup custard cups. Arrange cups in 13×9×2-inch metal pan. Pour enough hot water into pan to come halfway up sides of cups. Bake custards until gently set in center, about 25 minutes. Remove cups from water and chill uncovered until cold, at least 3 hours.

DO AHEAD *Can be made 1 day ahead. Cover and keep chilled.*

PREHEAT broiler. Place custards on baking sheet. Sprinkle ½ tablespoon brown sugar onto each. Broil until sugar starts to bubble and color, turning sheet often to prevent burning, about 2 minutes. Chill until topping is hard and brittle, at least 1 hour and up to 6 hours.

Lime fool with strawberries and kiwis

4 SERVINGS *Fools are light desserts made of fruit and whipped cream. They date back to fifteenth-century England, but white chocolate and kiwis give this one a contemporary twist.*

1   cup chilled heavy whipping cream, divided
¼   cup fresh lime juice
1   teaspoon finely grated lime peel
6   ounces high-quality white chocolate (such as Lindt or Perugina), chopped

3   tablespoons sugar

2   cups sliced hulled strawberries, divided
2   kiwis, peeled, thinly sliced

BRING ¼ cup cream, lime juice, and lime peel to simmer in heavy small saucepan. Reduce heat to low, add white chocolate, and stir until melted and smooth. Pour into medium bowl. Refrigerate until cool but not set, stirring occasionally, about 25 minutes.

BEAT remaining ¾ cup cream in another medium bowl until beginning to thicken. Add sugar and beat until peaks form. Fold cream into cool white chocolate mixture.

PLACE scant ¼ cup sliced berries in each of four 8- to 10-ounce wineglasses. Press 3 kiwi slices against sides of each glass. Spoon ⅓ cup cream mixture into each glass. Spoon scant ¼ cup sliced berries in center of each, so berries do not show at sides of glasses. Spoon remaining cream mixture over. Cover and chill at least 2 hours and up to 6 hours.

Vanilla pear clafouti

6 SERVINGS *Clafouti is a rustic, simple French dessert from the Limousin region that's a bit like a cross between a custard and a baked pancake. This version features wine-marinated pear slices. Peach or plum slices briefly soaked in the sweet wine would make excellent substitutions for the pears. You can serve the clafouti with vanilla ice cream.*

¾   cup sweet white wine (such as sweet Riesling)
3   large pears, peeled, cored, cut lengthwise into ½-inch-thick slices

4   large eggs
½   cup sugar
    Pinch of salt
6   tablespoons all purpose flour
1   cup whole milk
¼   cup (½ stick) butter, melted
1   tablespoon vanilla extract

    Powdered sugar

PREHEAT oven to 325°F. Butter 9-inch-diameter glass pie dish. Combine wine and pears in large bowl; let stand 10 minutes. Drain pears, reserving ¼ cup wine.

BEAT eggs, sugar, and salt in medium bowl to blend. Whisk in flour. Add milk, melted butter, vanilla, and reserved ¼ cup wine; whisk until smooth. Arrange pears in prepared dish. Pour batter over pears.

BAKE clafouti until center is set and top is golden, about 55 minutes. Cool 10 minutes. Sift powdered sugar generously over top. Cut into wedges and serve warm.

Cherry-almond clafouti

6 SERVING S *Cherries are the traditional ingredient in this classic French fruit-and-custard dessert. When fresh cherries are not in season, you can use two cups of drained jarred dark Morello cherries in syrup or frozen pitted sweet cherries that have been thawed.*

½ cup whole almonds (about 2 ounces)
1¼ cups whole milk

1 tablespoon plus ½ cup sugar
8 ounces dark sweet cherries, pitted, halved (about 2 cups)
3 large eggs, room temperature
½ teaspoon almond extract
   Pinch of salt
¼ cup all purpose flour

   Powdered sugar

BLEND almonds in processor until finely ground but not oily. Transfer to small saucepan; add milk and bring to simmer. Remove from heat; let steep 30 minutes. Pour through fine strainer, pressing on solids to extract as much milk as possible. Discard solids in strainer.

PREHEAT oven to 375°F. Butter 10-inch-diameter glass pie dish; sprinkle with 1 tablespoon sugar. Scatter cherries evenly in dish. Using electric mixer, beat eggs, almond extract, salt, and remaining ½ cup sugar in medium bowl until well blended. Add strained almond milk and beat to blend. Sift flour into egg mixture and beat until smooth. Pour batter over cherries.

BAKE clafouti until set and knife inserted into center comes out clean, about 30 minutes. Cool completely.

DO AHEAD *Can be made 6 hours ahead. Let stand at room temperature.*

LIGHTLY dust clafouti with powdered sugar.

Exotic fruit with ginger sabayon

2 SERVINGS; CAN BE DOUBLED *Known as sabayon in France and zabaglione in Italy, this is a lovely combination of egg yolks, wine, and sugar whipped into a warm, foamy custard; it's delicious on fruit. Here, a bit of ginger is added to the sabayon, which is served over a pretty tropical fruit compote.*

⅓ cup sugar
3 large egg yolks
3 tablespoons dry white wine
1½ tablespoons dry Sherry
½ teaspoon ground ginger

2½ to 3 cups diced peeled assorted tropical fruit (such as kiwi, mango, and papaya)
1 tablespoon chopped crystallized ginger

WHISK sugar, egg yolks, wine, Sherry, and ground ginger in top of double boiler to blend. Set over simmering water (do not let bottom of pan touch water). Whisk until thick and tripled in volume and thermometer inserted into sabayon registers 170°F, about 5 minutes.

SPOON fruit into 2 stemmed goblets. Spoon warm sabayon over. Sprinkle with crystallized ginger.

PUDDINGS

Sticky toffee pudding

MAKES 6 *In Britain, "pudding" simply means "dessert"—in this case, a moist cake with a caramel topping. The beauty of this recipe is that you really can't mess it up: It's easy to make and unbelievably delicious. Just watch the puddings while they're in the broiler, as broilers vary in intensity.*

Pudding

- ¾ **cup sugar**
- ¼ **cup (½ stick) unsalted butter, room temperature**
- 1 **large egg**
- 1½ **cups all purpose flour**
- 1 **teaspoon baking powder**
- 1¼ **cups boiling water**
- 1 **cup chopped pitted dates**
- 2 **teaspoons instant espresso powder or instant coffee powder**
- 1 **teaspoon vanilla extract**
- 1 **teaspoon baking soda**

Sauce

- ⅓ **cup (packed) brown sugar**
- 3 **tablespoons unsalted butter**
- 2 **tablespoons whipping cream**

FOR PUDDING: Preheat oven to 350°F. Butter six ¾-cup custard cups. Using electric mixer, beat sugar and ¼ cup butter in large bowl until combined. Add egg and beat 2 minutes. Sift in flour and baking powder and beat 1 minute. Mix boiling water, dates, espresso powder, vanilla, and baking soda in metal bowl. Add to butter mixture; beat until well blended. Divide batter among prepared custard cups. Bake until golden brown and tester inserted into center comes out clean, about 30 minutes. Transfer to rack; cool 10 minutes.

MEANWHILE, PREPARE SAUCE: Bring all ingredients to simmer in heavy small saucepan, stirring to dissolve brown sugar. Simmer 3 minutes, stirring occasionally.

PREHEAT broiler. Pour sauce over warm puddings. Broil until sugar melts and begins to brown, about 2 minutes. Serve immediately.

Bread and butter pudding

8 SERVINGS *Bread pudding is a great use for day-old bread. This classic English version features both raisins and currants, but you can use all raisins, if you prefer. Pressing the bread into the egg mixture with a spatula helps the bread absorb the liquid.*

- 8 tablespoons (1 stick) unsalted butter, room temperature, divided
- 14 white bread slices (about 13 ounces), crusts trimmed
- ½ cup dried currants
- ½ cup raisins
- ½ teaspoon ground cinnamon

- 6 large eggs
- 3 cups whole milk
- 1 cup heavy whipping cream
- ½ cup sugar
  Pinch of ground nutmeg

RUB 2 tablespoons butter over bottom and sides of 13×9×2-inch glass baking dish. Spread remaining 6 tablespoons butter thinly over both sides of bread slices. Arrange half of bread slices in bottom of prepared dish to cover, trimming bread as needed to fit. Toss currants, raisins, and cinnamon in small bowl. Sprinkle half of raisin mixture over bread in dish. Cover with another layer of bread slices, trimming to fit. Sprinkle remaining raisin mixture over.

WHISK eggs, milk, cream, sugar, and nutmeg in medium bowl to blend. Pour custard mixture evenly over bread. Let stand 30 minutes, occasionally pressing down with metal spatula to submerge bread.

PREHEAT oven to 350°F. Bake pudding until custard is set and top is golden brown, about 40 minutes. Cut into squares and serve hot or warm.

Sugar-crusted chocolate chip and cherry bread puddings

MAKES 6 *Semisweet chocolate chips and dried tart cherries add nicely contrasting flavors to this homey dessert, which you can get into the oven in just 15 minutes. Kirsch, an unsweetened clear cherry brandy, is sometimes labeled kirschwasser.*

- 3 tablespoons butter, room temperature, divided
- 3 slices white sandwich bread (each about 5¼x4¼ inches)
- 1 cup half and half
- 2 large eggs
- 1 teaspoon vanilla extract
- ⅓ cup plus 3 tablespoons sugar, divided
- ½ cup semisweet chocolate chips
- ½ cup dried tart cherries

- ½ cup chilled heavy whipping cream
- 1 tablespoon kirsch (clear cherry brandy)

PREHEAT oven to 375°F. Spread 2 tablespoons butter over bread slices. Cut bread into 1-inch pieces. Whisk half and half, eggs, vanilla, and ⅓ cup sugar in large bowl to blend. Add bread cubes, chocolate chips, and dried cherries; toss to coat. Divide mixture among six ¾-cup custard cups. Dot tops with remaining 1 tablespoon butter. Bake puddings 10 minutes. Sprinkle puddings with 2 tablespoons sugar. Bake until tops are browned, about 15 minutes longer.

MEANWHILE, whisk cream, remaining 1 tablespoon sugar, and kirsch in medium bowl just until slightly thickened. Serve puddings warm with cream.

Banana pudding

6 TO 8 SERVINGS *To make this meringue-topped, southern-style pudding even easier, prepare the custard a day ahead and refrigerate it overnight. An equally delicious version can be made with thin slices of pound cake in place of the vanilla wafers.*

¾ cup plus 6 tablespoons sugar
6 large egg yolks
3 tablespoons cornstarch
2½ cups whole milk
1 teaspoon vanilla extract

46 (about) vanilla wafer cookies
3 bananas, peeled, sliced

2 large egg whites
¼ teaspoon cream of tartar

PREHEAT oven to 400°F. Whisk ¾ cup sugar, egg yolks, and cornstarch in heavy medium saucepan to blend. Gradually whisk in milk. Cook over medium heat until pudding boils and thickens, whisking constantly, about 10 minutes. Remove from heat. Mix in vanilla.

ARRANGE enough cookies side by side in 8-inch square glass baking dish to cover bottom, trimming to fit, if necessary. Cover with half of banana slices, then half of warm pudding. Repeat layering with remaining cookies, banana slices, and pudding.

BEAT egg whites and cream of tartar in medium bowl to soft peaks. Gradually beat in remaining 6 tablespoons sugar. Continue beating until whites are stiff but not dry. Spoon meringue over pudding, sealing to edge of dish. Bake until meringue is light brown, about 10 minutes. Cool. Chill uncovered until cold, at least 3 hours and up to 6 hours.

Amaretto chocolate pudding

6 SERVINGS *Amaretto, an almond-flavored liqueur that's actually made from apricot kernels, adds sophistication to chocolate pudding from a mix. Serve the pudding with amaretti cookies (Italian macaroons), which you can find at some supermarkets and at Italian markets.*

2½ cups whole milk
1 5-ounce box (cook-and-serve) chocolate pudding mix
½ cup bittersweet or semisweet chocolate chips (about 3 ounces)
5 tablespoons amaretto, divided

½ cup chilled heavy whipping cream
1 tablespoon sugar
Fresh raspberries (optional)
Chocolate curls (optional)

COMBINE first 3 ingredients and 4 tablespoons amaretto in heavy medium saucepan. Whisk mixture over medium heat until chocolate melts and pudding comes to boil and thickens. Divide pudding among six ¾-cup ramekins or custard cups. Chill until cold, at least 1 hour.

DO AHEAD *Can be prepared 1 day ahead. Cover and keep chilled.*

WHIP cream, sugar, and remaining 1 tablespoon amaretto in small bowl until peaks form. Top each chilled pudding with large dollop of flavored whipped cream, then with raspberries and chocolate curls, if desired.

Coconut rice pudding

6 SERVINGS *Serve this creamy rice pudding on its own or top it with a mixture of sliced tropical fruits, such as mango, lychee, and papaya. Be sure to cook the pudding until the rice is very tender—actually overcooked—so that the grains will stay soft when the pudding is chilled. Unsweetened coconut milk is available at many supermarkets and at Southeast Asian and Latin markets.*

- 2 cups reduced-fat (2%) milk
- ⅔ cup basmati rice
- ½ cup sugar
- ½ cup sweetened flaked coconut
- 2 14-ounce cans light unsweetened coconut milk, divided

COMBINE first 4 ingredients in heavy large saucepan. Stir in 1 can coconut milk. Bring just to simmer over medium-high heat, stirring occasionally. Reduce heat to very low and simmer gently, uncovered, until pudding is thick and rice is very tender, stirring occasionally during first 45 minutes of cooking, then stirring often during last 15 minutes, about 1 hour total. Stir in second can of coconut milk. Transfer rice pudding to bowl; press plastic wrap directly onto surface and chill until cold, at least 4 hours.

DO AHEAD *Can be prepared up to 2 days ahead. Keep chilled.*

Turkish coffee pudding

6 SERVINGS *Cardamom, native to India, is a wonderfully aromatic spice with a citrusy-spicy flavor. The ground spice is added to baked goods in Scandinavia and to coffee in the Middle East—just a bit gives this dessert its exotic flavor. The puddings can be prepared in about five minutes but do need to chill for about five hours before serving.*

- 2¼ cups heavy whipping cream, divided
- 3 tablespoons Kahlúa or other coffee liqueur, divided
- 2 tablespoons instant espresso powder plus additional for garnish
- 1 teaspoon (scant) ground cardamom plus additional for garnish
- 4 large egg yolks
- ½ cup (packed) golden brown sugar

COMBINE 1¾ cups cream, 2 tablespoons Kahlúa, 2 tablespoons espresso powder, and 1 scant teaspoon cardamom in heavy medium saucepan; bring to simmer. Whisk egg yolks and brown sugar in medium bowl to blend. Gradually whisk hot cream mixture into yolk mixture; return custard to saucepan. Stir over medium-low heat until pudding is thick enough to coat back of spoon (do not boil), about 5 minutes. Strain through fine-mesh sieve into medium bowl. Divide pudding among 6 demitasse (2- to 3-ounce) cups. Chill until set, about 5 hours.

DO AHEAD *Can be prepared 1 day ahead. Keep chilled.*

WHISK remaining ½ cup cream in medium bowl until peaks form. Whisk in remaining 1 tablespoon Kahlúa. Top each pudding with whipped cream. Sprinkle with additional espresso powder and cardamom.

Strawberry, mascarpone, and Marsala budini

6 SERVINGS *This is an excellent example of desserts served in Italy: simple, not too sweet, delicious. These parfaits (or budini—Italian for "puddings") feature ultra-creamy mascarpone cheese layered with Marsala-soaked strawberries. Mascarpone (Italian cream cheese) and amaretti cookies are available at many supermarkets and at Italian markets. To retain some crunch, don't crush the cookies too finely.*

1 8-ounce container mascarpone cheese

6 tablespoons sweet Marsala (preferably imported) or other sweet dessert wine (such as Essensia), divided

3 tablespoons heavy whipping cream

3 tablespoons sugar, divided

3 cups sliced hulled strawberries (about 15 ounces)

2¼ cups coarsely crumbled amaretti cookies (Italian macaroons; about 4½ ounces)

COMBINE mascarpone, 3 tablespoons Marsala, cream, and 2 tablespoons sugar in medium bowl; stir gently until blended. Combine strawberries, remaining 3 tablespoons Marsala, and remaining 1 tablespoon sugar in another medium bowl; toss to blend. Cover mascarpone and berry mixtures; refrigerate 30 minutes.

PLACE 2 tablespoons crumbled cookies in each of 6 goblets. Divide strawberry mixture with juices among goblets. Top berries with mascarpone mixture, then remaining cookies. Cover and chill at least 30 minutes and up to 2 hours.

Meyer lemon buttermilk pudding cake with fresh berries

6 TO 8 SERVINGS *As it bakes, this dessert forms a light sponge-cake-like layer on the top and a smooth pudding layer on the bottom. Meyer lemons are tender skinned, juicy, and sweeter than regular Eureka lemons. You can substitute regular lemon juice—just decrease the amount of juice by 1 tablespoon.*

1½ cups buttermilk

1 cup sugar, divided

4 large egg yolks

⅓ cup fresh Meyer lemon juice

¼ cup all purpose flour

¼ cup (½ stick) unsalted butter, melted

⅛ teaspoon salt

3 large egg whites

Chilled heavy whipping cream
Assorted fresh berries

PREHEAT oven to 350°F. Butter 8×8×2-inch glass baking dish. Blend buttermilk, ½ cup sugar, egg yolks, lemon juice, flour, melted butter, and salt in blender until smooth. Transfer buttermilk mixture to medium bowl. Using electric mixer, beat egg whites in large bowl until soft peaks form. Gradually add remaining ½ cup sugar and beat until stiff but not dry. Gently fold buttermilk mixture into whites in 3 additions (batter will be runny).

POUR batter into prepared dish. Place dish in roasting pan. Pour enough hot water into roasting pan to come halfway up sides of dish. Bake until entire top is evenly browned and cake moves very slightly in center but feels slightly springy to touch, about 45 minutes. Remove dish from roasting pan.

COOL cake completely in baking dish on rack. Chill until cold, at least 3 hours and up to 6 hours. Spoon pudding cake into shallow bowls. Pour cream around cake. Top with berries.

30-minute rice pudding with dried fruit

8 SERVINGS *Try replacing the raisins with different dried fruits, such as cherries or chopped dried apricots, prunes, or pears. A cinnamon stick would be a nice flavor addition to the vanilla and orange peel. Arborio rice is the short-grain rice from Italy that is used in risotto—it gives this pudding its creamy texture.*

1	cup arborio or medium-grain white rice
5	cups whole milk
¼	cup raisins
½	teaspoon finely grated orange peel
1	2-inch piece of vanilla bean, split lengthwise
½	cup sugar
4	large egg yolks

PLACE rice in strainer and rinse under cold running water until water runs clear; drain rice. Place rice, milk, raisins, and orange peel in large saucepan. Scrape seeds from vanilla bean into pan; add bean. Bring rice mixture to simmer over medium heat, stirring occasionally. Reduce heat to very low; cover and simmer, stirring occasionally, until rice is tender, about 23 minutes. Remove from heat.

MEANWHILE, whisk sugar and egg yolks in small bowl to blend. Whisk yolk mixture into hot pudding. Stir over low heat until thickened, about 1 minute. Divide pudding among eight ¾-cup ramekins or custard cups. Chill until cold, about 3 hours.

DO AHEAD *Can be prepared 1 day ahead. Cover and keep chilled.*

Dark chocolate mousse with sugared kumquats

4 SERVINGS *Kumquats are small orange citrus fruits with sweet, thin skin and sour pulp. Cooked with a little sugar, they add an exotic touch to this rich, dark chocolate mousse. Be sure to use a high-quality chocolate for the flavor to really come through, and the freshest eggs possible.*

6	ounces bittersweet or semisweet chocolate, chopped
¼	cup water
3	large egg whites
½	cup sugar, divided
½	cup sliced fresh kumquats
⅓	cup chilled heavy whipping cream

COMBINE chocolate and ¼ cup water in heavy small saucepan. Whisk over low heat until melted and smooth. Cool to just barely lukewarm, about 10 minutes.

USING electric mixer, beat egg whites in medium bowl until soft peaks form. Gradually add ¼ cup sugar, beating until stiff but not dry. Pour cooled melted chocolate over egg whites and gently fold together. Divide mousse among 4 parfait glasses or small dessert bowls. Cover; chill at least 6 hours or overnight.

MIX kumquats and remaining ¼ cup sugar in small saucepan; let stand 10 minutes. Stir slowly over low heat until sugar dissolves. Cover; chill at least 2 hours and up to 1 day.

BEAT chilled whipping cream in small bowl until peaks form. Spoon whipped cream over mousse. Top with sugared kumquats and syrup.

Mom's blender chocolate mousse with lemon cream

4 SERVINGS *Only five ingredients go into this silky mousse, which gets whipped up in the blender. The lemon-flavored whipped cream provides a lovely contrast to the chocolate, but if you prefer a vanilla cream, use ½ teaspoon vanilla extract instead of the lemon juice and peel.*

 1 **cup bittersweet or semisweet chocolate chips (about 6 ounces)**
 ¾ **cup water**
 3 **tablespoons sugar, divided**
 ¼ **teaspoon instant espresso powder or instant coffee powder**
 3 **large egg whites**

 ⅓ **cup chilled heavy whipping cream**
 1 **teaspoon fresh lemon juice**
 ½ **teaspoon finely grated lemon peel**

PLACE chocolate in blender. Bring ¾ cup water, 2 tablespoons sugar, and espresso powder to simmer in medium saucepan, stirring to dissolve sugar. Pour over chocolate in blender. Cover tightly; blend 5 seconds. Add egg whites. Cover tightly; blend on high 1 minute. Divide mousse among 4 small bowls. Chill until firm, about 2 hours.

WHISK cream, lemon juice, peel, and remaining 1 tablespoon sugar in small bowl until very soft peaks form. Spoon over mousse.

Simplest chocolate honey mousse

8 SERVINGS *Mousse is a French term for "foam". Here, whipped cream adds a fluffy texture to the chocolate dessert, and honey adds flavor and smoothness. After the mousse is set, cover the ramekins; the mousse will keep in the refrigerator for up to four days.*

 2½ **cups chilled heavy whipping cream, divided**
 12 **ounces bittersweet or semisweet chocolate, chopped**
 5 **tablespoons honey**

STIR ¾ cup cream, chocolate, and honey in heavy medium saucepan over low heat until chocolate melts and mixture is smooth. Let cool, stirring occasionally.

BEAT 1¼ cups cream in large bowl until soft peaks form. Fold cream into cooled chocolate mixture in 2 additions. Divide mousse among eight ¾-cup ramekins. Refrigerate until set, about 2 hours.

WHISK remaining ½ cup cream in small bowl until peaks form. Spoon cream over each mousse.

White chocolate mousse with dark chocolate sauce

4 SERVINGS *Fresh raspberries would be a delicious addition to this mousse—fold them into the mixture along with the whipped cream, and add a few more as a garnish.*

- 8 ounces high-quality white chocolate (such as Lindt or Perugina), chopped
- 1 cup plus 6 tablespoons chilled heavy whipping cream, divided
- 4 tablespoons light corn syrup, divided
- 3 ounces bittersweet or semisweet chocolate, chopped

STIR white chocolate, ¼ cup cream, and 2 tablespoons corn syrup in heavy small saucepan over low heat until chocolate is melted and smooth. Pour into medium bowl; cool to barely lukewarm. Using electric mixer, beat ¾ cup cream in another medium bowl until peaks form. Fold cream into white chocolate mixture in 2 additions. Divide mousse among 4 custard cups. Cover and chill until firm, about 4 hours.

DO AHEAD *Can made 2 days ahead. Keep chilled.*

BRING remaining 6 tablespoons cream and 2 tablespoons corn syrup to simmer in heavy small saucepan over high heat. Reduce heat to low; add bittersweet chocolate and stir until melted and smooth. Cool sauce to room temperature. Spoon enough sauce over each mousse to cover completely.

How to "fold" Using the side edge of a large, flat rubber spatula, cut through the mixture in the center of the bowl through to the bottom. Scrape across the bottom of the bowl and turn the spatula, using the flat side to lift some of the mixture up from the bottom and over onto the top. Repeat, turning the bowl slightly with each stroke, until all components of the mixture are blended.

FRUITDESSERTS

Tropical fruit kebabs with lime cream

8 SERVINGS *Try these fun and colorful kebabs as a light dessert, fruit salad, or even an appetizer—they'd be especially festive at a barbecue where shish kebabs are the main course. The fruit can be skewered up to an hour before serving, and the lime cream can be made one day ahead and refrigerated.*

1	cup sour cream
3	tablespoons fresh lime juice, divided
2	tablespoons sugar
1½	teaspoons finely grated lime peel

1	papaya, peeled, halved, seeded
½	pineapple, peeled, cored
3	large bananas, peeled
8	12-inch-long wooden skewers

COMBINE sour cream, 2 tablespoons lime juice, sugar, and lime peel in small bowl. Cover and refrigerate lime cream.

CUT papaya into 24 one-inch pieces. Cut pineapple into 24 one-inch pieces. Cut each banana crosswise into 8 pieces and place in small bowl; add remaining 1 tablespoon lime juice and toss to coat. Alternate fruit on skewers. Arrange on platter. Serve with lime cream.

Peaches in spiced red wine

2 SERVINGS; CAN BE DOUBLED OR TRIPLED *This is a lovely way to enjoy late-summer peaches. Serve the peaches on their own, or pair them with crème fraîche or ice cream. If you really want to go all out, top a slice of toasted pound cake with the peaches, maple syrup, and a big spoonful of whipped cream. For an interesting variation, substitute white wine for red.*

2	large whole peaches
½	cup dry red wine
3	tablespoons sugar
⅛	teaspoon ground cardamom

BLANCH peaches in medium saucepan of boiling water 30 seconds. Using slotted spoon, transfer peaches to bowl of ice water to cool quickly. Peel peaches, cut in half, remove pits, and slice. Combine all remaining ingredients in medium bowl and stir to dissolve sugar. Add peaches. Chill at least 20 minutes and up to 1 day, stirring occasionally.

Sherry-poached pears with Spanish turrón ice cream

6 SERVINGS *Turrón is a Spanish almond-based nougat candy that comes in hard and soft varieties. For this recipe, use the hard turrón for its crunchy texture. You can find it at Spanish food stores, at specialty markets, and online at tienda.com. Or you can use chopped almonds instead. Look for the full-bodied, semisweet oloroso Sherry at specialty foods stores and wine shops. Soften the ice cream in the microwave in 10-second intervals on a very low setting.*

- ½ cup plus 2 tablespoons oloroso Sherry
- ½ cup water
- ¼ cup (packed) golden brown sugar
- 1 3×¾-inch strip orange peel
- 3 firm but ripe large Bosc pears, peeled, quartered, cored

- 1 pint vanilla ice cream, slightly softened
- 1 cup chopped hard turrón (almond nougat; about 4 ounces) or ¾ cup chopped toasted almonds
- 1 generous teaspoon finely grated orange peel

COMBINE ½ cup Sherry, ½ cup water, brown sugar, and orange peel in heavy large saucepan. Bring to simmer over medium heat, stirring until sugar dissolves. Simmer 5 minutes. Add pears to syrup (pears will not be completely submerged). Cover pan, reduce heat to low, and cook until pears are tender when pierced with small sharp knife, turning pears occasionally, about 10 minutes. Transfer pears and poaching syrup to shallow glass dish and chill until cold, at least 30 minutes and up to 1 day.

STIR ice cream, turrón, grated orange peel, and remaining 2 tablespoons Sherry in medium bowl to blend, then freeze until firm, at least 1 hour.

SCOOP ice cream into shallow bowls. Top with pears and poaching syrup.

Blueberry crisp with cinnamon-streusel topping

8 TO 10 SERVINGS *Crisps are a simple and wonderful way to showcase summer fruit such as blueberries. The dessert is usually tossed together and popped into the oven, but you could prepare the crisp topping ahead of time and keep it covered and chilled until needed—up to 2 days.*

- 7 ½-pint containers blueberries (about 8 cups), divided
- ¾ cup plus 6 tablespoons sugar

- 1¾ cups all purpose flour
- 1 cup finely chopped walnuts
- 6 tablespoons (packed) dark brown sugar
- 1 teaspoon ground cinnamon
- ½ teaspoon salt
- ¾ cup (1½ sticks) unsalted butter, melted, cooled

    Whipped cream

PREHEAT oven to 350°F. Combine 2½ cups blueberries and ¾ cup sugar in large saucepan. Cook over low heat until berries soften and release juices, stirring frequently, about 8 minutes. Mix in remaining blueberries. Transfer mixture to 13×9×2-inch glass baking dish.

MIX flour, walnuts, brown sugar, cinnamon, salt, and remaining 6 tablespoons sugar in large bowl to blend. Gradually add cooled melted butter, mixing with fork until small moist clumps form. Sprinkle streusel over berries.

BAKE crisp until topping is golden and filling is bubbling thickly, about 45 minutes. Cool slightly. Serve with whipped cream.

Almond-peach crisp

2 SERVINGS; CAN BE DOUBLED OR TRIPLED *To peel the peaches easily, bring a large saucepan of water to boil. Place three or four peaches in the boiling water and blanch 30 seconds. Use a slotted spoon to transfer the peaches to a large bowl of cold water, and repeat the process with the remaining peaches. Cool peaches slightly and slip off the skins.*

1 pound peaches, peeled, pitted, cut into ¾-inch-thick slices
3 tablespoons sugar
2½ tablespoons all purpose flour, divided
⅛ teaspoon ground nutmeg
⅛ teaspoon almond extract

3 tablespoons old-fashioned oats
3 tablespoons (packed) golden brown sugar
Generous pinch of ground cinnamon
Pinch of salt
2 tablespoons (¼ stick) chilled unsalted butter, diced
2 tablespoons lightly toasted almonds

Vanilla ice cream or whipped cream (optional)

PREHEAT oven to 375°F. Butter two 1½-cup soufflé dishes. Combine peaches, sugar, ½ tablespoon flour, nutmeg, and almond extract in medium bowl; stir to blend well. Divide between prepared dishes.

COMBINE next 5 ingredients and remaining 2 tablespoons flour in processor. Blend, using on/off turns, until mixture resembles coarse meal. Add almonds and chop coarsely, using on/off turns. Sprinkle topping over peaches.

BAKE crisps until topping browns and peach mixture bubbles, about 35 minutes. Cool slightly. Serve warm with ice cream or whipped cream, if desired.

Mixed berry crisp

6 SERVINGS *Because this crisp uses frozen berries, you can always have the ingredients on hand for a quick dessert. While you're in the frozen-foods section, pick up some vanilla ice cream to serve with the crisp.*

2 12-ounce packages frozen unsweetened mixed berries (such as blueberries, blackberries, strawberries, and raspberries; about 6 cups), unthawed
¼ cup sugar
1 cup all purpose flour, divided
1 tablespoon fresh lemon juice
¾ cup old-fashioned oats
⅔ cup (packed) golden brown sugar
1 teaspoon ground cinnamon
½ teaspoon ground ginger
¼ teaspoon ground nutmeg
¼ teaspoon salt
7 tablespoons chilled unsalted butter, diced

PREHEAT oven to 375°F. Combine berries, ¼ cup sugar, ¼ cup flour, and lemon juice in large bowl; toss to blend well. Transfer berry mixture to 9-inch-diameter glass pie dish. Combine remaining ¾ cup flour, oats, brown sugar, all spices, and salt in medium bowl. Add butter; rub in with fingertips until small clumps form; sprinkle topping over berry mixture.

BAKE crisp until berry mixture bubbles thickly and topping is golden brown, about 1 hour. Let stand 15 minutes. Serve warm or at room temperature.

Double-cherry almond crisp

8 SERVINGS *A touch of kirsch, a clear cherry brandy, enhances the flavor of cherries. Here, the filling is baked before the almond-oat-brown sugar topping is sprinkled over—ensuring that the topping will stay crisp and not sink into the fruit. Ice cream is wonderful alongside.*

2¼	pounds Bing cherries, pitted
2	1-pound cans pitted red tart pie cherries in water, drained
¾	cup plus ⅓ cup (packed) golden brown sugar
3	tablespoons quick-cooking tapioca
1	tablespoon kirsch (clear cherry brandy) or brandy
⅔	cup whole almonds, chopped
¼	teaspoon almond extract
½	cup all purpose flour
⅓	cup old-fashioned oats
¼	cup (½ stick) chilled unsalted butter, diced

PREHEAT oven to 375°F. Generously butter 13×9×2-inch glass baking dish. Combine all cherries, ¾ cup brown sugar, tapioca, and kirsch in large bowl; toss to blend. Let stand 15 minutes, tossing occasionally. Transfer to prepared dish. Bake until fruit is tender and juices bubble thickly, about 50 minutes. Cool in dish.

DO AHEAD *Can be made 4 hours ahead. Let stand at room temperature.*

PREHEAT oven to 375°F, if necessary. Toss chopped almonds and almond extract in medium bowl to coat. Mix in flour, remaining ⅓ cup brown sugar, and oats. Add butter and rub in with fingertips until mixture resembles coarse meal. Sprinkle topping over fruit. Bake until fruit is heated through and topping is golden brown and firm to touch, about 25 minutes. Serve crisp warm.

Plum crumble

4 SERVINGS *A crumble is basically a crisp with a British accent. "Crumble" refers to the crumbly oat, sugar, and butter topping. Plum brandy is clear, quite potent, and most commonly imported from Eastern Europe, where it is called slivovitz. Find it at specialty wine stores, or use Port instead.*

1¼	cups all purpose flour
¾	cup old-fashioned oats
⅓	cup plus ½ cup sugar
½	teaspoon ground cinnamon
½	cup (1 stick) chilled unsalted butter, cut into pieces
2	pounds plums, halved, pitted, cut into wedges
1	tablespoon plum brandy or Port
	Vanilla ice cream or frozen yogurt

MIX flour, oats, ⅓ cup sugar, and cinnamon in medium bowl. Add butter and rub with fingertips until mixture begins to form moist clumps.

DO AHEAD *Can be made 1 day ahead. Cover and chill.*

PREHEAT oven to 350°F. Toss plums, remaining ½ cup sugar, and brandy in medium bowl. Transfer to 9-inch-diameter deep-dish pie dish. Sprinkle crumb topping over. Bake until fruit bubbles and topping browns, about 1 hour. Cool slightly. Serve with vanilla ice cream.

Apple crumble with vanilla ice cream

10 TO 12 SERVINGS *Make this super-easy, comforting dessert whenever you find yourself with a surplus of apples. Pippin, Cortland, and Winesap apples all make good substitutes for the Granny Smiths.*

2½ cups old-fashioned oats
1½ cups (packed) golden brown sugar, divided
1 cup all purpose flour
1 cup (2 sticks) chilled unsalted butter, cut into ½-inch cubes

4 pounds large Granny Smith apples, peeled, halved, cored, each half cut into 6 slices
3 tablespoons fresh lemon juice
1 tablespoon ground cinnamon

Vanilla ice cream

MIX oats, 1 cup brown sugar, and flour in medium bowl. Add butter; rub in with fingertips until topping comes together in moist clumps.

DO AHEAD *Can be made 1 day ahead. Cover; chill.*

PREHEAT oven to 375°F. Mix apples, lemon juice, cinnamon, and remaining ½ cup brown sugar in large bowl. Transfer fruit mixture to 13×9×2-inch glass baking dish. Sprinkle topping over.

BAKE crumble until apples are tender and topping is brown and crisp, about 55 minutes. Cool slightly. Spoon warm crumble into bowls. Serve with vanilla ice cream.

Nectarine cobbler

8 SERVINGS *A cobbler is a baked fruit dessert with a biscuit topping. Although peach cobbler is the best known, nectarine cobbler has one big advantage: Nectarines have thin, fuzz-free skin that does not require peeling. When making the biscuit topping, make sure that the butter and shortening are very cold. Ice cream (peach, vanilla, or butter pecan) would be great with this.*

4 pounds nectarines, halved, pitted, cut into wedges
¾ cup plus 8 tablespoons sugar, divided
⅓ cup plus 2¼ cups unbleached all purpose flour
2 tablespoons fresh lemon juice

1 tablespoon baking powder
¾ teaspoon salt
¼ cup (½ stick) chilled unsalted butter, cut into pieces
¼ cup chilled solid vegetable shortening, cut into pieces
1 large egg, beaten to blend
¾ cup plus 2 tablespoons chilled buttermilk

PREHEAT oven to 400°F. Toss nectarines, ¾ cup sugar, ⅓ cup flour, and lemon juice in 13×9×2-inch glass baking dish to blend. Bake 15 minutes.

MEANWHILE, mix remaining 2¼ cups flour, 6 tablespoons sugar, baking powder, and salt in large bowl. Using fingertips, rub in butter and shortening until mixture resembles coarse meal. Add egg and buttermilk; stir until batter forms.

REMOVE fruit from oven. Spoon batter over hot filling in 12 mounds, spacing evenly. Sprinkle with remaining 2 tablespoons sugar. Bake until juices thicken and topping is golden, about 30 minutes. Cool on rack at least 15 minutes. Serve warm.

Fresh fruit with mascarpone and white chocolate dip

4 TO 6 SERVINGS *This would be a fabulous dessert to take on a picnic. Transport it in a divided container with the dip in one compartment and the fruit in the other. Use any variety of fruit that is in season. Mascarpone, Italian cream cheese, is available at many supermarkets and at Italian markets.*

6 ounces high-quality white chocolate (such as Lindt or Perugina), chopped
1 cup heavy whipping cream, divided
1 8-ounce container mascarpone cheese
1 teaspoon vanilla extract
5 cups assorted fresh fruit (such as whole strawberries and cherries, and sliced peaches, nectarines, apricots, bananas, or melon)

STIR chopped white chocolate and ½ cup cream in medium metal bowl set over saucepan of gently simmering water until melted and smooth. Remove from over water and cool to room temperature. Whisk remaining ½ cup cream, mascarpone, and vanilla in another medium bowl until blended and smooth. Fold melted white chocolate into mascarpone mixture. Transfer dip to serving bowl. Serve with fruit.

Dark chocolate fondue

8 SERVINGS *Dipping bits of cake, cookies, and fruit into the rich fondue is fun for kids and grownups. Any leftover fondue would be great drizzled over ice cream for an easy sundae, or mixed with hot milk to make a decadent hot chocolate.*

½ cup unsweetened cocoa powder
2½ cups heavy whipping cream
12 ounces bittersweet or semisweet chocolate, chopped

24 ¾-inch cubes peeled cored pineapple
24 small strawberries, hulled
24 ¾-inch cubes peeled kiwis (from about 3)
24 purchased bite-size pastries, cookies, and/or petits fours

PLACE cocoa in medium saucepan. Gradually add cream, whisking until cocoa dissolves. Bring to simmer, whisking occasionally. Remove from heat; add chopped chocolate. Whisk until smooth.

DO AHEAD *Can be made 1 day ahead. Cover; chill. Rewarm over medium-low heat, whisking occasionally, until smooth.*

THREAD 1 pineapple cube, 1 strawberry, and 1 kiwi cube onto each of 24 short skewers. Arrange on platter with pastries, cookies, and/or petits fours. Transfer chocolate mixture to fondue pot. Place over candle or canned heat burner and serve with fruit and pastries.

Milk chocolate fondue with strawberries

2 SERVINGS; CAN BE DOUBLED OR TRIPLED *Milk chocolate, half and half, and a splash of crème de cassis are all it takes to make this luxurious dip. When strawberries aren't in season, substitute dark rum for the cassis and serve the fondue with sliced bananas.*

3 to 3.5 ounces high-quality milk chocolate (such as Lindt or Ghirardelli), chopped

2 tablespoons half and half

1 tablespoon crème de cassis (black-currant liqueur) or brandy (optional)

1 1-pint container strawberries (preferably with stems)

STIR chocolate and half and half in heavy small saucepan over low heat until melted and smooth. Mix in liqueur, if desired. Pour into heated bowl. Serve, passing berries to dip in chocolate.

Summer fruit with praline fondue

4 SERVINGS *This butterscotch-colored dip takes its flavor cues from the southern candy made with brown sugar and pecans. You can prepare the fruit and the sweetened crème fraîche one hour ahead. Spear the fruit with skewers and dip the fruit first into the fondue, then into the nuts and crème fraîche.*

½ cup crème fraîche or sour cream

½ tablespoon plus 1 cup (packed) dark brown sugar

½ cup chopped toasted pecans

6 tablespoons (¾ stick) unsalted butter

2 tablespoons water

2½ tablespoons dark rum

1 teaspoon vanilla extract

4 to 5 cups assorted fresh fruit (such as grapes, berries, cherries, and plum and peach wedges)

STIR crème fraîche and ½ tablespoon brown sugar in small bowl to blend. Place pecans in another small bowl.

MELT butter in medium nonstick skillet over medium-high heat. Add remaining 1 cup brown sugar and 2 tablespoons water; stir 1 minute (mixture will bubble up). Add rum and vanilla; stir until smooth. Transfer fondue to medium bowl. Serve sweetened crème fraîche, pecans, and fondue with fruit.

Berries in sweet Fragolino wine with biscotti

8 SERVINGS *Fragolino is a light, fizzy dessert wine with the flavor of strawberries—look for it at wine stores. If unavailable, use Moscato, a sweet white wine made in Italy and California—and in France, where it is called Muscat. Use any combination of fresh berries and serve with your favorite biscotti or other crisp cookies.*

- 2 ½-pint containers blackberries
- 2 ½-pint containers blueberries
- 2 ½-pint containers raspberries
- 3 cups halved stemmed small strawberries
- ½ cup sugar
- 3 cups (about 750 ml) chilled Fragolino or Moscato

   Biscotti or other crisp cookies

MIX all berries in large bowl. Add sugar; toss to coat. Pour wine over. Cover and chill at least 30 minutes and up to 1 hour.

DIVIDE berries and wine syrup among 8 dessert goblets. Serve with biscotti.

Mixed berries with mascarpone-limoncello cream

8 SERVINGS *Limoncello is a lemon-flavored liqueur made in Southern Italy, where it is served as a digestivo, or after-dinner drink. The liqueur adds sophistication to the mascarpone cream and berries. Enjoy the simple yet fabulous dessert alfresco with a small glass of the chilled liqueur, as they do on the Amalfi Coast. Mascarpone (Italian cream cheese) is available at many supermarkets and Italian markets.*

- ¾ cup chilled heavy whipping cream
- ½ 8-ounce container mascarpone cheese
- 3 tablespoons plus ½ cup sugar
- 3 tablespoons limoncello (lemon liqueur)
- 8 cups assorted fresh berries (such as raspberries, blueberries, blackberries, and hulled sliced strawberries; about 2 pounds)
- ¾ cup raspberry preserves
- 1 tablespoon finely grated lemon peel

COMBINE whipping cream, mascarpone, 3 tablespoons sugar, and limoncello in large bowl. Beat until soft peaks form.

COMBINE all berries, raspberry preserves, lemon peel, and remaining ½ cup sugar in another large bowl; toss gently. Divide berry mixture among 8 coupes. Top with mascarpone cream.

Caramelized chocolate, banana, and marshmallow sandwiches

4 SERVINGS *These gooey goodies feature toasted marshmallows, chocolate, and banana slices sandwiched between slices of bread, then grilled. Whip up a couple as a decadent after-school snack or a late-night movie treat.*

2 tablespoons (¼ stick) unsalted butter, room temperature
2 tablespoons (packed) dark brown sugar
4 slices buttermilk bread
8 large marshmallows
2 metal skewers
2 tablespoons semisweet chocolate chips
12 ¼-inch-thick banana slices

MIX butter and brown sugar in small bowl to blend. Spread over 1 side of bread slices. Place 2 slices, buttered side down, on plate. Skewer 4 marshmallows on each of 2 skewers; hold skewers over open flame and toast until marshmallows are blackened in spots, about 10 seconds. Divide marshmallows between bread slices on plate, leaving 1-inch border. Sprinkle chocolate chips over marshmallows, dividing equally. Top with banana slices. Cover with remaining 2 bread slices, buttered side up, pressing slightly to compact.

HEAT large nonstick skillet over medium-high heat. Add sandwiches; cook until brown, about 1½ minutes per side. Transfer sandwiches to work surface; cool 1 minute. Cut diagonally in half.

Strawberries with lemon sugar and lavender syrup

8 SERVINGS *You can make the syrup and slice the berries ahead of time, but be sure to toss them together at the last minute. Any remaining lemon sugar can be used to sweeten espresso or tea. Find the lavender blossoms at natural foods stores and at some farmers' markets.*

⅓ cup plus ½ cup sugar
1 teaspoon finely grated lemon peel

½ cup water
2 tablespoons honey
2 teaspoons dried lavender blossoms

3 1-pound containers strawberries, hulled, sliced
Crème fraîche or sour cream

MASH ⅓ cup sugar and lemon peel in small bowl to blend well.

BRING remaining ½ cup sugar, ½ cup water, honey, and lavender to boil in heavy small saucepan over medium-high heat, stirring until sugar dissolves. Reduce heat to medium and simmer until lavender flavor is pronounced, about 3 minutes. Strain syrup into small bowl.

DO AHEAD *Lemon sugar and lavender syrup can be made 1 day ahead. Cover separately and let stand at room temperature. Rewarm syrup before continuing.*

PLACE berries in large bowl. Pour warm syrup over berries; stir to coat. Divide berries and syrup among 8 bowls. Spoon crème fraîche over berries, sprinkle with lemon sugar, and serve immediately.

Grilled cardamom-glazed pineapple with vanilla ice cream

6 SERVINGS *Before grilling the pineapple slices, make sure that the barbecue is very clean and well seasoned (heated to remove any residue or solvents), so that the fruit doesn't pick up flavors from, or stick to, the grill. A light coating of nonstick spray formulated for the barbecue is a good precaution; spray it on while the grill is cold. To enhance the tropical theme, serve the pineapple with coconut ice cream.*

⅓ cup mild-flavored (light) molasses
3 tablespoons unsalted butter,
   cut into small pieces
8 whole cardamom pods, lightly cracked
2 teaspoons fresh lime juice

12 ¾-inch-thick rounds peeled
   pineapple (from 2 pineapples)
2 tablespoons peanut oil
   Vanilla ice cream

BRING molasses, butter, and cardamom to boil in heavy medium saucepan over high heat, stirring occasionally to melt butter. Reduce heat to low and simmer until slightly thickened, about 5 minutes. Remove glaze from heat. Stir in lime juice.

DO AHEAD *Can be made 1 day ahead. Cover and chill. Rewarm before using to melt butter; whisk until smooth.*

PREPARE barbecue (medium-high heat). Brush pineapple rounds with peanut oil. Sprinkle with salt and pepper. Grill until golden brown and slightly charred, brushing with glaze on each side during last 30 seconds of cooking, about 4 minutes per side. Divide pineapple among 6 plates. Top with vanilla ice cream; drizzle with remaining glaze.

Grilled nectarines with honey-balsamic glaze

6 SERVINGS *Honey and balsamic vinegar lend a unique sweet-tart taste to the lightly grilled fruit. To keep the nectarines from sticking, spray the grill with nonstick spray or rub with a paper towel that has been moistened with vegetable oil before lighting the barbecue. Peaches can replace the nectarines, and if crème fraîche isn't available at your supermarket, sour cream is delicious with the nectarines, too.*

½ cup plus 2 tablespoons honey
¼ cup balsamic vinegar
½ teaspoon vanilla extract
1 8-ounce container crème fraîche or sour cream

6 firm but ripe nectarines, halved, pitted

WHISK ½ cup honey, vinegar, and vanilla in small bowl for glaze. Whisk crème fraîche and remaining 2 tablespoons honey in medium bowl to blend.

DO AHEAD *Glaze and crème fraîche mixture can be made 1 day ahead. Cover separately. Chill crème fraîche mixture. Rewhisk both before using.*

PREPARE barbecue (medium-high heat). Brush nectarines generously with half of glaze. Grill until heated through, turning occasionally, about 4 minutes. Arrange 2 nectarine halves, cut side up, on each plate. Drizzle with remaining glaze. Spoon some crème fraîche mixture into center of each nectarine half.

Grilled brown-sugar peaches with white chocolate

4 SERVINGS *This is a sweet and simple finale to any barbecued meal. Rinse the peaches and wipe off any fuzz, if necessary. For a grown-up twist, serve the peaches in bowls and drizzle with amaretto or peach liqueur. Or sprinkle the peaches with chopped hazelnuts instead of the pistachios and drizzle with Frangelico, a hazelnut liqueur.*

- 4 tablespoons (½ stick) unsalted butter, melted
- 2 tablespoons (packed) dark brown sugar
- ½ teaspoon ground cinnamon
- 4 unpeeled peaches, halved, pitted
- ⅓ cup finely chopped high-quality white chocolate (such as Lindt or Perugina)
- 3 tablespoons coarsely chopped toasted salted pistachios

PREPARE barbecue (medium-high heat). Whisk first 3 ingredients in large bowl to blend. Add peach halves; toss to coat well. Place peaches, cut side down, on grill. Grill until slightly charred, about 1 minute. Using tongs, turn peaches over. Divide chopped white chocolate among peach cavities and drizzle remaining butter mixture from bowl over chocolate. Grill until chocolate just begins to melt and peaches are charred, about 2 minutes. Divide peach halves among bowls. Sprinkle with chopped pistachios.

Honey-roasted plums with thyme and crème fraîche

6 SERVINGS *Roasting at high heat intensifies the flavor of the plums and the thyme adds an interesting savory element. For extra color, use different kinds of plums, such as bright red-fleshed Elephant Hearts and yellow Shiro plums, as well as pluots. Avoid using Santa Rosas, which don't retain their shape when cooked.*

- ½ cup (packed) dark brown sugar
- ¼ cup honey
- 4 tablespoons (½ stick) unsalted butter
- ½ cup fresh thyme sprigs
- 6 assorted ripe but firm large plums (about 2 pounds), halved, pitted

  Crème fraîche or sour cream

PREHEAT oven to 475°F. Stir first 4 ingredients in large ovenproof nonstick skillet over high heat until butter melts. Cook 2 minutes, stirring constantly (mixture will bubble vigorously). Add plum halves, cut side down. Cook plums without stirring for 2 minutes. Turn plums over and transfer skillet to oven. Roast until caramel is deep brown, checking frequently to prevent burning, about 4 minutes.

DIVIDE plum halves among 6 plates. Spoon sauce from skillet over plums, leaving most of thyme sprigs behind. Drizzle plums with crème fraîche.

Apricot-raspberry Pavlovas with sliced almonds

6 SERVINGS *Both Australia and New Zealand claim to have invented this light meringue dessert named in honor of ballerina Anna Pavlova. The components can be made several hours ahead and assembled shortly before serving.*

4	large egg whites
1¾	cups plus 1 tablespoon sugar, divided
2	teaspoons cornstarch
¼	teaspoon almond extract
⅓	cup sliced almonds
1½	pounds apricots, halved, pitted, each half cut into 3 wedges
1	teaspoon vanilla extract
1	½-pint container raspberries
1	cup chilled heavy whipping cream

PREHEAT oven to 350°F. Line large rimmed baking sheet with parchment paper. Using electric mixer, beat egg whites in large bowl until soft peaks form. Gradually add 1 cup sugar, beating until mixture is thick and resembles marshmallow creme, about 5 minutes. Beat in cornstarch and almond extract. Drop meringue onto prepared sheet in 6 mounds, spacing apart. Using spoon, make indentation in center of each. Sprinkle almonds over meringues. Place in oven; immediately reduce temperature to 250°F. Bake until meringues are dry outside but centers are still soft, about 45 minutes. Cool on sheet on rack 30 minutes.

MEANWHILE, stir apricots and ¾ cup sugar in large nonstick skillet over medium-high heat until sugar dissolves and apricots are soft, about 5 minutes. Stir in vanilla. Transfer to bowl; chill until cool. Stir in raspberries.

USING electric mixer, beat cream and remaining 1 tablespoon sugar in medium bowl until peaks form.

PLACE meringues on plates. Spoon whipped cream in center of each. Top with apricot mixture.

Spiced rhubarb and pear compote

2 SERVINGS; CAN BE DOUBLED OR TRIPLED *This lightly spiced compote is wonderful with vanilla ice cream, but is also good with sweetened crème fraîche or sour cream. Add a slice of pound cake or angel food cake for a more substantial dessert. Any leftover compote would be good for breakfast with yogurt and granola.*

6	tablespoons sugar
¼	cup dry red wine
¼	teaspoon ground allspice
2	Bartlett pears, peeled, cut lengthwise into eighths, cored, cut crosswise into 1-inch pieces
10	ounces rhubarb, trimmed, cut into 1-inch pieces
	Vanilla ice cream

BRING first 3 ingredients to simmer in heavy medium saucepan over medium-low heat, stirring until sugar dissolves. Add pears and simmer 2 minutes. Mix in rhubarb. Cover and simmer until rhubarb and pears are just tender, stirring occasionally, about 8 minutes. Spoon warm compote into bowls. Top with ice cream.

Caramel oranges

2 SERVINGS; CAN BE DOUBLED OR TRIPLED *This is the perfect light dessert after a rich meal or following a cheese plate. The recipe doubles and triples easily and can be made in minutes. For an interesting variation, use pink Cara Cara oranges or raspberry-hued blood oranges.*

2   seedless oranges

¼   cup (packed) golden brown sugar

3   tablespoons water

1   tablespoon unsalted butter

1   cinnamon stick

CUT peel and white pith from oranges. Cut oranges into rounds; overlap on plates.

STIR all remaining ingredients in heavy small saucepan over medium heat until sugar dissolves and mixture is syrupy, about 3 minutes. Discard cinnamon stick. Drizzle caramel sauce over orange rounds.

Baked apples with mincemeat, cherries, and walnuts

4 SERVINGS *Chopped walnuts and dried tart cherries embellish purchased mincemeat in these old-fashioned baked apples that are perfect for fall. Look for the mincemeat in the canned fruit section or baking section of some supermarkets, especially at holiday time. Serve with vanilla or black-walnut ice cream.*

1   25.4-ounce bottle sparkling apple cider

¼   cup red currant jelly

2   tablespoons (¼ stick) unsalted butter

4   large Fuji apples (about 9 ounces each)

¾   cup purchased mincemeat with rum and brandy

¼   cup chopped walnuts

¼   cup dried tart cherries

1   tablespoon chopped crystallized ginger

PREHEAT oven to 400°F. Boil first 3 ingredients in large skillet until reduced to 1¼ cups, stirring occasionally, about 12 minutes.

MEANWHILE, cut cone-shaped piece from stem end of each apple, 2 inches wide at top and 1 inch deep. Using melon baller, core each apple, leaving bottom intact. Starting halfway down and using small sharp knife, make ¼-inch-deep slit all around each apple. Mix mincemeat, walnuts, cherries, and crystallized ginger in small bowl; spoon filling into apples, mounding in center.

ARRANGE apples in 11×7×2-inch baking dish. Spoon cider mixture over and around. Bake until apples are tender, about 45 minutes. Serve in shallow bowls.

Ginger baked apples

2 SERVINGS; CAN BE DOUBLED *These beauties are actually cooked in the microwave and browned briefly under the broiler—so you can enjoy the homey treat in minutes. Raisins or currants make an excellent addition to the ginger filling.*

- 2 large baking apples (such as Rome Beauty)
- 2 tablespoons chopped crystallized ginger
- 1 tablespoon butter, melted

- 6 tablespoons water
- 1½ tablespoons sugar
- 1½ teaspoons fresh lemon juice
- ¾ teaspoon finely grated lemon peel
- ½ teaspoon ground cinnamon

  Whipped cream (optional)

PEEL each apple halfway down from stem end. Using small melon baller, core each apple, leaving bottom intact. Place apples in broilerproof microwave-safe casserole dish. Mix ginger and butter in small bowl. Spoon half of ginger mixture into each apple.

STIR all remaining ingredients except cream in small saucepan over medium heat until sugar dissolves and syrup boils. Pour syrup over apples. Cover loosely with microwave-safe plate or glass cover. Microwave on high until apples are tender, rotating dish twice, about 6 minutes. Uncover; spoon juices over.

PREHEAT broiler. Broil apples until tops are glazed and syrup bubbles, about 2 minutes. Serve apples with whipped cream, if desired.

Hazelnut-stuffed pears with maple glaze

6 SERVINGS *Anjou pears are the large, round, green variety named for the Anjou region in northwestern France. The pears are very juicy, with a mild, delicate flavor. Choose firm, slightly underripe Anjou pears so that they will retain their shape while baking.*

- ⅓ cup hazelnuts, toasted, husked
- ⅓ cup (packed) golden brown sugar
- 1½ tablespoons unsalted butter, room temperature
- 2 teaspoons all purpose flour
- 2 teaspoons Frangelico (hazelnut liqueur), amaretto, or brandy

- 3 8-ounce Anjou or Bosc pears, peeled, halved lengthwise
- 6 tablespoons apple juice
- 6 tablespoons pure maple syrup

POSITION rack in center of oven; preheat to 375°F. Place hazelnuts in plastic bag; crush coarsely with rolling pin. Transfer to bowl. Mix in brown sugar, butter, flour, and liqueur.

USING melon baller, core each pear half, creating cavity. Arrange pears, cut side up, in 11×7-inch glass baking dish. Mound hazelnut mixture in cavities, dividing equally and pressing to compact. Pour apple juice into dish around pears. Drizzle pears with maple syrup.

BAKE pears until tender, basting occasionally with juices, about 45 minutes. Transfer pears to plates. Drizzle with juices from dish.

Fresh pears with Port zabaglione

2 SERVINGS; CAN BE DOUBLED OR TRIPLED *A warm, airy, soft custard, zabaglione is a classic Italian dessert from Northern Italy. Although traditionally made with Marsala, Port (the sweet fortified wine that originated in northern Portugal) goes particularly well with the pears. You can use an imported or a California tawny Port, or cream Sherry—or Marsala.*

1 large pear, halved, cored, sliced
2 large egg yolks
2 tablespoons sugar
¼ cup Port, Marsala, or cream Sherry

ARRANGE pear slices in fan pattern on plates. Whisk egg yolks and sugar in medium metal bowl until thick and pale yellow. Whisk in Port. Set over saucepan of simmering water. Whisk until mixture triples in volume and holds shape in spoon, and instant-read thermometer registers 160°F, about 5 minutes. Spoon warm zabaglione over pears and serve immediately.

Cinnamon apple ring fritters

2 SERVINGS; CAN BE DOUBLED OR TRIPLED *It's important to let the batter rest (but not too long), as a mild fermentation will tenderize the dough so it won't become tough when fried. Applejack and Calvados are apple brandies—they add flavor to the batter and help speed up the fermentation. Use a deep, straight-sided skillet for frying the fritters.*

⅓ cup half and half
1 large egg
1 tablespoon applejack brandy or Calvados (apple brandy; optional)
5 tablespoons sugar, divided
½ teaspoon vanilla extract
½ cup all purpose flour
½ teaspoon baking powder
⅛ teaspoon salt

½ teaspoon ground cinnamon

   Vegetable oil (for frying)
2 Golden Delicious apples, cored, cut into ¼-inch-thick rounds

MIX half and half, egg, brandy, 1 tablespoon sugar, and vanilla in processor to blend. Add flour, baking powder, and salt. Using on/off turns, blend until just smooth. Transfer batter to bowl. Let stand at room temperature at least 30 minutes and up to 2 hours.

MIX remaining 4 tablespoons sugar and cinnamon in small bowl. Set aside.

ADD enough oil to heavy large skillet to reach depth of ½ inch. Attach deep-fry thermometer and heat oil to 350°F. Working in batches, sprinkle apples with cinnamon sugar. Dip in batter and add to oil (do not crowd). Fry until golden brown, about 1 minute per side. Drain on paper towels. Sprinkle with more cinnamon sugar.

Dark chocolate–lime soufflés

MAKES 6 *Traditionally, sweet soufflés are baked in carefully buttered and sugared soufflé dishes. In this casual version, that step is skipped, cutting the prep time to just 20 minutes. The tart, refreshing lime flavor balances the richness of the dark chocolate.*

⅔ **cup sugar**

2 **tablespoons finely grated lime peel**

10 **ounces bittersweet or semisweet chocolate, chopped**

5 **large eggs, separated, room temperature**

⅛ **teaspoon salt**

½ **cup semisweet chocolate chips (about 3 ounces)**

1 **cup chilled heavy whipping cream**

1½ **tablespoons fresh lime juice**

PREHEAT oven to 400°F. Place six ¾-cup soufflé dishes on baking sheet. Thoroughly mash sugar and lime peel in small bowl to infuse sugar. Place chopped chocolate in medium bowl set over saucepan of simmering water; stir until melted. Remove bowl from over water; whisk in egg yolks, salt, and 2 tablespoons lime sugar (mixture will become thick). Beat egg whites in large bowl to soft peaks; add 2 tablespoons lime sugar and beat until stiff but not dry. Whisk ⅓ of whites into chocolate mixture to lighten; fold in remaining whites in 2 additions. Fold in chocolate chips. Spoon batter into dishes, dividing equally. Bake soufflés until puffed and softly set, about 14 minutes.

MEANWHILE, whip cream, lime juice, and 4 tablespoons lime sugar in medium bowl until peaks form.

TOP warm soufflés with whipped cream mixture. Sprinkle with additional lime sugar.

Beating egg whites The bowl should be spotlessly clean before you begin beating. Using a handheld or stand mixer set on high, move the beaters in a continuous circular motion through the egg whites in the bowl. Beat the whites from a loose foam to a firmer mixture with bubbles becoming progressively smaller and more opaque. To test, turn off the mixer and lift the beaters from the bowl—if the whites form soft peaks that hold their shape and appear glossy, you're done. Caution: Overbeating will cause the whites to dry out and begin separating.

Vanilla-infused Scharffen Berger bittersweet soufflés

4 SERVINGS *Scharffen Berger is an artisanal choco-late, and its taste really comes through in these soufflés—but if it's hard to find, you can use another premium chocolate. Be sure not to overbake the souf-flés; you want the center to remain soft.*

1½ cups water
 1 cup sugar
 1 large vanilla bean, split lengthwise, then crosswise

 5 ounces Scharffen Berger bittersweet chocolate (70% cacao), chopped
 3 large egg yolks
 4 large egg whites
    Pinch of coarse kosher salt

 ½ cup crème fraîche or sour cream

GENTLY simmer 1½ cups water, sugar, and vanilla bean in heavy small saucepan over medium-low heat until reduced to 1 cup, stirring until sugar dissolves, about 20 minutes. Cool vanilla syrup completely.

DO AHEAD *Can be made 1 week ahead. Cover and chill.*

GENEROUSLY butter and sugar four ½-cup soufflé dishes or ramekins. Combine chocolate and 5 tablespoons vanilla syrup in medium metal bowl. Set bowl over saucepan of simmering water and stir until chocolate melts and mixture is smooth. Remove from heat and stir in egg yolks. Whisk egg whites and salt in large metal bowl until foamy. Add 1 table-spoon vanilla syrup and whisk until soft peaks form. Whisk ⅓ of whites into warm chocolate mixture to lighten. Gently fold in remaining whites. Divide soufflé batter equally among prepared dishes, filling to rims.

DO AHEAD *Can be made up to 1 day ahead. Chill.*

STIR crème fraîche in small bowl with 2 teaspoons vanilla syrup (or more) to sweeten to taste.

POSITION rack in center of oven and preheat to 400°F. Place soufflés on rimmed baking sheet. Bake until soufflés rise about 1 inch above dishes but are still moist in center, about 12 minutes. Serve imme-diately with sweetened crème fraîche.

PREPARING SOUFFLÉ DISHES Using index finger or pastry brush, coat inside and top rim of each soufflé dish or ramekin with soft (room-temperature) unsalted butter. Spoon in 1 to 2 tablespoons sugar. Tilt and turn dish, coating inside and rim completely with sugar. Pour out any excess sugar.

Strawberry shortcakes with mint and whipped cream

6 SERVINGS *Mint updates this summer favorite. If you don't own a food processor, simply combine the dry ingredients in a bowl and blend in the butter by rubbing the mixture between your fingertips until it resembles coarse meal. Then stir the cream and orange peel into the flour-butter mixture with a fork.*

1¾   cups all purpose flour

8   tablespoons plus ½ cup sugar, divided

1   tablespoon baking powder

¼   teaspoon salt

¼   cup (½ stick) chilled unsalted butter, cut into ½-inch cubes

2   cups plus 2 tablespoons chilled heavy whipping cream, divided

1   tablespoon plus ½ teaspoon finely grated orange peel

3   1-pint containers strawberries, hulled, sliced

2   tablespoons thinly sliced fresh mint

1   teaspoon vanilla extract

PREHEAT oven to 375°F. Line rimmed baking sheet with parchment paper. Blend flour, 4 tablespoons sugar, baking powder, and salt in processor 5 seconds. Add butter. Using on/off turns, process until mixture resembles coarse meal. Add 1 cup cream and 1 tablespoon orange peel. Process just until moist clumps form. Gather dough into ball; gently knead 5 turns. Roll out dough on floured work surface to ¾-inch-thick round. Using 3-inch-diameter cutter, cut out 3 biscuits. Gather dough scraps and reroll as needed to cut out 3 more biscuits. Arrange biscuits on prepared sheet. Brush with 2 tablespoons cream; sprinkle with 1 tablespoon sugar.

BAKE biscuits until pale golden and tester inserted into center comes out clean, about 20 minutes. Cool 15 minutes.

DO AHEAD *Can be made 2 hours ahead. Let stand at room temperature.*

COMBINE berries, ½ cup sugar, mint, and remaining ½ teaspoon orange peel in medium bowl; stir to blend. Let stand at least 30 minutes and up to 2 hours, stirring occasionally.

WHISK remaining 1 cup cream, vanilla, and remaining 3 tablespoons sugar in large bowl until soft peaks form.

CUT biscuits horizontally in half. Place 1 biscuit bottom in each of 6 bowls. Top each with berries, then sweetened whipped cream and biscuit top.

Raspberry Salzburger nockerl

2 TO 4 SERVINGS *Salzburger nockerl are light, fluffy, soufflé-like dumplings from Austria. Here, they are baked atop a layer of raspberry jam. Any jam or preserves would work—lingonberry, blackberry, apricot.*

¼   cup raspberry jam

3   large eggs, separated
    Pinch of cream of tartar

¼   cup sugar

1   teaspoon vanilla extract

1   teaspoon finely grated orange peel

1½   tablespoons all purpose flour
    Powdered sugar

PREHEAT oven to 350°F. Butter 9-inch-diameter glass pie dish. Spread jam over bottom of dish. Beat egg whites with cream of tartar in large bowl until soft peaks form. Gradually add ¼ cup sugar and continue beating until stiff but not dry.

WHISK egg yolks, vanilla, and orange peel in medium bowl to blend. Whisk flour into yolk mixture, then mix in ¼ of whites to lighten. Gently fold yolk mixture into remaining whites in bowl. Spoon batter atop jam in 4 mounds. Bake until golden, about 15 minutes. Sift powdered sugar over.

drinks

ALCOHOLIC

Black and Tan

Peachy Mimosa Punch

Pimm's Cup

The Retro Cuba Libre

Vodka-Lime Cooler

Sazerac Cocktail

Cantaloupe-Mint Cooler

Cucumber Gimlet

Meyer Lemon Cosmopolitan

Mint Julep

Dark and Stormy Cocktail

Pamplemousse Cocktail

Classic Shaken Margarita

Jamaica Margarita

Pepper Martini

Rum Punch with Passion
Fruit and Lime

Cranberry, Gingerly

Ruby Champagne Cocktail

Blood Orange French 75

Pomegranate Mojito

Tangerine Mimosa

Citrus-Blossom Gin Fizz

Strawberry and Peach Sangria

Sake Sangria

Minted Mai Tai

Wasabi Bloody Mary

Plymouth Rock and Roll

Perfect Turkey

Blended Vodka Daiquiri
with Lime and Mint

Frozen Watermelon Daiquiri

Banana Colada

Koala Float

Delano Caipirinha

Hot Orange Mocha with Grand
Marnier Whipped Cream

Spiced Cherry Cider
with Kirsch Cream

Irish Coffee

Polar Bear

Mulled Cranberry, Apple,
and Rum Cider

NONALCOHOLIC

Cucumber Agua Fresca

Honeydew-Lime Quencher

Blueberry-Orange Smoothie

Spiced Mango Lassi

Vanilla-Date Breakfast Smoothie

Orange Sherbet Punch

Sparkling Cranberry
and Apple Punch

Sparkling Raspberry Lemonade

Fresh Mint and Ginger Lemonade

Watermelon Lemonade

Lavender Iced Tea

Caramel-Swirl Hot Chocolate

Spiced Apple Cider

tool kit When making cocktails, a little mixology know-how and a few simple recipes will make your drinks the life of the party.

FREEZING: Freeze glasses to help keep beverages cold longer; or try frosting them by dipping them in water, then freezing for 30 minutes before using. If vodka is the prime ingredient in your cocktail of choice, keep the bottle in the freezer so that it's icy cold and ready when happy hour strikes. (The alcohol will prevent it from freezing solid.)

MEASURING: Most of the recipes in this chapter use tablespoon and cup measurements. If you're playing bartender for the night, know that a jigger equals one and a half ounces or three tablespoons, which is about the size of most shot glasses.

MUDDLING: Pounding sugar with mint leaves for a Mojito, with lemon slices for fresh lemonade, or with bitters for a Sazerac not only dissolves the sugar and releases the juices from fruit and herbs, it also releases the flavorful oils from the leaves and peels.

RIMMING: Coating the rims of glasses with sugar or salt adds flavor to Margaritas and fun Cosmo-style drinks. The rims need just a light moistening— try a wedge of lemon, lime, or orange; a halved strawberry; or a piece of watermelon; even water will do the trick. But if the rims are moistened too much, the sugar or salt coating will be too thick and overwhelm the drink. (See "On the Edge" on page 683 for more suggestions for flavored rims.)

SHAKING: Shaking not only ensures that all the ingredients in the cocktail shaker are well blended, but also allows just enough ice to melt into the other ingredients, which helps round out the flavors and cut the sharp edges of the alcohol. Be sure to shake vigorously until the cocktail shaker is frosty. ➤

SIMPLE SIPS

— Blend fruit sorbets and frozen fruits with alcohol for icy Daiquiris. Try raspberry sorbet, frozen raspberries, Chambord, and clear rum for triple-raspberry Daiquiris.

— When making cocktails for a large party, use frozen lemonade, orange juice, and limeade concentrates instead of squeezing the fruits yourself. For example, just blend the limeade with tequila, triple sec, and ice for no-fuss Margaritas.

— Create easy Champagne cocktails by adding a splash of flavored liqueur—such as Chambord (black raspberry liqueur), crème de cassis (black currant), limoncello (lemon), or Grand Marnier (orange) to a glass of Champagne.

— Make your own fruit sodas by preparing fruit juice concentrates (such as passion fruit, peach, or raspberry) with sparkling water.

— Add an element of surprise to your next cup of hot cocoa by steeping cinnamon sticks, dried red chile peppers, orange peel, fresh mint leaves, or peppermint sticks in the milk as it comes to a simmer; then strain the milk before mixing it with chopped chocolate and topping with whipped cream. Add a hint of the flavor that lies within by dusting with ground cinnamon, cayenne, or crushed peppermint candies, or garnishing with fresh mint sprigs or orange twists.

— Blending frozen fruit and regular or frozen yogurt makes a hassle-free smoothie with the luxurious thickness of a shake. Try frozen blueberries and nonfat vanilla yogurt with a squeeze of orange blossom honey, or frozen tropical fruit (such as mangoes) with diced banana and grated nutmeg.

ALCOHOLIC

Black and tan

6 SERVINGS *Also called a Half and Half, this Irish drink consists of two different beers—dark stout and lighter ale or lager—poured one after the other into the same glass, creating a layered effect (the stout is heavier so it sinks to the bottom). Guinness is the traditional stout to use. Bass ale is the traditional accompaniment, but using lighter-colored lager makes for a more dramatic contrast.*

- 3 **12-ounce bottles chilled light lager (such as Harp)**
- 3 **12-ounce bottles chilled Guinness stout**

FILL 6 beer mugs halfway with lager. Pour Guinness stout over lager and serve drinks immediately.

THE LAYERED LOOK Here's another way to try it: Fill the glasses halfway with stout, then pour lager or ale into the glasses slowly over the back of a spoon. Splashing and foaming will be kept to a minimum and the layers will be clearly defined.

Peachy Mimosa punch

MAKES ABOUT 10 CUPS *This on-the-rocks version of a Mimosa adds vodka and peach schnapps, the color-less, intensely peachy liquor, to the usual Champagne-orange juice combo.*

- 4 **cups fresh orange juice**
- 2 **cups vodka**
- 1 **cup peach schnapps**
- 1 **750-ml bottle chilled brut Champagne or other sparkling wine**
  Ice cubes
  Fresh mint sprigs

MIX first 3 ingredients in large pitcher.

DO AHEAD *Can be prepared 4 hours ahead. Cover and refrigerate.*

ADD Champagne to orange juice mixture. Fill tall glasses with ice. Pour orange juice mixture over. Garnish with mint sprigs.

GOING SOLO If you'd like to pour these individually (rather than from a pitcher), make the base ahead as instructed, then pour some into each glass and top with chilled Champagne as guests arrive.

Pimm's cup

6 SERVINGS *We have the British to thank for this fruity, thirst-quenching gin concoction. A favorite at cricket matches and at Wimbledon, it's also a fun brunch drink and it pairs beautifully with spicy Indian food. All sorts of garnishes can be used: apple slices, citrus wedges, cucumber rounds, sliced grapes, you name it. The longer the fruit steeps in the mixture, the more flavor it will infuse.*

- 9 **ounces Pimm's No. 1 Cup**
  Crushed ice
- 18 **ounces lemon-flavored soda or ginger ale**
- 6 **orange or lemon slices**
- 6 **3×½-inch cucumber sticks**

POUR 1½ ounces (3 tablespoons) Pimm's into each of 6 tall glasses or balloon wine glasses. Fill with ice. Add 3 ounces soda to each. Add orange slice and cucumber stick to each.

NUMBERS GAME London oyster-bar owner James Pimm first invented the gin-based drink in the 1840s. His fruit-and-gin recipe became so popular that the base was bottled as Pimm's No. 1 (just top with ginger ale or tonic). Pimm's Cups were eventually made with other boozes, all the way up to No. 6 (with vodka), but Pimm's No. 1 is the only one that's available in the U.S.

Do the math If you're preparing for a cocktail party and don't know how many bottles to buy, the following guidelines will help:

One 750-ml bottle = 17 shots

One 750-ml bottle = 5 to 6 glasses of wine

One 1-liter bottle = 22 shots

One 5-pound bag of ice = rocks for 24 glasses

The retro Cuba libre

MAKES 1 *This takes the rum and Coke to a sophisti-cated new level. Coca-Cola prepared with cane sugar, rather than corn syrup, is made in Mexico. You can get it at a vintage soda shop if you're lucky enough to have one in town, or online from sodapopstop. com. Look for Matusalem Clásico rum—made in the Dominican Republic from a century-old, pre-Castro Cuban formula—at well-stocked liquor stores.*

- 1.5 ounces Matusalem Clásico rum
  or other gold rum
- 5 ounces cane-sugar Coca-Cola or other cola
  Lime wedges

POUR rum and cola over ice in glass; squeeze lime wedge into drink. Garnish with another lime wedge if desired.

Vodka-lime cooler

8 SERVINGS *This is a great, all-purpose cooler for summer parties. Vodka and lime are natural part-ners, and a little fizz from the club soda makes it festive. If you're having a big party, the recipe doubles easily.*

- 1 375-ml bottle vodka, gin, or tequila
- 2 12-ounce cans club soda
- 1 12-ounce can frozen limeade, thawed
  Ice cubes
  Lime slices

MIX first 3 ingredients in pitcher. Fill tall glasses with ice. Pour vodka mixture over ice. Garnish with lime slices.

Sazerac cocktail

MAKES 4 *This New Orleans native was first made with Cognac rather than bourbon. Here the swirl of Herbsaint or Pernod (originally absinthe) scents the glass with a spicy hint of black licorice. Peychaud's bitters are another New Orleans invention, created as a digestive aid. These bitters can be tough to find outside Louisiana; buy them online at sazerac.com or substitute angostura bitters, which are widely available but have an earthier flavor.*

- 2　teaspoons Herbsaint or Pernod
　　Ice cubes
- 1　cup bourbon
- ½　teaspoon Peychaud's bitters
　　or angostura bitters
- 4　teaspoons simple syrup
　　Lemon twist

SWIRL ½ teaspoon Herbsaint or Pernod in each of 4 small Martini glasses to coat inside of glasses. Fill cocktail shaker with ice; add bourbon, bitters, simple syrup, and lemon twist. Shake well; strain into glasses.

Cantaloupe-mint cooler

12 SERVINGS *Frothy and refreshing, this vodka cooler also provides a wonderful opportunity to try different types of melons from the farmers' market—Ambrosia, Charentais, and even honeydew. Choose whichever is ripest and most fragrant.*

- 8　cups chopped peeled cantaloupe
　　(about one 4-pound melon)
- 2　cups ice cubes
- 2　cups cold water
- 1　cup sugar
- 1　cup vodka
- 6　tablespoons fresh lime juice plus
　　12 lime wedges for garnish
- 4　teaspoons (packed) fresh mint leaves
　　plus 12 mint sprigs for garnish

PUREE half of all ingredients (except lime wedges and mint sprigs) in blender until smooth. Pour into 6 stemmed glasses; repeat. Garnish with lime wedges and mint sprigs.

Keep it simple Simple syrup is a mixture of sugar and water that's been heated until the sugar dissolves. It's best for sweetening cocktails because granulated sugar won't dissolve in cold liquid. You can buy simple syrup at some liquor stores, but it's truly as simple to make as the name suggests—and you can keep it in the fridge for weeks of cocktail-making. Bring a cup of water to a simmer over medium-high heat. Add a cup of sugar and stir until the sugar dissolves. Remove from heat and let cool. Store covered in the refrigerator. Makes about 1½ cups.

Cucumber gimlet

MAKES 4 *The gimlet goes to the spa: Adding strained cucumber juice is a super-fresh take on the classic gin-lime combination. Try to use English hothouse cucumbers, which have fewer seeds. These drinks mingle well with salmon, tuna, or caviar appetizers.*

 2 large cucumbers (1½ pounds total)

½ cup gin
 4 teaspoons fresh lime juice
 1 tablespoon sugar
 1 cup ice cubes
 4 lime slices

SLICE four ¼-inch-thick slices from 1 cucumber and reserve. Peel and coarsely chop remaining cucumbers; transfer to processor and puree until smooth. Pour through fine strainer set over large bowl, pressing on solids in strainer. Discard solids in strainer.

MIX 1 cup cucumber juice, gin, lime juice, and sugar in pitcher; stir until sugar dissolves. Add ice; mix well. Immediately strain mixture into 4 small Martini glasses. Garnish with lime and reserved cucumber slices.

Meyer lemon Cosmopolitan

MAKES 8 *The ubiquitous '90s cocktail is fun as a blonde: Sweet Meyer lemon juice stands in for the lime, and white cranberry juice takes the place of red.*

2¼ cups white cranberry juice
1¾ cups plus 2 tablespoons Absolut Citron vodka
 ¾ cup sweet-and-sour mix
 ¾ cup fresh Meyer lemon juice
    Ice cubes

MIX first 4 ingredients in large pitcher. Working in batches, fill cocktail shaker with ice cubes. Add cocktail mixture. Shake briefly, then strain into 8 Martini glasses.

Mint julep

MAKES 2 *The traditional beverage of the Kentucky Derby shouldn't be confined to the first Saturday in May: It makes for lovely sipping all summer long. Juleps are traditionally served in short pewter cups, but old-fashioned glasses will work as well. Definitely use a caramel- or brown-sugar–flavored bourbon, like Maker's Mark or Basil Hayden's.*

16 fresh mint leaves plus 2 fresh mint sprigs
 2 teaspoons (packed) dark brown sugar
 ½ cup bourbon
    Crushed ice

USING muddler or handle of wooden spoon, pound mint leaves and brown sugar in a glass or cocktail shaker. Add bourbon and stir. Pack 2 julep cups with ice until overflowing. Strain bourbon mixture into cups, dividing equally. Stir drink until outside of cup frosts. Top with more ice and garnish with mint sprigs.

MUDDLING THROUGH To properly release the flavor and oils of the mint, you'll need a muddler, a wooden pestle-type implement made for crushing the mint and sugar together in the bottom of a glass. If you don't have a muddler, the handle of a wooden spoon will do the job in a pinch.

Dark and stormy cocktail

6 SERVINGS *This classic rum cocktail from Bermuda is said to be the perfect antidote to the island's heat and humidity, and the ginger reportedly helps soothes the stomach. Ginger beer is similar to ginger ale except that it's fermented instead of carbonated. You can find it at well-stocked liquor stores and at some supermarkets and specialty foods stores.*

2 12-ounce cans ginger beer or ginger ale
1 cup dark rum
2 tablespoons fresh lime juice
   Ice cubes
6 thin slices peeled fresh ginger
6 lime wedges

COMBINE ginger beer, rum, and lime juice in large pitcher. Fill 6 tall glasses with ice. Add rum mixture. Garnish glasses with fresh ginger slices and lime wedges and serve immediately.

On the edge One of the best ways to add extra flavor—and flourish—to a drink is to make a special mixture for the rim, going beyond the customary salted rim of a Margarita. Consider the flavor profile of the drink you're making, and decide whether you'd like to go with a salt or sugar base (or a bit of each), then take a look at the possibilities below.

MIX WITH SALT:

— Finely grated lime peel (best with a Margarita)

— Finely grated lemon peel

— Ground cayenne pepper (fun for a Bloody Mary)

MIX WITH SUGAR:

— Finely grated lemon, lime, orange, or grapefruit peel

— Ground ginger

— Ground cinnamon

— Grated chocolate

— Cocoa powder

— Grated nutmeg

A FEW GUIDELINES:

— Mix the desired amount of add-in into the sugar or salt, then transfer to a small plate, leveling into about a ¼-inch layer.

— Run lemon or lime wedges around the rim of the glass to moisten.

— Turn the glass upside down, setting the top gently on the salt or sugar mixture and twisting until a good amount is clinging to the rim. Gently tap or shake off the excess.

— Keep in mind that coarse kosher salt is best, and either raw sugar or granulated sugar will work (but will result in different looks).

Pamplemousse cocktail

MAKES 6 COCKTAILS Pamplemousse *is French for "grapefruit," and in this lovely pink cocktail, grapefruit juice is enhanced by pomegranate juice, vodka, honey, and lime. After you've juiced the grapefruit, make a twist out of the peel—pink grapefruit would be especially colorful.*

7	tablespoons water
5	tablespoons pomegranate juice
¼	cup sugar
4	teaspoons honey
1½	cups vodka
¾	cup fresh grapefruit juice
¼	cup fresh lime juice
18	fresh mint leaves plus 6 mint sprigs for garnish
	Ice cubes

BRING first 4 ingredients to boil in small saucepan, stirring to dissolve sugar. Cool.

DO AHEAD *Can be made 1 day ahead. Cover and refrigerate.*

COMBINE pomegranate mixture, vodka, grapefruit juice, lime juice, and mint leaves in large pitcher. Fill pitcher with ice. Stir vigorously. Strain drink into Martini glasses. Garnish each glass with mint sprig.

MORE TO TRY The pomegranate-sugar syrup could be used in lots of other cocktails: Try it mixed with vodka and topped with tonic or soda, or mix with Champagne for a pomegranate version of a Kir Royale.

Classic shaken Margarita

MAKES 2 *These Margaritas come from the Too Hot Tamales—chef-restaurateurs Mary Sue Milliken and Susan Feniger, who clearly are as knowledgeable about Mexican drinks as they are about Mexican food. Use white or silver tequila; the more-expensive reposados and añejos are better for sipping straight. Use Mexican limes (also called Key limes) if you can find them. They're a little sweeter and milder than standard Persian limes. Look for Mexican limes at Trader Joe's markets, farmers' markets, Latin markets, or at melissas.com.*

1	lime, cut crosswise into 5 slices, divided
	Coarse kosher salt
1	cup ice cubes
½	cup premium tequila
¼	cup triple sec or other orange liqueur
2	tablespoons fresh lime juice

PLACE 3 lime slices in single layer on small plate. Pour enough coarse kosher salt on another small plate to reach depth of ¼ inch. Lightly press rims of 2 Margarita glasses onto lime slices, twisting to extract juices and coat rims. Dip moistened rims into salt to coat lightly.

COMBINE ice cubes, tequila, triple sec, and lime juice in cocktail shaker. Shake until outside of shaker becomes frosty. Strain mixture into prepared glasses. Garnish rims with 2 remaining lime slices and serve immediately.

Jamaica Margarita

8 SERVINGS *Jamaica flowers are red hibiscus blossoms used in Mexican cooking. They have a tart, slightly earthy flavor, but are mainly used for their stunning fuchsia color. Here they're infused into a simple syrup for a gorgeous pink Margarita with a delectable sugared orange-peel rim. You'll find Jamaica blossoms at Latin markets, or you can order them from melissas.com.*

Jamaica Tea

- **2 ounces Jamaica (hibiscus) flowers (about 2 cups)**
- **3 cups cold water**
- **½ cup sugar**

Margaritas

- **½ cup sugar**
- **1 teaspoon finely grated orange peel**
- **1 orange slice**
- **1½ cups silver tequila made from 100-percent agave**
- **½ cup fresh lime juice**
- **4 to 8 tablespoons Cointreau or triple sec**
  Ice cubes
- **8 lime slices, each cut from edge to center**

FOR JAMAICA TEA: Place Jamaica flowers in strainer and rinse briefly under cold water. Combine flowers, 3 cups cold water, and sugar in medium saucepan. Bring to boil over high heat, stirring until sugar dissolves. Reduce heat to medium and simmer 10 minutes. Strain; discard flowers. Chill tea until cold.

DO AHEAD *Jamaica tea can be made up to 1 week ahead. Keep chilled.*

FOR MARGARITAS: Rub sugar and orange peel together in small bowl to release essential oils from orange peel. Sprinkle orange sugar over small flat plate. Rub orange slice around rims of 8 old-fashioned glasses to moisten lightly. Dip rims in orange sugar to coat.

STIR Jamaica tea, tequila, and lime juice in pitcher. Add enough Cointreau to sweeten to taste. Carefully fill prepared glasses with ice cubes. Carefully pour Jamaica mixture over ice. Garnish each with lime slice.

FIZZY ICED TEA For a nonalcoholic version of this drink, pour the tea over ice in glasses rimmed with orange sugar, filling them halfway. Add enough sparkling mineral water to fill the glasses to just below the rims. Garnish with lime slices.

Pepper Martini

MAKES 8 *Give an ice-cold Martini a blast of heat with pepper jelly (a translucent, bright-green preserve made from jalapeño chiles). Tomolives—small, pickled green tomatoes you'll find jarred in the olive aisle at some supermarkets or at specialty foods stores—provide the perfect pungent bite to go with this drink. If you can't find them, regular pimiento-stuffed green olives can be substituted.*

2 **cups Plymouth gin**

4 **tablespoons dry Sherry (such as La Ina or Tío Pepe)**

8 **teaspoons pepper jelly**

4 **teaspoons orange bitters (such as Regans' No. 6)**
  Ice cubes

8 **tomolives**

COMBINE ½ cup gin, 1 tablespoon Sherry, 2 teaspoons pepper jelly, and 1 teaspoon orange bitters in cocktail shaker. Fill with ice cubes and shake vigorously. Strain into 2 Martini glasses. Repeat 3 times for 6 more drinks. Garnish each with 1 tomolive.

Rum punch with passion fruit and lime

4 SERVINGS *This taste-of-the-tropics drink would be great for an outdoor party, like a luau or other summer barbecue. If you're feeling whimsical, garnish with paper umbrellas or (unsprayed) orchids.*

1½ **cups gold rum**

1 **11.5-ounce can frozen passion fruit juice concentrate (such as Welch's)**

1 **cup water**

⅓ **cup fresh lime juice**

¾ **teaspoon grated peeled fresh ginger**

4 **long peeled pineapple spears**
  Ice cubes
  Fresh mint sprigs

MIX gold rum, passion fruit juice concentrate, 1 cup water, lime juice, and grated ginger in pitcher until concentrate dissolves. Place 1 pineapple spear in each of 4 tall glasses and fill glasses with ice. Pour rum punch over ice and garnish with mint.

SPEAR IT To make pineapple spears, use a large knife to slice off the top and bottom of a fresh pineapple. Stand the pineapple upright and slice off the rind. Quarter the pineapple lengthwise, and slice off the core from each piece. Then slice the pineapple pieces lengthwise into spear shapes.

Cranberry, gingerly

MAKES 1 *This elegant mix of vodka, cranberry juice concentrate, and ginger beer would make a gorgeous cocktail for holiday parties. Take it right over the top with a ginger-sugar rim (see "On the Edge," page 683) or garnish with a slice of crystallized ginger.*

Ice cubes
- ¼ **cup vodka**
- 2 **tablespoons ginger beer or ginger ale**
- 1½ **tablespoons thawed frozen cranberry juice cocktail concentrate**
- 1½ **teaspoons fresh lemon juice**
- ⅛ **teaspoon ground ginger**

FILL cocktail shaker with ice. Add remaining ingredients; shake vigorously. Strain into Martini glass.

Ruby Champagne cocktail

MAKES 4 *Here's a beautiful and innovative take on the Mimosa, using pink grapefruit juice rather than orange juice. A little sugar sweetens the deal.*

- 2 **Ruby Red pink grapefruits**
- ¼ **cup sugar**
- 1 **750-ml bottle chilled brut Champagne**

USING vegetable peeler, remove peel (pink part only) from 1 grapefruit; place peel in bowl. Cut both grapefruits in half; squeeze enough juice to measure ¾ cup. Mix juice and sugar in bowl with peel. Let stand 5 minutes. Strain syrup into small bowl, pressing on solids.

POUR 2 tablespoons syrup into each of four 6-ounce flutes. Fill each with ⅔ cup Champagne.

Blood orange French 75

12 SERVINGS *The name "French 75" comes from a French-made 75-mm field gun used during World War I, when this drink was invented. The original was reportedly a mix of gin, Calvados, and absinthe; today it's made with lemon juice and Champagne. We've upped the ante with blood orange juice and a dash of angostura bitters. The deep-red pigment of the blood oranges (look for them at some supermarkets and at farmers' markets in winter and early spring) makes for a striking drink, but regular oranges will still taste great.*

3 blood oranges (about 1 pound)

1½ cups gin

2 tablespoons sugar

½ teaspoon angostura bitters

2 750-ml bottles chilled brut Champagne

CUT 1 orange in half through stem. Cut each half crosswise into 6 slices; reserve for garnish. Using small knife, cut peel and white pith from remaining 2 oranges; chop oranges. Transfer chopped oranges with juices to bowl; mash with potato masher or wooden spoon. Stir in gin, sugar, and bitters. Strain into 2-cup measuring cup, pressing on solids to release liquid. Chill 4 hours.

POUR scant 2 tablespoons gin mixture into each of 12 Champagne coupes; fill with Champagne and garnish with orange slices.

Pomegranate Mojito

MAKES 1 *The Mojito is a favorite Cuban cocktail of muddled mint, sugar, and lime juice topped off with rum. This one, from the bar at the Four Seasons Hotel in Beverly Hills, calls for vivid red pomegranate juice in place of most of the lime.*

2 tablespoons raw sugar

1 tablespoon fresh lime juice

12 fresh mint leaves

6 tablespoons white rum

¼ cup pomegranate juice

Ice cubes

Soda water

COMBINE sugar, lime juice, and mint in tall glass. Using muddler or handle of wooden spoon, pound mint leaves. Mix in rum and pomegranate juice. Fill glass with ice. Top with splash of soda water.

Tangerine Mimosa

10 SERVINGS *Grand Marnier ups the orange quotient, both flavor- and color-wise, so this is a little sweeter, a little mellower, and a little prettier than the standard orange-juice version. You can find fresh tangerine juice at some supermarkets and at Trader Joe's markets in the wintertime, when tangerines are at their peak.*

1 750-ml bottle chilled brut Champagne

5 tablespoons Grand Marnier or other orange liqueur

2½ cups fresh tangerine juice

Tangerine peel twists (optional)

DIVIDE Champagne among 10 Champagne glasses. Add 1½ teaspoons liqueur, then ¼ cup tangerine juice to each glass. Garnish with tangerine peel, if desired.

Citrus-blossom gin fizz

8 SERVINGS *Fresh and aromatic, this is an eye-opener for brunch parties. The egg whites—whipped up with everything else in the blender—give this drink its fizz; be sure to use very fresh eggs. Orange-flower water contributes a floral complexity (you'll find it with the extracts in the baking aisle, in the Middle Eastern section, or in the liquor department of supermarkets, or at specialty foods stores). Lemon verbena (look for it at farmers' markets) is an aromatic herb that makes a beautiful and fragrant garnish. If you have extra citrus-blossom syrup, use it for seconds or for a different cocktail for your next party (it will keep in the fridge for two weeks).*

Citrus-Blossom Syrup

- **2 cups water**
- **2 cups sugar**
- **1 tablespoon loosely packed fresh lemon verbena leaves (optional)**
- **1 orange**
- **1 lemon**
- **2 teaspoons orange-flower water**

Drinks

- **6 cups ice cubes**
- **½ cup gin**
- **½ cup heavy whipping cream**
- **4 large egg whites**
- **4 tablespoons lemon juice**
- **Freshly ground nutmeg**
- **Fresh lemon verbena sprigs (optional)**

FOR SYRUP: Mix 2 cups water, sugar, and lemon verbena leaves, if desired, in medium saucepan. Using vegetable peeler, remove peel (colored part only) from orange and lemon; add peel to saucepan (reserve orange and lemon for another use). Bring sugar mixture to boil, stirring until sugar dissolves. Reduce heat to medium and simmer 5 minutes. Cool completely. Stir in orange-flower water.

DO AHEAD *Can be made 2 weeks ahead. Cover and refrigerate.*

FOR DRINKS: Combine 6 tablespoons syrup, 3 cups ice, ¼ cup gin, ¼ cup cream, 2 egg whites, and 2 tablespoons lemon juice in blender. Blend until smooth and foamy. Divide among 4 glasses. Repeat with 6 tablespoons syrup and remaining ice, gin, cream, egg whites, and juice. Sprinkle drinks with nutmeg; garnish with lemon verbena sprigs, if desired.

FRESH GROUND For the freshest flavor, grind your own nutmeg, rather than using pre-ground spice from a jar. Most supermarkets carry whole nutmegs (they look a little like walnuts) in jars in the spice aisle. Use a box grater or a Microplane zester to grate it.

drinks

Strawberry and peach sangria

8 SERVINGS *This is a white-wine sangria elevated by Essensia (sweet orange Muscat wine), peach liqueur, and strawberry liqueur. After you've mixed the fruit and wine in the pitcher and chilled it, and just before serving, slip a few more lemon slices down the side of the pitcher so the cross sections show through the glass.*

- 1 750-ml bottle dry white wine
- 1½ cups Essensia (sweet dessert wine)
- 1½ cups sliced strawberries
- 1 cup peach liqueur
- 3 peaches, each cut into 12 slices
- 1 large orange, cut crosswise into 6 slices
- 1 large lemon, cut crosswise into 6 slices
- ¼ cup strawberry liqueur (optional)
- 3 to 4 cups ice cubes

MIX white wine, Essensia, strawberries, peach liqueur, peach slices, orange slices, lemon slices, and strawberry liqueur in large pitcher, smashing citrus slices slightly. Let stand at room temperature at least 2 hours or chill up to 4 hours. Serve sangria over ice.

Sake sangria

8 TO 10 SERVINGS *Sangria goes east in this version, with sake, Asian pear, and lychees giving the drink a sophisticated spin. (A little warning: There's vodka in here, in addition to wine and sake.)*

- 1 cup vodka
- 1 cup sugar
- 3 oranges, peeled, segmented
- 1 large Granny Smith apple, halved, seeded, cubed
- 1 Asian pear, halved, seeded, cubed
- 1 15-ounce can lychees, drained
- ¼ pineapple, peeled, cored, cubed
- 2 750-ml bottles chilled Sauvignon Blanc
- 1 750-ml bottle chilled junmai sake
  Ice cubes

MIX first 7 ingredients in large pitcher. Cover; let stand 4 hours at room temperature. Mix in wine and sake. Fill glasses with ice. Ladle sangria over.

Beer or wine? *Sake* is technically rice beer, not rice wine, because it's brewed and made from grain, not fruit, although you'll often see it incorrectly labeled or categorized as wine. The junmai variety called for in this recipe is the purest style of *sake*, perfect for mixing with other flavors.

690

Minted mai tai

6 SERVINGS *Chopped fresh mint and a dash of almond syrup (which you'll find in the coffee aisle of the supermarket) take this classic drink up a notch. Tiki parties and luaus will never be the same.*

½ cup fresh lime juice
½ cup almond syrup (such as Torani)
½ cup chopped fresh mint leaves

2 cups pineapple juice
1½ cups orange juice
1½ cups dark rum
  Ice cubes
  6 fresh mint sprigs

STIR lime juice, syrup, and chopped mint leaves in heavy small saucepan over medium heat just until mixture simmers. Cool.

STRAIN syrup into pitcher. Add pineapple juice, orange juice, and rum; stir to blend. Fill 6 tall glasses with ice. Pour juice mixture over. Garnish Mai Tais with fresh mint sprigs.

OH, MAI Loosely translated, *mai tai* means "out of this world" in Tahitian. The drink was invented in 1944 by Victor Bergeron, owner of the Polynesian-themed Trader Vic's restaurant chain, at the original location in Oakland, California.

Wasabi Bloody Mary

MAKES 2 *Hot pepper vodka and wasabi powder really pack a punch in this version of the Bloody Mary. Wasabi powder is green horseradish powder, and can be found in the Asian foods section of some supermarkets and at Japanese markets. (When mixed with water, it becomes the green paste that's served with sushi.)*

6 tablespoons hot pepper vodka
4 teaspoons fresh lemon juice
1½ teaspoons wasabi powder
½ teaspoon ground black pepper
1½ cups chilled tomato juice
1 teaspoon Worcestershire sauce

  Ice cubes
  Celery stalks with leaves

STIR vodka, lemon juice, wasabi, and pepper in pitcher until wasabi dissolves. Stir in tomato juice and Worcestershire sauce. Chill at least 1 hour.

DO AHEAD *Can be made 1 day ahead. Cover and keep refrigerated. Stir before using.*

FILL 2 glasses with ice cubes. Pour tomato juice mixture over. Garnish with celery stalks.

Plymouth rock and roll

MAKES 1 *Shake things up on Thanksgiving with this autumnal rendition of the Martini. Use Plymouth Gin (a super-smooth English gin) in honor of the Pilgrims' arrival at Plymouth Rock. Skewering an olive on a rosemary sprig accentuates the herbal elements.*

- 1 fresh rosemary sprig
- 1 fresh thyme sprig
  Dash of dry vermouth
  Ice cubes
- ¼ cup Plymouth gin
- 1 green Martini olive, skewered on fresh rosemary sprig

USING MUDDLER or handle of wooden spoon, pound rosemary, thyme, and vermouth in a cocktail shaker. Add ice and gin. Shake vigorously, then strain into Martini glass. Garnish with skewered Martini olive.

Perfect Turkey

MAKES 1 *This is a Manhattan that calls for Wild Turkey bourbon. This version is slightly dryer than the classic, with a "perfect" balance of sweet and dry vermouth (rather than just sweet). The spice-sugared rim adds a seasonal note (pumpkin pie, anyone?), and it's garnished with that favorite of fall colors, orange.*

- 2 tablespoons sugar
- ¾ teaspoon ground allspice
- ¾ teaspoon ground nutmeg
- 1 orange wedge
- ¼ cup Wild Turkey bourbon
- 1½ teaspoons sweet vermouth
- 1½ teaspoons dry vermouth
  Ice cubes
  Orange peel twist

MIX sugar and spices on small plate. Rub orange wedge around rim of Martini glass; dip rim into spiced sugar mixture. Add bourbon, sweet vermouth, and dry vermouth to cocktail shaker; fill with ice. Shake vigorously, then strain into glass. Garnish with orange peel twist.

Blended vodka Daiquiri with lime and mint

6 SERVINGS *This refreshing drink would make a nice start to a Thai or Vietnamese meal, and it's also delicious alongside salty or spicy nibbles.*

3½ cups ice cubes
1 cup frozen limeade concentrate (do not thaw)
¾ cup vodka
⅓ cup fresh mint leaves
 Fresh mint sprigs

BLEND first 4 ingredients in blender until mixture has smooth slushy texture.

DO AHEAD *Daiquiri can be made 2 hours ahead. Place in freezer. Stir gently before serving.*

DIVIDE among 6 Martini glasses. Garnish each Daiquiri with mint sprig.

Frozen watermelon Daiquiri

MAKES 4 *Fresh watermelon and watermelon liqueur (available at supermarkets or liquor stores) give these a slightly mellower flavor than the typical frozen strawberry Daiquiri. Freezing cubes from a very watery watermelon before blending the drink eliminates the need for ice cubes. To save time, skip the skewers.*

4 strawberries, halved, plus
 ½ cup sliced strawberries
1 kiwi, peeled, cut into 8 wedges
4 4-inch-long lemongrass skewers
 or wooden skewers

5 tablespoons light rum
3 tablespoons sour watermelon
 liqueur (such as Pucker)
2 tablespoons sugar
2 tablespoons fresh lime juice
3 cups ¾-inch cubes seedless
 watermelon, frozen at least 1 hour

THREAD strawberry halves and kiwi wedges alternately onto skewers.

STIR light rum, sour watermelon liqueur, sugar, and fresh lime juice in small bowl until sugar dissolves. Transfer mixture to blender. Add frozen watermelon cubes and ½ cup sliced strawberries. Blend mixture well; pour into Martini glasses. Garnish with lemongrass skewers.

SKEWER IT Lemongrass, which is available in the produce section of many supermarkets (usually in plastic packages with the herbs) or at Asian markets, is a long, narrow, woody stalk with a lovely citrusy aroma. It makes a clever, fragrant skewer for the strawberry-and-kiwi garnish in this recipe. Just use the narrow tops and save the wider bottom sections for another use.

Banana colada

4 SERVINGS *This enhanced Piña Colada uses banana in addition to the requisite pineapple, and dark rum in addition to traditional light rum. You'll find canned cream of coconut (most typically, the Puerto Rican Coco López brand) in the liquor department of the supermarket or at liquor stores.*

20	ice cubes
3	ripe medium bananas, cut into chunks
1	cup canned sweetened cream of coconut (such as Coco López)
1	cup pineapple juice
½	cup dark rum
½	cup light rum
4	tablespoons fresh lemon juice
4	fresh pineapple wedges
4	fresh mint sprigs

PLACE 4 tall glasses in freezer. Combine 10 ice cubes, half of banana chunks, ½ cup cream of coconut, ½ cup pineapple juice, ¼ cup dark rum, ¼ cup light rum, and 2 tablespoons lemon juice in blender and blend until smooth. Divide between 2 frozen glasses. Attach pineapple wedge to side of each glass; garnish with mint sprig. Repeat as described above to make second batch of drinks.

Koala float

2 SERVINGS *Creamy, sweet, and cool, this drink is made for coconut and coffee lovers. It's a luscious treat any time of day, but would be particularly satisfying for dessert on a hot summer night.*

4	cups ice cubes
¾	cup canned sweetened cream of coconut (such as Coco López)
6	tablespoons coffee liqueur
6	tablespoons Irish cream liqueur
	Chocolate shavings

BLEND first 4 ingredients in blender until smooth. Pour into 2 tall glasses. Sprinkle with chocolate.

Delano Caipirinha

2 SERVINGS *The Brazilian cocktail (pronounced kai-pi-REEN-ya) comes to us by way of the Delano, a swanky Miami Beach hotel. Cachaça (ka-SHA-sa) is a dry Brazilian sugar-cane-based liquor, not dissimilar to rum but with a dryer bite. It's available at well-stocked liquor stores and at Latin American markets.*

- 1 large lime, quartered
- 2 tablespoons sugar
- ½ cup cachaça or white rum
- 2 tablespoons fresh lemon juice
  Ice cubes

DIVIDE lime quarters and sugar between 2 short glasses. Using wooden spoon, mash lime and sugar in each glass. Add ¼ cup cachaça and 1 tablespoon lemon juice to each glass; stir to blend. Fill each with ice.

Hot orange mocha with Grand Marnier whipped cream

4 SERVINGS *Coffee, chocolate, and orange come together in this delicious hot drink that could stand in for dessert. The sweetened orange whipped cream would also be delectable atop chocolate, coffee, or nut desserts.*

- ½ cup chilled heavy whipping cream
- 2 tablespoons brown sugar, divided
- 1 tablespoon Grand Marnier or other orange liqueur

- 2 oranges
- 4 cups whole milk
- 6 ounces bittersweet or semisweet chocolate chips
- 3 tablespoons instant espresso powder
- 1 tablespoon unsweetened cocoa powder
  Ground coffee beans (optional)

WHISK cream, 1 tablespoon brown sugar, and Grand Marnier in medium bowl to soft peaks; cover and chill.

USING vegetable peeler, remove peel (orange part only) from oranges in strips; add strips to medium saucepan (reserve oranges for another use). Add milk; bring just to simmer over medium heat. Add chocolate, espresso powder, cocoa powder, and remaining 1 tablespoon brown sugar; bring just to simmer, whisking to melt chocolate. Strain. Ladle mocha into 4 mugs. Top with whipped cream and ground coffee beans, if desired.

Spiced cherry cider with kirsch cream

4 SERVINGS *This ruby-red winter-spiced drink would be ideal for a Christmas open house or a Valentine's evening in front of the fire. Try a dollop of the kirsch cream on any cherry, chocolate, or almond dessert. You'll find cherry cider (usually a blend of apple and cherry juice) in the juice aisle at most supermarkets.*

4   cups cherry cider or cherry juice
2   cinnamon sticks, broken in half
15 whole cloves
2   tablespoons sugar, divided

⅓   cup chilled heavy whipping cream
5   teaspoons kirsch (clear cherry brandy)
1   2-ounce piece semisweet chocolate grated, (optional)

BRING cherry cider, cinnamon sticks, whole cloves, and 1 tablespoon sugar to boil in heavy large saucepan. Reduce heat and simmer until spiced cider is reduced to 2½ cups, about 10 minutes. Strain cider.

WHISK whipping cream, kirsch, and remaining 1 tablespoon sugar in medium bowl to very soft peaks. Ladle cider into glass mugs and top with kirsch cream. Garnish each serving with some grated chocolate, if desired.

Irish coffee

10 SERVINGS *What could warm up a cup of coffee better than a shot of Irish whiskey? This drink was born at Shannon International Airport in Ireland and soon made it to the Buena Vista bar in San Francisco, where locals in the chilly, foggy city embraced it.*

¾   cup chilled heavy whipping cream
1¾   cups plus 2 tablespoons Irish whiskey
10   tablespoons (packed) dark brown sugar
7½   cups freshly brewed strong coffee
     Grated semisweet chocolate

WHISK cream in large bowl until slightly thickened. Place 3 tablespoons whiskey and 1 tablespoon sugar in each of ten 8- to 10-ounce mugs. Pour ¾ cup coffee into each mug. Top each with dollop of cream; sprinkle with chocolate.

Polar bear

8 SERVINGS *This toasty—and potent—drink could fend off even arctic temperatures. It's a hot buttered rum taken up several degrees with brandy and butter spiced with cinnamon, nutmeg, cloves, and vanilla. For a traditional presentation, don't blend the butter into the rum mixture—just serve it as a pat floating on top and let your guests stir it in.*

1¼ cups (packed) golden brown sugar

½ cup (1 stick) unsalted butter, room temperature

½ teaspoon ground cinnamon

½ teaspoon ground nutmeg

½ teaspoon ground cloves

½ vanilla bean, split lengthwise

4 cups water

1½ cups dark rum

1½ cups brandy

8 cinnamon sticks

PLACE first 5 ingredients in food processor. Scrape in seeds from vanilla bean. Process until blended.

DO AHEAD *Butter mixture can be made 1 week ahead. Wrap in plastic and chill.*

BRING 4 cups water to boil in large saucepan. Add rum, brandy, and spiced butter mixture; stir until butter melts. Ladle into mugs and garnish with cinnamon sticks.

Mulled cranberry, apple, and rum cider

MAKES ABOUT 6 CUPS *Hot apple cider gets punched up with rum, and livened up with cranberry juice. Get this recipe going a little while before guests arrive: There's nothing better than walking into a holiday party and smelling the festive aroma of mulled cider.*

1 large orange

3 cups cranberry juice cocktail

3 cups apple cider

¾ cup (packed) golden brown sugar

4½ 3- to 4-inch-long cinnamon sticks

18 whole cloves

½ teaspoon ground nutmeg

6 tablespoons dark rum

6 additional 3- to 4-inch-long cinnamon sticks (optional)

6 orange slices (optional)

USING vegetable peeler, remove peel (orange part only) from orange in strips. Place strips in large saucepan; halve orange and squeeze juice into pan. Add cranberry juice cocktail, apple cider, sugar, cinnamon sticks, cloves, and nutmeg. Bring to boil over high heat, stirring until sugar dissolves. Reduce heat to medium and simmer 25 minutes.

DO AHEAD *Can be made 1 day ahead. Cover and chill.*

ADD rum to cider; simmer 5 minutes. Ladle into mugs. Garnish with cinnamon sticks and orange slices, if desired.

NONALCOHOLIC

Cucumber agua fresca

8 SERVINGS *In Mexico, aguas frescas—"cool waters"—can be made from just about any fruit or vegetable (watermelon, hibiscus blossoms, lime), plus water and sugar. This one is the coolest of them all: cucumber. It's great with tacos, quesadillas, chips and salsa, or guacamole.*

4½ cups coarsely chopped seeded peeled
    cucumbers (about 4 medium)
  4 cups cold water
  2 cups ice cubes plus more for glasses
  1 cup sugar
 ⅔ cup fresh lime juice
  2 large pinches of salt

COMBINE 2¼ cups chopped cucumbers, 2 cups water, 1 cup ice cubes, ½ cup sugar, ⅓ cup lime juice, and 1 pinch of salt in blender. Blend until sugar dissolves and mixture is smooth but slushy, about 2 minutes. Transfer mixture to pitcher. Repeat with remaining chopped cucumbers, 2 cups water, 1 cup ice cubes, sugar, lime juice, and pinch of salt. Place additional ice cubes in 8 glasses. Fill with cucumber drink.

Honeydew-lime quencher

8 SERVINGS *Make sure you find a super-ripe honeydew (it should give a little at the stem end and should be very fragrant). A bit of tang from the lime juice and a touch of heat from the jalapeño balance the sweetness perfectly.*

  5 pounds ripe honeydew melons,
    halved, seeded, rind removed, flesh
    cut into large pieces, chilled
 ½ cup water
  6 tablespoons fresh lime juice
  4 tablespoons honey
  2 tablespoons minced seeded jalapeño chile
12 ice cubes
  1 lime, cut into thin slices

COMBINE half of melon pieces, ¼ cup water, 3 tablespoons lime juice, 2 tablespoons honey, 1 tablespoon jalapeño, and 6 ice cubes in blender; puree until smooth. Pour into 4 glasses. Repeat with remaining ingredients to make 4 more drinks. Garnish with lime slices.

Blueberry-orange smoothie

2 SERVINGS *Antioxidants from the blueberries, vitamin C from the orange juice, and protein from the yogurt add up to a very nutritious breakfast smoothie. Frozen berries will result in a thicker smoothie.*

1½　cups fresh or frozen blueberries
　　　(about 8 ounces)
　1　cup orange juice
　½　cup low-fat frozen vanilla yogurt
　½　cup ice cubes
　¼　teaspoon finely grated orange peel
　　　Fresh blueberries for garnish

COMBINE first 5 ingredients in blender. Puree until thick and smooth. Pour smoothie into 2 glasses. Garnish each smoothie with fresh blueberries.

Spiced mango lassi

2 SERVINGS *A lassi is an Indian yogurt smoothie. This one would be fantastic with spicy Indian food: Cinnamon and cardamom complement the flavors of the cuisine, and the yogurt has a cooling effect.*

1½　cups diced peeled pitted
　　　mango (about 1½ large)
　1　cup plain nonfat yogurt
　1　cup ice cubes
　¼　cup low-fat (1%) milk
1½　tablespoons honey
　½　teaspoon vanilla extract
　¼　teaspoon ground cinnamon
　⅛　teaspoon ground cardamom

PUREE all ingredients in blender until smooth. Divide smoothie between glasses.

Vanilla-date breakfast smoothie

MAKES 2 *The date shake is a tried-and-true sweet treat; the ones from Hadley's Fruit Orchards near Palm Springs in California's date capital are probably the best known. This one gets extra depth from a dash of vanilla.*

　1　cup nonfat yogurt
　1　cup nonfat milk
　1　cup (packed) pitted Medjool
　　　dates (about 9 ounces)
　½　teaspoon vanilla extract
　2　cups ice cubes

PUREE yogurt, milk, dates, and vanilla in blender. Add ice cubes; blend until mixture is thick and smooth. Divide between glasses.

IT'S A DATE Medjool dates are a soft variety, and therefore the kind best suited to blending into a smoothie. Pitting dates is easy: Simply slice down one side of the date, open it up a bit, and pull out the pit (they're not bound to the date and will be easy to remove).

Orange sherbet punch

MAKES 12 SERVINGS *Fun for all ages, this is like a fizzy liquid Creamsicle. Sherbet is made from fruit juice and usually milk or egg whites (rather than water or whole eggs), placing it somewhere between ice cream and sorbet on the richness scale, and making it just right for this punch.*

 4 **cups chilled orange juice**
 1 **cup milk**
 3 **tablespoons sugar**
 2 **teaspoons finely grated orange peel**
 ½ **teaspoon ground nutmeg**

 1 **cup chilled sparkling water**
 1 **quart orange sherbet**

COMBINE first 5 ingredients in large pitcher. Mix until sugar dissolves.

DO AHEAD *Can be made 3 days ahead. Cover and refrigerate.*

POUR sparkling water into orange juice mixture and stir to blend. Scoop sherbet into large glass punch bowl. Pour punch over sherbet and serve immediately.

Sparkling cranberry and apple punch

12 SERVINGS *Cranberry-apple juice gets dressed up for a party in this gorgeous jewel-toned punch. It's a lovely nonalcoholic drink for the holidays, but substituting sparkling wine for the sparkling water is also an option. Using cranberry juice to make ice cubes is a brilliant idea: During the course of the party, as the ice cubes melt, the punch won't get watered down.*

 2 **quarts chilled cranberry juice cocktail, divided**

 3 **cups chilled sparkling apple juice or cider**
 2 **cups chilled sparkling water**
 ½ **cup fresh lemon juice**
 1 **orange, thinly sliced**
 1 **lemon, thinly sliced**

POUR enough cranberry juice cocktail into 2 ice cube trays to fill. Freeze.

DO AHEAD *Can be made 1 month ahead.*

PLACE cranberry ice cubes in punch bowl or large pitcher. Add remaining cranberry juice cocktail, apple juice, sparkling water, lemon juice, and orange and lemon slices; stir to combine.

On the rocks Orange, lime, lemon, grapefruit, cranberry, and tomato juices—all these liquids freeze as easily as water does. And these ice cubes won't water drinks down when they melt. So when preparing a pitcher of Sangria, use ice cubes made from red or white wine. Bloody Marys? Frozen cubes of pure tomato juice. A Greyhound? Grapefruit-juice rocks. And adding cubes of watermelon or frozen raspberries or blueberries to drinks provides both form and function: beautiful garnish, virtual ice cube.

Sparkling raspberry lemonade

6 SERVINGS *This colorful sweet-tart cooler would be a hit at any backyard summer party, but you can make it year-round, as it calls for frozen berries (just skip the fresh berry garnish). A shot of vodka or gin would probably be a hit with the grown-ups.*

1 12-ounce package frozen unsweetened raspberries
1 cup sugar
½ cup water
1½ tablespoons finely grated lemon peel

1 cup fresh lemon juice
1 1-liter bottle chilled sparkling water or club soda
   Ice cubes
   Fresh raspberries (optional)
   Lemon slices

COMBINE frozen raspberries, sugar, and ½ cup water in medium saucepan. Stir over medium heat until sugar dissolves and berries thaw. Increase heat and boil 3 minutes. Strain raspberry mixture into bowl, pressing on solids to extract as much liquid as possible; discard solids in strainer. Mix lemon peel into raspberry syrup in bowl. Chill until cold.

STIR raspberry syrup, lemon juice, and sparkling water in large pitcher to blend. Fill 6 glasses with ice cubes. Pour raspberry lemonade into glasses. Add fresh raspberries to each glass, if desired. Garnish with lemon slices.

Fresh mint and ginger lemonade

4 SERVINGS *Here's a fresh take on lemonade that is infused with the flavors of mint and ginger and sweetened with honey. Chill it and serve cold as the recipe instructs—or try it hot as a soothing drink on a chilly morning.*

½ cup (packed) chopped fresh mint leaves
⅓ cup chopped peeled fresh ginger
⅓ cup honey
2 cups boiling water
⅓ cup fresh lemon juice
1½ cups (about) cold water

   Ice cubes
   Fresh mint leaves
   Lemon slices

COMBINE chopped mint, ginger, and honey in medium bowl. Add boiling water. Let steep 30 minutes. Strain into 4-cup glass measuring cup, pressing on solids to extract liquid. Add lemon juice and enough cold water to measure 4 cups total.

DO AHEAD *Can be made 1 day ahead. Cover and chill.*

FILL glasses with ice cubes. Add lemonade. Garnish with mint leaves and lemon slices.

Watermelon lemonade

MAKES 9 CUPS *Pretty, refreshing, sweet, tart. Make a big batch and serve it at a party, or keep it in the fridge for a week's worth of refreshment. Or try it mixed with an equal part iced tea for a variation on an Arnold Palmer.*

- 8 **cups 1-inch pieces seedless watermelon (from about 4½ pounds)**
- 1 **cup fresh lemon juice**

- 3½ **cups water**
- 1 **cup sugar**
   Ice cubes
   Lemon wedges

WORKING in 2 batches, blend watermelon and lemon juice in processor or blender until smooth. Transfer to pitcher.

BRING 3½ cups water and sugar to boil in medium saucepan over high heat, stirring until sugar dissolves. Add hot syrup to pitcher with watermelon-lemon juice. Refrigerate until cold, about 2 hours. Fill tall glasses with ice. Pour lemonade over and garnish glasses with lemon wedges.

Lavender iced tea

MAKES 4 QUARTS *A sophisticated spin on iced tea, this would be perfect for afternoon tea or brunch, or alongside a lavender-scented dessert, like ice cream, custard, or cookies. Dried lavender blossoms, sometimes labeled culinary lavender buds, are available at natural foods stores, farmers' markets, and at surfasonline.com.*

- 17 **cups water, divided**
- 2 **cups sugar**
- 2 **tablespoons dried lavender blossoms**

- 12 **tea bags**

   Ice cubes

BRING 5 cups water, sugar, and lavender to boil in large saucepan, stirring until sugar dissolves. Boil until reduced to 4 cups, about 14 minutes.

BRING remaining 12 cups water to boil in large pot. Remove from heat. Add tea bags; steep 5 minutes. Strain into very large pitcher.

DO AHEAD *Syrup and tea can be made 1 day ahead. Chill separately until cold. Cover; keep chilled.*

FILL 10 glasses with ice cubes. Pour 1 cup tea into each glass. Stir in 4 to 6 tablespoons syrup, adjusting to taste.

Caramel-swirl hot chocolate

6 SERVINGS *Milk chocolate plus caramel whipped cream equals a molten Milky Way in a mug. Kids will go crazy for this, and it's a fun treat around the holidays or a warm-up after trick-or-treating. Make sure to just gently mix the caramel and whipped cream to maintain the swirl effect.*

5 cups water
5 3-ounce bars milk chocolate, chopped
¼ cup plus 1 cup chilled heavy whipping cream

1 tablespoon powdered sugar
3 tablespoons purchased caramel sauce

BRING 5 cups water and chocolate to simmer in medium saucepan, stirring to dissolve chocolate. Mix in ¼ cup cream.

DO AHEAD *Can be made 1 day ahead. Cover and chill. Bring to simmer, stirring frequently, before continuing.*

WHIP remaining 1 cup cream and powdered sugar in medium bowl until peaks form. Drizzle caramel over and swirl together, forming streaks (do not overmix).

DIVIDE hot chocolate among 6 mugs. Top with generous amount of caramel whipped cream.

Spiced apple cider

MAKES ABOUT 8 CUPS *The ultimate version of a fall classic: Cardamom gives this spiced cider an exotic new spin. You can find whole cardamom pods— they're pale green and about the size of a pistachio—at some supermarkets and at Indian and Middle Eastern markets. When you crush them for this recipe, you may release some of the tiny seeds inside. Be sure to use all of the pods and seeds for the most flavor.*

1 large orange
4 quarts apple cider
¼ cup (packed) golden brown sugar
2 tablespoons fresh lemon juice
15 whole cloves
10 whole allspice
8 whole green cardamom pods, crushed
5 cinnamon sticks, each broken in half

USING vegetable peeler, remove peel (orange part only) from orange in strips. Place orange peel in heavy large pot (reserve orange for another use). Add apple cider, brown sugar, lemon juice, cloves, allspice, cardamom pods, and cinnamon sticks to pot. Bring to boil, stirring until sugar dissolves. Reduce heat to medium-low; simmer until cider mixture is reduced to generous 8 cups, about 40 minutes. Strain cider into medium pot.

DO AHEAD *Can be made 1 day ahead. Cool slightly. Refrigerate until cold, then cover and keep refrigerated. Rewarm cider before ladling into mugs.*

CONTRIBUTORS

RECIPES

Joy Ackerman
Bruce Aidells
Luis Miguel López Alanís
Nancy Alexandroff
Al Fornello da Ricci, Ceglie, Italy
Alon's, Atlanta, Georgia
Amanwana, Moyo Island
José Andrés
Linda Archer
Arroyo Village Inn, Arroyo Grande,
     California
Peter Arvanitis
Atwood Cafe, Chicago, Illinois
Avoca Handweavers, Kilmacanogue,
     Bray, County Wicklow, Ireland

Mary Corpening Barber
Melanie Barnard
Nancy Verde Barr
Armandino Batali, Salumi, Seattle,
     Washington
Caroline Belk
Anna Bruni Benson
Peter Berley
Sondra Bernstein
Vern Bertagna
Davina Besford
Maurice Bessinger, Piggie Park,
     Columbia, South Carolina
Veronica Betancourt
Rosie Bialowas
Lena Cederham Birnbaum
Mark Bittman
Anthony Dias Blue
Frank Bonanno, Luca D'Italia, Denver,
     Colorado
Julia Boorstin

Daniel Boulud
Kimberly Boyce
Georgeanne Brennan
Joan Brett
Marilyn Bright
Frank Brigtsen, Brigtsen's, New
     Orleans, Louisiana
Jane Bronk-Gorman
Katie Brown
Lynn Brown
Rick Browne
Sharon Buck
Gertrude Burnom

Cafe Deluxe, Washington, D.C.
Lisa Caiazzo
Connie Capani
Camille's, Key West, Florida
Susie Campbell
Carla Capalbo
Carmelo's Italian Restaurant,
     Houston, Texas
Lucy Carney
Wendy Taylor Carroll
Penelope Casas
Mary Cech
Chameau, Los Angeles, California
Miriam Chandler
Charleston Grill, Charleston,
     South Carolina
Laura Christie
Bobbi Claibourne
Melissa Clark
Alain Cohen
Mindy Cohn
Gerald Colapinto
Stephanie Coon
Cat Cora
Agathe Corby

Patrick Corrigan
Patti and David Cottle
Courtney's Bistro, Caernarvon, Wales
Colin Cowie
Jameson Cox
James Cratin
Debra Creed-Broeker
Helen and Tony Crimmins
Russell Cronkhite
Marie Devito Crowley
Geoffrey Crowther
Lane Crowther
Liz Cullinane
Jane Cunningham
Leila Cuttino

Paula and Taras Danyluk
Gretchen Davis
Renee Davis
Dale DeGroff
Delano Hotel, Miami, Florida
Giada De Laurentiis
Lorenza de' Medici
Lori De Mori
Mary Demuth
Annie Denn
Joe Dion
Stefanie Dirienzo
Devora Disner
Brooke Dojny
Sue and Mark Dooley
Tom Douglas

Sheila Eaton
Elizabeth Ellis
Sue Reddin Ellison
Sandy Ercolano

Susan Elizabeth Fallon
Charlotte Fekete
Susan Feniger
Barbara Pool Fenzl
Fialho, Évora, Portugal
George Fike
First St. Cafe, Benicia, California
Louise Fiszer
Janet Fletcher
Fleur de Lys, San Francisco, California
Jamie Elizabeth Flick
Tyler Florence
Jim Fobel
Lucy Footlik
Fore Street, Portland, Maine
Four Season's Hotel, Beverly Hills,
    California
Clark Frasier
Robyn Fuoco

Mark Gaier
Gale Gand
Gayle Gardner
Jason Gareffa
Ina Garten
Joie Gaty
Hugh Garvey
Daryl Getman
Ann Gillespie
Gerri Gilliland
Todd Goddard
Suzanne Goin
Rozanne Gold
Darra Goldstein
Myra Goodman
Kathy Grady
Bill Granger
Rose Gray
Dorie Greenspan
Gresslin's, Hampstead, London,
    England
Sophie Grigson
Sherri Gugenheim

Anita Hacker
Ken Haedrich
Sara Hainsworth
Gordon Hamersley
Juliet Hardesty
Louisa Thomas Hargrave
Judy Harmon
Beverly Harvey
Katy Hees
Bev Heinecke
Sabrina Henderson
George Hendrix
Beth Hensperger
Mily Hernandez
Evelyn Herring
Cara Brunetti Hillyard
Susanna Hoffman
Ken Hom
Jill Silverman Hough
Michael Hunter
Selma Hurwitz
Barbara and Charlie O'Reilly Hyland

Ile de France, Hudson, Florida
Indigo, Honolulu, Hawaii
Inn of the Anasazi, Santa Fe,
    New Mexico
International Cafe, Santa Fe,
    New Mexico
Seemi Iqbal
Russell Ito
Diane Ives

Jack Fry's, Louisville, Kentucky
Doris Jacobson
Ruth Jacobson
Cheryl and Bill Jamison
Janos, Tucson, Arizona
Russell Jeavons, Russell's, Willunga,
    South Australia
Nancy Harmon Jenkins
Heidi and Ron Johnson
Kathy Johnson
Michele Anna Jordan

Karen Kaplan
Jacqueline Karamanos
Barbara Karoff
Paula Keener-Chavis
Karen Keisir
Amy Keller
Thomas Keller, Bouchon, Las Vegas,
    Nevada
Jeanne Thiel Kelley
George Kelso
Judi Kerr
Kristine Kidd
Lenore Klass
Ron Klein
Evan Kleiman
Elinor Klivans
Andrew Knowlton
Norman Kolpas
Jim Kronman
Patric Kuh

Carrie LaJeunesse
La Locanda, Scottsdale, Arizona
La Marmotte Restaurant, Telluride,
    Colorado
Susan Lasken
Josie Le Balch
Le Colonial, West Hollywood,
    California
Rosemary Leicht
Larry Leichtman
Ron Lento
Amber Levinson
David Lebovitz
Donald Link
Tony Litwinko
Joyce Litz
Locanda Veneta, Los Angeles,
    California
Michael Lomonaco
Deborah Lovely
Emily Luchetti

Andrew Mandolene

Tom Marady

Sal Marino

Tony Matranga

Janet Taylor McCracken

Michael McLaughlin

Chuck McNeil

Tory McPhail, Commander's Palace,
New Orleans, Louisiana

Tracey Medeiros

Medizona, Scottsdale, Arizona

Meridian Café, Louisville, Kentucky

David Meshell

Lucy Metcalf

Bonnie Wilkens Metully

Tina Miller

Mary Sue Milliken

Brenda and Scott Mitchell

Jinx and Jefferson Morgan

Diana Morrison

Selma Brown Morrow

Eleanor Moscatel

MV Mozart, Peter Deilmann Cruises,
Alexandria, Virginia

Doris Murphy

Antoinette Muto

Florence Myers

Erin Renouf Mylroie

Micol Negrin

Brandi Neuwirth

Nancy Oakes

Catherine Oettinger

Katie O'Kennedy

Joe Ortiz

James O'Shea

Joan and David Oswalt

Sri Owen

David Page

Carey Paquette

Federigo Pardini

Kristi Parnell

Sal Passalacqua, Dimaio Cucina,
Berkeley Heights, New Jersey

Jean Patterson

Alexandra Payard

Lisa Pendleton

Maureen C. Petrosky

Christine Piccin

Laurie Polansky

Marcia Porch

Rebecca Poynor-Burns

Lisa and Stephen Price

Anna Pump

Dave Purdy

Stephan Pyles

Susan Quick

Patricia Quintana

Rachel's Wood Grill, Portland, Maine

Peggy Reed

Renato's, Palm Beach, Florida

Victoria Abbott Riccardi

Rebecca and Ralph Riskin

Mary Risley

Ristorante Chianti, Geneva, Illinois

Tori Ritchie

Jackie Robin

Rick Rodgers

Ruth Rogers

Douglas Rodriguez

Marcela Valladolid Rodriguez

Peggy Ann Roege

Betty Rosbottom

Judy and Robbie Ross

Margaret Jane Ross

Sandra Rudloff

Naomi and Dan Sachs

Julie Sahni

Sally Sampson

Diane Brown Savahge

Richard Sax

Chris Schlesinger

Michael Schlow

Kay Schlozman

Jan Schroeder

Gemma Sanita Sciabica

Michele Scicolone

Sarah Patterson Scott

Barbara Scott-Goodman

Marika and Gianluca Seguso

Lillian Seieszka

Laurence Senelick

Lysa Senich

Paulette Sexton

Rachel Shakerchi

Barbara Shinn

Shorty's Mexican Roadhouse, Bedford,
New Hampshire

Michael Shrader, Nine Restaurant
Group, Palm Springs, California

Martha Rose Shulman

Sibling Rivalry, Boston,
Massachusetts

Stacey Siegal

Sally Siegel

Steve Silverman

Jeanne Silvestri

Marie Simmons

Susan Simon

Prem K. Singh

Maria Helm Sinskey

Kristin H.R. Small

Jennifer Smith

Mark L. Smith

Sally Anne Smith

Laurie Smolenski

Snake River Grill, Jackson Hole,
Wyoming

Scott Snyder

Southampton Princess, Hamilton,
Bermuda

Marlena Spieler

Susan Springob

Ilene Sterns

Molly Stevens

Joy and Alex Stewart

St. Orres, Gualala, California

Sumile, New York, New York

Christine Swanson

Polly Tafrate
Tartine, San Francisco, California
Marilyn Tausend
Todd Taverner
Mark Taylor
Frances Teasley
Julian Teixeira
Bill Telepan
Sarah Tenaglia
Teppo, Dallas, Texas
The Lodge at Koele, Lanai, Hawaii
The Porthole Restaurant, Lynn,
    Massachusetts
Cynthia and Dwayne Thomas
Michael Thompson
Thompson House Eatery, Jackson,
    New Hampshire
Beth and Tom Tiernan
Rochelle Palermo Torres
Laurent Tourondel, BLT Steak, New
    York, New York
Suzanne Tracht
Corinne Trang
Trattoria Bar Ligagin, Pannesi, Italy
Tres Joli Bakery Café, Oakton, Virginia
Rori Trovato
Nancy Tringali
Charlie Trotter
Juli Tsuchiya-Waldron
Brenda Tunstill
Turtle Bay Hilton and Country Club,
    Kahuku, Hawaii
Dave Tyson

Shula Udoff
Karen and Tom Uhlmann

Tom Valenti
Mark Van Wye
Nick Vidargas
Violet, Santa Monica, California
Viva Pizza & Fine Italian Food Res-
    taurant, San Francisco, California

Lovoni Walker
Ila Walrath
Diane Ward
Alexis Watson
Maria Watson
Renee Werbin
Sara Corpening Whiteford
Cynthia Wilson
Dede Wilson
Diane Rossen Worthington
Clifford A. Wright

Helen Yard

Zenzero, Santa Monica, California
Lisa Zwirn

FOR BON APPÉTIT

Zoë Adnopoz
Amy Albert
Lena Cederham Birnbaum
Melissa Brandzel
Frederika Brookfield
Susan Champlin
Nina Elder
Gaylen Ducker Grody
Camille Hahn
Evelyn Jacobson
Jeanne Thiel Kelley
Katie O'Kennedy
Kristine Kidd
Katy Laundrie
Matthew Lenning
Marcia Hartmann Lewis
Marcy MacDonald
Elizabeth Mathews
Janet Taylor McCracken
Selma Brown Morrow
David Nemetz
Dennis O'Brien
Rochelle Palermo
Monica Parcell
Amy C. Quick
Christine Schuchart
Amy Steinberg
Sarah Tenaglia
Victoria von Biel

INDEX

SERVING SIZES